D1211873

DEVELOPMENT

OF AMERICAN JOURNALISM

Larry Fried - Pix, Inc.

Publisher Alicia Patterson Guggenheim checks over Long Island Newsday with printers.

DEVELOPMENT OF AMERICAN JOURNALISM

Sidney Kobre
Community College of Baltimore

WM. C. BROWN COMPANY PUBLISHERS
Dubuque, Iowa

JOURNALISM SERIES

Consulting Editor
Curtis D. MacDougall
Northwestern University

Library of Congress Catalog Card Number: 68-28705

Printed in the United States of America

Perspective

The American Press, A Social Institution

Study of American journalism is both fascinating and useful. It is fascinating because the history of the press is filled with dramatic, exciting incidents and unusual, lively personalities. Examination of press history is useful because, to understand America's vast communication news network today, we must grasp yesterday's development of its communication system. From colonial days to the twentieth century, newspapers and magazines, radio and television, have played significant roles in the development of American life.

Development of American Journalism shows how American journalism as a social institution evolved. The interest is not only in painting in the historical background of the great press periods, but in showing the interaction of the press with changing American social forces. This sociological approach gives coherence to a multitude of complex facts about the press.

The emphasis here is on the basic factors which caused the press to develop and to change in each era. The concern is with the fundamental processes and cycles which occurred in the news-communications industry.

The newspaper was an integral part of its age, and the characteristics of the press can be understood best by reference to economic, political and social conditions of each major period in American history. Publications were also influenced by changing cultural and technological developments. Journalism, therefore, was related to the larger social trends of the nation. Publication of weeklies and dailies, for example, was closely linked with urban developments, the transformation of colonial towns to twentieth-century metropolitan areas having a million or more people.

The newspaper not only was influenced by these various factors in the environment; the press, in turn, affected them. Journalism became increasingly important as a vital force in the growth of these United States. As an agency of persuasion and control, the news industry was active in influencing people by means of emphasis, suppression, opposition and support of various political, economic and cultural movements and groups as well as their leaders. Through news and advertising columns, newspapers promoted commercial activity in the towns and states in which they were published. The publications took a determined part in political party battles over the control of America.

As do all other social institutions, the newspaper interacted with its environment. Conditions in the environment produced journalistic changes or new traits in the press; and, in turn, the press stimulated public interest in this activity. Sports is a prime example of this. As men became interested in football and baseball, the newspaper publishers recognized the small but growing public interest in these sports; consequently, the papers began to print a column of news about football and baseball. This news, in turn, stirred further interest in the games and the players. Entire sports sections eventually were devoted to this newly generated interest.

For each major journalistic era a picture is given of the broad national social trends which affected the news-communication facilities so profoundly. This was the social context in which newspapers were published and without which they cannot be fully understood.

In turning to regional journalism in each of the historical periods, there is discussion of some major developments in the various sections of the nation and in the cities where the weeklies and, later, the dailies were issued. The newspapers of the city of New York, the New England states, the Middle Atlantic states and the Southern region are discussed. Next the publications of the Midwest, the Southwest and the Rocky Mountain areas are presented. This treatment is completed by describing Pacific Coast journalism when it developed.

Although a social institution, the press operates and changes through alert, sensitive-to-the-age publishers, editors, reporters, photographers and other staff members. This volume describes and analyzes personalities of the press and contributions they made to the mainstream of journalism and to American life.

To explain changes in the communications industry and in individual newspapers one searches for causes so a richer understanding of the journalistic evolution can be obtained. The causes for changes in journalism were usually multiple and interacted on each other.

Some of the basic causes were external. Pressures originated in the public, outside the newspaper and in the social environment. Changing educational levels, changing public desires and wants in American history created alterations in the press and in its parts. Shifts in population from rural to urban, or the development of large cities with their changing patterns and problems, stimulated press change. This central urban thread is followed in the *Development of American Journalism.*

Other factors which spurred journalistic developments were internal. Pressures developed within the communications industry. Coverage of more and different "beats," for example, created the need for more reporters and more specialized and larger staffs. The desire for a faster means of printing greater quantities of newspapers to achieve large circulations in the growing urban population led to the invention of linecasting machines and larger, more automatic presses. The close relationship between the external factor and the internal cause is observed here.

The internal competition between individual newspapers, or created by other divisions of the news communication network, such as radio and television, resulted in changes. The original newspaper trait, worked out by one editor or reporter, moved to other newspapers or other regions. A publisher proved that a method was successful; other competitors "borrowed" or "acquired" this trait. Unless they did, they might be forced out of business. The trait might be a type of news, a style of writing or a kind of headline.

As a result of all these external and internal factors, the colonial weeklies evolved into the modern dailies supplemented and reinforced by magazines, radio and television news facilities.

CREDITS

The author is appreciative of the help given by Professor Maurice Vance, History Department, Florida State University, who provided many insights into the historical background of the journalistic developments. Also to be acknowledged is the value of the stimulating and useful discussions about press history with Professor Edwin Emery, School of Journalism, University of Minnesota; the late Professor Warren C. Price, School of Journalism, University of Oregon; Professor Harold L. Nelson, School of Journalism, University of Wisconsin.

The efforts of Richard B. Sessions, Press Bureau Staff of Colonial Williamsburg, have helped intensify the pictorial appeal of the early sections of the book. Also to be acknowledged is appreciation for the interest in this social history shown by Professor Curtis D. MacDougall, Medill School of Journalism, Northwestern University. The staffs of the New York Public Library, Columbia University Library, Enoch Pratt Free Library in Baltimore and the Library of Congress have been courteous and helpful.

Reva, my wife, has been a constant critic of the text, contributing much to its clarity of thought and expression. Ronald Guberman and Kenneth Kobre were helpful in giving the book its graphic and pictorial effectiveness.

Sidney Kobre

Contents

PART FOUR

GILDED AGE JOURNALISM (1865-1900)

PART FIVE

CHAIN AND SYNDICATE JOURNALISM (SINCE 1900)

List of Figures

List of Tables

Part One

Colonial and Revolutionary Press
(1690-1783)

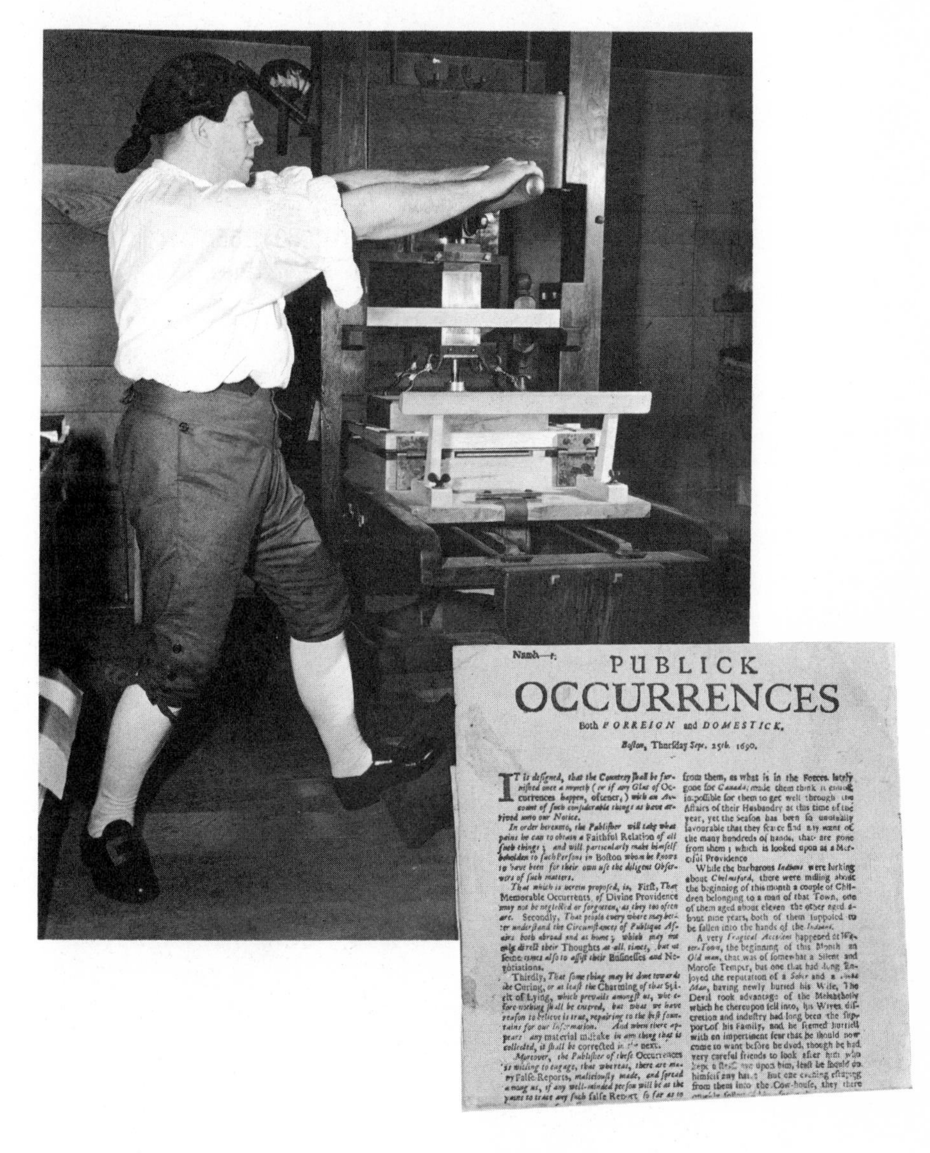

Printer Pulls Press—This was a typical scene in the printshop of the colonial newspaper. It was a handicraft age, and the type was set and the press operated by hand.

(Courtesy Colonial Willamsburg)

Chapter 1

American Colonial Beginnings

BUSY PRINTSHOP SCENE

Bustle and unusual activity occurred in the little dingy printshop of Richard Pierce in the narrow Boston street. The last piece of copy had been slowly set in type by hand. All the forms were fixed on the small, crude, wooden press. Pierce's apprentice had rubbed the inked deerskin balls over the type pages. He now stood ready to pull the heavy lever.

It was September 25, 1690. Bibles had been printed before in Massachusetts; sermons had been published; and laws of the colony issued. No newspaper, however, had been published on American soil. Now in this wooden shack in Boston, *Publick Occurrences,* the first attempt at a newspaper, was about to go to press.

The apprentice braced himself, grabbed the heavy press handle and pulled. The initial issue of *Publick Occurrences* was printed.

Who was the publisher? Who dared defy the wrath of the Puritan clergy and the royal governor in those troublesome times? Courageous Benjamin Harris. A former London publisher, he had issued there a newspaper and a seditious pamphlet. For this he was sentenced to prison but finally was illegally discharged. Again he went into printing, issuing *English Liberties,* which irritated the authorities. Warrants were issued for his arrest. As a result, Harris decided that England was "an uneasy . . . place for an honest man," and set sail for Boston.

When his boat docked at Boston in the fall of 1686, Harris walked through the bustling town and decided to open a coffeehouse at the corner of State and Washington streets. At his London Coffee House, he sold coffee, tea and chocolate. The place became a social center, even for women who were denied access to other shops. Here then was Harris, a trained newspaperman, with wide contacts for picking up news. He had both news experience and boldness.

CRITICAL SITUATION IN NEW ENGLAND

Critical political and economic conditions at this time led to publication of several near-newspapers in Boston. Reverend Increase Mather, colonial leader, had gone to London where he attempted to obtain a new and more just charter for the Massachusetts colony. In 1689 a printer, Samuel Green, obtained several letters which Reverend Mather had sent to Boston. Green published a news broadside, *Present State of New English Affairs,* with a subtitle *Published to Prevent False Rumors.* The newssheet told of Reverend Mather's efforts in England and the promise of King William to restore the rights of the colonists, who protested that their rights were being taken away by Governor Edmund Andros. The broadside also related that the king had ordered the offending Governor Andros and other officials to return to England. This was significant news.

Issuance of such a newssheet and other pamphlets in Boston revealed recognition of the need for a printed newspaper. They probably suggested to Harris the possibility of newspaper publication.

Most of the news Harris printed in the first issue of *Publick Occurrences* concerned Indian warfare about which the colonists were deeply disturbed. The following paragraph illustrates both the style of writing and the type of news found in the paper:

> Christianized Indians in some part of Plimouth have newly appointed a day of Thanksgiving to God for his Mercy in supplying their extreme and pinching necessities under their late want of Corn & for giving them a prospect of very Comfortable Harvest. Their examples may be worth mentioning.

Not all Indians were admirable, for *Publick Occurrences* also told about other Indians who kidnapped two children. This news was about a month old but was the best Harris could do; his readers were glad to get any news. Harris also published news about a suicide in nearby Watertown and told about the sickness, fever and smallpox in Boston. Readers of his *Publick Occurrences* also learned about a fire which broke out near the South Meeting House and lasted for six hours, and a massacre of sailors who landed in a port on the Maine coast.

It will be noted that Harris printed news of Boston and of other towns in Massachusetts and New England. This coverage was characteristic of later papers. They were issued for readers in the entire colony, not solely for the town in which the paper was published. Hence the name: *New-England Courant,* or *Pennsylvania Journal.* Use of the town name, *Boston,* in the title was exceptional.

TABLE 1

Social Forces Shaping the American Press in Colonial Times

Social Forces
Population grew in the colonies
Economy expanded
Handicraft technology prevailed
Transportation improved slowly
Political conflicts with England began
Predominately rural environment shaped lives, interests
Town growth was steady
Educational advancement made slowly
Religion still powerful, but changing
Literature religious, but secular writing began
Theatre reflected economic-political swirls
Scientific advance was slow, but beginning
Social classes emerged
Women's place was still in home

Unfortunately, two of Harris' news items caused the suppression of his paper after only one issue. The first news article charged that certain colonists had corrupted the Indians and that the "miserable" Indians had not carried out their promise to provide canoes and warfare against the enemy. The second article concerned a scandal in the French court. Harris reported that the French king had seduced his daughter-in-law. This was the first and last issue of *Publick Occurrences.* Publisher Harris eventually returned to his coffeehouse business and his bookselling, never to issue a newspaper again.

When *Publick Occurrences* came from the wooden hand press in Boston, it was born into a dynamic colonial milieu. *Publick Occurrences* grew out of the changing economic, social and cultural background, and was affected by it.

CONDITIONS RIPE FOR NEWSPAPER DEVELOPMENT

Although colonists had begun to settle the American seaboard a hundred years before, colonial conditions in the seventeenth century were not yet suitable for native periodicals. Population was too small and scattered to build up any sizable subscription list. The towns were still tiny seaports or crossroad communities. Illiteracy was too extensive for profitable newspaper publication.

Trade, commerce and industry were undeveloped. Settlers for a long time made their own clothes and furniture and raised their own foodstuffs. Advertising would not have been profitable, especially since money was scarce and the general income level low. For a century the postal system was poor because roads were bad and a system of regular riders had not been established to carry the mails. News of other colonies therefore was hard to obtain, and finished newspapers could not be easily delivered to outlying subscribers.

The royal government, representing the British Crown, had the power to license the press. Proprietary colonies, such as Pennsylvania and Maryland, also hemmed in the would-be publishers. In Virginia, the second largest colony, Governor Berkeley, in 1671, made this famous remark, and he wasn't jesting:

> I thank God we have no free schools or printing; and I hope that we shall not have them these hundred years.
>
> For learning has brought disobedience and heresy and sects into the world; and printing has divulged them and libels against the government. God keep us from them both.

All of these economic, political and social conditions combined to discourage publication.

Significant changes, nevertheless, were slowly taking place in American life, leading to the development of newspapers in every colony during the first half of the eighteenth century. On the seaboard, population reached three hundred thousand by 1700 and rose to 1.2 million by midcentury. Growth of such towns as Boston, New York and Philadelphia provided markets for newspapers.

Expanding farming and industry furnished more wealth while simultaneously the shipping business (exporting and importing food and merchandise) grew. All these commercial activities supplied colonists with money to purchase newspapers. They also created news of economic value and interest. Advertising of merchandise and services in a local publication became practical.

Postal service, born in the 1690s, improved, providing quicker delivery of news to publication offices and enabling publishers to get their printed papers to subscribers in rural areas and other colonies more readily.

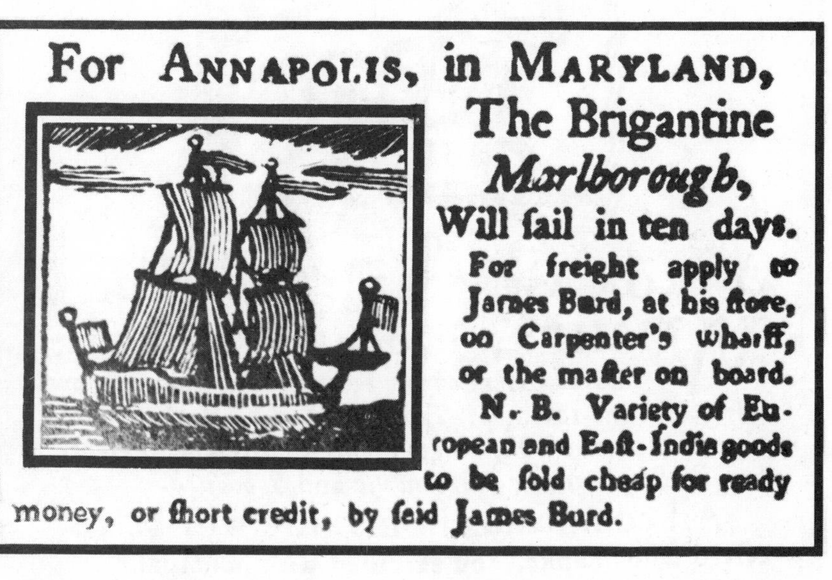

Figure 1. Freight Wanted. The owners of the brigantine *Marlborough,* sailing for Annapolis, Maryland, were seeking merchants and others who had freight to send to Annapolis. The shipping business was aided by advertisements such as the above. The advertisements helped the weeklies survive and succeed.

The political situation, once a hindrance to growth of the press, improved with the trend toward local self-government in the colonies. This trend, beginning after 1690, saw the power of the governor and his council partly offset by the representatives elected by the colonists. Independence from England was increased as the colonials developed their own commerce.

In England, the House of Commons, gaining power, had refused to renew the Crown's power to license the press. In America colonial governors felt that they, similarly, had lost such power of prepublication

NEWS! NEWS!!

AARON OLIVER, *Poſt-Rider*,

WISHES to inform the Public, that he has extended his Route ; and that he now rides thro' the towns of *Troy*, *Pittſtown*, *Hooſick*, *Mapletown*, part of *Bennington* and *Shaftſbury*, *Petersburgh*, *Stephentown*, *Greenbuſh* and *Schodack*.

All commands in his line will be received with thanks, and executed with punctuality.

He returns his ſincere thanks to his former cuſtomers ; and intends, by unabated diligence, to merit a continuance of their favours.

O'er ruggid hills, aud vallies wide,
He never yet has fail'd to trudge it :
As ſteady as the flowing tide,
He hands about ths NORTHERN BUDGET.

June 18, 1799.

Figure 2. Postrider Carries Packages and Mail, Brings News. Aaron Oliver had some additional towns. He brought packages and newspapers to customers along the route. Note the language of his advertisement and the poem.

censorship. They could, however, prosecute for seditious libel after the paper was pulled from the press. Juries, comprised of colonists who felt a growing independence, refused to convict publishers, a fact which gave them additional courage.

Culturally the colonists advanced. Some schools were established; consequently, the illiteracy rate was cut, providing more newspaper readers. Five colleges opened their doors to freshmen: Harvard was the first in 1636; then the College of William and Mary (1693); Yale (1701); Princeton (1746); and what was later to become Washington and Lee (1749). College graduates, in addition to becoming subscribers, developed into writers for the infant press.

Into the seaboard towns came the enterprising printers, who opened little commercial job shops. Printers saw economic opportunities in the growing communities. For the businessmen, printers produced business forms, account books and ledgers as well as stationery. Lawyers wanted legal documents such as deeds and contracts. Governors needed the colonies' laws printed. These officials also wanted proclamations, public notices and other legal documents printed. Each governor needed an official printer for the colony.

Printers helped support themselves by selling stationery, books and other merchandise. Some of them printed books, and they bound new and old sets of cherished volumes. Being somewhat better educated, printers also served as postmasters to the colonies.

The colonial printer was a craftsman in an age of craftsmen: weavers, hatters, cabinetmakers. From England the printer inherited his hand-operated press and his type, a part of the social heritage of the American colonies. He set all type by hand. His equipment, press and type, could be traced to Johann Gutenberg, German inventor of movable type in 1450 and known as "The Father of Printing." A few improvements had been made in the press since then, but the basic principle remained the same.

Four colonies had printing presses in operation by 1685. Chronologically, they were Massachusetts, 1638; Virginia, 1682 to 1685; Maryland, 1685; Pennsylvania, 1685. During the next decades, with increase in population and expansion of agriculture, commerce and industry, more job printers went into business, and busy printshops soon existed in every colony. Located on the main street or on a back street in the developing little towns, the printeries were available for printing regular weekly newspapers for other ambitious colonists or for the postmasters. The printers, themselves, also launched gazettes.

COLONISTS READ ENGLISH NEWSPAPERS

Colonists were not without newspapers in this early colonial period. In taverns, while the new Americans quaffed their ale, they read English weeklies, and after the turn of the century, London dailies which arrived months after publication. In their homes along tree-lined streets, men read avidly the columns of European news in the glow of lamp or fireplace.

When the first Englishmen came over to America in the early part of the seventeenth century, English newspapers were still in an embryonic state of development. The newspaper had not become an established and necessary social institution, such as the school and church represented in Britain. The king was supreme in England, and in those days a license system was established by the royalty to regulate printed matter. Under the circumstances, it was dangerous and foolhardy for any English printer to start a newspaper, although presses were available.

Early in the seventeenth century, newssheets about European continental affairs in which Englishmen were interested were printed in Holland and sent to England. The next step in the evolution of English journalism was the printing of such continental news in England. These *courantos* of foreign affairs, at first, were single newssheets, but they soon developed into twenty-page newsbooks. They followed the tradition of book format. The earliest of these, issued in 1622, was the *Weekly News from Italy, Germanie, Hungarie, Bohemia, the Palatinate, France, and the Low Countries,* indicating news sources of the day.

British readers were also interested in the news of their homeland, especially news about Parliament. Within two decades a publisher rose to fill this vacuum. John Thomas issued *Diurnall Occurrences* on November 28, 1641.

Desiring to lay before the public its side of the controversies with the king, Parliament ignored the long-established prerogative of the Crown to control and regulate printing. In effect, members of Parliament approved this publication and similar ones. Their growth was steady. The official newsbook founded to present the king's side in the current controversy was the *Mercurius Aulicus,* "Mercury of the Court," launched in 1643.

For the next half-century publication of news followed the vicissitudes of English political struggles; both Royalist and Parliamentary groups recognized the increasing value of newspapers in affecting public opinion.

When Charles I was beheaded and the followers of Oliver Cromwell came into power in 1649, only the official publications, the *Mercurius*

Politicus and the *Public Intelligencer,* were permitted to be issued until 1660. When all licensed newsbooks were suppressed, surreptitiously written newsletters developed. With restoration of the king in 1660, however, the royal license prerogative was renewed.

In 1665 the *Oxford Gazette,* later retitled the *London Gazette,* was founded as the official court publication. It became the first continuously issued periodical with a newspaper format. Distinct from a newsbook, the *London Gazette* consisted of a single sheet with only two sides. The reader found two columns of news on each page instead of the usual one column.

Bitter quarrels, meanwhile, continued between king and Parliament, the central issue frequently being the royal license over the press. In 1685 a license system was in force; but the House of Commons, jealous of its power, refused to renew the license law for the king in 1695. English newspapers were thus free from regulation of the licensor *before* publication. This eventually had an important effect on the American newspaper. English newspaper publishers, however, could be punished *after publication* for seditious libel.

With removal of press restrictions on prepublication material, English journalism entered a brilliant period in the Eighteenth century. The two-party system, Whigs versus Tories, led the party leaders and their supporters to seek aid of literary men to publish party newspapers. The first daily appeared in 1702 when Elizabeth Mallet established the *Daily Courant.* Other dailies followed.

Brought to the fore during this period were such popular writers as Daniel Defoe, Jonathan Swift, Joseph Addison, Richard Steele and Samuel Johnson. Journalistic writing was raised to a higher level than it had ever been before.

Addison and Steele were the greatest single journalistic force. They issued the two-page *Tatler,* a triweekly between 1709 and 1711; then they established the daily *Spectator* in 1711. Their lively, witty essays, revealing keen observation of the contemporary scene, attacked vice and folly, and appealed to both men and women. Commenting on modes and manners of the era, the *Spectator's* style was imitated widely and became a model for colonial American writers.

Daniel Defoe, called "the father of English journalism," was one of the first professional writers of major standing. A regular contributor to printed journals as well as an industrious pamphleteer, Defoe was the first journalist to make a wide, popular appeal. His *Robinson Crusoe* appeared originally in an English newspaper. However, Defoe had his troubles with the authorities, being arrested several times for his writings.

Paralleling development of the newspaper as a news and editorial medium, advertising proved its value and became a permanent part of the press institution. Advertisements of books, medical cures, lost horses, runaway apprentices, houses-to-let and professional services were offered through the pages of these papers. Various typographic devices were attracting attention: all-capital headlines, the symbol of the pointing finger, the long dash, the paragraph mark and the triple asterisk, all of which had been used by book printers before.

English newspapers were published weekly, semiweekly and triweekly before a daily newspaper made its appearance in 1702. Woodcuts of postmen and ships representing the facilities for distributing the newspaper appeared at the top of page one. A variety of newspaper names had been coined: *gazette, mercury, intelligencer, occurrences, post,* all of which the colonial publishers copied later.

The newspaper, consequently, had become a firmly established institution in England. The newspaper was becoming recognized as an effective medium for presenting a political party's viewpoint on controversial issues. London papers were subscribed to by colonial tavern owners for their customers. Wealthy colonial merchants and others who could afford the London papers also had them sent to their homes.

Thus, the newspaper was a ready-made social heritage, a news communication agency, brought over from England along with the language, religion, government, schools and the various other trades and crafts.

BOSTON BECOMES NEWSPAPER CRADLE

It was natural that the first regular American newspaper should make its appearance in Boston, a busy seaport. Boston was the largest town in colonial America, holding, at the end of the seventeenth century, first rank as the commercial and cultural center of the new country.

Emergence and later growth of the newspaper in the colonies can be best understood if its dependence on development of population, business and culture in the colonial town is understood; the newspaper was closely integrated with expansion of the small village into the large, bustling town.

Boston was typical of other northern towns; however, it led the other communities in growth. It grew so rapidly that between 1690 and 1725 four newspapers appeared there, while other centers struggled to produce one gazette, and some colonies issued none at all in this period. Boston's population increased steadily. By 1690 the community had seven thousand residents; in 1750 about twenty thousand. Economic, political and cultural attractions were concentrating colonists in Boston. More potential newspaper readers lived in town. Division of labor in such a center gave some persons leisure time to write. The larger population increased chances that residents with literary ability might appear in town. Also, such a place could support bookshops, printshops and even newspapers.

New England, from which Boston derived much of its economic sustenance, had a population of one hundred thousand by 1700. Pioneers in this region lived on small farms in the interior and in small villages and towns. All roads from these communities led to Boston, the hub of a large trading area. Farmers and lumbermen in the back country shipped their exports through Boston, and in turn received many European supplies through the seaport. This commercial activity contributed much to Boston's growth and economic prosperity, which in turn made newspapers profitable.

Figure 3. Shipbuilding Industry. Colonial America depended largely on rivers and on the sea for transportation of people and freight. The export and import businesses became more important each decade. Shipbuilding thus began to thrive in Boston, New York, Philadelphia and the eastern shore of Maryland, contributing to colonial prosperity.

Down at the Boston docks activity was furious. Into the harbor regularly sailed vessels that smelled of slaves, molasses, rum and tobacco. The ships, after a short stay, were reloaded with cod, rum, timber or furs. Anchors were cast and sail unfurled for another longer voyage. The tap, tap of ship carpenters' hammers could be heard as they built strong fishing ketches and sloops.

A newspaper could grow in this environment if its publisher could get advertisements from shippers who had room in their vessels for freight, the products of colonial farms, timberland and craftshops. Some of the merchants with cargoes of molasses, Madeira wine or English-styled cloth to sell might advertise. The newspaper could meet also the need for commercial and marine news created by the increased shipping and other commercial activity.

Catering to the Bostonians and the farmers and lumbermen in the outlying rural areas and small towns were the shopkeepers and craftsmen who began to hang out their shingles along the main streets. Every boat from England brought skilled artisans. Professional weavers, feltmakers and furriers opened shops behind the multiglassed windows. Instead of using homespun, many Boston families began to have their clothes made.

On the edge of town, too, were the flour millers who built their operations near a stream or waterfall. There, the farmer or city dweller took his grain to be ground into flour. Nearby the tanner was ready to provide leather shoes and high boots, or leather for harness and coach springs.

From any or all of these merchants and artisans with goods and services for sale, newspaper advertisements served as the necessary link between seller and buyer. The merchant could announce in the newspaper columns new merchandise from Europe or the West Indies. As the town grew and as settlers spread to the back areas, face-to-face contacts and word-of-mouth advertising decreased. Town dwellers and country residents made fewer of their own goods, depending increasingly on store-bought or artisan-made merchandise and services. The colonists needed a medium to tell them where to buy.

Besides being a commercial center, Boston was also a political capital. Here the governor and assembly met and quarreled. Their legislative acts were important to the lives of the colonists, hence the legislative sessions were news. When the governor issued an official proclamation and when he approved or vetoed legislation, these acts made significant news. Likewise, as a result of their controversies with the governor, the votes of the assemblies and their resolutions affecting the settlers became vital news. Colonists in Boston and other towns and country districts

Figure 4. Colonial Dames Purchase Merchandise. Women bought their household supplies from the general store. They purchased the food they did not raise and did not cook. They wanted European products and those from other colonies. For a long time, families did not have much money for store purchases. Merchants advertised their new products and wares in the local gazettes.

would subscribe to the newspaper carrying such information. As the colony's official printer, the printshop owner could print the record of the assembly sessions, the laws of the colony and other documents, all of which contributed to his income.

As a legal center where trials of varying importance were held, the town could furnish legal news. Lawyers with a ready pen might write for the newspapers. And, of course, a printer could issue a multitude of legal forms demanded by the profession.

The cry of the stagecoach driver and the crack of his whip were heard regularly now as he brought the mails to Boston. The town was the official mail stop. The driver brought news and letters containing news, and later, other colonial newspapers, all of which helped the local Boston publisher fill his newspaper columns with the freshest information.

Boston was also a rapidly growing cultural center. Churches of various denominations expanded, and their clergymen often had facile pens. Preachers were the most literary minded in the colony at this period. Various schools, including Harvard, were established in Cambridge across the river. These institutions could furnish news and advertisements; printers might even publish graduation theses of students. In Boston some scientists and doctors dwelt, and the scientists' experiments and the physicians' advice were news. Booksellers needed advertising space to tell these educated people about the latest issues of books and literary imports from London. With the spread of schools, literacy increased and the number of potential newspaper readers multiplied.

Boston was not without its social activities. Here the royal governor, his aristocratic council and the social elite among the merchants, distillers and shipbuilders lived in splendid houses. Their social activities were not as colorful and gay, perhaps, as such events in Annapolis, Maryland, and Charleston, South Carolina. In those places, such activities were the big news.

Taverns did flourish, however, in Boston. Here Bostonians and travelers got a variety of rum, punch and wine, met their friends and the strangers who just arrived by boat or stagecoach. They exchanged gossip and news and discussed political and economic issues of the moment before the roaring fire. Tavern frequenters were potential newspaper readers and writers. Clubs were formed and some of them wanted an organ of their own to publish their political and economic views.

Boston News-Letter Begins

The need for some media of news communication existed in Boston, but with the suppression of Harris' *Publick Occurrences* the vacuum remained for ten years. Then John Campbell, appointed postmaster of Boston in 1700, distributed by means of his mailing privilege *hand-written* newsletters to governors, shippers, farmers and merchants throughout the colonies. For the most part, these letters consisted of shipping and governmental news and laws, although some local news such as births, deaths and social events appeared occasionally.

It was logical for Campbell to become a newspaper publisher. The office of postmaster was closely linked to that of newspaper publisher throughout the colonial period, as the position had been in England. As the postmaster handled incoming and outgoing mails to foreign countries as well as to the American colonies, he had an opportunity to get news by asking the recipients what the incoming letters contained. Campbell also knew when official mail came to the governor.

The postmaster's office was often the gathering place for people to exchange news and gossip. His free "franking" privilege enabled him to send out letters and newspapers without cost. And, finally, the postmaster was a paid government official and was close to the administration. It would be natural enough for the postmaster to be under the thumb of the governor and his council.

N. E. Numb. 1.

The Boston News-Letter.

Published by Authority.

From Monday April 17. to Monday April 24. 1704.

London Flying-Post from *Decemb. 2d to 4th.* 1703.

LEtters from *Scotland* bring us the Copy of a Sheet lately Printed there, Instituted, *A seasonable Alarm for* Scotland. *In a Letter from a Gentleman in the City, to his Friend in the Country, concerning the present Danger of the Kingdom and of the Protestant Religion.*

This Letter takes Notice, That Papists swarm in that Nation, that they traffick more avowedly than formerly, & that of late many Scores of Priests and Jesuites are come thither from France, and gone to the North, to the Highlands & other places of the Country. That the Ministers of the Highlands and North gave in large Lists of them to the Committee of the General Assembly, to be laid before the Privy-Council.

It likewise observes, that a great Number of other ill-affected persons are come over from *France*, under pretence of accepting her Majesty's Gracious Indemnity; but, in reality, to increase Divisions in the Nation, and to entertain a Correspondence with *France*: That their ill Intentions are evident from their talking big, their owning the Interest of the pretended King *James* VIII. their secret Cabals, and their buying up of Arms and Ammunition, wherever they can find them.

To this he adds the late Writings and Actings of some disaffected persons, many of whom are for that Pretender, that several of them have declar'd they had rather embrace Popery than conform to the present Government; that they refuse to pray for the Queen, but use the ambiguous word Soveraign, and some of them pray in express Words for the King and Royal Family; and the charitable and generous Prince who has shew'd them so much Kindness. He likewise takes notice of Letters not long ago found in Cypher, and directed to a Person lately come thither from St. *Germains*.

He says that the greatest Jacobites, who will not qualifie themselves by taking the Oaths to Her Majesty, do now with the Papists and their Companions from St. *Germains* set up for the Liberty of the Subject, contrary to their own Principles, but meerly to keep up a Division in the Nation. He adds, that they aggravate those things which the People complain of, as to *England's* refusing, to allow them a freedom of Trade, *&c.* and do all they can to foment Divisions betwixt the Nations, and to obstruct a Redress of those things complain'd of.

The Jacobites, he says, do all they can to perswade the Nation that their pretended King is a Protestant in his Heart, tho' he dares not declare it while under the Power of *France*; that he is acquainted with the Mistakes of his Father's Government, will govern us more according to Law, and endear himself to his Subjects.

They magnifie the Strength of their own Party, and the Weakness and Divisions of the other, in order to facilitate and hasten their Undertaking; they argue themselves out of their Fears, and into the highest assurance of accomplishing their purpose.

From all this he infers, That they have hopes of Assistance from *France*, otherwise they would never be so impudent; and he gives Reasons for his Apprehensions that the *French* King may send Troops thither this Winter, 1. Because the *English & Dutch* will not then be at Sea to oppose them. 2. He can then best spare them, the Season of Action beyond Sea being over. 3. The Expectation given him of a considerable number to joyn them, may incourage him to the undertaking with fewer Men if he can but send over a sufficient number of Officers with Arms and Ammunition.

He endeavours in the rest of his Letters to answer the foolish Pretences of the Pretender's being a Protestant, and that he will govern us according to Law. He says, that being bred up in the Religion and Politicks of *France*, he is by Education a stated Enemy to our Liberty and Religion. That the Obligations which he and his Family owe to the *French* King, must necessarily make him to be wholly at his Devotion, and to follow his Example; that if he sit upon the Throne, the three Nations; must be oblig'd to pay the Debt which he owes the *French* King for the Education of himself, and for Entertaining his supposed Father and his Family. And since the King must restore him by his Troops, if ever he be restored, he will see to secure his own Debt before those Troops leave *Britain*. The Pretender being a good Proficient in the *French* and *Romish* Schools, he will never think himself sufficiently aveng'd, but by the utter Ruine of his Protestant Subjects, both as Hereticks and Traitors. The late Queen, his pretended Mother, who in cold Blood when she was *Queen of Britain*, advised to turn the West of *Scotland* into a hunting Field, will be then for doing so by the greatest part of the Nation; and, no doubt, is at Pains to have her pretended Son educated to her own Mind: Therefore he says, it were a great Madness in the Nation to take a Prince bred up in the horrid School of Ingratitude, Persecution and Cruelty, and filled with Rage and Envy. The *Jacobites*, he says, both in *Scotland* and at St. *Germains*, are impatient under their present Straits, and knowing their circumstances cannot be much worse than they are, at present, are the more inclinable to the Undertaking. He adds, That the *French* King knows there cannot be a more effectual way for himself to arrive at the Universal Monarchy, and to ruine the Protestant Interest, than by setting up the Pretender upon the Throne of Great *Britain*, he will in all probability attempt it; and tho' he should be perswaded that the Design would miscarry in the close, yet he cannot but reap some Advantage by imbroiling the three Nations.

From all this the Author concludes it to be the Interest of the Nation, to provide for Self defence; and says, that as many have already taken the Alarm, and are furnishing themselves with Arms and Ammunition, he hopes the Government will not only allow it, but encourage it, since the Nation ought all to appear as one Man in the Defence

Figure 5. First Regular Newspaper, The *Boston News-Letter*, April 17-24, 1704. It appeared fourteen years after Benjamin Harris' abortive attempt, *Publick Occurrences*. Observe the line, "Published by Authority." How much freedom could the printer-publisher have? Colonists were eager to get any news.

Four years after he became postmaster, Campbell found the demand for his hand-written *News-Letters* so great that he turned to a local printer, Bartholomew Green, for assistance in issuing the periodical. When the *Boston News-Letter* came from the press on April 24, 1704, it became the first American newspaper to be published regularly. The *News-Letter* was a single, small sheet with reading matter on both sides. Its style was crude as well as dull if compared to later colonial weeklies or even to *Publick Occurrences*. Campbell followed the earlier pattern of the English newspaper. The *News-Letter* received the official sanction of the government, and, almost throughout its career, the weekly avoided criticism of local government.

Campbell's news was divided into three types: local (Boston), colonial (domestic) and foreign. Local news received a minimum of attention, chronicling births, deaths and religious and political events around Boston. On the colonial (or domestic) level Campbell reported such varied events as piracy on the high seas and political and commercial events throughout the colonies. For his foreign news the *News-Letter* clipped from English journals. Because of slow communication facilities foreign news in the Boston paper was invariably dated by three months or more.

No consideration was given to literary style in the *News-Letter,* hence it was terse and drab. No headlines and only one illustration appeared in the paper, the latter, a woodcut showing the new English flag. It was the first picture in any American newspaper.

The second issue of the *News-Letter* carried the first paid advertisement. Advertisements in Campbell's *News-Letter* reflected the interest of people of that era, stressing some thefts and runaway slaves. Campbell recognized the value of his paper as an advertising medium and even offered a form of classified advertising. He had to depend primarily on subscription income for most of his revenue.

Campbell expressed his opinions, as Harris had, by tacking on a moralistic sentence at the end of a news item. Occasionally, he would write a paragraph about certain issues, but the idea of a newspaper as an organ for discussion of vital issues did not develop in this early period.

Even though by 1715 he had extended his circulation to include Rhode Island and New Hampshire, his subscribers totaled only two hundred to three hundred weekly, showing the lack of public interest in newspapers at this time. In the early 1700s Boston mail required a week to reach New York in the summer. About three days were necessary for the New York-Philadelphia journey. Bad roads and bad weather made this a slow, tedious trip.

TABLE 2

Colonial Publishers Obtained News from a Variety of Sources

1. Private letters, containing matters of general interest, sent to residents or publisher from abroad or other colonies
2. Ship captains and sailors from foreign and local ports found down at the docks or in taverns
3. Merchants receiving or sending goods
4. Travelers with news to tell
5. Soldiers and officers fighting wars
6. Postcarriers who picked up news on the route
7. Postmasters in other colonies
8. Governors and their officials
   a. News from other colonies, official and unofficial
   b. News from England, especially about Parliament
   c. State documents, addresses to the councils or assemblies
   d. Actions taken officially
9. Assemblymen with news
   a. Official news and actions taken on measures
10. Foreign newspapers (chiefly English)
    a. News about Parliament and king
    b. News of England
    c. European news
11. Colonial newspapers, as they were established in other communities in the colony or other colonies
    a. Local happenings
    b. Official actions of colonial lawmaking bodies

Boston Gazette: Competition Begins

In 1719 John Campbell lost the postmaster's position to William Brooker, but Campbell continued publishing his *News-Letter.*

Meanwhile, Postmaster Brooker believed that he might publish a newspaper profitably. It is likely that he was encouraged by the governor to continue the official organ, to give that official a regular periodical for government news and for his views. Accordingly, Brooker founded the *Boston Gazette* on December 21, 1719, naming it after the English royal newspaper, the *London Gazette.* Brooker gave the printing job to James Franklin, who operated a small Boston shop. The new postmaster did everything in his power to keep the rival *News-Letter* out of the mails, compelling the postriders under his supervision to discriminate against the paper of his rival. In spite of this obstacle both papers succeeded, showing the increased interest in newspapers.

Soon both newspapers became involved in the controversy between the governor and the local assembly. When Governor Shute attempted to suppress the publication of news about this fight, he was advised that he no longer had unrestricted power to grant a license to operate a press. As the king of England had lost his authority over the press to the House of Commons in 1695, the colonists maintained that the governor, as the king's representative, had also lost his authority over the colonial press.

Governor Shute still had as a weapon a legal device called "a bill of information," by which he could prosecute the rebellious publishers directly before the General Sessions Court, charging that newspapers were being published seditiously. But this method was cumbersome. Besides, the governor might lose his case in court.

Accordingly, in March, 1721, Governor Shute asked the House to give him control of the press, but the representatives refused. Enraged, the governor dissolved the assembly. His speech on that occasion appeared in his postmaster's *Boston Gazette.* The full text of the answer from the House of Representatives was published in Campbell's independent *News-Letter.*

Between 1695 and 1721 the rigid control over the press had been loosened somewhat. The battle was now between the assembly and the royal governor, with the press an important prize.

Despite Brooker's absorption with political affairs, he found space in his *Boston Gazette* for other matters of interest and attraction. He was the first to introduce a market or business feature called, "Prices Current," which proved valuable to the increasing number of farmers, shippers, tradesmen and merchants who wanted to know the prices of produce, textiles and raw materials. Brooker was the first to introduce front-page pictures. On the left of the *Boston Gazette*'s front page appeared the figure of a sailing vessel and on the right the picture of a postboy delivering the news. These and later front-page symbols, changing from age to age, reflected current technological devices and political issues of the day. Made from woodblocks, these illustrations appeared in the newspaper title and in advertisements.

New-England Courant, Crusader

Criticism was heaped on Postmaster Brooker for his poor printing of the *Boston Gazette,* and within a year he was removed. His successor switched printers, taking the job from James Franklin and giving it to Samuel Green who had a small printshop.

James Franklin, who had learned the printing trade in London, was therefore out of a printing job. He was intimately acquainted with members of a talkative, rebellious group of men who visited Richard Hall's Tavern to learn the news, argue and drink. This group was nicknamed later the Hell-Fire Club. Chief among these men were rebellious John Checkley, who had written anti-Puritan pamphlets and had been arrested for them before, and Dr. William Douglass, who had earned degrees at Edinburgh and had traveled much and read much. Franklin knew he could depend on these local litterateurs for contributions to a newspaper if he established one.

On August 7, 1721, he brought out the first number of the *New-England Courant,* a name previously used by London papers. The title, *New-England,* represented the region or area the publisher hoped to cover and from which he expected to draw advertising.

Franklin's *Courant* became the first fighting, rebellious periodical in America, expressing colonial resentment against the current religious and political order. The Franklin paper also mirrored other aspects of life of the growing commercial class in Boston. It will be recalled that in England, Addison and Steele in their *Tatler* and *Spectator* pages had sought to improve manners and morals of tradesmen in the towns. These clever writers served as models for others in England, and their influence spread. Franklin, while in London, had read their publications and recognized their popularity. Besides, he knew he had to have something more than official and commercial news, such as the *News-Letter* and the *Gazette* had in their publications, which stressed foreign, colonial and local news.

The important innovation of the *Courant* was its discussions of current issues and the small weaknesses and characteristics of people. In

THE [Nº 80

New-England Courant.

From MONDAY February 4. to MONDAY February 11. 1723.

The late Publifher of this Paper, finding fo many Inconveniences would arife by h s carrying the Manufcripts and publick News to be fupervis'd by the Secretary, as to render his carrying it on unprofitable, has intirely dropt the Undertaking. The prefent Publifher having rec eiv'd the following Piece, defires the Readers to accept of it as a Preface to what they may hereafter meet with in this Paper.

Non ego mordaci diftrinxi Carmine quenquam,
Nulla venenato Litera onifta Joco eft.

LONG has the Prefs groaned in bringing forth an hateful, but numerous Brood of Party Pamphlets, malicious Scribbles, and Billinfgate Ribaldry. The Rancour and bitternefs it has unhappily infufed into Mens minds, and to what a Degree it has fowred and leaven'd the Tempers of Perf ns formerly efteemed fome of the moft fweet and affable, is too well known here, to need eny further Proof or Reprefentation of the Matter.

No generous and impartial Perfon present Undertaking, which is defigned fion and Merriment of the Reader. and Mirth have a fecret Charm in th and Tumours of our Spirits, and to restlefs Refentments. They have a ftra harfh Diforders of the Soul, and reduc placid State of Mind.

The main Defign of this Weekly P tain the Town with the moft comical a of Humane Life, which in fo large a P fail of a univerfal Exemplification : N to fill up thefe Papers with a grateful ferious Morals, which may be drawn fr and odd Parts of Life.

As for the Author, that is t' e nex we profefs our felves ready to oblige th teous Reader with moft Sorts of Intellig a Referve. Nor will it be of any M either to them or to the Writers, that publifhed ; and therefore in this Matte of you to fuffer us to hold our Tong this Time of Day it may found like queft, yet it proceeds from the very H Servants.

By this Time the Reader perceives t engaged in the prefent Undertaking. fon, an Inhabitant of this Town of Bo as a Doctor in the Chair, or a perpetual

The Society had defign'd to prefent Effigies, but that the Limner, to whon a Draught of his Countenance, defcrye to offer upon Oath) Nineteen Features i ever he beheld in any Humane Vif raifed the Price of his Picture, that our the Extravagance of coming up to it. And then befides, the Limner objected a Schi m in his face, which fplits it from his Forehead in a ftrait Line down to his Chin, in fuch fort, that Mr. Painter protefts it is a double Face, and h 'll have *Four Pounds* foa the Pourtraiture. However, tho' this double Face has fpoilt us of a pretty Picture, yet we all rejoiced to fee old *Janus* in our Company.

There is no Man in *Bofton* better qualified than old *Janus* for a *Couranteer*, or if you pleafe, an *Obfervator*, being a Man of fuch remarkable *Opticks*, as to look two ways at once.

As for his Morals, he is a chearly Chriftian, as the Country Phrafe expreffes it. A Man of good Temper, courteous Deportment, found Judgment ; a mortal Hater of Nonfenfe, Foppery, Formality, and endlefs Ceremony.

As for his Club, they aim at no greater Happinefs or Honour, than the Publick be made to know, that it is the utmoft of their Ambition to attend upon and do all imaginable good Offices to good Old *Janus* the Couranteer, who is and always will be the Readers humble Servant.

P. S. Gentle Readers, we defign never to let a Paper pafs without a Latin Motto if we can poffibly pick one up, which carries a Charm in it to the Vulgar, and the learned admire the pleafure of Conftruing. We fhould have obliged the World with a Greek fcrap or two, but the Printer has no Types, and therefore we intreat the candid Reader not to impute the defect to our Ignorance, for our Doctor can fay all the *Greek* Letters by heart.

His Majefty's Speech to the Parliament, October 11. tho' already publifh'd, may perhaps be new to many of our Country Readers ; we fhall therefore infert it in this

racious SPEECH iament, on Thurs-

liged, at the Opening of you, That a dangerous t, and is ftill carrying on t, in Favour of a Popifh

here, the Informations I oad, and the Intelligences ance with me, rnd indeed ven me moft ample and n.

ir Emiffaries, made the from Foreign Powers, but ons: However, confiding raged by their former ill pon their own ftrength, to nment.

derable Sums of Money, rs from abroad, fecured mmunition, and thought t had not the Confpiracy l, without doubt, before d particularly the City of fufion.

he Bleffing of God, hith- their trayterous Projects. l this Summer; fix Regi- he Security of that Kingdom have been brought over from *Ireland*; The States General have given me affurances that they would keep a confiderable Body of Forces in readinefs to embark on the firft Notice of their being wanted here; which was all I defired

Figure 6. First Weekly Protester. James Franklin's *New-England Courant* was the first publication to oppose the Boston authorities. This issue, February 4-11, 1723, was edited by Benjamin Franklin, when his brother was given warning by officials about publishing and therefore turned the newspaper over to his young apprentice. Inset shows Benjamin Franklin, as painted by Benjamin Wilson.

their discussion-essays, the *Courant* writers employed serious, humorous and sarcastic styles. Franklin and his contributors did not sign their own names but used pseudonyms, partly because of the English newspapers' tradition and partly because of the fear of reprisal, for Boston was still a small town.

Campbell's *News-Letter* had little besides news because the publisher could not pay editorial contributors. Franklin, and other colonial publishers who followed, solved this problem by getting free literary contributions from men in the community who could write and who had an urge to express themselves in print. Most of the *Courant's* contributors were Episcopalians, a sect which had increased and had objected to Puritan control. In his announcement Franklin stated that the paper was to be published weekly. He declared that he earnestly desired his friends to furnish him with short pieces, "Serious, Sarcastic, Ludicrous or otherwise Amusing."

Among early essay writers was Benjamin Franklin, brother of James. A young apprentice then, Benjamin became one of the most famous colonial newspaper publishers later.

Born on January 17, 1708, Benjamin was an exceedingly intelligent and shrewd child. At ten, Ben's formal schooling was over, after about two years of classroom work. From this time on, Ben educated himself. He became a writer with a distinctive style. Through his own efforts he learned several foreign languages. Becoming interested in science, he later made contributions to scientific knowledge.

After his father withdrew him from school, Ben was taken in the parental tallow candle shop where he helped with the melting. He did not like the smell of the place and longed to sail the seas. Father Josiah Franklin tried to cure the wanderlust in Benjamin. Desperate, the elder Franklin turned to his son, James, who operated a printshop in Boston. Ben was apprenticed to his brother and at twelve learned the rudiments of the printing trade. The young apprentice spent his spare time reading. He studied and became a deist, a rationalist. Reading several bound volumes of the *Spectator* in the shop, he laboriously rewrote the essays to acquire the style of the English writers.

In his brother's printing shop, Ben did all the odd jobs of an apprentice: mixing ink and sweeping floors. He also set type, inked forms, pulled the lever on the hand press to print the job work and the books. After James recognized Ben's ability to write verses, the printer set his apprentice to writing a poem or ballad about current events which could be hawked about the streets.

When James started the *New-England Courant,* Ben helped with its production. He even delivered the *Courants* in town. Ben listened to the discussions of the Hell-Fire Club and knew what kind of essays the *Courant* would print. Having practiced the *Spectator* style for his own self-improvement, he decided he would try to write an essay or two.

Ben wrote the first letter and signed it "Silencc Dogood," as he felt his brother would not print the article if he knew the author. Late at night, when the Franklin printshop was locked, Ben slipped his essay under the door. The next day he watched the glow of interest shown by members of the Hell-Fire Club when they read the Dogood letter in the *Courant.*

He wrote more. Characteristic of him, these letters were interesting and were cleverly written. In his first letter, in which he posed as the virtuous widow, "Silence Dogood," Ben described the courtship and married life of "the young girl" and finally her husband's death. In subsequent letters Franklin ridiculed Harvard College as a citadel of conservatism, open only to the wealthy, full of corruption and bad manners, its students, insolent and idle. In this piece Ben was at once humorous and ironical, according to the *Spectator* tradition. The Dogood letter created a sensation, and in the *Boston Gazette* "John Harvard" replied.

In other letters Franklin satirized local foibles and weaknesses. His shrewd puppet character, Silence Dogood, commented on the nature of the weaker sex, danger of fashionable dress and the lamentable condition of widows. These letters, running from April to September, 1722, also demanded free speech when James was thrown into jail. The letters stopped abruptly in September, 1722, when envious James, recognizing his brother's hand, would not print any more of the clever articles.

The *Courant* did not live up to the last part of its opening announcement: that it would not reflect on the clergy or government. The weekly soon launched violent attacks on the Puritan clergy, particularly the Reverend Increase Mather and his son, Reverend Cotton Mather, and later aimed its pointed barbs at the governor himself.

The paper, in a series of articles signed with pseudonyms or unsigned, singled out for special attack the smallpox inoculation theories of Reverend Increase Mather. He had advocated inoculation, then spreading in Europe, to cure smallpox, which plagued the inhabitants of colonial Boston; Boston physicians opposed the new theory. The *Courant's* articles aroused the Puritan pastor's wrath. The *New-England Courant* created a sensation in Boston with its defiance of the established clergy, arousing many residents against Mather. The Mather supporters resorted to a broadside, *The Little Compton Scourge, or the Anti-Courant.*

James Franklin now launched a frontal assault on Governor Shute himself. On June 11, 1722, Franklin inserted a sly, unobstrusive bit of information:

> The Massachusetts government was not earnestly cooperating for the capture of a pirate vessel then reported to be off the coast of New England.

Before this Franklin had confined his attention to religious and medical questions. Now, for the first time, he attacked the government openly. It should be recalled that Bostonians and other residents in Massachusetts depended for their livelihood on shipping. Pirates were menaces because they captured both cargoes and ships and put sailors to death. Franklin thus was pleading the cause of the shippers publicly in his paper. The *Courant* thus became a political and economic organ, representing colonial economic interests.

The governor was furious at the implications in the Franklin weekly, and immediately the General Court, consisting of the House of Representatives and the Council, threw the publisher in jail for his high affront. He remained there during the session of the court, three weeks in June, 1722, until the General Court adjourned. The Governor's Council now attempted to suppress the *Courant* and established a censorship over the press, but the House, representing the colonists, again refused to be tricked and, therefore, did not concur in the order.

Although, while in jail, Franklin apologized for printing such scandalous material, he, in stinging doggerel verse, satirically attacked the General Court for imprisoning him. In the issue of July 30, 1722, he tried to prove from the Magna Charta the illegality of the government's action.

This did not finish his conflict with the authorities. On January 14, 1723, Franklin's *Courant* contained three attacks. The first of these was a mocking denunciation of religious hyprocrites, intimating that New England contained not a small number of these detestable human beings. Another article spoke of the "extraordinary manner of Governor Shute's absenting himself from the government" and suggested that he might be expected to labor in England against the interest of the province. The *Courant* even proposed that trusted agents be sent to England to vindicate the House of Representatives.

The two branches of the General Court resented these remarks bitterly; in the absence in England of Governor Shute, usually an agent of friction between the Council and the House, they united to do battle against the bold publisher. A joint committee of both bodies censured the *Courant* for its mockery of religion and its affront to the government. The committee recommended that the General Court forbid James Franklin to "print a paper of the like nature, except it be first supervised by the Secretary of this Province, and that bonds should be extracted from him for his good behavior."

Despite passage of this order, Franklin defiantly printed another satire on the government. The aroused Council promptly ordered Franklin's arrest for contempt of the General Court's order. To evade its requirements Franklin resorted to a subterfuge. He caused the name of his brother, Benjamin Franklin, 17-year-old apprentice, to be substituted as publisher of the *Courant*, beginning with the issue of February 11, 1723. James marked Benjamin's apprenticeship papers "finished" on the theory it would appear more legal if a journeyman rather than an apprentice was the *Courant*'s publisher. Meanwhile, James Franklin was put under bond to wait the action of the Grand Jury for publishing without receiving permission. The attempt to get the Grand Jury to indict him failed. He was discharged from his bond in May, 1723.

The *Courant* case was of importance in the development of the freedom of the press, for this was the last instance of an attempt to revive and enforce newspaper censorship by license in Massachusetts.

These events occurred in 1723, ten years before another important test case, the Zenger freedom-of-the-press trial in New York. The Franklin incident showed the direction the winds of independence were blowing. Franklin's *Courant,* itself a product of the changing forces, helped stimulate the movement toward independent religious and political thinking. It showed that, in addition to printing news, another legitimate function of the newspaper was publication of editorial opinion, or news discussion. This function was developed in critical periods when great issues faced the public and when press restrictions were removed. During these colonial years cost of establishing a publication, buying press and paper and hiring news-gathering and printing personnel, was not prohibitive and not a serious deterring factor in furnishing a variety of opinion on current issues.

Because of its sarcasm, its ridicule and satire and the discussion it provoked, the independent *Courant* was quite successful. Franklin declared that it had a far greater number of subscribers than any other paper and was also read by a larger number of persons who borrowed the weekly from their neighbors. The *Courant*'s circulation was concentrated in Boston, in Massachusetts and in Rhode Island.

The *New-England Courant* continued to be published until 1726 when James closed down the weekly. In 1728 he went to Rhode Island, a freer community, and set up a shop there. Convinced of the need for a paper, in 1732 he published the first issue of the *Rhode Island Gazette,* but the newspaper failed within a year.

During the next two decades Boston printers recognized the economic possibilities of publishing in the growing community, which by midcentury had reached fifteen thousand in population. They issued three more weeklies. Two of the papers, the *Boston Evening Post* and the *Independent Advertiser,* indicated that uniformity of opinion in religion and government belonged to a bygone day. The new publications gave expression to the growing independence of the colonists. Boston, with her five newspapers in the period 1725 to 1750, has been rightly called "The Cradle of American Journalism."

PHILADELPHIA, COMMERCIAL CENTER, GETS FIRST PAPER

Philadelphia was next to establish a colonial newspaper. The City of Friends was growing in both population and commerce. Trade routes on land connected Philadelphia with the north and the south, and it was both an import depot for European goods and an outlet for crops raised in the interior. Foodstuffs were brought to Philadelphia and shipped to foreign ports as well as to other colonial towns. The Pennsylvania hub was soon to rival Boston and New York.

Numerous foreign groups, such as the Germans, had come and settled in and around the town with the result that an old world liberal and cultural atmosphere was in the making. A center of politics, Philadelphia was also the capital of the Pennsylvania colony.

Pennsylvania, of which Philadelphia was the chief trading center, increased to one hundred ninety thousand persons by midcentury. Responding to the regional boom, Philadelphia grew from only a few thousand to thirteen thousand during this time. The Quaker town became large enough to support three newspapers.

The American Weekly Mercury (1719–)

When William Bradford, Philadelphia's first printer, quarreled in 1693 with the Quakers he departed for New York, leaving an apprentice in charge of this Philadelphia shop. His son, Andrew, worked in his father's New York printshop until 1712, when, sixteen years old, he returned to Philadelphia. Finding the Friends less strict than before, he took charge of his father's old printshop and became postmaster and also printer to the colony.

These jobs placed him in a strategic position to launch a newspaper; his *American Weekly Mercury* appeared on December 22, 1719, backed

TABLE 3

1650 Growth of Colonial Towns 1775

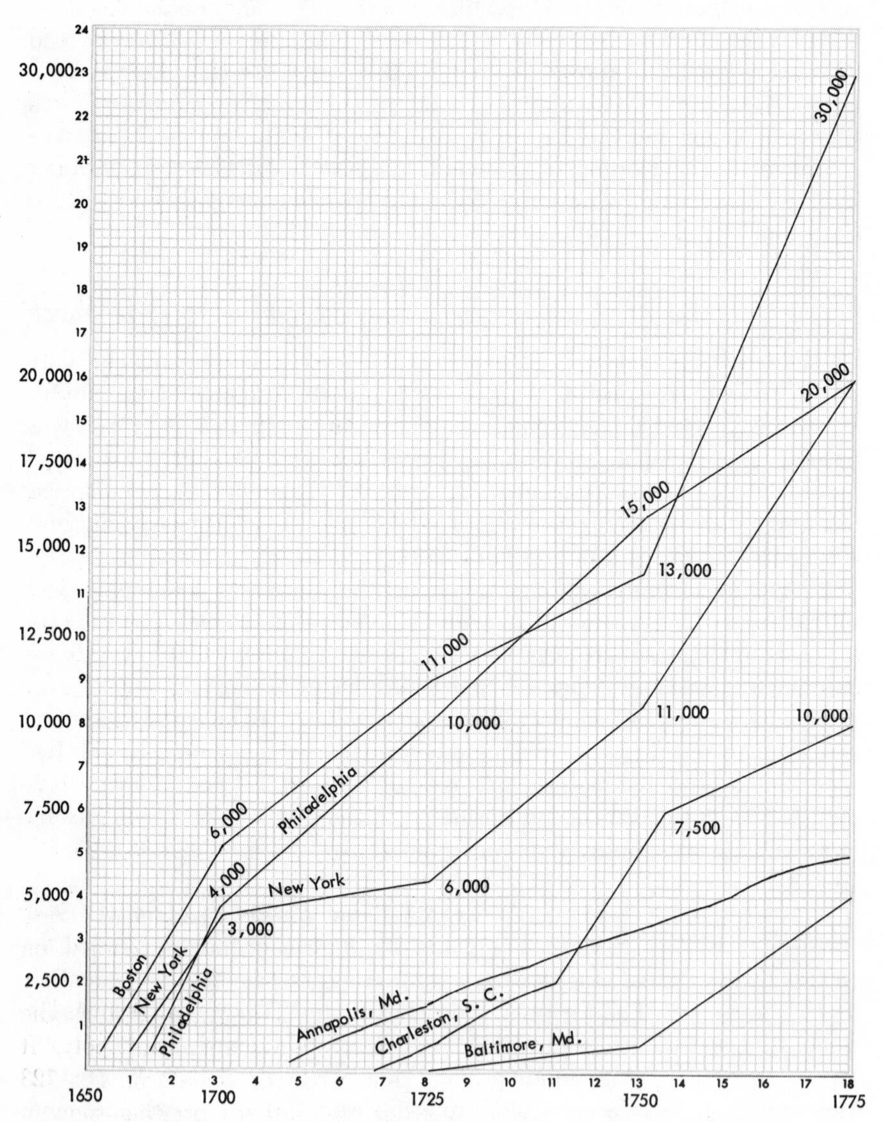

by John Copson, wealthy local merchant. Like all contemporary publishers, Andrew Bradford ran into political troubles. He published an announcement which reflected unfavorably on the General Assembly. This body called him before it for an explanation. He declared that a printer had put in the item without his knowledge, and so the Assembly excused Bradford with a warning to publish no more unfavorable news.

Later the implications of James Franklin's troubles with the Boston authorities were only too clear to Bradford, and so he immediately wrote an article defending the Boston publisher. The article itself was the first evidence of a developing bond between the various seaboard community publishers, a bond which resulted in far more extensive and regular exchange of news.

The Mercury followed the news pattern of the *Boston News-Letter* and the *Boston Gazette.* Bradford, however, published more local news, including accounts of fires, accidents, crimes, executions and the last speeches of criminals; he also imitated the *Boston Gazette's* business feature: current prices. *The Mercury,* however, was thinner in content than the Boston papers, perhaps because Philadelphia was neither as large a seaport nor as active a cultural center as Boston.

In 1717 the *Mercury* was combined with the *New York Gazette* and was published by the father and son in partnership until December 13, 1739, after which the *Mercury* was published by Andrew Bradford alone. This Bradford combination was the first example of chain journalism which, in the colonial period, was more or less limited to financial relationships and the exchange of essays with no centralized control.

With no copyright law, Boston publishers were soon reprinting articles from the *Mercury* to supplement news from ship captains and travelers about occurrences in Philadelphia. Other papers established along the coast followed this plan. Later, the various publishers not only revealed troubles between governors and assemblies but also fought for their collective right to publish their respective papers without interference.

In addition to the *Mercury,* two more successful papers were added to supply news, features and advertisements to the growing population of Philadelphia.

In 1728 events of importance in Philadelphia began to disturb the journalistic tranquility of Andrew Bradford's newspaper monopoly. It was the turbulent Benjamin Franklin who produced the storm. In 1723 Ben, who was seventeen, ran away from his brother's printing shop in Boston and came to New York where he called on William Bradford. Bradford could not give Ben a job but sent the young printer to see the publisher's son in Philadelphia. Ben made his way there and called on Andrew Bradford, who liked the lad sufficiently well to allow him to board at the publisher's home. Since, however, there was no job open at the *Mercury* office, Bradford sent Ben to Samuel Keimer, another Philadelphia printer. Franklin was hired. He worked hard and saved his few pennies. Soon, he struck up an acquaintance with a fellow printer, Hugh Meredith, a thirty-year-old farmer who was learning the printer's trade.

The Governor of Pennsylvania, William Keith, hearing about the learning and sharpness of young Franklin, came to the shop to visit him. Governor Keith wanted a printer under his control and suggested to Franklin that he acquire some money and start a shop and a newspaper. The governor promised that he would back the enterprise. Governor Keith promised to give Ben a letter of credit if he sailed to England and purchased a press and equipment from abroad.

Inexperienced Ben left for England. When he arrived in London he discovered that the governor had misled him. Ben could not get the expected credit. Franklin secured a job in a large London printing house and remained in the busy metropolis for eighteen months. In London, he became further acquainted with European thought and custom, particularly the deistic and scientific movements coming into fashion.

Franklin later returned to Philadelphia and again worked with Keimer for a short time. Then Hugh Meredith's father proposed that Benjamin go into business with his son, offering to supply at least part of the capital for the new enterprise. Equipment was ordered, and the firm of Franklin and Meredith began business.

Keimer Starts Universal Instructor

Philadelphia had grown to thirteen thousand, and its commercial development was accelerating. Among those who heard of Franklin's printshop and his proposal to issue a newspaper was Samuel Keimer, his former employer. Keimer also believed there was a place for a second newspaper in Philadelphia. Bradford's *Mercury* was as uninteresting as the editor was ignorant, and the paper included no sparkling essays. Samuel Keimer, therefore, decided to steal Franklin's idea, and on December 24, 1728 he issued the *Universal Instructor in All Arts and Sciences; and the Pennsylvania Gazette*, priced at ten shillings ($2.50) yearly.

Keimer was a bookseller as well as a printer, and on his shelves was a copy of *Chambers' Cyclopedia*: *Or An Universal Dictionary of the Arts and Sciences*. The publisher started to print long extracts from this work in his newspaper, the *Instructor*. At the same time he republished extracts from works by Daniel Defoe and others, thus introducing fiction for the first time in the American newspaper.

Thoroughly aroused by the theft of his newspaper idea, Franklin published several articles in the *Mercury* under the name "Busy-Body," attacking the *Instructor*. These articles were also modeled after the *Spectator's* style. In fact, Ben brought to the *Mercury* the essay technique, originated in England and later transferred to Boston.

Finally, the combined effect of Franklin's attacks and the dullness of the *Instructor* itself drove Keimer out of business. In the summer of 1729 Keimer's financial burdens increased, his circulation dropped to ninety, and he left for the Barbadoes in the West Indies. Franklin and Meredith took over the paper.

The Pennsylvania Gazette (1729–)

After Franklin and Meredith assumed control of the *Universal Instructor*, Franklin, one of the great geniuses of the eighteenth century, instituted radical changes in the newspaper which improved its quality immensely. Witty, urbane and exceedingly shrewd, he became one of the best newspaper publishers and editors in the colonies. He was the intellectual giant of his day. If any editor has reflected the major tendencies of his era, it was Franklin. He also foreshadowed the road America was to travel. A symbol of the rising tide of commercialism, he made a great financial success of the printing house and newspaper while other printers and publishers struggled.

Fortunately for Franklin, Meredith soon withdrew from the firm. Just as Franklin was a forerunner in other fields, so he was ahead of contemporary newspaper colleagues in journalism. Most of them in this period were not editors nor did they express their personality and ideas in their newspapers. Franklin, however, was the editor of the *Pennsylvania Gazette*, and he made his ideas and presence felt. Such editors became more prevalent in the revolutionary era and post-revolutionary period.

Though Franklin's *Pennsylvania Gazette* was distinguished by its clever essays, he published as much news as any other paper in the colonies. Restricted by technology and communication facilities of the colonial era, as were other publishers, his foreign news came three or more months late in summer and even later in winter. Many of his news items had an ironical ending which gave them a clever twist. For instance, this one was printed in the issue of March 6, 1732:

> A servant girl near Christian Bridge hanged herself lately with a design, as 'tis thought, to haunt a young fellow who refused to marry her.

Through philosophical articles by the "Plain Dealer," a special essayist, the *Pennsylvania Gazette* emphasized the necessity of reading good books and becoming inquisitive about the universe, stressed the function and necessity of doubting, and dealt with toleration, moderation and free-thinking. In this way the *Pennsylvania Gazette* encouraged its readers to join the rationalists of the eighteenth century in pursuit of knowledge and exercise of reason.

Franklin, because of his education and background in Boston and London, was able to appeal to and stimulate the scientific, literary, philosophic and humanitarian tendencies of his community. Philadelphia, influenced by Franklin and his *Pennsylvania Gazette,* became one of the most progressive centers of culture in the colonies.

Franklin, as he had done in Boston, attempted to control and affect the behavior of other colonists, both men and women. Reason was the watchword of many in the eighteenth century, and Franklin, since his early reading in Boston, had been a rationalist and had sought to stir his readers to become rationalists.

He influenced the community in other ways as well. In walks about Philadelphia he saw civic improvements which could be profitably made in the growing country town. Philadelphia was expanding from a village to a market town, the process of urbanization beginning. Through articles in his paper, Franklin was instrumental in effecting many improvements: establishing a fire department, obtaining cleaner streets, calling attention to danger of icy sidewalks, deepening the rivers and other projects. Franklin, although not a college graduate himself, urged people to promote a liberal college in Philadelphia. The college was launched in 1751 and later became the University of Pennsylvania. Franklin also founded an insurance company.

Science was another absorbing interest of Franklin, and scientific essays often appeared in the *Gazette,* contributing to colonial interest in science and later having a wide impact on American thought.

In the early 1750s colonists were faced with a national issue affecting the lives and businesses of all. Defense against both the Indians and the French was imperative. Franklin recognized the importance of the problem facing the disjointed colonists and drew the first political cartoon which was published in his *Gazette.* The cartoon represented a snake cut into eight parts. The head represented New England, and the other seven parts symbolized New York, New Jersey, Pennsylvania, Maryland, Virginia, North and South Carolina. The slogan "Join or Die" was printed under the cartoon.

Woodcuts had been used previously in books and in a few newspapers. *Boston News-Letter* had used one to show the pattern of the new English flag. There had been a map in Zenger's *Weekly Journal* in New York. But because of the expense involved, pictorial illustrations had not been used frequently in reinforcing the news. However, the defense problem was an exceptional issue and, as usual, Franklin led the way. In a month his snake device had spread to most of the other important papers in the colonies.

From October 16 to 23, 1727, Franklin made an attempt to issue a semiweekly, among the first, if not the first, in the American colonies. He announced:

> From this time forward, instead of publishing a whole sheet once a week, as the first undertaker engaged to do, we shall publish a half sheet twice a week . . . we think it will be more acceptable to our readers in as much as their entertainment will be by this means more frequent.

This attempt at semiweekly publication, reflecting increase of trade and improvement of the postal system which brought in news more quickly, did not succeed. Franklin reverted to weekly publication.

Franklin became official printer to the Pennsylvania colony, an enterprise which added to his revenue. He also became a clerk of the assembly, enabling him to get information firsthand about actions and bills of the lawmaking body. When Franklin became postmaster of Philadelphia, he was placed in a strategic position for securing news for his newspaper. He also kept rival publishers from sending their papers through the mails.

Franklin's commercial abilities and farsightedness became evident soon after he assumed management of the *Pennsylvania Gazette.* He recognized the value of his newspaper as an advertising medium. Grouping advertisements together on one page, he then separated them from each other with lines, or gave them plenty of white space to set them off. He printed the first few words of the advertisements in 14-point type to make them stand out, and later put short headlines over some advertisements, such as:

JUST IMPORTED ANOTHER PARCEL OF SUPER CROWN SOAP

Illustrations, consisting of small woodcuts which pictured merchandise to be sold, were taboo in England at this time. Franklin, however, recognized their strong advertising value. Soon his *Gazette* boasted a variety of illustrations.

Franklin backed at least six other newspapermen in their ventures, thus starting an early type of chain journalism. His action was similar to the steps taken by some of the richer businessmen of Boston, New York and Philadelphia, who invested surplus money from their businesses into other enterprises. Franklin trained Thomas Whitemarsh in the *Pennsylvania Gazette*'s shop, and in 1731 sent him to South Carolina, where a printer was needed. There Whitemarsh established a press, the following year publishing the *South Carolina Gazette*. Franklin gave financial backing to another apprentice, James Parker, to open a print-shop in New York in 1741, when the *New York Gazette and Post Boy* was published. Franklin also helped Lewis Timothy in publication of the first German newspaper in America, the *Philadelphia Zeitung* in 1732. Only a few numbers appeared. Franklin likewise encouraged Christopher Sowers in issuing another German newspaper, the *Germantown Zeitung* in Philadelphia twelve years later.

This did not end his assistance to other printers. He backed his nephew, James Franklin, Jr., in Rhode Island with his printing enterprise, and another nephew, Benjamin Mecom, who issued his paper in New Haven, Connecticut. Franklin's operations extended as far as Jamaica, where he loaned money to William Daniell.

Franklin made a profit, too, by supplying publishers and printers with ingredients to make ink. An excellent source of income to Franklin was his clever *Poor Richard's Almanac,* which sold ten thousand copies each year. Franklin became interested financially in eighteen paper mills in the vicinity of Philadelphia.

The usual colonial publishers struggled along on profits from their newspapers and commercial and government printing, and from their book and stationery selling. In some instances, as indicated, they also derived incomes from their postmasters' jobs. From all these sources their incomes averaged between £100 and £500 yearly, the latter figure being unusually high. But between his commercial and official printing, Franklin earned about £2000 a year during his first twenty years in the printing business and £1000 annually after he offered David Hall a partnership in 1746.

Franklin brought Hall, an excellent printer, from England in 1744. Two years later Franklin offered Hall a partnership. Then, in 1748, Franklin turned over the business to Hall, withdrawing himself from active participation in the firm. Hall operated the printing house, which now employed five men and did work in German, French, Swedish and English. Franklin attended only to the writing of the newspaper. Hall agreed to pay Franklin £ 1000 each year for eighteen years; by 1776 Hall owned the entire plant.

Franklin moved away from busy downtown Philadelphia and lived in a house near the water's edge, where he carried on his electrical experiments. Franklin did not remain long at his scientific work. Public affairs claimed his interest six years after his retirement. During the remainder of his life, he engaged in politics and diplomacy. In 1754 he represented Pennsylvania in the Albany Congress, called to unite the English colonies against the French and Indians. His plan for unification was adopted by the Congress, but the colonial assemblies did not ratify the proposal, Franklin said, because they thought the plan had too much authority; England did not agree to the proposal because it was too democratic.

New disputes sent him to England, where he was a sort of ambassador extraordinary from the colonies. During the critical period when relations were strained between England and the colonies, he worked hard for a reconciliation. In 1775 he was chosen a member of the Second Continental Congress. The following year he was sent to France as a committee member to negotiate a treaty with France. His simple dress, his fur cap, his unpretentious manner, his wit and wisdom won him a wide circle of friends. When the other commissioners fell out among themselves, Franklin was the sole diplomat. He was successful in his mission. Later he served on the commission to negotiate the peace treaty with Great Britain.

This many-sided, self-educated genius, therefore, was a printer, postmaster, philosopher, writer, scientist, inventor and diplomat. Because of his fine literary touch and the sparkle of his clever mind, Franklin produced the most interesting newspaper in the colonies. He had to work with a paucity of materials, and he was part of the colonial newspaper system, with all its restrictions. He could not rise far above it, but he tapped its wells more deeply than other persons. He sensed the need for educated editors, and he attempted to speed up publication of news by publishing a semiweekly. Both of these two institutional characteristics became a part of the newspaper machinery within the half-century.

The Journal and Weekly Advertiser (1742–)

During the entire colonial period journalistic history of the two metropolises, New York and Philadelphia, was intertwined with the lives of the members of the Bradford family. William Bradford, Sr., had been publishing the *New York Gazette* since 1725. He had two sons: Andrew, publisher of the Philadelphia *American Mercury*, and William, Jr., a sickly young man who after his marriage and the birth of a son, William Bradford, III, had gone to sea. William, III, later worked on the *Mercury*, expecting in due time to become a full-fledged partner.

After his uncle's death, William Bradford, III, purchased a press, probably with the aid of his grandfather in New York, and set up a shop in Philadelphia on December 12, 1742, in competition with both his uncle's widow and Benjamin Franklin. Bradford made a bid for the old *American Mercury* readers, offering the *Pennsylvania Journal* for ten shillings per year. William Bradford, III, was one of the earliest editors to issue postscripts. These consisted of extra sheets with two sides of news and a few advertisements and were added to the newspaper whenever a ship arrived with English news after the paper had been made up.

By the middle of the century the *Journal* had grown and was occasionally being issued as a six- or eight-page paper. Both Bradford and Franklin issued magazines in this period. These publications will be discussed in the special section on magazines.

NEW YORK FIGHTS OVER A FREE PRESS

New York: Growing Farm Market, Seaport

Four years after his son established the *Mercury* in Philadelphia, William Bradford, realizing that a similar newspaper in New York might be a profitable source of income, started his *New York Gazette* on November 8, 1725. Conditions were becoming more opportune for a successful publication there.

New York, like Philadelphia, was growing as a commercial and political center. The town of New York served as a market for the farmers and livestock raisers in the Hudson and Mohawk valleys of the New York province, East New Jersey and Long Island. New York's position was further strengthened by lack of deep harbors along the Jersey coastline. All produce from the surrounding farm area was shipped through New York. Horses and livestock were raised on nearby Long Island, and the city served as a marketplace for them. An extensive fur trade was built, but this had declined somewhat. New York, too, was the port of entry for manufactured articles from England, for West Indies rum and salt and for Virginia and Maryland tobacco. New York's riverfront also was the scene of bustling shipyard activities, for a number of businessmen began to build ships for the ocean-going and inland-river trade.

Politically, New York, seat of colonial government, was having the same type of friction that existed in Boston and Philadelphia between the English government officials and local assemblies. The key issue was the dispute over the right of newspaper publication.

Population growth for the New York trading area was steady, the New York colony alone increasing from twenty-five thousand in 1725 to one hundred thousand by midcentury. The town of New York reached four thousand at the beginning of this period; fifty years later it attained ten thousand, making the town one of the largest in the colonies.

Reflecting this population and commercial expansion and the current political controversy, by midcentury four newspapers were launched in New York.

New York Gazette (1725–), Government Organ

Because of the favorable economic conditions for newspaper publication, the *New York Gazette* emerged in 1725 with William Bradford as publisher and printer to the governor.

Like the *Boston Gazette* and the Philadelphia *American Mercury*, the *New York Gazette* was a governmental organ. It consisted of little more than a dry recital of facts: colonial news from Boston and Philadelphia, scanty local news, foreign information reprinted from European papers and a few essays and letters to the editor. The paper carried advertisements for slaves who had escaped from their masters in the South. Bradford faced the obstacles to newspaper publication typical of the colonial period: financial stringency, lack of facilities for gathering news, poor distribution, bad debts and costly paper.

As official printer for the colony, Bradford was under the thumb of the governor. Gagged by this official, no opposition to him could be expected to come from the *New York Gazette.* Nor was there in existence any other organ through which factions opposed to the government could express themselves, for the governor's power was still strong in New York. Rebellious colonists, therefore, resorted more and more to pamphlets in which they charged the colonial government with bribery and oppression.

Zenger's Weekly Journal: Colonial Voice

New York's second newspaper, the *Weekly Journal,* reflected the turbulent political atmosphere. Its publisher, John Peter Zenger, had been a German immigrant of ten when his mother apprenticed him to William Bradford in 1711 to learn the printing trade. In 1726 Zenger opened his own printshop in New York.

Political conditions in the colony became critical when King George appointed William Cosby as Governor of New York in 1732. Pending Governor Cosby's arrival, Rip Van Dam, a Dutch merchant, served as governor. Van Dam relinquished the office when Governor Cosby arrived but flatly refused to surrender half of his salary as demanded by the new governor. Governor Cosby, deciding to sue for the salary, ordered Chief Justice Lewis Morris to decide that the New York court should have jurisdiction over the case. Morris ruled otherwise, so Governor Cosby removed the justice from the bench! Morris then became a candidate for the colonial assembly, but an attempt was made to checkmate

Numb. 18.

THE

New-York Gazette.

From *February* 28. to Monday *March* 7. 1725-6.

Continuation of the Treaty of Commerce between the Emperor of Germany *and the King of* Spain.

Article 27.

THE Subjects on both Sides shall be allowed to chuse, at their own Pleasure, Councils, Agents, Attornies, Solicitors and Brokers.

28. In all the Ports and trading Cities which both their Majesties shall agree upon, National Consuls shall be established to protect the Merchants on both Sides, and they are to enjoy all the Rights, Authorities, Liberties and Immunities the most befriended Nations do enjoy.

29. Those Consuls shall be empowered to take Cognizance of the Differences and Disputes between the Merchants and the Masters of the Ships, and between the latter and their Crews, to decide them; so that there shall be no Appeal from their Sentence to the Judge of the Place of their Residence.

30. As to the Judges Conservators, who in the former Reigns were a considerable Magistracy in *Spain*, which the most favoured Nations were allowed to chuse for themselves, with a Power to judge peremptorily in Civil and Criminal Cases, among those of their own Nation, it has been agreed, That in case his Royal Catholick Majesty grants for the future this Privilege to any Nation, the same shall be likewise granted to his Imperial Majesty's Subjects: Mean while, impartial & speedy Justice shall be done by the ordinary Magistrates and Judges, from whose Sentences no Appeal shall be made but only to the Council of Commerce at *Madrid*.

31 The Escheat, or any Right of the like Nature, shall not be made use of with Respect to each other's Subjects, but the Heirs of the Deceased shall succeed them, either by Will or *ab Intestato*, without any Lett or Hindrance; and in Case of Dispute among two or more Heirs, the Judges of the Place are to decide the Matter peremptorily.

32. If a Merchant or other Subject of either of the contracting Parties should chance to die within the other's Dominions, the Consul or some other of their publick Ministers, if there be any, shall repair to the House of the deceased, and take an Inventory of all his Merchandizes and Effects, as likewise of his Books and Papers, in Order to secure them for the Heirs of the Deceased.

33. In case any Ship belonging to the contracting Parties or their Subjects should be wrecked upon each other's Coasts, the Fiscal Officers shall claim no Right to it, and all plundring shall be severely forbidden; moreover, Assistance is to be given to those who suffer Shipwreck, for saving and securing all they can.

34. His Catholick Majesty shall, under no Pretext whatsoever, set a limited Price to the Merchandizes belonging to his Imperial Majesty's Subjects, but they shall be at Liberty to sell them at the current Price: The same Liberty is granted to the Spanish Subjects in the Emperour's Dominions.

35. If the Effects of some of either Parties Subjects, should be confiscated, and that some Goods belonging to any other Person should happen to be among them, they shall be restored to the Owners, &c.

36. His Imperial Majesty's Ships and Subjects shall be allowed to carry and bring from the *East-Indies* into all the King of *Spain*'s Dominions, all sorts of Fruits, Effects, and Merchandizes, provided it appear, by Affidavits of the Deputies of the *India* Company established in the *Austrian Netherlands*, that they come from the conquered Places, Colonies or Factories of the said Company, in which Case they shall enjoy the same Privileges granted to the Subjects of the United Provinces, by the Royal Letters of the 27*th* of *June*, and 3d of *July* 1663: Moreover his Catholick Majesty declares, That he grants to the Imperial Subjects whatever has been granted to the States-General of the United Provinces by the Treaty in 1648, both with respect to the *Indies* and any other thing applicable to the said Treaty, as likewise to the present Peace concluded between their Majesties.

37. As to what relates to the Commerce of the *Canary-Islands*, the Imperial Subjects shall enjoy the same Advantages with the *English* and *Dutch*.

[*To be Continued in our next.*]

Remonstrance of the General Assembly of the Clergy of France, *as presented to the King, against the* New Tax *of* Two per Cent.

SIRE,

THE Clergy of *France*, who have always esteem'd it their Glory to give your Majesty, and the Kings your Predecessors, Effectual as well as publick Proofs of their most profound Submission and Obedience, find themselves constrained to accompany the new Homage, which they have the Honour to pay you this Day, with just Complaints and most humble Remonstrances.

The Edict which your Majesty has been pleas'd to publish, for raising *Two per Cent.* upon all your Subjects Estates, seems indeed not to include the

Figure 7. Organ of Officials. The *New York Gazette*, the first publication in the New York colony, was a vehicle for news and for the views of the officials. William Bradford, publisher, had left Philadelphia because of the Quaker interference. Now he was a printer to the New York colony and a conservative publisher. He printed foreign news on page one. Note New York seal at top on left and postrider, Bradford's carrier, on the right.

him. Local Quakers were refused the vote when, following their religious principles, they would not swear to the oath. Candidate Morris won the seat in the assembly anyway.

All the governor's high-handed methods, which colonists thought violated their rights, fed the fires of resentment. Justice Morris, a rich landowner, and other wealthy men who opposed the governor felt the need for presenting their side of the issues. Since the *New York Gazette,* official governmental organ, was gagged these critical colonists went to the printshop of John Peter Zenger and arranged to finance his *New York Weekly Journal,* the second newspaper in the colony. Zenger issued the *Weekly Journal* on November 5, 1733.

Aims of the newspaper, it stated, were "to expose him [the governor] and those ridiculous flatteries with which Mr. Harrison loads our other newspaper which our Governor claims and has the privilege of suffering nothing to be in but what he and Mr. Harrison approve." The Mr. Harrison mentioned was the recorder and a council member, and the paper referred to was, of course, the *New York Gazette.* News of the election of Morris and the political trickery attempted by the sheriff, an appointee of the governor, was printed in the *Journal* but not in the *Gazette.*

The *New York Weekly Journal* was the first newspaper in America to be established as an organ of a political party. This paper became popular, for it championed the cause of colonial economic and political groups opposing the governor and his council. In the *Journal* the opponents of the governor discussed liberty of the press, trial by jury and other fundamental rights of the people.

The *Journal,* on December 3, 1733, attacked Governor Cosby for permitting French warships to enter the harbor and spy on the fortifications of New York. Writers criticized the governor for allowing only a few favorite members of the New York governor's council to sit in on the meetings and declared that the official dominated the council.

Zenger also printed a letter attacking the maladministration of the governor. The *Journal* declared that he arbitrarily displaced judges and erected courts without consent of the legislature. The administration was charged with depriving freeholders of votes, as in the Morris election. The governor, further, was attacked for abusing his power in dismissing the representative assembly. The *Journal* cried out that people were about to lose their liberties and that slavery was to be imposed on New Yorkers!

Governor Cosby was enraged. He characterized the printed material as "scandalous, virulent and containing seditious reflections upon the government." The *Journal* was ordered burned in public by the common whipper. Zenger continued publication.

The chief justice then attempted to obtain an indictment against Zenger for treason, but the grand jury refused to indict him. The governor's council sought support of the assembly in prosecuting Zenger. The colonial representatives, however, would not concur in the prosecution. The council charged the printer with "raising sedition," inflaming the minds of the people and holding His Majesty's government in contempt by casting reflections on the officials.

As the grand jury had blocked prosecution, the attorney-general now filed a bill of information against Zenger. This was a legal device to bypass the grand jury. Zenger was arrested on November 17, 1734.

Unable to raise bail, he was jailed in the local lockup, where he remained for nine months. During this time the paper missed only one issue; Zenger's wife took the copy he wrote in his cell, listened to his printing directions, and with the aid of the paper's supporters issued the *Journal* regularly.

On August 4, 1735 the day of the trial, the New York courthouse was packed; among the spectators was Mrs. Zenger. Zenger's two counselors questioned the legal right of Judge Delancey to sit on the bench since he had been appointed by Governor Cosby to replace Chief Justice Morris. Defense lawyers were immediately disbarred by the enraged judge, and the case looked hopeless for Zenger. John Chambers was appointed his legal counsel and the trial continued.

While the trial was in progress, Andrew Hamilton, an eighty-one year old Philadelphian and one of the foremost and wealthiest attorneys in the colonies, appeared and acted as Zenger's lawyer. He had been secretly hired by Zenger's backers.

Hamilton maintained that publication of a truthful complaint was the right of every freeborn citizen. Zenger, he admitted, was guilty of printing the papers, but no crime, he argued, had been committed in the process.

Hamilton knew the difficulties he had to overcome to get an acquittal. It was a well-established English legal principle that the truth of a printed or spoken statement in a seditious libel against the government had nothing to do with the guilt or innocence of the accused person. In fact, it was an axiom that "the greater the truth, the greater the libel." Therefore, if John Peter Zenger had actually printed the utterances against the government, no matter how much evidence he had for his statements, he was guilty. And English law declared *that the jury could decide only the facts in the case,* that is, whether Zenger published the newspaper containing the libel. The *judge alone had the right to decide whether the articles were libelous.*

Brilliant attorney Hamilton argued that the English law regarding "the greater the truth, the greater the libel" should be set aside. Judge Delancey overruled this point on the usual grounds, the request was contrary to English law. Then Hamilton insisted that the *jury should have a right to decide whether the statements were true or false.* The attorney was bold enough to assert that English law did not apply in America. He argued that unless men could tell the truth about governments, people would have no way to redress wrongs.

In addressing the jury, Hamilton finally declared:

> The question before the Court and you, Gentlemen of the Jury, is not of small or private concern. It is not the cause of the poor printer, nor of New York alone which you are trying. No! It may, on its consequences, affect every freeman that lives under a British government, on the mainland of America. . . .
>
> As old and weak as I am, it is my duty, to go to the utmost part of the land, if my service would be of any use, to stop prosecutions set on foot by government, to deprive people of the right of remonstrating and complaining against the arbitrary actions of men in power.
>
> It is the best cause; it is the cause of Liberty, and I may not doubt but your upright conduct, this day, will not only entitle you to the love and esteem of your fellow-citizens, but every man who prefers freedom to a life of slavery, will bless any attempt of tyranny.

These were strong, emotionally charged statements, constituting attacks on the Crown. But, in spite of Hamilton's eloquence, the judge's instructions to the jury were to find a verdict of "guilty" or "not guilty" purely in respect to the question of whether Zenger actually had published the statements referred to. The jury, however, brought in a verdict of "not guilty." The jury said, in effect, that *Zenger had a right to publish what he pleased.*

Zenger became a hero and for a time was given the job as public printer of New York and New Jersey. He died in 1746, but the *Journal* was continued by his widow and son, John, for five years before expiring.

Zenger's trial did much to determine the right of colonial newspapers to criticize the government. As this right was not established in the colonies by law, the immediate legal effect of the case should not be overestimated. The trial *did set, however, a legal precedent for other cases of printers and publishers* because the case received excellent publicity through reprinted news articles and pamphlets. Similar cases may have been tried, but attention was focused on this one. A publisher had dared defy the government!

Although an information, or indictment was filed against Zenger, a jury had refused to convict. Other juries in later cases followed this precedent and would not convict printers. The Zenger trial had indirectly warned the governors not to attempt to gag the press. The press now could mirror changing economic interests and political views of the colonial party. And, as an agency of control, the newspaper could fight the colonists' battles.

Other precedents were set by the trial. It did much to break down the legal rule that the jury could not decide the question of whether the printer published a seditious libel. This was important for it gave the jury greater power in press and free speech cases than ever before.

The second contention of Hamilton, that the truth should determine whether printed statements were seditious libel, was not established as an official law until almost sixty years later.

A significant aspect of the Zenger case was that the colonial commercial and political groups in time of trouble and controversy turned to the newspaper's news columns and its political essays. Lifting of censorship and possible reprisal made publishing less hazardous. Colonial printers with less to fear launched new publishing enterprises.

The Zenger trial was brought to the attention of many persons in the colonies and in England. The story was printed in journals along the American coast, and pamphlets giving the entire case were issued by many printers. After reading about the case, many colonists recognized the Zenger trial as a test of strength, a test not only of the press but of their own interests and colonial rights.

News and comments about Zenger stirred resentment against the Crown and gave the colonists courage. Outcome of the trial strengthened the colonists' critical opposition to England. The Zenger case contributed to the fight to establish certain constitutional principles—freedom of the press, independence of the judiciary, freedom of elections and independence of the jury—all of which were later incorporated into the United States Constitution. Principles expressed in the Declaration of Independence were the results of a century of colonial developments. Zenger aided in that development. The American Revolution could not have been won had not men like Zenger prepared the way for it by challenging the might of a tyrannical government.

Other New York Papers Begin

Bradford's *New York Gazette* died in 1743, but two new journals were launched in its place by printers who had been apprenticed to William Bradford. Chief claim for one of these, the *New York Evening Post,* was that it was the first evening newspaper printed in New York.

TABLE 4

Milestones in Fight for Free Press in American Colonies

I. License Power Period (1600-1696)

1. English king had license power; passed on to governors in colonies
    - a. William Bradford, 1692, harassed; case dropped, settled out of court
2. Parliament refuses to renew license in England (1695)
3. Colonial governors now lost power to license (control before publication)

II. Governors Could Prosecute for Seditious Libel after Publication (1695-)

1. Governor had certain powers:
    - a. Could punish for seditious libel
    - b. Could seek to get grand jury indictment (cumbersome; and jury may not indict)
    - c. Could file Bill of Information through his attorney-general, bringing case directly to trial
2. English law stated:
    - a. Jury decided whether libel had been printed
    - b. Judge determined whether material was libelous or not
    - c. "Truth is not a defense" was prevailing legal principle

III. Governor Attempted to Renew License Power in Courant Case (1723)

1. Governor attempted to invoke old license power, but House of Representatives denied it and defied him
2. Governor asked for license power but formally refused by house
3. Governor ordered James Franklin to refrain from seditious libel; Franklin defied the order and was sent to jail
4. Grand jury, although requested, refused to indict Franklin; no genuine court test yet
5. Result of the Franklin incident showed growth of colonial and newspaper publisher's independence

TABLE 4 (continued)

IV. New York Weekly Journal Test Case (1733-35)

1. Information filed by attorney-general with charge of seditious libel against Zenger
2. Jury declared John Peter Zenger not guilty
3. Trial established precedent for future cases of free speech and free press
4. Afterwards, governors could not get grand jury indictments against printers for seditious libel
   a. Governors knew they could not get convictions, even through informations filed directly by their attorney-generals
5. Basic law of libel not affected
   a. Prosecution after publication; judge decided on question of libel; jury determined only if libel was published or not

V. Colonial Assemblies Upheld Independent Printers and Newspaper Publishers (1735-1783)

VI. Law Establishing Free Press Principles Established Much Later (1785-)

1. In England, new libel act passed in 1792
   a. Truth became a defense in libel suits
2. In America constitutions of new states after revolution guaranteed free press (1785-)
3. First amendment to federal constitution provided for no abridgement of freedom of speech
4. Alien and sedition actions (1797-98) provided for truth as a defense in libel cases
   a. Acts lapsed in 1800; return to old principle
5. Cromwell Case, in 1804, sought to establish truth as a defense, with jury deciding both fact of publication and libel
   a. Case lost, but drew much attention and led to action by state legislators
6. State legislatures enact both Cromwell Case principles into law
   a. Foundation laid for U. S. libel law

The second, the *New York Weekly Post-Boy,* was issued by James Parker, who, from 1747 to 1748, became involved in a quarrel between Governor Clinton and the assembly. The governor objected to Parker's publication of the assembly's side of the controversy and rebuked him. Parker published the news anyway and was vindicated by the assembly, a further example of the growing power of the press and the esteem with which it was being held.

NEWSPAPERS SPREAD TO THE SOUTH

Press Reflects Southern Living

Maryland, Virginia and South Carolina reached the point in their social and economic development where they could support gazettes before the mideighteenth century. Their format and makeup were like the Boston, New York and Philadelphia journals. Southern weeklies carried foreign and domestic news, particularly information about agricultural crops, tobacco and rice. Because southern seaports were not as active as Boston's, the press did not carry as much shipping news as found in papers of that northern capital.

Southern newspapers, however, differed chiefly from those in the North in their stress on cultural and social news. Publishers were aware that in order to be successful their papers had to appeal to the aristocratic, wealthy, pleasure-loving planters as well as to their wives, who, with slaves to do the work, had time to cultivate the arts and read the news. Entertainment was on a more lavish scale. The governors, who lived in the capitals, set the standards. This southern social life, including long accounts of marriages of the socially prominent, was duly reported in the gazettes.

Because southerners enjoyed horse racing, their gazettes gave space to this sport. The local weeklies also published reviews for their theatre-loving readers. Thus, local conditions caused regional variations of the press.

Maryland's First Paper

In 1726 William Parks descended from the boat, which had just borne him from England, and walked up the main street of Annapolis. Annapolis, with its excellent harbor, was the leading community in the Maryland colony. Although it had had printers for forty years, on and off, it never had a newspaper.

Parks had previous newspaper experience in England; now he was in America as public printer to the Maryland colony. He began publication of the first southern newspaper, the *Maryland Gazette,* on September 19, 1729. In his *Maryland Gazette,* Parks printed both sides of all controversies, especially those relating to disputes between tobacco planters and their English commission merchants who sold products for them. His reporting of the conflict between Lord Baltimore, proprietor of the colony, and the local residents irritated the gentleman, and the governmental heel was put on Parks' press. After 1730 Parks printed few of these disputes, indicating that restrictions were still harassing the southern printers.

Distinguishing features which raised Parks' paper above the level of other newspapers of the time were his literary articles, philosophical essays and poetry. Publisher Parks imported from England two innovations to colonial journalism. First, he adopted the English practice of giving a specific title to periodical essays, heading those in the *Maryland Gazette,* "The Plain Dealer." This device featured one writer and created a serial interest in his work over a period of time. This method was widely copied in other colonial newspapers. Parks' second innovation was use of new journalistic forms. Fables, allegories, legends and fairy tales were having their day in England. These were sermons in disguise: warning against vice and other evils, praising virtue and morality. No doubt much of this journalistic writing was reprinted or adapted from English publications, but a considerable portion was produced by Parks or his local contributors. When material in the *Maryland Gazette* is considered together with the prose and poetry of the *Virginia Gazette* and the *South Carolina Gazette,* the score for the southern papers reveals a high literary standard.

Parks eventually found the restrictions on his paper obnoxious. His debts increased. Receiving a good offer in Virginia, Parks closed his Maryland paper in 1735.

For ten years Maryland was without a newspaper. Then, on January 17, 1745, Jonas Green, who had worked on both Andrew Bradford's *Mercury* and Benjamin Franklin's *Pennsylvania Gazette,* issued another *Maryland Gazette.* Four years later Green took William Rind into partnership with him, and their paper continued through the revolutionary period.

Virginia Falls Into Line: Virginia Gazette

Parks was lured to Williamsburg, Virginia, when he was offered the job of public printer at the salary of 200 pounds of tobacco a year. Williamsburg, with a population of about five thousand, was a political, cultural and social center rather than a commercial metropolis or hub of export-import activity. Tobacco was shipped to England directly from the wharves of the planters; consequently, Williamsburg did not develop into the bustling commercial metropolis that Boston, New York or Philadelphia did. Williamsburg was the seat of the second college in America, William and Mary, established in 1693.

Parks issued his first *Virginia Gazette* on August 6, 1736. Situated in the Virginia capital, Park's *Gazette* naturally contained much news of the legislature and royal governor. In addition to the usual social news published by the other southern papers, the *Virginia Gazette* also gave much space to the Virginia Sweepstakes Race and cock fighting, the principal sports of the day. The little paper also devoted regular notices to plays at the Williamsburg theater. Prose and poetry filled Parks' columns, in fact, often taking precedence over news on the front page.

Parks continued his *Virginia Gazette* until the middle of the century, when he died almost penniless. Immediately another *Virginia Gazette,* published by a new group of printers, appeared to take its place.

South Carolina Gets First Paper

Charleston, South Carolina, a busy seaport for West Indies and English shipping, produced its first newspaper a few years earlier. Charleston's streets were colorful with sailors and ship officers and crowds of traders. All this commercial activity meant news and advertisements. In Charleston's muddy streets also was heard much political discussion, for it was the capital of this southern colony. South Carolina's population increased from five thousand in 1700 to about sixty thousand in 1750 when Charleston had seven thousand inhabitants.

By 1731 Charleston boasted three printers, a bookbinder and an engraver. Eleazar Phillips, a New England printer, had come to South Carolina as the official printer for this province. Eleazar Phillips, Jr., his son, soon after began to publish the *South Carolina Gazette.* The paper suffered many vicissitudes, since the successive publishers lived only a short time. Benjamin Franklin backed several of these printers financially. Elizabeth Timothy, widow of Lewis Timothy, became the first woman editor, publishing the paper after her husband's death. There appeared to be a need for the little journal, for in spite of the death of its publishers the *South Carolina Gazette* survived.

During this time the *South Carolina Gazette* published shipping lists, court news and foreign news, as did its northern contemporaries;

it catered to, reflected and stimulated the community's agricultural and trade interests. In the absence of farm newspapers and magazines, the *Gazette* also served the agricultural functions of specialized journals.

The *South Carolina Gazette* was rich in advertising. Announcements of sales of all sorts of products, including the seeds of the indigo plant, appeared. Books published in Franklin's shop were also advertised. As midcentury approached, advertisements multiplied. Sometimes two pages of announcements appeared; and, occasionally, the advertising amounted to more than 65 per cent of the paper. This growth showed the need for a medium for farmers, shippers and tradesmen to advertise their wares and services.

The *Gazette* also mirrored the cultural activities of Charleston. The paper contained a considerable amount of literary material, reprints from English magazines and newspapers. A study shows that the amount of this material was unusually large. Like the *Maryland Gazette,* the *South Carolina Gazette* appealed to the aristocratic wives and daughters of southern planters.

Interest in the theater was considerable, and, here again, an attempt at original literature was made.

PRODUCING THE NEWSPAPER

To produce these gazettes, courants and journals, the publisher-printer had simple equipment and tools. Colonial printing was in the small craftshop stage with all the machinery being hand-operated. The printing press, however, was an early mass-production machine, turning out duplicate copies faster, cheaper and in greater quantities than a publisher could have produced by writing each copy by hand with a quill. The printer also faced problems of securing supplies, such as ink, paper and new fonts of type. As his business expanded, he needed to secure printers to help him.

Built of wood, the colonial press was a cabinetmaker's product, simply constructed. The press was hand-operated. The apprentice used two big deerskin balls to ink the type. He placed a sheet of paper on top of the type. Next he pushed the forms containing the type into the middle of the press between the upright wooden beams. Now the apprentice pulled an iron lever which forced a heavy plate, or platen against the paper resting on top of the type.

The "printer's devil," as the apprentice was called, pulled back the lever and removed the printed sheet. He then hung it up to dry. When dry, the paper was turned over and placed on the press again; a second

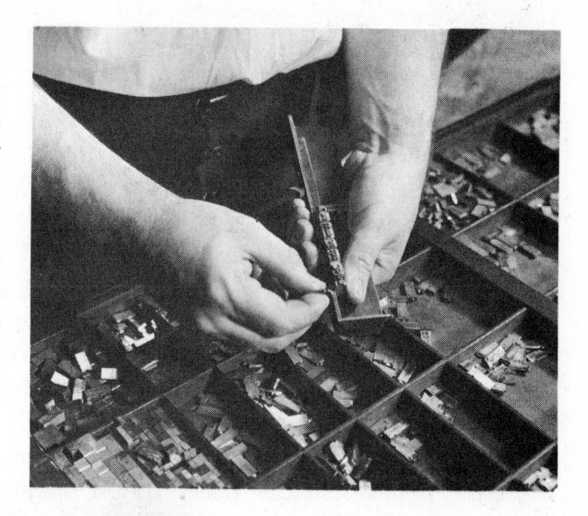

Figure 8a. Setting Type by Hand. The colonial printer, as his ancestors since Gutenberg's day, set type by hand. The printer had to pick up each letter and fit it into his "stick," a small printer's device made of metal, to hold a line of type firmly. He then transferred the type to an iron frame. (Courtesy Colonial Williamsburg, Williamsburg, Va.)

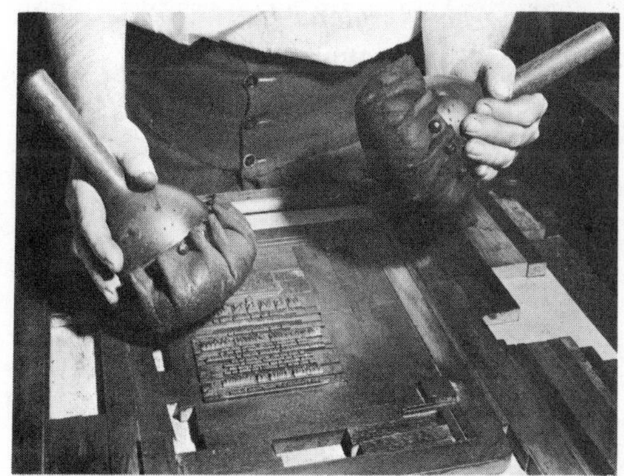

Figure 8b. Inking the Form. The printer or his apprentice inked the form, or frame of type with a deerskin dauber. His motions with two daubers were rapid, but the ink had to be put on smoothly for attractive printing. (Courtesy Colonial Williamsburg, Williamsburg, Va.)

Figure 8c. Printing the Newspaper. The entire page form was transferred to the press for the final printing stage. The printer pulled the lever which pushed the iron plate, or platen against the paper and the type. He could produce two hundred to two hundred fifty impressions an hour. The paper was hung up to dry and then printed on the opposite side. (Courtesy Colonial Williamsburg, Williamsburg, Va.)

impression was made on the reverse side of the sheet. The printer produced two hundred fifty impressions an hour, waited for them to dry and then printed two hundred fifty more impressions.

All the type was set by hand by a compositor. The colonial printer had difficulty in getting the necessary type. Typefaces wore out regularly, and the newspaper often showed the results in poor printing. In the first half of the eighteenth century, type had to be imported from England; native typecasters had not yet learned the art. Some printers cast their own type, but it was a tedious job.

Cost of equipping a printshop in the colonial period varied depending on whether the press and equipment were new or secondhand and also on the amount of type in the shop.

Printshops were generally characterized as one-press, two-press and three-press shops. Three-press shops, such as Franklin and Hall later had, meant that a large and flourishing printing business was being conducted. On an average, cost of various shops were:

One-press shop .... 85 £ sterling
Two-press shop ....160 £ sterling
Three-press shop ....236 £ sterling

A secondhand press could be obtained for about 50£.

Though colonial money hardly can be compared in purchasing power with money of later periods, it was relatively inexpensive to establish a printshop and publish a newspaper in colonial days, if this cost is compared to the thousands, then the hundreds of thousands, and the millions of dollars required in later periods in metropolitan centers. Though the 85 £ needed for a small shop may have loomed large to an apprentice, or journeyman with ambitions, many printers often did accumulate enough money to start their own shops. Journeymen also borrowed from entrepreneurs, such as Benjamin Franklin, to begin printing businesses.

Securing raw materials, such as paper and ink, was one of the acute problems colonial printers and newspaper publishers faced. During the seventeenth and eighteenth centuries, the printer's supply of paper came largely from England. In 1693 in Germantown, Pennsylvania, William Rittenhouse, experienced German papermaker, established his paper mill on a creek. Very slowly, paper mills were started in other colonies whenever the demand grew sufficient. New England obtained its first mill in 1728. Other colonies followed.

In spite of establishment of various mills, there was a constant scarcity of paper. Printers and publishers began to go into the papermaking business to supply themselves with paper. Papermaking even then did not keep pace with growing demands. English dealers wanted to sell to the colonies but could not supply enough paper. Linen rags, from which paper was made, were hard to get. Housewives did not have rag bags to save scraps. Thrifty women threw away only a few scraps. Newspaper publishers had to exhort and appeal to colonial housewives to save their rags. By holding contests and offering premiums and prizes, printers sought to stimulate rag saving.

Paper manufacturers were also faced with the problem of getting proper equipment. Vats, pots and a few knives were the simple tools for making paper, but these were scarce. Skilled labor was required, and for many years trained men were not available. Because of scarcity of paper and its high cost, newspaper publishers were restricted in the number of pages they printed.

Another important raw material was ink, and printers also imported it from England until local factories were started. Ingredients of ink were lampblack and linseed or flaxseed. Lampblack had an unpleasant smell. Much labor was required to make it. The printer, therefore, purchased the lampblack ready-made if he could and then did the mixing himself. In his spare time the printer's devil churned the ingredients.

Like other colonial businesses, printing was in the household stage, and wives and children, both boys and girls, helped operate the shop. If women could weave cloth and tan leather, they could set type. When their husbands died, widows of the publishers carried on the printing for many years.

The publisher supplemented his own and his female relatives' work with that of an apprentice, usually a neighbor's son. This was the chief source of labor supply outside his own sons. Some apprentices began to learn types when they were six-years old; others began at twelve. Contracts ran until the boys were twenty-one years old.

Frequently, conditions of work for the apprentice were bad. Poor and meager food, cruelty of the printshop proprietor, long hours, severe work and menial service all irked the printers' devils. Runaway apprentices were commonplace. Many found the highway more pleasant than their masters' dingy shops.

Value of the apprenticeship arrangement was undeniable, however. It was the only way to learn in the absence of vocational schools. While boarding and clothing the boy, the printer agreed to teach the mystery of his art in exchange for the apprentice's services. Almost all famous colonial printers and publishers secured their training in this fashion. Labor costs were the most important item in the publishers' expense account. Throughout the colonial period, securing of skilled printers was one serious problem the publishers faced. The apprenticeship system helped the publisher solve this problem. Journeymen from England were hired later. Experienced printers worked nine hours daily, fifty-four hours weekly. They earned eight dollars for a week's work. Employer-employee relationships in the small printshops were close and personal; consequently, there was little class stratification. Printers' unions were organized at the end of the colonial period.

FIFTY-YEAR SUMMARY SHOWS NEWSPAPER GROWTH (1700-1750)

Developing from the increase in population, expanding economy and emergence of a native culture, growth of the newspaper was steady during the first half of the eighteenth century. The newspaper had won a measure of publication freedom which made it easier for alert printers to establish and operate the journals.

Only one newspaper was being published in 1704; by 1725 five papers had appeared in three colonies. Although some of the weeklies had been started but died, by 1750 a 100 per cent increase was recorded, with twelve newspapers being issued in six colonies.

Newspapers not only reflected the economic, political, cultural and population growth of the English colonies along the Atlantic seaboard; the press also stimulated business, spurred political independence and contributed to the cultural advancement of the emerging Americans.

Chapter 2

The Revolutionary Press

NEWSPAPERS EXPAND AS COLONIES DEVELOP (1750–)

After 1750 colonial population multiplied and economic and cultural life expanded at a more rapid rate. After 1765 the country's temper became revolutionary, the air tense with excitement. All the submerged resentments, all the quiet conflicts that before seeped occasionally above the surface, now became openly articulate and swollen. When they finally burst, they swept the colonies into war. Newspapers, as expressions and stimulants of the conflict, played a significant role in the era.

As the revolutionary temper mounted, newspaper publishers were drawn into the conflict. They lined up on the colonial side or in the British camp, depending on (1) their own background, (2) clientele to which they appealed, (3) amount of money received from the British government. The British government recognized the value of the press in influencing colonial public opinion and spent, it was said, 50,000 guineas on American newspaper publishers and pamphleteer writings in 1780. In the following year twice as much was spent, according to one of the Patriot gazettes.

In some instances publishers tried to straddle the conflict and succeeded in doing so until the British or Patriots learned their tactics. Sharpening issues demanded that definite sides be taken, and as the spirit of the revolution sparked and tension became acute, clear decisions had to be made. "Tory or Patriot? Which?" the excited colonists demanded.

After the midcentury the newspapers multiplied. They increased in the colonies where they had been established already, and they spread to the few remaining colonies which did not have journals. Some centers, such as Boston, had as many as eight newspapers. In 1750 twelve newspapers were being published on the seaboard; in 1775 there were forty-eight.

The average circulation doubled, reaching about five hundred. In the critical war years after 1765, some papers in the larger towns recorded circulations between one thousand and three thousand. This metamorphosis was not an overnight change. There were twenty-five years of development from midcentury to the opening of the Revolutionary War, as Table 5 shows:

TABLE 5

Colonial Newspaper Growth Accelerates

Date	Number of Newspapers	
1703	0	
1704	1	
1725	5	
1740	12	
1750	12	
1764	24	
1770	29	Period of War Tension;
1774	37	Stamp Act Passed 1765;
1775	48	New Papers Sprang up

Not only did newspapers increase in number and circulation, but they were published more often. Not one semiweekly had been successfully established by the middle of the century, although some were attempted. During the next few decades, semiweeklies, triweeklies and even a daily were founded, though the latter, not succssfully. Expanding business conditions, greater flow of news caused by the establishment of newspapers in other colonies, the desire of readers to get the vital news more quickly, all produced more frequent publication. Now, even postscripts and extraordinaries (EXTRAS) were issued. Many newspapers increased their page size. This was a result of the increasing flow of news and the expanding number of advertisements resulting from the development of trade and commerce.

Newspaper methods were altered. Publishers introduced newspaper techniques they had not tried, or which they attempted only sporadically before. Political essays, crusades, cartoons and even headlines were instituted to serve the newspaper's editorial purpose more effectively.

The growth of newspapers in the third quarter of the century can be attributed to a number of social and economic conditions and to changes within the newspaper business.

Population of each of the colonies grew, and the total population of the embryonic nation jumped from 1.2 million persons in 1750 to 2.5 million at the opening of the war with England. The ever-increasing population demanded more newspapers, and more newspapers grew. During the war subscriptions increased nine times as fast as before the conflict began.

Catering to the merchants, farmers, shippers, fishermen, and depending on them for advertising and subscriptions, the colonial newspaper kept pace with the prosperity of these farmers and businessmen. All along the seaboard, agriculture, industry, shipbuilding, fishing, foreign and domestic commerce accelerated after the middle of the eighteenth century, but growth was not at a uniform rate throughout all the colonies.

Nevertheless, expansion of American capitalism was one of the notable characteristics of this period. Many enterprising merchants, manufacturers and planters made more money than they could use in the purchase of consumption goods, such as food, shelter and clothing, for themselves. They turned their surpluses into capital goods: ships, tools, mills, iron furnaces and land. This commercial activity meant that money was being ploughed back into business to expand the economy.

Agriculture continued to expand and pour forth rich and abundant harvests. Growth of the colonial population by natural increase and by immigration, along with constant demand for farm products in Europe and the West Indies, created a need for larger crops of foodstuffs, and, of course, tobacco. Colonists now pushed back the line of settlement from the coast. They cleared the land and cultivated more acreage with improved farming methods. Wherever possible, settlers followed rich river valleys which provided easy waterway navigation to the East.

Certain industries, which had secured only a foothold in previous years, forged ahead. Partnerships were formed to build larger shops and to purchase more machinery for mills, ironworks, distilleries, breweries and furnaces. The leather industry went from home to shop for production of leather goods, particularly shoes. The production of rum, which continued to be New England's chief manufacturing industry, expanded.

Merchants in seaboard towns profited particularly by the general improvement of American business. Many merchants in these thriving towns owned both ocean-going ships and coastal vessels in which they brought cargoes from foreign lands and from other American colonies. Retail stores multiplied. Weavers, tailors, cabinetmakers and carpenters, who had been in business before, expanded. New craftsmen opened stores to catch the growing trade.

Truly, American business, in spite of many temporary setbacks, was expanding. Newspapers, as in the previous century, fed on this business system and its prosperity. This was reflected as indicated in (1) the increase in the number of newspapers being issued, (2) the expansion of newspaper circulation, (3) the multiplication of advertising. Printers also enlarged the page size of weeklies and stepped up the frequency of their publication to semiweeklies and triweeklies.

The press helped promote the commerce and prosperity of the new Americans. Through its news columns, its list of ships clearing and entering and its notes about the West Indies, colonial newspapers acquainted businessmen with facts and information pertinent and valuable to their commercial enterprises. As a part of the machinery of economic distribution, newspaper advertisements helped sell farm products as well as merchandise of retail stores. Some advertisements helped catch runaway slaves, part of the labor force. Feature articles on fire prevention, hempmaking, and rice and indigo planting aided business and agriculture. Newspaper circulation was relatively small compared to that in later periods, but colonial papers reached the more enterprising businessmen and farmers who recognized the publications' news and advertising value.

An important factor in the acceleration of the economic system was improvement of intercolonial land transportation and communication; these facilities were identical then. Improvement of transportation services began toward the middle of the century, many travelers commenting favorably on the roads which were cleared through the forests and made more passable, while stronger bridges were constructed. Horses traveled about 8 miles per hour. Still it took two days to travel from New York to Philadelphia. A new epoch came with the establishment of stagecoach and boat lines, running on regular schedules and carrying passengers at moderate rates. James Wells, for instance, undertook the operation of a combined stage and boat line twice a week between New York and Philadelphia. One or two other routes were added, and in 1757 the line was extended to Annapolis. Travel by water became easier with increased size of the vessels.

The postal system, on which the newspaper depended for gathering news and for distributing finished papers, was now overhauled. How much of this improvement was a result of nagging by publishers is hard to say. Postmasters in Boston and elsewhere who were or had been newspaper publishers wanted better service. The postmaster-publishers actually improved service in some instances.

Most important of the postmaster-publishers was Benjamin Franklin, appointed in 1753 Deputy Postmaster General, jointly with William Hunter of Virginia, also a publisher. To make the trip between Philadelphia and Boston before had required six weeks, and in winter the post set out fortnightly. Franklin, the new postmaster, established weekly posts and cut delivery time in half. By 1757, during the summer, the mails passed between New York and Philadelphia twice a week and were used more frequently than ever before. Franklin was interested in developing the postal service not only for the commercial benefit of the country but for the advantage which would accrue to newspapers. By 1775 a complete chain of post offices existed between Portsmouth, New Hampshire and Williamsburg, Virginia.

When Franklin came into office no rates had been established for newspapers and no provision had been made in the postal laws for carrying them. He saw it would be better if newspaper publishers paid for carrying their weeklies. Hitherto, postmasters who also published newspapers compelled postal riders to take only their own newspapers, keeping out rival journals. Now, if publishers paid the fee, the rider was forced to admit the papers to his bag. Riders, seeing commercial advantage, were apt to make exorbitant charges on subscribers for delivering their papers.

Franklin solved these difficulties by establishing a definite newspaper rate in 1758. For newspapers not going over 50 miles, the rate was nine pence sterling per year; for 50 to 100 miles, one shilling six pence. Proportionate rates were charged for papers going further. The effect on the newspaper of laying out new routes, increasing the regularity of postal service and standardizing rates can be readily understood. Franklin permitted publishers to exchange issues free of any postal charge for carrying them.

Many educational and cultural activities of the colonists made headway between midcentury and the outbreak of the revolution, and these had their effects on the newspaper.

Educationally, the colonists continued their advance. More private academies and elementary schools were established. Colleges were founded in eight of the ten colonies north of the Carolinas by the 1780s. The developing educational agencies helped diminish illiteracy and hence to produce more newspaper readers. Educational institutions, particularly the colleges, also furnished writers for the Patriot and Tory newspapers. Samuel Adams, M.A., from Harvard, became an outstanding newspaper writer of the revolutionary period; and many others with college degrees penned Patriot essays.

With pioneering days well behind them and with more leisure, money and education, colonists bounded forward in many cultural activ-

TABLE 6

Establishment of American Colleges Before the Revolution

1636 Harvard (Mass.)	1751 Pennsylvania
1693 College of William & Mary (Va.)	1754 King's (Columbia) (N. Y.)
1701 Yale (Conn.)	1764 Brown (R. I.)
1746 Princeton (N. J.)	1770 Dartmouth (N. H.)
1749 Washington & Lee (Va.)	

ities. A greater demand was generated for reading matter. This resulted, in part, because of the heating and lighting devices. The Franklin stove and the spermaceti candles, made from whales, were such improvements. Colonists thus began to read more. With their intense interest in religion diminishing, they turned to political and economic affairs, to literature and to the newspaper. Numerous excellent private libraries with a variety of books existed.

In music, the theatre, painting and other arts, activity of this period was marked. Plays and concerts were advertised in the local press, and contributors stimulated interest in these cultural pursuits by writing their criticism for the local gazettes. The newspaper thus profited by the general cultural progress, and publishers, in turn, aided this development by publishing news, advertisements and reviews.

Also reflecting cultural growth were the new magazines started at this time. They will be discussed in a later section.

A number of strands had been weaving the colonists together for some years. Colonists in the previous century lived in isolated settlements. In such communities they had no bonds of sympathy or of interest with neighboring seaboard colonists since little trade and only limited transportation and communication facilities existed. Now the webs of trade and cultural ties bound them together. The newspaper served to link the colonists more closely because it was a regular means of printed communication. The newspaper told news about people in other colonies who became acquainted with each other. This regular communication of printed news had begun as early as Campbell's *Boston News-Letter* in 1704.

Newspapers also helped prepare the way for the cooperative effort needed in the American Revolution. Newspapers, pouring from the presses weekly, filled with political essays and news, told what was happening in other communities and acquainted the colonists with each other's problems and conflicts with the Crown. The bitter political essays were reprinted widely, and leaders in the colonies kept in touch with revolutionary thought elsewhere.

Because of the newspaper, the colonists' problems appeared to be similar; their fights with the royal governors, and finally with the Crown, seemed identical. The press helped develop "a consciousness of kind," an emotional, intellectual and economic sympathy for distant colonies. The many newspapers aided in unifying the thirteen separate colonies into one nation and in promoting the social solidarity required for a war of revolt.

Newspaper Problems and Advances

Colonial publishers had certain favorable factors which aided in the growth of their newspapers. Newsmen also faced certain problems in getting the news, printing the newspaper and distributing it.

During this period the principle of a free press was more firmly established and led to further growth of the press. The colonists and their representative assemblies increasingly recognized the need for newspapers which would fight their battles. In all conflicts with the Crown's agents, the Patriots supported the newspaper publishers. The British governor and his council understood the temper of the people and made few attempts to punish contrary publishers for sedition or libel. When such attempts were made, grand juries refused to indict, and court juries would not find verdicts of guilty.

As the revolutionary tide came to a crest, the Crown lost all control over newspapers with Patriot sympathies. Elimination of this important obstacle to publication of newspapers encouraged more publishers and political groups to establish gazettes and gave them broader leeway in printing news and essays of a controversial character. Further interest in the newspaper thus was aroused because it contained information of significance and value and was not a pale reflection of the British officials' views. The newspaper publisher was not rid of all attempts to control him, however. Freedom from British punishment, nevertheless, was gained in greater measure than before. Local Patriot groups still sought to restrict publishers' freedom.

To understand the growth of the newspaper, an additional factor, tension created by the Revolutionary War, must be added to the foregoing factors. The colonial newspaper thrived on new conflict-situations. The journals were in demand when people wanted news involving matters with which they were vitally concerned. The preliminary Stamp Act controversy of 1764 to 1765 jabbed them sharply: emotionally, politically, commercially. News acquired a new and more acute significance. The situation and feeling were heightened immediately before the outbreak of hostilities. The war news itself, of course, meant to the colonists, life or death: the prevailing of American freedom or the continuation of English control over the political and commercial life of the colonies. The war was the first great news event for the American newspaper to report. Subscriptions jumped.

Newspapers were pulled violently into this vortex of news events. Newspapers presented news; they gave opinions about news. The papers reported startling events. Publishers could not hold aloof in scornful disdain. The newspaper could be utilized as an agency to sway others: British Tory or American Patriot. The effect of all this was vitalizing to gazettes, journals and mercuries everywhere.

As new newspapers were launched in each of the colonies, the problems of gathering news lessened. The postrider, or mail coach arriving in town more frequently brought a constant flow of exchanges as well as travelers from other provinces. All this contributed to a steadier flow of news.

Still other factors within the newspaper industry operated favorably for the rapid growth of publications. With continued expansion of the colonial population and commerce and consequent development of job printing and newspaper publication, the need for paper became sharper. As a result, paper mills multiplied in Pennsylvania, and they developed in other colonies where they had not been attempted before.

Boycott of English goods in 1765 slowed or completely stopped the importation of paper. Now, colonial assemblies encouraged establishment of mills and purchase of locally made paper. When the revolution began ten years later, a sharp paper stringency was produced. Newspaper publishers faced troublesome paper shortages. Legislative and army officials needed paper for correspondence, military and legislative orders, documents and records. General Washington recognized the paper need; consequently, he freed certain papermakers and skilled artisans from military duty so that they could continue their business.

PRINTERS ON THE MOVE

In moving from town to town printers were motivated by various considerations. If there were no printer in the new settlement, economic opportunity beckoned. Some colonies had a more favorable intellectual climate and a more liberal attitude toward printers. A yearning for change and adventure lured some printers to new communities. The possibility of securing financial backing from the governor or from merchants led other printers to establish papers. When apprentices were beaten or in other ways badly treated by their masters, the young printers watched for an opportunity to slip away, and did so.

Although a variety of individual motivations existed, the migrant printers had the enduring effect of spreading the use of the printing press. The printers gained fame and prestige from publishing newspapers; the publishers became important members of the community, often influencing the economic and political destinies of the colonists.

High tribute should be paid to the colonial tramp printers. Arriving in a colony with a press to establish his shop and newspaper, each printer brought enlightenment and information wherever he hung his printing shop sign. The weekly newspaper publishers kept colonists in touch with the mother country and with other American communities. The publishers offered to the storekeepers and craftsmen a regularly printed media for the sale of their products and services. Moreover, when the printer-publishers established their four-page papers, primitive though they were by modern standards, the publications afforded literary-minded and politically-inclined citizens the opportunity to express themselves in writing.

In the early eighteenth century printers imported their presses from England. These were expensive and the freight charges were high. It was not until 1750 that Christopher Sower, mechanical genius, made his own press in Germantown, Pennsylvania, probably copying English models. He fashioned the press for his own use. Nineteen years later, in 1769, the first American press was made to be sold. It was made by Isaac Doolittle for William Goddard, Connecticut publisher. Now, others turned to the trade of building presses in Philadelphia and in Hartford, Connecticut.

Development of local typecasting was also accelerated after the turn of the midcentury, particularly when the colonists' boycott of English goods began. In the 1750s Adam Bell, Connecticut silversmith, experimented with typecasting, but it was not until 1768 that he received a loan from the local assembly for a foundry. Other typecasters soon began to supply the demand. Christopher Sower, Jr., established the first successful foundry in 1770. During the war, colonial assemblies recommended that American types be bought.

The newspaper by its subscriptions and advertising produced a small income for the printer; he supplemented this with governmental and commercial printing. Bad debts (subscribers who did not pay) plagued him. With the rising economic trend of the country reflected in increased subscriptions and advertisements, the printer-publisher likewise gained and received more income, although his business was still limited.

Uniformities and Differences Develop

Uniformities developed throughout the newspaper institution along the colonial seaboard because various groups in the colonies had similar political, economic and cultural interests; because the methods for gathering, printing and distributing news were similar; because techniques and traditions for writing and presenting news and comment were alike. The content of one newspaper, therefore, bore striking resemblances to the content of others; publishers reprinted from each other and from the same foreign publications.

In spite of general similarities, distinguishing characteristics could be noted in the various papers. Many groups in the colonies developed specialized economic and political problems or distinctive cultural and religious backgrounds and attitudes, which, when reported, gave newspapers different flavors. These issues often split towns, causing differences in the community's newspapers. Regional differences, such as those in the South, led to additional press variations.

Difference of a sharp character developed particularly after 1765, based largely on the split between the Tory and Patriot publishers who, in turn, reflected economic and political conflicts. Within each political group, further differences appeared. Front page symbols, occasional illustrations and other typographical devices produced further variation. Ability and training of publishers and printers also caused differences to appear in their newspapers.

Newspapers' External Structure Differentiates from Political State

Not only did the internal organization of the newspaper as a social institution alter, but simultaneously the external structure began to separate from the political institution, the government. With the royal governor in power, the newspaper was closely identified with the state. From the Crown's executive, the printers derived income as well as authority to print a newspaper.

With expansion of business, new printers established printshops and issued newspapers supported by advertising and subscriptions from readers. In an increasing number of colonies, the colonial assembly won power over the purse strings and consigned the public printing. Freed economically, the newspaper thus began to separate from the state. The newspaper became a critical organ of comment in proportion to the press' economic freedom. Rising revolutionary temper gave newspaper publishers support and built up their courage.

This did not mean that the newspaper was completely free from government domination or control or the control by Tory or Patriot parties. "Liberty of the press" was a changing concept; it was not a fixed legal principle at any time in the colonial era. It depended on the attitude of the people of the period and on the views of reigning authorities. The newspaper publisher had to bend to whatever group was in power.

Rising commercial and professional classes in the colonies fought for a free press, free from political restrictions and control by the Crown. The press was, they declared, the bulwark of their own liberty. The press helped them achieve their own political and economic desires and ends.

The time when the legal principle of a free press in America was established came later. Then, the publisher could print news or comment directed toward any party, if he could prove the truth of his statement and justify his motive.

REVOLUTIONARY TEMPER MOUNTS

In the years preceding the American Revolution, some newspapers helped stimulate and crystallize the economic and political resentments of the colonists and serve as powerful propaganda media. Other newspaper publishers still fought valiantly for the British cause. By tracing the underlying and fundamental dissatisfactions which led to the war, one can picture more clearly the part the newspaper played in the revolutionary drama.

The American Revolution was caused not solely by the tyranny of King George III of England, who suddenly pushed his heel into the face of the colonists. This revolt began when settlers first stepped on these shores. Economic and social forces and conflicts had been accumulating for more than a hundred years.

The American View

Economic conditions were the critical factor which directly affected certain groups: merchants and shippers, industrialists and planters. Others, who had different reasons for hating the British, were carried along by the economic revolutionary tide.

When colonial commercial activities continued to swell during the seventeenth and eighteenth centuries, American business entrepreneurs came into sharp conflict with English businessmen, ably represented in Parliament. This conflict grew out of the application of the English mercantile doctrine to the colonists. Parliament passed a number of acts designed to strengthen the British Empire and to control colonial shipping more closely. England sought to develop home manufacturing so that she would not have to depend on other countries.

A series of enactments by Parliament enforced the mercantile philosophy. The Navigation Acts of the seventeenth century generally aimed to divert colonial trade to English ships and to build up the British fleet. As the Acts were evaded, Parliament in 1695 tightened its control still further. American newspapers reported that Parliament passed the Molasses Act of 1733, which imposed a tariff on rum, molasses and sugar coming from non-English islands in the West Indies.

Although the Molasses Act was practically ignored, the weeklies reported how irritating it proved to the colonials. If enforced, the measure would have seriously crippled northern industry, which was largely dependent on this trade. The Act turned New England merchants, shippers and ship captains into smugglers and law breakers. Respect for the law and the English diminished.

Manufacturing Acts passed by Parliament were additional sources of irritation. In 1699 English legislation prohibited any woolen goods from being shipped out of the colony manufacturing them. The weeklies also told readers about the Hat Act of 1732 which forbade shipment of American-made hats to foreign ports. Similar legislation regulated the iron and lumber industries.

Newspaper columns were filled with accounts which described the newly passed English laws affecting currency and financial matters. As protection to the English merchants, to whom many colonists were in debt, Parliament prohibited the issuance of paper money in America. The English lawmaking body also suppressed a colonial Land Bank which would have eased the money situation. Colonial merchants, shippers and manufacturers were affected directly by these measures.

Other American groups were irritated by the actions of the British or by the English attitudes. Colonial tradesmen, mechanics and small farmers expressed their irritation about taxation by writing letters to the colonial press. They could not vote because they did not have sufficient property. Toward them, both the wealthy colonist and English officials assumed a snobbish attitude. Lower economic groups in America felt that by throwing off the English yoke, they might destroy the social, economic and political grip of both England and the ruling colonials.

American colonists also had built up a basic spirit of independence as a result of being separated by 3000 miles of ocean for one hundred fifty years. The colonials had weaned away from England. Possessing their own representative assemblies to control their purse strings, colonists felt they had certain political rights in deciding how they should be governed and taxed. They had secured extensive control over their own destinies in spite of the fact that the governors had the right to veto colonial legislation and the British Parliament legally had the final authority over colonial Acts.

Although colonists in a new country, they considered themselves Englishmen and, as such, entitled to the same rights as those in the mother country; among those rights were the jury trial and taxation only with proper representation.

The British View and British Acts

Many British statesmen, meanwhile, believed that the English colonial policy badly needed reform. The time had come for a centralized control of the trans-Allegheny country, newly acquired in the French-Indian War. A closer association of the colonies for administrative purposes was essential. English officials, moreover, wanted to impose a greater share of the expense of administering the empire on colonial shoulders. A number of Acts were passed by Parliament to carry out these objectives. None perhaps was of greater importance in disrupting the Empire than the Proclamation of 1763 relating to the northwest lands which closed the trans-Allegheny region to settlement and prohibited trade with the Indians except to licensed commissioners.

This legislation was followed by the Quebec Act in 1774. This Act recognized the Catholic church officially; it also extended the boundaries of Canada to the Ohio and Mississippi Rivers. The measure aroused great hostility, as it disregarded the territorial claims of the eastern colonies and disappointed land speculators.

Parliament had enacted the Sugar Act in 1765, lowering the duty on molasses but adding duties on several other imports including sugar. When the newspapers reported this, deep resentment resulted because the prosperity of New England depended on its foreign trade. Merchants were pinched. Formal protests followed.

In 1765 the military Quartering Act was passed. The law required colonists to maintain British soldiers in public hostelries whenever barracks were insufficient and to supply the troops with candles, vinegar, salt and small quantities of rum, beer and cider, reimbursements to be made at a later date.

Stamp Act Stirs Mighty Protest

Short-sighted Chancellor of the Exchequer, George Grenville, planned to raise part of the American defense fund for soldiers by means of a Stamp Act. In 1765 the new Stamp Act was passed, imposing taxes on commercial and legal documents and on licenses, playing cards and dice. A tax was also placed on newspapers. The law required every advertisement to be taxed two shillings, amounting to about 50 per cent above the original cost. Actually, the Stamp Act of 1765 marked the time when the temper of the colonists began to mount to the revolutionary breaking point.

It is significant that, on two other occasions previous to the passage of the Stamp Act of 1765, colonial taxes had been imposed on newspapers. Designing its tax to raise revenue for the military, Massachusetts passed a half-penny tax on newspapers in 1755. During the life of this Act, a small red stamp appeared on the *Boston News-Letter*, the *Gazette* and the *Post*. Similarly, the New York legislature a year later passed a Stamp Act, placing a half-penny tax on newspapers in that colony. Since both of these taxes could be easily passed onto the readers, publishers made no protest.

A howl of indignation, however, accompanied passage of the Stamp Act by the British government in 1765. No colonial newspaper carried the required stamp. Publishers objected because the present tax was passed by the British Parliament where they were not represented. And the publishers thought they could not pass the English stamp tax onto their readers as readily as if the tax were locally imposed.

The tax also affected commercial groups on which newspapers depended for advertising. Now came the critical test of the newspaper's power to act as advocate of the colonists. All through the colonies, publishers expressed resentment in no uncertain terms in their editorial columns.

In place of weather reports, shipping news and literary essays, papers became galvanized with activities of the various classes of society, responding to the first of a series of "tyrannies." Artisans and laborers formed the Sons of Liberty and leaped over boundaries of polite ceremony. Mobs of them razed the offices of stamp agents and burned stamps in the streets. Artisans pried open the residences of lieutenant-governors in Boston and New York, sacked their chambers and pitched property into the streets. Occupying many columns of space, news of the activities of the Sons of Liberty produced an effect more powerful than the legal arguments concerning the unconstitutionality of the Act.

More sober resolutions of protest passed by the representative assemblies, and merchant organizations were also published. Not content with formal protests, the Massachusetts Assembly appealed for concerted action. In the autumn of 1765 the Stamp Act Congress was called to order in New York. Typical of other newspapers, the *New York Mercury* published the first news of the Congress on an inside page under its "New York News." Hugh Gaine, the publisher, merely printed an announcement of the opening of the Congress and the list of members.

Congress passed resolutions that Englishmen could not be taxed without their consent and that they could be taxed only by local legislatures. With some finality, congress proposed a general boycott on English goods.

Until this time newspapers had been printing columns of news concerning the reaction of the rioters, the assemblies and the Stamp Act Congress. Many papers had carried inflammatory essays denouncing Great Britain for its tyrannical action. Readers of the newspapers must have felt a rising temperature as the day when the Stamp Act was to be enforced drew near in the fall of 1765.

As a climax to this swollen resentment, publishers now were stirred violently in behalf of the colonists and particularly of their readers, advertisers and themselves.

The *New York Mercury* printed this bitter paragraph when it was learned that the hated stamps had been brought to the New York port:

> Alas! What have we done to merit such treatment from our Mother Country, and our Brethren? Have we deserved to be thus degraded and dishonoured, and used by them, as the most inveterate Enemies? What strange infatuation has prevailed in their Councils:
>
> To distress, ruin, and enslave us, when our rights and privileges are precisely the same, and our Interests inseparably united.

Lieutenant-Governor Colden said in a letter that the council, considering "the present temper of the people," did not think it "a proper time" to prosecute printers and publishers of seditious libels. The attorney-general likewise did not deem it a "safe time" to commence any such prosecution.

In Philadelphia, William Bradford, III, publisher of the *Pennsylvania Journal,* issued a striking edition on the occasion of the imposition of the Stamp Act. Typography of the issue on October 11, 1765, resembled a tombstone, with page one having heavy black borders and black lines between columns. A skull and crossbones adorned the top of the paper and also appeared in the lower right corner. The top line read:

EXPIRING: IN THE HOPES OF A RESURRECTION TO LIFE AGAIN

Bradford also tried to arouse the colonists with a stirring article on liberty. Probably a reprint from a Boston newspaper, the article argued: "Liberty is one of the greatest blessings which human beings can possibly enjoy." The writer then pointed out that "Liberty of the Press has been esteemed one of the main pillars of the Liberty of the People. While if it is maintained, the first steps of oppression are detected and the Attention of the people are seasonably awakened . . . all attempts to curtail Liberty even in the smallest degree have always been strenuously opposed or rigorously punished."

Other newspapers in the colonies used similar methods to arouse readers. The *Maryland Gazette* appeared October 10, 1765, in deep mourning, with skull and crossbones where the stamp should have been. This alliterative line was printed prominently:

THE TIMES ARE DREADFUL, DISMAL, DOLEFUL, DOLOROUS, DOLLARLESS

While newspapers, such as the *Maryland Gazette* and the *Pennsylvania Journal,* announced that they would not appear again unless the Stamp Act was lifted; nevertheless, they published their regular issues. To avoid trouble they omitted their customary titles and substituted these: *Recent Occurrences* or *No Stamped Paper To Be Had.*

Technically, publishers wanted to avoid publishing a newspaper which according to law had to be printed on stamped paper. By changing the name, they issued, technically, or legally a broadside or newssheet.

Some papers suspended briefly. Upon resuming, the Annapolis paper carried the line: *The Maryland Gazette Reviving.* After a few weeks all the colonial newspapers resumed their old titles. The snake cartoon, which Franklin had originated ten years before to consolidate the colonists against the French, appeared again during this period.

Meanwhile, merchants boycotted English goods. The protests on all sides had the desired effect on the English merchants. American newspapers began to publish articles about the curtailment of trade in England. Whereupon, with a cry of despair, English merchants descended on Parliament, and the Stamp Act was repealed.

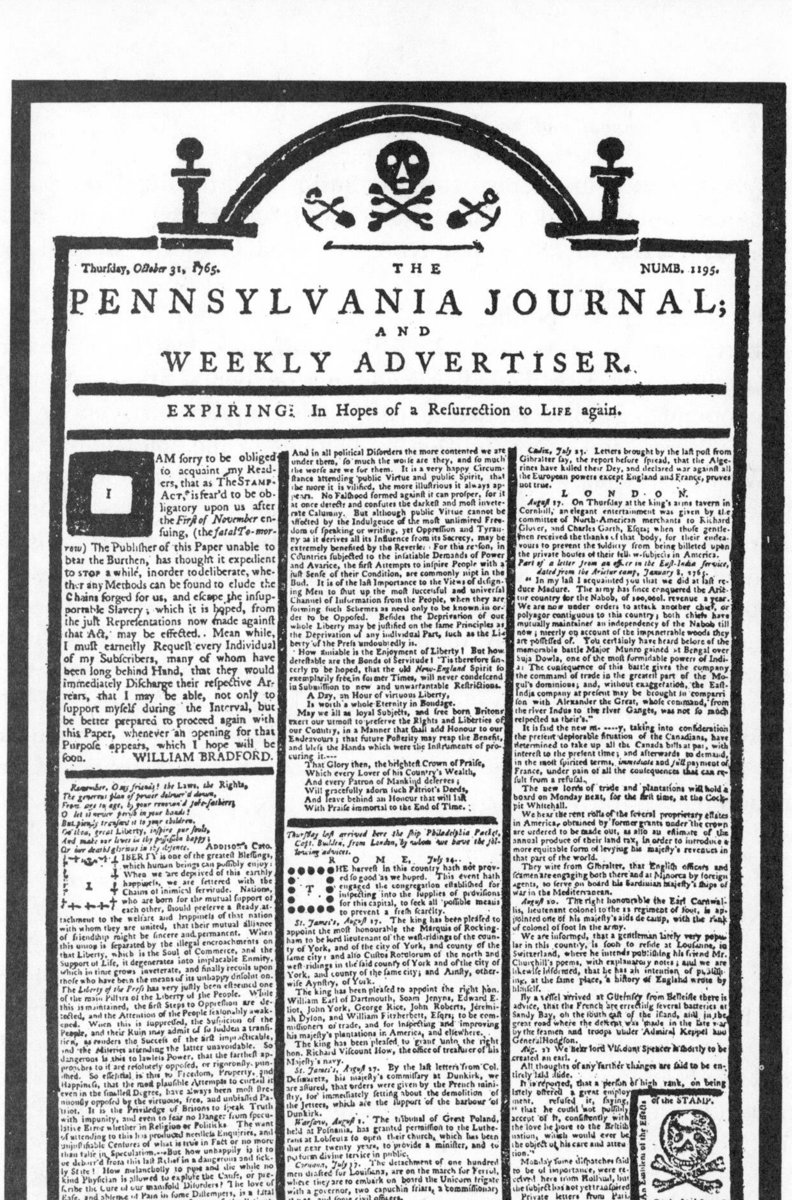

Thursday, October 31, 1765. THE NUMB. 1195.

PENNSYLVANIA JOURNAL; AND WEEKLY ADVERTISER.

EXPIRING: In Hopes of a Resurrection to LIFE again.

I AM sorry to be obliged to acquaint my Readers, that as The STAMP-ACT, is fear'd to be obligatory upon us after the *First of November* ensuing, (the *fatal To-morrow*) The Publisher of this Paper unable to bear the Burthen, has thought it expedient to STOP a while, in order to deliberate, whether any Methods can be found to elude the Chains forged for us, and escape the insupportable Slavery; which it is hoped, from the just Representations now made against that Act, may be effected. Mean while, I must earnestly Request every Individual of my Subscribers, many of whom have been long behind Hand, that they would immediately Discharge their respective Arrears, that I may be able, not only to support myself during the Interval, but be better prepared to proceed again with this Paper, whenever an opening for that Purpose appears, which I hope will be soon. WILLIAM BRADFORD.

Remember, O my friends! the Laws, the Rights,
The generous plan of power deliver'd down,
From age to age, by your renown'd forefathers,
O let it never perish in your hands!
But piously transmit it to your children.
Do thou, great Liberty, inspire our souls,
And make our lives in thy possession happy;
Or our deaths glorious in thy defence. ADDISON's Cato.

LIBERTY is one of the greatest Blessings, which human beings can possibly enjoy: When we are deprived of this earthly happiness, we are fettered with the Chains of inimical servitude. Nations, who are born for the mutual support of each other, should preserve a steady attachment to the welfare and happiness of that nation with whom they are united, that their mutual alliance of friendship might be sincere and permanent. When this union is separated by the illegal encroachments on that Liberty, which is the Soul of Commerce, and the Support of Life, it degenerates into implacable Enmity, which in time grows inveterate, and finally recoils upon those who have been the means of its unhappy dissolution. The *Liberty of the Press* has very justly been esteemed one of the main Pillars of the Liberty of the People. While this is maintained, the first Steps to Oppression are detected, and the Attention of the People seasonably awakened. When this is suppressed, the Suspicion of the People, and their Ruin may admit of so sudden a transition, as renders the Success of the first impracticable, and the Miseries attending the latter unavoidable. So dangerous is this to lawless Power, that the farthest approaches to it are resolutely opposed, or rigorously punished. So essential is this to Freedom, Property, and Happiness, that the most plausible Attempts to curtail it even in the smallest Degree, have always been most strenuously opposed by the virtuous, free, and unbiassed Patriot. It is the Priviledge of Britons to speak Truth with impunity, and even to fear no Danger from speculative Error whether in Religion or Politicks. The want of attending to this has produced needless Enquiries, and unjustifiable Censures of what is true in Fact or no more than false in Speculation.---But how unhappily is it to be debarr'd from this last Relief in a dangerous and sickly State! How melancholly to pine and die while no kind Physician is allowed to explore the Cause, or prescribe the Cure of our manifold Disorders? The love of Ease, and absence of Pain in some Distempers, is a fatal symptom of the desperate Circumstances of the Patient.

And in all political Disorders the more contented we are under them, so much the worse are they, and so much the worse are we for them. It is a very happy Circumstance attending public Virtue and public Spirit, that the more it is vilified, the more illustrious it always appears. No Falshood formed against it can prosper, for it at once detects and confutes the darkest and most inveterate Calumny. But although public Virtue cannot be affected by the Indulgence of the most unlimited Freedom of speaking or writing, yet Oppression and Tyranny as it derives all its Influence from its Secrecy, may be extremely benefited by the Reverse. For this reason, in Countries subjected to the insatiable Demands of Power and Avarice, the first Attempts to inspire People with a just Sense of their Condition, are commonly nipt in the Bud. It is of the last Importance to the Views of designing Men to shut up the most successful and universal Channel of Information from the People, when they are forming such Schemes as need only to be known in order to be Opposed. Besides the Deprivation of our whole Liberty may be justified on the same Principles as the Deprivation of any individual Part, such as the Liberty of the Press undoubtedly is.

How amiable is the Enjoyment of Liberty! But how detestable are the Bonds of Servitude! 'Tis therefore sincerely to be hoped, that the old *New-England* Spirit so exemplarily free in former Times, will never condescend in Submission to new and unwarrantable Restrictions.

A Day, an Hour of virtuous Liberty,
Is worth a whole Eternity in Bondage.

May we all as loyal Subjects, and free born Britons exert our utmost to preserve the Rights and Liberties of our Country, in a Manner that shall add Honour to our Endeavours; that future Posterity may reap the Benefit, and bless the Hands which were the Instruments of procuring it.---

That Glory then, the brightest Crown of Praise,
Which every Lover of his Country's Wealth,
And every Patron of Mankind deserves;
Will gracefully adorn such Patriot's Deeds,
And leave behind an Honour that will last
With Praise immortal to the End of Time.

Thursday last arrived here the ship Philadelphia Packet, Capt. Budden, from London, by whom we have the following advices.

R O M E, *July* 24.

THE harvest in this country hath not proved so good as we hoped. This event hath engaged the congregation established for inspecting into the supplies of provisions for this capital, to seek all possible means to prevent a fresh scarcity.

St. James's, August 17. The king has been pleased to appoint the most honourable the Marquis of Rockingham to be lord lieutenant of the west-ridings of the county of York, and of the city of York, and county of the same city; and also Custos Rotulorum of the north and west-ridings in the said county of York and of the city of York, and county of the same city; and Ainsty, otherwise Aynstry, of York.

The king has been pleased to appoint the right hon. William Earl of Dartmouth, Soam Jenyns, Edward Elliot, John York, George Rice, John Roberts, Jeremiah Dyson, and William Fitzherbert, Esqrs; to be commissioners of trade, and for inspecting and improving his majesty's plantations in America, and elsewhere.

The king has been pleased to grant unto the right hon. Richard Viscount How, the office of treasurer of his Majesty's navy.

St. James's, August 27. By the last letters from Col. Desmaretz, his majesty's commissary at Dunkirk, we are assured, that orders were given by the French ministry, for immediately setting about the demolition of the Jettees, which are the support of the harbour of Dunkirk.

Warsaw, August 1. The tribunal of Great Poland, held at Posnania, has granted permission to the Lutherans at Lobseutz to open their church, which has been shut near twenty years, to provide a minister, and to perform divine service in public.

Corunna, July 17. The detachment of one hundred men drafted for Louisiana, are on the march for Ferrol, where they are to embark on board the Unicorn frigate with a governor, two capuchin friars, a commissionary at war, and some civil officers.

Cadiz, July 23. Letters brought by the last post from Gibralter say, the report before spread, that the Algerines have killed their Dey, and declared war against all the European powers except England and France, proves not true.

L O N D O N.

August 17. On Thursday at the king's arms tavern in Cornhill, an elegant entertainment was given by the committee of North-American merchants to Richard Glover, and Charles Garth, Esqrs; when those gentlemen received the thanks of that body, for their endeavours to prevent the soldiery from being billeted upon the private houses of their fellow-subjects in America.

Part of a letter from an officer in the East-India service, dated from the Arictur camp, January 8, 1765.

"In my last I acquainted you that we did at last reduce Madure. The army has since conquered the Arictur country for the Nabob, of 100,000l. revenue a year. We are now under orders to attack another chief, or polyagor contiguous to this country; both chiefs have mutually maintained an independency of the Nabob till now; meerly on account of the impenetrable woods they are possessed of. You certainly have heard before of the memorable battle Major Munro gained at Bengal over Suja Dowla, one of the most formidable powers of India: The consequence of this battle gives the company the command of trade in the greatest part of the Mogul's dominions; and, without exaggeration, the East-India company at present may be brought in comparison with Alexander the Great, whose command, from the river Indus to the river Ganges, was not so much respected as their's."

It is said the new m----y, taking into consideration the present deplorable situation of the Canadians, have determined to take up all the Canada bills at par, with interest to the present time; and afterwards to demand, in the most spirited terms, *immediate* and *full* payment of France, under pain of all the consequences that can result from a refusal.

The new lords of trade and plantations will hold a board on Monday next, for the first time, at the Cockpit Whitehall.

We hear the rent rolls of the several proprietary estates in America, obtained by former grants under the crown are ordered to be made out, as also an estimate of the annual produce of their land tax, in order to introduce a more equitable form of levying his majesty's revenues in that part of the world.

They write from Gibralter, that English officers and seamen are engaging both there and at Minorca by foreign agents, to serve on board his Sardinian majesty's ships of war in the Mediterranean.

August 20. The right honourable the Earl Cornwallis, lieutenant colonel to the 12 regiment of foot, is appointed one of his majesty's aids de camp, with the rank of colonel of foot in the army.

We are informed, that a gentleman lately very popular in this country, is soon to reside at Lousanne, in Switzerland, where he intends publishing his friend Mr. Churchill's poems, with explanatory notes; and we are likewise informed, that he has an intention of publishing, at the same place, a history of England wrote by himself.

By a vessel arrived at Guernsey from Belleisle there is advice, that the French are errecting several batteries at Sandy Bay, on the south east of the island, and in the great road where the descent was made in the late war by the seamen and troops under Admiral Keppel and General Hodgson.

Aug. 21 We hear lord Viscount Spencer is shortly to be created an earl.

All thoughts of any farther changes are said to be entirely laid aside.

It is reported, that a person of high rank, on being lately offered a great employment, refused it, saying, "that he could not possibly accept of it, consistently with the love he bore to the British nation, which would ever be the object of his care and attention."

Monday some dispatches said to be of importance, were received here from Holland, but the subject has not yet transpired.

Private letters from Paris mention that the true reason

An Emblem of the Effects of the STAMP.
O! the fatal STAMP.

Figure 9. Stamp Act Edition. Colonial publishers expressed their opposition to the hated British Stamp Act of 1765 with words and strong typographical display. The *Pennsylvania Journal and Weekly Advertiser* used a tombstone effect the day before the Stamp Act went into effect. Note the skull and crossbones at the top of the page, along with the graveyard pick and shovel. Instead of an official government stamp, the publisher printed a skull and crossbones stamp at the bottom of column three. Rules between the type were turned backward in mourning.

When news of the repeal reached Boston on May 16, 1766, papers of that city united and published an EXTRA, carrying the headline, **GLORIOUS NEWS,** in the largest type ever used in the press until that time.

The Stamp Act reporting was the first genuine test of the strength of American newspapers. Until 1765 their influence had been indirect, and in only a few cases had they made any deliberate attempt to mold public opinion. Publishers had been merely middlemen who printed news of interest and essays written by factions in the communities.

With the struggle against the Stamp Act, colonial newspapers developed a new strength and began to assert positive, conscious influence. Publishers realized that their papers could be utilized to protest injustice. Merchants, shippers and wealthy farmers also were aware of the growing power of the press. Those with revolutionary drives (those persons, like Sam Adams, against any form of tyranny) recognized the value of the newspaper. It also became clear that the newspapers' effects were achieved by regularity of publication. Week after week, protests and "liberty essays" had hammered home their points. Unlike public addresses, which had to make their points in one thrust, newspapers had won acceptance for their ideas by the cumulative effect of their repeated weekly appearances.

Other Irritating Incidents and Acts

Now, other parliamentary acts and local incidents stirred the colonists to revolutionary pitch. Parliament passed the Townshend Acts of 1767, imposing a tax on tea, lead and glass. By this time colonists resented all taxes which they claimed were imposed without their consent. Then, English troops were brought into Boston. In this tense atmosphere it did not take much to provide the fuel for a clash. British soldiers on guard duty were pelted with snowballs by a group of citizens in March, 1770. The soldiers called for assistance. The crowd of Bostonians was fired on and the Boston Massacre occurred, five Bostonians being shot and killed. All this was reported in many colonial newspapers with the necessary anti-British emotional slant.

In 1773 Parliament gave the British East Indian Company a preferential position in the tea trade in America, making it difficult for colonial merchants to compete. Colonists became angry and staged a party, dumping the tea in the harbor of Boston and preventing the tea from being sold in other seaports. All this exciting news the newspapers reported.

The British were indignant and followed by passing the Intolerable Acts (Coercive Acts) in the summer of 1774, measures which united the colonists. The legislation closed the port of Boston until the tea was paid for. A military governor was appointed for Massachusetts. The Boston Town Meeting could assemble only with permission. More troops were brought in. The Quartering Act was reenacted for all thirteen colonies. Royal officers accused of capital offenses, such as murder, committed in enforcing the law, could be tried elsewhere. These Acts resulted in an outpouring of relief for Boston. Soon the Continental Congress was convened. A declaration of war followed.

Newspapers' Power Recognized; Take Sides

As the revolutionary temper mounted, newspapers played an even more significant role both in reporting and in stimulating the conflict. Quickly, publishers lined up on one side or the other, reflecting and expressing the new political and economic alignments of the people. The publishers' selection of the group they decided to support depended on their own background and sympathies. The publishers' affiliation also reflected the section of the public to whom they catered. In some instances publishers were influenced by the amount of money they were offered by the British government, either as salaries for printing or as direct subsidies for publishing pro-English newspapers. The English helped the *News-Letter* in Boston and Rivington's *Gazetteer* in New York. They also supplied funds for Robertson's *Royal American Gazette* in New York, the *Royal Pennsylvania Gazette* in Philadelphia and the *Royal South Carolina Gazette* in Charleston. In New Jersey, on the other hand, the Provincial Assembly established and subsidized a paper to give the Patriots a publication. The New Jersey Assembly supplied money to issue the *New Jersey Gazette* in 1777 in Burlington.

The British recognized the value of the press in influencing public opinion. One of the patriot papers, the *New Jersey Gazette* of July 4, 1781, claimed that the 100,000 guineas ($500,000) was spent by the British on American newspapers and pamphlets.

War tension, with its vital exciting news, accelerated newspaper growth. While the newspaper fed on the war conditions, at the same time it stimulated and promoted the war fever.

In this critical war era, the *news-letters, gazettes, journals, post-boys* and *mercuries* helped unify the thirteen separate colonies into one nation. Committees of Correspondence also were at work, sending information and letters to each other throughout the colonies. Many committeemen took their information to the newspapers where the news was printed, and the Patriots also wrote for their cause essays which were published in the gazettes. Because of the newspaper the fight of each colony with the Crown became the concern of all the colonies.

The older, traditional pamphlet continued to be a potent force, but the weekly newspaper began to supplant it. The political essay could be printed in the newspaper without cost to the writer; moreover, the newspaper was sent out regularly and had a ready-made audience. The newspaper brought news about current events more quickly and regularly; hence, it was awaited eagerly.

NEW ENGLAND'S REVOLUTIONARY PRESS GIVES LEADERSHIP

Boston's Revolutionary Press

During this period Boston, because of expansion of agriculture, business and trade throughout Massachusetts, became a hustling little metropolis, reaching thirty thousand by the opening of the revolution. By this time the Massachusetts population had grown to nearly four hundred thousand.

Boston was the center of revolutionary activity; Massachusetts residents had been quarreling with their governors for many decades and had learned the fine art of disputation, carrying on their government in the form of town meetings. They had become politically minded as well as independent. Boston patriot papers became leaders of the revolutionary movement, goading and stimulating colonists and publishers in other districts of the country. Several new papers originated in the growing city to reflect the new political and economic viewpoints, while older-established newspapers began to stir with the infiltration of new blood, both Tory and Patriot.

Three papers favoring the British side at the beginning were the *Boston News-Letter, Boston Post-Boy* and the *Boston Chronicle.* The *Boston Evening Post* claimed neutrality, but Patriots thought otherwise. At the other end of the scale were the outright Patriot newspapers, the *Boston Gazette* and the *Massachusetts Spy.* During the war other newspapers arose to defend the Patriot cause. Some publishers desired to be neutral, but the dominating public opinion, being Patriot, led them gradually to the colonial side of the fight. Some of the more conservative found prestige, money and revenue from official printing more magnetic.

The Boston News-Letter, Royal Mouthpiece

The *News-Letter* continued on its vigorous way but always in a conservative vein. John Draper, printer to the government and council who had inherited the paper in 1733, published it weekly for thirty years. Upon his death the paper passed to his son, Richard Draper. Chiefly a businessman's newspaper in its early days, the *News-Letter* had carried only bare news accounts. However, competition compelled it to add new techniques.

The decades after 1750 began the period of newspaper enlargement, and the *News-Letter* increased from two to three columns on a page, and the page itself, from 8 3/4 by 14 1/2 inches to 9 3/8 by 14 1/2 inches. On occasion, the publisher added supplements, extraordinaries and postscripts, bringing the number of pages to five or six. Publication of these additional pages sometimes resulted from late news or an abundance of it, but they were also inserted when advertising increased. Eventually, the publishers were compelled to issue a larger size paper.

Draper was a staunch defender of the King; and, as the revolutionary movement swept on, the *News-Letter* showed its strong Tory predilections. Symbolizing the changing economic and psychological conditions, the publisher inserted the king's arms at the head of his newspaper and changed its title to the *Massachusetts Gazette and Boston News-Letter.* Movement to the British side was a gradual but unmistakable transition. In the early part of the period Draper printed a few essays protesting "The Tyranny of the British," but even these essays seemed to favor the English. Draper published one Tory article from an English paper so that, he said, the colonists might understand the British arguments in support of the tax.

Few protests against the Stamp Act appeared in the Draper paper. After the tide had swung against England and colonists were making open protestations against the Stamp Act, Draper did print some essays in opposition to it. Draper reported in full the meeting of the Boston merchants who decided against importation of British goods. The *News-Letter* also carried an account of the Boston Massacre, but it was simply a straight news story. The *News-Letter* helped consolidate Tory sentiment in Boston and Massachusetts.

When Draper died in 1774, his widow, Mrs. Richard Draper, carried on the paper, and the *News-Letter* continued to move with the Tory cause. A month before the British troops were evacuated from Boston, the paper ceased circulating. Mrs. Draper left town. For her work on the *News-Letter*, she later received a life pension from the British government.

Boston Post-Boy (1757-1775)

Mirroring the commercial trend and revealing the press as a selling medium, John Green and Joseph Russell on August 22, 1757, established the *Boston Weekly Advertiser.* However, two years later the traditional title of *Post-Boy* was substituted. The paper continued publication under its old owners until 1773, and became, with the aid of the British, an outright Tory paper, for it was the first to be financially supported by the British. The *Post-Boy* folded in April, 1775.

The Boston Chronicle, Tory Organ (1767-70)

John Mein, one of the publishers of the *Boston Chronicle,* had been a successful bookseller and had started the first circulating library in Boston. Mein saw the necessity for the British to have an organ to represent their cause, especially after the trouble experienced in the enforcement of the Stamp Act. Accordingly, on December 21, 1767, the *Boston Chronicle* was launched, the third paper in Boston to favor the British cause. The *Chronicle* was the second semiweekly to be published in New England.

When it was first issued the *Chronicle* seemed favorable to the Patriots. Among other items it included the famous "Letters From a Farmer in Pennsylvania," by John Dickinson, a writer who, in the *Pennsylvania Chronicle,* first stated his grievances against the British in such beautiful, simple language that his work was reprinted in twenty-one papers. Besides these letters, the *Boston Chronicle* also published excerpts from John Wilkes' essay on "Liberty." Wilkes was an outspoken British newspaper publisher who was jailed for sedition in the 1760s.

The *Boston Chronicle,* however, showed its British leanings when the publisher refused to join other Boston merchants in their boycott of imported English goods. For his violation of the boycott, Mein, along with other Royalists, had his named printed in large type, week after week, on the front page of the patriot *Boston Gazette,* a journalistic device developed in the revolutionary period.

In retort, Mein jabbed his attackers with a skilled and satirical pen. In the *Chronicle* of August 7, 1769, he charged that John Hancock and other "well-disposed merchants" who had signed the boycott agreement were violating it for their own profit; and, in further retaliation, he printed their names at the top of the *Chronicle's* first page for many weeks. Mein became so unpopular with the Patriots that he was hanged in effigy. His partner, John Fleeming, was attacked on Boston streets. In 1776 the *Chronicle* was forced to discontinue. Publisher Mein fled to England.

The Boston Evening Post, The Neutral (-1775)

While the *News-Letter, Post-Boy* and *Chronicle* followed the right of the revolutionary road, the *Boston Evening Post* pursued a middle-path policy and succeeded in maintaining its neutrality for sometime.

This newspaper gained popularity under management of Thomas Fleet, who published both sides of controversial issues. When he died in 1768 his sons, Thomas Fleet, Jr. and John Fleet, continued the neutral policy. In April, 1775, the Fleets were forced by the Patriots to suspend publication. The Fleets turned to job printing for a livelihood.

Boston Gazette, Samuel Adams' Revolutionary Organ

Sharply to the left was the outstanding Patriot newspaper, the *Boston Gazette and Country Journal*, printed by Benjamin Edes and John Gill, and supported chiefly by Samuel Adams and a group of merchants and lawyers. Adams grew up in a cultured, prosperous family with a touch of radicalism and a love for political argument. Samuel listened to many exciting political discussions in his home. The Adams family felt bitter toward the British because a land bank, of which the senior Adams was a director, was closed by Parliament.

Figure 10. Samuel Adams, Pioneer Propagandist. America's first genius of propaganda, Samuel Adams was a staunch exponent of the colonial cause. He stirred newspaper readers to a revolutionary pitch. He wrote for the *Boston Gazette* and sent his news to other colonial newspapers. Copley, J. S., Courtesy, Museum of Fine Arts, Boston, lent by the City of Boston.

To a colonial with deep resentment against the British, the times gave such a person the opportunity to become a leader; as a result, Sam Adams, operating through the *Gazette*, became the firebrand of the American Revolution and the outstanding revolutionary editor. A master at understanding the needs of colonists, Adams stirred them to a high pitch. His aims were to destroy British prestige, unshackle English bonds and make America free. The *Boston Gazette* was unquestionably the most vigorous organ of anti-British propaganda in the colonies. Chief devices for its Patriot propaganda were political essays, reprints from anti-British pamphlets and republication of the colonial charters and Bills of Rights.

While contributing to the *Independent Advertiser,* a short-lived publication issued from 1748 to 1750, Adams had taken the measure of the men who would stand with him in a crisis and aid in fighting the British. Consequently, he was in a position to assemble, as his editorial associates, such men as Joseph Warren, James Otis, Josiah Quincy and John Adams, all skillful, both in attacking the ideas of others and in defending their own views.

When news of the Stamp Act came, Adams, under a pseudonym, blasted away at England. The tax measure, he declared, was an example of British tyranny. A mob aroused by Adams' agitation, forced Oliver, the local tax collector, to resign.

When the British government later sent troops to Boston to quell riots and keep order, the *Boston Gazette* waged a grueling campaign against the English soldiers. Articles attacking the constitutionality of the order providing for soldiers' presence appeared in the *Gazette* from October to December, 1768. Between September, 1768, and August, 1769, Adams wrote a series of articles entitled, "Journal of the Times, or Journal of Events," including some of the most effective propaganda against the British he had yet manufactured. He sent the articles to the *New York Journal,* copies of which were distributed to every American weekly, with many of the publishers reprinting the Adams' articles. Some articles were even sent to England.

Adams followed with a number of "piping-hot atrocities" supposedly committed by British soldiers in Boston. He described blood-curdling incidents in which British regulars allegedly beat small boys in Boston's narrow streets, desecrated the Sabbath and violated matrons and young girls. English officials indignantly denied these charges, the soldiers claiming that they had no need for force since plenty of Boston women of easy virtue walked the streets.

These lurid descriptions led directly to bloodshed. Bostonians began to resent bitterly the presence of the soldiers, looking on them as undesirable guests who had no right there.

When the Boston Massacre, which involved the shooting of a number of Bostonians by British soldiers, occurred, Adams had an unparalleled opportunity to inflame the already outraged feelings of the people. On March 12, 1770, a week after the incident, the *Boston Gazette* used deep mourning borders on its inside pages; and, on page three, printed a picture of four large coffins. Upon each coffin were the initials of one of the men shot to death by the soldiers, together with a skull and

Figure 11. Boston Massacre. When the British soldiers killed Boston citizens in March, 1770, the newspapers had a cause célèbre. The editors told the story in detail and commented on it fully. (From Paul Revere's original engraving)

crossbones. The accompanying story was an editorial expression of rancor and bitterness, starting with a blast against the quartering of British troops. This article was sent to all the colonial publishers, many of whom reprinted it.

Adams next attempted to prove that Bostonians were innocent of any blame and that the soldiers were guilty. He also pressed for a trial of the redcoats. After some delay a civil trial was actually held; curiously enough, the evidence revealed that a wide-spread plot had been afoot to attack the soldiers and that warning had been given to be ready for an emergency. Adams, it is believed, was the chief instigator of the attack on the soldiers which led to the "instruments" used to bring about the explosion. At any rate, the soldiers were acquitted by a jury of Massachusetts citizens.

In the office of the *Boston Gazette* on Court Street, Adams and his associates planned the Boston Tea Party. Adams had long hoped to produce an emergency that would force Bostonians to show their mettle; and the Tea Party incident provided the explosive incident.

In the *Boston Gazette* of September 27, 1773, Adams, as an instigator of the American Revolution, proposed that a Congress of American States be called to set forth a Bill of Rights and publish it for the world. A few weeks later, on October 11, 1773, he suggested that an American commonwealth be established. Following the Bostonian's plea for an American independent nation, the First Continental Congress was called in Philadelphia. A set of resolutions was drawn up to boycott English goods. It was a definite step toward unification of the American colonies.

In the *Massachusetts Gazette* and *Boston News-Letter,* a series of articles written by Loyalist Daniel Leonard found fault with the First Continental Congress and attacked it sharply. John Adams defended the Congress in the *Boston Gazette.* This was a sharp, interesting newspaper debate, focusing attention on the crucial issues. The articles in both papers attracted much attention and were later reprinted in pamphlet form.

From the middle of 1774 to April, 1775, the *Gazette* sold two thousand copies weekly, one of the largest circulations of that time. But the paper's influence extended far beyond Boston so that when its stories about British atrocities, highly dramatic and editorially colored accounts, were reprinted along the seaboard, the British put a price on the heads of Edes and Gill, its printers, and on Adams. They were to be executed. Adams has been called the promoter of the American Revolution; he was certainly the publicity man and the propagandist of the revolutionary cause which erupted into a fighting war in the hills of Lexington and Concord in Massachusetts, April 19, 1775.

Like other colonial publishers, Adams was greatly handicapped in reporting the war. He had to depend on indirect sources for news of battles and progress of the war. Reporting was fragmentary, irregular and late. One source of news consisted of letters and reports George Washington sent to Congress. Other information came from the colonial generals' reports to the officials of their respective states. News could be reprinted from the newspaper in the locality where a battle had been fought.

Whenever news arrived after publication date, the *Gazette* issued a broadside, for a penny. During the war many essays were published to bolster the courage of the people. Most important of these were Thomas Paine's series entitled, "The American Crisis," reprinted from a Philadelphia paper. Paine's work will be referred to later.

Like other Boston Patriot printers, Benjamin Edes, now sole publisher of the *Gazette,* as Gill had withdrawn, was forced to move his press out of town in April, 1775, when the British began their occupation.

When news of the English surrender of October 19, arrived in Boston on October 26, 1781, publishers joined to immediately issue a broadside containing one of the few headlines printed in the colonial period: CORNWALLIS TAKEN!

Massachusetts Spy: Labor Press

The first "labor newspaper," catering to the growing class of workers in Boston, began with the issue of the *Massachusetts Spy, or Thomas' Boston Journal* on August 7, 1770. Isaiah Thomas, the publisher, had learned the printing art in Boston but had run away to work on newspapers in Canada, New Hampshire and as far south as South Carolina. Early in his career he revealed his rebellious, independent nature and was fired from at least one of his newspaper jobs. In 1770 he returned to Boston where he joined Zachariah Fowle in a partnership and published the *Massachusetts Spy.*

Appealing to Boston workers, the *Spy* sold at five shillings a year, half the price of other Boston newspapers. Twice a week the *Spy* was printed "on a quarter sheet and once on a half sheet." The *Spy* was the first triweekly in the colonies, but as a triweekly the paper lasted only a short time.

When Fowle withdrew from the paper, Thomas, borrowing money, reissued the paper in November, 1770, as a semi-weekly. This too failed.

Cornwallis TAKEN!

BOSTON, (Friday) October 26, 1781.

This Morning an Expreſs arrived from Providence to HIS EXCELLENCY the GOVERNOR, with the following IMPORTANT INTELLIGENCE, viz.—

PROVIDENCE, Oct. 25, 1781. Three o'Clock, P. M.

This Moment an Expreſs arrived at his Honor the Deputy-Governor's, from Col. Chriſtopher Olney, Commandant on Rhode-Iſland, announcing the important Intelligence of the Surrender of Lord CORNWALLIS and his Army; an Account of which was Printed this Morning at Newport, and is as follows, viz.—

NEWPORT, October 25, 1781.

YESTERDAY Afternoon arrived in this Harbour Capt. Lovett, of the Schooner Adventure, from York River, in Cheſapeak Bay, (which he left the 20th inſtant,) and brought us the glorious News of the Surrender of Lord Cornwallis and his Army Priſoners of War to the allied Army, under the Command of our illuſtrious General; and the French Fleet, under the Command of His Excellency the Count de Graſſe.

A Ceſſation of Arms took Place on Thurſday the 18th Inſtant in Conſequence of Propoſals from Lord CORNWALLIS for a Capitulation.—His Lordſhip propoſed a Ceſſation of Twenty-four Hours, but Two only were granted by His Excellency General WASHINGTON. The Articles were compleated the ſame Day, and the next Day the allied Army took Poſſeſſion of York Town.

By this glorious Conqueſt, NINE THOUSAND of the Enemy, including Seamen, fell into our Hands, with an immenſe Quantity of Warlike Stores, a Forty-Gun Ship, a Frigate, an armed Veſſel, and about One Hundred Sail of Tranſports.

Printed by B. Edes and Sons, in State Street.

Figure 12. Revolutionary Extra. Benjamin Edes, publisher of the *Boston Gazette,* was so excited about the surrender of General Cornwallis that the printer brought out an Extra. Note the large headline at the top of the page. This is one of the few headlines printed during the colonial period. It was not a label head, as it contained a noun and a verb. Cornwallis surrendered on October 20; the news was published in Boston six days later.

A few months later, the *Spy* appeared as a weekly and was successful. Thomas appealed to the working class of Boston and other towns. Analyzing the population, he found that a large group of literate artisans, shipbuilders, ropemakers, cobblers, tailors and blacksmiths had no newspapers. Thomas used a simple, direct style for the colonist-on-the-street. He directed his news to the new group of workers who wanted short, nutshell statements of events.

The *Spy* did not advocate labor measures or make the popular appeal characteristic of the penny press of the 1830s. Conditions were not ripe for the emergence of a laboring class or a popular press. Yet, Thomas eventually reached with his *Spy*, thirty-five hundred workers, one of the highest circulations in the colonial period.

As a neutral printer the *Spy's* young publisher at first let both the Tories and the Patriots present their arguments, despite his own leanings. His determination to support the revolutionaries was in accord with his psychological makeup and his early leaning toward the Patriot cause. He was supported by Joseph Greenleaf, a strong Patriot who financed the young Thomas when Fowle withdrew.

Soon Patriot writers for the *Spy* were overwhelmingly in the majority; and the Tories began an attack on Thomas. Then Thomas' paper became emotional and violent. Thomas and his contributors in strong, bitter, yet simple language, characterized the British as monsters and tyrants.

Joseph Greenleaf's writing, accusing Governor Hutchinson of being paid by the Crown, enraged the governor and council, which sent a messenger to summon Thomas in his "sedition foundry," as his printshop was called.

An indictment was drawn up. At the crowded courthouse trial the grand jury refused to cooperate and returned the bill ignoramus ("we don't know"). The charge was dropped. Thomas, rejoicing, reprinted a disloyal address to the king; again the governor and the council attempted court action. A second failure was recorded, for again no jury could be found to indict Thomas. Seeing how powerful a weapon they now had in the press, the Patriots instructed their representatives to the Assembly of Massachusetts to take care of the "liberty of the press."

Thomas withdrew from Boston when the British entered it in 1775, and he transferred his newspaper to Worcester, Massachusetts. Here he symbolically called his weekly the *Massachusetts Spy, or the American Oracle of Liberty,* immortalizing his first issue with his excellent eyewitness account of the Battle of Lexington. However, Thomas' wartime struggles were severe. He went deeply into debt, and paper was almost impossible to secure.

In 1773 Thomas, like Franklin and Bradford, became interested in the possibility of "chain newspapers." With Henry Walter Tinges, he established the *Essex Journal and Merrimack Packet, or the Massachusetts and New Hampshire General Adverstiser* in Newburyport, Massachusetts, on December 4, 1773. He sold out after a year.

Other New England Papers

While Boston remained the hub of New England newspaper activity, other colonies were falling into a similar pattern. New Hampshire issued three newspapers, Vermont produced one, Rhode Island published three and bustling Connecticut issued five. These New England journals followed the lead taken by aggressive Boston newspapers, reprinting essays and news from them. Both Patriot and Tory papers were established.

The Green family of printers, originating in Boston, was responsible for several of the five Connecticut papers produced during this period. The Greens extended their operations through Massachusetts, Connecticut and Maryland. In Connecticut, Thomas Green brought out the first issue of the *Connecticut Courant* in Hartford in 1764. It became one of the outstanding Patriot papers.

NEW YORK KNOWN AS CENTER OF TORY PRESS

New York became the center of Tory influence and activities in this period. Here lived wealthy royalist sympathizers and many of the king's own representatives. By 1775 the town of New York had twenty thousand people, and the colony of New York had one hundred eighty thousand.

With the death of Mrs. Zenger in 1751, the *Weekly Journal*, which had fought so courageously for press liberty, also died; and a year later, Henry DeForest's *Evening Post* expired, leaving only James Parker's *New York Gazette*, or *Weekly Post-Boy*. However, seven new papers appeared during this period. In New York the assembly, composed of conservative, wealthy colonists, put a curb on unfavorable utterances.

Holt's New York Journal, Patriot Organ (1766–)

Born in Williamsburg, Virginia, John Holt received a good education and was trained for a merchant's career. In 1749 he married Elizabeth Hunter, a sister of William Hunter, the public printer, from whom Holt learned the trade. After business reverses, Holt went to New York in 1753 with an introduction to James Parker. From this association arose all of Holt's publishing ventures. He published the *Connecticut Gazette* in 1755, then issued Parker's *Post-Boy* in New York five years later. Holt's *New York Journal* was first published in 1766.

His *New York Journal* was a readable colonial newspaper with an excellent balance of news, editorial material and advertising. Throughout the critical prelude to the war, Holt's *Journal* supported the Patriot's cause. During the early revolutionary era, Holt presented news relating to the growing "distemper" of the people rather than violent essays on "liberty." However, he did publish Sam Adams' propaganda articles.

Newspaper quarrels revealed the resentment between Tory and Patriot factions in New York at this time. The *Journal* violently attacked "Rivington's Lying Gazette." In retaliation, Holt was assailed in the Tory *New York Mercury*. When the British army invaded New York in 1776, Holt was forced to move his newspaper to Esopus, New York (now Kingston). There he published the *Journal* until three days before the king's soldiers burned the town. Later, he published in Poughkeepsie, New York; and in 1783 he returned to New York town.

Holt's *Journal* was considered a profitable colonial newspaper. Many issues between 1770 and 1775 ran six or eight pages on account of the pressure of increased advertising. Size of the pages increased from 15 1/2 by 9 3/4 to 18 1/2 by 11 3/4 inches, and the number of columns per page, from three to four. Advertising rates were figured on the basis of a square, 2 1/2 inches by 2 1/2 inches, the width of the newspaper column. The charge was five shillings for four weeks, with one shilling for each week afterward, and larger ones (than the square) in proportion.

Gaine's New York Gazette and Mercury (1752-1783)

One Patriot paper in New York, the *New York Gazette and Mercury*, was edited by Irish-born Hugh Gaine. When he came to New York in 1740, he found employment with James Parker. After Gaine learned the local printing and publishing business, he launched his own newspaper, the *New York Gazette and Mercury* in 1752. During the Stamp Act fracas he was one of the loudest protesters against the hated measure. The *Gazette and Mercury's* temper was inflamed by this conflict, and the paper became a forceful sheet. Its attack, although slow in getting under way, became violent after the Stamp Act Congress met in New York.

Tories, ever alert to enemies in the local press, recognized Gaine as hostile. When the British captured the city, he fled with part of his printing equipment to Newark, New Jersey, where he edited his paper for some months. Meanwhile, British General Gage appointed an editor, Ambrose Serle, to publish Gaine's *New York Gazette and Mercury* to spread British propaganda. That the British recognized the power of the press is evident from one of Serle's letters in which he declared that, next to preachers, "newspapers had done the most to fire up the colonists."

Serle's method of attacking the colonists through essays and news stories is revealed in the following item, setting forth the characteristic British view of the rebellion:

CONSIDERATIONS OF THE PRESENT REVOLTED STATE OF AMERICA, ADDRESSED TO ITS INHABITANTS AT LARGE

> . . . The deluded colonists running wildly after the shadow of liberty have lost the substance. The present armament will restore Americans to Freedom—to that freedom which is enjoyed under the British constitution. It will relieve them from the most degraded species of tyranny, Republican Tyranny.

Gaine continued to publish in Newark a paper bearing the same name as the New York organ: the *New York Mercury.* In November, 1776, he returned to New York and once again became publisher of the *New York Mercury.*

From then on, his paper was a Royalist sheet which attacked everything the Patriots attempted. Gaine never quite won the confidence of the British generals. His smooth ways and honeyed tongue enabled him to remain in America after the revolution, when many Tory editors had to leave the country. Gaine, however, abandoned his paper and turned to bookselling and job printing. He not only made peace with the Patriots, but actually was one of the marshals of the parade when New York celebrated adoption of the Constitution on July 23, 1788.

Rivington's New York Gazetteer, Tory (1773-1783)

Unlike the vacillating Gaine, James Rivington was a staunch British champion. Born in England in 1724, James was given a good education there. As a member of a famous English printing house bearing his name, he became wealthy. He lost more than $50,000 on horse races in England, and, although able to pay his debts, his fortune collapsed and he came to America. In 1760 Rivington established a bookstore in Philadelphia with the aid of partners, and later he branched out into New York and Boston. Rivington liked to travel in aristocratic society and to indulge himself in the royalist costume of the era. It was natural for him to lean to the English cause.

Recognizing a need for a New York newspaper with British sympathies, aristocratic Rivington launched his *New York Gazetteer* on April 12, 1773, and the paper soon became very influential. Its circulation reached more than thirty six hundred, and it was distributed throughout the colonies wherever there were Tories. He also claimed a foreign circulation, with subscribers in the West Indies, Great Britain, France and Ireland.

Rivington proved to be a thorn in the side of the Patriots, who hated and feared him. A man of keen literary talent, he presented the cause of the Tories with skill and force. Writers in the *Gazetteer* were constantly attacking the Patriot party. Rivington and his Tory writers felt that the British government with all its faults was best for the colonies. The government system could be modified and changed. The pro-Tory writers in the *Gazetteer* objected to colonial rule by inexperienced, uneducated rabble.

Late in 1774 Rivington's interest in the British cause became even more pronounced. He no longer presented both Patriot and Tory news and opinion. In November, when most American publishers were withdrawing from their front pages British headings and coats-of-arms surrounding the newspaper titles, Rivington inserted the English symbols in place of his illustration of a ship. Material inducement by British officials combined with his aristocratic British background and his confidence in the success of the British regulars over the provincial army, influenced Rivington more and more strongly. He began to specialize in lies and false rumors about the Patriots.

On May 10, 1775, a mob attacked Rivington, but through the efforts of two friends, he found refuge on a warship in the harbor. After declaring officially that he would be fair to all, Rivington was allowed to publish again, but the feeling of Patriots against Rivington was strong. On November 23, a raiding party of Liberty Boys with the rebellious Patriot, Alexander MacDougall, in their midst, galloped down from Connecticut and destroyed Rivington's plant.

Returning to England, Rivington was appointed king's printer for New York. Upon returning to New York with new equipment, he resumed publication on October 18, 1777, calling his paper *Rivington's New York Royal Gazette*. With the May 19, 1778 issue, the paper changed from a weekly to a semiweekly.

In 1783, when the British evacuated the city, his paper dropped the royal title, resuming the old name. However, his paper expired at the end of the year. Rivington was permitted to remain in New York because, according to unsupported evidence, he had been a spy for General George Washington and had supplied the general with important information, for which, of course, he had been handsomely paid.

Typographically, Rivington's *Gazette* was one of the best papers in the colonies, with ornamental borders, woodcuts and attractively arranged advertisements.

Four Tory papers were issued in New York at this time. So that the people might have fresh news everyday of the week, military authorities in May, 1778, arranged a schedule by which each paper appeared on a different day. This arrangement foreshadowed the daily newspaper in postwar America.

In New York as well as in other towns, Tory newspapers were suppressed after the war. Along with the American government, newspapers as an institution of control passed into Patriot hands.

PHILADELPHIA'S NEWSPAPERS DIVIDED OVER WAR

Pennsylvania, of which Philadelphia was the capital, was one of the largest colonies in rising colonial America. Having only twenty thousand settlers in 1700, Pennsylvania reached three hundred thousand by the beginning of the war. By this time Philadelphia had twenty thousand residents. With an improved intercolonial transportation system, Philadelphia was linked with New York and Boston on the North, and with Baltimore and Williamsburg, Virginia on the South. Philadelphia was also a center of expanding cultural activity.

Accompanying this growth came rapid development of the newspaper. At midcentury, only two Philadelphia newspapers were being published; by 1775 there were nine, although several of these were short lived. Here, too, all shades of political complexion from deep revolutionary red to Tory blue were revealed.

The Pennsylvania Gazette, Under New Management

By 1750 the *Pennsylvania Gazette* (issued continuously since 1727) was a respectable, well-established and prosperous sheet. Its distinguishing philosophic and moral essays had been eliminated, and the paper contained only news and advertisements. Several factors may have been responsible for the changed policy. Possibly, Franklin, busy with other activities, was devoting less time to the *Gazette*. Again, many other newspapers, as well as magazines, had sprung up along the seaboard, and, aided by improved transportation services, could publish literary material.

In 1766 Franklin withdrew from the publishing business and his partner, David Hall, continued the paper. Franklin, however, was to receive £ 1,000 annually from the *Gazette*. Hall was a native of Edinburgh, Scotland, and joined Franklin in 1743. He was an excellent typographer. When he assumed control of the Franklin publishing house, he took a journeyman, William Sellers, into partnership; and in May, 1766 the firm of Hall and Sellers began to publish the *Gazette*. Their business was lucrative; in addition to job printing, book printing and newspaper publishing, the partners had government work including the printing of paper currency.

While the *Pennsylvania Gazette* leaned to the Patriot side, it was not a flaming revolutionary organ. During the period preceding the Stamp Act, conservative influence of Franklin restrained the editors. Hall printed protests and resolutions of the colonies; and when the Stamp Act finally went into effect, he avoided the tax entirely by substituting the title *Remarkable Occurrences* for the *Pennslyvania Gazette*. The printer's name also was omitted.

During the Revolutionary War the *Gazette* supported the Patriots and obtained its war news in the same indirect manner employed by other papers, frequently publishing information about battles weeks after they had been fought. Reaction of the British Parliament to the outbreak of hostilities was published. Actions, proceedings and addresses of Congress were reported and commented on favorably in the *Gazette*.

In 1777 when the British entered the city, the *Pennsylvania Gazette* was moved to York, Pennsylvania, where it was issued from December, 1777, until June, 1778. In January, 1779, the *Pennsylvania Gazette* returned to Philadelphia where Hall began publishing again.

Bradford's Revolutionary Journal

William Bradford, III, was not only publisher of the *Pennsylvania Journal and the Weekly Advertiser;* he was also tied closely with the commercial life of Philadelphia and the other colonies. In addition to his printshop, he was also proprietor of the London Coffee House, a popular resort and merchants' exchange.

In partnership with John Kidd, he established the Pennsylvania Insurance Company in 1762. Bradford's violent protest in his *Journal* against the Stamp Act characterized him as a strong fighter for the Patriot cause. He continued his revolutionary work, becoming known as the "Patriot Printer." On December 19, 1776, the *Journal* published the first of Thomas Paine's "Crisis" series. During the war Bradford lost his large fortune, and in September, 1777, when the British occupied Philadelphia, he had to cease publication altogether. He returned to Philadelphia in December, 1778, and his son, Thomas Bradford, assumed management of the resuscitated *Journal,* continuing it as a semiweekly for some years after the Peace Treaty had been signed.

Paine as Journalist-Pamphleteer

Writing for the *Pennsylvania Journal* was Thomas Paine, one of the great revolutionary propagandists, who was born in England in 1737. Poverty forced the family to withdraw Thomas from school at thirteen and apprentice him to a corsetmaker. Like Franklin, Paine was self-educated. He sailed for a time, taught school and served as tax collector. Reading widely, he became a deist and a student of science.

Figure 13. Revolutionary Writer. Thomas Paine was one of the most forceful of the revolutionary writers. He contributed to the Philadelphia press and wrote pamphlets for the Patriot cause. (After the portrait by Romney)

Making the acquaintance of Benjamin Franklin, then in Europe, Paine decided to try his fortune in America. Arriving in Philadelphia in 1774 with a recommendation from Franklin, he served as editor of Robert Aitken's *Pennsylvania Magazine* and began his pamphlet writing. Revolutionary spirited, Paine felt that something was wrong with the world. In America Paine found soil where his genius as a political writer could develop.

Paine seems to have been a natural-born writer, writing easily and well from the moment near middle age when he decided to make writing his career. He was always pleading a cause, and his brief sentences were filled with telling, quotable phrases. Paine was a propagandist through whom ideas of original thinkers were transmitted to the crowd.

Paine's pamphlet, *Common Sense,* issued in 1776, attained quick success. It hit the market at the right time. Excerpts were printed in many colonial newspapers. Paine urged in *Common Sense* an immediate declaration of independence. This action would serve, he argued, not only to unite the colonies but to secure French and Spanish aid. America had an obligation to the world which she should fulfill by revolt. Success of the pamphlet was amazing. It sold one hundred twenty thousand copies in three months; eventually, five hundred thousand copies were sold. *Comomn Sense* had a strong effect in arousing public opinion against England. The essay appeared as a series in the *Pennsylvania Packet.* As an effective journalist, Paine had expressed vividly what the common man thought.

Paine now wanted to get into the middle of affairs, and he enlisted in the colonial American army. Observing the condition of the army, especially its low morale, he wrote *The Crisis,* which first appeared in the *Pennsylvania Journal.* The lines which have become famous began:

> These are the times to try men's souls. The Summer soldier and the Sunshine Patriot will, in this crisis, shrink from the service of their country; but he that stands now, deserves the love and thanks of men and women. . . .

Washington received a copy and read it to his soldiers. The appeal was reprinted in many other colonial newspapers and in pamphlet form.

Peace found Paine honored but poor. When the French Revolution broke out, he returned to Europe and wanted the revolution to spread to England. Edmund Burke condemned the excesses of the revolution, and Paine replied in *The Rights of Man.* He appealed to the English to set up a Republic. This pamphlet sold three hundred thousand copies. Tried for treason in England, Paine was outlawed.

The journalist-pamphleteer was made a French citizen in 1792 and was elected to the French Convention. Later, with a change in regime, he was deprived of citizenship and imprisoned. Eventually, he was freed and reelected to the Convention. Upon returning to America in 1802, Paine was caught in the conflict between the Federalists and the Republicans.

The Pennsylvania Packet, Patriot (1771–)

John Dunlap, an Irish-born immigrant who arrived in Philadelphia in 1757, learned the printing trade thoroughly. When his uncle, William Dunlap, postmaster and printer, joined the ministry, he left the printshop in his nephew's charge. Two years later, William sold the shop, then merely a job printery, to John. On October 28, 1771, John Dunlap began publication of the *Pennsylvania Packet.* Paine's *Common Sense,* as indicated, first appeared in the *Packet.*

When the British captured Philadelphia, Dunlap had to move his press to Lancaster, Pennsylvania, where he remained until the British withdrew. Returning from Lancaster to Philadelphia in July, 1778, Dunlap served as printer to Congress, meeting then in Philadelphia. Dunlap took David C. Claypoole into partnership in October, 1780, another indication of the expansion of the printing and publishing business. The *Pennsylvania Packet* later became the first successful daily in America.

The Pennsylvania Chronicle (1766-1774)

William Goddard was one of the most colorful and distinctive personalities among colonial newspaper editors. Wherever he went, he stirred up a storm of controversy, usually centering about himself. He was restless and unsteady, moving from town to town, but in his travels, he launched more newspapers than any other publisher of his day.

He made enemies in both Patriot and Loyalist camps. Lorenzo Sabine, in his sketches of *Loyalists in the American Revolution*, characterized Goddard as a Tory; Isaiah Thomas considered him a Patriot. Evidence seems to point to the conclusion that Goddard was a good Patriot. But his tactlessness and his obstinacy were combined with an irreverence for public opinion and its current idols. Goddard was willing to fight and suffer for the right to print whatever views he thought should have a hearing. This embroiled him constantly with the Patriots and indicated to them that he leaned to the Tory side.

Goddard's career carried him through New England and the Middle Colonies. He was born in New London, Connecticut, in 1740. Goddard was apprenticed to James Parker who, with John Holt, had established the *Connecticut Gazette* in New Haven. In 1762, on termination of his apprenticeship, Goddard became the first printer in Providence, Rhode Island. Then, on October 2, 1762, he issued the *Providence Gazette and Country Journal*, a paper which lived only a few years. After working for a time in New York, issuing the *Constitutional Courant*, Goddard moved to Philadelphia.

Here, in June, 1766, he opened a printshop with the aid of Joseph Galloway and Thomas Wharton, rich, influential members of the Philadelphia community; on June 26, 1766, he issued the first number of the *Pennsylvania Chronicle and Universal Advertiser*. Goddard hoped to win the *Pennsylvania Gazette* readers, since the partnership of Franklin and Hall was terminating.

In Philadelphia Goddard took issue with Galloway, the *Chronicle's* backer, when Galloway attempted to use the paper to advance his political fortune. Galloway, increasingly conservative, objected to Goddard's publication of John Dickinson's famous "Letters from a Farmer" as well as the reprinting of Sam Adams' "Journal of Occurrences." Goddard, therefore, objected to Galloway's dictatorial tactics, called him a Tory and attempted to prevent Galloway's reelection to the assembly.

Wharton sided with Galloway, and the two partners withdrew their financial support of the paper. The last issue of the *Pennsylvania Chronicle* appeared February 8, 1774, but by that time Goddard had launched his *Maryland Journal, or Baltimore General Advertiser.*

Dickinson's letters which represented the conservative American businessman's views of the English-American struggle, were widely reprinted. The eleven letters, which began in 1767 and continued in 1768, hammered away at the unfairness of British laws restricting American business interests. Such laws gave English merchants an untold advantage over colonial businessmen, Dickinson wrote. He opposed "taxation without representation." The writer was not especially interested in liberty as an abstract principle nor was he concerned with the colonist-on-the-street as Adams was. Dickinson gave articulate expression to the businessman and convinced many colonial readers of the soundness of his views.

In keeping with his conservative background and viewpoint, Dickinson opposed any violence, any attempt to discard the English bonds forcibly. He advocated change through regular, orderly, constitutional methods. But the trend, of course, was not in this direction, as men like Adams came to the fore and the bugles of war sounded. Faced with the dilemma, Dickinson refused to take part in demonstrations, but at the same time would not become a Loyalist. He was criticized sharply by the Patriots. In defense of his home, he did take up arms. Dickinson emerged in the postwar era as a Federalist.

Philadelphia Evening Post, Tory (1775-1783)

The *Evening Post* was the only paper continuously issued in the town throughout the war. Established by Benjamin Towne in 1775, the *Post* first appeared as a triweekly. Towne, who had been a partner in the *Chronicle,* began as an ardent Patriot and helped put a Tory paper out of business. However, in September, 1777, when the British army occupied Philadelphia, Towne became a Royalist, the *Evening Post* reflecting his views.

Towne was proscribed by the Patriots for high treason, but four days before his scheduled trial, he shouted his Patriot fervor; not only was the treason charged dropped, but he was also permitted to continue publication.

He had alienated confidence, nevertheless, by his change of views; and his sales fell off. Before his *Evening Post* finally died in 1784, he established it as the first daily in America (May, 1783), although it was irregularly published. Towne's idea was sound and the time ripe for a daily in America, but his effort was abortive. After less than a year, the

Pennsylvania Packet, the first regularly issued daily in America appeared in September, 1784.

Three other Tory papers began publication in Philadelphia to support the British cause. They were all short lived.

SOUTHERN NEWSPAPERS FIGHT FOR FREEDOM

In the southern colonies newspapers continued in towns where they had already been established. Printers saw opportunities in new towns removed from the seaboard. These inland towns became the stronger centers for newspaper growth. In Maryland, Baltimore began to take precedence over Annapolis and produced three newspapers; while in Virginia, Richmond rather than Williamsburg became the center of journalistic activity.

With expansion of their population and their further economic development, North Carolina and Georgia saw their first newspapers established. The *North Carolina Gazette* was launched in 1751, and the *Georgia Gazette* in 1763. Some publishers were Patriot sympathizers; others, however, lined up on the British side. Most southern publishers lacked the great zeal of such revolutionists as Samuel Adams, Jr., and Isaiah Thomas. They, however, reprinted extensively from their northern contemporaries' publications.

BEGINNING OF MAGAZINE COMPETITION

Some competition was afforded the newspaper with establishment of local magazines in the 1740s. The magazine idea, like the idea for the newspaper, spread from England where magazines had been published earlier in the century. Although it was that enterprising newspaper publisher, Benjamin Franklin, who first envisioned a monthly periodical for colonial circulation, credit for bringing out the first American magazine must go to publisher Andrew Bradford.

Bradford learned that Franklin planned to publish a magazine and, realizing the potentialities, offered his *American Magazine, or A Monthly View of the Political State of the British Colonies* on February 13, 1741, ahead of Franklin by three days. Franklin entitled his periodical the *General Magazine and Historical Chronicle for all the British Plantations in America.* It contained about seventy-five pages. With all the high ambitions of the publishers these two magazines did not last long. Bradford published only three issues. Franklin stopped after the sixth. The potential public need for such magazines existed and conditions for their publication appeared to be improving, for another similar periodical was attempted by midcentury.

In Boston, center of newspaper activity, Jeremiah Gridley, a young lawyer with literary leanings who had attempted a newspaper, issued the *American Magazine and Historical Chronicle.* Gridley published this magazine for three years, between 1743 and 1746. The magazine idea did not die, and other periodicals sprang up after the midcentury. These monthly periodicals represented something culturally American. Their broad scope indicated the intellectual change which colonists were undergoing.

These colonial periodicals were intended to be storehouses or magazines of varied information gathered from books, pamphlets, newspapers and political documents. The publishers reprinted lengthy extracts from new colonial history books and from colonial and English newspapers. The magazines contained political information and resumés of English parliamentary proceedings affecting the colonies. Publishers allotted space to actions of local assemblies concerning such economic questions as issuance of paper money and international trade. Discussions of these issues which appeared in the newspapers and originl essays about these matters were published in the magazines. Current disputes between governors and assemblies over taxes to be used to equip armies were aired.

Economic news, such as lists of current prices of foodstuffs and other products in trade, was given. Much space was devoted to current religious controversey aroused by the revival meeting of Reverend George Whitefield, English divine traveling in America. In addition, colonial magazines printed a considerable number of general essays on manners of the times and poetry relating to current events as well as love themes.

Certain functions of these colonial magazines were similar to those performed by the newspaper. With more space, however, magazine publishers could print longer, more complete and varied articles; with more time for publication, they could offer a selection of reprints from books.

While the newspaper stressed the latest news, magazines could gather and assemble significant news and documents and discussion for the reader. Readers might not have the opportunity to get the complete news in their thin, local papers. It was too expensive to subscribe to several newspapers. Magazines, in a sense, were periodicals of current history, or as they said in their titles, "historical chronicles." They were monthly news and discussion periodicals.

New Magazines Established

In the period after 1750 five magazines, almost twice as many as in earlier decades, were established. Boston and Philadelphia continued to be the centers of magazine journalism. In Boston, Isaiah Thomas, newspaper publisher, issued the *Royal American Magazine* in 1774 but soon turned it over to his friend, Joseph Greenleaf. Paul Revere produced a series of anti-British cartoons on copper engravings for the periodical which was abandoned, however, at the beginning of the revolution.

In Philadelphia there was even more magazine activity. William Bradford, III, issued the *Monthly Magazine for the British Colonies* in 1757. The magazine's editor was Reverend William Smith, provost of the College of Philadelphia. The *Monthly Magazine* offered political material, satirical essays and poetry to the readers. The Bradford periodical lasted only a year, but it had obtained a thousand subscribers.

Robert Aitken issued one of the best publications, the *Pennsylvania Magazine,* in 1775, employing Thomas Paine, recently arrived from England, to edit the periodical. The last magazine to appear was H. H. Brackenridge's *United States Magazine.* The former president of the College of New Jersey wrote for it. The magazine, which made its appearance in 1779, continued only a year. Mortality of colonial magazines was high, but attempts at publication reflected the rising cultural interests of the colonists.

BIRD'S EYE VIEW SHOWS PRESS ON SOLID FOUNDATION

The colonial newspaper was now on a firm, solid foundation. A press was established in every colony, while several newspapers were competing with each other in some of the busy colonial capitals. Printers saw the satisfactory income to be derived from establishing weeklies or even dailies because of increasing subscriptions and multiplying advertisements.

The newspaper was regarded with considerable respect by many of those in the general public and by colonial leaders for the part the journals had played in the recent revolution. For, as no other agency of communication, the newspaper reported the news and fought for colonial economic and political rights. Liberty of the press was tied up with the colonial struggle to obtain freedom from tyranny.

Easy to establish because of the low capital investment required and easy to continue because of small operating costs, the newspaper was ready to play an important role in the birth of the young nation.

Five magazines, some of which dealt with current events, added to the news media of this time, giving colonial readers an opportunity to obtain a summary of the news of the month and a fuller discussion of current economic and political issues. Foundations for American magazine journalism were laid at this time.

References

English Newspapers

BLEYER, WILLARD G., *Main Currents in the History of American Journalism,* Boston: Houghton Mifflin Company, 1927. (Has excellent summary chapter on English journalism, with considerable detail to round out the picture.)

Cambridge History of English Literature, New York: The Macmillan Company, 1907-1933. (Covers specific topics in various volumes. See J. B. Williams, *Beginnings of English Journalism* Vol. VII, pp. 389-415; W. P. Trent, *Defoe, The Newspaper and the Novel* Vol. IX, pp. 1-28.

FOX-BOURNE, HENRY RICHARD, *English Newspapers* 2 vol., London: Chatto and Windus Ltd., 1887. (An early study, but thorough.)

FRANK, JOSEPH, *The Beginnings of the English Newspaper,* Cambridge, Mass.: Harvard University Press, 1961. (A newer, worthwhile study combining old material and new research findings.)

HERD, HAROLD, *March of Journalism,* London: Allen & Unwin, 1952. (Brief, swift-moving account of history of press. Highlights emphasized.)

NOAH, JAMES E., "Oliver Cromwell, Protector and the English Press," *Journalism Quarterly,* 39:57ff, Winter, 1962. (Throws further light on the dictator and his relations with newspapers.)

MOORE, JOHN ROBERT, *Daniel Defoe, Citizen of the Modern World,* Chicago: University of Chicago Press, 1958. (Tells of Defoe as journalist.)

MORISON, STANLEY, *The English Newspaper,* Cambridge, England: Cambridge University Press, 1932. (Excellent reproductions of newspapers.)

SHAABER, MATTHIAS A., *Some Forerunners of the Newspaper in England, (1476-1622),* Philadelphia: University of Pennsylvania Press, 1929. (Sheds light on prejournalism period before newspapers were issued.)

SIEBERT, FREDRICK S., *Freedom of the Press in England, 1476-1776,* Urbana: University of Illinois Press, 1952. (A highly detailed legal study showing changes in controls over the press.)

WERKMEISTER, LUCYLE, *The London Daily Press 1772-1792,* Lincoln: University of Nebraska Press, 1963. (A scholarly study of important papers from the time of the *Morning Post;* their interaction discussed.)

WILLIAMS, J. B., *History of English Journalism to the Foundation of the Gazette,* London: Longmans, Green and Co., Ltd., 1908. (Has history in great detail.)

Useful General Histories of American Journalism

BLEYER, WILLARD G., *Main Currents in the History of American Journalism,* Boston: Houghton Mifflin Company, 1927. (An earlier study, well-organized, interestingly written. Has strong sections on each period.)

DANIELS, JONATHAN, *They Will Be Heard,* New York: McGraw-Hill Book Company, 1965. (Biographical approach.)

EMERY, EDWIN and HENRY LADD SMITH, *Press and America*, Englewood Cliffs, N.J.: Prentice-Hall, Inc., 1954. (Revised edition, 1962, with Emery as sole author. Blends historical background with press.)

KOBRE, SIDNEY, *Foundations of American Journalism*, Tallahassee: Florida State University Press, 1958. (Study of early forms of news communication in Egypt, Europe and America. Follows U.S. press until 1865.)

LEE, ALFRED MCCLUNG, *Daily Newspaper in America*, New York: The Macmillan Company, 1937. (Analyzes press by departments. Has wealth of useful statistics of growth. Gives some information on colonial and revolutionary press but Lee's best sections deal with dailies.)

LEE, JAMES MELVIN, *History of American Journalism* rev. ed., Boston: Houghton Mifflin Company, 1923. (An older volume but has many details on territorial journalism.)

MCMURTRIE, DOUGLAS, *A History of Printing in the United States*, New York: R. R. Bowker Company, 1936. (Presents spread of printing by colonies, states. Largely chronological.)

MOTT, FRANK L., *American Journalism. A History of Newspapers in the United States Through 270 Years: 1690-1960* rev. ed., New York: The Macmillan Company, 1962. (Has much rich detail on each period; is largely chronological in approach but is valuable for newspaper contents in each period.)

STEWART, KENNETH and JOHN TEBBEL, *Makers of Modern Journalism*, New York: Prentice-Hall, Inc., 1952. (Has some outstanding colonial publishers analyzed. Covers all periods with emphasis on personalities.)

WEISBERGER, BERNARD A., *The American Newspaperman*, Chicago: University of Chicago Press, 1961. (A concise, overall account of press history.)

The above books may be used for the Colonial and Revolutionary Period as well as later eras in American journalism.

Reference Volumes

CANNON, CARL L., *Journalism, A Bibliography*, New York: New York Public Library, 1924. (One of first attempts to compile extensive bibliography on newspapers. Still highly useful.)

FORD, EDWIN H., *History of Journalism in the United States, A Bibliography of Books and Annotated Articles*, Minneapolis: Burgess Publishing Co., 1938.

JOHNSON, ALLEN and DUMAS MALONE, *Dictionary of Modern Biography, Under the Auspices of the American Council of Learned Societies*, New York: Charles Scribner's Sons, 1928-1958.

KOBRE, SIDNEY, *Journalism History Guidebook*, Tallahassee, Florida: National College Press, 1955. (Has bibliographies by periods; gives progressive teaching methods for journalism history.)

PRICE, WARREN C., *The Literature of Journalism*, Minneapolis: University of Minnesota Press, 1959. (A recent and valuable contribution. Volumes are classified in various ways and annotated fully.)

SWINDLER, WILLIAM F., *Contributions to Bibliography in Journalism, No. 3, Journalism Subjects in American Historical Reviews*, Lincoln: University of Nebraska School of Journalism, July, 1954. (Very useful for cross-reference work.)

WOLSELEY, ROLAND E., *Journalists' Bookshelf* 6th ed., Chicago: Quill and Scroll Foundation, 1955. (One of the best of its kind. Tells the contents of each volume.)

Colonial and Revolutionary Press

General

BARNES, VIOLA F., *Dominion of New England,* New Haven: Yale University Press, 1923. (Discusses early political history in England, leading up to publication of *New English Affairs.*)

COOK, ELIZABETH C., *Literary Influences in the Colonial Newspaper,* New York: Columbia University Press, 1912. (Deals with influence of *English Spectator* and *Tattler* and other British papers on colonial publishers and their writers.)

DAVIDSON, PHILIP, *Propaganda in the American Revolution, 1763-1783,* Chapel Hill: University of North Carolina Press, 1941. (An illuminating study of the subject; has a section on the press.)

DOWNS, ROBERT B. (ed.), *The First Freedom,* Chicago: American Library Association, 1960. (A collection of essays about freedom to publish.)

DUNIWAY, CLYDE, *Development of the Freedom of the Press in Massachusetts,* Cambridge: Harvard University Press, 1906. (One of the first books on the subject.)

KOBRE, SIDNEY, *Development of the Colonial Newspaper,* Pittsburgh: Colonial Press, 1944. (Considerable detail for each newspaper and section; has sociological approach, giving background of period. Reprinted by Peter Smith, Gloucester, Mass., 1960.)

LEVY, LEONARD W., *Legacy of Suppression,* Cambridge: Harvard University Press, 1960. (A critical study of free press issue, showing pressure on publishers from all sides. Reprinted as Torchbook by Harper & Row, publishers, 1963 as *Freedom of Speech and Press In Early American History.*)

SCHLESINGER, ARTHUR M., *Prelude to Independence,* New York: Alfred A. Knopf, Inc., 1958. (Paperback edition, Harper Torchbook, 1963. Contains many details about the role played by the newspaper and other agencies in bringing on the revolution.)

WROTH, LAWRENCE C., *The Colonial Press,* New York: Grolier Incorporated, 1931. (Has the best account of the mechanical and financial operations and problems of the early printer-publishers.)

Individual Publishers and Presses in Colonies

Peter Zenger

BRUNELLI, VINCENT, *Trial of Peter Zenger,* New York: New York University Press, 1957. (Has reprint of trial, biographies of principals and discussion.)

GAULT, TOM, *Fighter for Freedom,* New York: Thomas Y. Crowell Company, 1951. (A popular, fictionalized biography of Zenger but follows the known facts about the publisher closely.)

RUTHERFURD, LIVINGSTON, *John Peter Zenger,* Gloucester, Mass.: Peter Smith, 1941. (Has detailed account of life of Zenger and reproduction of *New York Journal.*)

Benjamin Franklin

FAY, BERNARD, *Franklin, the Apostle of Modern Times,* Boston: Little, Brown and Company, 1927. (An interesting interpretation by a French writer.)

VAN DOREN, CARL, *Benjamin Franklin,* New York: The Viking Press, Inc., 1948. (The most thorough and readable of the many volumes on this genius. See also Benjamin Franklin, *Autobiography,* Frank Pine, Ed., New York: Holt, Rinehart & Winston, Inc., 1916.)

Isaiah Thomas

MARBLE, ANN R., *From 'Prentice to Patron,* New York: Appleton-Century-Crofts, 1935. (A readable life of Isaiah Thomas, Boston revolutionary publisher.)

SHIPTON, CLIFFORD, *Isaiah Thomas: Printer, Patriot, Philanthropist,* Rochester: Leo Hart, 1938. (A useful study. Can be followed in conjunction with Marble's biography.)

Thomas Paine

BEST, MARY A., *Thomas Paine,* New York: Harcourt, Brace & World, Inc., 1927. (A lively study of this revolutionary writer.)

FAST, HOWARD, *Citizen Tom Paine,* New York: Modern Library, Inc., 1946. (A stimulating study, showing Paine's interest in common man.)

WOODWARD, WILLIAM, *Thomas Paine, America's Godfather,* New York: E. P. Dutton & Co., Inc., 1945. (An informative study in Woodward's readable style.)

Other Publishers

BRIGHAM, C. S., *Journals and Journeymen,* Philadelphia: University of Pennsylvania Press, 1950. (Has a variety of biographies.)

DEARMOND, ANNA J., *Andrew Bradford, Colonial Journalist,* Newark: University of Delaware Press, 1949. (One of the few detailed studies of colonial publishers.)

MILLER, JOHN CHESTER, *Samuel Adams, Pioneer Propagandist,* Boston: Little, Brown and Company, 1936. (A thorough, reliable study, giving all aspects of Adams' life and his work.)

MINER, WARD L., *William Goddard, Newspaperman,* Durham, N. C.: Duke University Press, 1962. (Excellent, detailed study of this independent-minded publisher.)

OSBORNE, J. A., *Williamsburg in Colonial Times,* Richmond, Va.: Dietz Press, 1935. (Excellent for a picture of what the colonial newspaper contained; many excerpts from *Virginia Gazette.*)

Connecticut Press

MCNULTY, JOHN BARD, *Older Than The Nation,* Stonington, Conn.: Pequot Press, Inc., 1964. (A solid history of *Hartford Courant.*)

Maryland Press

WHEELER, JOSEPH T., *The Maryland Press (1777-1790),* Baltimore: Maryland Historical Society, 1938. (An informative book, continuing Wroth's study.)

WROTH, LAWRENCE C., *History of Printing in Colonial Maryland, (1686-1776)*, Baltimore: Typothetae of Baltimore, 1922. (Highly useful account of origins of printing and newspapers in Maryland.)

Press and Other Mechanical Developments

LEE, ALFRED McCLUNG, *Daily Newspaper in America,* New York: The Macmillan Company, 1937. (Has detailed chapters on press, paper, etc.)

OLSON, KENNETH E., *Typography and Mechanics of Printing,* New York: Appleton-Century-Crofts, 1930. (Tells of operations of various early presses.)

SUTTON, ALBERT A., *Design and Make-Up of the Newspaper,* Englewood Cliffs, N.J.: Prentice-Hall, Inc., 1949. (Gives useful details of press developments.)

WROTH, LAWRENCE C., *The Colonial Press,* New York: Grolier Incorporated, 1931. (Unusually complete detail on press costs, operations, employees and problems. Reprint, Portland, Me., Southworth-Anthoensen Press, 1938.)

Freedom of Press

FOGEL, HOWARD H., "Colonial Theocracy and a Secular Press," *Journalism Quarterly* 37:525, Autumn, 1960.

See Zenger entries and General entries, Barnes, Duniway, Levy.

Reprints of Front Pages

EMERY, EDWIN, ed., *The Story of America As Reported In Its Newspapers From 1690 to 1965,* New York: Simon and Schuster, Inc., 1965. (A voluminous work with representative newspapers' front pages reprinted; interpretation of periods given too.)

———, and WARREN C. PRICE, *A Century of American Journalism by Publishers' Auxiliary,* Washington, D. C.: Publishers' Auxiliary, 1965. (A useful, informative compilation of articles and pictures which appeared in the trade newspaper on its one hundredth anniversary.)

Part Two

Young Nation's Newspapers (1783-1830)

Gazette of the United-States.

NUMBER II. From WEDNESDAY, April 15, to SATURDAY, April 18, 1789. PRICE SIX PENCE.

[The Revolution of America, it was very early predicted, would have a great influence upon the political affairs of the European World—but the most sanguine advocate for the Liberties of Mankind, could not have anticipated those surprising Events, which have already transpired to distinguish the annals of the present age.—Our generous, and magnanimous Allies, the French nation, in their publications upon laws, government, and Freedom, discover a noble ardour in the best of causes—and the following communication will shew, that under the Auspices of the best of Kings, they are on the eve of establishing a new, and a free Constitution.]

FOREIGN INTELLIGENCE.

LONDON, DEC. 20.

POLITICAL STATE OF FRANCE.

[TRANSLATED FROM THE FRENCH.]

THE warmth and zeal with which some provinces have of late reclaimed their ancient privileges, though hostile to the general welfare of the kingdom, has reached the municipalities, and even a great number of individuals, who have been considerably alarmed: but all at once, and at a most unexpected period, the eyes of all the good citizens have been turned with affection and complacency towards the Dauphinians, who by means of a noble and steady conduct have obtained from the government whatever they have solicited: their neighbours, the States of Bearn, filled with admiration, and willing to follow their steps, tho't proper to consult them on this momentous subject; but the new States of Dauphine, not having as yet met, and their Syndics not being elected, a Committee appointed for that purpose was ordered to send them the following truly patriotick answer, which has been much applauded throughout the kingdom, and has been read by all ranks of people.

"ANSWER from the STATES of DAUPHINE to the SYNDICS of the STATES of BEARN.

"GRENOBLE, 28th Sept. 1788.

"GENTLEMEN,

"We take on ourselves to answer your letter, though addressed to our Syndics who have not as yet been chosen, as our new States are not entirely organized. The three orders of this province presented some time ago to his Majesty, a new provincial Constitution, free from the many errors of the obsolete one, which has since received his most gracious approbation and sanction.

"You ask us, gentlemen, what were the motives which formerly determined the inhabitants of this province to send deputies to the States General, as you seem to fear lest the right of granting subsidies in our provincial assemblies, which you hold in common with us, should be infringed.

"The people of Dauphine represented in their provincial states, it is true, have the right of withholding or granting subsidies to the monarch; it is equally true that we might find in our ancient charters some plausible pretence for not sending deputies to the States General, and perhaps for exempting ourselves from paying our share of such general taxes as are imposed by the majority of national deputies: but fortunately the inhabitants of this province have never thought it would be advantageous not to assist the nation with their councils, whenever she is deliberating on her most important concerns. Whether the ancient States of Dauphine have ever recorded their reasons for so doing, is more than we can say, the States having never been called since the year 1628, and though this period is not very distant, yet we have observed nothing in their proceedings relating to those deputies; but we find in those of the States General, held in 1484, 1588 and 1614 manifest proofs that we were then represented. Those who think they held a seperate meeting as deputies from an independent State, entertain a most palpable error; they voted with those of the other provinces in 1484, as well as in the three last ones.

"Dauphine is not the only province, which tho' it enjoyed the rights of granting or withholding subsidies in its particular States, yet submitted to the national deliberations: Provence, Languedoc, Bretagne, Normandy, &c. have formerly given the same example.

What advantage could this province reap from not sending deputies to the States General? Could its inhabitants flatter themselves with the idea of possessing more wisdom and pursuing the steps of a sounder policy, than the whole nation assembled? Are we not obliged to contribute our share of the expenses necessary to the preservation of order and publick tranquility, as well as to the safety of the kingdom? Became independent, could we find among ourselves a greater degree of strength, with which to oppose the snares of intrigues, and repel the encroachment of authority?

"Whilst an individual may hold up his charters, and sometimes oppose them successfully to the rapacity of power, can he at the same time dispense with attending national assemblies, met to deliberate on the remedies required by the calamities and general distresses of the nation?

"Until now, gentlemen, France has not had a positive, nor a fixed Constitution, sufficiently defined to guarantee the respective rights of the sovereign and of the subjects; hitherto the provinces, the different orders, nay the very individuals have been too widely separated; no bond of real union has ever existed between the parts of this vast whole. Each, circumscribed within the narrow circle of their own private concerns, have not reflected how much their division led them to inability and weakness, and how much their exclusive attention to their particular privileges, made them neglect national and individual liberty, as well as the rights of private property; hence the strong tide of power has progressively swallowed up every thing.

"Provinces ought never to have separate interests but when they form federal republicks, each possessing a sovereign power: In a monarchy, we never can be free, unless impelled by the same views and closely united, in order to maintain in its full vigour, the general Constitution.

"Let us forget what we have been, in order to think more attentively on what we wish to be; Frenchmen enjoying under a King a proper share of freedom; when the Representatives of this great nation are met to deliberate on the best means of healing her wounds, on those of preserving to the throne, that necessary share of splendour and dignity; on those of paying the debts of the state; on those in short of leading France towards that summit of power and glory to which nature has raised her; we are well assured, gentlemen, that then both the Bearnois and Dauphinians, will not be the last to appear and offer their honest tribute of councils and personal services.

"We are of opinion, gentlemen, that you ought

cipal aim of all my actions, and of my best wishes.

"But before the Convocation of those States is to take place, I wish to consult you, gentlemen, on the most eligible mode of rendering that important meeting as useful to my kingdom as possible. For that purpose, I have ordered, that every information, and papers which may tend to elucidate the principle object of your meeting, should be laid before you. I am confident that your zeal, the celerity of your debates and deliberations, will hasten the completion of this important task, for which I have called you together, and that your labours will deserve all my confidence, and answer the expectations of the publick."

SPEECH of the KEEPER of the SEALS.

"GENTLEMEN,

"THE Notables of the kingdom have never been called but on the most urgent occurrences, and in consequence of the most important circumstances, it is in those momentous ones, that a monarch, whose first wish is the publick good, loves to meet the wise councils of his people, and to surround himself with the light of their knowledge.

"Such has been the conduct of those of our sovereigns whose names have been handed down, and are exhibited to their successors, as patterns of good kings; such was the conduct of that magnanimous one, whose memory becomes dearer every day, as we trace his virtues in the heir of his throne.

"The convocation of the States General will become one of the most memorable events of his reign; what greater boon could the nation expect from his goodness and justice? But the tender solicitude of his Majesty is not limited to the mere calling of this great assembly; he wishes also to remove every obstacle, to smooth every difficulty which can possibly be foreseen. He wants to know which is the most perfect mode of calling them, and that which may become the most useful to the people. Instead of trusting to his own wisdom, or

Federalist Exponent—The Federalists needed a newspape voice, and the *Gazette of the United States* filled this need. This was the period of the party press newspapers. Brilliant Alexander Hamilton, Federalist leader, was the power behind the *Gazette of the United States*, published in the capital at Philadelphia.

Chapter 3

Launching the New Nation

PRESS PLAYS SIGNIFICANT ROLE

With the end of the Revolutionary War, Americans faced the problem of launching their young nation. Monumental tasks of building a strong, workable government and of resolving internal economic and political issues also confronted the founders of the republic. They had to develop their agriculture, commerce and native industry. Abroad, they had to cement good foreign relations.

The press played a significant role in the founding of the young nation and its subsequent development. The Revolutionary War had demonstrated that the newspaper possessed barely tapped persuasive power. With growth of new political parties, the Federalists (Hamiltonians) and the Anti-Federalists (Jeffersonians or Republicans) turned to the newspaper to fight political party battles in early decades of the republic. As parties developed and grew more powerful, so did newspapers. Editors not only mirrored party battles but stimulated interest in government and aided leaders in consolidating their followers, the voters.

While the nation was being launched politically, its population boomed and the country expanded commercially, industrially and financially. Western lands beyond the Alleghenies were opened for further settlement by farmers and for the building of towns. These trans-Allegheny farms began to supply an abundance of foodstuffs for the eastern seaboard. Internally, trade improved. Coastwise shipping and foreign exports continued to mount. Established colonial seaports became bustling cities, and new towns were born at strategic locations in the interior. By means of its news, editorials and advertisements, the press played an important role (1) in telling the story of this economic expansion and (2) in spurring the development of the hustling economy.

Educational progress and cultural advancements were marked in this period. Newspapers, which mirrored the changes, benefitted from the rising cultural level. This trend produced greater literacy, boosting press circulation.

As a result of all these economic, social and cultural factors, the news media became stronger, with newspapers increasing the frequency of publication to triweeklies and dailies and enlarging their page sizes. Publisher-editors improved news coverage, while adding regular editorials. City newspapers expanded their staffs. Soon advertising filled 50 per cent of the pages. For many dailies, circulation doubled and quadrupled. To take care of this expansion mechanical facilities for producing newspapers were revolutionized with introduction of the cylinder press.

First will be surveyed the political developments because of their strong influence on the character and development of the news media.

A NEW NATION IS BORN

In the post-Revolutionary War period, newspapers reported the severe depression felt by financiers, farmers and returning soldiers. The journals told how the weak Continental Congress, operating under the Articles of Confederation, could not cope with the problem of English goods being dumped in America. Weeklies also published articles which showed that the Congress had not taken any steps to avoid curtailment of trade with the West Indies, an action enforced by the British fleet.

Equally important, the Articles of Confederation gave no power to Congress to impose taxes or regulate commerce. Soon a national debt of seventy-five million had accumulated. The country was depressed economically and psychologically. Some states defaulted their debts. Mortgages were foreclosed. Shays' Rebellion broke out in Massachusetts in 1787 when local citizens closed the courts and would not let the legal machinery operate.

Recognizing the need for drastic action, business leaders called the Philadelphia Constitutional Convention in 1787 to revise the old Articles of Confederation or to draw up a new constitution. Members of the convention were appointed by state legislatures. The great majority of those who journeyed to Philadelphia were lawyers, merchants, moneylenders and real estate speculators. Small farmers, mechanics, and laborers were not represented. Democratically inclined men such as Samuel Adams, Tom Paine and Thomas Jefferson were absent. The members of the convention believed that the only way to promote their hard-won economic interests and to save the country from ruin and possible civil war lay in establishing a strong centralized system of government.

Newspapermen did not cover the proceedings; the convention worked behind closed doors. If reporters had been allowed to report the debates and actions taken, the outcome of the work of the convention (the Constitution) might have been different. After laboring for four months, the members drafted a new federal Constitution, reprinted in the weeklies. Nearly all the framers of the Constitution agreed that democracy was a dangerous institution and that the majority's will should be limited as much as possible. A system of checks and balances formed the basic framework of the new governmental machinery, with executive, legislative and judicial branches. The document established a Senate and a House of Representatives.

Framers of the Constitution did not include any guarantee of a free press which had helped the colonists win the battle with the British. No one knows exactly why the guarantee was omitted, but various reasonable explanations have been offered. By the time the argument over details of the national constitution was underway, nine of the thirteen states had already incorporated in their state constitutions such a press protection. Some political leaders at the Philadelphia constitutional convention may have believed this state protection was sufficient. Others remembered radical Patriot newspapers and their incitement to violence. Since the general tone of the Constitution was conservative, emphasizing the need for controls and brakes over the will of the people, the business and professional men may have deliberately refrained from including a safeguard for newspapers.

Hamilton later defended omission of the press guarantee. Writing in Federalist papers, he said,

> What signifies a declaration that the Liberty of the Press shall be invariably preserved? What is Liberty of the Press? Who can give it any definition which does not leave the utmost latitude for evasion?
>
> I hold it to be impractical. And from this I infer, that its security, whatever fine declarations may be inserted in any constitution respecting it, must altogether depend on public opinion, and on the general spirit of the people and of the Government.

This was a sound, philosophical point, for interpretation of "liberty" depended on the kind of government and the attitude of the people. A protective law, however, would establish certain legal safeguards which many others thought later were essential. Hamilton, however, revealed the constitutional framers' conservatism and lack of concern over the free press principle. James Madison, whose minutes of the convention were preserved, tended to confirm this view because only occasional and casual references were made to the press in his records of the proceedings.

JOURNALISTIC BATTLE OVER RATIFICATION

Securing ratification of the Constitution was the next great problem. The liveliest kind of journalistic campaign arose between those who favored its adoption and those who opposed it. The former, styling themselves Federalists, were propertied businessmen and their lawyers who had worked for a central government. Federalists also included the clergy, physicians and merchants.

Anti-Federalists, who came to be known as Jeffersonians or Republicans, were recruited mainly from small-farmer, nonpropertied groups. They mistrusted men of superior education and property. The nonpropertied citizens felt their liberties were endangered by the new Constitution. The document, for instance, did not guarantee any rights for which the colonists had fought in the revolution: rights of free speech and press.

Between the Federalists and Anti-Federalists were many middle-grounders who did not know which party to support. Both Federalists and Anti-Federalists, therefore, made every effort to win the undecided. During the campaign over adoption of the Constitution, newspapers from Maine to Georgia were flooded with slashing, acrimonious attacks on the upholders of the Constitution and with counterattacks on the opponents of the document. Arguments for ratification of the Constitution were set forth in *The Federalist,* a collection of eighty-five essays written by Alexander Hamilton, James Madison and John Jay, and published first in the *New York Independent Journal.*

Authors of the *Federalist Papers,* addressed to the "People of the United States," knew the essays would be reprinted in many journals along the seaboard. The *Federalist Papers* were reprinted later also in pamphlet form. As Hamilton anticipated, the articles were copied widely in American newspapers, for the essays were strong, convincing arguments for a national government with central control. It is believed that the Federalist essays had much to do with the adoption of the Constitution, providing the framework of the United States government.

Richard Henry Lee in his *Letters from the Federal Farmer* to the Republicans proved to be one of the strong leaders of the opposition to the adoption of the new document. Lee claimed that the Constitution was undemocratic and that it was planned to serve the interests of the propertied minority.

Strength of the Federalists lay in seacoast towns. Back portions of the various states, settled mainly by small farmers, were overwhelmingly opposed to ratification. In some states, widespread debate occurred over the omission of a free press guarantee. The states refused to ratify unless free press provisions were made.

Hamilton, as indicated, made the point that the "liberty of the press" phrase was too vague as a principle and that press freedom depended entirely on the will of the people. Thomas Jefferson, on the other hand, was very concerned that the Constitution had omitted a bill of rights, providing clearly for freedom of religion and freedom of the press. He wrote to James Madison, of Virginia, that he thought James Wilson, of Pennsylvania, was wrong when he said that a bill of rights was not necessary because the federal government had no power not expressly delegated to it and therefore could not interfere with press rights. An amendment to the Constitution forbidding the federal government to restrict press freedom was useless and not needed, opponents had argued. Jefferson and his followers declared, however, that without an expressed guarantee of liberty of the press, the federal government through implied powers might seek to control the newspapers.

Recognizing that the controversy over the free press issue might endanger adoption of the Constitution, the framers decided to compromise. They promised to include a people's bill of rights in the Constitution shortly after it was adopted. These rights would be in the form of amendments. It is believed by historians that if the Founding Fathers had not made this proposal and promise, the states might have rejected the document, so fierce was the feeling. After a strong fight by the Federalists and their promise to pass a protecting bill of rights, the states finally approved the Constitution.

Congress, upon convening, passed the first ten amendments quickly. The first article provided that Congress shall make no law abridging the freedom of speech or of press. The amendment was ratified by the states in 1791. The article represented a great legal milestone in the struggle for a free press in the United States. It expressed nationally what the Zenger case had established by principle, and it confirmed what some of the states already had established on a state-wide basis by law.

DOMESTIC PROBLEMS CHIEFLY ECONOMIC

The new Federalist government had to face certain economic and political issues in domestic and foreign areas. A division of interest on these major issues led to formation of the two political parties: the Federalists, led by brilliant Secretary of the Treasury Alexander Hamilton;

and the Anti-Federalists, whose guiding light was Secretary of State Thomas Jefferson. As issues sharpened and divided the country into political-economic groups, many newspapers lined up with the Federalists or Anti-Federalists. A number of papers, as before, did not take a great part in the party battles of the era.

Hamilton's program became the battleground on which the forces contended. Newspapers printed his historic report on public credit, a document issued to Congress in January, 1790. In the report, Secretary Hamilton proposed that the new nation take over the entire national debt and state debts. Federalists also favored the establishment of a national bank, which Hamilton said was needed to put more currency into circulation and make use of idle funds. Also the bank would enable the government to make loans to commercial concerns more easily. Hamilton's proposals for raising internal revenue were supported by the Federalist press and strenuously opposed by the Anti-Federalist papers. Hamilton, not wanting to impose direct taxes and thus alienate the business-propertied class, recommended excise taxes which could be passed on to the consumer. Distilleries had to pay an excise tax on liquor, a tax which their customers would not readily pay. This measure stirred up a hornet's nest and led to open rebellion in Western Pennsylvania, a protest known as the Whiskey Rebellion. Hamilton's arguments in favor of a protective tariff for manufacturers were set forth in his Report on Manufacturers in 1791. It was reported in newspapers of all political inclinations.

Although the Federalists had won the first round on domestic problems, the Jeffersonians did not sit idly by but continued their opposition throughout the 1790s. Through the press they continued to express the feeling that the Hamiltonian legislation was designed to aid the wealthy at the expense of the farmer and laborer. The Financial Acts involving the national government's assumption of state debts and payment of securities at face value antagonized those whose securities had passed to the hands of speculators. Anti-Federalists also claimed that the Hamiltonians condemned democracy and equalitarianism.

FOREIGN AFFAIRS STIR PARTIES, PRESS

The French Revolution had a profound effect on America. When the journals reported that in France the old regime had been overturned, the common people were overjoyed. To them, the Old World upheaval was similar to their own struggle against wealth and privilege. Many colonials who had left their homes to fight for the rights of man had become somewhat disillusioned since ratification of the Constitution. News of the French Revolution came as a pleasant and hope-inspiring surprise. Perhaps the rights for which colonists had battled might be realized. The Americans put on festivals, sang songs, gave speeches and participated in riotous parades. Jacobin Clubs sprang up in this country in support of the French radicals.

Newspapers reported that the Hamiltonians feared the French Revolution with its defiance of authority and its emphasis on the common man. They feared the "rabble" in America might overturn the government and destroy the Constitution. Every sympathizer was called a Jacobin. Federalists called the Jacobin Clubs demoniacal societies and raised the cry, "Down with the Democratic Clubs." Washington implied they were back of the Whiskey Rebellion.

Relations with England also became strained and developed into an issue over which Federalists and Anti-Federalists fought through their newspapers. No sooner did England and France become involved in a war in 1793 than English naval commanders proceeded to destroy the French merchant marine. The British even attacked shipping of neutral countries if their ships carried French goods. Many American vessels were captured and crews taken. Chief Justice John Jay was sent to England to work out what became known as the Jay Treaty. The British agreed to evacuate the Northwest Territory but insisted the Mississippi River be opened to English ships for trading. When terms of the Jay Treaty were made public through newspapers, rage swept the country: The Anti-Federalists charged the British were getting too many privileges.

POLITICAL PARTY PRESS DEVELOPS

For the upper-class public of farmers, shippers, manufacturers and bankers interested in these foreign and domestic problems, newspapers devoted increasing attention to political news. The party press grew in this country, reflecting a situation similar to the two-party struggle in England which produced the Tory and Whig newspapers. Sharp divisions into two distinct party newspapers developed gradually here.

Established publishers at first loudly avowed their nonpartisanship. Eventually, some of these publishers, because of their own political and economic convictions, began to align themselves with one or the other of the parties. Then, new local papers were established by some printers and writers to espouse a partisan stand. If a town had a Federalist paper but no Anti-Federalist sheet, or at least not a strong one, a printer or editor soon saw the opportunity to fill this vacuum, and a weekly paper representing the Anti-Federalist appeared. The reverse political situation also called for a new journal: A Federalist organ came from the press. Cost of founding a newspaper in this era was still not large; the paper could be operated as a part of a job-shop business.

Contributed essays continued to serve as a source of published opinions in some of these gazettes, but both Hamiltonians and Jeffersonians soon realized that they needed a more systematic, effective way to present party views. These national and other local political leaders began to help young men found new journals to promote the Federalist or Anti-Federalist party's political and economic views.

As economic and political issues grew *national* in scope, political leaders, instead of having to influence only people of one colony, needed to interest those in distant states in the parties' political programs. So politicians established or helped found national journals in the capital. The national newspapers reflected the transition from the era when Americans lived in separate colonies to the new period when they were welded together into one united nation.

Jeffersonians and Hamiltonians in each state and in the nation's capital continued to offer inducements to printers, publishers and editors to become partisans. Political leaders furnished funds to launch newspapers. Parties also subsidized established editors to keep them operating when their income was insufficient. Party leaders also gave publishers jobs as postmasters or government printers. Some politicians in office appointed editors to other governmental positions, such as clerking in state or federal departments, or translating foreign documents for the government. Frequently, friendly newspapers received legal government advertising from officials or members of the legislature. On all levels government officials and party leaders gave exclusive news to papers representing the party's views. Businessmen who had advertisements to insert in a weekly or daily gave their patronage to their party newspapers.

Editorials Begin in Newspapers

Instead of waiting for contributors to send in news articles or essays favoring their party, as in the colonial period, partisan publisher-editors themselves regularly wrote items reflecting the party's viewpoints. This gave rise to the editor as a person distinct from the printer of the newspaper.

News commentary, inspired by the publisher's political beliefs, also became an integral part of the newspaper and was the forerunner of the editorial. The editorial function had always been present in embryonic form; in the colonial period essays and letters written by prominent lawyers and businessmen were published. The editorial which now developed was shorter and more direct than the colonial essays. Newspapers, indeed, had evolved into political and economic organs.

FEDERALIST PRESS EXERTS INFLUENCE

In cities of the seaboard a number of Federalist papers were launched. Since New York became the first capital of the young republic, it was natural that a strong Hamiltonian organ would develop there.

NEW YORK FEDERALIST PRESS

Fenno's Gazette of the United States (1789–)

Federalist Party leaders felt that a strong publication was needed in New York to plead the Federalist cause consistently. The party did not have a national organ to uphold its program. In April, 1789, Federalists launched the *Gazette of the United States* in New York, with John Fenno as editor. The paper became the Federalists' recognized organ. Its articles were widely quoted in party papers and bitterly attacked in Republican organs.

John Fenno, the *Gazette*'s editor, was born in Boston in August, 1751. During the Revolutionary War his writing ability was recognized and he served as secretary to American generals. After the Revolution he entered the importing business in Boston. When Fenno's venture failed he sought to retrieve his fortunes in New York.

If Fenno had not made his appearance there at that time, some other Federalist organ would undoubtedly have been started by wealthy merchants and financiers. They backed not only Fenno's *Gazette of the United States* but also, somewhat later, the *American Minerva* and the *Evening Post,* both issued in New York. On the other hand, Jeffersonians secured expatriated Englishmen and Irishmen to fight their journalistic battles.

Since the *Gazette of the United States* was intended to be the central organ of the Federalist Party, Fenno wished the paper to circulate in every state to serve as a guide for other Federalist editors. Fenno proposed to publish news of politics and commerce; and if any space were left a few odds and ends about science, art and education. There was no conception of news as "human interest," no appeal to the emotions of the masses. As an upper-class paper, the *Gazette* was slanted toward merchants, manufacturers, shippers and wealthy farmers, in other words, those who could vote. It was a semiofficial government organ designed to promote the Federalist viewpoint.

Among the paper's contributors were Alexander Hamilton, Rufus King and John Adams, with Hamilton the guiding genius. Fenno described how, late at night, he would go to Hamilton's library where the chief of the Federalist forces would dictate articles with great precision and rapidity. Historian Claude G. Bowers has also paid tribute to Hamilton's newspaper ability:

> He was a natural journalist and pamphleteer—one of the fathers of the American editorial. His perspicacity, penetration, powers of condensation, and clarity of expression were those of a premier editorial writer.

While the *Gazette* of the United States led the Federalist newspaper clique, the Fenno publication was less vituperative than some others. Despite government backing the *Gazette of the United States* had only fourteen hundred subscribers at the close of the second year. Neither was there much advertising because Fenno believed advertisements would militate against circulation. Fenno supplemented his income by acting as a printer to the United States Treasury. Despite lack of financial success the *Gazette of the United States* made its influence felt; Jefferson, to counteract Fenno's paper, founded the *National Gazette*.

In late 1790 Fenno transferred his paper to Philadelphia, the capital, where he first issued it on November 3. Originally a semiweekly, the *Gazette of the United States* became a daily after 1793.

The American Minerva-Federalist (1793—)

With removal of the *Gazette of the United States* to Philadelphia, New York was without a strong Federal organ. At this point, Noah Webster, former school teacher and writer, began the *American Minerva* with Federalist support.

Noah Webster entered Yale College in 1774. Later he supported himself by teaching and by obtaining royalties from a spelling book. He also studied law. He acquired his earliest newspaper training on the *Hartford Courant*, where he first actively fostered nationalism and its twin, the American character.

In 1787, after unsuccessfully attempting to edit the *American Magazine* in New York, he returned to Hartford. His arrival coincided with the shift of the *Gazette of the United States* to Philadelphia. The national political situation was fast becoming unfavorable to the Federalist Party. Federalist leaders turned to Noah Webster; it had become vital that a party organ have a full-time New York editor. Webster returned to New York to edit the new Federalist journal.

Webster was a genuine American nationalist who believed that Federalism represented the best plan for the American nation. On December 9, 1793, Webster established the *American Minerva* as a daily. His Federalism was staunch; his personal loyalty to Washington undeviating.

Ten well-known Federalists contributed a temporary loan to start the *American Minerva*: John Jay, Rufus King, James Watson, James Greenleaf, Alexander Hamilton and five others gave one hundred fifty dollars each, a total of fifteen hundred dollars.

In emphasizing a desire to keep his *American Minerva* free from personalities, Webster reacted against the vituperative Republican organs in Philadelphia. He even refused to answer personal attacks.

Webster was one of the first to issue a weekly, the *Herald*, as an adjunct to a daily. The *Herald* was designed to appeal to farmers in northern and western New York and other sections where Federalist newspapers had not been established. This new journalistic technique was born of the spread of population westward. Instead of local store advertisements the *Herald* printed announcements of farm implements and essays on agriculture.

For his European news coverage Webster used American representatives abroad. He refused to rely on the clippings from the foreign press, arguing that America ought to be intellectually free of all bonds attaching her to Europe. He helped prepare the way for an intellectual change in the next century, one which was to have repercussions on all American newspapers.

Webster was also active in diffusing education through the newspaper. In the first issue of the *Minerva* he discussed his ideas of journalism, ideas well in advance of those of his contemporaries:

> . . . newspapers are not only the vehicles of . . . news. They are common instruments of social intercourse, by which the Citizens of this vast Republic constantly discourse and debate with each other on the subjects of public concern. . . .

Alive to issues of the day as well as those foreshadowed, he was quick to see the perils underlying slavery, and he wrote essays attacking it from an economic standpoint. He also proposed unemployment insurance, city planning, street cleaning, improvement of penal laws, investigation of diseases, collection of statistics and organization of charitable societies.

The *American Minerva* reached a circulation of seventeen hundred while other New York papers were printing about ten hundred copies. In 1794 the paper became the *American Minerva and the New York Evening Advertiser*, and in 1796, the *Commercial Advertiser*.

On April 1, 1798, Webster withdrew from active editing of the paper. It was believed he was dissatisfied with the "personalities" of daily journalism as well as with the Federal bungling and self-seeking. At any rate, he placed his nephew, Ebenezer Belden, in charge of the paper and returned to Hartford, where he devoted himself to his monumental project, the dictionary.

After his withdrawal the *Commercial Advertiser* developed into a purely commercial newspaper. Its national circulation began to dwindle partly because of the rise of other Federal organs but it continued to have a steady audience.

Lewis, New Publisher

In 1803 Zachariah Lewis became publisher of the *Commercial Advertiser* and later purchased the paper, paying Webster about one-half the five thousand dollars he asked—an indication of the financial value of a New York paper at that time. The new publisher continued Federalist policy. Lewis began to use the headline technique proved effective by the *Boston Centinel.* His bias was plain in such headings as:

REAL PIRACY—BLOODY BEACONS—LOOK OUT
FOR FRENCH TORIES

By 1812 the *Commercial Advertiser* had acquired both Washington and Albany correspondents, and in the same year William Leete Stone, an upstate New York Federalist publisher, became one of the proprietors of the paper, adding his editorial power and literary strength to those of the other editors.

It had been said of the *Commercial Advertiser* that wars might be fought and won, dynasties rise and fall, quakes and floods ravage the earth, without getting a word in the *Advertiser*, but that should it fail to list a single ship's arrival or departure the editor would immediately blow his brains out. Under Stone's direction the *Advertiser* began to emerge from its commercial doldrums. The *Commercial Advertiser* used satire against the three democratic movements of the time: public schools, trade unions and emancipation of women.

The New-York Evening Post (1801–)

Establishment of the *New-York Evening Post*, which developed into the strongest arm of the Federalist Party, grew out of a political and journalistic setting adverse to that organization. Spring of 1801 was the blackest the Federalists had ever known. Republican Thomas Jefferson became President. Governor DeWitt Clinton was wielding the guillotine in New York state politics, cutting out every Federalist. Many New York Federalists watched the turn of events with alarm, believing the state was on its way to ruin.

Federalists needed an organ to defend their cause more vigorously than the *Commercial Advertiser,* the only New York Federalist paper. Democrats already had a vitriolic sheet, the old *Argus,* now the *American Citizen.* Other advertisers and gazettes were largely commercial journals. So Hamilton met and discussed the situation with William Coleman, a New England Federalist lawyer and newspaper writer.

After graduation from Andover Academy, Coleman studied law. From his practice he made a considerable amount of money. After a term in the legislature and loss of his money on some ventures, however, he moved to New York to seek better opportunities. There he came under the magnetic influence of Alexander Hamilton, and through him Coleman was appointed clerk of the circuit court.

Realizing the need for a newspaper, Coleman proposed to the Federalists that he establish one; his offer was accepted. Plans for the *Evening Post* were drafted during May and June, 1801, with the founders' list being circulated among trusty Federalists, each of whom was expected to contribute one hundred dollars toward the initial capital required. Hamilton himself furnished a thousand. This transaction indicated that by 1801 ten thousand dollars capital was needed to start a first-rate metropolitan daily, although smaller papers were undoubtedly launched on less. The *New-York Evening Post* appeared in November, 1801.

Although Coleman declared he was openly attached to Federalism, he said he disapproved of political dogmatism. The *Post* however was strictly Federalist for many years; it was rarely open to Democratic views and news. In this period the conception of a newspaper reporting news and opinions of both parties was unknown.

Coleman received articles and many advertisements from members of the party. The marine list, vital to the shipping business, stock quotations, advertisements of new lands being opened, editorial advocacy of the interests of large commercial groups, all indicated that it was the Federalist class to which Coleman made his appeal. Coleman's articles were reprinted in many Federalist newspapers.

The question has often been asked what connection Hamilton had with the *Evening Post.* Certainly, some of the *Post*'s articles were beyond Coleman's writing ability. While the editor admitted that the Federalist

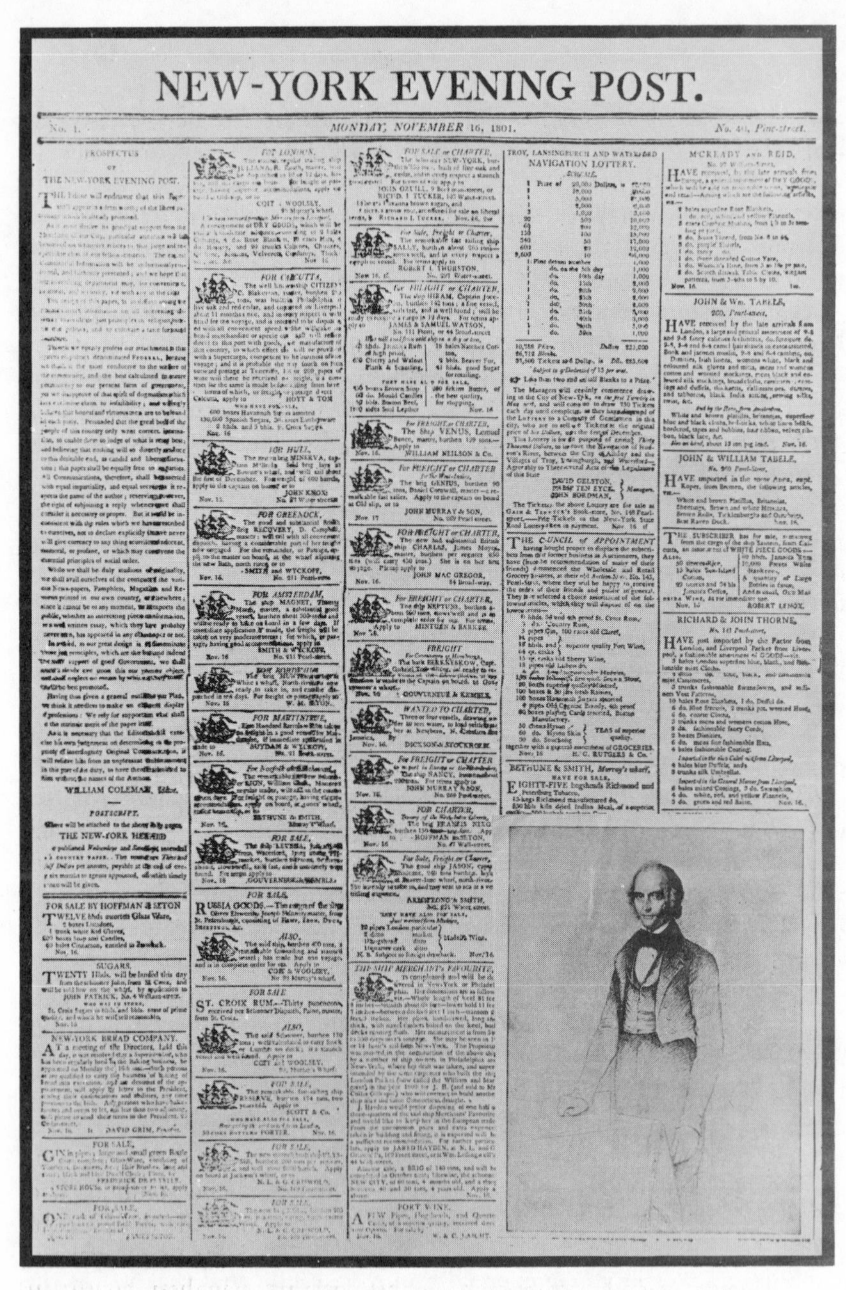

NEW-YORK EVENING POST.

No. 1. MONDAY, NOVEMBER 16, 1801. No. 40, Pine-street.

PROSPECTUS OF THE NEW-YORK EVENING POST.

WILLIAM COLEMAN, Editor.

POSTSCRIPT.

FOR LONDON.

FOR CALCUTTA.

FOR HULL.

FOR GREENOCK.

FOR AMSTERDAM.

FOR MARTINIQUE.

FOR SALE.

RUSSIA GOODS.

ST. CROIX RUM.

FOR SALE or CHARTER.

For FREIGHT or CHARTER.

FREIGHT

WANTED TO CHARTER.

FOR CHARTER.

PORT WINE.

TROY, LANSINGBURGH AND WATERFORD NAVIGATION LOTTERY.

THE COUNCIL of APPOINTMENT

BETHUNE & SMITH, Murray's wharf,

M'CREADY AND REID,

JOHN & Wm. TABELE,

JOHN & WILLIAM TABELE,

RICHARD & JOHN THORNE,

SUGARS.

NEW-YORK BREAD COMPANY.

FOR SALE.

Figure 14. New York Federalist Daily. The Federalists needed a powerful organ to represent their cause in New York, and John Fenno obtained backing from wealthy business and professional men to launch the *New-York Evening Post* in 1801. William Cullen Bryant, a New England poet, joined the staff and later became editor of this distinguished newspaper.

leader "assisted him," Coleman insisted that Hamilton did not write a word. Hamilton probably wrote, however, under the penname Lucius Crassus, attacking President Jefferson's first annual message.

Coleman blasted Jefferson's administration with vigor, accusing the President of immorality, charges as indecent as they were false. Yet, curiously enough, when Jefferson was negotiating for purchase of the Louisiana territory, a move opposed by the Federalists, the *Post* took a sympathetic stand, declaring that the purchase was essential to peace and prosperity. The *Post,* nevertheless, did discredit Jefferson's role in the negotiations. The *Post,* as leader and spokesman for commercial interests, bitterly opposed the embargo against European goods and shipping imposed by Jefferson in 1807 during his second term.

It was not Coleman's intention to make the *Evening Post* a purveyor of general news. Coleman lacked news sense. The *Post* was incredibly blind to important events. One searches in vain for an account of the first trial of Fulton's steamboat, the *Clermont,* the paper's brief references being meager and unsatisfactory despite the fact that on July 22, 1807, sixteen days before the steamboat news, the *Post* reported Fulton's experiment with torpedoes.

Explanation lies in the fact that the *Post,* as other newspapers of the day, concentrated on a different kind of news. Whenever an important event, such as the steamboat's trial, was missed, omission was because of a lack of a systematic method of gathering such news. The full implications of the steamboat's possibilities also were too difficult for the paper's commercial reporter to grasp. In 1828 the *Post* carried an advance notice of the opening of the Baltimore and Ohio Railroad, the beginning of American railroad traffic; yet the paper gave no report of news of the progress of inventions. Such news was not sought out; if the editor published any such news, it was because someone brought the information to him.

In the colonial period newspapers devoted little space to the existing civic problems. The towns were small; the problems few. New York, however, was becoming a metropolis. New buildings were constructed; the city was spreading. Pressing civic problems demanded solution. The *Post* responded effectively to these new urban conditions; the daily established a tradition for civic consciousness that endured for many generations. Coleman waged a campaign against locating slaughter houses in the city and also against the presence of hogs in main streets. He battled for street cleaning and repairing; he was among the first to argue that the water system should be owned by the city. Interestingly enough, he opposed the city aldermen in 1820 when they decided that no more burials should take place at Canal, Sullivan and Grand streets. Always a defender of the merchants, he knew it would be inconvenient for them to travel some distance to bury their dead!

Coleman's editorial column was embryonic and experimental; sometimes he published a paragraph of comments, sometimes two columns of editorials. Often he reprinted the same articles in several different issues. The short editorial essay, complete in itself, discussing a single idea, had not yet come into its own. The editor did not clearly identify the editorial from other material. The personal pronoun "I" which crept slowly into the newspaper editorial indicated that the standardized, impersonal era when publisher kept behind editorial doors was passing.

When New York became a theatrical center the *Post* reviewed and criticized plays. A group of laymen comprised the *Post's* critics. Most of the criticism was leveled at performers. Theatrical folks did not relish the severe criticisms appearing in the *Post.* Dramatic reviews usually were written in other papers by the performers themselves to insure proper newspaper notices. When the *Post* articles started, some of the actors contended with the paper. In January, 1802, the actors' guild produced a satire called "The Wheel of Truth," which concerned the *Post*'s theatrical reviews; Coleman devoted five columns in rebuttal.

Bryant Joins Staff

In 1826 William Cullen Bryant, poet, lawyer and magazine editor, joined the staff of the *New-York Evening Post,* almost by accident and certainly without any intention of making journalism his profession. A New Englander, he had attended Williams College but lacked money to complete his academic training. He studied law, later practicing that profession in Great Barrington, Vermont. The praise he received for his famous poem, "Thanotopsis," and for a thin volume of poetry he published encouraged him to accept the position of co-editor of the *New York Review.* When the magazine was consolidated with other publications, he accepted the position of co-editor of the *United States Review and Literary Gazette.* About the same time *Post* editor Coleman was so severely injured in an accident that his recovery was in doubt, and his son took charge of the *Post.* Someone was needed at once to assist temporarily with the *Evening Post.* Bryant accepted the position. Soon the *Post*'s readers were aware of the new and vigorous hand in the management of the paper.

Despite the *Post*'s past inclination toward a low tariff policy, its editorials had been weak. Bryant favored free trade. His views stamped him as an ardent member of the Democratic Party which eventually was the successor to the Anti-Federalist Party. The paper finally supported Andrew Jackson for the presidency.

Bryant, too, suggested many local municipal improvements. He denounced lotteries, even turning down lottery advertisements, and advocated a bankruptcy law, frowned on by New York merchants.

Bryant, a literary man, devoted much space to book notices and reviews. Coleman and Hamilton had started the literary tradition of the *Post,* but it was Bryant who developed it, another illustration of how the personal background of the editor shaped the course of a paper. Regular and better poetry appeared. Bryant was interested in painting; patrons of the *Post,* therefore, were presented with critical reviews and descriptions of new canvasses.

No previous American editor had made as good use of the editorial page. Bryant had a keen sense of the dignity of his profession. Under Coleman the *Post*'s circulation reached fifteen hundred by 1815; within the following five years it boasted two thousand readers, although other papers arising in New York were giving the *Evening Post* keen competition.

Philadelphia's Federal Party Journalism, The Porcupine's Gazette

Most violent of the Federalist papers, *Porcupine's Gazette and United States Advertiser* was started by William Cobbett on March 4, 1797. Cobbett was an adventurer, son of English peasants. When he was twenty he left the family farm in England and later enlisted in a regiment going to Canada. In the army he learned grammar, sitting on the edge of his bed with a board on his lap as a writing table. Two years after his regiment arrived in Nova Scotia, he became sergeant-major. When he discovered that the quartermaster for several years had been keeping one quarter of the provisions' money for himself, Cobbett gathered enough evidence to indict a number of officers; and in 1792, with supreme courage, he placed charges with the War Office in London.

Powerful interests were arrayed against him, for he had uncovered a whole system of army graft. Although it was planned to court-martial the accused men, fake charges were lodged against Cobbett, and soon thereafter he left for America.

Settling near Philadelphia, he taught English to French emigrés with such success that he was able to support himself and his family. In the following years he attracted considerable attention with a series of pamphlets. He attacked Dr. Joseph Priestley, scientist, educator and political writer who sided with the Democrats. Cobbett thus won the approbation of the Federalists.

Federalists turned to him to supplement Fenno's conservatively pitched *Gazette of the United States,* for Cobbett could reply to the rough-and-tumble methods of Republicans. Cobbett, therefore, launched the new Federalist newspaper, *Porcupine's Gazette,* its title from a nickname applied to the editor by a Republican.

Cobbett's style of writing was plain and simple yet stimulating. Never trite, he had the power of invective and was a master of literary invention and biting humor. Cobbett became one of the most violent newspaper editors on the Federalist side. His vituperative attacks on the French people caused so much scandal that early in 1799 President John Adams, although himself a Federalist, considered ordering Cobbett to leave the country under provisions of the Alien Act.

He made a personal and vicious attack on Benjamin Bache, a rival editor, caricaturing "Benny" with his "sleepy girl's eyes," Bache's emphatic Republicanism and his manners of an artistocratic-turned-market-gardener. After this, even Noah Webster, also a staunch Federalist, rebuked the vehement, low-grade Cobbett methods. In Boston publisher Benjamin Russell, whose invective carried a hornet's sting, reminded the party of Cobbett's value as stated in the following paragraph in the *Columbian Centinel,* April 10, 1799.

> Cobbett was never encouraged and supported by the Federalists as a solid, judicious writer in their cause; but was kept merely to hunt jacobin foxes, skunks, and serpents. . . . It was . . . tho't necessary that the . . . party should keep and feed a suitable beast to hunt down these skunks and foxes; and the "fretful porcupine" was selected for this business.

Eventually, Cobbett found himself involved in a lawsuit for libel. A verdict against the editor for five thousand dollars in damages nearly ruined Cobbett. Before the end of the trial Cobbett moved to New York, taking with him as much of his property as he could. The remainder of his effects in Philadelphia were sold by auction to defray damages and costs, and *Porcupine's Gazette* was suspended on October 26, 1799.

In New York, Cobbett edited the *Rushlight,* but only five numbers of this periodical were published. He then returned to England, where he launched Cobbett's *Political Register,* which gained him a wide reputation for its liberalism. He led in the fight which brought about the Reform Bill of 1832 in England.

Boston, Federalist Center, Massachusetts Centinel

An outstanding Federalist publisher in Boston, indeed the one who built up a national influence, was Benjamin Russell. He had gained his newspaper experience with Isaiah Thomas in Worcester, and he had served in the Continental Army. In 1784 he turned to publication of his own newspaper, the *Massachusetts Centinel.* The name *Centinel* struck the new note, "guardian of the welfare of the community, always alert for news." The newspaper was no longer a mere newsletter, gazette, or chronicle. It had become a herald, an argus, or a centinel.

Russell's prospectus priced his paper at twelve shillings a year, adding that single issues could be had for twopence each according to the custom in London, New York and Philadelphia. The *Centinel* was established as a semiweekly. Russell's credo as well as his stress on sprightly style was announced in this way:

> Variety shall be courted in all its shapes, in the importance of political information—in the sprightliness of mirth—in the playful levity of imagination—in the severity of satire—in the vivacity of ridicule—in the luxuriance of poetry, and in the simplicity of truth. We shall examine the regulations of office with candor—approve with pleasure—or condemn with boldness. . . .
>
> Uninfluenced by party, we aim only to be just.

The *Massachusetts Centinel* became a most powerful organ for the Federalist side and achieved a national reputation for the vigor with which it expounded the Hamiltonian viewpoint. Russell crystallized and united the strong Federalist tendencies in his community.

Effectiveness of the *Centinel* to the Federalists was limited because it was published in Boston, northern outpost of the new country. Russell would have wielded a stronger influence had he been located in New York or Philadelphia, capital cities of the young republic.

American news flowed regularly into the *Centinel* office from postriders and ship captains. On occasion, domestic news was more important than foreign, so Russell presented it on page one, breaking an old precedent. A versatile publisher, Russell supplemented straight news with a multitude of anecdotes, gathering them from other newspapers. Above his news items and anecdotes, Russell published catchy headlines, sometimes satirical, sometimes factual, a departure from usual journalistic practice. As examples:

Melancholy Accident
Sagacity of Rats

He refrained from printing anecdotes about local residents because he faced the small-town psychology of the times. Bostonians were not yet on an impersonal basis in their relationships, and an editor could not afford to offend his neighbors.

Despite Russell's cleverness in all phases of journalism, his variety of essays was the outstanding feature vitalizing the *Centinel.* These essays appeared under the column, "The Observer," with topics ranging from woman's vanity to the importance of philosophy.

Russell's versatility was comparable to Benjamin Franklin's. Russell used many devices to stimulate interest in the *Centinel,* one device being humorous and pointed allegories on various themes and topics in the news. When Washington was inaugurated, Russell's well-known "Federal Ship" was published, revealing the publisher's imagination and wit:

> Just launched on the Ocean of Empire, the Ship Columbia, George Washington commander, which, after being thirteen years in dock, is at length well-manned, and in very good condition. The ship is first-rate—has a good bottom, which all the builders pronounced sound and good.
>
> Some objection has been made to part of the tackling, or the running rigging, which, it is supposed, will be altered, when they shall be found to be incommodious, as the Ship is built to make good headway with them as they are. A Jury of Carpenters have this matter now under consideration. . . .

A special "Poet's Corner" on the back page of the *Centinel* usually concerned the ever-recurring love theme. Russell reported on literature, music, drama and science regularly. Although he had no science reporter, Russell presented scientific articles whenever he could obtain them.

Around 1790, however, a definite cultural decadence began to seep into the *Centinel,* a degeneracy which also affected other newspapers of the day. Essays on life were gradually eliminated as newspapers became commercial journals and party organs. Both readers and editors turned to, or were absorbed by, political and economic controversies of the period. Russell at this time seemed bent solely on arguing the Federalist viewpoint. It was many years before the American newspaper recovered from the bog into which political parties and businessmen had driven it.

Russell had to increase the size of the *Centinel* four times by the turn of the century to accommodate his news and advertising. Also, in 1790 he changed the paper's name to the *Columbia Centinel and Massachusetts Federalist.*

REPUBLICAN PAPERS PROVIDE STRONG OPPOSITION

Just as in each city there were Federalists who were represented by newspapers, so the Anti-Federalists had their organs directly or indirectly controlled by party leaders.

New York's Anti-Federalist Press, The Independent Gazette

John Holt was one of the two prewar Patriot publishers who came back to New York to reestablish his journal. To catch the new independent spirit in the air, he changed the name of his weekly, the *New York Journal* to the *Independent Gazette or the New York Journal Revived,* published again on December 13, 1783. Holt died soon afterward. His wife, Elizabeth, ran the paper alone and then with partners for a few years. The name was changed to *New York Journal and State Gazette.* Thomas Greenleaf acquired the paper in 1787. A New Englander, Greenleaf had obtained his knowledge of printing in Isaiah Thomas' printshop in Boston and later as owner of his own shop. When he was thirty years old, Greenleaf came to New York and went to work for the *New York Journal.* Two years later, Greenleaf purchased the weekly.

The *New York Journal* was strongly Anti-Federalist in sentiment and ridiculed the pageant celebrating ratification of the Constitution. As a result, Greenleaf's machinery was destroyed by some of the paraders. Greenleaf later fought Washington's Federalist administration.

On May 11, 1795, the publisher entered the daily field with publication of the *Argus, Greenleaf's Daily Advertiser.* At the same time, the old paper became a semiweekly edited for country circulation. When yellow fever swept New York and Philadelphia in 1798, Greenleaf himself was stricken and died. His widow, Ann Greenleaf, continued to publish the paper two years longer, after which it was sold to David Denniston who continued its Republican policies and changed its name to the *American Citizen.*

American Citizen

Denniston, however, lost party patronage in 1799 when Federalists came into power; although he put three thousand dollars in the paper, his circulation fell to two hundred seventy. On May 1, 1801, he admitted James Cheetham into partnership to bring the Anti-Federalist (Republican) paper new blood, a change which coincided with birth of the *New York Evening Post,* Federalist mouthpiece.

Born in England, Cheetham, in his youth, became a member of the English Constitutional Society, an organization to protest antiindustrial measures of the government. In 1793 Cheetham was charged with conspiracy to overthrow the government but was freed for lack of evidence. An outbreak of rioting forced him to come to America in 1798.

The *American Citizen,* of which he became editor, was backed by Aaron Burr, at that time a leader in the Republican Party in New York.

Cheetham's prospectus announced that the paper would be published "every morning on good quality paper at $8 a year, paid in advance by distant subscribers, and in quarterly payments by city residents." The *Citizen,* Cheetham added, would be "decidedly Republican, a defender of liberty, and an advocate of the constitution. . . . Nor shall our attentions be directed any less to the concerns of agriculture, manufacturing, and commerce." Cheetham's *Citizen* soon became the outstanding Republican paper in New York. The *American Citizen* gave support to DeWitt Clinton and attacked the Federalists and their newspapers. Cheetham was the first publisher to print editorials regularly, of which most were assaults on prominent Federalist politicians and editors.

In his issue of October 14, 1801, Cheetham defended Mary Wolstonecraft's book, *The Rights of Women,* ridiculed in the *Commercial Advertiser.* Cheetham declared that the *Advertiser's* writer actually attacked Republicanism under the guise of book reviewing; Cheetham added a powerful discourse on the need of freeing women's minds from the slavery to which they had been subjected. His articles, far ahead of public opinion, prepared the way for the later change in viewpoint toward women and their political and economic rights.

Instead of attacking principles, Cheetham hurled his thunderbolts at political leaders. The *Citizen's* editor paved the way for the even more personal journalism of the next period. Cheetham had close contact with President Jefferson, from whom he received firsthand information about governmental affairs.

Philadelphia's Anti-Federalist Press
The National Gazette,
Freneau's Influential Republican Organ

The leading Republican newspaper, destined to set the pace for the Anti-Federalist press throughout the nation, was the *National Gazette* established by Philip Freneau, poet and ship captain. Freneau was born of a French Hugenot family in New York in 1752, a year later than Fenno and Webster. Son of a wealthy importer, Philip attended the College of New Jersey where both teachers and students opposed England. Freneau wrote sparkling verse at college. He also became the lifelong friend of James Madison and Hugh Brackenridge, a Jeffersonian who became a Pennsylvania judge. Later Freneau attended Princeton, a center of anti-British feeling.

After leaving college he read law and taught school. Freneau loved the sea, and in 1776 he sailed to the West Indies. Returning to the United States, he became involved in the struggle for independence. He loved liberty as a principle of government and life and was one of

Figure 15. Leading Republican (Jeffersonian) Editor. Philip Freneau, the poet of the American Revolution, turned to journalism after the war. He became editor of the *National Gazette,* which had the backing of Thomas Jefferson, Secretary of State.

those intellectuals who get into a revolutionary movement because of principle. He had no personal business interest to further. Many of his revolutionary poems were published in the *United States Magazine and Repository of History, Politics, and Literature.* Freneau ventured to sea again during the Revolutionary War but was captured by a British cruiser. When he finally escaped his health was greatly impaired.

From 1781 to 1784 he was employed by the Philadelphia post office and contributed poems satirizing the Loyalists to the *Freeman's Journal.* On April 25, 1789, Freneau came to New York for Washington's first inauguration. In New York Freneau found himself among his old college companions: James Madison, the unscrupulous Aaron Burr and Henry B. Livingston. He obtained employment as a writer for the Republican *New York Daily Advertiser* and brought more vigor to this paper. He soon became recognized in political circles as a strong ally of the Anti-Federalists.

With the opening of the new government in 1790, Thomas Jefferson came to New York as Secretary of State. Monarchial forces represented by the Federalist Party were getting the upper hand. Each of Hamilton's measures, in Jefferson's opinion, threatened the rights of the comman

man. Jefferson, therefore, set out to build up the Republican Party. In Freneau, Jefferson found a congenial spirit. He felt that Freneau was the man to edit a newspaper to oppose Fenno's *Gazette of the United States.* Highly articulate, Freneau could fight the Federalists with their own weapons. An editorial organ was needed to arouse and consolidate the widely scattered Republicans so that the farmer of Georgia, the planter in Virginia, the frontiersman in western Pennsylvania, the mechanic in Boston, the shopkeeper in Rhode Island and the men of Tammany sipping their ale in a New York tavern, might all talk the same language at the same time. There were some independent Republican papers, but there were no party organs; an effective organ was needed. In August, 1791, Jefferson arranged to have Freneau appointed translator in the State Department in Philadelphia with the understanding that, at the same time, he was to issue a Republican newspaper.

Freneau, then called the "Poet of the American Revolution," issued the *National Gazette* on October 31, 1791, as the voice of the Republican, or Jeffersonian Party. According to the publisher's plans, the *National Gazette,* appearing semiweekly, on Wednesdays and Saturdays, was to cost three dollars a year. Francis Childs, publisher of the *New York Daily Advertiser,* agreed to print the new paper in his Philadelphia shop and to assume financial responsibility.

News in the *National Gazette* was to be of a national character, according to the prospectus: "Columns were opened to all original and interesting productions, whether of prose or verse." Political discussions were to be conducted "with perfect fairness and the greatest latitude." Debates of Congress would be printed. Freneau promised that all important books would be reviewed. Then, counteracting the tendency of many prosperous commercial papers, he said that "advertisements would not encroach on general reading matters."

Freneau's newspaper, like the Federalist *Gazette of the United States,* was to become an organ of national influence, reflecting transition of the country from thirteen individual colonies to a single nation. Recognizing the value of the *National Gazette,* both Thomas Jefferson and James Madison, Republican Party leaders, aroused interest in the paper whenever they could and obtained subscriptions for it. The *National Gazette* ultimately reached between fourteen hundred and seventeen hundred subscribers.

During the first four months of its existence, the *National Gazette* was mild in tone. Republican opinions were restrained. By February, 1792, however, the Freneau paper had become more controversial, more bitter. Its principal target was Hamiltonian schemes. When the House

National Gazette

By PHILIP FRENEAU.

Vol. I. THURSDAY, November 3, 1791. Numb. 2.

CONGRESS.

HOUSE OF REPRESENTATIVES OF THE UNITED STATES.

MONDAY, *October* 31.

NATHANIEL NILES and Ifrael Smith, from Vermont; Upton Sheredine, from Maryland; William Barry Grove, from North-Carolina; and Robert Barnewell, from South-Carolina, appeared and took their feats.

Several petitions were read, viz. From James Beers, Leonard Walter, Margaret Flour, Ifaac Richards, Jedidiah Brown, William Haburn, John Fox, and Elizabeth Eafton, praying compenfation for wounds received and fervices rendered in the army of the United States, during the late war.—Said petitions were feverally referred to the Secretary at War.

A petition from Richard Blackledge, praying compenfation for a quantity of leather, furnifhed in the late war; which was referred to the Secretary of the Treafury.

A memorial from Jofeph Cerecchi, an Italian Sculptor, propofing to execute on a certain defign, and conditions, a monument to perpetuate American liberty and independence.

According to the order of the day, the Houfe refolved itfelf into a committee of the whole on the fchedule of enumeration of the inhabitants of the United States.—In debating upon this fubject,

Mr. Lawrance obferved, that the ratio of reprefentation and fome provifion refpecting S. Carolina were the principal objects in view. He meant to propofe a refolution relative to the reprefentation, after which he thought the committee might defer the further confideration of this fubject for fome days that gentlemen might have time to make up their minds upon the bufinefs. He then moved, that till the next cenfus be taken, one member fhould continue to be the reprefentative of thirty thoufand inhabitants.

Mr. Livermore thought that the determination of their conftituents ought to be previoufly known on the amendment to the conftitution, propofing that the reprefentation of one for every thirty thoufand do continue until the number of Reprefentatives fhall amount to one hundred. The people's agreeing to that amendment would oppofe the motion before the Houfe. If the people rejected the amendment, he fhould oppofe fo large a reprefentation as one for every thirty thoufand.

Several other gentlemen having fpoken on the fubject,

Mr. Sedgwick, after reading to the Houfe a calculation he had made, ftating the number by which each ftate would be reprefented, according to the feveral ratios of reprefentation, obferved, that the general fenfe of the people feemed to be that the number of reprefentatives fhould be one hundred until increafed by the ratio of one to forty thoufand. He thought the ratio of 33 or 34,000 more conformable to public opinion than any other number; but that on this fubject the Houfe had nothing whereon to found their conclufions: for his own part he wifhed the Houfe of Reprefentatives always to confift of about one hundred members.

Mr. Livermore was for the ratio of one to forty thoufand. The Houfe would then confift of about eighty members. This would give lefs occafion for complaints of expence, and the public, in his idea, would be equally well ferved. He wifhed the Houfe, if they fettled any ratio might adopt that of one to 40,000.

Mr. White, faid that the general voice of the people was for an increafed reprefentation at certain ftated periods. One to thirty thoufand feemed to be the general idea. The amendment propofed might not always give one to thirty thoufand, but it would fecure an increafe of the reprefentation as the population of the country increafed. He concluded with wifhing the Houfe would not immediately decide on the fubject.

Mr. Dayton wifhed the motion to lay over till tomorrow for further confideration. He thought the general fentiment to be in favour of thirty thoufand, but as a medium between the oppofite

Upon motion of Mr. Smith, the queftion was taken and carried, that the whole houfe be difcharged from farther proceeding on the Prefident's fpeech, and that to-morrow be affigned for the confideration of the fame. Adjourned.

TUESDAY, *Nov.* 1.

Two other members appeared and took their feats, viz. Jofiah Parker, from Virginia, and Anthony Wayne, from Georgia.

A meffage in writing was then received from the Prefident of the United States, by Mr. Secretary Lear, as follows—

United States, *Nov.* 1, 1791.

Gentlemen of the Senate and of the Houfe of Reprefentatives,

I received yefterday from the judge of the diftrict of South-Carolina, a letter inclofing the prefentment, of the grand jury to him, and ftating the caufes which have prevented the return of the cenfus from that diftrict, copies of which are now laid before you.

G. WASHINGTON.

Another meffage was received from the Prefident, viz.

United States, Oct. 31, 1791.

Gentlemen of the Senate and of the Houfe of Reprefentatives.

I fend you herewith the arrangement which has been made by me, purfuant to the act, entitled, "An act repealing, after the laft day of June next, the duties heretofore laid upon diftilled fpirits imported from abroad, and laying others in their ftead; and alfo upon fpirits diftilled within the United States, and for appropriating the fame," in refpect to the fub-divifions of the feveral diftricts, created by the faid act into fur-

ment of a militia, magazines, arfenals, and fortifications, be referred to Mr. Wadfworth, Mr. Dayton, Mr. Giles, Mr. Ward, Mr. Gordon, Mr. Wayne, and Mr. Steele, with inftructions to bring in a bill, or bills, providing for the fame.

Mr. White moved for the appointment of a committee, to report a bill for the eftablifhment of a land-office.—Mr. Williamfon, Mr. White, and Mr. Boudinot, were chofen a committee.

Mr. Lawrance moved for the appointment of a committee, to report a bill for the regulation of the trade and intercourfe with the Indian tribes—committed to Mr. White, Mr. Lawrance, and Mr. Steele.

It was then ordered, that the Secretary of the Treafury, be directed to report to the Houfe, fuch information as he may have obtained, refpecting any difficulties which may have occurred in the execution of the act, "repealing, after the laft day of June next, the duties heretofore laid upon diftilled fpirits imported from abroad, and laying others in their ftead; and alfo upon fpirits diftilled within the United States, and for appropriating the fame;" together with his opinion thereupon. Adjourned.

WEDNESDAY, Nov. 2.

A petition of John Torrey was read, praying to be reimburfed a fum of money which he had been compelled to pay for waggonage on account of the United States.

Ordered to lie on the table.

A petition of Robert Conyngham, praying compenfation for fervices rendered in the navy of the United States, in the late war.

Ordered to lie on the table.

The feveral petitions of John Cooper, [R]obert Crooke, Robert Hodge, Ofwald Keffelbaugh, and Abraham Levi, [re]fpectively praying compenfations for [w]ounds received or fervices rendered [in] the army or navy of the United [S]tates during the late war. Referred to [th]e Secretary at War.

Petitions of Robert Aitken and Tho[m]as Bradford, printers, praying to be [em]ployed in the public printing bufinefs [o]f the United States.

Ordered to lie on the table.

Petition of Nicholas F. Weftfall, [p]raying compenfation for fervices ren[d]ered in the American army, in the [la]te war.

Ordered to lie on the table.

Mr. Dayton moved the following re[fo]lution:

That the Secretary of the Treafury be [di]rected to report to this houfe whether [an]y, and what alterations, in favor of [th]e fpirits which fhall be diftilled from [a]rticles of the growth or produce of the [U]nited States, or from foreign articles [w]ithin the fame, can, in his opinion, [b]e made in the act for laying duties upon [fp]irits diftilled within the United States, [c]onfiftently with its main defign, and [w]ith the maintenance of the public faith.

[O]rdered to lie on the table.

Mr. Giles called the attention of the [H]oufe to a meffage from the Prefident [o]f the United States, containing a re[p]refentation from the officers and fol[d]iers of the Virginia line on conti[n]ental eftablifhment refpecting bounty [la]nds, &c. The papers accompanying [fa]id meffage being read, Mr. Giles mov[ed th]at the fame be referred to a felect [c]ommittee, to report their opinion [u]pon, which motion was ordered to lie [o]n the table.

Mr. Giles moved a refolution in fub[ft]ance, that the Secretary at War be in[ft]ructed to lay before the Houfe a ftate[m]ent of all balances of pay which ap[p]ear by the books in his office to be [d]ue to the officers and foldiers. Order[e]d to lie on the table.

Mr. Vining moved a refolution, that a committee be appointed to prepare and bring in a bill to eftablifh an uniform fyftem of bankruptcy throughout the United States, which was read and ordered to lie on the table.

Mr. Dayton moved a refolution, that the board of commiffioners for fettling the accounts between the United States and individual ftates, be directed to report what progrefs they have made, and what profpect of the bufinefs being finally completed. Ordered to lie on the table.

Purfuant to the order of the day, the houfe refolved itfelf into a committee of the whole, to take into confideration the bill granting further time for making returns of the enumeration of the inhabitants in the diftrict of S. Carolina; after fome time the committee rofe, and reported the bill with fundry amendments, fome were agreed to, and others rejected, and the bill was then ordered to be engroffed.

A meffage was received from the Senate, informing that the petition of

Figure 16. Voice of the Republicans (Anti-Federalists). The *National Gazette,* established in Philadelphia, the capital, in October, 1791, became the leading organ of the Republican (Jeffersonian) Party. The paper obtained a national influence and was quoted widely by other papers which followed the party line. Secretary of State Thomas Jefferson (insert) backed Philip Freneau in the publication.

of Representatives debated Hamilton's proposal that a picture of George Washington be stamped on coins of the United States, Freneau asked on March 29, "Shall Washington, my favorite child, be ranked 'mongst haughty kings?" Resenting the opinions in Freneau's paper, Fenno wrote in his *Gazette of the United States* that Republican writers were "mad dogs" and "audacious scribblers."

Hamilton, seeing that the *National Gazette* would have to be discredited if Federalists were to retain their power, replied on July 25 in the *Gazette of the United States.* "If Jefferson was opposed to every measure of government, why did he not resign as Secretary of State," Hamilton wrote. "Moreover," the Federalist leader asked, "How much was Freneau being paid for the dirty work he was doing?"

In return, Freneau in the *National Gazette* characterized Fenno as a vile sycophant "who finds his interest in attempting to poison the mind of the people by propagating and disseminating principles and sentiments utterly subservient to the true interests of the country. . . ."

Controversy between the two cabinet secretaries caused a public scandal, and Washington requested that Jefferson dismiss Freneau. Jefferson refused, declaring that he had never written anything for the *National Gazette* except trivial pieces and that he had furnished Freneau only with some Leyden (Holland) papers, at that time, the best newssheets in Europe. He asserted that Freneau was trying to expose the monarchical tendencies of the government.

The Fenno-Freneau battle was symptomatic of the controversy created whenever the newspaper changed its character and moved into a new era. Within a few years support of a newspaper by a political party became commonplace.

Late eighteenth-century newspaper publishers were beset with considerable financial difficulties. Advertising was weak; newspapers relied on subscriptions, not paid in advance and hard to collect. After four years of publication, for example, Fenno was carrying twenty-five hundred dollars in bad debts. Political parties often rescued financially shaky newspapers, supplying capital or granting to editors subsidies in the form of printing work and governmental jobs. For a newspaper to exist independently, free from political party influence, the paper's publishers had to develop other sources of revenue: more subscriptions and additional advertising.

Influence of the Republican (Anti-Federalist) organ, the *National Gazette,* increased. Freneau became the leading Republican editor, with copies of his paper being sent to all sections of the country. Anti-Federalist editors in various towns reprinted the *National Gazette*'s aggressive articles, caught some of Freneau's audacity and thus strengthened their own papers.

Freneau's paper not only attacked Hamilton but also Vice President John Adams and even President George Washington. In spite of the fact that Federalist John Adams was reelected, he lost prestige; and decline of Adams' popularity was attributed to Freneau's *National Gazette.*

The attack on Washington stemmed from the editor's foreign policy. Of French ancestry, Freneau believed that if France failed every Republican in America would be crushed too. In his mind, American interests were identified with those of France. Consequently, when Citizen Edmond C. Genêt came to America to represent the French nation, Freneau supported him. When Washington declared the neutrality of the United States in the conflict between England and France, an article in the *National Gazette* accused Washington of double-dealing in issuing the proclamation.

This outspoken opposition to the President created an uproar. Resenting Freneau's violent language, Washington called him a "rascal" at a cabinet meeting; he again requested Jefferson to dismiss Freneau. The Secretary of State replied that Freneau had saved the nation when it was "fast galloping towards monarchy."

While accusing Hamiltonians of governing the country for the benefit of manufacturing classes, the *National Gazette* nevertheless published articles on manufacturing and encouraged commerce. The *National Gazette* also printed articles on improvements in farming as well as on scientific agricultural experiments.

Readers in farming regions frequently wrote to the paper attacking the policies of Hamilton. These farmers played an important role in the Republican Party. John Dickinson, the Pennsylvania farmer who had written such eloquent letters during the revolutionary era, contributed a series, "To the Yeomanry of the United States," in which he told American rulers to "Beware! For governments are tranquil when they are adapted to the ideas and lights of the age and are in turmoil when they are ill-adapted. . . . Rulers should not assume arbitrary power and make the name of a free government a mockery!"

The *National Gazette,* with its superior facilities for getting foreign news through the Secretary of State, published columns about French developments, supplementing these with essays by French writers.

The *National Gazette* also campaigned for open Senate sessions. In an appeal to the public, Freneau asked: "Why all the secrecy?" Within a year his onslaughts had taken effect; Senate doors opened to the public, and capital newspapermen could report the meetings, an important contribution to development of American journalism.

News from the West came in constantly and steadily. Hugh Brackenridge, Freneau's old friend now a jurist in Pittsburgh and a frontier novelist, contributed a flow of articles about Indians and disposal of western lands, stating that Americans were justified in attacking the Indians and taking away their land; Freneau, however, also printed the other side to these questions. Other domestic news in the *National Gazette* was obtained from personal letters.

Freneau reserved the fourth page of the *Gazette* to express his views in verse. One of his most interesting poems was "The Country Press," which dealt with tribulations of a rural editor.

Another lively poem replied to Fenno's attacks:

> Since the day we attempted the *Nation's Gazette*
> Pomposo's dull printer does nothing but fret;
> Now preaching,
> Now screeching,
> Then nibbling,
> And scribbling,
> Remarking,
> And barking,
> Repining,
> And whining,
> And still in a pet,
> From morning till night, with the *Nation's Gazette*. . . .

In the field of invention the *Gazette* described attempts being made to propel a boat by steam and included suggestions for mechanical improvements of the vessel.

One of the causes for expiration of the *National Gazette* was the deadly yellow fever which spread through Philadelphia in autumn of 1793, a disaster which closed several Philadelphia papers temporarily. The *Gazette* might have been crushed anyway. Many subscribers failed to pay. Moreover, when Thomas Jefferson resigned as Secretary of State, Freneau lost his job, and the *National Gazette*'s printer could not carry the paper alone.

The *National Gazette* ceased publication in October, 1793. For several critical years it had been a powerful influence throughout the nation. The paper helped counterbalance the strong Federalists who controlled the government, schools and church, and when most papers were pro-Federalist, for their income depended on the Federalist shippers, merchants and manufacturers. Frequent attacks on Federalists made by the *National Gazette* certainly contributed to eventual unseating of the Federalist Party.

Freneau later started the *Time Piece* in New York and also attempted to launch a paper in New Jersey. Both came to nothing. During the latter part of his life he lost most of his money. He died in 1832 in a snowstorm near his New Jersey home. In addition to his fame as a journalist, Freneau is also known for his poetic gifts and is called the most significant American poet before William Cullen Bryant.

Bache's General Advertiser, Republican (1790–)

Benjamin Franklin Bache, although neither so clever nor so gifted as Freneau, was a persistent man; the paper he founded was longer enduring. A grandson of Benjamin Franklin, Bache at the age of ten had been taken by the scientist-diplomat to Europe. Young Bache was educated in France, receiving his training in printing from Firmin Didot, one of the foremost Parisian printers of the day. By the time his grandfather took him back to Philadelphia, Bache had drawn away from American influences.

In the States he decided to open a bookshop and publish a gazette. He first asked support from Robert Morris, a Federalist leader in Philadelphia. Morris, however, felt that others had prior claim for newspaper support; then Bache presented himself to Jefferson to ask for support. The Secretary of State already had Freneau in mind as editor of a Republican paper.

Turned down by leaders of both Federalists and Republicans, Bache nevertheless launched his *General Advertiser* on October 1, 1790, backed by the American Philosophical Society, a hotbed of radicalism and opposition to Federalism. Facing keen competition from well-established journals, Bache had day-to-day patience, courage and honesty, qualities which brought success. The newspaper business called for systematic intelligence even more than for flashes of genius, and Bache was better suited for editing than either Webster or Freneau. When Freneau's paper expired, Bache stood out as leader of Anti-Federalist journalism.

Typical of a hard-working publisher of the era, Bache arose before daylight to distribute his papers to news agents and newsboys. He received orders, advertisements and complaints, edited the news and supervised printing. In between, he covered various news sources: the docks and the City Tavern. Back in his office, he translated French newspapers. Sometimes he worked at his table for eighteen hours at a time. Aside from an apprentice learning the trade, Bache had no printers or editorial assistants.

When Citizen Genêt came to America representing revolutionary France, he expected to use this country as a base for operations against the Spanish and British colonial empires. In these schemes he found a willing collaborator in Bache, whose *General Advertiser* became Genêt's mouthpiece. Bache was also a politician, and he began to organize the

American people behind Genêt. Bache and Genêt formed the Society of St. George for the Scotch, the Society of St. Patrick for Irish immigrants and the Democratic Society for all other persons in Philadelphia. The founders expected all members to support the Republican Party, Genêt and the *Advertiser.*

General Advertiser Becomes Aurora

Shortly, Bache changed the name of his paper to the *Aurora* and proceeded to attack the Jay Treaty with England. Through Senator Mason, Bache managed to obtain a copy of the treaty which had been locked in Washington's desk. On the morning of June 29, 1795, the *Aurora* circulated this exclusive political news, with its vast implications, carrying a complete summary of the document. Philadelphians read it in amazement. Some accused Bache of faking; others said he had garbled the account for political reasons. To counter these charges, Bache obtained Mason's authorization to publish the whole text as a pamphlet; this was offered to the public on July 2.

He organized a protest meeting which was attended by six thousand people. The meeting closed with public burning of the treaty. With this dramatic stroke Bache aroused the people so effectively that President Washington hesitated to sign the treaty. When public opinion shifted momentarily, Washington quickly took advantage of this situation to sign the treaty; nevertheless, Federalist prestige had definitely suffered.

Bache was persistent and tenacious. His next move was an attack on Washington himself. Republicans hoped to force Washington to quit political life. The campaign against Washington bore fruit. The General was dragged into party strife and ceased to be the supreme arbiter and model. He refused a third term, influenced not only by his convictions that an individual should not hold office too long, but also by violent editorial abuse heaped on him. Even after he had given his farewell address, Bache printed the following scurrilous letter "from a Correspondent":

> If ever a nation was debauched by a man, the American nation was debauched by Washington.
>
> If ever a nation has suffered from the improper influence of a man, the American nation has suffered from the influence of Washington.
>
> If ever a nation was deceived by a man, the American nation has been deceived by Washington. . . .

Finally, when Washington turned over the presidency to John Adams on March 4, 1797, the following infamous attack was published:

> "Lord, now lettest Thou Thy servant depart in peace for mine eyes have seen my salvation"; was the pious ejaculation of a man who beheld

> a flood of happiness rushing in upon mankind. If ever there was a time that would license the reiteration of the exclamation, that time is now arrived.

Even after Washington retired to Mount Vernon, Bache continued to attack him occasionally.

William Duane, English newspaperman, joined the *Aurora* staff in 1798. After learning the printing trade in London, Duane journeyed to Calcutta where he established the *Indian World* and made a fortune. For criticizing the East India Company and for espousing the cause of army officers, the publisher's property was confiscated and he was deported. Duane next worked in London as parliamentary reporter on the *General Advertiser*. From there he came to the United States.

After serving as editor of the Philadelphia *Federal Gazette* for a short time, Duane, in common with other expatriated Englishmen and Irishmen, joined Republican newspaper forces. Before the yellow fever epidemic spread to Philadelphia, he entered into partnership with Bache in publication of the *Aurora*. When Bache died, Duane married the widow of the former publisher and continued the paper.

It was against Duane more than any other editor that the Alien and Sedition Laws were directed. Jefferson described him in this way: "I believe Duane a very honest man and sincerely Republican; but his passions are stronger than his prudence, and his personal as well as his general antipathies render him very intolerant."

When he exposed the brutality of the undisciplined and idle volunteer soldiery, mobilized for the war with France, Duane was assaulted murderously by a group of armed men. Only the timely arrival of a group of Republicans saved his property.

Duane's most important service to the nation was his exposure of the Federalists' plan to prevent election of Jefferson through the notorious Ross Election Bill. A copy of this measure, then pending in the Senate behind closed doors, was sent to Duane secretly. He published it with vigorous comment, thereby so arousing the public that the bill was defeated. As Bache had earlier, Duane "scooped" the country with his political "newsbeat." In an era of political party organs this was the only kind of "newsbeat" of significance.

In the fall, 1799, Duane was indicted under the Sedition Law. His trial, however, was first postponed and then, when Jefferson became President, dismissed. But the publisher's career now moved toward an anticlimax. When in 1800 Washington became the capital, the *Aurora* lost its influence. A printing project in Washington failed to materialize, and the *Aurora* folded in 1822. Duane died in 1835.

FEDERALISTS PASS ALIEN AND SEDITION LAWS

By a curious and sardonic turn of events, the Federalists sponsored the Alien and Sedition Laws designed to curb Republican editors, but the measures acted as political boomerangs. Eventually, the measures contributed to the downfall of the Federalist Party responsible for them.

When Washington had sent commissioners to negotiate a treaty with France and when news of the subsequent "shakedown" of American representatives by Tallyrand, French minister, had appeared in American papers, Republicans who had favored the French lost public confidence. Federalist John Jay won the governorship of New York, and Republican newspapers lost support all through the country.

Federalists seized the opportunity to pass the Alien and Sedition Laws in 1798. They were fostered by Adams and other Federalist leaders apparently to prevent sedition in a war period, but actually they were designed for revenge against Republican editors. Former President Washington, now ill, saw the evil that could arise from such measures and warned against them. Hamilton likewise was very concerned, but other leaders of the Federalist Party prevailed.

The Alien Act permitted the President (1) to order out of the country all aliens thought to be dangerous to the peace and safety of the United States; (2) to imprison for three years any alien found in the country after receiving such an order. This law was aimed at Irish and English political refugees editing Anti-Federalist newspapers. To make it more difficult for these refugees to become citizens, the period of naturalization was extended from five to fourteen years.

To include American-born editors also in the net, Federalists passed the Sedition Act of 1798, making it a misdemeanor (1) to conspire against the government, or (2) to print, publish or quote any false scandal or scurrilous writings against the government of the United States, the President, or either House of Congress. Such action was punishable by a fine of five thousand dollars and five years imprisonment. This law was intended to intimidate writers who had subjected Federalists to unwelcome criticism.

The Alien and Sedition Acts, however, included legal principles: (1) that juries could decide whether printed matter was libelous, (2) that truth was a valid defense in libel cases. Thus, if editors could prove the truth of their remarks, the newsmen would be freed. Federalist judges said such proof was very difficult to produce in court.

Under these new measures, a number of persons were arrested. Ten of them were found guilty, of whom seven were newspaper editors.

Federalist editors were not prosecuted, only Anti-Federalists. They were given stiff sentences and fined. The first editorial witchhunt in the United States was carried out against respected editors, poor printers, mere printshop employees and prominent citizens.

In New England, the fury of the Federalists was especially strong. In Boston, publishers of the old revolutionary paper, the *Independent Chronicle,* were indicted. They had criticized the Virginia and Kentucky resolutions against the Alien and Sedition Laws. One of these critical publishers, Thomas Adams, was not prosecuted because he was ill. Abijah Adams, his partner, was tried and convicted for publishing a libel against the government. The judge sentenced Adams to thirty days in jail.

In New York, authorities proceeded against the famous Republican sheet, the *Argus.* This paper had reprinted an item that Hamilton was back of the plot to try to silence the Philadelphia *Aurora.* Hamilton insisted on prosecution. The publisher, Greenleaf, meanwhile, died. His widow and a printer, David Frothingham, were arrested. The case against Mrs. Greenleaf was dropped, but the prosecution tried the printer. Frothingham was fined one hundred dollars—he made only eight dollars a week—and was sentenced to prison for four months.

James Thompson Callender, an English political refugee and editor of the *Richmond Examiner,* was an outstanding Republican editor who was convicted. Judge Samuel Chase, a violent Federalist partisan, presided at the trial and sentenced him to four months in prison, fining him two hundred dollars. Callender was pardoned by Jefferson when he became President.

Public storm against the Alien and Sedition Acts grew. Many persons saw the measures were a subterfuge; the public recognized that the intent was to carry on a campaign of intimidation against all persons who criticized the administration. Resolutions against the Acts were drawn up by James Madison and adopted by the Virginia legislature. In Kentucky, similar resolutions, drawn up secretly by Jefferson, were passed by the legislature. They emphasized the fact that a state could nullify a law which was obnoxious. Many newspapers reprinted the resolutions although the editors' comments were not favorable to them. The large majority of editors, perhaps as many as three-fifths, according to Jefferson, were Federalist in their leanings. News of the resolutions and news of the trials were influential in determining public opinion.

The Alien and Sedition Acts lashed back at the Federalists and helped unseat them. The Federalists could not agree on a successor to Washington. Distrusting the common people, Federalists failed to see the growing demand for social and political democracy. Moreover, Republican newspapers, through their persistent attacks, had weakened the Federalist cause. The Federalist Party never regained its political power. The Alien and Sedition Acts were allowed to lapse when Jefferson became President in 1801. Clauses in the Acts relating to libel also lapsed. They were reestablished later as a result of the Croswell case.

Jefferson's Views on the Press

The Federalist press turned on Jefferson when he became President. His firm belief in the free press principle remained. He declared that errors may be made by the public, but the way to correct them was to give full information to people through newspapers which should be obtained by everyone. Showing what leaders thought of the press at this time, Jefferson said finally in a quotation which has become famous:

> If it were left to me to decide whether we should have a government without newspapers, or newspapers without government, I should not hesitate a moment to prefer the latter.

Even when, as chief executive, the Federalist press blasted him, he still maintained his belief in the need for press freedom. He said in 1802 he would protect the editors in their right to lie, for he believed the people would eventually be governed by reason. Pressured no doubt by his less intellectual party followers, Jefferson did allow certain editors to be prosecuted under state law for seditious libel. It was not a general campaign of intimidation because editors were singled out individually for prosecution.

Harry Croswell, editor of an insignificant paper, the *Wasp,* provided the country with the most famous of free press cases at this time. Croswell reprinted an article from the *New York Evening Post,* saying that Jefferson paid money to Callender, editor of the Richmond, Virginia, *Enquirer,* to villify Washington. It was reported that Callender was given money to call Washington a robber, traitor and perjurer.

In 1804 Croswell of the *Wasp* was tried and found guilty, but he appealed the case. Alexander Hamilton, leader of the Federalist Party, was his lawyer. In a brilliant address in court, Hamilton argued that *truth should be a valid defense in libel cases* and that the *jury should determine fact and law.* These were the same doctrines that Andrew Hamilton contended for in the Zenger trial in 1735 and which had been written into the Alien and Sedition Acts in 1798 but had lapsed with that law in 1800.

The judges decided against Croswell, but state legislatures recognized the essential value of these press doctrines and soon passed laws providing for them.

WASHINGTON BECOMES CENTER OF POLITICAL JOURNALISM

Influential National Intelligencer

With removal of the seat of government to Washington in 1800, the capital became headquarters for administration organs. Although Washington was but a muddy little town on the banks of the Potomac, with a few nondescript buildings, a number of politicians and publishers recognized the importance of establishing papers there. Consequently, there was a flurry of journalistic activity in Washington. Several local papers were established both in Georgetown, adjacent to Washington, and in the capital itself. Most important of these papers was the *National Intelligencer,* which began as a triweekly on October 31, 1800, with Samuel Harrison Smith as editor.

Although the public was admitted to the Senate beginning in 1795, no special facilities were provided for the press. This made it difficult for reporters to hear debates, and poor reporting resulted. On petition of Samuel Harrison Smith, the Senate adopted a resolution in 1801 providing for a special place for reporters in the Senate chamber at the discretion of the President of the Senate. Again in 1827 a resolution was passed to give facilities to reporters on the Senate floor or gallery where they could hear.

It was not until eight years later in 1835 that specific provision was made in the rules of the Senate for reporters to have desks on the floor of that chamber. Reporters from both Washington and out-of-town papers were given these privileges; however, in 1838, floor privileges were restricted by Senate rule to reporters of Washington newspapers. The out-of-town newspapers' fight against this rule will be discussed later.

In 1810, when Smith retired, Joseph Gales, Jr., and William W. Seaton, also shorthand reporters, assumed management of the paper as well as the stenographic reporting. Gales and Seaton were printers to both houses of Congress and also did a large amount of government printing since no official governmental printing office had been established. When John Quincy Adams became President in 1824, the *National Intelligencer* was displaced as administrative organ by the *National Journal.*

Jacksonian Organs

The Kitchen Cabinet

For many years Washington newspapers were largely political footballs. Papers were established to advocate candidacy of party leaders for President, and the journals went out of favor when these officials lost power. The administration organs were given public printing contracts.

When Andrew Jackson came to Washington as President in 1828, a change in administration papers occurred. The rise of the Jacksonian movement, representing a coalition of small farmers in the West and city workers in the East, meant emergence of the common man, a significant trend followed in more detail in the next era. President Jackson relied for advice not so much on his official cabinet as on his unofficial Kitchen Cabinet. The cronies in this cabinet had been, or were at the time, newspaper editors who had met Jackson on a keel boat while on their way to Washington.

United States Telegraph Established

Friends of Jackson established the *United States Telegraph* in 1820 with Duff Green as editor-in-charge. When Jackson was elected President, the *Telegraph* became the administration organ. Green continued on the editorial job during the new president's first administration but lost his position when his loyalty swung to John Calhoun. The influence of the *United States Telegraph* diminished. Then the Washington *Globe* was launched by the Jacksonians in 1830 with Amos Kendall, Francis P. Blair and James Rives in charge. Five hundred thousand dollars in government printing contracts were given to the paper.

Both Kendall and Blair were experienced newsmen. Kendall, as editor of the Frankfort (Kentucky) *Argus of Western America,* had become very influential nationally in the Democratic Party, which had evolved from the Anti-Federalist or Republican Party. He was asked, therefore, to come to Washington where he was given a job in the Treasury Department. In the *United States Telegraph* he exposed the corruption in the previous administration and became President Jackson's righthand man. Giving Jackson ideas, Kendall also helped the President write his official speeches.

A banker and plantation owner, Francis Blair had taken over Kendall's position on the Frankfort *Argus* but in 1830 was also called to Washington to edit the new *Globe.* He wrote vigorous editorials advocating Jacksonian measures. John C. Rives joined the staff as Blair's assistant two years later. These editors, Kendall, Blair and Rives, planned political moves and strategy for the Democratic Party. "Old Hickory"

TABLE 7

The Young Republic

The Newspaper and the Changing Social Setting

1. Economic-political groups contend for control
   Rise of two contending groups: farmers vs. businessmen
   Federalists battle Anti-Federalists
2. Population grows steadily
   Spreads beyond Mississippi
3. Rural environment still prevalent
   Older towns grow steadily
   New towns established beyond Alleghenies
4. Agricultural-mercantile economy dominates
   Farming, shipping, trading, chief forms of making living

YOUNG REPUBLIC'S NEWSPAPER

5. Handicraft technology continues
   Industrial Revolution gets under way at end of period
   Some factories established
6. Transportation-community facilities still slow
   Speeds up at end of period
   Roads improved, extended, canals constructed, pony express, clipperships, steamship lines start; railroads begin
7. Science makes advances slowly
8. Old colleges grow; new colleges established
   Popular elementary education not part of scene
9. Religion changes
   Church influences lessen
   Nation becomes secular-minded
10. Recreation modes change slowly
    No large-scale sports developed
11. Literature and theatre portray swirl of life
    Federalist and Anti-Federalist conflicts reflected
    Indian life portrayed
12. Social classes change slowly
    Working class begins to emerge at end
13. Women's place still in home

would lie on a couch, smoking and dictating in his crude style to Kendall and Blair. Later they rewrote and polished the paragraphs which appeared next day in the *Globe.*

Blair carried at the head of each issue of the *Globe,* the Jeffersonian slogan, the epitome of the frontier philosophy of government, "The World is governed too much." As editor, his problems were to persuade the warring factions to reelect Jackson in 1832 and to defeat Henry Clay's aspiration to become political leader in the West. Aiming to popularize any measures of the Jacksonian administration, he appealed to laborers, frontiersmen and partisans. Senator Henry Clay delivered an oration against him from the floor of the Senate, declaring the *Globe* a dirty, filthy sheet, publishing "muckraking scum of the earth." But the *Globe*'s influence continued; Jacksonians everywhere subscribed to the daily, and Blair's party editorials were reprinted widely.

Blair's influence lessened after the close of President Van Buren's administration. Internal party conditions and the dying influence of Jackson forced Blair to sell the *Globe* in 1845.

Chapter 4

National Expansion Stimulates Press

While these political developments occurred and the party press grew, other social and economic changes were influencing the character of American journalism.

No longer were there thirteen colonies with sparce populations and small newspaper circulations. By 1830 new businessmen, lawyers, farmers and doctors were ready to subscribe not only to weeklies and semi-weeklies but to triweeklies and dailies. The three million population at the end of the Revolution was now twelve million, a 400 per cent increase.

New York, Baltimore and Philadelphia were becoming truly large cities as a result of commercial and industrial expansion. New York was already a metropolis in 1830, with two hundred thousand people living there. Boston, however, had not grown to the same extent. Located too far from the midwestern granaries, Boston did not profit by the new western expansion.

AGRICULTURE STILL DOMINATES ECONOMY

America remained chiefly agricultural. After the Revolutionary War, vast areas beyond the Alleghenies were opened to the American farmer. At first settlers subscribed to hometown papers along the seaboard. Gradually, they began to shift to local journals which wandering printers started. By 1820 more than three million settlers had trekked westward.

In 1803 President Thomas Jefferson purchased the vast Louisiana territory for fifteen million dollars and thus acquired more than a million square miles of new land. New states were added. In 1791 Kentucky joined the Union. Mississippi (1803), Louisiana (1812), Alabama (1812), Indiana (1816), Illinois (1818) and Missouri (1821), all became part of the United States.

Many settlements in these states grew into thriving towns and cities such as New Orleans, Cincinnati and St. Louis. Publishers were quick to realize opportunities for newspapers in these and other new centers; small weeklies began to appear. They contributed to growth of these areas and became important parts of their economic and political life.

INDUSTRIAL DEVELOPMENT AFFECTS ECONOMY

Manufacturing began to affect every phase of American life including printing. After centuries of handloomed materials and homemade crafts came the invention of machines. About 1800, inventors began to design and build automatic machines. Inventors harnessed them to water and steam for power. The Industrial Revolution spread to America from

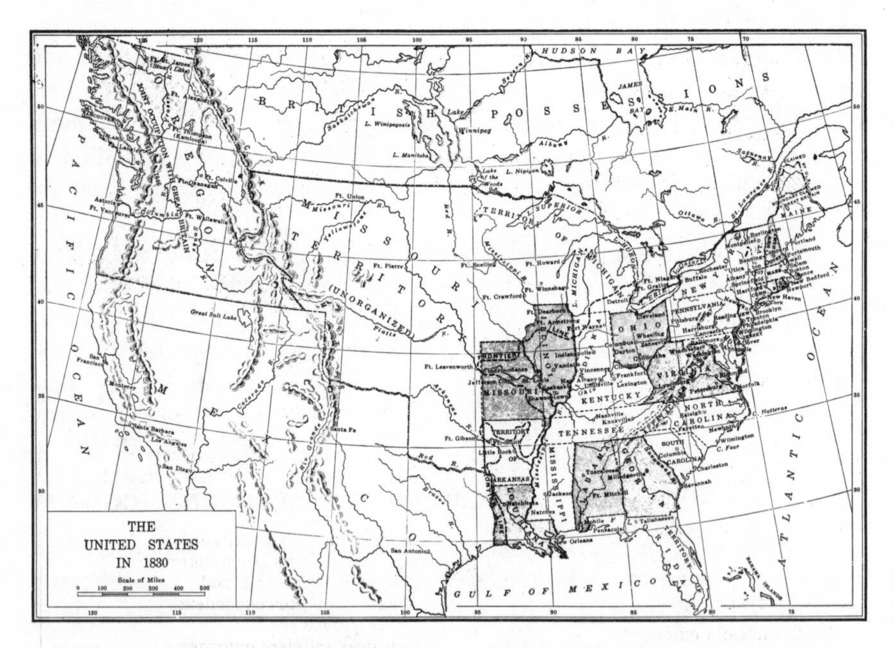

Figure 17. The United States Moved West. By 1830 population had pushed across the Alleghenies as well as the Mississippi River. New territories and states were added to the original thirteen colonies. President Thomas Jefferson's purchase of the Louisiana Territory added vast lands to the nation's possessions. New towns were born, and newspapers, weeklies and dailies were launched.

TABLE 8

Overall View: Environmental Changes Affect Press

U. S. CHANGES	NEWSPAPER EFFECTS
Population Expansion	Newspapers Multiply
Overall growth of nation	Eastern cities increase supply
Intensification in East	New trans-Allegheny papers begin
Spread West of Alleghenies	
Economic Developments	Circulation Expands
Agricultural expansion	Eastern metropolitan papers increase subscribers
Eastern seaboard improvements	
Eastern acreage added	Frequency Increases
Louisiana Purchase (1803)	Triweeklies increase
	Dailies begin, spread
Industrial Change	Size of Publication Enlargens
Old companies expand	Page size expands
New companies begin	Advertising Multiplies
Industrial Revolution starts	More products available for sale
More factory-made goods produced	Old advertisers have more money
Commerce Improves	New stores go into business and advertise
Interstate commerce accelerates	New types of advertisers begin
Foreign trade increases	
Transportation Progresses	Greater Profits Obtained
	Revenue obtained from (1) subscriptions (2) advertisements
Coastwide ships multiply	
Canals to West open	a. Publishers can hire more personnel
Steamboats on rivers	
Railroads begin	b. Can buy better machinery
Retail Trade Improves	c. Can establish better, faster news-gathering facilities: pony expresses, newsboats
Stores increase in cities	
Stores grow larger	
Urban Changes	Newspaper Contents Reflect U. S. Changes
Old eastern cities grow	Political news from parties published
New western towns start	Increased shipping news appears
(See Retail above)	Cultural news and reviews printed
	Editorials develop
Political Developments	Personnel More Specialized
Rise of political parties	Publisher no longer printer
	Shipping reporter hired
Cultural Advances	Washington correspondent employed
Public schools extended	Editor-Publisher emerges
Colleges grow	Directs policy, writes editorials
New colleges in West	
Theatre productions offered	
Musical concerts given	

England, and all phases of American life felt the changes. First, textile, and later, wool and metal manufacturing were influenced by the Machine Age.

The northeastern section of the nation became a huge workshop. Humming factory towns dotted the New England and Middle Atlantic states. People clustered in cities to work in factories; cities carried every type of provision they needed.

Families turned more and more to newspapers for advertisements telling where purchases could be made. Businessmen, too, recognized the medium of the newspaper as an effective vehicle for advertising their new wares. And what a supply of new articles began to come from the factories: shoes, hats, cloth, household articles, furniture, hardware!

The farmer, too, was affected by the new machines. He began to bring his load of vegetables to the city and found workers ready to buy. This led him to become more of a specialist in farming. The farmer saw that he could raise more profitably certain crops, depending on his soil. He looked in advertising columns for useful factory products for his home and his family's use. He bought furniture, pots, pans, hats, suits, dresses and shoes. He also purchased food he did not raise.

Old businesses were growing; new businesses began to mushroom. City dailies felt the results of this sharp expansion. They became sounder financially. The sheets became larger, and more personnel were needed to staff the paper.

Some journals grew large enough to hire special Washington correspondents. New and larger presses were needed to handle added news and advertising. A few larger newspapers with growing subscription lists began to use steam presses.

TRANSPORTATION FACILITIES IMPROVE

Improved transportation speeded transmission of news to newspaper offices and distribution of finished newspapers to readers of distant communities. Transportation was a more pressing problem than it had been in colonial days when farms were near the market town and seaport. With movement of population across the Alleghenies, agricultural produce was shipped down the Ohio and Mississippi rivers to New Orleans and then transferred to larger boats bound for Charleston, Baltimore, Philadelphia, New York and Boston. It was a long, roundabout route. Early attempts to ship by overland routes failed because of poor roads. Seaboard cities, such as New York, Baltimore and Phila-

Figure 18. Newsmen on Roof. Newsmen climbed to the top of a house or shop in the harbor to discover as soon as they could the approach of a boat bearing merchandise, news and newspapers from other ports along the coast and from foreign lands. Rowboats and fast-sailing vessels were dispatched to the incoming vessels as soon as they appeared around the bend.

delphia, strongly desired to capture western trade. Turnpikes, canals and finally railroads proved to be the answer.

Beginning with the Philadelphia and Lancaster Turnpike through Pennsylvania in 1792, numerous turnpikes were built in every state. These were followed by canals which cheapened transportation, the most successful canal being the Erie Canal in New York State.

In 1807 Robert Fulton ran his steamboat up the Hudson River, inaugurating a new era on the rivers of America. Soon steamboats were puffing on the Ohio and Mississippi rivers, carrying farm and manufactured goods. New settlements began and old towns grew with the region.

Railroad development began with chartering of the Baltimore & Ohio Railroad in 1826. Full effects of the railroad on the country and on the newspaper were felt in the next decade when rails were extended into many states.

Extension of postal service naturally resulted in more rapid exchange of news. In some cities, better mail service enabled newspaper publishers to turn weeklies into triweeklies and even into dailies. Postal rates for newspapers of one cent for 100 miles and one and a half cents beyond that distance were established in 1792, and being well below cost, the low rates contributed significantly in building up newspapers. Of even more importance was the practice of free exchange of copies between publishers. Struggling western papers thus were able to receive free news from the East. But often the United States mails were too slow for the larger aggressive papers which developed pony relays to bring the latest news.

FOREIGN TRADE MOVES IN NEW DIRECTIONS

Development of western agricultural regions sowed the seeds of a strong export and import business. The Embargo of 1807, imposed by President Jefferson, and the War of 1812 resulted in temporary checks and restrictions on American shipping. However, between 1820 and 1830, American shipping underwent a second period of growth and prosperity. Trade with China increased export-import business, New York and Boston shipowners having begun to trade with Asia in 1784.

One of the most notable developments was organization of the Black Ball Packet Line in 1816, the ships of which were considerably faster than any previously built vessels. Within the next few years running time between England and America was reduced to eighteen to twenty days. Just as road improvement of the era enabled news to be transmitted quickly, packet service brought news more swiftly across the ocean.

Expansion of export, import and coastwide business soon resulted in a demand for more shipping news as well as reports on foreign nations. Shippers of this era made extensive use of newspaper front pages to advertise their freight services, another example of the close relationship between the press and the economy of the nation.

CULTURAL CHANGE AFFECTS PRESS

American culture was also moving forward. New universities, colleges and academies as well as new elementary schools were established, and the newspaper reading public increased accordingly. College-bred readers wanted news, not only news of political and commercial developments, but news of the literary and theatrical worlds. Moreover, an increasing number of college graduates became editors and writers, such as Noah Webster, Philip Freneau, John Fenno; it will be recalled that William Coleman and William Cullen Bryant of the *New York Evening Post* were also college men.

Colleges remained the outstanding educational institution. Between 1783 and 1800, twenty-one institutions came into existence; by 1820, the number had approximately doubled. Like their older counterparts, all were founded and managed by churches, with heavy emphasis on morals and religion. By 1820, liberalism had gained momentum. Private academies, or high schools offered a broad course of study free from theological influences. Soon they were founded in almost every state. By 1830, high schools had increased to six hundred. They were patronized largely by sons and daughters of merchants, lawyers, doctors and well-to-do farmers.

Educational opportunities for children of artisans, mechanics, fishermen and poor farmers were still limited. Jefferson, Rush and other leaders worked diligently for universal, state-supported education, but progress was slow. Prevalence of agriculture, unwillingness of property owners to bear additional taxation, tradition that education for the rank and file was a matter of benevolence, all contributed to public indifference toward education.

In cities, elementary education was in the hands of parochial and pauper schools together with a few philanthropic agencies. In 1791 the First Day, or Sunday School Society, had been organized in Philadelphia to give instruction to children of the poor. The idea had spread to other cities. While the Sunday School was entirely religious in scope, it nevertheless provided elementary instruction for thousands.

The infant school, founded by Robert Owen to provide elementary instruction for poor children in New England, soon spread. It was not until the early nineteenth century that female academies began to assert their influence. Among the best known were the Female Academy opened by Moravians at Salem, North Carolina, and the Troy Seminary in New York.

Libraries reflected the changing era. In 1820 there were fourteen college libraries and nine free libraries, while many of the well-to-do also owned private libraries. Population growth, economic advancement and educational developments created a greater market for books. This does not mean that writers sold thousands of copies of their books. On the contrary, 90 per cent of the nation's inhabitants were provincial farmers uninterested in books.

Nevertheless, the upper-economic cultured class furnished a growing market for books, and a number of writers developed. It was inevitable that social and political struggles should impress themselves on the literature of the day. Although severe opposition was expressed to novel writing, native novelists made their appearance. The pioneer writers were mostly women. Mrs. Sarah Wentworth Morton of Boston produced *The Power of Sympathy,* this nation's first regular novel. The men writers of fiction ranged from conservative to liberal. Leaning well to the conservative right was Royall Tyler, dramatist and novelist, who published a two-volume novel called *The Algerine Captive.*

To the left of Tyler and occupying a middle ground was Hugh H. Brackenridge. A western Pennsylvanian of Scottish birth, Brackenridge, in his novel, *Modern Chivalry,* satirized the shortcomings and absurdities of the young republic. More radical was Charles Brockden Brown, the outstanding novelist of his time, who decried the struggle of the Hamiltonians for power. He expressed his views in *Alcuin: A Dialogue, Clara Howard* and *Arthur Mervyn.*

Washington Irving turned from law to literature for expression. With publication of his *History of New York* by "Diederich Knickerbocker," he satirized local history, gaining an American reputation for being an excellent writer. He created two characters from the American soil, Rip Van Winkle and Ichabod Crane of the *Legend of Sleepy Hollow.*

Concentrating more on American life, James Fenimore Cooper wrote on America's epic conquest of the wilderness. *The Spy* (1821) was his first success. *The Last of the Mohicans* (1826) told of the forest clashes between frontiersmen and Indians. In his subsequent writings Cooper attacked Jacksonianism.

Some newspapers with an upper-class audience responded to the developing interest in literature by reviewing books, by hiring special editors and by establishing departments devoted to literature, while book publishers began to advertise in these publications.

Many people, particularly the clergy, opposed the theatre on moral grounds. The press in Boston, New York and Philadelphia was unremitting in its opposition to the theatre.

Native writers now began to develop a dramatic style reflecting the manners, morals and conflicts of the day. Little of importance was produced until 1787 when Royall Tyler's comedy, *The Contrast,* was presented in New York. To Tyler belongs much credit for the changed public attitude toward the theatre. William Dunlap, "The Father of American Drama," was the first to make playwriting a profession. He wrote more than sixty plays, including tragedy, comedy and melodrama. His plays were intended not only to amuse his audiences but to inspire Republican ideals.

Some newspapers began to print reviews of plays as regular publication features. These reviews dealt primarily with the actors because many of the plays were performed over and over again. Readers knew the plots.

As part of the general cultural expansion, several magazines were launched. It was indeed a mark of distinction to be a magazine reader in this period. Although they reprinted much from English newspapers, American publications began to carry more products of local pens. Content of magazines will be considered in a later chapter.

DAILY NEWSPAPER EMERGES IN CITIES

Newspapers reflected the dynamic changes wrought through growth of strong political parties, expansion of commercial activity and general cultural advancement. The number of weekly papers multiplied. Many of them became dailies.

The daily newspaper had its start, in embryonic form, during the Revolutionary War, when British officers occupying New York decided on continuous publication rather than issuance of semiweeklies and triweeklies. The officers rearranged the dates of publication of various weeklies to avoid overlapping. A newspaper thus appeared every day although each issue bore a different name. When hostilities ceased, publishers lost no time in converting their semiweeklies and triweeklies into true dailies, for the people continued to look for their quota of the latest news each day.

People have always wanted news as quickly as possible. The speed of news transmission from event to reader depends on several key factors: (1) facilities needed to transmit news rapidly to news-media offices; (2) presses and other mechanical devices to print news and pictures in a hurry; (3) facilities to distribute the finished product quickly. In the faster-moving age at the end of the eighteenth century and beginning of the nineteenth, news-communication facilities improved and made daily publication practical.

As a result of increasing commerce, a psychological change began to appear; an increased tempo of the American people was reflected in the newspaper essays. Some writers indicated regretfully that the leisurely pace set by agricultural areas and small-town living belonged to the remote past. Readers wanted to learn the latest news quickly; they didn't want to wait a week or even several days until the next edition came out.

With the number of people increasing from three to twelve million, more events were happening. More commercial news was available: news of foreign and interstate trade, news of removal of state tariffs, news of development of turnpikes and canals, news of arrivals and departures of ships.

Important political news also was breaking. Events occurring in the early years of the young nation during the critical period under the Articles of Confederation and the battle over the Constitution all stirred deep interest. When the Constitution was ratified the new government assumed special significance because of the power given Congress and the President to pass domestic, political and economic measures, to approve foreign treaties and even to declare war. This political news was of importance, and people wanted to learn about it quickly.

Public demand for a daily paper had an economic basis. It was cheaper for readers to buy one daily than to subscribe to two or more semiweeklies or triweeklies to get the latest news every day.

Economic conditions led publishers to establish permanent dailies. Publishers found they could derive a larger income from daily newspapers by securing additional subscriptions and advertising. The increased income offset the extra expenses: cost of buying more paper and hiring more personnel. Full use of the printing shop, likewise, was an important economic consideration for the publisher. If he printed a weekly or triweekly, on certain days the shop would be idle. If he published five or six days each week, his downtime, the period when the machinery would be idle, would be reduced. Because of his press he could produce one daily, with a large circulation, more efficiently and cheaply than several shops could turn out separate weeklies. Here was the first demonstration of mass production in the news industry.

Transportation facilities brought in news in greater quantities and more frequently than before. Instead of weekly or triweekly, stagecoaches pulled up to the taverns every day with passengers, baggage and newspapers from far-off places. New stage lines were established, going to towns in all directions, and on their return, carried a steady stream of news and exchanges to be clipped. The postal service was improved, with mail being delivered more frequently. Vessels from foreign and American ports docked more often, bringing information about current affairs and newspapers which could be scissored for news.

News of the arrival and departure of ships with cargoes of merchandise for sale was supplied by some coffeehouses in seaport towns. Knowing the value of such commercial information, proprietors of these establishments had shipping facts on file for their customers. Newsbooks, containing such commercial information, were drawing features for taverns and coffeehouses. Successful businesmen recognized the value of learning the latest commercial news, for their profits depended on knowing when to buy or when to sell. Businessmen wanted to learn, too, where merchandise was available and to whom consigned so they might make profitable purchases. Shippers desired to find out also what trade conditions were in certain regions or countries since these conditions affected business. Taverns in the ports of Boston, New York and Philadephia furnished such useful commercial news daily.

Editors of newspapers recognized that such news, if published in their papers, would lead shippers and merchants to subscribe to their newspapers, especially if they were issued daily. The papers would also become effective advertising media for these businessmen who now obtained a fresh supply of merchandise more often than before and desired to tell their customers about these goods. The daily newspaper would have greater facilities for gathering commercial news and would reach a larger audience than the coffeehouses. Reading the paper with the news at home or in the office would prove more convenient, too. Daily newspapers, then, could supplant the tavern's shipping *news*-books as *news*-media.

It should be remembered that England, which matured economically before America, had successful dailies as early as 1702, eighty years before, thus setting a precedent for United States publications.

Emergence of the American daily, therefore, was not the result of an accident or a fortunate inspiration by a publisher. The daily appeared almost simultaneously in three Atlantic coast cities. It was a natural journalistic evolution, growing out of increasing news desires and economic needs of certain groups in the population and the publishers' better facilities to satisfy these wants.

The first daily appeared in 1783 in Philadelphia, then the largest metropolis, with thirty-five thousand inhabitants. *The Pennsylvania Evening Post,* a triweekly described before, had been published since 1775 in that city by Benjamin Towne, a turncoat. After the war he attempted to reverse his policies, and he initiated daily publication in 1783, renaming his paper *The Pennsylvania Evening Post and Daily Advertiser.* It did not last long.

The Pennsylvania Packet (described in the chapter on the revolution) appeared in September, 1784, as a daily, having changed from a weekly to a semiweekly to a triweekly before it became a daily. It was the first successful American daily newspaper. It succeeded because Philadelphians generally were more favorable to the new paper than to Towne's *Post.*

The next daily developed in Charleston, South Carolina on December 1, 1784, when John Miller issued the *South Carolina Gazette.* Charleston had a population of twelve thousand.

Two months later, on February 23, 1785, William Morton and Samuel Horner changed their *New York Morning Post,* a semiweekly, to the *New York Morning Post and Daily Advertiser;* six days later, March 1, Francis Childs issued the second daily in that city, *The New York Daily Advertiser.*

Boston did not get its first daily until John D. Burk issued the *Polar Star and Boston Daily Advertiser* on October 6, 1796, but this paper lasted less than a year.

By 1800 twenty American dailies were being published, six of them in Philadelphia and five in New York. By 1820 the number of United States dailies rose to twenty-seven; the next decade produced rapid growth, so that in 1830 there were sixty-five dailies being issued. Semiweeklies had not dropped out of sight but were on the increase in western settlements and in eastern rural areas. From eighty-five in 1790, the number of weeklies and semiweeklies reached three hundred forty-three in 1810.

Newspaper circulation was also growing. Total annual output between 1775 and 1778 was 2,004,000, whereas annual output of the years 1810 to 1828 increased to 45,617,798 because of expanding population, increased education and eagerness with which papers were read.

IMPROVEMENTS MADE IN NEWS COVERAGE FACILITIES

The newspaper did not develop at once facilities for covering a wide variety of news. Those who bought newspapers were primarily interested in commercial and political affairs. Slowly, publishers improved their facilities for gathering such news for upper-class readers.

In earlier days they secured reports from the nation's capital, Philadelphia, by subscribing to the leading party organ there: the Federalist

Fac-simile of the first daily newspaper published in America—now THE NORTH AMERICAN. Published at 701 Chestnut St., Philadelphia.

The Pennsylvania Packet, *and Daily Advertiser.*

Price Four Pence.] TUESDAY, SEPTEMBER 21, 1784. [No. 1755.

For Liverpool.

For Dublin,

For CORK,

For Gottenburgh,

For LONDON,

FOR SALE, Bermudas Packet

Sixty Dollars Reward.

Peter Whiteside & Co.

Muscovado Sugars of the first

DELAWARE STATE,

Jones and Foulke,

German DOWLAS,

The Sale of Public Stores

History of the Bible

To BE SOLD, The Island of Bombay-Hook,

Isaac Franks, Broker,

Well Assorted MERCHANDIZE,

Benjamin Nones & Co.

Lion Moses, Broker,

Grand Lodge.

Reed & Forde

For SALE by LACAZE *and* MALLET,

P. D. Robert,

Onfray Painniere,

Matthew M'Connell,

Two Dollars Reward.

Five Pounds Reward.

This Morning

PUBLIC GOODS

Jackson & Dunn

To be sold by public Vendue.

PROCLAMATION.

GOD SAVE THE COMMONWEALTH!

Lotbe D'Orliere,

LOTS to be LET

Figure 19. First Regular Daily. Because of improved commercial conditions and the population growth of Philadelphia and Pennsylvania, the *Pennsylvania Packet and Daily Advertiser* was launched in September, 1784, as the first successful daily newspaper in America. The *Packet* began as a weekly, shifted to semiweekly, and then triweekly before publication as a daily.

Gazette of the United States or the Republican *National Gazette.* When the capital was transferred to Washington, the *National Intelligencer* became the official source of governmental news.

Later, as newspapers in New York and other towns grew financially, they established their own correspondents in Washington. Although roads were improved and coaches carried mails and newspapers, certain publishers in the 1820s and 30s organized their own pony relays in order to beat the United States mails bringing the Washington economic and political news to their competitors. Newspapers had to be large enough financially to pay for this special pony service.

For news from abroad, publishers continued to rely on clippings and summaries from foreign newspapers, as well as on letters from Europe. Fast packet ships on fixed schedules brought European news more regularly and quickly. Nevertheless, in the 1820s and 30s, publishers, rather than wait for the ships to dock, went out a hundred miles in the sea to meet them: first, by rowboat for short distances; later, by schooner, and finally, by clipper for the longer distances. They then hastened back to their offices and attempted to beat their rivals with foreign news. Most of such exclusive newsbeats dealt with commerce and politics. Again, some dailies had money to meet these added costs of news gathering, for subscriptions and advertising had multiplied enough to furnish the added revenue.

SUNDAY NEWSPAPERS ARE LAUNCHED

During the Revolution newspaper publishers issued only occasional extras on Sunday. Important battles or treaty negotiations were reported in these issues. But strong religious tradition forbade regular Sunday editions.

England set the Sunday precedent. The *London Observer* had been issuing on Sundays since 1791. In America, Philip Edwards, who merged the *Baltimore Daily Advertiser* with the *Maryland Journal,* was the first to publish a Sunday paper. His shop was swept by fire in 1796, and he conceived the idea of a Sunday paper to retrieve his losses. Realizing that he was violating the mores of the community, he took care to include religious discourses, but the paper appeared for only one issue.

The idea was not lost; in 1809 the *New York Observer* appeared, priced at two dollars a year or six cents an issue. The paper's first editor is not known; but after a few numbers had been published, William Elliot, a bible printer, assumed management. News in the *Observer* was mostly clipped from the *Daily Mercantile Advertiser.* Since the *Ob-*

server's publisher had to overcome objections of the religious people to publication, some defensive paragraphs were mixed with regular news. For example:

> But, say you bigots, you break the Sabbath by publishing his paper on that day. This is not true. This paper is printed late on Saturday night; and we no more break the Sabbath by the delivery of it on that day, than the minister who delivers his sermon.

The *Observer* was suspended on August 6, 1809; but three months later, on October 14, it was revived by William Elliot and James Crissy. The major difficulty of *Observer* publishers was that of inducing newsboys to distribute the paper on Sunday mornings. During the next decades a few attempts at Sunday publishing were made by enterprising newsmen in New York and Philadelphia, but Sunday papers did not last long. The public was not ready for them.

PRESS ADVERTISING IMPORTANCE RECOGNIZED MORE

Increased advertising revenue during this period resulted from a number of factors. New kinds of advertisers were created. Insurance companies began to insert advertisements regularly. By means of advertisements new stock companies appealed for investors. Manufacturers, now increasing in number, emphasized in their advertisements "American" goods for sale rather than those "recently arrived from London," for the American economy began to shift from homemade goods to factory-made products. American industrialization was accelerated by the growth of the city where residents worked in commerce and industry and manufacturing. City workers purchased rather than made most of their necessities. Responding to this increased consumer demand, new merchants appeared in the cities and towns and advertised; well-established merchants became more prosperous and were able to advertise.

The newspaper was becoming necessary for those who wished to keep abreast of the news. Merchants recognized this fact and the corollary one that such people would also read their advertisements. Circulations, which had in 1776 averaged six hundred, now reached two thousand, and in some instances, four thousand.

Merchants in the city used newspapers to reach customers out of their neighborhood and to procure new customers. Pages grew larger to accommodate more advertising. Publishers narrowed their columns, cramming four columns instead of three onto a page. By 1790 publishers were printing five columns to the page, reducing the size of type and heads. Weeklies became dailies, partly because of advertising growth.

Publishers were more interested in many short advertisements than in one large advertisement. Newspapers charged about forty dollars a year for an advertisement of whatever length desired, or fifty to seventy-five cents for an occasional announcement. Usually, an annual subscription and an advertisement both could be purchased for forty dollars, publishers requiring advertisements to remain the same for periods varying from seven weeks to one year. Advertisements generally appeared on pages one and four, sometimes overflowing to pages two and three, where the advertisements were printed alongside the editorial matter.

HEADLINES EMERGE IN DAILIES

Seeking to call attention to the news, editors began to top their items with larger headlines, giving summaries of the events. This headline trend was accelerated during the War of 1812. There was evident a distinct sense of something that must be told quickly. Editors had an inner push to convey with a blurt news to their readers. One publisher topped a war story with:

DETROIT IS TAKEN!
Our Brave Volunteers and the
Heroes of Tippecanoe, Are
Prisoners of War

Newsmen had a feeling that news would cease to be of value when it ceased to be new. This idea was opposed to the mere communication of news in colonial times when information could be printed at one time as well as another, now or later. Headlines in dailies were usually in 8-point or 9-point capitals, with the second deck in 6-point italic. Varied and graded types of headlines appeared only infrequently. Bias in headlines was evident. Makeup of front pages and inside pages presented a solid gray appearance, punctuated with small headlines. As papers were sold by yearly subscription, editors exerted no effort to make headlines attractive and appealing for individual street sales.

PRESS IMPROVEMENTS INCREASE SPEED, PRODUCTION

Newspapers remained in the handicraft stage beyond the turn of the nineteenth century, although some manufacturing improvements were made in the colonial press with its capacity of two hundred fifty impressions, or one hundred twenty-five small papers per hour. When press improvements came they were the result of pressure on the publishers.

The pressure developed from increase in newspaper circulation, especially that of the dailies.

The first cast-iron press was produced in 1789 under the direction of the Earl of Stanhope. Although it retained the principle of the screw, the Stanhope press operated by a combination of levers to afford greater pressure with less effort. It printed a more readable newspaper than the wooden press. In spite of being heavy and cumbersome, the Stanhope press found favor among printers.

In 1816 George Clymer improved on the Stanhope machine by introducing a combination of levers instead of the century-old screw to raise and lower the platen, or heavy impression plate. This made the press easier to operate. The first genuine American printing invention, the Clymer press afforded a better method of taking impression, and it was larger and stronger than those preceding it. Decorating it with a cast-iron American eagle, Clymer called his machine the Columbian Press. The press could print a larger-size newspaper than the previous printing machines.

As the superiority of cast iron proved itself, a number of inventors began working on ideas to make the iron press more efficient. Peter Smith substituted for the old screw method a toggle joint operated by a single lever. Although a simple change, this represented a clear-cut departure from the screw-type press which had been used since the middle of the fifteenth century.

In 1827 Samuel Rust employed the new principle also, but introduced a machine that was greatly superior to the Smith Press. Known as the Washington Hand Press, it was used widely by editors and publishers for years. A few of these presses were found in some newspaper offices two centuries later, standing as reminders of the old days. Instead of being cast in one piece, the Washington Hand Press was constructed so that it would give extra strength. Strong springs of this press caused the impression platen to be lifted after the hand lever had been pulled and the page printed. The press, therefore, was easier to operate than previous machines. The type form also was inked automatically by rollers operated by a weight. When the weight descended the ink rollers were drawn over the type. A printer then lifted the weight for the next operation.

It was not until the 1820s and 1830s that American newspapers began to use cylinder presses operated by steam. These presses came from England. The same technological forces of the Machine Age affecting industry likewise influenced the printing and newspaper businesses. Faster and more automatic printing machines producing copies of newspapers in greater quantities more quickly and at lower per unit cost were needed. Inventors responded.

During the fifteenth century, printing of copper-plate engraving was done on presses using the principle of a revolving cylinder. Paper was placed on the cylinder and when it turned the copper plate underneath moved in and was pressed against the paper, producing the impression. Several attempts to adapt such a press to newspaper and book publishing were made.

The Napoleonic War stimulated the demand for news and newspapers in Europe and was largely responsible for ushering in a new era in printing presses. Credit for the first practical cylinder press using type goes to Frederick Koenig, a Saxon printer, who in 1812 patented in London a steam-driven press with an impression cylinder and an automatic inking roller. This came to be known as a flat-bed cylinder printing press.

This machine presented a revolutionary departure from the old hand press with its upright beams. On Koenig's press, printers fed the press sheets of paper, hooking them onto pins attached to a revolving cylinder. The moving cylinder pressed the paper against a flat form, or bed containing type. Another rotating movement of the wheels brought the cylinder around again, with the type returning to its original position. The paper, now printed, was forced out of the machine. A second cylinder was added later, so that the paper, after being printed on one side, was brought by a series of tapes to the second cylinder, where the reverse side was printed.

Koenig's early press could produce about eleven hundred impressions on one side of a sheet, or five hundred fifty finished copies (both sides of a sheet) in an hour, as compared with two hundred or three hundred impressions turned out with the old Stanhope iron press. By 1824 Koenig's press was producing two thousand impressions, or one thousand completed copies per hour.

Meanwhile, in 1822, Daniel Treadwell invented the first power press in America. It did not use the cylinder principle. Constructed of wood, it was improved by Isaac Adams after 1827 and was widely used by newspaper publishers in the United States. It was not as fast or as efficient as the Koenig machine.

Similar to Koenig's, a press invented by David Napier in England used automatic grippers instead of pins to convey the paper around the cylinders. The press had a capacity of two thousand impressions an hour and cost forty-five thousand dollars. A number of American publishers used the Napier cylinder press, the first of which reached Boston in 1824.

In 1830 Richard Hoe, after studying the Napier machine, brought out in New York his first power-driven cylinder press, and thus began production of a number of rapid, effective presses for American newspapers. Hoe's two-cylinder models claimed a speed of four thousand impressions or two thousand papers an hour. Printing facilities for mass production of cheap newspapers were in the process of being perfected.

Top circulation in 1800 for a daily was eight hundred to one thousand. By 1830 circulation of some dailies reached four thousand; consequently, publishers turned to the new steam-driven cylinder press since it was far more economical than the hand press. A publisher would need seventeen hand presses and many operators to produce four thousand sheets in one hour. The cylinder press needed only two or three men to operate it.

PAPERMAKING MACHINES PUT ON MARKET

Improvements were made in the manufacture of paper. The ancient handicraft process of making paper was replaced by the Fourdrinier automatic machine. The colonial papermaker made each sheet by hand, a costly and slow method. The Fourdrinier machine fabricated paper in an endless sheet. The long sheet was then cut into small sheets for use on the press. Chlorine bleaching process, also introduced about this time, enabled mills to make use of colored rags, rope and other scraps.

As a result of introduction of the Fourdrinier machine and the bleaching process, the price of newsprint dropped. Publishers increased the size of the paper by doubling the measurements of the sheets. This expansion reached the "blanket-size" stage within a few years.

PRESS READERS STILL RESTRICTED

The newspaper did not penetrate to the people-at-large. For the most part, it was read by, as far as numbers were concerned, influential but minority groups, such as the upper social classes, wealthy town dwellers, plantation owners and, of course, the clergy, doctors and lawyers. These groups were better educated, and in most instances were in the upper economic level. For the time being they controlled the newspaper market.

Circulation under these conditions was naturally limited. Even though potential newspaper readers increased, they were not immediately sought by publishers. Federalists, whose political control lasted from Washington through John Adams, who left office in 1800, had only contempt toward the masses. Even the Jeffersonian Republicans, who defeated the Federalists in that year, were chiefly interested in the agrarian class, not the city workers who were unable to vote unless they owned property.

AGGRESSIVE MERCANTILE DAILIES DOMINATE JOURNALISM

Various strategically located cities reflected this national growth, and their newspapers revealed the aggressive, commercial spirit in the air. New York, though the largest, was typical.

In 1800 there were influences in New York which foreshadowed its future as a national metropolis. Most important was its commercial enterprise. Beginning with Dutch traders, business had always been uppermost for New Yorkers. At the time of the Revolution, the commercial class was prosperous and influential, and Alexander Hamilton achieved no little of his fame by acting, during Washington's administration, as spokesman for this group.

Wall Street had gained its reputation by 1800. Yet banking and trade were not the only aspects of business enterprise in New York. The phenomenal rise of manufacturing soon brought the city scores of factories with their attendant problems of wages, working hours and living conditions. And financial interests and factories combined to make New York a great commercial city.

Keen New York businessmen had foreseen that leadership would go to the city which could control the trade of the upper Mississippi and Ohio valleys. The Hudson River was easily navigable to Albany. From that city to Buffalo, the state constructed the Erie Canal, completing the work by 1826. Within a few years farm products were pouring through the canal to New York and then were exported to Europe. Concurrent with this huge increase in foreign trade, the city became the chief port of entry for immigrants.

New York was never as cultured a capital as Philadelphia. Grafted onto the solid Dutch stock, the city's ambition now was to acquire commercial and financial dominance. A new acquisitive and aggressive spirit for moneymaking began to creep over New Yorkers, replacing the plodding methods of getting money which had satisfied an earlier generation.

City and commonwealth, at the turn of the century, were ruled by a small group of old-fashioned gentlemen who upheld the rigid Federalism of the tie-wig school. Political leaders of the state were men of long-established reputations: Hamilton, Jay, Gouverneur Morris and Rufus King, together with the brilliant lawyer, James Kent. But the political field was disturbed by bitter schisms and vindictive struggles for the spoils of office. The Democratic Party, which grew out of the Anti-Federalists, briefly called Republicans, at the time was led by the Livingstons and the Clintons; and outside both factions was the ambitious Aaron Burr who played a lone hand. All of this political controversy and dissension was mirrored in the press.

In 1789, when Washington came to New York to assume the presidency, the town had approximately twenty-nine thousand inhabitants. By 1800, it had sixty thousand residents; but in 1830 its population reached two hundred thousand. New York State also became the largest in the union, drawing up from fourth place in 1790.

Old Papers Continue

Benefiting by ever-increasing prosperity, the old papers (the *Mercantile Advertiser,* the *Daily Gazette,* the *Daily Advertiser* and the *Commercial Advertiser*) continued to cater to shipping, manufacturing and retail groups in New York. With political factions battling for control and spoils in the Democratic Party, new papers were launched while some of the older papers were reinvigorated by the new aggressive spirit. The five dailies issued in 1800 increased to nine by 1830. Following party lines of the era, some publishers grouped themselves into Federalists and Republicans (or Democrats) to do journalistic battle for the political and economic doctrines of their parties. Others were purely commercial publications. Some, such as the *Evening Post,* were a combination of commercial and political journalism.

Journal of Commerce, Strictly Commercial

The *Journal of Commerce* became one of the strongest of the New York mercantile journals. Its founder, Arthur Tappan, was a New Englander whose father and mother planted a deep religious consciousness in their son. He came to New York in 1815 to establish the firm of Arthur Tappan and Company, building up a mercantile business of more than one million dollars annually. He devoted himself also to religious work.

His next idea was to spread religion through a commercial daily newspaper. He thought it would exert a wholesome moral influence, with the publisher refusing advertisements relating to liquor, circuses and theatres. Tappan therefore launched the *Journal of Commerce,* one of the most vigorous newspapers to be established after the first quarter of the nineteenth century. The *Journal of Commerce* came from the press on September 1, 1827. Its enterprise in news gathering and its strenuous efforts to get the latest economic and political information marked the start of a significant change in American newspaper methods.

Tappan, with his single-minded religious purpose, probably had little idea that he would contribute to the development of journalism. One of the first strictly businessmen to own and publish a paper without doing any of the writing or printing, he chose for his assistant a man who later became a minister, at the same time selecting a literary writer of Virginia for his editor-in-chief. The business department was in the hands of David Hale, also a New Englander of strong religious feelings. Hale had once assisted his uncle, Nathan Hale, on the *Boston Daily Advertiser* and had drawn considerable attention with his attacks on Boston newspapers and theatres.

After announcing the paper's religious purpose, the first issue said:

> To avoid a violation of the Sabbath Day . . . the paper on Monday morning will be issued at a later hour than usual.
>
> Like other commercial papers, it is the design of the Journal of Commerce to exhibit improvements in literature, science and the arts, such as shall be acceptable to the statesman, the scholar and especially the merchant.

The *Journal*'s daily circulation was about three hundred; its columns principally were concerned with business; and its few editorials concentrated on literary subjects. Politics were avoided.

The *Journal of Commerce* did not prove to be the moral influence Tappan had hoped. Before the end of the year the proprietor had to invest thirty thousand dollars in his enterprise. He now decided to sell out to David Hale, his business manager, and to Gerard Hallock, then co-editor of the *New York Observer.*

Hallock had a New England background similar to that of Tappan's. His father was a pastor who supplemented his income by farming. Hallock was graduated from Williams College in 1819 and opened a private school in Salem in 1822. He borrowed two hundred dollars from David Hale to establish the *Boston Telegraph.* In 1827 Hallock bought a half-interest in the *New York Observer.*

Then he joined David Hale in publication of the *Journal of Commerce.* Several New York merchants underwrote the paper for twenty thousand dollars. The new proprietors actually paid Tappan six thousand dollars for his equipment, indicating the rising costs of establishing and operating a newspaper. The *Journal*'s main contributions were to extend and to perfect news-gathering facilities. Marine news had always been a part of the American newspaper so it was natural that the first advancement should grow out of the effort to obtain marine intelligence quickly.

Samuel Topliff, son of a sea captain who worked in a newsroom owned by Samuel Gilbert, established a Marine and General News Book in 1811 at the Exchange Coffee House in Boston. Instead of waiting for marine reports to come in, he engaged a small boat to meet arriving ships in the harbor. After picking up the news he posted the information where it could be read. An annual subscription of ten dollars enabled merchants and shippers to peruse his books. Boston newspaper publishers caught the idea from Topliff. The Boston *Palladium* featured shipping news in a department uniquely developed by Henry Ingraham Blake.

Blake's achievement was so outstanding that it was thought by some newsmen that this reporter might almost be said to have invented "the present universal mode of reporting, clearances, arrivals, disasters, and various incidents connected with the shipping interests of the country." Blake preferred walking around the wharves, visiting merchant's offices and picking up items of shipping news rather than being confined all day in an office. Later Blake was lured to New York to handle shipping news for the *Journal of Commerce* and, afterward, for the *Express*. He did not make a success of his New York venture.

Newspaper Association Begins

Although Topliff's method of meeting incoming ships spread to New York, expense of maintaining separate boats proved excessive for each publisher. Sometime between 1820 and 1827, therefore, the Association of New York Newspapers was founded, the first organization of newspaper publishers in the United States. Nine publishers joined the organization, forerunner of the later Associated Press. The early organization was probably called New York Harbor Association.

Newspapermen who had been copying and reprinting each other's news and editorials for many years were now making their first conscious effort to coordinate reporting activities. While this did not stop their quarreling and competing, it nevertheless showed that they could join together for mutual advantage. The expense borne by New York newspapers for this rowboat news service amounted to $2,500 a year, another indication of the increasing operating costs.

The *Journal of Commerce* was not part of the association. Two explanations have been offered for this situation. The association's boat operated on Sundays, but Tappan had strong religious scruples; consequently, he did not join the organization. The second explanation states that members of the association did not want the newcomer in. Tappan, therefore, couldn't get past the harbor combine to gather his news from Europe. His boatmen regularly came back from the waterfront with their heads bashed in. As soon as they set foot on a ship's ladder, they were knocked back into their rowboats. If the *Journal of Commerce* could not obtain such news, it could not survive for long. Tappan sold out to Hale and Hallock.

Early one morning in October, 1828, a small sloop sailed down the East River. The boat slipped past the spot where the Brooklyn Bridge now stands and headed toward the entrance of the lower harbor and Sandy Hook. On the side was painted the legend: *Journal of Commerce, 1828.*

The *Journal of Commerce* editor, Hale, had fitted the craft in a desperate effort to beat the harbor combine. He wanted to keep the plan a secret, but word leaked out. Other papers in the news organization accepted the challenge by rigging out a fast sloop they called the *Thomas H. Benton.*

The two boats raced the 18 miles to Sandy Hook on Long Island, and when the *Journal of Commerce* stopped in the rolling swells, the combine craft was far behind. News gatherers never had ventured that far before, but Hale saw that it was an excellent spot. Arriving merchantmen from foreign ports started to trim their sails there, and Hale's sailboat could obtain whatever news they brought and then scuttle back to port.

The success of the *Journal of Commerce* jolted rival editors out of their lethargy and set the whole town talking. The *Journal of Commerce* had introduced the vital stimulant of competition into the world of news gathering.

The daily's schooner frequently went out as far as 100 miles. The harbor combine fought back with all its resources. The association made use of a new marine telegraph constructed between the harbor entrance and the battery at the lower end of Manhattan. The marine telegraph was a semaphore device with flagstaff stations. A man at Sandy Hook identified incoming boats and signaled word to the next station where the information was picked up and resignaled to stations along the route all the way to the city. A shortcoming of the system was that it could transmit little more than the name of the ship.

Hale wanted to get and convey complete news. The editor devised another system. His boat now picked up the news packet from the incoming vessel at the tip of Long Island, raced to Fort Lafayette and handed the parcel to a waiting horseman who spurred his steed for a quick run to the Fulton Ferry. It was a short ride from the ferry slip to the *Journal of Commerce* building.

The contest with the association continued. Soon the organization broke up and every newspaper fought for itself.

Before long, Hale and Hallock added a second schooner, calling the new 90-ton boat, *The Evening Edition.* These *Journal* newsboats soon established a reputation for speed. News of the French Revolution of 1830 arrived in this way, and the *Journal* got out an extra to report the news quickly.

The first by-lines were given to the marine reporters of the *Journal of Commerce,* the paper carrying the line: "Marine News—Abraham Bancker, collected under supervision for *New York Journal of Commerce* only."

Newspaper wars and competition during the colonial period centered around obtaining superiority by publishing well-written, forceful literary essays, or letters to the editor on current issues. Colonial publishers had neither money nor facilities to obtain news quickly. They had to wait for ships to bring foreign and colonial news, and for post-carriers and stagecoaches to arrive in town with news and newspapers from other colonies. Publishers were fortunate when the latest news was brought just before the weeklies' press time. Generally, publishers had their own steady clientele; it was not dignified to seek new subscribers.

In the commercial atmosphere which pervaded New York in this new era, daily publishers sought special favor with the merchants; consequently, publications began to compete with each other in quickly obtaining commercial news and political news with economic implications. They fought sharply for subscribers. This was a new, aggressive business age with publishers reflecting this spirit of enterprise. To compete, they required enterprise, energy and more capital than ever before.

Success of the *Journal of Commerce* fleet so strengthened their newspaper that Hale and Hallock introduced a similar news service on land. In 1833 they established a horse express from Philadelphia to New York with eight relays en route, enabling the publishers to print congressional news and southern news a day in advance of their competitors.

During the excitement of President Jackson's administration, the *Journal of Commerce*'s rival established an opposition pony express from Philadelphia to New York. Not to be outdone, proprietors of the *Journal* extended their relays to Washington. Although competition developed the facilities of journalism, at the same time, it drove up the costs of establishing and operating a newspaper. By 1831 maintenance of six newsboats cost all the publishers twenty-five thousand dollars a year.

The National Advocate

When the *Columbian* supported DeWitt Clinton for president in 1818, Tammany Hall broke with the paper and launched a rival, the

National Advocate, with Henry Wheaton, a native Rhode Islander, as editor. His successor as editor of the paper, Mordecai Manuel Noah, had a strange career behind him. He received his first taste of journalism as a news correspondent at the legislature in Harrisburg, Pennsylvania. Later he also gained newspaper experience in Charleston, South Carolina. In 1813, when he was only twenty-eight, he was appointed United States Consul at Tunis. After returning to the United States six years later, Noah settled in New York and embarked on a literary career, writing *Travels in England, France, Spain, and the Barbary States,* the first book of travel by an American citizen. He later became one of the first American playwrights.

His career with the *National Advocate* did not last long. Henry Eckford, Jacob Barker and John Targee became the secret proprietors of the *National Advocate.* Eckford, an exceptionally successful shipbuilder, then purchased the paper in order to support Crawford for President. Noah was thus removed from his editorial chair.

In 1826 Noah established another paper bearing the same name, *National Advocate.* Eckford, however, legally restrained Noah from using the title, so he changed it to *Noah's National Advocate.* Again enjoined, Noah finally altered the name to the *New York Enquirer.*

The New York Enquirer (1826)

Noah established the *New York Enquirer* on July 6, 1826, with the motto "A Free Press, the Ark of Public Safety," and a picture of a canal boat on the masthead, undoubtedly reflecting the interest in the new Erie Canal. Noah declared that the *Enquirer* would be an "entirely new paper; it will support the old Republican principles of '98, and the system and usages of the Republican Party."

Noah followed the growing tradition of New York publishers to print congressional news on page one. He also printed "Post Office News" describing the brawls of New Yorkers, a type of news which later became the main feature of the penny press. Noah carried on an extensive crusade against speculators, stock market operators and manipulators of life insurance and real estate. The editor was reacting to the financial situation of the period. Banks were started with little capital or specie; yet they issued quantities of notes and made loans freely. Between 1829 and 1837 the number of banks increased from three hundred twenty-nine to seven hundred eighty-eight.

Noah found himself blocked at every turn. Noah always defended the South, and he supported slavery. He was a Jacksonian but because of his views was later attacked by other Jacksonian papers.

The *Enquirer's* ace Washington correspondent was newspaper adventurer James Gordon Bennett, destined to make his mark later as a penny press editor. Bennett wrote for the *Enquirer* in a breezy, gossipy style, getting away from the old stereotyped form of reporting. The *New York Statesman* and the *Philadelphia National Gazette* also had Washington correspondents, but many editors still relied on scissoring the columns of the *National Intelligencer,* the *United States Telegraph* or the *Washington Globe.* Elias Kingman operated the first Washington News Bureau, supplying papers from 1822 to the Civil War.

Bennett was the first to realize that the *Enquirer* and the *Courier,* owned by James Watson Webb, were duplicating each other. The amalgamation effected was largely the result of Bennett's wise counseling.

Courier and Enquirer (1829–)

Belligerent, aggressive and energetic, James Watson Webb was another publisher to respond to the new journalistic conditions and competition. Webb was born in New York, son of an aide-de-camp of Washington at the Battle of Bunker Hill. James' mother was of Dutch ancestry.

At age twelve, the boy went to live with his brother-in-law and guardian, Judge George Morrell at Cooperstown, New York, in the Mohawk Valley. Webb ran away from the judge's home. Later James managed to get a commission in the army, served in the artillery and became an adjutant. Webb was called "fearless and courageous," but his belligerency led him into many duels.

In September, 1827, Webb turned in his commission, resigning from the army. He became editor and principal proprietor of the *Morning Courier* in December. His other partners were James Gordon Brooks and James Lawson, commercial editor of the paper.

In May, 1829, on suggestion of Bennett, Webb combined the *Courier* with Noah's *Enquirer.* The new publisher of the combined daily estimated the annual expenditure of the journalistic venture at thirty thousand dollars, "which it is necessary to incur in publishing a morning paper in a manner correspondent with the improvements of the age. . . . ." Bennett became an editor but spent most of his time reporting.

Merger of the two papers, each with about three thousand subscribers, meant that the circulation of the *Courier and Enquirer* could now top that of other papers. Advertising increased considerably with the merger. The publisher issued a two-page supplement on some days and a four-page supplement regularly on Saturdays. When, on October 6, 1829, the *Courier and Enquirer* increased its size, it also printed a story of its new steam press and included a bid for patronage in the aggressive commercial spirit of the day. This was an early attempt at newspaper promotion.

Newspapers thus began to take on the characteristics of large-scale business, with several partners owning stock and enjoying profits.

What drove Webb's costs of operation up? At first, he joined the Association of New York Newspapers. Then, when his rival, the *Journal of Commerce,* was admitted, he withdrew. Webb had to beat his rivals if his prestige was to grow. He secured the news schooner *Eclipse* and a fleet of small boats. The schooner and fleet cost him about $4,300 annually to maintain.

Webb went further. He contracted with a famous shipbuilder, Isaac Webb, to build for the paper a 100-ton clippership which "should beat every pilot boat and schooner in the harbor or he would not be compelled to take her." The schooner *Courier and Enquirer* put Webb so far in front in the news competition that often his rivals had to buy their news from Webb. A three-cornered rivalry was set up among the boats of the *New York Harbor Association,* the *Journal of Commerce* and the *Courier and Enquirer.*

The rivalry resulted in publication of extras at any time of the day, whenever important foreign news arrived. Large, boldface type was employed for display. Webb, for example, headed his news with this:

> WEDNESDAY MORNING
> *Half Past One O'clock*
>
> Our boat has this moment arrived, having boarded the ship Britannia, Captain Marshall from Liverpool, whence he sailed on 6th of June, bringing the London, Liverpool and Glasglow papers, with Lloyd's and shipping lists to the latest dates. At this hour we have barely time to glance at their contents. . . .

In these extras of the *Courier and Enquirer,* foreign news appeared on the front page, displacing the usual advertisements and miscellaneous reprints. Front-page display of news was exceptional in this period because with flat-bed presses it was still necessary to run each sheet through the press twice. The first and fourth pages were printed first, leaving the second and third pages, containing news and editorials, for last. New cylinder presses enabled the publisher to print both sides of the paper more quickly.

Mails, at that time, left Washington in the morning and arrived in New York on the night of the following day; therefore, Monday's congressional proceedings appeared in Thursday's New York papers. Determined that the capital news appear in the *Courier and Enquirer* on Wednesdays, Webb contracted for a daily horse express from Washington to New York during the entire session of Congress, agreeing to pay $7,500 a month. New York merchants thus received their news twenty-four hours before the regular mails.

Webb called attention to his quick news gathering and transmission facilities by placing this announcement above his regular heading:

BY EXPRESS
IN ADVANCE OF SOUTHERN MAIL

And, later in the day, he printed:

SECOND EDITION
New Schooner Courier and
Enquirer Arrived in Town
at 9 o'clock This Morning

With the new system of rapid collection and transmission of news, employment of additional editors and reporters and discussion of subjects never before touched on by the press, daily expenses of newspapers more than quadrupled. Four of the older morning papers died out.

Bennett and the *Courier and Enquirer* conducted a violent campaign against the Bank of the United States. President Andrew Jackson attacked the institution and wanted to let its charter expire because he thought it was too powerful.

Realizing the bank would soon be put out of business, its directors began to seek to influence the press. In March, 1831, the officials authorized Nicholas Biddle, president, to get probank news and opinions into newspapers. Between 1831 and the end of 1834, President Biddle spent without vouchers $29,600 on newspapers.

When Biddle was accused of using the whole press of the country to aid in his fight with President Jackson and when he was charged with pouring money illegally into newspapers which favored a new charter for the bank, he pointed to the number of papers to which loans were given, yet which opposed rechartering the bank. Among these papers were the Washington, D.C., *United States Telegraph* and the New York *Courier and Enquirer.*

The *Courier and Enquirer,* in a brutal assault, charged the bank with buying men and votes as "cattle in the market" and with "withering as by a subtle poison the liberty of the press." Bennett began his series of articles on February 5, 1831. Thereafter, they appeared daily for the next two months. Bennett charged that the Bank of the United States was using its money for political purposes and for building up one party over another. The bank sought to control the government, the newsman contended.

After these charges had been made, the Bank of the United States continued to loan money to the Webb paper until the notes totaled $52,975. The bank claimed the loans were considered a safe and legitimate business transaction. The *Courier and Enquirer* thus found itself attacked for criticizing the bank while at the same time being its debtor.

The Bennett articles suddenly vanished from the *Courier and Enquirer*. The reporter was ordered to cease his attacks on the financial institution and to turn to other matters. Bennett did not know of certain transactions which took place during April, 1831. Daniel Tylee, half-owner of the daily, sold his stock in the *Courier and Enquirer* apparently to Mordecai Noah. Noah had borrowed fifteen thousand dollars from Silas E. Burroughs, a wealthy friend of Biddle. Burroughs' chief desire was to shift the position of the paper away from Jackson. Burroughs had obtained the money from President Biddle by advancing the argument that Noah would be able to change the daily's position. Even publisher Webb did not know what was taking place at that time.

Later, with increased pressure Burroughs and Noah brought on Webb, the *Courier and Enquirer* publisher went completely over to the

TABLE 9

Income and Expenses
Courier and Enquirer

On one occasion Publisher James Watson Webb gave this account of his newspaper finances:

Annual Income	$65, 000
Expenses	35, 000
Profit	$30, 000 annual

On another occasion, Publisher Webb listed these items of income:

Daily subscribers	3, 300 × $10	$33, 000
Weekly, Semiweekly	2, 300 × $4.50	10, 350
Advertising revenue	275 × $30	8, 250
	Income	$51, 600

From statements made by Publisher James Watson Webb

anti-Jacksonites on the bank issue. Bennett parted company with the *Courier and Enquirer*.

A congressional committee later looked into the daily's shift of viewpoint and allegiance, unearthing the fact that fifty-three thousand dollars in loans had been made by the bank to the paper in one year. Webb launched attacks on his former associate editor, but Bennett did not reply. He said the shift in the *Courier and Enquirer*'s policy was made by Noah "who saw the paper's financial difficulty and the breeches pocket of Mr. Biddle open."

Similar mercantile papers appeared in such eastern seaboard cities as Boston, Philadelphia and Baltimore.

Chapter 5

The Press Moves West

EARLY TRANS-ALLEGHENY NEWSPAPERS STRUGGLE TO SURVIVE

Wagons loaded with people and plows for farms of the West crawled along the rough Pennsylvania trail leading from Philadelphia. Sometimes wagons bore printing presses and type for newspapers yet to be born in new territories. From Pittsburgh, presses were floated on flatboat, down the Ohio to points nearest their destinations. Then they were conveyed along rough roads to printshops where they were set up to spread the news. Thus journalism moved west across the Alleghenies.

No other single factor has so profoundly affected American development and shaped American ideals as the West and its frontier. It influenced politics, industry, education and literature. Little weeklies issued on hand presses under great difficulties contributed much to western development.

Long before the outbreak of the revolution the mighty movement destined to carry the white man over the slopes of the Alleghenies was already under way. Soon after the end of the Revolutionary War, the ring of the axe and the crack of the rifle of the American frontiersman resounded along the eastern fringe of this same region. So rapid was migration after 1780 that, within two generations, the frontier of civilization had advanced beyond the Mississippi. To the struggling eastern farmer, the dissatisfied tradesman, the religious dissenter, the oppressed mechanic or the ambitious young lawyer, the West was the promised land. The gates were open always.

Journalism moved along with these eastern settlers into the trans-Allegheny region. Printers were not the first group of settlers to come to these new sections. First were the frontiersmen who explored, built

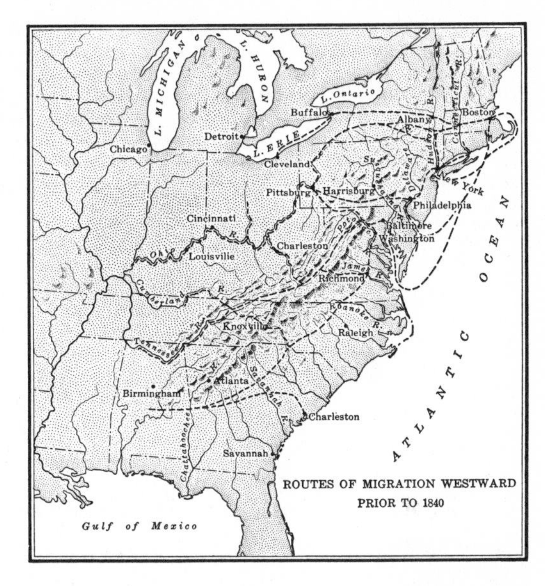

Figure 20. Westward Ho! Migrants heading west had several choices of routes open to them. The great barrier was the Allegheny Mountains. Those in the New England States could avoid them by cutting across Albany and New York State. The Middle Atlantic group traveled the Philadelphia-Harrisburg-Pittsburgh route. Other families followed the Potomac River route, and then could either take the Pittsburgh path or travel down the Shenandoah Valley. The James River and the Roanoke Rivers in Virginia provided access.

cabins, trapped and hunted. Then came the real pioneers who cultivated a truck patch and a crop of corn and then moved on. This group was succeeded by the third group who purchased lands, cultivated larger farms and became more permanent settlers. Then the fourth group appeared, the men of capital and enterprise who concentrated in villages and towns. There preachers founded frontier churches, housing their congregations in simple wooden structures, improving the facilities as the parishioners multiplied and became more affluent. With experience in stores back East, other settlers opened up general merchandise stores, while blacksmiths and harnessmakers began to cater to the needs of town dwellers, farmers and ranchers. Also, on the main street a barber opened his one-chair shop, where a customer could get a shave, haircut or even a bath. Professional men followed, with physicians putting out their shingles to prescribe pills for the sick, set broken bones and deliver pioneer babies. Litigation over land sites in the new territory, making of wills and defense of thieves and murderers, all called for the knowledge and skills of a lawyer. He might aspire to be a judge or to represent the district in the territorial or state legislature, or later even in Congress in Washington. Soon a printer saw possibilities for his special abilities and hauled his press into town. When economic conditions were favorable and population of village and countryside grew, he ventured to publish a weekly newspaper.

Printers came for various reasons. They hoped to benefit by the opening of new territory and the growth of a prosperous farming region, of the timber or cotton area, or of the riverboat town. Some eastern printers had been unsuccessful in the seaboard towns; they reasoned that perhaps they would issue weeklies and prosper in western communities now developing. Printers could become territorial printers, too, and receive extra revenue. Governors invited some of the publisher-printers to the new territories. Many sons of established printers on the Atlantic seaboard, desiring to make their own way, turned westward. They were joined by journeymen who had worked long for printer-publishers in Boston, New York, Philadelphia or Baltimore.

Any western hamlet or town which looked economically promising beckoned the printer to set up his shop. In addition to printers, some lawyers, finding little need for their professional services, turned to newspapering. Frequently politicians became editors to control public opinion and to get elected to office.

The frontier newspaper cycle, in many respects, was a repetition of what had occurred during the colonial period on the seaboard. The printer could not survive with his newspaper alone. He became a job printer, and sometimes was appointed territorial printer and later state printer. He served as postmaster, sending his paper free to subscribers by virtue of his franking privilege. Other printer-newspaper publishers sold merchandise and real estate.

Many restless printers moved a number of times, always westward. When the town they first settled in did not grow, they looked for a more progressive one or one more favorably situated. Establishment of a capital in the new territory led to a printer-publisher's decision to transfer his operations. He moved sometimes within the state, but he might shift also to a new territory with good prospects.

Problems of Pioneer Printer

The printer-publisher faced many problems in the pioneering environment. First he had to secure a press and equipment from the East. He could have them shipped or he could bring hand press and type and cases with him over rivers, through the mountain gaps and across the land.

Securing white paper from eastern mills was another major problem of the frontier printer. The first paper mill in the trans-Allegheny region was constructed in 1792 near Georgetown, Kentucky, but the mill could not supply all the needs of pioneer printers in the region. They had to obtain paper from eastern sources of supply. For many years poor roads also handicapped publishers and delayed newspapers from the East. Often the pioneer publisher had no skilled help who knew the printing trade, and he advertised in large city papers for able printers. Desperate, the publisher sometimes announced he would teach a man or boy the types.

European news took two or three months to reach western papers, and even dispatches from the East were more than a month old. Nevertheless, when they did arrive, the news absorbed more than two-thirds the available space in the newspapers. For years revenue from advertisements was small because communities had not advanced commercially.

As postal service improved, news arrived more rapidly. Washington and other leaders were anxious to ease the publishing situation. So in 1792 Congress officially admitted papers to the mails. New postal laws also permitted free carriage of exchanges between publishers. In no part of the country were results of this ruling more noteworthy than in the western territory. Whenever exchanges failed to arrive on time, local publishers were forced to use old clippings over again. Some newspaper operators even reprinted George Washington's will to fill up space.

At the beginning of 1800 there were two important postroads to the West: one from Wheeling, West Virginia, along Zane's Road to Lewistone, or Maysville, Kentucky, and thence to more important places in the northern and central parts of the state; the other road from the Shenandoah Valley in Virginia, through Knoxville, Tennessee, as far as Nashville in that same territory. Additional routes and crossroutes were soon established.

These weekly newspapers, in their influence on backwoods communities, were most important in this pioneer period. Only a skilled orator could hope to rival the editor of a weekly gazette in his ability to shape the popular will. Crude as they undoubtedly were, these papers brought news-hungry pioneers information about events back home and reported events of the national capital as well as the world.

Matters of local interest, other than political and personal quarrels, occupied only limited space in these publications and other pioneer papers. A unique frontier feature carried in the *Kentucky Gazette* for a number of years was its narratives of Indian atrocities. Foreign coverage, at first, consisted of attacks England and other countries made on revolutionary France. Writers called loudly for American participation on the side of France.

Pioneer newspaper publishers had a sublime faith in their sections. Such a belief was necessary to survive. They expected the area to grow, and they believed in its agricultural and commercial future. Newspapers played an important role in territorial and later state development and advancement. In their newspapers, publishers pictured their settlements as something of a paradise. Sometimes the purpose for establishing the paper was to advance the area and to lure settlers to it. Pioneer papers were advocates of internal improvements and usually were Democratic and Jacksonian in politics. When opposition parties developed, newspapers were born to express this opposition.

With growth of population and commercial advancement in the community, the publisher was faced with a new rival, a printer who believed the town or territory could support an additional newspaper. Sometimes he guessed correctly. In other instances he closed up shop or merged with his rival. As population spread back from the main turnpikes and rivers, new communities multiplied and many acquired their own weeklies. Eventually some of these became semiweeklies, triweeklies and even dailies.

NORTH CENTRAL NEWSPAPERS SPREAD

PITTSBURGH'S PIONEER PAPER

Pittsburgh was the first community west of the Alleghenies to get a newspaper. The town was strategically located at the junction of the Allegheny and Monongahela rivers, forming the Ohio River at that point. Pittsburgh was the stopping-off place for settlers traveling west. At Pittsburgh they could mount a flatboat, keelboat or other craft made there and sail down the Ohio River to the Mississippi River, and later to New Orleans.

Beginning as a trading post in the colonial period, Pittsburgh was fought over by the French and English for many years. When the French captured it, they called it Fort Duquesne; the English later named it Fort Pitt, the name being changed later to Pittsburgh. Following the Revolutionary War the state bought all lands still claimed by the heirs of William Penn who owned a manor of several thousand acres. The land was surveyed and offered for sale in small lots.

Settlers arrived in a steady flow and among them, in 1786, were two printers from eastern Pennsylvania. John Scull and Joseph Hall were only twenty-one years old. They set up their printing equipment at Water Street and Chancery Lane, and on July 29, 1786, they issued the first *Pittsburgh Gazette*. They were encouraged to come to western Pennsylvania by Hugh Brackenridge, litterateur, lawyer, and later judge.

New publishers faced many obstacles in this wilderness. Pittsburgh had only three hundred residents. Subscribers and advertisers were sorely limited. Paper had to be brought over the mountains by wagon and packhorse. When the supply of paper was short, cartridge paper from the adjacent garrison was used. The publishers did not find this satisfactory and were happy to announce in the June 14, 1797 issue that the

Gazette had been printed on paper manufactured on Redstone Creek in Fayette County nearby.

Scull and Hall had guessed right about the future of Pittsburgh. It grew steadily. In 1787 the Pittsburgh Academy was opened to furnish higher education to young men. A year later the settlement was made the seat of the newly organized Allegheny County and chartered as a borough a few years afterward. Industrial advance was made. The borough began to manufacture furniture, hats, leather goods, whiskey and flour. A boat-building industry was begun, and a glassworks was started. Opening of the Mississippi River to trade after the American Revolution and opening of the vast land west of Pittsburgh to settlement made Pittsburgh an important trading and manufacturing center. Ironmasters in the back areas produced the primary iron, while Pittsburgh built mills and factories which fashioned the iron into utensils and implements needed by the pioneering family and trader. Turnpikes soon linked Pittsburgh to other western Pennsylvania towns and, meanwhile, the road to Philadelphia was improved.

The *Pittsburgh Gazette* survived its early pains and difficulties and expanded with growth of the town and the region. Following the usual pattern, publisher Scull became Pittsburgh's postmaster in 1790, an office he held for seven years. He retired in 1816, turning over the printing and publishing company to his son and a partner. Extended scope of the weekly and changing economic environment were noted in the new name given the paper: the *Pittsburgh Gazette and Manufacturing and Mercantile Advertiser.*

Scull was also a book printer, issuing in 1793 one of the first books printed west of the mountains. It was the third volume of a novel, *Modern Chivalry: containing the adventures of Captain John Ferrago and Teague O'Regan, his Servant,* written by Brackenridge.

Meanwhile, seeing opportunities in the community for a second paper, some printers issued the *Commonwealth* in 1805. It continued for thirteen years.

With growth of Pittsburgh, Brackenridge, always a politician, backed a third newspaper, *Tree of Liberty,* in 1810. He had as his editor and printer, John Israel. The paper was a political organ, lasting about ten years.

Kentucky Newspapers

Meanwhile settlers began to push west. Although Kentucky was first organized as a part of Virginia, it sought admission to the Union as a state soon afterward. The area was first called Kentucke. To promote its admission, Lexington, the largest town, voted a free lot in July, 1786, to John Bradford, a Virginia printer who had come to Kentucky after the war. He bought his equipment in Philadelphia. Paper, type and press came by wagon over postroads to Pittsburgh and then by flatboat down the Ohio to Maysville, Kentucky. The equipment was brought by wagon over the trail blazed recently to Lexington.

The initial number of the *Kentucke Gazette* was a single sheet with two pages (10 x 9 1/2 inches) and three columns to a page. John Bradford and his brother, Fielding Bradford, were co-publishers but the latter soon withdrew. John Bradford made an attempt to issue the *Kentucke Gazette* as a semiweekly in January, 1797, but the times were not ready, as the increased frequency lasted only a year. The publisher now extended the scope of his weekly, with *General Advertiser* being added to the title in 1803. Again efforts were made to transform the paper into a semiweekly, but they were not successful. The *Kentucke Gazette* passed through the hands of a number of proprietors, ceasing entirely in 1848.

Meanwhile, other journals were founded as the state grew in population and commerce. Thomas H. Stewart started *Stewart's Kentucky Herald* in 1795, but ten years later it was absorbed by the earlier-founded *Kentucke Gazette*. As other towns in the state developed from hamlets, they acquired weeklies. At Frankfort, Benjamin J. Bradford issued the *Kentucky Journal* in 1795; A. Hunter, the *Palladium* in 1798 and William Gerard, the *Argus of Western America* in 1808.

Louisville on the Ohio River was to develop into the leading Kentucky town and newspaper center, but its first newspaper, the *Louisville Gazette and Western Advertiser*, did not appear until 1807, with Joseph Charless as publisher. Irish-born, he had lived in France and then, on arriving in the United States, established in 1790 the *Mifflin Gazette* in Lewistown, Pennsylvania, but this venture failed. He next joined Matthew Carey, another Irish refugee, in the latter's printshop in Philadelphia. While in that community, he became acquainted with the nation's leaders, Benjamin Franklin, Alexander Hamilton and others.

Charless decided to seek his fortunes on the frontier. In 1803 he moved to Lexington, Kentucky; his effort to establish a newspaper there never materialized. Then he moved to Louisville, where in November, 1807, he started the *Gazette and Western Advertiser*.

Tennessee Gets First Newspaper

George Roulstone brought out on November 5, 1791, the first number of the *Knoxville Gazette* in Rogersville, Tennessee, then the county seat. Roulstone's moving about as a printer was typical of many others at this time. A native of Salem, Massachusetts, he learned the printing business and issued a weekly there. Roulstone then moved south to Fayetteville, North Carolina, where he published several newspapers. The governor of Tennessee persuaded him that the opportunities for a printer were better in a western pioneer state like Tennessee. Yielding to the suggestion, Roulstone took his press apart and packed his equipment into a wagon. He trekked over the trail of the Blue Ridge Mountains into Holston Valley, where Kingsport, Tennessee, now stands. There on the banks of the Holston River he loaded his equipment on a flatboat and went down river to Rogersville.

In that community he set up again and started to print the *Knoxville Gazette,* the first piece of printing ever attempted in Tennessee. The *Gazette's* office was in a log hut, a one-room affair about 16 by 12 feet. In this one-room office and home, Roulstone worked, ate and slept, his press at one end, his bed at the other.

Roulstone called his journal after the town of Knoxville because he planned to move there as soon as the Indians were put under control. This soon was the situation, for in October, 1792 the publisher again took his press apart, put it on another flatboat and drifted down the Holston River to Knoxville where he began to publish.

His subscribers, short of funds, brought him a bag of potatoes or a ham in lieu of cash payments. Roulstone became official printer to the territory, an office which paid six hundred dollars yearly. Later he was elected clerk of the territorial court and senate. When the mails began to come through in 1797, he was elected postmaster. He closed down his paper. Two other weeklies soon started in Knoxville, steadily but slowly progressing. In Nashville, Benjamin J. Bradford launched the *Tennessee Gazette* in 1797.

Population spread and business, meanwhile, began in the western part of the state. Long before Daniel Boone started opening the eastern end, De Soto and LaSalle found the Mississippi and paddled down its immense distances. Settlers started a trading post at Chickasaw Bluffs, later called Memphis, where traders stopped. Economic opportunities for printers beckoned. The empire of printing moved westward. In Jackson in 1823 Charles McLean started the *Gazette,* the first newspaper in west Tennessee. Two years later, the *Memphis Advocate and Western District Intelligencer* made its appearance.

Ohio Press

With a Ramage press and a few fonts of type, William Maxwell issued the first paper in Ohio, the *Centinel of the Northwestern Territory,* on November 9, 1793. Maxwell, originally from New Jersey, had settled in Pittsburgh but saw opportunities for journalism in the new Ohio country. He set up his log cabin printshop at the corner of Front and Sycamore streets in Cincinnati. Cincinnati reached twenty-five thousand by 1830. It was clear Maxwell's paper was not going to be a strictly local one, for he called it *Centinel of the Northwestern Territory* with the slogan, "Open to All Parties—Influenced by None."

In his opening issue Maxwell indicated that he was going to publish a "News Paper." "The country is in its infancy," he said, asserting that the big menace was the Indian who swept away whole families in the fields and burned their houses. He declared the want of trade down the Mississippi deprived the country of money, for the French owned the territory. From the first, editor Maxwell advocated opening the Mississippi River to navigation and never ceased his plea.

"Western" often appeared in the titles of these trans-Allegheny weeklies. The second paper in Ohio, *Western Spy and Hamilton Gazette*, appeared in 1799 also in Cincinnati. Other Ohio papers were issued during the next decade in Chillicothe, Marietta and Dayton. With expansion of population and building of towns, by 1800 Ohio had fourteen papers and by 1819 published thirty-three journals. Dailies were established in the next decade.

Michigan's Spoken Newspaper

Michigan did not have enough population or commerce to warrant a printed newspaper for some time. The need for news communication, however, was present and was recognized by the Reverend Father Gabriel Richard, a priest of the Order of Sulpice, who came to Detroit in 1798 as a resident pastor of the Roman Catholic Church. Father Richard began his "spoken newspaper." He appointed a crier to stand on the church steps to tell the public about such "news as was fit to speak." Advertising had its place because the crier told of objects for sale. For benefit of those absent when the crier appeared, a written newspaper was developed and publicly posted near the church. Father Richard had the help of one of his parishioners, Theopolis Metz, who later became a newspaper publisher.

From this spoken and later written newspaper grew the first printed sheet in Michigan, the *Michigan Essay, or Impartial Observer.* It appeared on August 31, 1809. Father Richard appointed an editor and publisher among his flock. Detroit's population was a combination of French and English, consequently the *Michigan Essay* carried a French section written by Father Richard.

This was the only paper for eighteen years. The *Detroit Gazette* was established July 25, 1817, the first permanent paper in Michigan. The *Detroit Gazette* served the English and French population, with a proportion of one page devoted to French and three to English. Times were difficult for newspapering in this region. In 1820 the *Gazette* editor asserted that only ninety of its one hundred fifty-two subscribers had paid their bills, and not a single advertiser had paid his. The *Detroit Gazette*, however, survived for ten years more. Detroit continued to grow; a competitive newspaper, the *Michigan Herald*, arose from the improved conditions in 1825.

Indiana and Illinois Journalism

Hardship, privation and Indians could not stop migration of population into Indiana and Illinois and even into Missouri. These new territories got their first weeklies now.

Elihu Stout pulled Indiana's first newspaper, the *Indiana Gazette*, from his hand press in July, 1804. The newspaper came out after great difficulties. Paper was brought to Vincennes on a packhorse which followed the old Buffalo trail. Printing equipment was carried from Frankfort, Kentucky, down the Ohio River and up the Wabash in piroques or canoes. After it was established, the *Indiana Gazette* was burned out, but the publisher was dauntless and started again under a new name, the *Western Sun*. Stout, by this time, became territorial printer. A competitive paper, the *Gazette*, was launched in Vincennes in 1817.

During this period, whenever towns grew in Indiana, enterprising printers started their weeklies. Papers came from presses in Brookville, Madison, Vevay, Lawrenceburg and Charleston during the next decades. By 1831 a directory listed twenty-nine different papers in Indiana.

It was not until 1814 that Matthew Duncan made a first newspaper attempt in Illinois with his *Illinois Herald*. Duncan, typical of many pioneer printer-publishers, came originally from Virginia and had worked first on a Kentucky paper. Recognizing the opportunity in the newly settled territory, he moved to Kaskaskia. He became territorial printer, thereby receiving a steady income. He issued the *Illinois Herald* on or about June 24, 1814. Two years later the paper became the *Western Intelligencer*. When Vandalia became capital of the new state in 1820, Duncan's weekly, which had changed its name to *Illinois Intelligencer*, was moved there too. Meanwhile a second paper, the *Illinois Immigrant*, appeared in Shawneetown in 1818, the "immigrant" part of the title reflecting the frontier environment.

Subscribers Pay for Paper in Pork

The hardships of publishing a frontier paper and the method by which the publisher survived may be seen in the following item typical of others:

> Persons expecting to pay for their papers in produce must do so soon, or the cash will be expected. Pork, flour, corn and meal will be taken at the market prices. Also, those who expect to pay us in firewood must do so immediately—we must have our wood laid for the winter before the roads get bad.

Bloomington, Indiana, *Post*

Louisiana Purchase Opens New Area to Settlement and Press

Strategically located in the upper Mississippi Valley and a gateway to the West, St. Louis became the center of active weeklies. Settled first by the French, St. Louis developed into an important center for the fur trade west of the Mississippi River. For many years after its founding the community's manufacturing was on a small but substantial scale: it included lumber, bricks, flour, foundry products, shoes and leather goods. Because St. Louis was located at the juncture of the Ohio and Mississippi rivers, boats sailed from Pittsburgh and other Ohio and Kentucky ports to St. Louis, and from there moved south to New Orleans. The population of St. Louis was larger than that of Chicago until after the Civil War. In 1810 St. Louis had twelve hundred; this increased to sixty thousand by 1830.

Foundations for cultural institutions of St. Louis were laid during this time. Early settlers were members chiefly of the Roman Catholic Church, which provided instruction in elementary subjects given in the French language. The first English-speaking private school was opened in 1804, but the public school system did not begin until 1833.

Analyzing the economic possibilities in St. Louis, Joseph Charless, who had established the *Louisville* (Ky.) *Gazette and Western Advertiser,* launched also the first paper in St. Louis. Governor Merewether Lewis offered Charless encouragement and patronage if he would establish a journal in St. Louis. Charless received $225 as an advance. In Lexington, Kentucky, Charless secured an old, secondhand Ramage press and a few fonts of type and shipped his equipment down the Ohio River to St. Louis.

There, aided by another Kentucky printer, he launched the *Missouri Gazette* on July 12, 1808. The first issue of the weekly appeared on foolscap paper, 8 by 12 inches, twelve columns in all. The *Missouri Gazette* had a total of one hundred seventy-two subscribers at first. The weekly cost twenty dollars a week to operate. Charless complained frequently about his supplies of paper which failed to arrive. Often when the mail failed to come, he printed only two pages. Charless reached five hundred subscribers by 1814 and a thousand by 1819, which was excellent considering the community had only four thousand residents. No doubt many of his subscribers lived out of town.

As did his colonial predecessors, Charless conducted a number of sidelines to keep alive. He was territorial printer, and he conducted a boarding house and livery stable, dealt in old brass, and sold land, town lots and slaves.

Charless clipped much of his news from eastern papers and picked up other information from travelers going through St. Louis and from letters. *Missouri Gazette* carried accounts of Indian traders and their business activities, judicial proceedings and army news. Charless printed little local news since he felt readers would know about these events anyway. The publisher attempted to advance agricultural knowledge of his farmer-readers by printing farm news and the latest developments in crop and sheep raising.

Charless was independent minded. He opposed local politicians and others. Charless objected to the military for permitting excessive drinking and gambling among soldiers. He also objected to the United States' handling of the War of 1812 and did not like the leniency with which the local courts treated Indian cases. Charless supported the antislavery cause in Missouri. As his paper caught on and as the community's commercial life expanded, the *Missouri Gazette*'s advertising increased.

To counteract the influence of the *Gazette,* political opponents of Charless raised a fund of one thousand dollars to start a Republican paper in St. Louis. They advertised in the *Lexington* (Kentucky) *Reporter.* Attracted by the large amount of money offered, Joshua Norvell of Nashville, answered the advertisements. After arriving in St. Louis, he started a rival sheet, the *Western Journal,* in May, 1815. Norvell was unsuccessful as an editor, however, and within a year moved to Arkansas. The new proprietors changed the *Journal* to the *Emigrant and Western Advertiser* in May, 1817, and a year later the weekly changed hands and its name to *St. Louis Enquirer.* Thomas Hart Benton served as editor of the *Enquirer,* using it to place himself before the public and to discuss the issues of the day. Benton urged better roads, protection of the frontier and the fur trade. During the next decade various partners joined the *Enquirer.* Duff Green, who was one of these, was later chosen to become editor of the Jacksonian organ, the *United States Telegraph,* in Washington, D.C.

As Missouri advanced agriculturally and economically, population spread and new communities grew. The press developed, too, in the outlying villages and towns in the interior, for population of Missouri climbed from nineteen thousand seven hundred in 1810 to one hundred forty thousand by 1830. Nathaniel Patten became Missouri's first publisher outside of St. Louis when he launched in February, 1819 the *Missouri Iintelligencer and Boone's Lick Advertiser* in Franklin, about 160 miles in back country. By 1828 six towns outside of St. Louis had weekly newspapers.

SOUTH CENTRAL PRESS LAUNCHED

To the south, the pressure of population was also felt. Seeking better cotton lands, families from the Carolinas and Georgia began settlement of Alabama, Mississippi, Louisiana, Arkansas and Texas.

Alabama Press Begins

Papers were printed at the United States fort in Alabama even before the territory was ceded by the Spanish government. Samuel Miller and John B. Hood issued the *Mobile Sentinel* at Fort Stoddert on May 23, 1811. They were so determined to be the first in Mobile journalism that they started south before the city was annexed. They were stopped and began printing in the neighborhood of St. Stephens. Sixteen issues of the paper were brought out there.

Mobile was surrendered to General James Wilkinson April 13, 1813. On April 28, a *Mobile Gazette* with an account of the surrender was published with George B. Cotton as publisher. The paper endured for six years. Two years later the *Commercial Register* appeared.

Arkansas Journalism

Arkansas journalism was begun by a former Long Islander. William W. Woodruff arrived at the United States Post in Arkansas in October, 1819, bringing a press and some type in a canoe from Franklin, Tennessee. He issued the first number of the *Arkansas Gazette* on November 20, 1819. Two years later when he became printer to the territory, Woodruff abandoned the paper and moved to Little Rock, which had been made the capital. There he revived the *Arkansas Gazette.* He had strong political ambitions and used his paper to promote his own candidacy for office. A second paper, the *Advocate,* did not appear until later.

Louisiana Press

Since Louisiana was under control of the French until the sale of the vast area to the United States, it was natural that the first and subsequent newspapers in New Orleans should be published in French. *Le Courier du Vendredi* was the first, issued on May 26, 1785; it later became the *Louisiana Courier,* a triweekly published in French and English.

Monsieur L. Puclot, a San Domingo refugee who settled in New Orleans, persuaded Governor Carondelet of the value of the journal in his territory. Puclot issued the *Moniteur de La Louisiana* on March 3, 1793. A year later J. B. L. Fontaine took over editorship and held the position also as publisher. In 1797, four years after its founding, the *Moniteur* became the official state paper. Most of the facts obtainable about the history of Louisiana are found in its pages. It was filled with government news, decisions of the New Orleans city council, lists of baptisms and marriages. A third French weekly, the *Telegraphe,* came from the press in 1803, later becoming a triweekly, issued in French and English.

Soon after the Louisiana territory was purchased by the United States in 1803, the *Louisiana Gazette* was established by John Maury on July 27, 1804. He began with nineteen subscribers who paid ten dollars each. Several attempts were made to issue a daily, but they did not succeed. The fact that there were not enough readers who knew English was given as the main reason for the daily's failures.

Texas Newspapers

Several attempts were made to publish newssheets in Texas before a genuine newspaper appeared. When Commodore Aury and others were stationed at Galveston Island in 1816, a wandering printer from Baltimore, Samuel Bangs, issued a newssheet containing military orders and other news. When the United States Army reached Nacagodoches, Texas, in 1819, a small printed sheet was published more or less regularly.

The first genuine newspaper in Texas, however, was the *Texas Gazette* established by Goodwin B. Cotton in San Felipe County on September 28, 1829. The paper had its first rival when the *Texas Gazette and Brazoria Commercial Advertiser* appeared in 1830.

Chapter 6

Magazine Expansion

FACTORS FAVORING MAGAZINE GROWTH

As part of the general cultural expansion a number of magazines were started. Magazine publishers continued to aim at the educated and upper economic classes. With expansion of population, widening of education and improvement of business, the magazine market was improved and circulations increased. The number of magazines grew from five in 1794 to twelve in 1800 and by 1825 reached one hundred. Financially stronger, they remained in business longer than during the colonial era.

Postal laws passed in 1794 proved more favorable for magazine publication. Rates for carrying magazines through the mails were decreased, which contributed toward magazine popularity.

LITERARY FLAVOR

While some periodicals contained news, magazines began to veer in other directions. Magazines became more distinctly literary and took this function away from the newspaper which had stressed literature in the absence of news. The magazine served as a repository for all kinds of writing. Some periodicals dealt with current political and social questions. A considerable amount of space was devoted to historical articles, extracts from books. Much attention was devoted to poetry.

In absence of schools and public libraries, magazine editors considered themselves educators-in-print, bringing information and knowledge to readers. Some publishers supplied a kind of literary entertainment for their public. Magazines began to feature illustrations on copper plates, showing maps, buildings and some portraits.

MATHEW CAREY'S MUSEUM

One of the most successful publishers in the post-Revolutionary period was Mathew Carey. A firebrand printer in Ireland, he was jailed there for printing material criticizing British policy. He fled to Philadelphia where he established a newspaper, the *Pennsylvania Herald,* which did not last long.

Carey and three others then started the *Columbian Magazine* in 1786. The editor clipped many articles from English magazines, but he stressed native works. Inaugurating a new method in magazine publishing similar to the one begun in the newspaper offices, Carey employed an editor and a chief contributor.

Soon after establishing the *Columbian,* Carey withdrew and issued a second magazine, the *American Museum.* He intended this periodical to be a museum of American writing worth preserving. Now with a history of its own, America was already becoming historical minded; Carey, therefore, reprinted from documents of the American Revolution.

The *Museum*'s articles on business were especially noteworthy. Carey printed articles favoring elimination of tariffs between the states but advocating tariffs on imports. Other articles urged government and private enterprise to join forces and encourage American industry. While newspapers might give the news about congressional actions, Carey's *American Museum* furnished ideas and discussion of current political problems. Although it started with only a score of subscribers, the *Museum* soon reached more than twelve hundred. The magazine came to an end in 1792.

THOMAS' MASSACHUSETTS MAGAZINE

Newspaper publisher Isaiah Thomas, who saw the need for a newspaper to appeal to lower economic groups and the less educated, also recognized a similar market for a magazine. In 1789 he launched the *Massachusetts Magazine,* which was to be a "Museum of Knowledge as Rational Entertainment." He sought original writings but was forced to rely on his scissors.

He presented news, procedures of the Massachusetts legislature and the national Congress. He gave readers serious discussions of contemporary problems by Franklin, Jefferson and others. Thomas printed literary essays and poetry for his readers, but he also furnished them with sentimental stories, articles and melodramas filled with villains and seductions. The *Massachusetts Magazine* was published for eight years, much longer than the colonial publications.

WEBSTER'S AMERICAN MAGAZINE

While Thomas was issuing his Boston publication, another New Englander with literary leanings launched a magazine in New York. Noah Webster, ambitious school teacher and later publisher of the newspaper in New York, the *American Minerva,* had an interest in national affairs and saw possibilities in a magazine publication. He issued the *American Magazine* in 1787, the first monthly publication in New York. Webster meant his magazine to be the expression of sound, conservative ideas on politics and education. He favored adoption of the new Constitution and wrote about the need for education in America. He carried several pages of current news for his readers, showing that magazines had not completely broken away from newspapers. Webster's magazine lasted only a year.

DENNIE'S PORT FOLIO, POPULAR FEDERALIST

Called the American Addison, Joseph Dennie was one of the most colorful and skillful magazine editors of that era. Dennie established the *Port Folio* in 1801, aiming it at "men of influence, men of liberality, and men of letters." Dennie was a Federalist and one of his objectives was to combat democratic tendencies in the Jefferson administration. The publisher asserted that the American separation from England was a mistake. Although indicted in 1803 for seditious libel, he was acquitted. Dennie's *Port Folio* drew on the Tuesday Night Club for contributions. All members were university graduates and Federalists, but it was Dennie who gave the publication its dash and brightness.

Dennie started with a circulation of two thousand, an indication that magazines were gathering a larger audience than during the revolutionary period. Dennie died in 1812, and although the magazine continued until 1829, it became more of a literary review under the subsequent editors. The great force of the publisher was lost.

BROWN'S LITERARY MAGAZINE

Called the "first professional man of letters," Charles Brockden Brown established the *Literary Magazine and American Register* in 1803 in

Philadelphia, a growing center of the magazine business. Brown asserted that he would record domestic matters, but he would handle in a systematic, orderly way news which newspapers commented on in a vague and indiscriminate fashion. His efforts, however, were short lived; his magazine lasted only a few years.

SATURDAY EVENING POST

One of the most important weeklies issued in America at this time, the *Saturday Evening Post,* proclaimed itself as a "Family Newspaper, Devoted to Literature, Morality, Science News, Agriculture, and Amusement." Although the claim was made that, when issued in 1821, it was a continuation of Benjamin Franklin's *Pennsylvania Gazette,* this has been disputed since a six-year interval elapsed from the time when the *Gazette* folded to establishment of the new *Post.*

Priced at two dollars a year, the *Saturday Evening Post* sought a popular appeal. Edited by Thomas Cottrell Clarke and published by Atkinson and Alexander, it was printed on a large sheet folded to make four pages. It contained essays, poetry, obituaries, a moral and religious column, and an appeal to women readers. The *Post* published William Cullen Bryant's poems; Edgar Allen Poe's "Black Cat," the famous short story; and it had, as its contributors, James Fenimore Cooper, James Russell Lowell and Nathaniel Hawthorne. The *Saturday Evening Post* had a popular formula, and it absorbed other less substantial magazines. It reached a circulation of ninety thousand before the Civil War.

NORTH AMERICAN REVIEW

Each section of the country began to produce its regional magazines. In Boston, however, the *North American Review,* first launched in 1815, sought to be a national magazine. Its object was to provide the best ideas of American thinkers to those who affected the thinking of America. The *North American* aimed to be a literary, historical and critical review, and during its long career it published many of the outstanding American writers.

NILES WEEKLY REGISTER

Performing an invaluable service to serious readers and to newspaper editors and later to historians, the *Niles Weekly Register* printed news of current events but especially stressed statistics and factual material and state papers.

TABLE 10

Contributions Made by Young Nation's Newspapers to Stream of Journalism (1787-1830)

News Coverage Expands

Development of Political News

- News of political parties developed intensely
- News of state legislatures increased
- News of U. S. capital expanded
- Partisanship in the news shown

Development of Newspaper as a Party Organ

- Gives news of parties
- Pleads party cause in news and editorials

Development of Commercial News

- News of domestic and foreign shipping, and of trade widened

Some Development of Court News

- Court news related to business printed
- Some criminal court news presented

Editorial Function Develops

Editorial Becomes Definite Part of Journalism

Editorials Published Regularly

Editorials Largely on Political and Economic News

Personnel Expansion

First Washington Correspondents Hired

Ship Reporters Added to Staffs

Beginnings of Development of Editor as Personality

Format Changes

Some Development of Headlines Occurred

More Columns to a Page Printed

Live News on Front Page Introduced

Increasing Size of Newspapers

More News Forced Increased Newspaper Page Size

Additional Advertisements Compel Publishers to Expand Size

Number of Newspapers Multiplied

New Newspapers Published in Older Towns

New Papers Appear in New Territories, States

TABLE 10 (continued)

Increased Circulation

Total Number of Copies Increased

Eastern Cities Have Larger Dailies with Growing Circulations

News-Gathering Facilities

Use of Schooners to Get News from Boats Quickly

Use of Fast Pony Expresses to Get Washington News

Formation of Harbor Association to Cut News-Gathering Costs

Editions

Development of Daily Editions Now

Some Development of Sunday Issues

Advertising

Development of Newspaper as Better Advertising Medium for:

- Shippers
- Insurance companies
- Book sellers
- Theatres
- Retail stores

Financial, Business Side

Development of Newspaper as a Profitable Business Enterprise

- Revenue increased from subscriptions, ads
- More funds to buy larger presses and news schooners and to hire reporters
- Still a small enterprise, not requiring tremendous amount of capital
- Cost for large metropolitan paper increased because of news-gathering and production facilities

Mechanical

Development of Steam, Cylinder Press in Large Cities

- Speed of production increased
- Mass production of newspapers possible
- Mechanical personnel increased
- Costs of starting, operating publication increased

Magazines

Numbers Multiplied

Circulation Increased

Founded in 1811 in Baltimore, Maryland, by Hezekiah Niles, an editor of a daily newspaper, the *Register* ran sixteen pages and was enlarged after the first year. Although Niles had his own views, he impartially printed speeches and important documents, giving both sides of controversies of the time. Readers and newspaper editors came to depend on the *Register*'s reliability and reporting in an age when most political reporting was bitter and partisan. The elder Niles died in 1839; the publication lasted only another ten years.

References

Papers, Publishers and Editors

ANDREWS, J. C., *Pittsburgh's Post-Gazette,* Boston: Chapman and Grimes, 1936. (A good study of this trans-Allegheny newspaper and its publishers.)

AXELRAD, JACOB, *Philip Freneau, Champion of Democracy,* Austin: University of Texas Press, 1967. (Detailed biography written in literary style.)

BELL, EARL and KENNETH CRABBE, *The Augusta Chronicle,* Athens: University of Georgia Press, 1960.

BIGELOW, JOHN, *William Cullen Bryant,* Boston: Houghton Mifflin Company, 1890. (An early biography of the *New York Post*'s editor.)

BOWEN, MARJORIE, *Peter Porcupine: A Study of William Cobbett, 1762-1835,* New York: Longmans, 1935. (See Pearl entry.)

BOWERS, CLAUDE, *Jefferson and Hamilton,* Boston: Houghton Mifflin Company, 1933. (Has excellent detail on the conflict between these two political giants and their papers, *Gazette of the United States* and the *National Gazette.*)

ELLIOTT, ROBERT NEAL, JR., *The Raleigh Register, 1799-1863,* Chapel Hill: University of North Carolina Press, 1955. (A worthwhile study of a state capital political paper.)

FAY, BERNARD, *The Two Franklins,* Boston: Little, Brown and Company, 1933. (Tells about Benjamin Franklin and Benjamin Bache.)

GOLDBERG, ISAAC, *Major Noah, American-Jewish Pioneer,* Philadelphia: Jewish Publication Society of America, 1937. (A good piece of work on an unusual editor of the era.)

GOLDSMITH, ADOLPH O., "Roaring Lion of Vermont," *Journalism Quarterly* 39:179ff, Spring, 1962. (Tells about a victim of Alien and Sedition Acts.)

HALLOCK, WILLIAM H., *Life of Gerard Hallock,* New York: Oakley, Mason, 1869. (Only one available.)

KENDALL, AMOS, *Amos Kendall Autobiography,* William Stickney, ed., Boston: Lee Shephard, Dillingham, 1872.

LEARY, LEWIS, *That Rascal Freneau,* New Brunswick, N.J.: Rutgers University Press, 1941. (The early volume on the Jeffersonian editor. See Axelrad entry.)

LUXON, NORVAL NEIL, *Niles' Weekly Register,* Baton Rouge: Louisiana State University Press, 1947. (A thorough study.)

LYON, WILLIAM H., *The Pioneer Editor in Missouri, 1808-1860,* Columbia: University of Missouri Press, 1965. (Excellent analysis of problems of frontier publisher; discusses in detail content of weeklies.)

MARBUT, FREDERICK B., "Early Washington Correspondents: Some Neglected Pioneers," *Journalism Quarterly* 25:370, December, 1948.

———, "The United States Senate and the Press," *Journalism Quarterly* 28:342, Summer, 1951.

Mott, Frank Luther, *Jefferson and the Press,* Baton Rouge: Louisiana State University Press, 1943. (Informative with many quotations.)

Nevins, Allan, *The Evening Post,* New York: Boni and Liveright, 1922. (An unusually good study of the newspaper and its times and the city in which it was published.)

Pearl, Morris Leonard, *William Cobbett,* London: Oxford, 1953. (A useful study of a controversial editor. See also Bowen entry.)

Scott, F. W., *Ohio Valley Press Before War of 1812,* Worcester, Mass.: Davis Press, 1909.

Taft, William H., *Missouri Newspapers,* Columbia: University of Missouri Press, 1964. (First complete study of the Missouri press. See Lyon entry.)

Tappan, Lewis, *Life of Arthur Tappan,* New York: Hurd, Houghton, 1870. (Only one in print.)

Warfel, Harry R., *Noah Webster, Schoolmaster to America,* New York: The Macmillan Company, 1936. (An informative, readable account.)

Bill of Rights, Alien and Sedition Acts

Rutland, Robert Allen, *Birth of the Bill of Rights, 1776-1791,* New York: P. F. Collier, Inc., 1962. (An authoritative, lively account of the first ten amendments.)

Smith, James Morton, *Freedom's Fetters: The Alien and Sedition Laws and American Civil Liberties,* Ithaca, N.Y.: Cornell University Press, 1956. (An exhaustive study of the Alien and Sedition Acts.)

Magazines

Mott, Frank Luther, *A History of American Magazines* vol. I, Cambridge: Harvard University Press, 1938-1957. (Is an exhaustive study.)

Wood, James Playsted, *Magazines in the United States,* New York: The Ronald Press Company, 1956. (Useful, but briefer account than Mott's work.)

Press and Mechanical History

See Sutton, Olson, Lee entries in Colonial Section.

Advertising

Presbrey, Frank, *The History and Development of Advertising,* Garden City, New York: Doubleday & Company, Inc., 1929. (Very thorough, with many examples.)

Ransome, Frank, *They Laughed When I Sat Down,* New York: McGraw-Hill Book Company, 1959. (A popular history of advertising.)

Wood, James Playsted, *Story of Advertising,* New York: The Ronald Press Company, 1958. (A standard, short work of the subject.)

See encyclopedias for bibliographies at end of English Press for additional references.

Part Three

Popular Penny Press (1830-1865)

THE  SUN.

NUMBER 1.] NEW YORK, TUESDAY, SEPTEMBER 3, 1833. [PRICE ONE PENNY.

PUBLISHED DAILY,

AT 222 WILLIAM ST .... BENJ. H. DAY, PRINTER.

The object of this paper is to lay before the public, at a price within the means of every one, ALL THE NEWS OF THE DAY, and at the same time afford an advantageous medium for advertising. The sheet will be enlarged as soon as the increase of advertisements requires it—the price remaining the same.

Yearly advertisers (without the paper) Thirty Dollars per annum—Casual advertising at the usual prices charged by the city papers.

☞ Subscriptions will be received, if paid in advance, at the rate of three dollars per annum.

FOR ALBANY—PASSAGE ONLY $1.

The large and commodious steamboat COMMERCE, Capt. R. H. Fitch, will leave the foot of Courtlandt street on Friday, at five o'clock P. M. for Albany, stopping at the usual landing places to land and receive passengers. Passage $1. For particulars apply to the Captain on board.

REGULAR DAYS.

From New York, Mondays, Wednesdays, Fridays.
From Albany, Tuesdays, Thursdays, Saturdays. s29

FOR NEWPORT AND PROVIDENCE.

The splendid steamboat BENJAMIN FRANKLIN, Capt. E. S. Bunker, and the PRESIDENT, Capt. E. S. Bunker, will leave New York at 5 o'clock, P. M. and Providence at 12 o'clock, M. every Monday, Wednesday and Friday. For further information apply to the Captain on board, foot of Courtlandt-st. or at the office 11 Broad-st.

FOR HARTFORD—PASSAGE 1 DOLLAR.

THROUGH BY DAYLIGHT.

The splendid low-pressure steamboat WATER WITCH, Capt. Vanderbilt, leaves the foot of Catherine street every Tuesday, Thursday and Saturday mornings, at 6 o'clock, and arrives in Hartford at 7 o'clock the same evening. Passage One Dollar—meals extra.

The above boat leaves Hartford on Mondays, Wednesdays, and Fridays, at the same hour. s2 tf

FOR LONDON.—To sail 10th of Sept.—The new packet ship Montreal, Champlin, Master, will sail on the 10th inst. For freight or passage, having elegant accommodations, apply to the captain, on board, Pine-st. wharf, or to
s2 JOHN GRISWOLD, Agent, 70 South st.

FOR LIVERPOOL.—The fast-sailing ship Tallahassee, S. Glover, Master, will be ready to receive cargo in a few days, and have despatch. She has excellent accommodations for both cabin and steerage passengers. For freight or passage, apply to
s2 WOOD & TRIMBLE, 157 Maiden-lane.

FOR HAVRE.—The Packet ship Formosa, Orne, master, will sail on the 8th Sept. For freight or passage apply to the captain on board, or to W. H. WHITLOCK, Jr. 46 South st. s2

FOR LIVERPOOL.—Packet of the 8 Sept.—The packet ship Roscoe, J. C. Delano, master, is now in readiness to receive cargo. For freight or passage apply to the captain on board, foot of Maiden lane, or to
s2 tf FISH, GRINNELL & CO. 134 Front st.

FOR KINGSTON, JAM.—Packet 10th Sept. The elegant coppered ship Orbit will sail as above. For freight or passage, having splendid accommodations, with state rooms, apply to
s2 B. AYMAR & Co. 34 South st.

FOR NEW ORLEANS.—Packet of the 8th September, the very fast-sailing coppered ship, Nashville, Capt. Rathbone, will sail as above.—For freight or passage, having handsome accommodations, apply to E. K. COLLINS, 68 South st.
N. B. A lighter is in readiness to receive cargo at Pine street wharf. s2

FOR NEW ORLEANS—Packet of Sept. 15. The ship Tennessee, Capt. Sears, will sail as above. For freight or passage, having handsome accommodations, apply to
SILAS HOLMES & CO. 62 South st.
N. B. A lighter is in readiness to receive cargo. s2

AN IRISH CAPTAIN.

"There are as sweet a pair of pistols as any in the three kingdoms," said an officer, showing a pair to a young student of his acquaintance, "and have done execution before now; at the slightest touch, off they go, as sweet as honey, without either recoiling or dipping. I never travel without them."

"I never heard of highwaymen in this part of the country."

"Nor I," replied the officer, "and if I had I should not trouble myself to carry the pistols on their account—Highwaymen are a species of sharks who are not fond of attacking us lobsters; they know we are a little too hard to crack. No, my dear sir, highwaymen know that soldiers have not much money, and what they have they fight for."

"Provided you had a good cause," replied the young student.

"I should not be squeamish respecting the cause, provided I had a good battle: that, my dear, is what is the most essential to a conscientious officer, who wishes to improve himself in his profession. I have much reason, therefore, to wish for a war; and at the present juncture, it would be much to the advantage of the nation in general, as it is dwindling into a country of ploughmen, manufacturers, and merchants. And you must know, too, that I am pretty fortunate, having already stood thirteen shots, and I never was hit but once."

"Thirteen! what, have you fought thirteen duels?"

"No, no!" replied the captain, "the last shot fired at me completed only my sixth duel."

BENJAMIN H. DAY
Founder of *The Sun*

Mass Appeal—Benjamin H. Day sized up the New York newspaper market and found that the vast majority of people were not reading the daily press. He launched *The Sun* on September 3, 1833, as a cheap paper with a wide appeal. *The Sun* was a breakthrough in publishing, with many imitators following Day's venture. He established a new era in journalism—the popular press period.

Chapter 7

Expanding Democracy and the Press

SIGNIFICANT SOCIAL CHANGES SHAPE AMERICA

On September 3, 1833, Benjamin Henry Day looked at the first issue of the *New York Sun.* It was crude and small, about the size of commercial letter paper. The publication had only four pages, but it was a great achievement. With a journeyman printer and an apprentice boy, Ben Day had worked all night in his one-room office to produce the first thousand papers. The type page measured about 7 1/2 by 10 inches. A hand-operated press printed two hundred copies an hour. Day had little capital, but he had a big idea.

Early the previous morning he had bought several six-penny papers, had copied news items, a bank note table and even some advertisements, the last named a "front" to present an appearance of prosperity. Humorous anecdotes, a suicide story and lively police court news which he added, did not appeal to the merchant who subscribed to the *Journal of Commerce,* but to his clerk; not to the banker or shopkeeper who read the *Evening Post,* but to the office employee and dockworkers hired by these businessmen. To make its appeal more certain, the little *Sun* was priced at one cent. This price was constant even through the Civil War.

These were the inauspicious beginnings of the newspaper which was to revolutionize the six-penny sheets, the prevailing type for more than forty years. Before the *Sun* was a decade old, it had many imitators and had altered the whole course of American journalism.

Underlying social, economic, political and cultural conditions of the age actually bred the new journalism. Profound changes occurred in American life, making this one of the most colorful and dynamic periods.

The Machine Age came to America. This was also the age of the rise of the common man and the extension of political democracy. Newspapers reflected these changes. Becoming an instrument for the spread of democracy, the press played an important economic and political role in these decades.

As America was being transformed from an agricultural, small-town economy to an industrial and urban civilization, the press too was fast becoming a product of the Machine Age and the metropolis. Great editorial personalities arose to express these changes through journalism and to meet psychological and economic needs and wants of the various publics.

NATION'S POPULATION, TERRITORY INCREASE RAPIDLY

Families continued to be large, and easier living conditions enabled more children to reach maturity than ever before. Two and one-half million English, Irish, Welsh and German immigrants also poured into the country. Many became factory hands and dockworkers, and others dug ditches for gas and water mains, and worked on railroad gangs. Some immigrants became politicians, policemen and newspapermen. Between 1830 and 1860 the nation's total population increased from twelve million to thirty million.

Heaviest concentration of population remained on the Atlantic slope, where more than fourteen million, or 54 per cent of the population lived. At the same time development of agriculture both in the East and in the Ohio and Mississippi valleys made growth of cities possible by furnishing food to urban dwellers and factory workers. Cities became marketplaces for the agricultural products.

The late 1840s also saw acquisition of Texas, Oregon and the great Southwest. During the pre-Civil War generation, the entire West was explored in its general outline. This development, especially such spectacular events as discovery of gold in California in 1848, made Americans aware that they were living in stirring times. Few eastern papers were sold west of the Mississippi, but western events made news for all dailies and helped sell papers to subscribers in the Atlantic seaboard cities.

The increase in population produced more potential subscribers for existing papers and likewise increased the number of newspapers. In 1830 1,300 newspapers were published; by 1860, the year Lincoln was elected, newspapers had increased to 4,051. Dailies had multiplied during this time from twenty-five to three hundred eighty-seven. Not only were new newspapers launched along the eastern coast, but strong newspapers developed in Cleveland, Cincinnati, Detroit, Chicago, St. Louis and other midwestern cities. Some dailies appeared on the West Coast.

Circulation of individual newspapers also mounted. Responding to the amazing but natural growth of seaboard cities with their prosperous seaport businesses and their factories, circulation of some dailies jumped very rapidly. Instead of 1,000 or 4,000 readers, top circulation in the previous era, new urban dailies with popular appeal now attracted 30,000; one paper had as many as 60,000 readers.

The increase in population affected not only circulation but the business side of newspaper publication. Through advertising, larger sales markets were created for products of factories, wares of retail stores, skills of craftsman and the services of professional people. The wealth of the nation was mounting, and the newspapers prospered along with the nation.

AGRICULTURE MECHANIZED, COMMERCIALIZED

The amazing economic activity of the American people supported this rapid population growth. Farmers worked with better tools and machines. The new steel plow, seed drill for planting, reaper, mower, hayrack and mechanical thresher enabled one man to do twice the work he could do before. Profits from his farm made possible the purchase of manufactured goods. The Industrial Revolution had changed household crafts to factory production, especially for cotton and wool goods.

Because of westward expansion and increasing markets, wheat, corn, oats and rye were produced in great quantities to swell the farmer's income and supply food for urban dwellers, which was now increasing. These years also saw the beginnings of livestock improvement. With growth of urban markets, demand for wool and hides had to be met. Further development of railroads, canals and river steamboats made it possible for the farmer to move his products more easily and cheaply to market. The Industrial Revolution, bringing more factories into cities and producing a greater quantity of manufactured products, enabled the farmer to purchase rather than make these by hand as he once did.

INDUSTRIAL REVOLUTION CHANGES UNITED STATES ECONOMY

Accelerating forces of the Industrial Revolution changed the economic face of America profoundly. The Machine Age had several identifying characteristics. Machinery was used more extensively. The ma-

Figure 21. Iron Horse Comes to Town. The coming of the railroad to town was one of the most important events of the day. The railroad brought manufactured products and farm foods, and it carried out the local produce and other freight. The train conveyed passengers to far-off places. The rails were the ties with the outside world. They brought news and newspapers. Scene shows a stop for passengers and mail near Stone Mountain on the Georgia Railroad.

chinery, operated by waterpower or steam, was housed in large factories. The trend, therefore, was to larger manufacturing units. Company owners now had to distribute their products on a mass scale to operate their businesses profitably. Hundreds of workers were employed in factories. The growing cities were filled with factories and with workers. These effects, of course, were gradual and were felt more at the end of the period than at the beginning. Extensive industrialization came after the Civil War, but the beginnings were made in this era.

Instead of Farmer Brown slaughtering his stock and shipping it to market for sale, pork and beef packing now were beginning to become large-scale industries. In place of small, water-operated mills, larger flour mills began to centralize in towns with access to wheat-growing areas as well as to good rail and harbor facilities. By the fifties the sewing machine had been adapted to shoemaking, and the 105,000 workers in this industry were no longer apprentices at the shoe trade but had become specialized operators. Men's clothing was made in hundreds of factories by tailors working at sewing machines. Similar specialization spread through many industries.

At first power to work at the new machinery was derived by damming streams and rivers. Then in the 1840s the water wheel utilized

TABLE 11

Significant Changes in American Life (1830-1865)

1. Introduction of Machinery
   a. Mass production made practical
   b. Lower costs result
   c. Wider distribution of merchandise feasible
2. Spread of Factory System
   a. Manufacturing spreads to many industries
   b. Development of factory-owner groups rapid
   c. Expansion of factory-working class steady
   d. Need for larger markets for goods observed
   e. Creation of advertising need results
3. Rapid Growth of Cities
   a. Towns become metropolises for commerce and manufacturing
4. General Increase in Population
   a. Natural increase expands population
   b. Immigration adds people
   c. Economic conditions provide basis for more children, large families
5. Expansion in West
   a. Midwest settled more heavily
   b. Farmlands multiply, foodstuffs increase
   c. New towns and cities grow
   d. Pacific Coast settled
6. Democracy Broadened
   a. Emphasis put on the common man
   b. Greater political rights gained
   c. "Education for all" is slogan
   d. Other cultural institutions broadened
   e. Many reforms of old social order advocated
7. Political Suffrage Extended
   a. More people able to vote
8. Cultural Changes Many
   a. Urban, paid sports develop
   b. Theatre made popular

more force and turned more rapidly. The steam engine answered the demand for more power and faster-turning machines. Imported from England and adapted to American conditions by Oliver Evans, the steam engine soon provided power for sawing lumber, grinding grain, manufacturing cloth and building machinery.

In 1833 the Reverend Dr. Frederick W. Geissenhainer patented his method of smelting iron by the use of anthracite coal, and production of furnaces leaped ahead. The voracious demand for iron, a need created by expansion of railroads, served as a stimulus. Steam engines as well as hardware, stoves and household utensils were now made from iron casting.

Among the many improvements of the period which directly aided the newspaper and culture generally was the kerosene lamp. This lamp, an advance over the tallow candle and whale oil lamp, gave better light and permitted reading later into the night. The kerosene lamp also helped develop "night life" in America, making it possible to have entertainment at night, including serious plays, burlesque and cheap melodramas.

In 1840 the value of manufactured products reached $483,000,000. Twenty years later the figure was almost four times as great ($1,885,000,000). Nonagricultural employees grew from one million to four million. This latter figure represented about 40 per cent of the working population.

How did this industrialization affect the country and the press? Mass production lowered costs. In 1815 cost of weaving cotton was forty cents a yard; in 1820 it dropped to seven cents. Thousands of families who could not afford to buy merchandise before could do so now. The national wealth rose from three billion to sixteen billion dollars. Higher standard of living for many resulted although factory workers did not share proportionately in the economy. But generally there was more money in their pockets with which to buy goods.

Expanding purchasing power developed a sales market for the products of industry: clothing, stoves, wallpaper, nails, pots, pans and farm implements. These could be sold through advertising placed in newspapers. Retailers had many products and a steady supply of them. Aggressive selling was needed. Customers for goods were not centered around the general store as in previous eras. Families now lived in all parts of the growing, spreading cities. They had to be reached by some printed advertising media. Fewer families made their own clothes or household goods. They were in the market for factory-made articles sold in stores, but they had to be informed through advertising; therefore, newspaper advertising grew.

TRANSPORTATION FACILITIES IMPROVE, SPEED UP

Transportation facilities improved with extension of railroads. Railroad mileage jumped. These decades also marked growth of both coastal and foreign shipping. Exports and imports each increased fivefold. Steamboats and railroads, in addition to creating a national market for food products of the farm and manufactured goods, also lowered the cost of transportation, thus reducing the price of merchandise.

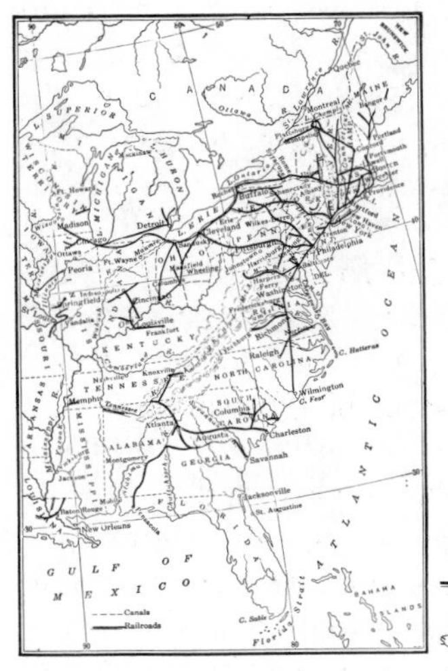

Figure 22a. Canals and Railroads Operated in 1850. The canals and railroads furnished the transportation and communication arteries of the expanding nation. The heaviest concentration of railroads was in the North. Continuous lines extended from Main to Wilmington, North Carolina, and from New York and Philadelphia to as far west as Madison, Wisconsin.

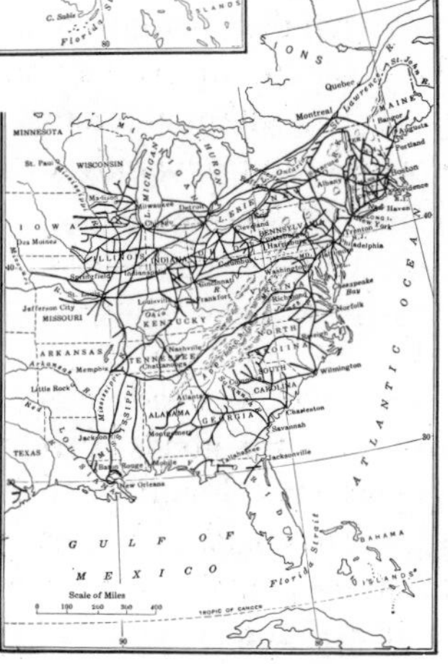

Figure 22b. Canals and Railroads in 1860. The decade between 1850 and 1860 saw a rapid extension of the railroad lines. A rapid building plan added to railroad routes in the North, Northeast and Northwest. The southern states increased mileage on the main lines and also added feeders, especially in South Carolina, Georgia and Alabama. The web of railroads furnished a speedier means of transporting goods, news and newspapers.

Figure 23. Trans-Atlantic Travel. Transportation across the Atlantic Ocean from Europe to America was hastened with the coming of the steamboats. This side-wheeler still had sails for emergencies, but the steam in her boilers drove the paddlewheels steadily. The steamboat cheapened transportation. The steam-driven vessels soon pushed the fast clipper ship from its top place. (Courtesy of Cunard)

New facilities also brought news more quickly. Publishers of dailies used these conveyances to reach subscribers in outlying regions. This was particularly true in the Ohio and Mississippi valleys where large local dailies had not developed. Trans-Atlantic steamboats began regular operation in the 1840s, bringing European news more quickly.

POSTAL SYSTEM EXTENDED

An expanding postal system aided news gathering and newspaper delivery. Between 1820 and 1860 mail routes were extended from 72,000 miles to 240,000 miles, and the number of post offices multiplied six-fold. Cheap postal rates for newspapers had been in existence since colonial times. One cent was charged for delivery of each newspaper anywhere in the state where the paper was published. These publication

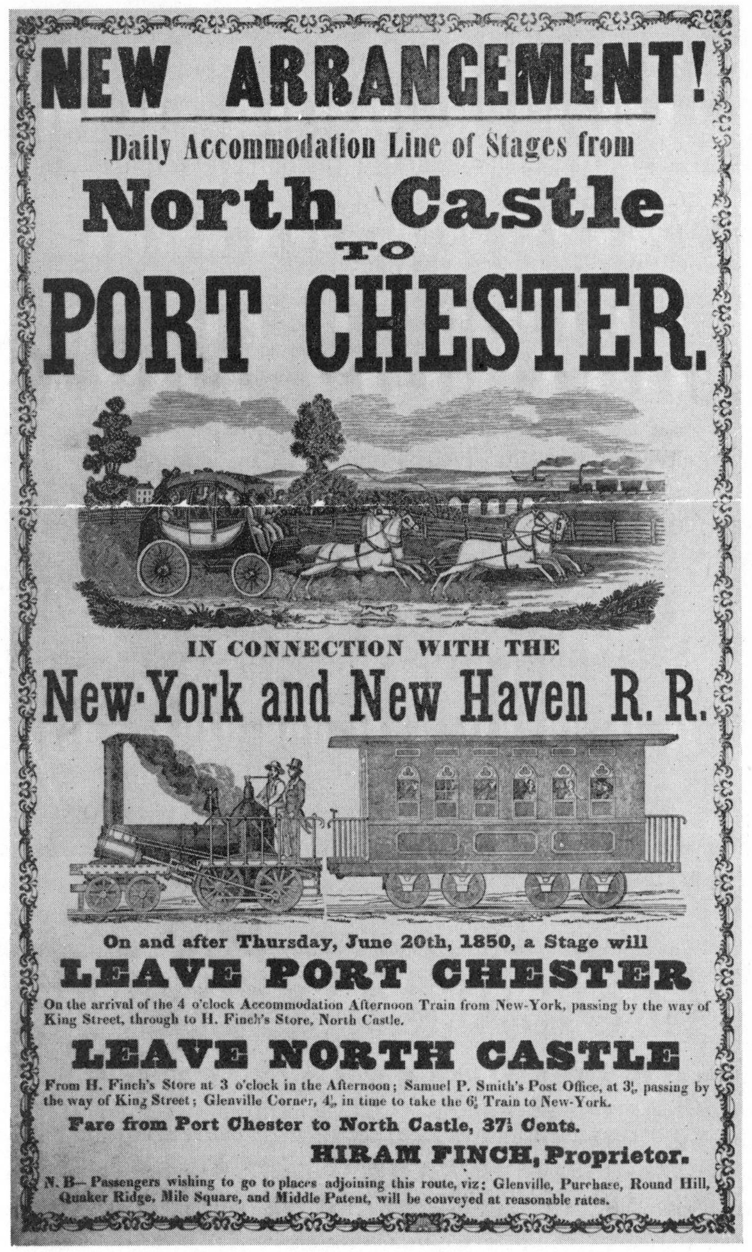

Figure 24. Old and New Means of Transportation Connect. The travelers on the North Castle, Connecticut to New York run had to take the stagecoach from North Castle to Glennville, then switch to the New York and New Haven Railroad to reach Manhattan.

postal rates, materially less than for letters, were of special aid to struggling frontier editors.

Eventually, in 1845, various rates for newspapers were established. One rate was for newspapers of not more than 1900 inches and another rate for those journals exceeding that figure. Rates on postal weights as well as those on distance were raised. United States Postmaster Johnson recommended that postage for newspapers should be prepaid, for the government was losing revenue; consequently, the Act of 1852 provided for prepayment of postage by the publisher.

TELEGRAPH SPEEDS NEWS

It took a painter to solve the public's demands for faster news-transmission facilities. In 1844 Samuel F. B. Morse introduced the era of electric telegraph transmission when he strung a wire from Baltimore to Washington. In 1846 a line from Fort Lee, New Jersey through Philadelphia to Baltimore extended the chain. In 1861 establishment of a wire from New York to San Francisco added to the 50,000 miles already in use. Newspapers began using these facilities. In frontier areas newspapers developed when townspeople learned a telegraph wire would pass through their town.

URBAN EXPANSION CREATES NEW PROBLEMS

Into towns and cities on the Atlantic coastline came thousands of factory workers and their families. Addition of manufacturing enterprises, wholesalers, distributors and other merchants brought new prosperity to these cities.

New York, still thriving, reached about two hundred thousand in 1830, while a large number lived in Brooklyn. By the time the first shots were fired in the Civil War, New York had about a million residents. Equally spectacular increases were noted in other seaboard cities, such as Boston, Philadelphia and Baltimore. With the spread of population to the Mississippi Valley and the expansion of its economy, other towns, strategically located, grew rapidly. Soon Cincinnati, St. Louis, Chicago and New Orleans each had more than one hundred thousand people.

In the cities lived the wealthy, the middle class, the workers and the poverty stricken. The city was filled with slums, disease and crime. Many fires and accidents occurred. The growth and changing character of cities had important effects on the character and appeal to the press. Large circulations were possible. Many urban activities created news.

TABLE 12

Growth of Large Cities (1830-1860)

	1830	1860
New York	202,589	1,000,000
Brooklyn	20,535	279,122
Baltimore	80,620	212,418
Boston	61,392	177,840
Philadelphia	80,462	565,529
New Orleans	29,694	168,000
Cincinnati	24,831	161,044
St. Louis	14,125	160,773
Chicago	4,000 (1840)	109,260

Newspapers had to deal with many civic and social problems not found in colonial towns. Crime increased. Transportation problems became more critical. Political corruption multiplied. During the economic depressions of the Industrial Age, widespread unemployment was felt, creating labor news and leading to expressions of editorial opinion about the news.

The metropolitan newspaper replaced the sober and serious rural or small-town papers of the young nation. A different character, a different appeal and a different psychology characterized the new age being reflected in the press.

LABOR EXPANDS AND ORGANIZES LOCALLY

A swelling army of workers recruited from farm families was joined by an increasing number of immigrants. They worked in commercial businesses and factories from twelve to fourteen hours a day for twelve dollars to fifteen dollars a week. Industrial and other employees increased from one to four million in these decades. Although not rich and powerful individually, their numbers made them a growing market for food, clothing, entertainment and newspapers. A number of alert printers and newsmen developed the right combination of appeals for these workers and prospered.

TABLE 13

Social, Cultural Preparation for Emergence of Penny Press (1800-1830)

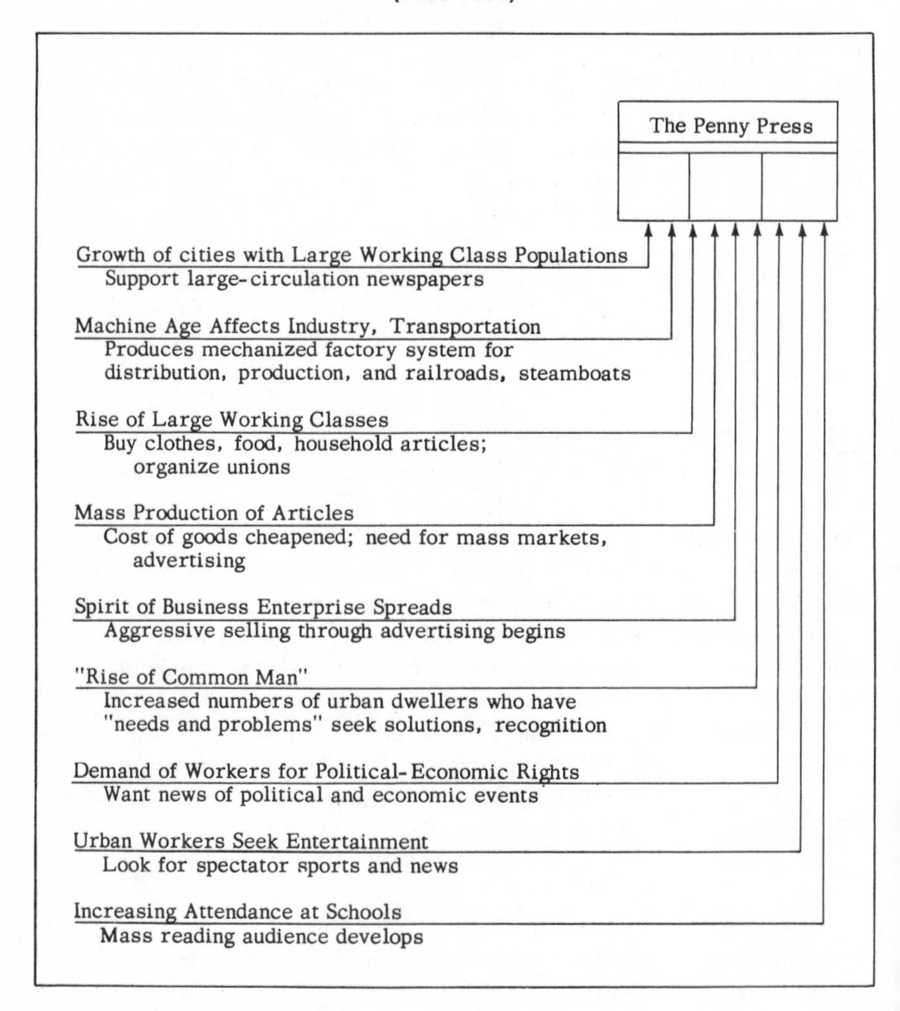
The Penny Press
Growth of cities with Large Working Class Populations
Support large-circulation newspapers
Machine Age Affects Industry, Transportation
Produces mechanized factory system for distribution, production, and railroads, steamboats
Rise of Large Working Classes
Buy clothes, food, household articles; organize unions
Mass Production of Articles
Cost of goods cheapened; need for mass markets, advertising
Spirit of Business Enterprise Spreads
Aggressive selling through advertising begins
"Rise of Common Man"
Increased numbers of urban dwellers who have "needs and problems" seek solutions, recognition
Demand of Workers for Political-Economic Rights
Want news of political and economic events
Urban Workers Seek Entertainment
Look for spectator sports and news
Increasing Attendance at Schools
Mass reading audience develops

Because of bad working conditions, short mealtimes, poor ventilation and unsanitary restrooms, workers began to organize. The American labor movement got underway in 1827 when labor parties started in both Philadelphia and New York. These parties focused attention on the demands of workers.

Labor became a force to be reckoned with. Mechanics' lien laws to protect wages were enacted, and imprisonment for debt was abolished. Most important for the newspaper was establishment of free schools, resulting from an aroused and insistent wage-earning class. Newspapers reported the news of labor and took stands on the union issue. Some publishers called trade unions dangerous conspiracies. Horace Greeley, however, met the issue by publishing articles advocating measures to improve the lot of employees. Several labor papers were begun but were short lived; other dailies catering to the growing working class's psychological and economic desires succeeded.

COMMON MAN GETS THE VOTE

Political parties began to recognize the potential votes among the workers. Property restrictions on voting and other barriers to political suffrage for the masses were wiped away, and during the 1820s and 1830s thousands of men voted for the first time. Between 1830 and 1860 the population doubled while the number of voters also doubled and in certain states tripled.

Effects of the new political currents of the era on newspapers varied. As a result of the widening of the suffrage, many men who had not been able to vote before now demonstrated an increased interest in voting and consequently in political news. Alert political leaders had seen in the common man a potential supporter, and having made it possible for him to vote tried to make sure he voted "correctly." In attempting to influence new voters, political parties held rallies and issued pamphlets and posters.

The factory hand, the dockworker, the carriage driver who could now vote became more and more concerned about who was running for office and possibly the issues involved. Many of the issues affected him. These new voters wanted news written in a style they could understand.

Newspapers making a popular appeal catering to this interest increased their circulations. Politicians attempted through the press to win new voters. The first popular papers of the period were exponents of the Democratic Party and advocated measures of concern to the workers. With rise of the Whig Party, popular Whig papers catering to the masses were established.

Thus the press, reflecting new currents of the time, marched along with the extension of democracy. Cost of establishing a paper even in large cities was relatively low; therefore, journals sprang up to mirror the varying political-economic viewpoints and promote an interest in political parties.

REFORM MOVEMENTS BETTER CONDITIONS

Utopian reformers like William E. Channing, Theodore Parker, Robert Owen and Francis Wright urged shorter hours, higher wages and better working conditions for laborers. They launched self-contained, self-organized communities, such as Brook Farm, near West Roxbury, Massachusetts to carry out their ideals. This group practiced cooperative living, with the property being held in common and work tasks shared. Much time was allotted to social and literary activities. Horace Greeley, founder of the *New York Tribune,* along with Charles A. Dana, his managing editor, were reformers who reflected these ideas in their paper, stimulating public interest in humanitarian movements.

The word *reform,* however, applied to many phases of American life. The term *reform* played much the same part in the life of that era that *progressive* did in later periods. The general objective was to improve the lot of the common man, the helpless child and the unfortunate adult. Social problems produced by the Machine Age became acute in the urban environments.

Dorothea L. Dix sought to change the inhumane treatment of dependents. She fought against indifference of the public toward its care of prisoners, paupers and the insane. A number of insane asylums were established, and prison associations were formed to improve conditions. The temperance movement was also launched.

One of the striking anachronisms of American life was the legal and political position of women. In no state or locality could they vote. Although they desired to cooperate in reform movements, they soon discovered they were unwanted. Lucretia Mott, Elizabeth Carey Stanton, Margaret Fuller and Lucy Stone persisted in their demands for women's civil rights and suffrage. A Women's Rights Convention, first of its kind, was held in 1848.

Greeley, of the *Tribune,* was one of the few editors who championed the women's cause. Most newspapers, still male institutions, ridiculed the women. As a result of the newspaper and other opposition, women were usually unsuccessful in this age in getting political and economic rights.

PUBLIC SCHOOLS OPEN DOORS; COLLEGES MULTIPLY

Most significant educational advance of this age was development of tax-supported, public school systems which were adopted in most states. By 1850 about three million pupils were attending elementary schools. The high school movement now began and spread. By mid-century, 250,000 were attending secondary schools. Eight new colleges and universities were founded between 1830 and 1850. The greater number of educated persons combined with improved economic conditions contributed to rising newspaper circulations.

SCIENTISTS MAKE CONTRIBUTIONS

Advancement of applied science was notable. Benjamin Silliman assembled a chemical laboratory at Yale. Progress was especially marked in geology, and the coast and geodetic survey was founded in 1815. The interest in science led to establishment of the American Society of Geologists and Naturalists which became the American Association for the Advancement of Science in 1847. The Smithsonian Institution was originated in Washington by the federal government with funds given by an Englishman.

The United States excelled in application of scientific discoveries to the uses of mankind. Many Americans became interested in inventions. In America S. F. B. Morse introduced the daguerreotype, invented by the Frenchman, Daguerre, and photos became very popular. The growing scientific interest was reflected to some extent in newspapers of the day. The more serious papers printed scientific articles. Inexpensive popular papers printed distortions and fakes because of their sensational character.

Science also had a direct effect on newspaper publication. Application of science and invention to solving newspaper problems in transmission of news and printing of newspapers was notable. These advances will be described later.

LITERATURE REFLECTS CURRENT CHANGES

Literature manifested the various currents of the day and showed the close association between American life and American letters. New publishing houses were launched; printing of publications became an important business. The steam engine helped produce books economically. The literary profession was put on a sounder economic basis, and many writers of novels, stories, essays, reviews and histories could count on respectable incomes. More than ever before, sons of families, made wealthy by professional and mercantile and now by shipping and manufacturing pursuits, had leisure and money to attend college and embark on literary careers. Responding to the rising interest in books, more newspapers published book reviews. Some newsmen became literary editors and reviewers for their publications.

New England had a great intellectual revolution between 1820 and 1850. The region had been dominated by the minister, the merchant and the lawyer. The area was smug, oligarchic and conservative. With the coming of the Industrial Revolution, old barriers began to give way and traditional theology was gradually forced to yield to the attacks of romantic philosophy and science. Much of the literature reflected the changing scene. Although sharp differences marked the writers, William Wadsworth Longfellow, Ralph Waldo Emerson, Henry D. Thoreau, Theodore Parker, Margaret Fuller, Nathaniel Hawthorne, Harriet Beecher Stowe, all were products of the same social upheaval. They were all moralists, devoting themselves to reform.

In the Middle Eastern States, the literary capitals were New York and Philadelphia. Writers like Walt Whitman and Herman Melville were rebels of the spirit. Others, notably Washington Irving, James Fenimore Cooper and James K. Paulding, concerned themselves with frank expressions of their individual temperament and taste.

Southern writers, surrounded by a plantation system, few large cities and practically no industrialism, did not share in the revolutionary utopianism of the day. Social criticism was unwelcome. The writers spent much of their energy defending slavery. William Gilmore Sims was the most popular writer in Charleston, South Carolina, at that time the mecca of southern writers and the intellectual capital of the South. Brilliant Edgar Allan Poe, though neither a typical southern writer nor concerned with reform movements, was applying his talent to poetry, criticism and short stories. Plantation life was depicted by John Pendleton Kennedy; frontier life by David Crockett; and the southern lower classes by August Baldwin Longstreet, who was also a strong defender of slavery.

Many "serious" writers also turned their talents to journalism. Whitman, for instance, served as editor of the *Brooklyn* (New York) *Eagle,* and Poe, editor of the *Southern Literary Messenger,* published in Richmond, Virginia.

NATIVE THEATRE PORTRAYS CONTEMPORARY PEOPLE

As other institutions in American life, the stage widened its audience. Puritanical taboos, which checked the development of the theatre in the eighteenth century, definitely passed, except for strictly evangelical sects which continued to oppose plays as sinful.

To attract lower economic classes in the cities, theatre prices were reduced to meet the urban-dwellers pocketbook limitations. Plays were written by American writers using American themes to appeal to this new audience. Newspaper editors recognized this growing interest, and news, reviews and theatre advertisements appeared with greater frequency. Stock companies were formed to give a variety of plays, and entire companies of actors and actresses moved from city to town wherever theatres were built. Increasing in popularity were dramatists who turned their attention to the portrayal of contemporary American types and situations: the man of the frontier, the farmer, the Yankee peddler, the fireman. Some plays poked fun at society people who were aping foreign manners. Others drew contrasts between the rich and the poor.

Circuses brought an equally vicarious existence to the people in rural areas. P. T. Barnum, a former newspaper man, made a fortune with his American Museum in New York, appealing to the ageold love of city and country people alike for the bizarre and unusual.

URBAN AMERICA TURNS TO SPORTS

As the agricultural era made way for the Machine Age, America turned to spectator sports. While the farmer and the huntsman could go outside the village or beyond the hills to hunt and fish, the city dweller had to sit behind a desk, stand behind a storecounter or operate a machine. All these occupations were carried on inside and from dawn to sundown. For these city workers there were no winter-long seasons and weekends when little farm work was to be done, and they could enjoy the outdoors in a sport in which they participated.

Commercialization of sports began because enterprising sportsmen found money in the new crowds seeking relaxation and fun. Newspapers had carried sports news before, but now an opportunity existed for the publisher of a cheap newspaper, seeking large circulations, to capitalize on the sports interest. This created the beginnings of systematic coverage, with more extensive space being given to sports.

The first sports reporter made his appearance, and the first magazine devoted to this activity was issued. Widespread opposition to sports as an activity of the devil and therefore connected with sin and laziness dissolved rapidly in this period. Although many papers continued to oppose sports the popular press was equally persistent in its efforts to cover these events.

Diversions such as hunting, fishing, boating and backgammon continued, especially in rural areas; but spectator sports, such as horse racing, cockfighting, boxing, cricket, and, later, baseball and football, moved into popularity.

Magazines had led the way in sports reporting, and it is likely that newspaper editors followed the interest the magazines were creating. English periodicals on sports had already appeared when John Stewart Skinner, Baltimore postmaster, thought the American public might be interested in a similar venture. He established the *American Farmer* in 1819 and included in this publication the results of hunting, fishing, and shooting matches. He did much to overcome the opposition to sports, keeping in front of his readers the value of sports as health giving. A competitive publication was the *Farmers, Mechanics, Manufacturers, and Sporting Newspaper* issued in 1827. But it was the *Spirit of the Times,* published by William T. Porter in New York in 1831, which became the first sports periodical devoted exclusively to that subject. It was the beginning turf magazine of its day and reflected the growing interest in sports activities.

Thus the changing economic, political and social conditions created by a dynamic democracy provided the factors essential for the birth and growth of a popular type of newspaper appealing to masses.

IMMEDIATE FACTORS PRODUCE POPULAR PRESS

A number of immediate, internal conditions in the newspaper industry also contributed to development of the new type of publication. These factors joined with the underlying and external ones in the social environment previously described to produce the popular papers. Internal factors included:

1. The potential market of readers;
2. The current newspaper situation;
3. The printing technology available for the mass production of dailies;
4. The English precedents which paved the way for the American popular paper;
5. The earlier United States attempts at cheap newspaper production.

Established daily advertisers, couriers and enquirers and evening posts attracted only the upper business and professional classes. These dailies sold for six cents a copy, but individual sales were discouraged. A family bought its paper by the year, and it was delivered to the home or office. These papers were serious, sober publications carrying economic and mercantile news, shipping information and political events. City news, if it appeared at all, was reduced in size. The writing style was heavy, laborious.

For the increasing numbers of workers now crowding into urban centers, such established papers were too expensive and their appeal too limited. The subjects covered and the style of writing were not geared to the level of thousands of city dwellers. These workers would have had to work a whole week for a newspaper subscription. Newspaper vacuum was thus created.

To appeal to the worker, the popular paper had to be low in cost, easily available and aimed at a tired, nonserious employee seeking entertainment rather than information. This type of news was not emphasized or featured by standard papers. The new journals succeeded because they published news dealing with small happenings and problems of the average man. These papers featured crime or sex news in the metropolis, now shedding its small-town intimacy and conventionality. Amusing news which drew a laugh made the front page. Sports news received consistent coverage. Political news, presented brightly and concisely, interested the newly enfranchised voters. The worker in the city was more concerned with local events happening all around him than with affairs in far-off places. Consequently, local news was stressed in the new dailies.

Three other factors in the social environment swelled the potential newspaper-reading market. The spread of mass education provided more readers, and the rising economic level of many workers enabled them to buy newspapers. The newspaper filled a need for an advertising medium to reach men and women to whom old-style papers did not appeal. City dwellers did not make their own clothes, household furniture, kitchen utensils. Families now bought them from stores, but which stores? Advertising of merchandise and services in a mass media was the answer to the needs of buyers and sellers. With the expansion of cities, business and industry, and the need for employees, publications which brought employer and employee together through help-wanted advertising also served an economic need.

Publishers of the new dailies used existing press technology to produce newspapers inexpensively and in large quantities. Several significant technological improvements were made in this period, contributing further to development of the newspaper. These improvements speeded production, made possible the printing of a large number of newspapers quickly and reduced the cost per unit. Mass production was applied for the first time on a large scale to the newspaper.

Technological advances included:

1. Manufacture and development of better printing presses;
2. Introduction of the stereotyping process;
3. Development of papermaking machines.

Cylinder presses which could produce newspapers quickly and in large numbers were available, for in the 1820s they had been used already by the established standard papers, circulations of which were growing.

In the 1830s popular cheap paper publishers first used the Napier hand-cranked single cylinder presses. The type was placed on a flatbed which moved under the cylinder. Paper was fed into the machine in sheets. The cylinder, or drum revolved, pressing the paper against the type. Then the cylinder spun around again, and the newspaper was printed. Two thousand impressions could be printed in an hour. The paper was then turned over and the other side printed. A second cylinder was added which doubled the previous capacity. Steam was added to power the press in 1835, enabling the publisher to further speed production.

When circulations of popular, cheaper newspapers continued to mount, Richard Hoe, an American, set to work to improve the speed and capacity of the press to meet the urgent needs of publishers. The new Hoe revolving press, invented in 1840, turned out nineteen thousand impressions an hour in contrast to the earlier Napier machine which printed four thousand an hour. The Hoe press enabled publishers to increase their newspapers from four to eight pages and permitted late-night news to be printed for delivery the following morning.

This revolving machine operated on a new principle. Instead of being placed on a flatbed as before, the type was now held together tightly on forms which were fitted around the cylinder. V-shaped column rules, tapering toward the bottom, held the type to the cylinder. Automatic rollers spread ink on the type. Pressmen fed in single sheets which were printed rapidly.

Four small impression cylinders brought the paper in contact with the type on the big central cylinder. Each small cylinder had its own feeder and delivery table. One revolution of the type cylinders printed four sheets. This machine could now turn out eight thousand sheets an hour, printing on one side of the paper only, pages one and four. Then

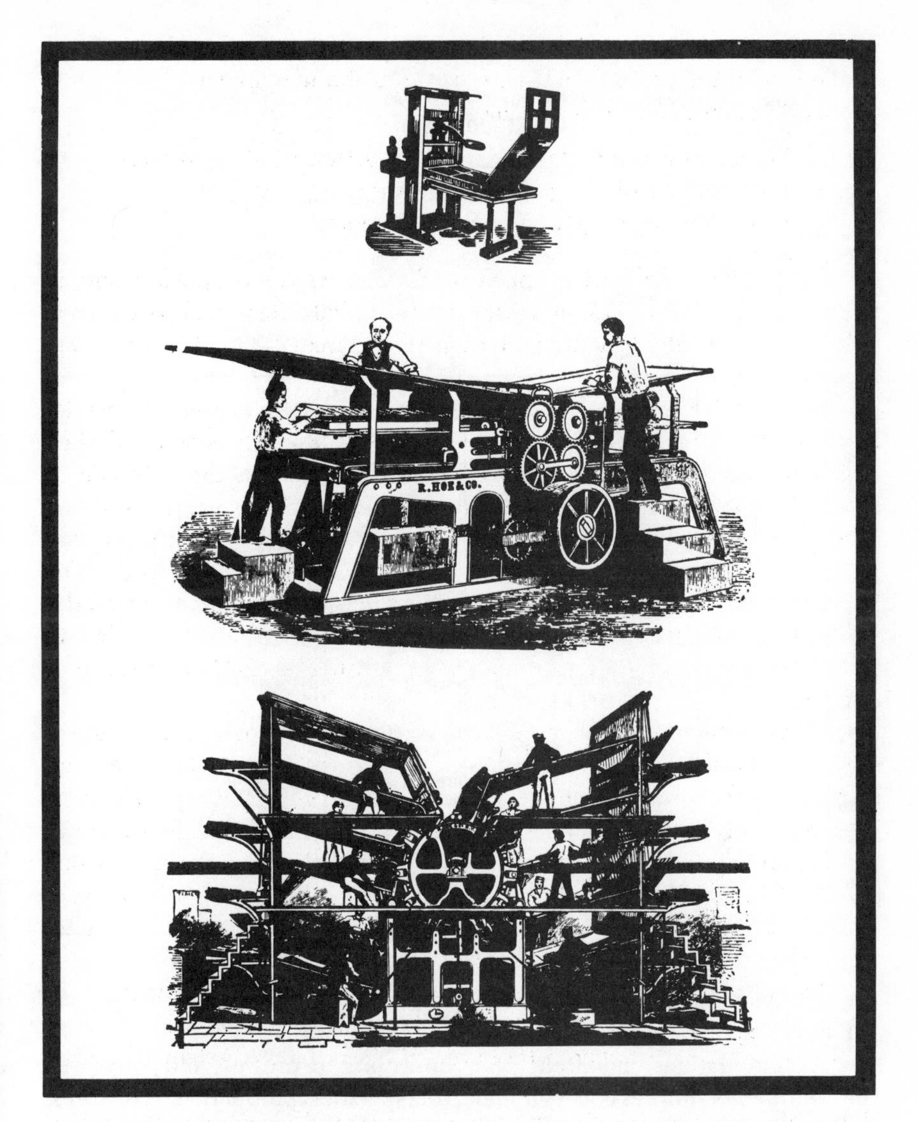

Figure 25. Printing Press Development. Printing technology developed rapidly to accomodate the demands of publishers and their growing army of readers. (Top), The *Sun* was printed on the hand press in 1833. (Middle), The double-cylinder press which was installed at the *Sun* produced 4,000 four-page papers an hour in 1840. (Bottom), A marvel of printing machinery in its day, the ten-cylinder press was invented by R. H. Hoe to meet the need of eighteen thousand copies an hour for the *Sun*'s circulation of fifty-two thousand. This was in 1851.

TABLE 14

Rapid Development of Machinery for Mass Communication in U. S. (1800-1865)

	Gathering News, Transmitting to Newspaper		Newspaper Technology			
	Land Travel, Communication	Water Travel River, Ocean	Typesetting	Printing	Pictorial	Paper
1800	Stagecoach Pony rider	Sailing Vessels	Handset	Handpress	Woodblocks (Few)	Handmade (Rags)
1810		Steamboats				
		STEAM POWER—FACTORY AGE—MASS PRODUCTION				
1820	Railroad	Riverboats		Napier flatbed cylinder press Steam press		Fourdrinier Papermaking machine
1830		Trans-Atlantic steamships		Hoe steam flatbed cylinder press Revolving cylinder press [type fixed on cylinder]	Camera used More woodblocks	
1840	Telegraph			Double cylinder press Ten cylinder steam press		
1850				Web-perfecting press		
1860				Stereotyping		
1865						

the type was removed, new type inserted, and pages two and three were printed.

As circulations mounted, Hoe built larger presses and increased the number of impression cylinders for speedier production. The press builder added cylinders until they reached ten. The Hoe press then had a capacity of twenty thousand sheets per hour. After the run, old type was replaced by the type for pages two and three, the inside pages. Printing began again. A second press might have been installed to print these inside pages as quickly as they came from press number one, but this would have been costly.

The next development in press machinery was introduction of the web-perfecting press which printed both sides of the paper in one operation without changing the type. Paper came in a roll which unwound from a reel; paper manufacturers were now making rolls instead of single sheets. The continuous sheet was a "web," hence the name. As the press completed both sides of the paper at once, it was called "perfecting."

Introduced by William Bullock in 1863, the Bullock press, first of these new machines, consisted of two pairs of cylinders. Each pair consisted of one printing cylinder on which a stereotype plate was fastened and one impression cylinder. The paper was fed from a roll and cut into sheets by knives in the cylinders before the impression was taken. After the sheets had been cut, they were carried through the press by means of tapes and grippers. The sheet emerged from the second press printed on both sides. Because of its unreliability at first, newspapers abandoned the web-perfecting press; as improvements were made, it gained popularity. The Hoe Company introduced a superior web-perfecting press in 1871.

Stereotyping, meanwhile, was introduced in the 1850s to decrease costs of printing and to speed publication of newspapers. As early as 1721, stereotyping had been used in Scotland. Edward Cowper succeeded in making curved stereotyped plates for book printing in England by 1816. Many American firms were producing page molds for job printers. When the penny papers found they had to replace their type every three months because of the wear, James Gordon Bennett, publisher of the *New York Herald*, decided to make use of the stereotyping process. In 1854 he pioneered with plates made by Charles Craske. Stereotyping also enabled the publisher to make duplicate plates for two presses, increasing his output according to his growing circulation. People marveled at the speed and economy of the press. In a few minutes a few men could do what previously had required many hours to do.

News of the stereotyping process leaked out, and other popular papers, the *New York Tribune* and the *Times* in 1861 and the *Sun* in 1862, took advantage of its speed and economy. Stereotyping also eventually revolutionzied advertising. Column rules, necessary during the days of the type-revolving press to hold forms on cylinders, gave way. Whole pages rather than single columns now became units in advertising. Stereotyping also had an effect later on headlines. Two, three and more column headlines were possible.

Another factor contributing to success of the inexpensive popular paper in this era was the Fourdrinier automatic papermaking machine introduced in 1820. This ended the manufacture of handmade paper. The price of a ream of paper was cut 25 per cent. Paper manufacturers produced single sheets until the 1860s when they began to deliver in rolls.

English journalism which had always served as a model for American editors had its popular two-cent paper as early as 1830. The English had established, as a feature, the reporting of criminal trials. It was only a matter of time before this police court reporting technique was adopted by American publishers. Within the old-fashioned newspapers, there existed the germ of a feature which caught and held the attention of a large group of workers.

Between 1830 and 1833 some attempts at small, cheap newspapers were made. Keen-minded, socially sensitive publishers saw the potential market and adapted their newspapers to march with the parade. Attempts were made by some papers to sell for half the usual price, but they failed to include the appealing elements of other later penny papers and so did not succeed.

In New York Dr. Horatio D. Sheppard broke the six-penny tradition and launched his *Morning Post* on January 1, 1833. It sold for two cents. On the last two days of its short life, the *Post* sold for a cent, and the readiness with which it was purchased convinced Dr. Sheppard that if it had been started at that price it would not have been a failure.

Nine months later Day's *Sun* appeared: a penny paper and a dingy sheet. Its success demonstrated, however, the correctness of Sheppard's calculations and justified his enthusiasm.

Chapter 8

Penny Press Leaders

NEW YORK, LEADING AMERICAN METROPOLIS

In 1833 bustling, enterprising New York was the best place to launch a penny newspaper. During the next decades New York retained its position as the center of newspaper publication in the United States. New York led all other cities in population, commerce and industry. Population increase was amazing. It passed the one hundred thousand mark about 1815, reaching two hundred thousand in 1830. By the opening of the Civil War, one million persons resided in the metropolitan area. New York was a great magnet which drew the enterprising from farms and from other towns. Thousands fleeing from Europe's poverty and persecutions docked at and stayed in New York.

New York attained its leadership in the western hemisphere as a result of a combination of geographic, historical and social factors. Above all, it possessed a great natural port, which contributed much to its natural growth. Establishment of the Black Ball Line of packet boats with regular sailings between New York and Liverpool in 1818, and a similar packet line between New York and Le Havre, France, now brought additional prosperity. New York shipowners managed even to capture the cotton freight business, picking up cotton in the South, bringing the goods to New York for European shipment. On the return trip from Europe ships carried millions of dollars worth of imported merchandise. The Hudson River continued to enable the city to tap the rich hinterland: New York State. Descendants of Dutch colonists were now being edged out by New Englanders, fleeing from the rocky soil of the eastern seaboard to the fertile Mohawk Valley.

Figure 26. New York, American Metropolis. New York became the metropolis of the United States. By 1830 it had twenty thousand persons; by the opening of the Civil War, it had a million residents. Note the improvement in houses and the solid blocks of three-story residences in the vicinity of Broadway and Bowling Green.

Now the full benefits of the Erie Canal, opened in 1825, were felt. New York had an advantage in attracting flour and other products of the West while providing easy distribution of imports in turn. When pushed by rival cities which opened railroads, New York responded with its own New York Central and Erie railroads.

The decades which saw the tremendous expansion of commerce and trade also saw establishment of banking institutions. By 1850 the city was already the nation's financial center, its banking houses dealing with sister institutions in all world capitals. The New York Stock Exchange, founded in the previous century, traded in stocks of the states and of private corporations. The Exchange sold the bonds of the Erie Canal successfully and helped many western states get loans for improvements.

Shipbuilding and ship repair boomed in the New York harbor, this city getting the major volume of such business. New York at this time became a workshop where hundreds of products were manufactured.

The city began to spread northward. By 1820 the residential section reached Fourteenth Street, and by 1850 it extended to Forty-second Street. Everything north was open country. Retail trade followed the population spread. Many new stores were opened and carried a wide variety of merchandise. As evidence of the spread north, the New York and Harlem Railroad was incorporated in 1831. Two years later the single track extended to Murray Hill (Thirty-fourth Street), and horse-cars inaugurated a rapid transit system. A ferry connected the city with the population expansion in New Jersey, just across the Hudson River.

As a cultural center, the city fell short of her competitors, largely for want of institutions of higher learning. Columbia University was the only New York City college until 1831 when New York University was established, followed by Fordham four years later. By 1853 New York had its first World's Fair in the Crystal Palace erected in the square (now Bryant Park). The city that year boasted five theatres, two music halls, twenty-five Broadway hotels and others scattered about the city. Officials purchased the site of Central Park in 1856 as a result of prodding by the *New York Evening Post*.

Until some years after the War of 1812, New York had few Roman Catholics. The first Roman Catholic church had opened in 1786 and was sufficient for the needs of the city for thirty years. During the second quarter of the nineteenth century, there began a great influx of Roman Catholics from Europe. New York became a European melting pot. Many Germans poured into the city and settled in certain sections, opening up restaurants and *turners*, or social clubs catering to the newly arrived immigrants.

After widespread voting rights were given in 1827 Tammany Hall political organization developed a system of recruiting aliens, in contrast to the indifferent or hostile attitude of the Whigs. Immigrants were met at the dock, assisted in finding jobs and rushed through naturalization. New York abounded in saloons, and the Democratic politicians organized the Irish, volunteer fire companies and social organizations, such as the Chowder Club.

Urban growth meant emergence of severe urban problems in New York. The newly rich real estate proprietors, shipowners, factory owners, bankers, merchants lived in better sections and developed a "society." The city also had its criminals and its slums. The Five Pointers, the

Bowery Boys and the Cherry Hill gangs robbed, raped and killed citizens and fought each other. Such crime increased as waves of industrial depression and unemployment struck the city. Houses of prostitution ranged from fancy bordellos to waterfront dives, the girls drifting into New York from farms and from other cities.

NEW YORK SUN BECOMES TRAIL BLAZER

In this bustling, expanding metropolis, Benjamin Day issued his thousand new, shining *Suns* on September 3, 1833. A New Englander, Day had learned the printing trade on the *Springfield* (Massachusetts) *Republican.* Coming to New York in 1831 when he was twenty, he opened a printshop, doing commercial job work. Alert for business, Day studied attempts made by others who tried to launch cheap papers. A workman himself, he sensed the reading needs of employees working in factories, behind counters and on the docks of New York. An inexpensive daily newspaper, geared to the needs of these persons who did not buy or read the big dailies, seemed to him a practical idea. When he talked over this idea with two friends, Arunah S. Abell and William M. Swain, printers, they said they "couldn't see it." They laughed at his foolish notion and discouraged him.

Day had little to lose. Job printing was slow anyway. The new publication would help his business. Day went ahead, therefore, and published his *Sun.* His salutation to the public was modest and reticent:

> The object of this paper is to lay before the public at a price within the means of everyone, ALL THE NEWS OF THE DAY, and at the same time afford an advantageous medium for advertising . . . .

Day stretched the definition of news and placed more emphasis on news in his publication than the established journals had done. His paper was a step ahead of the six-pennies which were almost entirely political and economic sheets.

Day's first *Sun* featured on page one a story entitled "An Irish Captain." Written in dialogue and describing a conversation between an old captain and his young admirer, the anecdote was easy to read. Another story told of a clever thief. "A Melancholy Suicide" was the title of another piece of news; another article concerned Fred A. Hall who took poison as a result of a disappointing love affair.

But the feature of the *Sun* to appear regularly was the column entitled "Police Office." These news stories ran a paragraph or less in length. The publisher hired George Wisner to write this news, and he became the first police reporter in American journalism.

Day discovered the human side of the news: murder, catastrophe and love, blended with elements of pathos and humor. Light in tone and selling for a penny, the *Sun* amused and aroused the large urban masses. Such items and features were what Day had meant by news. Mechanics and laborers soon demonstrated that they liked the little *Sun*, and its circulation, therefore, rapidly mounted. The *Sun*'s publisher sought such news wherever he could find it: in New York streets, in other cities, in London newspapers and magazines. Such news became a traditional part of American journalism. Reprints from books also helped Day fill his columns.

Crime dealt with weaknesses and errors that comprised human life, arousing pity, anger and sorrow, and affording various thrills. What matter if the people were drunkards, prostitutes, frauds or unemployed factory workers? They were human. Almost every day the editor of the *Sun* found some bawdy feature or news story to publish. An outstanding example was the sensational Robinson-Jewett murder case. Ellen Jewett, a New York prostitute, was murdered in 1835, and Richard P. Robinson was indicted for the crime. For two months New York was flooded with a steady stream of salacious matter. The three penny papers, the *Sun*, and its new competitors, the *Herald* and the *Transcript*, in hot rivalry, searched all aspects of the case that would make exciting reading for the masses. After the trial opened the papers reported verbatim the various accounts of the murder as given by the witnesses.

Penny paper publishers discovered that day-by-day running accounts of popular stories attracted and held readers, and hiked circulation. When one story was completed publishers had to round up another to replace it.

An outstanding sex murder occurred in 1841. The dead girl was Mary Cecilia Rogers, the "beautiful cigar girl," who had been the magnet at John Anderson's tobacco shop. The murderer was never apprehended. The mystery was played into a sensational crime story. The *Sun* condemned employment of girls as attractions in retail stores. Using the story as a basis, Edgar Allan Poe wrote *The Mystery of Marie Roget,* veiling the names and resetting the locale in Paris.

Sensationalism of such stories was not their only appeal. The trend of the period, a growing emphasis on the common man, was reflected in the political, educational and social life of the day. The fact that most of this news concerned the underdogs of society, butchers, shoemakers, carriage drivers, mistresses and prostitutes, heightened public interest. The result was to make the *Sun* a mirror of life of the urban masses.

The first serial printed by the *Sun* concerned the pioneer, David Crockett. Another feature described the adventures of Daniel Boone, a reprint from the *Western Methodist Review.* Even then the West had a strong appeal for the city-bred easterner. The *Sun* also made an appeal to the unusual, the bizarre, the variation from normal in animal and human life. The psychology peculiar to people of that day made such features particularly popular. This was the era of the circus and the museum. Few Americans had gone far in school, and facts about animal life were generally unfamiliar. Science, too, had just begun to examine the universe and its inhabitants and to make known scientific findings. Museum advertisements, with their copy and exciting pictures of monstrosities and wild animals, were the most persistent and prominent advertisements in the paper.

The "moon hoax" which the *Sun*'s reporter Richard Adams Locke perpetrated on its readers demonstrated this kind of appeal. In reading about science Locke learned of the possibility of communicating with the moon. The *Sun* broke his story on August 25, 1835, and it appeared to be genuinely authentic. The next day the daily devoted four columns to describing the moon's extraordinary vegetation and animal life which Locke reported a scientist had seen through his high-powered telescope. Locke portrayed winged men and women living on the lunar body. Other editors, even those of high-priced dailies, were fooled by the hoax. Then the *Journal of Commerce* exposed it.

Clearly, the old tradition that people were not interested in local news was broken. That belief grew up in a period when towns were

Figure 27. Sun Staff. The *Sun* began to acquire a staff of competent employees. Richard Adams Locke (left) was an excellent reporter and was responsible for the Moon Hoax story. The *Sun* developed its street circulation successfully, and Bernard Flaherty (right) was one of its first newsboys.

small and every resident of a community knew his neighbor's business. Now, however, New York had reached the status of America's leading city, and the sphere of acquaintances of each resident was limited. So the newspaper stepped in to perform the function of contact agent binding people together and enabling them to act as a unit. The newspaper became a metropolitan substitute for face-to-face contacts; it printed local news regularly.

Day's paper could not use long articles since the *Sun* contained only four pages. Yet the editor believed that he needed to publish some political news in addition to crime and court news. When Jackson addressed Congress the *Sun* devoted many columns to the speech, for the *Sun*'s readers were Jacksonians.

Unlike the six-penny dailies, the *Sun* in its early period did not regularly have editorials dealing with economic and political news. Politics was not an all-absorbing topic; in fact, for many people violent partisanship was passé. The *Sun* sold news, not editorial views.

The *Sun*'s revenue amounted to two hundred dollars a day for advertising. Its net income was about twenty-six thousand a year. The penny newspaper became a highly profitable business enterprise.

Despite the fact that the *Sun* was read largely by Jacksonians, the editor did not defend the party nor attack its opponents. The *Sun*, however, was generally proworkingman. The paper fought against imprisonment of debtors and attacked the filth in the city's Bridewell jail. When the cost of flour rose the *Sun* fought for a price reduction, charging that "combination" was pushing the price up. The aristocratic *Journal of Commerce*, representing conservative interests, charged the *Sun* with inciting trouble for business, even suggesting that the grand jury investigate Mr. Day.

The *Sun*, in turn, attacked the six-pennies for their conservatism. To bolster its argument the *Sun* described its favorable effects on the public, particularly the working-class segment:

> Already we can perceive a change in the mass of the people. They think, talk, and act in concert. They understand their own interest, and feel that they have numbers and strength to pursue it with success. The *Sun* newspaper has probably done more to benefit the community by enlightening the minds of the common people than all the other papers together.

The *Sun* had no experienced editorial writer. Nevertheless, there were strong paragraphs on abolition, pieces written by Day's reporter, George Wisner. Day devoted little attention to sports although horse racing flourished and was later exploited by other penny editors.

Evidence that the six-pennies had overlooked a large, potential reading population is seen in rising circulation figures of the *Sun.* Within four months the *Sun* reached four thousand readers, as many as the *Courier and Enquirer* had attained at its highest circulation level. By June, 1839, six years after it was launched, the *Sun* sold fifty thousand copies daily. Mass production had now affected the newspaper. "Now every individual, from the rich aristocrat who lolls in his carriage, to the humble laborer who wields a broom in the streets, reads the *Sun,*" the editor boasted.

Without the technological advance of the new Machine Age, Day could not have produced so easily his thousands of papers. The hand-press on which he had launched his first thousand *Suns* was an old-fashioned machine capable of printing only two hundred copies per hour. When circulation reached ten thousand in 1834, the daily edition would have consumed 80 hours if Day had to depend on one press. By then Day had purchased a Napier hand-cranked cylinder press which produced one thousand copies per hour. In 1836 the proprietor ordered two new steam-driven Napier presses at $3,500 each and was able to run off thirty-two hundred copies an hour on each press.

The *Sun* introduced the cash-in-advance policy of advertising. In the old papers advertisements were sold on an annual basis, along with subscriptions, for thirty or forty dollars. Day insisted on a cash policy, influenced probably by the success of London papers. He encouraged small advertisers with "wants" or merchandise to exchange. He instituted "Help Wanted" columns for factory workers. In this way advertising reached out to appeal to the masses. The *Sun* instituted display type, capital letter headlines and tiny cuts, or illustrations.

The first issue of the *Sun* contained only four columns of advertising of a possible twelve. By 1839 the proportion was seventeen of twenty-four columns, forcing the publisher to increase the paper's size. In 1833 the *Sun* was a tabloid, 7 5/8 by 10 1/2 inches; by 1836 it measured 12 by 14 inches.

Concomitant with growth of the *Sun,* its personnel became specialized. When Day issued the first *Sun,* he was editor, reporter, advertising manager and mechanical assistant. He hired George Wisner as reporter. Later, Locke was employed as reporter and feature writer. To operate the Napier printing machines, Day also expanded his mechanical staff, driving up his costs.

A new aggressive business spirit was reflected in Day's scheme of selling papers. Until then papers were delivered to homes, and it was considered undignified to be aggressive about increasing the number of readers. Day sold directly to the man on the street.

Beach Buys the Sun

A new era in the *Sun*'s history began in 1838 when the paper was sold to Moses Y. Beach. Under Beach's guidance the *Sun* reached new circulation heights, became more respectable and more enterprising in gathering news. Beach bought the *Sun* for forty thousand dollars when Day was still a young man, twenty-eight. With forty thousand dollars and the profits he had accumulated, Day believed he could live comfortably. Later, however, he regretted selling the *Sun*.

Spurred on by the sharp competition of Bennett's *Herald*, which had now entered the field, Beach began publishing serious editorials on vital issues of the era. He also printed a greater variety of foreign, national and local news, and he published occasional pictures. Beach sought to build a reputation for being first with the latest news.

The new owner of the *Sun* turned to every quick means of transportation and communication available. He used express services, trains, steamboats, pigeons and telegraph. The *Sun*'s editorial page, becoming stronger, commented on outstanding news happenings and dealt with problems facing workers as well as the issues with which merchants, now beginning to read the *Sun*, were concerned.

The Mexican War, begun in 1846, was generally the result of a desire for territorial expansion by the United States. Specifically, Mexico and the United States split over the boundary line of Texas. The war, which lasted two years, was stimulus to newspaper enterprise. All Mexican news came by steamer to New Orleans, Louisiana or Mobile, Alabama, and was forwarded from those ports by railroad or other means to the nearest telegraph station. Beach was instrumental in speeding service from the South by establishing a special railroad news system from Mobile, where a telegraph station had been established. The *Sun* did not have a correspondent in Mexico as did the *Herald;* most of the *Sun*'s big news stories were those first used in the *New Orleans Picayune*. Keen news rivalry actually led to financial losses. Toward the end of the Mexican War, editors of various New York papers formed a newsgathering association, the Associated Press, which will be described later.

On August 6, 1860, Beach sold the *Sun* for one hundred thousand dollars to a group of religious people. They paid rent on the building and equipment. During the new regime the paper did not change radically. As expected, religious articles were included, and some of the news and features that did not coincide with religious policies of the new owners were rejected. The coins in the *Sun*'s cashbox did not tinkle as loudly as they had during Beach's regime, and circulation losses and high cost of running a daily paper caused the religious group to sell the paper back to Beach.

While in 1836, steam-driven presses had been purchased and had produced thirty-two hundred copies per hour, the *Sun*'s increasing circulation demanded faster presses. In 1842 Beach bought two printing machines for twelve thousand dollars. These machines were able to print six thousand papers an hour. The *Sun* printed directly from type, and the publisher was forced to buy a full new set of type six or eight times a year at an annual cost of six thousand dollars. In 1861 Beach adopted the stereotyping process by which the type was first cast into a curved plate and then fitted on the press cylinders. This increased speed, and it enabled duplicate plates to be made readily. The *Sun* could stereotype a plate in seventeen minutes.

With the *Sun,* Benjamin Day proved that a penny newspaper with a few simple appeals could reach out and secure thousands of readers who found little interest in the old standard newspapers. In the footsteps of the pioneering *Sun* came a number of penny papers catering to the urban masses. More than fifteen publishers attempted such publications in the next few years, yet only a few dailies were successful. In the following chapters those papers which substantially influenced the course of journalism in New York and other centers will be described.

NEW YORK HERALD HAS NEWS FOR SALE

James Gordon Bennett, a squint-eyed Scotchman who had been mistreated by old-line publishers, watched the *Sun*'s success carefully. As a result, in 1835, he started the *New York Herald,* a saucy, independent penny paper which reflected Bennett's catchy, humorous style and demonstrated his alert news-gathering abilities. Benjamin Day had started a revolution in journalism. Bennett pushed the revolution further, laying the foundations for a wider-scoped popular newspaper.

What the merchant-capitalist was to manufacturing, Bennett was to newspaper publishing. He sold a commodity: news. News was current information on every human activity. As the manufacturers of other products, Bennett used the latest and most efficient technological devices and machinery to produce his newspapers quickly, cheaply and in great quantities. He installed the best printing presses and other equipment and made full use of the new telegraph for rapid news transmission.

Bennett's opinions on the news were usually shifty, inconsistent and not particularly weighty. The commodity he specialized in was timely news—at the beginning, mostly light and bawdy. Later he furnished serious economic and political news about current affairs to a news-hungry population.

Born in Banffshire, Scotland, on September 1, 1795, Bennett was of French ancestry. He was trained for the Catholic priesthood, but with the independence which characterized his entire life, he turned his back on Catholicism and left home in 1815. Four years later he shipped to America. Arriving in Halifax, Nova Scotia, in April, 1819, he tried to make a living by school teaching. When this did not pay he moved to Maine then later to Boston. Still later he traveled to Charleston, South Carolina where he worked for the *Charleston Courier.* There, Bennett learned the newspaper business, particularly the technique of sending out boats to meet incoming trans-Atlantic sailing vessels. After trying various occupations in Charleston, Bennett returned to New York where he reverted to his earlier interest in journalism.

For a few short weeks in 1825 Bennett published the *New York Courier,* an early attempt at Sunday publication, but he found the times not ripe for a Sunday edition. Then Manuel Mordecai Noah hired Bennett as the Washington correspondent of the *New York Enquirer.* From the capital Bennett sent dispatches that were light and lively. They had sauciness and sting, Bennett laying bare Washington's social and political life. He was largely responsible for the merger of the *Courier* and the *Enquirer;* and he became associate editor and Washington correspondent of the combined journal. When he wrote a series of critical articles on the United States bank, in February, 1831, he was shifted to other jobs, then dismissed.

Still desiring to establish a newspaper for himself, where he could be independent of bosses, Bennett published the *New York Globe* in October, 1832. Although half as large as other standard papers and selling at a reduced price, it did not succeed. A similar venture with the *Pennsylvanian* in Philadelphia, where he expected to get support from the Democratic politicians, also was doomed.

Penniless, an outcast from his own Democratic Party, and for the third time a failure as a newspaper publisher, Bennett returned to New York. He was convinced that politics and journalism did not mix. He applied to the *Sun* for a job as a reporter but was not hired.

Now forty years of age and disillusioned with traditional journlism and ungrateful politicians, Bennett used his remaining five hundred dollars to launch his own penny paper, the *New York Herald.* Although

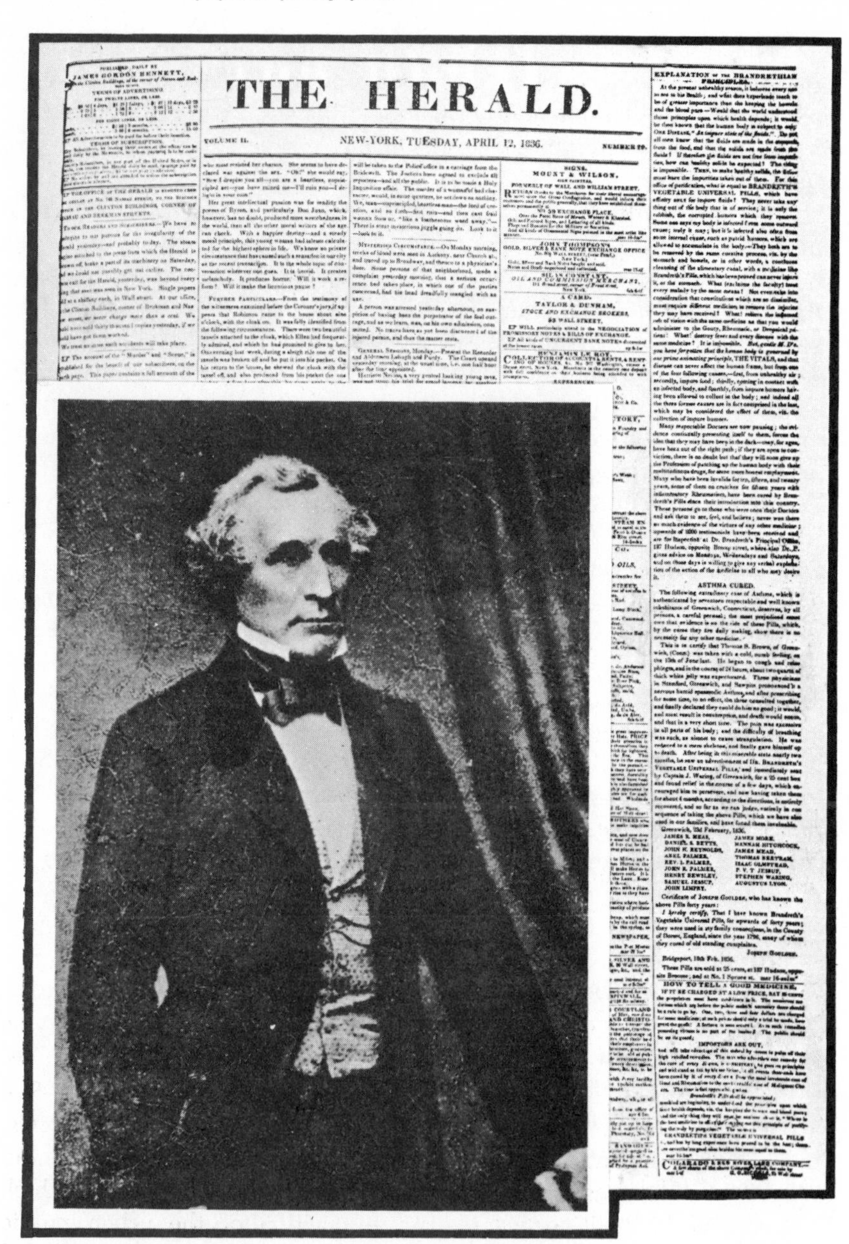

THE HERALD.

VOLUME II. NEW-YORK, TUESDAY, APRIL 12, 1836.

EXPLANATION OF THE BRANDRETHIAN PRINCIPLES.

ASTHMA CURED.

HOW TO TELL A GOOD MEDICINE.

IMPOSTORS ARE OUT.

Figure 28. Top Newsman. James Gordon Bennett saw the success of the New York *Sun* and launched the *New York Herald,* which specialized in thorough coverage of every type of news: crime, sex, sports, politics, business. Bennett opened new paths of news coverage.

he was middle aged, his head was buzzing with ideas. Bennett had considerable experience as a newsman; his writing style was lively and provocative. He saw the success of the *Sun,* and he believed he could do a better job of news gathering and writing than Day and his associates.

Bennett found a cellar at 20 Wall Street for his publication office. He rolled two barrels down the stairs. Then he connected the barrels with a long board to make a table. A couple of chairs completed his office. Bennett's printing was done by Anderson and Smith who also printed the *Sun* and the *Transcript.*

A specimen copy of the *Herald* was issued on May 6, 1835, with an outline of Bennett's aims. He said that he had fifteen years experience in publishing, experience which taught him how to build up a reputation and an establishment of his own.

> We openly disclaim all steel-traps, all principle, as it is called—all politics. Our only guide shall be good, sound, practical, common sense, application to business and bosoms of men engaged in everyday life. We shall support no party—be the organ of no faction or coterie, and care nothing for any election or any candidate from President down to a constable.

He promised "to record facts on every public and proper subject, stripped of verbiage and coloring, with comments when suitable, just and independent, fearless and good-tempered."

Bennett declared that the *Herald* was intended equally for the great masses of the community; merchants, mechanics, working people; the private family and the public hotel; the journeyman and his employer; the clerk and his principal. Thus Bennett intended to broaden the appeal of the *Herald* to include not only the working class but those who read the standard papers. The *Herald* was to be sold for ten dollars a year, and single copies could be purchased also.

New qualities, "variety, point and piquancy," that Bennett said he would use represented a protest against the heavy, sober style of news and editorial writing in commercial and political newspapers. The *Sun* was handicapped because publisher Day was not primarily a newspaperman but a printer. Bennett, however, was a skilled newswriter and understood politics as well as business. The sparkle and wit with which he endowed his writings constituted a reaction of the urban public against the provincial, repressed, humorless, all-work-and-no-play colonial heritage.

In an urban environment more activities were going on than in the small town. City residents had a greater variety of interests and amusements than those who lived in the smaller communities and villages of America. Politics in the big city was not the all-consuming topic of the day. The *Sun*, and more specifically the *Herald*, reflected the new, expanding metropolis, while the six-penny newspapers, with their heritage from an agricultural regime and small-town era, overlooked the metamorphosis.

Bennett made gathering of news in the New York metropolis an industry. News became a report of any event or idea, no matter how important, which the reader had not previously heard about. Bennett was not interested in helping or changing New York or its people. His paper, which merely reported the news, served primarily as a reflector of the metropolis.

Needing to get attention for a new daily, Bennett thought one of the best ways to do this was by attacking current established opponents, the *Sun* and the *Transcript*, as well as by assailing the standard papers. He called them all "blockheads" and "garbage of society." Day after day Bennett lashed out at his opponents. He cried, "Get out of my way, ye driveling editors." He compared himself to Socrates, Luther, Moses, and he referred to himself as "The Napoleon of the Press."

Publication of police court news, initiated by the *Sun*, was copied by Bennett. Although he first decided against such material, he later advertised for a police reporter. When the *Herald* was beaten in getting a crime story Bennett faked a rewrite of it. In exploitation of sex, Bennett went much further than Day, utilizing the same devices and appeals but giving his readers greater doses of certain types of news. If the *Sun* was sexy, the *Herald* was sensational. On page one Bennett presented his readers with spicy stories of seduction, crimes which never reached the courts. He used fictitious names. Bennett reprinted parts of the Maria Monk stories and others telling of alleged immoralities of priests and nuns in Montreal. He found, he said, similar conditions in New York and described the activities of a licentious clergyman in the metropolis.

Bennett exploited to the full the Ellen Jewett-Richard P. Robinson murder case and, later, the trial. This was the most sensational story the penny press had ever featured. By his extensive coverage, Bennett forced other papers to follow his lead. The story broke on April 11, 1836, and was headlined by Bennett in the *Herald* in this fashion:

MOST ATROCIOUS MURDER

Bennett described how the murderer killed Ellen Jewett, a prostitute, then set fire to her bed. Police identified Richard P. Robinson's cloak found in the girl's room and soon arrested him at home. A wealthy New Yorker, Robinson denied everything.

This story had many human interest angles: a rich, handsome young man; a prostitute who was his girl friend; a cruel type of murder and an attempt to burn the body in the bawdy house. Here was mystery, tragedy! Bennett saw possibilities in this news and went to the bawdy house to see for himself what happened and to report the story. In the following issues of the *Herald,* the publisher gave background stories about Ellen Jewett, who had drifted into prostitution in Boston.

The trial of Robinson began on June 2, 1836. Streets surrounding the court were packed with surging mobs, aroused by the sensational reporting. Interest was high and the *Herald* grew in advertising and in circulation. The publisher proved that the quick way to a quick rise in circulation was by obtaining and featuring a sensational murder story. Robinson was acquitted because of conflicting testimony.

Bennett often denounced licentious books while quoting, at the same time, long passages from them. Both Catholics and Protestants heaped abuse on the *Herald,* but they read the daily to see what Bennett had to say about other religions as well as their own.

The theme of a hundred *Herald* editorials during the early years was that all public men were knaves—politicians, lawyers, stockbrokers —with "clergy probably the greatest knaves of all." Bennett stressed the fact that he was a firm believer in the Gospel of Jesus, but his belief was based on a new principle, he said, and came "from the impulse of a fresh spirit."

Bennett went beyond the scope of the penny papers, his goal being to attract businessmen as well as workers. American journalism thus acquired a new department: Wall Street, a product of changing economic conditions. Interested in political economy before he became a publisher, Bennett sought to inform his readers about the fine points of business and finance. He desired to tell the truth about stockbrokers and to protect the public from swindlers.

Many bankers and speculators objected to the *Herald's* Wall Street reports, particularly when Bennett exposed some of their schemes. One of the *Herald's* greatest offenses was printing a list of bankrupts. Once Bennett was beaten by publisher Webb for publicizing financial manipulations of that aristocratic newsman for whom Bennett had formerly worked. The *Herald's* articles on Wall Street were widely quoted in other papers.

Bennett not only sold news of commercial value to businessmen, he also peddled entertainment to the masses. The *Herald* uncovered sources of entertainment entirely overlooked by the ten-dollar sheets. For the first time the fancy dress balls, given by the growing group of wealthy socialites, as well as the less elaborate dances at Tammany Hall, were covered by the paper's reporters. A colorful column about a brilliant social function was of interest to thousands of readers, many of them women.

Bennett reported news of the public conventions, a growing activity of American life. All kinds of like-minded persons began to join organizations and flock together at conventions. Bennett saw the news value of these meetings, attended by hundreds of members of organizations who would read the reports. Such news would be of interest also to thousands of other persons who did not come to the sessions.

Exploitation of sports received its first newspaper impetus from Bennett. Though some news about horse races had appeared in six-penny papers, Bennett gave the horses even more attention. Lacking Greeley's moral scruples and wanting to report events of public interest, Bennett seized on the sports activities of the changing environment. Americans needed diversion from factory life, and the aristocrats of the machine society had enough money to make racing profitable. Bennett recognized and responded to the potential interest of the wider public in sports by publishing racing news. Thus he further stimulated sports-news reading.

Forever driving onward to outdo his "despised" opponents, the "trashy penny papers" and the "blockhead Wall Street organs" as he called them, the editor of the *Herald* sought to illustrate the news, a difficult and expensive process then. In 1835, when the business section of lower New York burned, the *Herald* printed a two-column woodcut of the fire. The picture created a sensation and won the *Herald* many new readers. After that Bennett became more ambitious with his pictorial experiments. He published one-column pictures of criminals. Beginning in 1848 he issued an annual pictorial section of eight pages.

Bennett made a strong appeal in the *Herald* to women readers. Not only did he publish a weekly fashion article describing the latest modes, but even his Washington correspondence and reports of social affairs portrayed feminine apparel. Some of his articles recounted the love problems of girls, their disappointments and disillusioning experiences. During leap year Bennett printed an article on the right of women to propose.

Bennett, who had been a Washington correspondent, paid special attention to the capital news, hiring a correspondent the first year the *Herald* began publishing. Bennett found certain barriers to effective news coverage of Congress. In the House of Representatives the chamber was equally open for news gathering by Washington reporters as well as out-of-town correspondents. In the Senate, however, only newsmen from Washington papers were permitted on the floor.

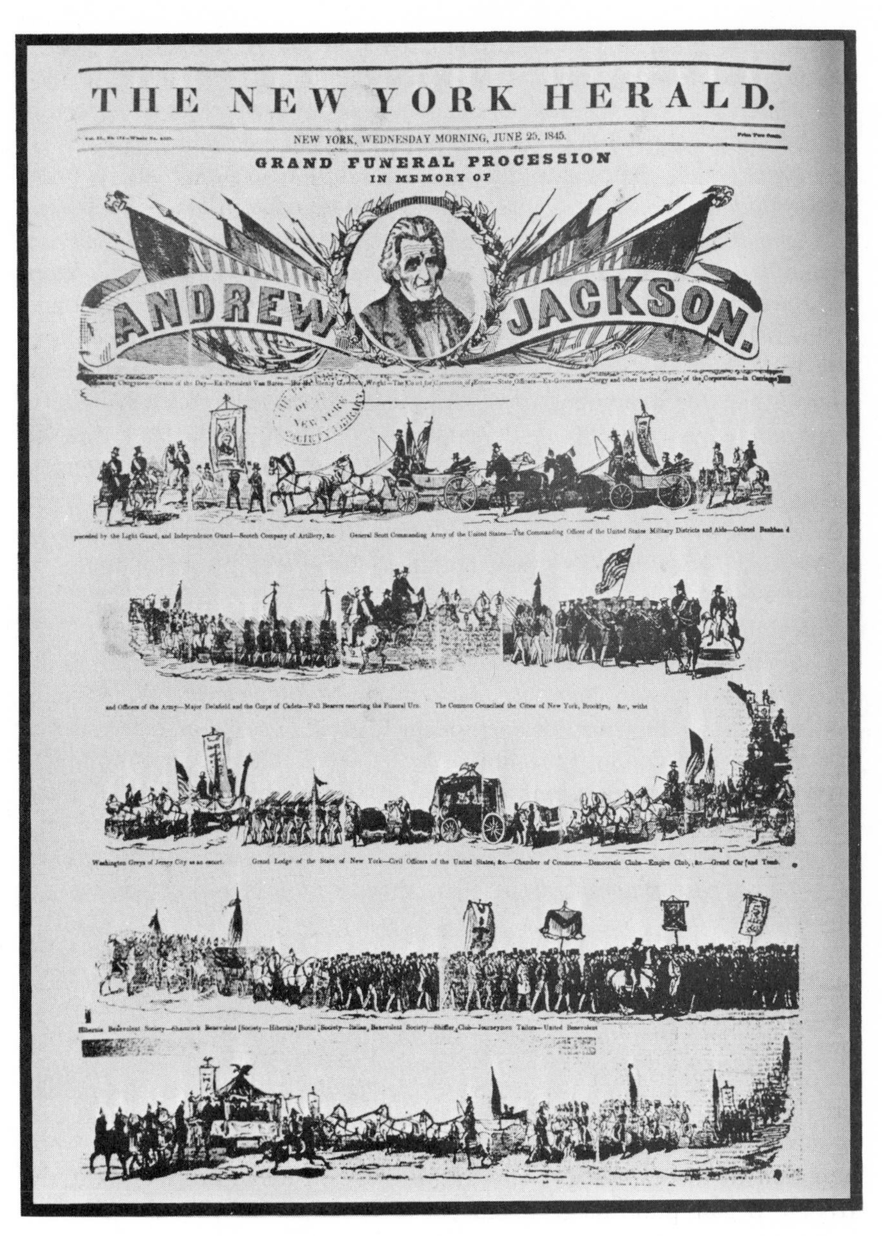

THE NEW YORK HERALD.

NEW YORK, WEDNESDAY MORNING, JUNE 25, 1845.

GRAND FUNERAL PROCESSION IN MEMORY OF ANDREW JACKSON.

—Orator of the Day—Ex-President Van Buren—Governor Wright—The Court for Correction of Errors—State Officers—Ex-Governors—Clergy and other Invited Guests of the Corporation—in Carriages

preceded by the Light Guard, and Independence Guard—Scotch Company of Artillery, &c. General Scott Commanding Army of the United States—The Commanding Officer of the United States Military Districts and Aids—Colonel Bankhead

and Officers of the Army—Major Delafield and the Corps of Cadets—Pall Bearers escorting the Funeral Urn. The Common Council of the Cities of New York, Brooklyn, &c, with

Washington Greys of Jersey City as an escort. Grand Lodge of the State of New York—Civil Officers of the United States, &c.—Chamber of Commerce—Democratic Clubs—Empire Club, &c.—Grand Car and Tomb.

Hibernia Benevolent Society—Shamrock Benevolent Society—Hibernia Burial Society—Italian Benevolent Society—Shiffler Club—Journeymen Tailors—United Benevolent

Figure 29. Picture Page. The *Herald* anticipated later tabloid and standard newspapers with its picture page. This was the first full-page illustration in an American newspaper, printed in the *New York Herald,* June 25, 1845 and *Weekly Herald,* June 28, 1845.

In 1841 Bennett wrote a strong letter to Senator Henry Clay, powerful political leader, asking that the regulation be changed. Bennett editorially attacked the restriction on out-of-town correspondents, with other papers soon joining in the protest.

As a result, the Senate adopted a resolution to admit all reporters to the floor of the Senate. Special desk accommodations for all reporters in the eastern gallery of the Senate were provided. Correspondents remained there until construction of the capitol extension in 1859, when they were moved into the new gallery provided especially for them. Bennett had won another fight to break down barriers to effective news coverage. Now he seized on leadership of Washington news gathering and kept it for a number of decades. His expanded news coverage of the capital increased his readership.

Bennett was no great editorial leader. If he had strong convictions he kept them to himself. He was interested only in news and in circulation, and declared that he could not afford to alienate anyone by expressing his (Bennett's) own opinions. Greeley, long an opponent of Bennett, said of him, "Editorially, he was cynical, inconsistent, reckless, easily influenced by others' opinions, and by his own prejudices."

Frequently, however, Bennett sent up a shower of editorial squibs and sometimes even giant firecrackers aimed at aspects of life which pleased neither him nor his Jacksonian readers. The labor movement at this time was becoming an editorial issue, and Bennett's views on unions were thoroughly inconsistent. He tried to play both sides at once. Trade unionism, he said, was an abstract principle not to be questioned. But when specific instances of strikes appeared in the news, he said workers could not raise wages by coercion; they rose because of supply and demand.

Bennett gave this prescription for trade union problems:

> We would advise all mechanics and journeymen to pay no attention to the incendiary scoundrels of the Sun and Transcript. Let the mechanics do as we do—rise early—be always at work—take what wages you can get— don't quarrel—stick to your porter houses—stick to your own wives, you that are married—you that are single seduce not your own sweethearts, or if you do, go to Alderman Brady, and make the weeping girls (poor things!) honest at once. . . . Go to bed at half past nine o'clock and get up early and read the *Herald*.

In July, 1836, printers in the *Herald* plant struck, demanding more wages. Bennett reported the incident with the headlines: "A Gross Outrage—Law Violated." Bennett charged conspiracy on the part of his rivals, particularly Colonel Webb.

Throughout his news and editorial columns, Bennett was anti-abolitionist, characterizing slavery reformers as fanatics. He reported their meetings with a decided bias. Presumably, Bennett's attitude toward the Negro developed from his early associations in Charleston. But New York was closely allied with the South commercially, and Bennett printed many business stories relating to the South. He boasted that as a result of his efforts more southern merchants were trading with New York. His southern sympathies led him later to favor the South in the war between the states.

While dueling was frowned upon, Bennett was horsewhipped with unfortunate regularity. His sharp editorial bite and his news inquisitiveness into hitherto sanctified realms made such beatings inevitable. When he accused Colonel Webb of being a tout for Wall Street, Webb beat him twice. Bennett was assaulted also by a Bowery Theater manager and by a Wall Street broker because of unfavorable news the *Herald* printed about them. The theater manager finally sued Bennett because the publisher ruined his show business, he charged.

Bennett was the high priest of newspaper promotion and self-advertisement, daily hammering away about his own and the *Herald*'s greatness but meanwhile denouncing the penny papers and ten-dollar sheets. He was apparently so sincere, so confident of his own ability, that *Herald* readers undoubtedly believed his paper superior. Like P. T. Barnum, Bennett was a master of the art of advertisement and did not care whether he was praised or denounced so long as he was noticed. Bennett anticipated the later development of promotion departments of daily newspapers.

Bennett followed a policy of cash-in-advance except for certain yearly advertisers. Early in 1847, however, he started an innovation with the announcement that advertising insertions could run for two weeks only. Later he refused to print for longer than one day ads without changes. This invested the *Herald*'s advertising with the same lively interest as its news columns. Display type, pictures and two-column advertisements were included in the *Herald*, thus breaking with tradition. When this policy brought complaints from small but regular advertisers, who claimed that their announcements could not be seen, Bennett banned advertising display type and pictures; advertisements were printed then in agate type. The "agate rule" became prevalent in large eastern papers, but in the western dailies was broken.

Between 1835 and 1840 the *Herald* mounted to seventeen thousand circulation; and in 1840 Bennett boasted that he was earning about $25,000 a year. Then the "moral war" on Bennett began. His attacks on other newspapers had aroused their jealousy; his salacious sex stories and quack advertisements had shocked the pious. His prolabor, anti-banking views had aroused conservative businessmen. In May, 1840, these moral and aristocratic groups began unmerciful assaults on the *Herald* and Bennett. He had touched economic and moral nerve centers, and his enemies opened fire on him. An attempt was also made to strike at Bennett by getting both readers and advertisers to boycott him, but this did not work.

Bennett fought back with consummate skill. Then he decided to get married, announcing his intention in characteristic style on June 1, 1840:

> **TO READERS OF THE HERALD —DECLARATION OF LOVE—CAUGHT AT LAST—GOING TO BE MARRIED —NEW MOVEMENT IN CIVILIZATION**
>
> I am going to be married in a few days . . . . . times are getting so good; . . . . that I cannot resist the divine instance of honest nature any longer; so I am going to be married to one of the most splendid women in intellect, in heart, in soul, in property, in person, in manner, that I have yet seen. . . . .
>
> James Gordon Bennett

Although the presidential campaign of 1840 closed the "war" on Bennett, the *Herald* had received a blow. Circulation dropped from seventeen to fourteen thousand within two years. By 1849, however, circulation had increased, reaching thirty-three thousand partly as the result of Bennett's expert coverage of the Mexican War. Another result of the moral war was that his struggling scandal sheet, with its wit and sparkle, was transformed into a mature newspaper, almost as lacking in color as its ten-dollar rivals but filled with news on a variety of subjects.

Interest in the Mexican War and the Civil War was another factor which changed the *Herald*. The wars forced scandal into the background. Controversy over slavery cut the nation into two warring groups, with nearly everyone interested in the current issue, rather than sex news.

Bennett was one of the first to grasp the significance of the telegraph to journalism, just as he recognized the value of trans-Atlantic steamboats. "The magnetic telegraph at Washington has totally annihilated what there was left of steam and locomotives and steamships," he said. Soon New York was connected with Washington via Philadelphia, Wilmington, Delaware and Baltimore. By May 23, 1846, the *Herald* was able to get Mexican news from Washington by this new telegraph. New York and Albany were not joined by telegraph until 1847. By January, 1848, the *Herald* was printing ten columns of telegraph news.

When the Mexican-Texas question became vital news in 1844, Bennett established a horse express between New Orleans and New York, getting an exchange of news with the *Crescent City*, an enterprising daily in New Orleans. Bennett's six-day "express" beat the United States mails by one to four days. When the Mexican War broke out, Bennett joined other penny papers, the Baltimore *Sun* and the Philadelphia *Public Ledger*, in establishing a pony express to get the news faster than by United States mail.

The *Herald* was the only New York paper to send a correspondent to report the *Mexican War*, thus inaugurating modern war correspondence. Of the entire country's press, only the *Herald* and the New Orleans journals, the *Picayune* and the *Delta*, engaged correspondents for the Mexican War. The *Herald* published the peace treaty with Mexico before any other paper, even printing the news before the government wished it made public.

Besides development of faster news service and utilization of the telegraph, the Mexican War also contributed to the emergence of spectacular headlines. Headlines summarized the content of the news. Successive subheadlines described details. Headlines, first applied only to news, now appeared above governors' speeches and outstanding criminal cases. The entire front page of the *Herald* changed from a dull, solid sheet with one or two headlines, to a lively, attractive page with many headlines. The headline technique soon spread through the entire American newspaper world.

Bennett saw the potential public desire to get news quickly; therefore, he tried several afternoon publications. He published the *Evening Herald* for a few issues in 1835 but discontinued it. He entered the afternoon field again with the *Evening Chronicle* a few months later. Believing he could get more ads he had merely changed the name of the paper. This afternoon paper lasted two years. Bennett did not give up easily. He remade his *Morning Herald* as often as three times in a single night. He would stop the press at the end of a two-hour run and insert the latest information about an important event. These late editions then began to be issued in the afternoon, competing with the regular late afternoon papers published a distance from New York. By 1848 the *Herald* divided its daily output into a "Before Breakfast" and two afternoon editions at one o'clock and three o'clock. These multiple editions long hampered the growth of distinctly evening sheets.

In 1841 Bennett broke tradition again; he issued his *Herald* on Sundays.

Every day, hundreds of politicians, business men, farmers and laborers would scan the columns of the *Herald* for news of interest and importance. Rival editors waited expectantly for the earliest edition of the *Herald* so they might cull, clip and crib many items of news which only the *Herald* had been able to acquire.

By the end of this era Bennett's income was between $25,000 and $30,000 yearly. He emerged from the dark and dingy cellar where he first scribbled his news items and editorial squibs. His *Herald* was housed now in an imposing brick and granite structure at the corner of Nassau and Fulton streets. The name of his paper and his own name were stretched in huge letters across the building. The basement was filled with printing presses and folding machines, the latest and best that money could buy. The street floor was devoted exclusively to business offices where Mrs. Bennett's brother, Robert Crean, supervised sixty cashiers, bookkeepers, advertising solicitors and others. The second floor housed the large and busy editorial offices of Frederic Hudson, managing editor. There were located also the reference library and publisher's private office. Directly above was the job-printing office. The top floor housed compositors sometimes as many as one hundred who translated hand-written scrawls of reporters into type. The composing room was a beehive of activity day and night, workday, holiday and Sabbath.

TABLE 15

James Gordon Bennett's Contributions to American Journalism

Positive	Negative
1. Developed new concept of news	1. Encouraged haste
2. Began aggressive news coverage on all levels, national, state, local	2. Promoted cynical attitude toward people
3. Widened news coverage—police, Wall Street, sports, society, conventions	3. Stressed emotional feelings
4. Put liveliness, color in newswriting	4. Promoted news fakes
5. Promoted political independence	5. Misused humor in serious news
6. Issued many editions with latest news	6. Degenerated editorial page and function
7. Used communication facilities—pony express, telegraph—more fully	
8. Widened newspaper audience	
9. Improved advertising methods—forced advertisers to change copy	
10. Put newspaper on better financial base	

Bennett set a fast pace for American publishers, both standard and popular. He took the Day formula and expanded it, adding successful innovations of his own. While making positive contributions, he also emphasized some negative ones. Both became a part of the newspaper pattern and heritage for many publishers.

NEW YORK TRIBUNE, POWERFUL HUMANITARIAN WHIG PAPER

A gawky New England country boy, Horace Greeley, walked down the streets of New York in August, 1831. With twenty-five dollars in his pocket and five years of experience on country weeklies, he was looking for a job as a printer. Ten years later he was to found the *New York Tribune,* a great social and communication instrument of democracy.

Although James Gordon Bennett pretended to be a reformer, it was Horace Greeley, the brillant New England farm boy, who actually produced a humanitarian newspaper to fit the acute social needs of the hour. Greeley listened to the whisperings and shouts of the impoverished "mechanics," and he pleaded their cause in a clear, persuasive voice. Greeley and his *Tribune* were actually journalistic expressions of social, economic and reform movements of the period. Greeley responded to all progressive movements in the American environment. He was not an original thinker. In his *Tribune* he gave expression to the ideas of reformers and other minority groups. This was a real contribution to journalism, developed by a mind incapable of rejecting a thought just because it was new, in an age of new ideas and untried ways.

Greeley invited opinion, opening his columns to every shade of economic, social and moral improvement. The penny press offered Greeley the chance to promulgate unorthodox democratic programs for the common man. He reflected aspirations of the common man, and at the same time spurred his readers on to seek reforms for the social and economic ills of the era.

Born on a farm near Amherst, New Hampshire, on February 3, 1811, Greeley's interest in learning was awakened by his mother, while he derived his sympathetic, kindly nature from his father. The elder Greeley could not make the farm pay, and in 1821 finally declared himself bankrupt and fled to Vermont to escape creditors. This experience made Horace, at the time ten years old, ultrasensitive to problems of workers and farmers.

The Greeleys settled in Westhaven, Vermont, where Horace began school again. He was a quick scholar, and by the time he was thirteen his teacher reported that Greeley knew more than the teacher himself. The farm boy quit school and did his reading at home. Because of poor health Greeley was never much at sports, a fact that later influenced the *Tribune*'s antisports policy. Journalism attracted him, and he learned the printing trade on the *Northern Spectator*, East Poultney, Vermont, and later worked in a print shop in Erie, Pennsylvania. Greeley early joined the Whig Party, never outgrowing his early political leanings.

Greeley went to New York, the metropolis, in 1831 and worked on various weekly papers. In December, 1832, Greeley and Francis V. Story, foreman on *Spirit of The Times*, started the printing firm of Greeley and Story. For three weeks the firm printed the *Morning Post*, an early attempt at a popular newspaper, and thereafter *Sylvester's Bank Note Reporter*. Then Story drowned while swimming, and Greeley found himself a new partner, Jonas Winchester.

In 1834 Greeley and Winchester established the weekly *New Yorker*, indicating the direction the daily *Tribune* was to take a few years later. He published a number of articles on the conditions of the poor. The articles grew out of conditions which Greeley observed; in 1838 unemployment was high; many families were destitute. Greeley became known for his journalistic ability. Thurlow Weed, Whig political boss of the state of New York and editor of the influential *Albany Evening Journal*, at this time needed state-wide publicity for the Whig Party. He asked Greeley to edit the *Jeffersonian*, a political organ, which Greeley consented to do.

In 1840 Greeley edited another Whig campaign weekly, the *Log Cabin*. The paper at one time sold nearly ninety thousand copies. The *Log Cabin* was not financially successful, showing that Greeley was not a good businessman. All his experiences with political weeklies, however, gave him confidence in his editorial ability and provided him with the courage to start a daily. He had $2,000, half of that in printing materials, and obtained a loan of $1,000 for his venture. His partner McElrath contributed $500 at first, then $1,500 more. The total capital was about $5,000.

Begins New York Tribune, 1841

On April 10, 1841, five months after the campaign of 1840, Greeley launched the *New York Tribune* with the aid of some Whig members. Later he revealed the economic, political and journalistic conditions which led to the new paper, thus:

> I had been incited to this enterprise by several Whig friends, who deemed a cheap daily, addressed more specifically to the laboring class, eminently needed in our city. . . .

New-York Daily Tribune.

Vol. XXIII....No. 6,950. NEW-YORK, TUESDAY, JULY 14, 1863. PRICE THREE CENTS.

THE DRAFT.

The Riot in the Ninth Congressional District.

Headquarters of the Provost-Marshal Burned.

The Draft Slips Destroyed.

SEVERAL OTHER BUILDINGS FIRED.

Telegraph Wires Cut and Fire Bells Not Allowed to Ring.

Firemen Obstructed in their Duty.

Pavements and Railroad Tracks Torn Up.

Police Superintendent Kennedy and Several Policemen Badly Injured.

SOLDIERS MOBBED.

PRIVATE HOUSES SACKED.

Figure 30. Horace Greeley. The founder-editor of the *New York Tribune* created a militant, reformist paper.

> My leading idea was the establishment of a journal removed from servile partisanship on the one hand and from gagged mincing neutrality on the other . . . I believed there was a happy medium between these extremes.

In this declaration of party independence, Greeley was merely reechoing the views laid down by his penny press predecessors, Day and Bennett. In his *Tribune* prospectus, published in the *New Yorker,* Greeley promised to:

1. Appeal to the laboring class;
2. Advance moral, social and political well being;
3. Advocate the principles of the Whig Party;
4. Be a slave to no party;
5. Publish political, literary and general intelligence;
6. Omit degrading police reports since the *Tribune* was to be family newspaper.

The Whigs represented primarily the manufacturing classes. Nevertheless, trade unions had been developing for fifteen years, and labor, now armed with the vote, could no longer be ignored. Labor had established a workingman's political party, launched newspapers, such as the *Workingman's Advocate,* the *Sentinel* and the *Man,* and struck for better working conditions. All these facts, as well as the business depression of 1837 to 1838, had prepared the way for the *Tribune.* Greeley's paper was the answer to labor and machine-age problems. Day's *Sun* and Bennett's *Herald,* penny papers, also appealed to workers but were Democratic. Other Whig papers were published in New York, but they were ten-dollar sheets, so could not reach the laborers, also now a voting class. Greeley's *Tribune,* a good, Whig, penny daily with prolabor bias, filled the journalistic vacuum.

Although disagreeing on some Whig policies and candidates, Greeley followed the party line for more than fourteen years. Nevertheless, not being financially tied to the Whig Party, he was able to advocate many, at the time, radical doctrines to which conservative Whigs objected. Greeley was an active supporter of the Whig Party and took part in every political convention and campaign during the 1840s and 1850s. His was an influential voice, and the *Tribune,* a leading exponent of the Whigs. Greeley was in a close alliance or "partnership" with Thurlow Weed, Whig political boss of New York state, and Governor William H. Seward. Greeley broke with these leaders in 1854 when they rejected his request to be nominated as governor. They thought he had advocated too many "isms" and was a prohibitionist, hence could not win.

The *Tribune* was a success from the start. By the end of the first year, ten thousand subscribers were purchasing the paper; it created keen competition for other penny papers. Moses Y. Beach, then proprietor of the *Sun,* tried in vain to crush his rival, bribing carriers and urging them to beat the *Tribune* boys. Actually, these attacks served to draw attention to the Greeley paper.

As editorial spokesman of the rising northern industries, Greeley advocated a group of well-defined policies. These doctrines were primarily: (1) a protective tariff for industry; (2) a national bank and sound currency; (3) internal improvements, such as highways, canals and railroads; (4) land reform, the opening of cheap western lands to eastern settlers.

In Greeley's *Tribune* the protective tariff became a noble measure. The only way to protect the American worker against low-paid workers in foreign countries was to protect the capitalist, he declared. Greeley further argued that the protective tariff would stimulate industry. Labor, too, would benefit indirectly through more and regular employment.

In 1845 Greeley committed himself to the Workingman's Party, guided by George H. Evans, editor of the *Workingman's Advocate.* Greeley embraced the party's land reform idea, the proposal that freedom of land was necessary to the emancipation of labor from misery. When Greeley went to Congress for a three-months' term in 1848, he introduced the first homestead bill. Six years later he prepared the way for the new Republican Party's acceptance of the platform plank to open land in the West.

In spite of his Whig views on protection, he was not merely the spokesman of northern business entrepreneurs. He had a keen social sense and was the first American of reputation and influence to give serious consideration to the effects of the Industrial Revolution on the working class.

Many humanitarian movements for amelioration of labor's conditions were organized at this time, and Greeley became the leader and spokesman of these groups. It was a happy conjunction of "the times and the man." Just as Webb, in his *Courier and Enquirer,* reflected the manufacturing classes, Greeley consolidated the interests of the working classes.

There was always a split in the economic viewpoint of the *Tribune,* even though its editor was unconscious of it. In one part of the paper he upheld the profit system and was eloquent for the capitalistic Whigs, while in other sections, he exposed the evils of a capitalistic society, seeking socialistic remedies. Greeley was looking for a solution to economic confusion and in his search wove together theories which made him a puzzle to both radicals and conservatives. Whigs and protectionists alike used him, but they both dreaded him. In his efforts to harmonize the opposing classes, Greeley was a hybrid and, therefore, was attacked by papers of both sides.

On July 12, 1841, Greeley started a series of articles "What Shall be Done for Labor?" advocating establishment of reading rooms, lyceums, scientific lectures and free libraries. The *Tribune* later ran another series of feature articles on workers of New York, describing conditions in factories, low wages and long hours of work for seamstresses and similar "female operators."

To Greeley, education and regular employment were foundation stones for a better social order. He recognized that if workers were to raise their standards they needed background and information; he turned the *Tribune* into a vehicle for the promotion of education and for stressing the dignity and rights of labor. He favored labor unions, believing that employers also should belong to them. Greeley, however, was opposed to strikes.

In early years of the *Tribune,* Greeley offered the Fourier scheme of forming small communities and living in a communistic state of barter and exchange. In 1840 wealthy, aristorcratic Albert Brisbane came back from Europe where he had been saturated with the ideas of the French philosopher, Charles Fourier. Greeley met Brisbane from whom he learned about the French reformer. The *Tribune* publisher absorbed many of Brisbane's ideas. Finally, the publisher sold Brisbane and his followers a front-page column in the *Tribune,* a special feature which began to appear on March 1, 1842, a year after the paper's establishment. The Brisbane articles, written in a simple yet penetrating fashion, exposed working conditions as much as they set forth the utopian principles of the "Association." Therefore, Greeley was dubbed a visionary whose paper struck at the foundations of the old political parties and economic system. The *Tribune* articles constituted one of the first newspaper exposés of American politics and were among the first analyses of the social and economic effects of the Industrial Revolution to appear in a popular daily American newspaper.

Greeley also became a propagandist for other "isms" of the period. Advocating prohibition of liquor, he was also against capital punishment and the practice of flogging in the navy. Joining the movement to reform insane asylums, Greeley carried on crusades against barbaric treatment of inmates. He was a follower of Sylvester Graham, a dietary reformer, who suggested the Graham cracker.

Greeley was active in popularizing inquiries into politics, economics, penology, labor and science. Because of his personal interest in reform, he was able to stimulate and arouse a potentially interested public in the need for change. Having neither party nor financial strings tied to his paper, he could use it as a sounding board for new ideas.

Greeley was attacked from all sides and made many enemies; even his friends pointed out that the *Tribune* lost many subscribers because of its "isms." The *New York Times* was established in 1851 as a conservative Whig newspaper to offset the influence of the *Tribune*. Nevertheless, the *Tribune* was able to withstand criticism, while Greeley, reflecting and expressing labor's most acute problems, became a great editorial leader.

The 1840s and 1850s might be considered an age of lectures, and the *Tribune*'s advertising columns were filled regularly with six or more such announcements.

Add the total effect created by lectures, book reviews and magazine condensations to that of the news of reform organizations which secured a hearing through the *Tribune*, and it is easy to understand why the paper was characterized by Professor John R. Commons as the "first and only great vehicle this country had known for the ideas and experiments of a constructive democracy." All ideas, except those of the Democrats, got a hearing in the *Tribune*.

The Greeley paper in early years did not stress live, urgent news as the *Herald* did. Following the newspaper pattern already cut in the penny papers, Greeley ran a column labeled "City Intelligence." The column at first consisted chiefly of scraps of information and little gossipy items. The *Tribune*, however, was conscious of the great city that was beginning to stretch out on all sides. The editor expanded his coverage of metropolitan city news. An excellent picture of New York in the 1840s was presented in the *Tribune* in a series of colorful articles, "Slices of New York." The reporter caught the spirit of this new metropolis of a half million people as he walked about town, and selecting one section after another, he described its peculiar features: Wall Street, Broadway, Chatham, Five Points, Bowery. These articles criticized people, architecture, methods of doing business and exploitation of labor. In the 1850s Solon Robinson wrote human interest sketches of New York streets after the manner of Dickens. These articles were very popular.

Greeley entered popular journalism after crime news had already become a part of the pattern. In his prospectus, however, he announced that he would not emphasize crime. He criticized other penny sheets for

Figure 31. Busy New York. New York was a busy, busy metropolis, with traffic and transportation becoming a critical problem. Horse-drawn buses were used to carry passengers from one end of town to the other. This was how Broadway, south of Barclay Street, looked in 1850. (From a watercolor by A. Köllner, New York Historical Society)

printing horrid murder news. From time to time, however, the *Tribune* could not escape the popular excitement and interest in notorious murders and had to cover them. Like other penny papers, the *Tribune* reported in full the trials in which prominent people were involved. Murders were usually headed: MOST HORRIBLE TRAGEDY, or HORRIBLE TRAGEDY.

Greeley's New England background was revealed in the *Tribune*'s attitude toward the theatre. He never refused advertisements of theatres, but he neither sought nor desired them. He believed the stage to be socially harmful. Dramatic criticism in the *Tribune,* therefore, was weak. Similarly, Greeley was uninterested in sports, which he considered stimulated gambling.

Greeley responded favorably to the women's suffrage movement of the day. The *Tribune* was in favor of opening professions to women and giving them control of their property after marriage.

While Greeley's *Tribune* was distinctive it was also caught in the main stream of American journalism and had to respond to new developments and newspaper competition. Greeley had to obtain news and distribute it quickly for he was competing with the low-cost, popular *Herald*, the *Sun* and the *Times* (after 1851), and even with ten-dollar papers.

As Bennett did, Greeley also published the *Tribune* in various editions to give news when it was alive. The age was speeding along. From the earliest years papers changed from weeklies, semiweeklies and triweeklies to dailies. Now there were both morning and evening dailies and extras. Also New York newspapers were specializing their appeal. Not only were there Whig and Democratic papers, but sharp contrast was noted in the penny paper group as represented by the flashy *Herald* and the sober *Tribune*.

Headlines and front-page display showed the public's desire for news. Greeley once published his Washington news on inside pages, but this news and the local articles forced their way now to page one. Greeley apologized for this transition.

His paper adopted the technique of the headline along with the *Herald*, the *Sun* and the ten-dollar papers. First came the usual labels: HORRIBLE MURDER, NINE DAYS LATER FROM EUROPE, DETECTED ATTEMPT AT DECEPTION, A CRUEL FATHER. Then when the telegraph arrived the nervous speed of the age was shown:

BY TELEGRAPH TO THE NEW YORK TRIBUNE
Highly Important
RATIFICATION OF THE TREATY CONFIRMED

The Mexican War, other important foreign news and the opportunity to editorialize in headlines made them bigger and longer. Here is an example of the new headline type and the bias:

GLORIOUS NEWS!
Down with the Compromise
The House Laid the Senate's
Slavery Compromise on the Table
112 to 97!
Motion to Reconsider Made and
Defeated by
18 Majority
HUZZA FOR FREEDOM AND FREE SOIL

Weekly Tribune, Popular in the West

This was an expanding business period when manufacturers in the Northeast sought markets in the expanding Northwest, and New York editors were not blind to the possibilities of the reading public market in the West, where papers were still crude, had little news and were poorly edited. Great masses of settlers were pouring into the Northwest. Wealth was increasing, and farmers were bound by commercial and psychological ties to the metropolis. All these conditions proved favorable to circulation of a New York weekly. Ten-dollar papers had long been issuing weekly editions for rural consumption. The *Log Cabin,* with its eighty to ninety thousand circulation, proved to Greeley the tremendous market possibilities in the Northwest.

On September 29, 1841, Greeley launched the *Weekly Tribune,* merging the *New Yorker* and the *Log Cabin* into the new venture. The *Weekly Tribune* contained articles, reprinted from the daily, with added agricultural material. Solon Robinson was the editor-in-charge.

In spite of other features in the paper, readers watched most eagerly for what "ole Horace" had to say on the editorial page; his simple, clear and picturesque way of expressing himself held a strong appeal. This appeal of the weekly *Tribune* was reinforced by occasional lectures by old Horace himself, looking something like a tall, tow-headed corpse. Farmers wrote him for advice or dropped by to visit him when in New York.

United City Worker and Farmer

Interested in city worker and farmer, Greeley brought the two together in his *Weekly Tribune.* Protective tariffs, he argued, as well as internal improvements would benefit both the farmer and the urban worker.

Most of all he hated slavery. Whatever psychological preparation there may have been for consolidation of the Northeast and Northwest into a single group opposing the southern cotton plutocracy and the spread of slavery, this movement was at work almost twenty years before the first gun of the Civil War was fired.

James Ford Rhodes, historian, takes the measure of the *Weekly Tribune's* influence as follows, in his *Historical Essays* (p. 90):

> . . . if you want to penetrate into the thoughts, feelings, and grounds of decision of the 1,866,000 men who voted for Lincoln in 1860, you should study the New York *Weekly Tribune.* . . .
>
> The greatest single journalistic influence was the New York *Weekly Tribune* which had in 1854 a circulation of 112,000 and many times that number of readers. . . . The questions were discussed in their family circles, and with their neighbors, and, as differences arose, the *Tribune,* always at hand, was consulted and re-read. There being few popular magazines during this decade, the weekly newspaper in some degree, took their place. . . .

In 1854 Dana wrote that the daily *Tribune* had never made a cent but existed solely to help along the weekly and the semiweekly, started in 1845.

By attracting a brilliant group of newsmen and writers, Greeley built up a highly capable staff which increased the readability of the *Tribune.* Charles A. Dana and George Ripley came from Brook Farm. Ripley in 1849 established the first regular department in any American daily newspaper devoted to the reviewing of current books and periodicals. Margaret Fuller, a woman writer of distinction, joined the staff in 1846. Bayard Taylor was commissioned to go to Europe to write special correspondence for the *Tribune.*

Elected to Congress

In 1848 Greeley was elected to Congress, and within a short time had created a sensation with his mileage exposé in which he pointed out that congressmen were making out travel expense sheets on the basis of old railroad rates, taking the longest way to and from home and pocketing large sums of money.

In the 1850s the *Tribune* had become too big for one man. Combined revenue from daily, weekly, semiweekly and California editions had transformed the paper into a large business enterprise, requiring hundreds of men and hundreds of thousands of dollars to operate it. Greeley now had a managing editor, Charles A. Dana, as well as capable assistants in each department. Expanding to a twelve page paper, the *Tribune* carried many advertisements in its two morning and two evening editions.

The desire for quicker and more abundant news was an outgrowth of changing economic and psychological conditions of readers themselves who were now living in a rapidly paced world. Small-town folks no longer had minds hermetically sealed against all but local interests. A network of railroads, steamboats, expresses and telegraph wires wove the sections into one unit, and changes taking place in one region were recorded almost simultaneously in all the others. It was natural that such an issue as the value of phalanxes of the Association and the problems of socialism were superseded by the fight over free soil and slavery.

With the change from a four page to an eight page issue, sometimes expanded to twelve pages, the *Tribune* acquired the characteristics of a newsy metropolitan newspaper. A greater variety of news was printed. More local coverage was given, and a larger stream of news, sent in by the special *Tribune* correspondents and the AP, from other American cities and from Europe was published. The literature department was reduced and the paper no longer stressed labor or Association news.

The greater abundance of news was made available by the strengthening and expansion of the news-communication facilities—United States mails, express companies, telegraph, trans-Atlantic, coastwise and inland river steamships and railroads. Many advertisements appeared, some on each page, all testifying to the *Tribune*'s prosperity. Greeley, as indicated, issued two morning and two evening editions. By 1855 circulation reached 35,000.

Greeley's *Tribune* was a medium of expression for European liberals not well liked on their own continent. Economist Karl Marx wrote from London. His correspondence on European affairs was often printed as editorials. When Charles A. Dana traveled in Europe, he reported the revolutions of 1848 for the paper. Bayard Taylor made a reputation as the *Tribune*'s European correspondent. Readers of the Greeley newspaper who read the foreign news and interpretation were kept well informed on European affairs.

Greeley's attitude toward Lincoln and the Civil War will be discussed in a later chapter dealing with the conflict.

Figure 32. Home of the Tribune. The large imposing building was needed to house the many editorial, reportorial, printing staffs of the *New York Tribune*. The five-story building reflects the rapid growth of the *Tribune* and the expansion of the newspaper business, now becoming more prosperous.

The *Daily Tribune* and the *Weekly Tribune* proved profitable. Starting with about $5,000, Greeley and his able partner McElrath built the papers steadily. Greeley turned the enterprise into a $100,000 joint stock-ownership company in 1849. He issued 100 shares of stock at $1,000 a share. The Tribune Company prospered. By 1851 it declared an annual dividend of $25,000. Value of the stock mounted, and within the next few years the company was valued in excess of $300,000. Personnel was added, the *Tribune* employing 125 persons.

TABLE 16

Greeley's Contributions to American Newspapers

1. Greeley was the first American editor to demonstrate that it was possible to publish successfully a cheap daily paper without depending on sensational news.
2. The Tribune editor proved that a cheap, popular paper need not be politically neutral, as were the first penny papers.
3. Greeley showed that the newspaper could mirror the needs and reflect the problems of the urban commercial and industrial worker.
4. Greeley sought to solve, through the popular press, the problems of the fast-advancing Machine Age in America.
5. He revealed how the newspaper might channel new ideas and viewpoints to the public in a democracy.
6. Greeley's vigorous editorial writing reestablished the value of the editorial page for the cheap, popular paper.
7. Greeley acquired an outstanding editorial staff, perhaps the best in America at the time.
8. He managed to maintain a literary character in the Tribune, unusual in a daily newspaper.
9. He set for the press a high standard and spirit of reform which have served as an inspiration for newspapermen since Greeley's day.

RAYMOND'S NEW YORK TIMES FOLLOWS MIDDLE-OF-ROAD POLICY

In 1851 conservative Henry J. Raymond, formerly a member of the *New York Tribune* staff and associate editor of the *Courier and Enquirer,* recognized the need for a new conservative Whig newspaper to sell for one cent. He had discussed the possibilities of such a paper with George Jones, of the business staff, when both previously were employed on the *Tribune.* Now Raymond considered the time ripe to launch a new publication. Jones had become a small-loan banker since leaving the paper. The *New York Times* began with $100,000 capitalization, of which $69,000 was immediately available.

Rapid growth of the *New York Times* demonstrated that Henry J. Raymond and George Jones had found a public for their paper, which was moral in tone and conservative Whig in politics. They found a newspaper market because other standard papers and penny papers did not fill the needs of certain groups. Among the old-time standard sheets, the *Courier and Enquirer* was conservative and dull; the *Journal of Commerce* consisted primarily of market reports and news of the personal quarrels of James Watson Webb. Among the inexpensive new papers the *Sun* was Democratic but did not take strong political stands, and the *Herald,* which seemed to be Democratic, had not yet lived down its early unsavory reputation. What about Greeley's *Tribune*? Its Whig policies were in line with the political thinking of Raymond and Jones, but the *Tribune* had opened its columns to socialism and identified itself with other reforms, unacceptable to many persons.

Raymond was in many respects like Greeley. But Raymond's college training gave him more polish than Greeley. Raymond was also more of a conformist and a shrewder politician. Born in Lima, New York, January 24, 1820, Raymond attended Wesleyan Seminary there; after clerking in a store and teaching, he enrolled at the University of Vermont. While there Raymond did some writing for Greeley's weekly *New Yorker.* When Raymond was graduated from the university in 1840, he went to New York City. Greeley hired him for reportorial work on the *New Yorker* at eight dollars a week. More important, Raymond learned the art of publishing a newspaper. Ambitious Raymond wrote for several out-of-town papers, and in spare moments studied law, which also affected his later writing career.

When Greeley launched the daily *Tribune* he made Raymond an editor, and Raymond's tireless work won him a raise to twenty dollars a week. He stayed with Greeley until Webb lured Raymond to the *Courier and Enquirer.* Raymond tried to blow life into the *Courier and Enquirer,* carrying on extended debates with Greeley over political and economic issues.

In 1849 Raymond ran as a candidate for the New York State legislature on the Whig ticket, winning the election and thereby becoming associated with Thurlow Weed, New York State political boss and Albany editor. Raymond expected to make this first attempt in politics his last; at the close of the session he returned to the *Courier and Enquirer.* But the pull between politics and journalism continued throughout his life. He ran again in 1850 for the New York legislature, and again he won. Later he was elected Speaker of the State House of Representatives.

Meanwhile Raymond had been discussing his plans for a new daily paper with George Jones of the *Tribune's* business office. The two men contemplated purchase of the *Albany Evening Journal* from Thurlow Weed, but the project fell through. When, in winter of 1851, Raymond and Jones, now a banker, met again, Jones casually observed that Greeley's *Tribune* had reputedly made a profit of sixty thousand dollars in the previous year. This revived the discussion of publication of a New York newspaper. Raymond and Jones were joined by E. B. Westley.

Although a series of more or less accidental circumstances precipitated the founding of the *New York Times,* its success was not accidental. The prosperity of New York State and New York City increased along with their population growth, and the new journal flourished on these conditions. The New York City newspaper situation had created a vacuum for a cheap Whig daily with a conservative economic, political and social policy. The *Times* filled this vacuum. The daily, of course, had the able Raymond as editorial director and also had two astute businessmen, Jones and Westley, as its financial directors, who, experienced in the newspaper business as well as in the banking, incorporated for $100,000 with 100 shares at $1,000 par value.

Raymond's prospectus, published in various newspapers in August, 1851, reflected not only the key and tone of the new age of journalism but also the principles and aims of the *Times.* At that time the *Sun* was the only other newspaper selling at a penny; the *Times* declared it, too, would sell for a cent. In announcing issuance of a morning as well as evening edition, the *Times'* publishers were following the new trend, calling for even faster news dissemination. The prominence of Henry J. Raymond's name was an indication of the entry of the personal element into journalism.

The *Times* said its editorial function would be to present news of the day with special attention given to reports of legal, criminal, commercial and financial transactions in New York; to political and personal movements in the United States; and to early publication of reliable intelligence from both continents. Raymond planned to send reporters to get political, religious, agricultural, scientific and mechanical news. He also promised to publish news of literature, music, drama and art.

Editorially, the *Times* intended to discuss all questions of interest and importance, political, social and religious. In spite of its declaration

The New-York Times.

VOL. XIII—NO. 3794. NEW-YORK, FRIDAY, NOVEMBER 20, 1863. PRICE THREE CENTS.

IMPORTANT FROM EAST TENNESSEE

The Rebels Advancing upon Knoxville.

THE PLACE COMPLETELY INVESTED.

HEAVY SKIRMISHING YESTERDAY.

The Position Very Strongly Fortified.

THE REBEL FORCES UNDER LONGSTREET

Knoxville, Thursday, Nov. 17.

The enemy began skirmishing from their position on Kingston Road at 10 this morning. [illegible]

A MORE DETAILED ACCOUNT

[illegible]

LATE FROM CHATTANOOGA.

[illegible]

REPORTS FROM REBEL SOURCES

[illegible]

THE ARMY OF THE POTOMAC.

[illegible]

THE HEROES OF JULY.

A Solemn and Imposing Event.

Dedication of the National Cemetery at Gettysburgh.

IMMENSE NUMBERS OF VISITORS.

Oration by Hon. Edward Everett—Speeches of President Lincoln, Mr. Seward and Governor Seymour.

THE PROGRAMME SUCCESSFULLY CARRIED OUT

[illegible]

PRESIDENT LINCOLN'S ADDRESS

[illegible]

DEPARTMENT OF THE GULF.

ARRIVAL OF THE CREOLE FROM NEW-ORLEANS.

The Attack upon Gen. Washburn's Column.

Our Entire Loss Six Hundred and Seventy-seven.

[illegible]

THE DELAWARE ELECTION.

[illegible]

GREAT BRITAIN AND AMERICA.

Welcome to Rev. Henry Ward Beecher.

Demonstration at the Brooklyn Academy of Music.

A GREAT SPEECH.

His Impressions of British Feeling Toward America.

[illegible]

MR. BEECHER'S ADDRESS

[illegible]

Figure 33. Henry J. Raymond, Co-Founder of the *New York Times*, and Front Page of *Times*, November 20, 1863. Raymond became the paper's distinguished editor. He struck a middle ground between the *Sun* and *Herald* on the one hand and the *New York Tribune* on the other. Note the vertical one-column headlines and the numerous cross-lines, or decks. Columns five and six run solid.

of independence, the *Times* proved to be consistently Whig, but its editorials and news were not violently partisan. Space was given to other political parties, although with a bias.

Reform was in the air, and Raymond had to take a stand. Looking at the *Tribune* with its string of "isms," Raymond expressed himself with obvious sincerity:

> In political and social discussions, the Times will seek to be conservative, in such a way as to best promote REFORM. . . .

A cool and deliberate policy guided the *Times*. Raymond was admired by all for his moderation, impartiality and courtesy.

Raymond had been deeply influenced by the democratic and humanitarian trend in society. He wanted to alleviate the condition of the poor and spread education, all along conservative lines. He declared:

> We shall be CONSERVATIVE in all cases where we think CONSERVATISM necessary to the public good, and we shall be radical in everything which may seem to us to require radical treatment and radical reform. We do not believe that everything in society is either exactly right or exactly wrong; what is good we desire to preserve and improve; what is evil, to exterminate, to reform.

As he had promised, the *Times* had a wider coverage of news in many departments than its contemporaries. The column and a half of city news which developed rapidly is typical. The *Times* seized on various catastrophes, such as fires, panics and accidents, and reported them thoroughly, building them up as "big news," an innovation of which the ten-dollar papers had never dreamed.

Unlike the rapid news presentation to develop later, the *Times* story of a public school fire first recounted previous catastrophes and then described the structure of the destroyed school. Unusual for the era, the reporter listed the dead. The sharp division between news and editorials had not yet been completely achieved, for the story's last paragraph contained an exhortation by the editor to start an investigation of the "murder."

This function of the press, to urge officials to correct abuses, developed slowly. The *Evening Post* was something of a civic crusader for the upper classes; the *Tribune,* a labor crusader; and the *Times* was becoming a popular paper crusading for the betterment of New York City.

The newspaper was fittingly designed to assume the role of local crusader. It had its news fingers on everything that occurred. The first two decades in the life of the *Times* saw the paper develop from a passive news organ to a newspaper "exposing" facts and calling for "righting of wrongs" and "elimination of the causes" of catastrophes.

In connection with the accident at a public school, the *Times* printed an editorial urging authorities to provide better stairways and fire escapes. Railroad accidents were frequent occurrences in the early days, and *Times'* editorials asked: "Where Lies the Blame?" Reporters would answer: "Upon the directors because they did not provide sufficient protection for the passengers."

Reporters of the *Times* tackled crime news with similar zest, going behind the scenes to picture the incidents leading to the trial of the criminal. Aggressiveness of *Herald* reporters in getting into meetings where they were not welcome was duplicated by the news hawks of the *Times*.

While the *Times* did not exploit criminal news nor emphasize sex crimes, it reported criminal trials consistently. More significant was the *Times'* scientific approach to crime, showing a genuine concern for causes and punishment of crime, especially in regard to juveniles.

The *Times'* later interest in scientific advance dates back to its early days when conventions of the American Association for the Advancement of Science were reported at length. Though the editor had declared he would conduct his journal along "Christian Lines," his policy of presenting all the news led him to go far in the opposite direction. On September 22, 1860, the Jewish day of Atonement, he published on page one an entire column about the holy day, giving the meaning of the occasion, a list of synagogues and translations of some of the prayers.

Whether the *Times'* policy of publishing news impartially extended to political news is an open question. Some Tammany Hall news was given a twisted headline and the members' activities held up to ridicule. It was difficult for Whig politician Raymond to be impartial when reporting Democratic news.

While conservative in economics, Raymond was conscious of the poor and the unemployed. The paper carried a series of sketches on the miseries of poor children, a series that probably squeezed the hearts as well as the pocketbooks of the rich in New York. The paper was sympathetic toward the poor, but it had no patience with those who would alter the system of the American economy. The *Times* also pointed out the need for giving work to men instead of offering charity. When the unemployed gathered in the park, carried banners and demanded relief, the *Times* said on January 8, 1855:

RELIEF FOR THE POOR
The Unemployed
The Park Meeting

> It was the old story to be repeated—ignorant vituperation of capitalists, ill-timed and unmeaning cries of Land Reform and what not. All supported by purposed misquotation and powerful distortions of Scripture. . . .

Raymond kept his promise to present literary intelligence. In his first issue he ran a column called, "Snap Shots at Books, Talk, and Town," written in a witty, racy style. He also gave his readers serious reviews of books, but neither the *Times* nor the *Tribune* attempted to popularize these features as did later publishers.

Just as Raymond's news policy was a broad one, with the announced intention of being impartial, so his editorial page followed the same pattern. Editorials covering many interests were written with a clear, lucid pen, most of the editorials following a middle-of-the-road policy. The *Times* followed the policies of the Whigs; yet nowhere could be found a rabid expounding of the virtues of that political organization.

The *Times* grew steadily from its start. By November, 1851, it claimed sixteen thousand circulation; in January, 1855, it reached thirty-six thousand. Yet during the *Times'* first year, it had rough sledding in spite of its mounting circulation. The cost of getting started was high. At the end of the first year the *Times* price was raised from one to two cents, and the paper enlarged from four to eight pages. This price hike cut circulation one third; the editors, however, had more room for advertising and news, and they soon began to rebuild the circulation.

Within five years the paper was able to pay to stockholders $20,000 a year in dividends; *Times* stock rose from $1,000 to $1,666 a share, making the company worth $166,600. In 1858 the paper moved into its own building, its five stories rising to a dizzy height. The *Times'* structure was far superior to anything ever before built for the housing of a newspaper. The increased dividends, the improved value of the stock, the construction of a large building to house the *Times'* operations, all reflected the growing stability of the metropolitan daily newspaper and its growth as a large and profitable business enterprise.

OTHER POPULAR PAPERS ESTABLISHED

New York's Popular Press

Benjamin Day's New York *Sun* developed the right formula for cheap newspapers appealing to the larger public that standard-sized papers had not touched. In New York a number of cheap popular publications were launched between 1833 and 1859. Most of them failed. They reflected various political, economic and social currents of the day. Some had an impact on their era and died. Others continued publication.

Among the more important papers was the *Evening Transcript* started by Dr. Asa Green in 1834. It was a close imitation of the *Sun* in size and content, specializing in sex news and sporting events such as horse racing, prize fights and foot races. It changed to a morning paper as the *New York Transcript,* but even so, lasted only five years.

Reflecting the new movement for emancipation of women, William Newell established the *Ladies Morning Star* in 1836. Although Newell sought to improve the female mind, he aimed particularly to improve the physical, moral and pecuniary condition of women factory workers. Editorials with a dull, heavy flavor were written on sensational sex murders. After six months' struggle, the publisher found New York merchants did not include his newspaper in their advertising budgets. He finally failed. Newell's idea was sound, but he was ahead of his time. James Brooks founded in 1836 both the *Morning Express* and the *Evening Express,* the former continuing until after the Civil War. In 1855 the *New York Daily News* was launched as an organ of Tammany Hall and made headway among the poor.

Penny Papers Elsewhere

The cheap penny newspaper idea spread to other urban centers where population was growing and social and economic conditions were suitable. In Boston, in Philadelphia, in Baltimore and in New Orleans, where enterprising publishers successfully issued inexpensive sheets to appeal to large numbers of readers, such newspapers dealt death blows to conservative standard journals as they had done in New York.

New England Popular Papers

In 1836, three years after the New York *Sun* was born, Boston had its *Daily Times.* This was patterned closely after New York penny papers, publishing scandal news. Boston *Daily Times* reached a circulation of twelve thousand in four months.

Another inexpensive paper in Massachusetts was the *Springfield Republican;* however, this newspaper differed from other penny papers in being free from scandal. The *Republican* stressed news, especially local news, and sold for two cents a copy. On March 27, 1844, Samuel Bowles and his son, Samuel Bowles, Jr., brought out the first issue of the *Springfield Daily Evening Republican,* which grew out of a weekly which the elder Bowles had established twenty years before. By now

Springfield had grown to the point where a daily could be supported. The *Springfield Republican* was an example of the decentralizing tendencies in American journalism. Boston, New York, Philadelphia and Washington were centers of journalism during the first part of the century. Now other cities were growing, developing strong newspapers.

Philadelphia Penny Journalism

Also in 1836 Philadelphia saw the *Public Ledger* launched by three compositors of the *New York Sun,* William M. Swain, Arunah S. Abell and Azariah H. Simmons. Although they followed the same news policy as Day did in the New York *Sun,* their editorial policy was stronger. Russell Jarvis, an experienced newspaperman, who became editor of the *Public Ledger,* attacked the six-penny papers as being venal and corrupt, and he fought for the laboring classes. In eighteen months the *Public Ledger* reached twenty thousand readers.

Baltimore Sun Rises

One of the *Ledger*'s partners, Arunah S. Abell, saw newspaper possibilities in the fast-growing town of Baltimore, Maryland, a seaport, railroad and manufacturing center with thousands of workers. Baltimore had six dailies, but all appealed to the leading commercial and financial classes, and as elsewhere these papers were restricted in circulation.

Abell launched the Baltimore *Sun* on May 18, 1837, using the same pattern he had worked with both in New York and Philadelphia. Democratic in tone, the *Sun* advocated all measures which would contribute toward the well being of the workingman.

The *Sun* caught on. Within a year the paper had twelve thousand subscribers, which was more than triple the circulation of any other paper in the city. Abell cooperated with the *Picayune* publishers in New Orleans to establish a pony news-express service from that city, as railroads had not been constructed all the way.

Baltimore, by the time of the Civil War, attained a population of 212,000, doubling its figure of thirty years before. The *Sun*'s circulation tripled, reaching about thirty thousand. The *Sun* became a profitable publication.

New Orleans Picayune

The penny press pattern was carried into the Deep South by two eastern printers, Francis Asbury Lumsden and George Kendall. Recognizing that conditions in New Orleans were similar to those in New York, Philadelphia and Baltimore, they established the *New Orleans Picayune* in 1837.

TABLE 17

Influence of Popular Press on Journalism

1. Made Many News and Editorial Improvements

    Popular press broadened concept of news

        All kinds of criminal trials covered by popular press
        Political speeches covered more fully
        Annual church meetings and conventions reported regularly
        Social world covered
        Sports news covered more thoroughly
        Wall Street reported more fully, objectively
        Local or city news reported more fully
        Humorous events covered

    Penny papers condensed long-winded news

    Popular press "humanized" journalism

2. Advanced News Transmission Facilities

    Used pony express to relay news quickly

    Employed steamships to bring news across Atlantic, and used boats on U. S. rivers

    Used telegraph extensively when introduced

3. Made Typographic Improvements

    Developed single column headlines

    Used decks

    Used banks to tell the news

    Gave variety to front page

4. Developed Pictorial Journalism

    Made use of woodblocks more extensively to illustrate news

5. Strengthened Advertising Department

    Encouraged small advertisements, especially "classifieds"

    Changed advertising daily, made ads newsier, timelier

    Gave advertising impact and pulling power

6. Improved Distribution or Circulation Departments

    Instituted selling of individual copies on streets

7. Expanded Staffs and Added Specialized Personnel News, Editorial

    Hired city editor; managing editor emerged

TABLE 17 (continued)

Hired police reporter

Increased number of editorial writers

Added foreign correspondents

Hired Washington correspondents

Business

Developed business manager

Circulation

Added newsboys

Printing

Increased production staff

8. Achieved Greater Independence

    Free newspaper from political controls

    Drew revenue and support from subscriptions and advertising

9. Stimulated Improvement of Press Equipment

    Revolving cylinder press improved

    Faster press machinery developed

    Stereotyping process first used

10. Competitive Spirit Intensified

    Spurred competition in all news coverage

    Accented drive for circulation

11. Expanded Newspaper Readership

    Dropped prices to meet more readers' pocketbooks

    Gave more pages to readers; printed more appealing news (see above)

    Employed newspapers to sell copies in streets (see above)

    Increased readership by tens of thousands

12. Metropolitan Newspaper Became Large-Scale Business

    Newspaper became more profitable—increased circulation and subscription revenue

    Newspaper operated by stock company

    More funds needed to launch and operate city newspapers

TABLE 18

Influence of Popular Press on Public

1. Popular Penny Press Proved a Concomitant of Democracy
   a. Popular press developed with rise of common man
   b. Press was part of social movements of the time
      (1) Population growth, urban expansion
      (2) Political changes
      (3) Economic revolution
      (4) Education advancement
      (5) Dissatisfaction with old form of life

2. Penny Press Stimulated New Segments of the Public to Become Interested in Public Affairs
   a. Informed workingman about politics
      (1) Workingman given vote, needed to know news of government and political parties
   b. Advocated measures for worker and his wife
   c. Stirred vigorous interest in reform of all kinds
      (1) Penology
      (2) Diet
      (3) Liquor

3. New Ideas, Viewpoints Found Space in Some Penny Papers

4. Popular Press Stirred Emotions About Crime, Sex, Disaster

5. Popular Press Served as Critical Organs of Common Man
   a. Publisher freed from financial ties to parties
   b. Criticized economic and political systems

6. Popular Press Advocated City Improvements

7. Mass Press Served as Mass Advertising Media
   a. Stimulated sales of merchandise, services
   b. Served useful purpose in industrial economy—provided wide outlet for factory-made products

The *Picayune* was a four page newspaper with four columns on a page, measuring 10 by 13 1/2 inches. The paper sold for a picayune, or Spanish half reel, equivalent to six and a half cents. This seems higher than the price of eastern tabloids, but prices were higher in New Orleans than in New York. In format, in news content and in news-gathering aggressiveness, the *Picayune* reflected the new type journalism. The Lumsden and Kendall paper also carried on campaigns for the common man and for civic improvements. When yellow fever killed several thousand residents in 1852 and 1853, the paper advocated a Board of Health and use of quarantine to prevent repetition of the awful epidemic.

The new paper caught on and soon was pressing its five established competitors. The *Picayune*'s circulation mounted and within two years it had two thousand readers. The publisher saw possibilities in a weekly for outlying regions and launched one in 1838, the paper soon attaining ten thousand circulation.

Size of the *Picayune* expanded. Because of pressure of additional advertising and news, its over-all size was doubled by the time of the Civil War. It grew to seven columns, and published twelve pages, sometimes jumping to sixteen. Kendall and Lumsden moved to larger quarters. In 1850 they built a four-story building to house the *Picayune*'s operations, reflecting the prosperity of the penny papers.

Chapter 9

Standard Papers Change, Merge, Expire

Newborn popular papers shook conventional newspapers loose from their old traditions and forced them to modify their news, editorial and advertising policies. Well-established publications, however, did not fail immediately when threatened by new upstarts because standard journals satisfied and continued to satisfy economic, political and cultural needs of certain segments of the public. Some of these conservative dailies were edited by able newsmen and had strong financial moorings.

Traditional newspapers reflected the interests of merchants, manufacturers and professional people who continued to play a strong role in shaping the course of the nation. For a complete picture of American journalism, these newspapers and their contents should be considered.

POPULAR TABLOIDS HAVE MANY EFFECTS

The directory of six-cent newspapers published in New York at the beginning of the 1820s when the popular press introduced its new style of journalism included eight newspapers which were reduced to three within the next few decades.

What happened to them is typical of what occurred in other cities.

1. Some of these standard dailies weathered the storm, grew stronger because they adopted in modified form new journalistic methods.
2. Other publications without changing appreciably continued in business but retained a small circulation among upper-class readers.
3. Some conservative newspapers merged soon with older conservative papers and continued in a strong position into the twentieth century.
4. Several conservative newspapers merged with new, popular dailies.
5. Still other old standard dailies failed within a decade or two.

Thinking of the Democratic Party as attracting largely working men is fallacious; actually, it contained many diverse groups including big city merchants. Thus the *Sun* and *Herald* represented the working class element in the Democratic Party; the *Evening Post* and *Journal of Commerce* reflected upper-class economic, political and cultural groups in the Democratic Party.

Likewise, Whig readers could choose the *Tribune* and *Times* among penny newspapers; members of the Whig Party could turn also to the *Courier and Enquirer* in the six-cent class. Nearly all phases of American life were represented by the press since it was relatively inexpensive to issue a paper, especially in the 1830s and 1840s. The page size of the *Journal of Commerce* and other six-cent dailies grew larger and larger with the coming of the cylinder press. The *Journal of Commerce* reached 3 by 5 feet, with eleven wide columns on a page. The "blanket sheets" increased their size to show their respectability because the popular two-cent papers were small.

NEW YORK EVENING POST WEATHERS STORM

The *New York Evening Post*, an example of the older type of newspaper, proved its qualities during this period, continuing in the face of penny press competition. By 1833, when the *Sun* appeared, the *Post* had a well-established reputation and was ably edited by William Cullen Bryant who had forsaken poetry for journalism. The *Post*'s appeal was strictly to mercantile and professional classes.

Though local, its news coverage was scanty. The *Post* had a strong editorial page and followed the Democratic Party. The paper's income was about ten thousand dollars yearly, and it had a small editorial staff of three. Bryant, a reserved, scholarly man, did not go out and gather news as Bennett did. The *Post*'s circulation was between fifteen hundred and two thousand.

Bryant was not too concerned with the upstart popular press. His paper was earning a good income, and he had William Leggett as his able assistant. In 1834 Bryant decided to travel to Europe. He left William Leggett in charge. Then the *Post* began to reflect the new political and economic winds of the time.

Liberal Leggett in Charge

Although the *Post* had been Democratic, Leggett's views were sharper and his pen struck with greater force at old aristocratic traditions and institutions. *Equality* was his catchword, and he poured invective on all who opposed removing property restrictions on voting. The *Evening Post* attacked current inflation, gambling and unsound business. Opposing particularly the great speculation in real estate in western lands and in the vicinity of New York, Leggett was also spokesman and leader of those who wanted to reform the new industrialism. He became a prophet of the Loco-Focos, or workingman's wing of the Democratic Party of New York.

Leggett's views naturally brought on attacks from more conservative Democrats as well as merchants. Some were advertisers, and they began to boycott the old, established daily. The *Evening Post* was heading for financial bankruptcy. Net profits fell from about $10,000 to $5,671 in 1836, and to $3,242 the next year. Bryant returned from Europe to rebuild the lost confidence in the paper and to regain advertising which had drifted away.

Faced with competition of new penny papers, Bryant improved his city news coverage and his Washington and London correspondence. He increased his staff. The *Post* now reported as news, lectures by famous men. The editor hired a special reporter to write market news, following Bennett's footsteps in financial journalism.

Bryant, always civic minded, conducted many persistent editorial campaigns for city projects and improvements. New York had many parks but not a single large open-air recreation facility. The *Post* in 1844 began a twelve-year fight for establishment of Central Park. Violent opposition came from many real estate operators. But after legislative action and various court battles, victory was won by the paper in 1856.

Although the penny papers are credited too with campaigns for a larger, well-paid city police and paid fire departments, the *Post* argued consistently for these improvements also. The need for these improvements marked the transition of New York from a country town to a metropolis. The *Post* noted the corruption in city government and sought a change in the charter.

Persons desiring to know about new books turned to the *Post,* reflecting the growing interest in literature in America. Bryant campaigned for an international copyright.

With respect to national issues the *Post* remained in the Democratic column during the 1830s and 1840s.

Circulation of the paper reflected the hold Bryant had on his part of the public and the needs he satisfied. In the 1830s the *Post* had sixteen hundred readers. By the time the Civil War was under way the paper reached twenty thousand. Pressure of advertising forced the *Post* to enlarge its size several times.

Some idea of the growth of the *Post* as a business enterprise can be seen in these figures: In the 1830s the *Post*'s return to the owners was about $10,000 yearly; by 1860 it reached $68,000. Value of the *Post* as a business property jumped from about $50,000 to $300,000 during this period. This growth demonstrated that standard-size papers, too, could be profitable in the metropolis.

COURIER AND ENQUIRER PRODUCE OUTSTANDING MERGER

The *Courier and Enquirer* was one of the most vigorous of the six-cent dailies, and it too weathered the newspaper storm for a number of years. Published by the fiery James Watson Webb, the *Courier and Enquirer* was a flag-waver for the Democratic Party and upheld Jackson in his fight with the Bank of the United States. But Webb had borrowed more than $52,000 from the bank.

Under the thumb of the Bank of the United States Webb shifted his allegiance and eventually became spokesman for the Whig Party. He had led the way in securing political, commercial and foreign news quickly, and he sought to keep up with the penny papers. Recognizing that they were a threat, particularly Bennett's *Herald,* Webb attempted to crush the new publications. He beat Bennett with his walking stick and carried on the moral war against that publisher.

The *Courier and Enquirer* eventually lost its hold. In 1861 it was merged with the *World* and lost its identity in this new religious and moral paper which had been established as an inexpensive paper the year before. Alexander Cummings, a Philadelphia newsman, the first editor, was backed by businessmen who contributed $200,000 to found the *World* as a religious and highly moral paper. The New York public, however, was not yet ready for a popular, religious daily.

The *World* was soon sold to a group of Democratic financiers and politicians, who included August Belmont, banker, and Fernando Wood, mayor. They chose as the new editor, Manton Marble, who steered the paper into the Democratic column, condemning Lincoln.

Chapter 10

Beginnings of Press Associations

HALE TAKES INITIATIVE

David Hale, publisher of the *New York Journal of Commerce,* watched the *New York Herald's* expensive activities in reporting the Mexican War in 1847. Hale realized the time had come to end cut-throat competition in which New York papers had so long indulged. He was convinced that no one paper could continue indefinitely to meet the multiplying problems of individual news collection. The Harbor Association of the New York press had succeeded for a time but had broken up. Cost of pigeon expresses, pony expresses, newsboat systems and telegraph increased operating costs. There had to be a solution. Cooperative effort to gather and transmit news was badly needed in 1847.

Hale put on his tall hat, left the *Journal of Commerce* office and soon knocked on the door of the Herald building at Nassau and Fulton streets. Hale proposed that he and Bennett pool resources to cover the Mexican war and other big news of the day. Bennett, a Scotsman, saw advantages in this economic arrangement and accepted the plan.

FIRST MEETING HELD

A few months later, in May, 1848, ten men representing the six most important New York newspapers, sat at a table in the *New York Sun* office. The meeting was the outcome of Hale's efforts to bring competing publishers together.

Bennett was there with his assistant, Frederic Hudson, for the *Herald;* James Watson Webb attended with his managing editor, Henry J. Raymond, of the *Courier and Enquirer.* Representing the *Journal of*

Commerce were Gerard Hallock and Hale. Horace Greeley of the *New York Tribune;* Moses Y. Beach, publisher of the *Sun;* and Eustace and James Brooks of the *Express,* completed the ten.

Hale knew how difficult it was to persuade publishers to forget their hostility to each other. He talked of problems they all faced and offered a proposal to establish an organization to gather and distribute news. He indicated that the present method of getting telegraph news was inefficient and costly. Telegraph companies were stealing news before transmission and selling to anyone who could pay. Hale also mentioned that telegraph officials were considering even setting up their own news-distribution agencies because they owned the wire facilities. They would become competitors of the press.

After listening to arguments and proposals Raymond called aside Webb, his employer, convincing him of the wisdom of the proposal. All the publishers realized the dangers ahead, and they recognized, if vaguely, the benefits of a news organization to them. They decided to organize the Associated Press of New York. The publishers, let it be said, thought only of benefiting themselves; they did not look on collection and transmission of news as a great public service. It was a good business arrangement. The idea of a cooperative service for all papers in the United States came later.

The Associated Press now elected Hale as the first president. The office of general agent was created, to be filled later. A committee, consisting of Hudson, of the *Herald,* and Raymond, of the *Courier and Enquirer,* were to make arrangements for collecting and distributing news. They arranged to get news from Boston in uninterrupted transmission over telegraph wires. Soon the Philadelphia *Public Ledger* and the Baltimore *Sun* also began to receive dispatches. Although they were not members of the association they were its first paying clients.

APPOINTS GENERAL AGENT

The Associated Press appointed as its first general agent, Dr. Alexander Jones, graduate in medicine, whose early interest in writing led him into journalism. The agent's salary was twenty dollars a week, and the entire cost of operations for the first year was between ten thousand and twenty thousand dollars. Dr. Jones opened an office at the top of a long, dim flight of stairs at the Northwest corner of Broadway and Liberty streets, which served as the AP headquarters in New York for more than two decades.

At first the entire New York staff consisted of Jones and one assistant; later, a second was added. Jones was kept busy engaging correspondents, or agents to obtain and telegraph news to New York. Sufficient copies of each incoming dispatch to the New York office were made on tissue paper and sent to the list of subscribers.

Associated Press correspondents covered the gold rush in California and a women's rights convention in Rochester which was demanding equal suffrage. The wires told of President Polk's offer to buy Cuba for one hundred million dollars. Foreign news was the biggest item in the AP budget. Jones worked day and night. Often on stormy nights in winter, when his errand boys were ill or absent in Jersey City, still the New York terminus of the telegraph lines, Jones went out at midnight and later to deliver news messages with a snow or sleet storm beating in his face. He had to climb three flights of stairs to reach the composing rooms of some of the newspapers.

A month after the organizational meeting, President Hale had a stroke and died. Dr. Jones lost a strong supporter. In May, 1851, the strain of the news work began to tell; Dr. Jones resigned. The Associated Press then promoted Daniel Craig, its foreign correspondent at Halifax, Nova Scotia, to the job of general agent.

CRAIG NEW GENERAL AGENT

Craig had been in the news-gathering business before being hired as AP correspondent. The AP had exerted every ounce of energy and initiative to beat him, but couldn't. So the association hired him as its first regular correspondent on foreign soil. He operated out of Halifax because that had been the first stopping place of the new Cunard steamers which replaced sailboats. By boarding the craft there, Craig obtained the news and rushed it to Boston and New York, first by pigeon post and by pony express, and then by telegraph as the lines expanded north. He sent the AP's first all-wire message of European news in November, 1849. Craig advocated the first AP controlled wire from New York to Boston, to St. John, to Halifax, so news could be sent quickly and without interruption.

Craig was a stickler for correctness and insisted that his men carry out this policy. He knew it was a general practice for a reporter in one city to telegraph a few lines about the main facts of an event, leaving it to an imaginative editor on the receiving end to "blow up" the story into several hundred words. The editor would fit in any details he imagined. Craig issued orders that if a story was important enough to warrant details, the details were worth the wire costs.

Craig also instituted other procedures which streamlined the organization. In 1856 the AP was formally reorganized. It was emphasized that the AP was a union of seven New York morning papers, and the news collected was designed to meet their needs. Desires of subscriber papers outside the city were not considered.

WASHINGTON BUREAU OPENED

The first Washington Bureau, or agency as it was called, was established, with Lawrence Augustus Gobright, who had been reporting for the Associated Press since 1848, in charge. A second AP bureau was established in Albany, New York, the capital.

Meanwhile the number of subscriber papers increased, as urban areas in the South and West expanded and their papers grew stronger. Payments from these outside sources supplied funds for AP expansion. The income, too, enabled the seven New York papers to receive a steadily larger report at a fraction of the expense that would have been necessary had the news organization in New York paid the entire bill.

REGIONAL GROUPS ORGANIZED

Gradually subscriber papers outside New York began to form loosely knit geographical groups. Their news was distributed to them on a regional basis, and by combining, these papers could deal better with New York AP officials. Thus the Philadelphia Associated Press, the New York State Associated Press, the Southern Associated Press and the Western Associated Press began.

The western group was particularly strong and vocal. Some of the publishers believed they were paying heavy charges for whatever the New York managers desired "to dole out" to them. A committee of the western publishers went to New York in 1863 and wrung some concessions. They succeeded in getting a special news agent in the New York office, and the AP, composed largely of morning dailies, agreed to send an extra dispatch to afternoon papers and a one thousand word message to be put on the wire after 10 P.M. The western publishers were satisfied temporarily.

Chapter 11

Dixieland's Newspapers

PRESS REFLECTS SOUTHERN PATTERN

Newspapers in Dixieland took on the distinct character of the southern pattern of living. While the North developed large cities and turned more and more to industry and manufacturing, the South clung to its farms and plantations. Agriculture was its chief means of livelihood, and southern towns, with few exceptions, continued to be small agricultural marketplaces. The South depended increasingly on the more than three million slaves to till and harvest crops.

Although the total number of all kinds of newspapers south of Pennsylvania grew, fewer newspapers were published, and their circulations were less than in northern towns and cities. This was especially true of dailies. Some southern states, such as North Carolina, did not get dailies until the 1850s, while Arkansas and Florida publishers did not attempt this type of publication until after the Civil War. Virginia in this period led with fifteen dailies, being followed by Georgia which had twelve, and by Tennessee where eight were issued.

Although the South's population grew steadily it was diffused over thousands of square miles, for the people lived on farms. Concentration was on staples: cotton, tobacco, rice, sugar and hemp. The sparse industrial efforts were largely associated with agriculture and lumbering. Most of the great banks, with facilities for money and credit, were centered in the North but had to be used by southerners.

In spite of population growth, therefore, relatively less money was available than in the North for such purchases as newspaper subscriptions. Fewer stores were found in southern rural communities and small towns, and fewer were able to place advertising, hence contribute to the prosperity of the papers.

In the North a new and large reading public had been found in lower-income groups. In the South plantation owners at the top of the social hierarchy furnished a potential readership, but their numbers were small in spite of the fact that their intellectual interests and economic and political views set the southern pattern.

Below the planting group, but closely allied to it, were the professional class and middle class farmers, both groups owning only a few slaves. At the bottom of the economic and social scale were the Negro slaves. About three and one-half million of these slaves, nearly one-third of the total population, worked on plantations and farms. The Negroes there had little or no buying power. Thus, the newspaper market was restricted to plantation owners and to professional and middle classes, a comparative minority.

Lack of education also adversely affected circulation of newspapers. Prior to 1850 university and college training was limited to children of planters who had means to educate their children in private institutions, or who had tutors and then sent the children to northern schools. Free public-supported high schools were unknown except in Baltimore and New Orleans. Even free elementary education came to the South belatedly, with South Carolina making the first effort in 1811.

The South had half of the one million illiterate whites in the country, and practically the entire slave population was illiterate; thus four times as many illiterates resided in the southern region as in the rest of the United States.

Southern roads were generally crude and primitive. Railroads were slow in coming. The South depended on its many rivers and the sea for much of its transportation needs. Wagons hauled produce to the nearest river or seaport where it was reloaded on larger vessels bound for northern and European ports. The method was slow.

Railroads and the telegraph came eventually, but the initial service of both was poor. By 1860, however, the telegraph followed every railroad in the South and brought practically every locality into communication with the outside world. Operation of daily newspapers was aided somewhat by these facilities.

As the Whig Party superseded the Federalist, some old conservative newspapers shifted to this new group, and other new Whig papers were established. The Whig press was largely found in seaports along the coast, but other party publications were found inland along the fall line. As the population moved westward and as frontier democracy expressed itself, the press in these communities advocated Jacksonianism. They desired improved inland transportation and help from the federal government so that they could get their produce to market more easily. Many Whig papers remained to oppose secession.

LEADING SOUTHERN NEWSPAPERS

Each large town and city developed its own journal. Size and influence of the individual newspapers depended on the population and economic growth of the towns and the vigor of their editor.

Richmond Enquirer

South of Baltimore the best-known paper was the *Richmond* (Virginia) *Enquirer.* Thomas Ritchie, who became its editor in 1804, gave it both fame and notoriety during the forty years he remained in charge. A strong states' rights Democratic journal, the *Enquirer,* under Ritchie's direction, came to be called the Democratic Bible. The *Enquirer* claimed the largest circulation of the southern newspapers and was one of the few southern papers circulated beyond the home community. Historians believe that the *Enquirer*'s influence on political development of the South was widespread. Ritchie was known for his vituperation, and even Andrew Jackson, who belonged to the same party, called him the "greatest scoundrel in America." Horace Greeley, a northern opponent, characterized him as the "Talleyrand of the Press."

With rise of the Whig Party in Virginia, Richmond, like other towns, saw establishment of a strong paper representing that conservative political group which absorbed the old Federalists. The *Richmond Whig* was established in 1824 and ably edited by John Hampden Pleasants, who originally had started a Whig paper in Lynchburg, Virginia. Ritchie and Pleasants, editors of opposite political faiths, fought each other for twenty years with every verbal weapon they could command. The war remained in the verbal stage until Ritchie was called to Washington to edit the *Union.* Then his son, more impetuous than the elder Ritchie, wrote some bitter articles which led to a challenge from Pleasants. In the fight which followed, Pleasants was so badly wounded that he died a few days later.

South Carolina Press Pattern

A similar newspaper pattern developed in Charleston, a busy southern economic, cultural and social metropolis of 18,033 people. Charleston was the intellectual capital of the slavery belt, which extended to Texas. The proportion of slaves to whites was greatest in this region, and the plantation system most profitable. Charleston became headquarters for southern militarists and "free editors." At the same time, other conservative business elements had close connections with the North and urged a moderate course of action.

Charleston developed two outstanding newspapers. Fiery Robert Barnwell Rhett edited the *Charleston Mercury,* the states' rights paper in the Deep South. It was a fire-eating nullification journal whose chief purpose was to "fire the Southern heart" and "to nerve Southerners to rid themselves of their subserviency to the North."

Under Rhett's guidance, the *Mercury,* reflecting views of southern plantation owners, became one of the earlier leading spokesmen for nullification of federal laws and later an advocate of secession. Rhett believed strongly that South Carolina should get out of the Union for the North was growing more powerful economically and politically. He and the *Mercury* were to the South what William Lloyd Garrison and the *Liberator,* the abolitionist sheet, represented to the North. Like Garrison, Rhett was ignored at first because he was too extreme, and southerners did not look on northern states with such fierce enmity. As the positions consolidated and as the abolitionists stirred hatred, South Carolinians turned to Rhett and the *Mercury.* He was sent to the United States Senate in 1851, succeeding John C. Calhoun. Rhett did not believe the North would fight and thought the South could get out of the Union without bloodshed.

The *Mercury* was opposed even in Charleston by the *Charleston Courier,* a conservative and moderate Whig paper. Lorring Andrews, Aaron Smith Wellington of Massachusetts and Stephen Cullen Carpenter of Ireland, who had become a London newsman, established the *Charleston Courier* on January 10, 1803.

The proprietors were strong Federalists, so the *Courier* followed the Federalist standard for many years. After his partners left for the North, in 1813, Wellington became sole owner. He continued publication for twenty years, when Richard Yeadon and William S. King joined him as co-partners and editors.

The *Courier* exemplified Wellington's concept of what a newspaper should be, a commercial enterprise, presenting the news fully, accurately and impartially, letting its readers form their own judgments and opinions. In the middle and late 1850s the *Courier* was wholly committed to this ideal.

Its huge pages were devoted primarily to those statistics of commerce, shipping and markets which the business community required. The *Courier* carried a considerable volume of advertising. As many other papers, the *Courier* neglected local news. It was not until 1857 that a local reporter was hired. Before that time the *Courier* obtained its local news from the *Times.* With the *New York Sun* the *Courier* developed the pony express, bringing news from Mexico during the Mexican War.

King, one of the partners, became proprietor in 1833 and assumed direction of the editorial policy after Yeadon left.

Louisville, Kentucky Newspapers

Ranking with the southern leaders were three Louisville, Kentucky papers, each giving various shades of opinions on the slavery issue. George D. Prentice, originally a Connecticut man, made the *Louisville Journal* an outstanding Whig newspaper in growing Louisville, a tobacco center on the Ohio River. Prentice specialized in ridicule, and his most effective weapon was the short, pungent paragraph, each word biting and vitriolic. He became a staunch Union man.

The *Louisville Courier,* the Democratic states' rights organ, was well edited by Walter N. Haldeman, one of the most vindictive of the secessionists. Since the large majority of the 40,501 residents in town were pro-Union, Prentice, with his *Journal,* had a larger audience. Union Democrats were represented by the *Democrat,* which opposed secession.

Tennessee Journalism

In Tennessee the *Knoxville Whig* was one of the outstanding papers. It was edited by William Brownlow, who, in addition to his editorial duties, filled a Methodist pulpit and was both nationalistic and antislavery. The *Whig* was edited in a section which had Union sympathizers but which also had many advocates of the South who became exasperated at Parson Brownlow.

In the Gulf States, commercial centers such as Montgomery and Mobile, Alabama produced strong newspapers. In the latter city the *Advertiser* divided the field with the *Register.* Two penny newspapers were also started.

New Orleans Journalism

Outside of Baltimore, New Orleans was the largest southern seaport. The city was an entry port for the entire Mississippi Valley; four hundred fifty steamboats and four thousand flatboats docked there yearly. By 1860 New Orleans had a railroad penetrating into Ohio. With this commercial background, the city's population reached one hundred twenty thousand. Here the *Picayune,* mentioned before as the first penny press in the South, became the outstanding paper.

Chapter 12

North Central States' Journalism Expands

While the penny press was revolutionizing journalism in large cities of the eastern seaboard, and southern newspapers struggled to gain a foothold, newspapers were also developing in the valleys of the Ohio and Mississippi, in the Southwest, in the Mountain States, and in the Far West.

The role of the press in this mighty westward expansion was significant. Weeklies, and later the dailies, reflected the regional interests of their readers and advocated economic and political measures of benefit to them. The press brought settlers news of other sections and the outside world. As each area grew strong economically and politically, so did its journalism, playing a greater role in shaping the destiny of the country.

SOCIAL AND ECONOMIC DEVELOPMENT

During this period population in the Mississippi Valley region multiplied enormously, representing about a third of the nation's population. The great prairie states and the land westward to the crest of the Rockies, however, were more sparsely settled Indian Territory. A thin layer of pioneers also lived along the Pacific Coast from Washington to California. Yet by the time of the Civil War continental territorial expansion was completed, with the population filling in from Canada to Mexico and extending from the Mississippi River to the Pacific Ocean.

Agriculture was the mainstay of the Mississippi Valley region with production of wheat, corn, hogs and cattle the chief source of income. Canals and rivers were used to transport products to the East. Railroads soon became an important transportation link east of the Mississippi.

A distinct democratic viewpoint characterized settlers in this new western territory. They did not have the traditions of the East to hamper them. The rigid hierarchy of social and economic classes was not present. Economic opportunities on farms and growing cities beckoned, and a man could rise if he had the ability, energy and vision. Schools were soon available and colleges were established by the states. Politically the West was Democratic in this period. It wanted internal improvements, such as canals and roads built, furnishing farmers with access to eastern markets.

The West exerted a growing influence on national affairs because, as territories entered the Union and population grew, states were created. These new states sent representatives to the United States Senate and the House of Representatives; the western congressmen began to exert a strong influence on legislation. The western vote in presidential elections, too, became important. The West helped elect Andrew Jackson to presidency in 1828. Close ties between the agricultural Northwest and the manufacturing Northeast were effected.

PRINTERS FACE OBSTACLES

From this town and regional population expansion and economic development, newspapers grew and multiplied. The frontier printer-editor-publishers of these four page sheets had the same tough experiences as frontier farmers, ranchers and miners. Wherever a prairie corntown, a cowtown or a mining camp arose, there was a job-and-newspaper printshop. Inside the shop was a printer-editor from the East, writing his news, setting it in type and printing the paper on the old handpress. Often the editor had to sit with his rifle across his knee while he wrote his hell-fire editorials blasting the rustlers.

In addition to local items, editors printed, as quickly as they could, important news from Washington and big eastern centers. Publishers with sufficient funds employed pony expresses and later used the telegraph. The little gazettes also published whatever advertisements came their way.

These papers, naturally enough, were not as strong as those in eastern metropolitan centers. Frontier publishers had neither large numbers of subscribers nor many advertisers to support the weeklies. The publishers had small staffs for some time. New York newspapers sent California editions to the West Coast to supply news-hungry westerners with more complete news. Greeley's weekly *Tribune* had a large following in the Midwest.

After the population began to fill in the open areas, and farming or ranching began, weeklies were issued. As the population grew and as the economic development of the region continued and accelerated, publishers launched dailies, bold undertakings which showed courage and daring.

OHIO JOURNALISM

Ohio, Indiana, Michigan and Illinois made some of the greatest gains in population and economic development in this era. Of these areas, Ohio, at midcentury, had the largest number of newspapers and the greatest total circulation. Located just beyond the Alleghenies, Ohio was the first place of settlement for pioneers who left the seaboard. The Ohio River was one of the main water arteries to the West and Southwest.

Cincinnati's Strong Papers

Because of its strategic position on the Ohio River, Cincinnati became the commercial and journalistic center of the territory. When steamboats came Cincinnati prospered because of the immense freight and passenger traffic. The Queen City began to manufacture steamboats, with more than a third of the boats built on western waters constructed in Cincinnati. The town also became a market for agricultural products of the region. Flour mills were built, and Cincinnati was called Porkopolis because of the great number of hogs butchered there. Population reached twenty-four thousand in 1830, but multiplied more than sixfold in the next three decades, when 161,000 residents lived in the city.

One of the older dailies, the *Cincinnati Gazette*, established in 1815 as a weekly then transformed into a daily in 1827, continued to flourish and to lead. Its distinguished Whig editor, Charles Hammond, directed the paper until 1840.

Another of the city's outstanding newspapers was the *Cincinnati Commercial*, edited by Murat Halstead. When he entered Farmers' College near Cincinnati he was drawn to newspaper writing, becoming a correspondent for several papers. After Halstead was graduated from the college, he abandoned law, his first choice in a profession, for journalism. By March, 1853, Halstead was working on the *Cincinnati Commercial*, founded ten years before. Soon he was able to purchase a sixth interest in the paper, and later, when the publisher died, Halstead succeeded him. The *Cincinnati Commercial* gained considerable influence before the opening of the Civil War, exceeding the *Cincinnati Gazette*'s circulation. After the war began Halstead traveled to the front where he reported the conflict firsthand.

John and Charles H. Brough saw possibilities in the afternoon newspaper field and in 1841 launched the *Cincinnati Enquirer*. The time was not ripe for an afternoon paper so they shifted to a morning edition two years later. A succession of owners published the *Enquirer,* but a new regime began in 1852 when James J. Faran and Washington McLean bought the daily. Faran had been mayor of Cincinnati, and McLean was interested in steamboat building among other enterprises. Newspaper business offered some economic possibilities to these men. The two enterprising owners gathered a staff of newspaper workers of unusual ability. The partners also developed, on the side, a successful commercial printing business.

Calvin W. Starbuck also recognized the value of an afternoon newspaper in Cincinnati and issued the *Cincinnati Daily Times* in 1840. He made a fortune by publication of this daily and its weekly edition.

Toledo's Blade

The *Toledo Blade,* established as a weekly in 1838, was transformed into a daily and became known for its humorous and satirical writer, David R. Locke, known as "Petroleum V. Nasby." Locke learned the printer's trade in the office of the *Courtland* (New York) *Democrat.* Becoming a traveling journeyman, he visited and worked in several cities, gaining experience which helped him later. On his way to Ohio he stopped in Pittsburgh where he was employed by the *Chronicle.* He then moved on to various papers in Ohio, establishing with a partner, the *Plymouth* (Ohio) *Advertiser* in the early 1850s. In Findlay, Ohio he began for the *Jeffersonian* a series of articles written under the pseudonym of "Petroleum Vesuvius Nasby," a caricature of a whiskey-drinking, illiterate crook who denounced the perpetuation of slavery. The letters leaped into popularity and were printed widely. President Lincoln read the Nasby articles, saying that for the genius who wrote them he would gladly give up his office. The *Blade* won a readership far beyond the town in which it was published.

CHICAGO'S BUSTLING NEWSPAPERS

Chicago was the core city of the Mississippi Valley, a halfway point between East and West. Underpinning the economic foundation of Chicago was its grain trade. The city became the greatest corn market in the country in 1851 and the greatest wheat center by 1854. Closeness to source of supplies combined with peerless transportation facilities assured Chicago of leadership in the grain business.

The network of railroads carrying the grain included the Chicago and North Western and the Chicago, Burlington & Quincy. In spite of rival towns such as Milwaukee and Minneapolis, Chicago continued to lead as the grain center, tapping the lush lands of the North Central States. Chicago also drew on timberlands of the Lake States, which lay close at hand, building up an important source of wealth: lumber. From about 3,000 persons in 1830, the city's population reached 109,000 during the Civil War.

As Chicago emerged into national prominence during and after the Civil War, so did its newspapers. Beginning to rival New York journals, Chicago dailies exerted particularly strong influence in the Midwest. With its expanding commerce and growing population, Chicago, which supported a half-dozen dailies, some of which grew particularly strong, gained regional and even national influence.

Chicago Democrat

After John Calhoun, a 25-year-old printer and editor in Oswego, New York, heard about the economic and journalistic possibilities in Chicago, he closed his own newspaper and hauled his press and type to Chicago. In a single frame house, at what is now Clark and Wacker drive, Calhoun issued the weekly *Democrat,* named because the publisher-editor was a Jacksonian. The *Democrat*'s first issue, dated November 26, 1833, had six columns on each side of its four pages. Calhoun's early difficulties can be seen when it is observed that at the end of the first year he had seven hundred subscribers who paid $12.50 a year or bought single copies at 12 1/2 cents a copy. Calhoun had four hundred fifty of his subscribers living outside Chicago. He delivered the *Democrat* to them by horseback and stagecoach, but his Illinois subscribers were happy to get the papers even though they were late. With no telegraph to bring news to his office, Calhoun filled the empty spaces with poetry and reprinted essays.

Calhoun had selected a growing community, suitable for journalistic enterprise. Within two years Thomas O. Davis also saw possibilities in a weekly which would follow the banner of Henry Clay and the new Whig Party, opposing the Democrats. Davis therefore launched the *American* in 1835. The weekly changed owners, but in 1839 the proprietors believed Chicago could support a daily, and the *American*'s frequency was stepped up, thus making it the first daily in town.

Meanwhile, Calhoun, publisher-editor of the *Democrat,* became ill and put his weekly up for sale. The paper now entered a new phase of its history. Horatio Hill, formerly of New Hampshire, purchased the *Democrat* for $2,800 as a downpayment, and appointed as editor John Wentworth, recently arrived from New Hampshire. When Hill could not raise enough money to complete his payment for the *Democrat,* Wentworth borrowed the money from Ebenezer Peck, Democrat Party leader. Wentworth profited by his political associations and became official printer for the city, publishing tax bills and notices of letters awaiting citizens in the post office. Realizing the value of a daily and seeing the need to meet the opposition of the *American,* Wentworth turned his *Democrat* into a daily in 1840. Not satisfied with being an editor under political domination, Wentworth sought to pay off his debt and did so by the time he transformed his paper into a daily edition.

Wentworth became a close friend of Stephen Douglas, legislator, Illinois Supreme Court Justice and later a member of the United States House of Representatives and then senator. When Douglas introduced his Kansas-Nebraska Bill in 1854, Wentworth disowned him, as Wentworth did not agree with Douglas' solution to the slavery issue in the new territory. Looking for consistent newspaper support, Senator Douglas founded the *Chicago Times.*

Chicago Tribune, Vigorous Republican Voice

The Chicago Daily Tribune, destined to become a dominating force in midwestern American journalism, was established on June 10, 1847, by three businessmen, James Kelly, a leather merchant; John E. Wheeler, former New York newspaperman; and Joseph K. C. Forrest, a newsman who had worked on other Chicago papers. These enterpreneurs previously established the *Gem of the Prairie* and expected the *Tribune* would be used to feed news into the *Gem.* The *Chicago Tribune* changed hands several times between its founding and 1855 when two forceful men purchased a majority interest. After Joseph Medill and Charles H. Ray took over management, the *Tribune* got a new charge of energy and able operators who led the paper to the top. Somehow they expressed the vigor and enterprise and the political outlook of the midwest.

Medill had newspaper experience in the East before arriving in Chicago. His father had settled on a farm near New Brunswick, Canada. When the Medill family moved to Stark County, Ohio, Joseph helped on the farm. The boy devoured books, especially history, biography and travel. His early interest in journalism began when he sold subscriptions to Greeley's weekly *Tribune.*

At 21, Joseph studied law in Canton, Ohio, and after passing the bar practiced in New Philadelphia, Ohio. Attracted to journalism again, he spent his spare time at the local newspaper office. There lawyers, politicians and teachers gathered to talk about their favorite subject: politics. Joseph even set type and operated the handpress. Journalism had caught him with its peculiar fascination.

After publishing the *Coshocton* (Ohio) *Whig* and the *Cleveland Daily Forest City,* which became the *Cleveland Leader,* Medill concluded that Chicago offered better journalistic opportunities for him. Chicago had eighty-five thousand residents by this time. Through Horace Greeley, Medill learned that Charles H. Ray, editor of the *Jeffersonian* in Galena, Illinois, was considering publication of a Chicago paper.

Ray had been a doctor, but the practice of medicine did not appeal to him as strongly as journalism did. In addition to being editor of the *Jeffersonian,* Ray was a correspondent for Greeley's *Tribune.* Ray wrote to the New York editor, asking advice about establishing a paper in the West. Greeley suggested that Ray begin a penny paper in Chicago, one that would appeal to the workingman and to the large number of Irish and Germans pouring into that city.

After corresponding with Medill, Ray met him in Chicago. It was an historic moment. The two were ideal partners. Medill was a business and editorial genius; Ray, an ardent reformer. Both were skilled newsmen. Instead of establishing a newspaper, they decided to buy the *Chicago Tribune.* The eight years the paper had been in existence were but a prelude to what it was to become. The *Tribune* helped to shape American history and by 1859 was surpassed in influence only by Greeley's *New York Tribune.*

The *Chicago Tribune* soon completely dominated its region. The two partners lacked money for an outright purchase of the *Chicago Tribune.* Medill bought one-third interest; Ray purchased one-fourth. The remainder was still owned by previous publishers. Ray became editor-in-chief; Medill, managing editor. Alfred Cowles, who had worked for Medill in Cleveland, was brought in as cashier.

The partners found the *Tribune* to be a temperance organ, opposed to liquor. The paper also followed the Know-Nothing Party line and objected to Roman Catholic immigrants. Ray and Medill proceeded to change slowly the paper's policies. For a time, however, they supported the party's nominees and candidates, which led to trouble. The editors backed Dr. Levi D. Boone for mayor. After winning, he proceeded to close beer gardens and saloons on Sunday. The *Tribune* also supported a state prohibition law, but this was defeated. An angry mob descended on the *Tribune* office, but no damage was done.

Medill eventually cut down on temperance and anti-immigrant emphasis while increasing coverage of the struggle against slavery. He hired James Redpath as correspondent and sent him to Kansas to report warfare between Free Soilers and slaveholders. Medill went to Washington to report congressional debates on the slavery issue.

In 1857 Chicago faced a depression, and the *Tribune* was in weak financial shape. The *Tribune* merged with the *Press* in 1860, a fortunate move. The consolidation added two excellent newsmen to the paper's staff: John Locke Scripps, lawyer, teacher and trenchant writer, and William Bross, New England school teacher, alderman and later lieutenant governor of Illinois.

The *Tribune* and its editors played an important role in formation of the Republican Party. Ray attended the convention in Bloomington in May, 1856 when the party was created. Ray convinced Abraham Lincoln that he should be the Republican candidate to oppose Senator Douglas in 1858 when he was to run for reelection as senator on the Democratic ticket. Meanwhile publisher Wentworth of the *Democrat,* as mayor of Chicago, tried to get votes for himself as party nominee for the Senate. He failed. Wentworth now supported Lincoln. Lincoln thus had the support in Chicago of the *Tribune,* the *Democrat,* the *Press* and the old Whig organs, the *Journal* and the *American.*

Later Medill in Washington sent correspondence about Lincoln to the *Tribune* and wrote editorials favoring him. All this contributed to bringing Lincoln before the public. Medill was able to secure Chicago as the site for the Republican convention of 1860.

During the Civil War the *Tribune* pressed forward as journalistic and political leader in the region. From 1861 to 1865 Medill and his *Tribune* preached the Union and emancipation with an increasingly powerful voice. Lincoln found that Medill was a strong supporter, but heaven help the president if he opposed the *Tribune*'s wishes! In 1862 the *Tribune* helped form the Western Associated Press and demanded and obtained better service from the Associated Press of New York.

Following a dispute between Ray and Medill over General John C. Fremont's critical defeats in the Civil War, Ray resigned and Medill became editor-in-chief of the *Tribune.* Circulation of the paper jumped from eighteen to forty thousand during the war years.

McCormick Buys Times

When Senator Douglas decided to sell the *Chicago Times,* he found a purchaser in Cyrus H. McCormick, inventor of the reaper and head of a large company manufacturing this farm implement. A former Virginian, McCormick was pro-South in his political and economic views. He thought some kind of compromise would head off the Civil War.

Storey New Times Owner

When the war broke out McCormick sold the *Chicago Times* to Wilbur F. Storey, more recently publisher of the *Detroit Free Press* and a pro-southern sympathizer. His earlier history will be told more fully in the Detroit section.

With $30,000 he received for his Detroit publication, Storey invested $17,000 in the *Chicago Times,* leaving $13,000 for operating expenses. His general philosophy was "to print the news and raise hell." For twenty-three years he practiced what he preached. He sought to give full coverage to war news, telling his correspondents, "Telegraph fully all the news, and when there is no news, send rumors."

Because Storey was strongly pro-South, northern generals prohibited circulation of the *Chicago Times* in their camps. During the Civil War Storey added Franc B. Wilkie, correspondent for the *New York Times,* as his assistant, and hired two war correspondents.

When Lincoln issued the Emancipation Proclamation, the *Chicago Times* abandoned the lip service the daily had given to the Union. Storey thundered that the war aim had been perverted. He went all out in his attack on Lincoln. In its account of the Gettysburg speech, the *Times* stated, "The cheek of every American must tingle with shame as he reads the silly, false and dishwatery utterances of the man who has been pointed out to intelligent foreigners as the President of the United States."

DETROIT'S JOURNALISM

Detroit had a slow but steady growth. Situated on the Detroit River which connects Lake St. Clair with Lake Erie, Detroit started as a lakeport and tapped the vast lake region consisting of thousnds of miles of rich land and forest. Detroiters dealt in grain, lumber, meat, fish, flour and skins, and the city became the greatest shipbuilding center on the lakes. Regular lines of steamers ran to the lakes' ports from Detroit, bringing raw materials and products to be transshipped or processed. With coming of the railroads in 1831, Detroit was linked with other Michigan cities. The Michigan Central and the Pierre Marquette railroads eventually gave Detroit access to Indiana, Ohio, and the West, as well as Ontario, Canada to the north.

When the *Detroit Gazette* was burned out in 1830, Joseph Compaur, wealthy merchant, and his partner, John R. Williams, Detroit's first mayor, did not want the town to be without a newspaper. They went to the tiny hamlet of Pontiac, Michigan where they purchased type and equipment of a struggling weekly publication. Loading the equipment into a single wagon, they hauled the type and press to Detroit, turned it over to Sheldon McNight, whom they selected as editor. These enterprising men gave Detroit a journalistic voice heard ever since then. The first issue of the weekly *Detroit Free Press and Michigan Intelligence* was dated May 5, 1831. McNight published it for four years as a weekly publication; then economic conditions improved in the community, and he issued the *Free Press* as a semiweekly in July, 1835. In September his enterprise led to his converting the *Free Press* into a daily.

In the years that followed several changes were made in management of the paper. Wilbur F. Storey, fiery Democrat mentioned in the Chicago section, purchased the *Free Press* in 1853. Storey was a New Englander, born near Salisbury, Vermont, in December, 1819. He became a printer's devil at the *Middlebury Free Press* when he was twelve; he next worked at the New York *Journal of Commerce* where he absorbed strong anti-Negro views from the publisher.

A restless soul, Storey moved to Indiana. With a partner he founded the *LaPort Herald*, investing his whole two hundred dollars in the enterprise. The partnership broke up in a conflict and the paper went on the rocks by March, 1841. Afterward Storey published other papers in Indiana and Michigan.

It was in Detroit that Storey's superior news ability and publishing skills flowered. He bought controlling interest in the *Detroit Free Press* in February, 1853. At the time the *Free Press* was a weak Democratic newspaper. It needed funds and strong news and editorial direction. Storey transformed it, injecting his great energy and political philosophy into the paper.

The new publisher enlarged the paper, printed more news and issued a Sunday edition. By 1860 he published a page of local news and used telegraph news more fully than before. The *Free Press* covered the courts thoroughly. A printing craftsman, Storey produced an attractive newspaper for his readers.

As a result of improvements he made in the news and editorial columns, by 1861 the *Detroit Free Press* became the most prosperous and best-known Democratic paper in the Old Northwest. Storey, forever restless, saw greater possibilities in Chicago. He sold the *Detroit Free Press* in 1861 and moved to the Illinois metropolis where he purchased the *Chicago Daily Times*.

Storey's successor on the *Free Press* was William E. Quinby, under whose direction the paper continued to prosper.

To the west and across the Mississippi was territory which had been opened more recently to settlement. Much of this land, now the states of Wisconsin, Missouri, Kansas, Nebraska and North and South Dakota, was still Indian country.

WISCONSIN PIONEER PAPERS

Wisconsin was settled slowly. In 1830 it had 130,000 settlers and grew to 775,000 at the time of the Civil War. Although the first newspaper in the territory, the *Green Bay Intelligencer* was issued in 1836, this semiweekly did not continue. It eventually merged with a second paper, the *Wisconsin Free Press,* the united paper becoming the *Democrat.*

The newspaper which became a dominating factor in the region was the *Milwaukee Sentinel.* It was established on June 27, 1837, when Milwaukee was a town of six hundred persons. Milwaukee was nine years away from city status, and Wisconsin eleven years from statehood. John O'Rourke, the first editor, stated his aims:

> We shall strive to make our paper a disseminator of facts . . . a censor of vice . . . a promoter of harmony and social order in the community . . . a detector of fraud, imposture, and crime, as a vigilant sentinel on the ramparts of liberty and democracy.

O'Rourke was not the owner of the *Sentinel.* He was backed by Solomon Juneau, husky fur trader and land speculator, who was Milwaukee's first white settler and later its first mayor. He provided the cash to establish the *Sentinel.*

Editor O'Rourke did not live long after the *Sentinel* was established. He had tuberculosis and operated the paper from a cot in the composing room. O'Rourke died in December, 1837. He was succeeded by Harrison Reed who struggled with the weekly, laboring eighteen to twenty-four hours daily, serving as both editor and printer. A series of financial reverses caused the paper to change hands several times. David M. Keeler, one of its editors, established a reading room and newsroom. He suggested the formation of a young man's library association.

Keeler turned the *Sentinel* into a triweekly in May, 1843 and a daily in December, 1844, as economic conditions were improving and the town was growing. The *Sentinel* was the first daily in the state. The paper introduced the New York technique of circulating the paper by newsboys who shouted the headlines on the streets. In 1846 the *Sentinel's* circulation had expanded to the point where improved printing machinery was needed; the owners bought the first power press in the Northwest. Two years later the *Sentinel* received its first telegraph dispatch. One of the *Sentinel's* most distinguished editors in this period was Rufus King, who had been editor of the *Albany* (New York) *Evening Journal.* He became one of the owners of the *Sentinel.*

Mirroring the population expansion and the economic growth of the state by 1850 a half-dozen dailies were being published in Wisconsin, but a decade later this number had increased to fourteen.

MINNESOTA GETS STRONG PRESS

Intense rivalry broke out between the *St. Paul Pioneer* and the *St. Paul Press.* St. Paul was the gateway to the Northwest and profited by extension of railroads into the region. There was a great demand for the wheat and timber of the region. The town was also the center of steamboat navigation on the Mississippi. Minnesota reached about fifteen thousand population and St. Paul experienced parallel expansion. The papers cultivated intensely the journalistic soil of subscribers and advertisers in the twin cities of St. Paul and Minneapolis, but the publications also fed news to surrounding communities which were developing. For decades the papers penetrated as far west as Orgeon when towns in the territories and states in between had no strong weeklies or dailies to serve the population.

St. Paul Pioneer Begins as Weekly

Roots of the *St. Paul Pioneer* extend into the era when Minnesota, although settlers were pouring in, had not secured even territorial status. James Madison Goodhue, graduate of Amherst College in New England and a lawyer by profession, published the *St. Paul Pioneer* on April 18, 1849. Goodhue built the reputation of the weekly, advocating town and territorial improvements. Becoming a leader in politics, he was also publicist for the territory, seeking to attract new settlers. The founder of the *St. Paul Pioneer,* however, died two years after he began publication of the weekly. A later publisher combined the *Pioneer* with the *Democrat,* a rival newspaper. By 1862 economic conditions in the area were suitable for publication of the *Pioneer and Democrat* as a daily.

St. Paul Press Under Strong Leadership

Meanwhile the *St. Paul Press* had been launched in 1861 and developed into a strong newspaper under the leadership of Joseph Wheelock. Moving to Minnesota from the East, Wheelock served as clerk in an Indian trading post. He received his first taste of journalism in 1856 when he was employed as editor of the *St. Paul Real Estate and Financial Advertiser.*

The *Advertiser* did much to promote the territory. At various times five thousand copies of the paper were sent to prospective settlers in the East. Wheelock wrote sparkling articles about the woods, hills and lakes of Minnesota and preached a thrilling gospel to unhappy easterners. The *Advertiser* did not prove to be a profitable publication, and after two years it was merged in 1858 with the *Pioneer and Democrat,* which had recently been combined. Wheelock now worked as associate editor, writing about half the news and three editorials a day. In the fall of 1858 Wheelock left the *Pioneer and Democrat* to write a book on Minnesota. He became State Commissioner of Statistics in 1860, serving in that position for several years.

Wheelock was drawn back to journalism, and with William R. Marshall, a leader of the Republican Party in the area, and J. Jay Knox, bought the equipment of the *St. Paul Times,* a nearly defunct Republican newspaper. The partners now founded the *St. Paul Press.* Marshall was editor and Wheelock his assistant. By making Marshall nominal head of the *Press,* Wheelock hoped to secure the public printing of the state. Republican policy, then adopted by the paper, was maintained by Wheelock throughout his career. Soon after the paper began, Knox, the third partner, sold his interest to Newton Bradley who became business manager.

The Civil War changed the situation further at the *Press.* Marshall left the paper in January, 1863 to recruit men, taking with him even personnel from the printing and accounting departments of the daily. Wheelock now became editor-in-chief, soon buying Marshall's interest. During the Civil War Wheelock devoted columns of the paper to the Union cause. Lincoln, to him, represented the genius and spirit of American institutions and democracy. The old *Republican Minnesotian* was now absorbed by the enterprising Wheelock.

Union Merger

Competition also appeared on the St. Paul journalistic scene. A Republican, Frederick Driscoll, established the *St. Paul Union* to compete with the *St. Paul Press* and its faction in the Republican Party. Upon the election of his candidate as governor, Driscoll became state printer. He then bought a half interest in the *St. Paul Press* and merged his *St. Paul Union* with it. Driscoll became general manager and continued with Wheelock as a perfect newspaper team for forty years. The *St. Paul*

Press was the only Republican journalistic survivor in St. Paul, and Minnesota was becoming a strong Republican state.

Wheelock was sympathetic to Indians in the area. During the Civil War Wheelock said the Indians' troubles were a result of frauds perpetrated in the Indian Bureau. He called the bureau men thieves and urged their punishment. Wheelock became secretary to the governor's commission sent to conclude a treaty with the Indians. The editor became a public figure, speaking at the St. Paul winter series of lectures.

ST. LOUIS PRESS COMPETITIVE

Down the Mississippi lay bustling St. Louis which surpassed even Chicago in size and commercial activity. New Englanders who favored free labor and southern Democrats who clung to the idea of slavocracy worked alongside a large German and Irish population. The town spread along the river for miles; steamboating was a big business. The great market lay to the South and Southwest. St. Louis had mercantile stores, markets and warehouses. It also boasted attractive hotels and theatres. Its earlier population of 77,000 ballooned to 160,000 by the opening of the Civil War.

St. Louis Union and the Democrat

The *Union* had been established in St. Louis before. Now up-and-coming was the *Missouri Democrat.* Its first editor was Francis B. Blair, son of Francis Preston Blair who was prominent in the Washington political and journalistic scene in President Andrew Jackson's administration. Young Blair was a lawyer and a leader in the Free Soil branch of the Democratic Party in 1848. He had written hard-biting editorials for three papers. Now he saw journalistic potential in this community.

He persuaded a group of businessmen that the *Missouri Democrat* could help Missourians determine whether the state should be free or slave. Joining him in the journalistic enterprise were Thomas Hart Benton and B. Gratz Brown, a cousin. The three issued the four-page, seven-column *Democrat* in the printshop of the *St. Louis Union.* This arrangement did not last long because the editors of the papers fought each other.

Within a short time Blair took a step which shaped the future course of the *Democrat.* He walked to the printshop of William McKee and William Hall and told them they could have the paper if they would print it every week. Apparently Blair was seeking only political expression through the *Democrat.*

McKee, an experienced newspaperman who had worked in New York, saw the value of the arrangement. McKee had been known as a Free Soil advocate. Soon he was able to buy for sixteen thousand dollars the *Union*, a competitor, and he merged the two journals. When Hall, the printing partner, quit later, he sold his interest to Francis Blair. A *Weekly Democrat* was issued, soon attaining a circulation of one thousand.

The *Democrat* was largely a political sheet, and the great issue of the time was slavery. The paper gradually shifted to the Free Soil side. Hesitating to declare openly for abolition, B. Gratz Brown favored colonization of Negroes. When Brown left the daily after some argument, Peter Foy became editor, strengthening the political writing in the *Democrat*, which became known as the leading Republican paper of the West. The paper played a major role in placing the Republican Party in power in Missouri. The *Democrat* helped establish the new state constitution freeing the slaves. Blair was always close to Lincoln and assisted strongly in his nomination and election. Lincoln persuaded several businessmen to raise a fund of five hundred dollars to promote the *Democrat* in southern Illinois.

While heavy emphasis was on political news the *Democrat* provided much European news for its German and Irish readers. As St. Louis was growing the *Democrat* instituted a city news column and reported local events. As soon as finances permitted, the paper broadened its news coverage and used telegraphic dispatches.

The paper served commercial news to merchants and riverboat men; and for those interested in literary affairs, it furnished some book news. Social news also crept into the paper. By December, 1858 the proprietors issued the *Sunday Democrat*. The *Democrat* slowly gained prestige and earned profits, particularly after advertising rates were raised. The proprietors were able to pay the sixteen thousand dollar debt incurred in purchase of the *Union*.

The *Democrat's* chief opponent now was the *Republican*, which, by a peculiar set of circumstances, favored the Democratic Party.

Meanwhile, George W. Fishback, a lawyer-turned-newspaper-writer, saw commercial possibilities in the *Democrat* and bought an interest in it. Owners now were Blair, McKee and Fishback.

The papers were suppressed in St. Louis by the Union army. The *Democrat* editor was arrested for printing a letter sent by President Lincoln to a local general, but the editor was soon released. During the war the *Democrat* experienced genuine difficulties as advertising fell off.

The *Democrat* partners had to mortgage the equipment for eight thousand dollars at one time to get sufficient revenue.

Westliche Post

With many of the German immigrants drifting to St. Louis, possibilities for publication of a German-language newspaper increased. The *Westliche Post* (*Western Post*) was established and became the greatest antislavery organ among the German-speaking Americans.

Kansas-Nebraska Weeklies and Daily

So thinly settled was some of the Kansas territory that weeklies could not survive. Recognizing the need for a newspaper for Shawnee Indians, Reverend Johnston Lykins published the *Shawnee Sun* on March 1, 1835. The paper was printed on the mission press. A small quarter sheet, the *Sun* was published in Indian language for four years. The press was later used to print another paper.

It was not until fifteen years later, in 1854, that the *Kansas Weekly Herald*, the first English newspaper, was begun on September 15. Settlement in Leavenworth was just beginning when Osborn Adams began to set type under the old elm tree. He corrected proof sitting on the ground with a big shingle of wood for a table. Five years later the *Weekly Herald* became a daily but on the death of its owner soon suspended.

Kansas journalism reflected the slavery controversy of the border state. Each faction sought to influence public opinion through publication of a newspaper. The *Kansas Free State* and the *Herald of Freedom* were launched in 1855 at Lawrence, both opposing slavery. The *Squatter Sovereign*, issued at Atchison, became an organ of the Border Ruffians and fought their opponents bitterly. Great fertile land attracted many easterners and Kansas filled up steadily, so that by 1860 three dailies were being published in the state.

Nebraska, meanwhile, began to be settled and acquired its first weeklies during the 1850s. The first Nebraska papers, however, were published in Iowa. The *Nebraska Palladium* was issued in Iowa in June, 1854, but later was removed to Nebraska. Other weeklies followed the same pattern.

SOUTH DAKOTA'S EARLY PRESS

The South Dakota territory during this period was inhabited largely by the Indians, and a strange fate befell the one newspaper attempting publication. In 1862 Indians sacked the town of Sioux Falls where the *Democrat* had been established four years earlier. When the Indian wars broke out the settlement was abandoned.

Indians rode into town, entered the *Democrat*'s office and carried off the metal type. Later they remelted the fonts of type, fashioned them into ornaments for pipes. These pipes were sold afterward to settlers when peace came. Several other weeklies were established in the Dakota Territory before the Civil War, but no dailies appeared.

Chapter 13

Southwest and Rocky Mountain Regions Get First Newspapers

INDIAN PAPERS IN OKLAHOMA

In Oklahoma Indian territory, two weeklies in Indian dialect were issued. To the Cherokees goes credit for printing the first of many papers published there. Issued in August, 1844, by the Cherokee Baptist Mission, the *Cherokee Messenger* was the earliest in the region. The *Messenger* was more a religious and temperance publication than a regular newspaper. It continued for about two years. The *Cherokee Advocate,* also issued in Indian dialect, began as an organ of the Cherokee Nation. The Cherokees in their national council in October, 1843, passed an act to establish a printing press and publish a newspaper. The first number of the *Cherokee Advocate* appeared under the editorship of William P. Ross on October 25. It was printed in English and Cherokee languages. The price was three dollars a year except to Cherokees who paid only two dollars. The *Cherokee Advocate* continued for ten years; however, it was revived after the Civil War.

The Choctaws and Chickasaws were not to be outdone journalistically, and in 1872 the *Vindicator* was established to advocate their interests. Still another Indian newspaper was established when the *Indian Journal* appeared in May, 1876, as an official organ of the Creek Nation. The first English newspaper was not issued until the 1880s in Oklahoma.

TEXAS PRESS ORGAN OF NEW SETTLERS

The *Telegraph and Texas Register* was the organ of American settlers who wanted to revolt against the Mexican rule. Published by Gail Borden, Joseph Baker and Thomas H. Borden, the weekly first appeared in San Felice on October 10, 1835. The editors moved the *Telegraph and Texas Register* to Austin, where it was issued for about a year. General Santa Anna ordered an advance guard to Austin where Mexican troops forced the staff to take the press apart, break up the forms, pi the type. The staff now moved to Harrisburgh, where another attempt was made to print the *Telegraph.* One issue was put into type when another troop from Santa Anna's army pushed its way into the office, seized the press and pied the type. The printers and newsmen were held as prisoners.

Later the troops threw the press and type into the Buffalo Bayou. The equipment was later rescued, cleaned and used in Houston, Texas to print the *Morning Star* on April 8, 1839. This became the first daily newspaper in the Republic of Texas.

Meanwhile Borden, after the battle of San Jacinto, went to Cincinnati where he bought another printing press and type. He hauled the equipment back to Texas and began publication of the *Telegraph* again in October, 1836, at Columbia, on the Brazos, temporary seat of government. When the capital was moved to Houston, the *Telegraph* was transferred too. Gail Borden sold his interest in the paper and returned to his native state, New York, where he established a milk company.

While the new owners continued the *Telegraph* at Houston, they also established the *Texas Sentinel* in Austin, the new capital, in January, 1840.

Galveston News Launched

When Samuel Bangs started the *Galveston News,* he had not the slightest idea that it would be more than another of the short-lived publications he had begun and was later destined to abandon. His first issue of the *Galveston News* appeared on April 11, 1842. A puny, four page sheet, measuring 8 1/2 by 12 inches, the *News* was printed in a one-room, unpainted shack. The *Galveston News* would have folded had it not been for Willard Richardson. Although a native of Massachusetts, Richardson had drifted to South Carolina and then his adventuresomeness had led him west to Texas in 1837. Richardson became a follower and friend of President Mirabeau B. Lamar of the Republic of Texas. Eventually the young easterner settled in Galveston to become publisher of Bangs' ailing *Galveston News.* To any but a hardy character, the scene in Texas in 1843 would have been discouraging. In the wilderness the few dim lights of civilization showed only in some towns along the Gulf Coast and the Rio Grande River. Indians ranged at will over eighty per cent of the country. The Republic of Texas' financial condition was shaky.

The Dixie-Yankee, Richardson, immediately launched his newspaper on a multifold program aimed at the economic and civic development of Texas. He drove hard at annexation of Texas to the United States of America. Richardson sought the solution of the Republic's monetary and public debt problems. By giving adequate transportation through building of railroads, the editor aimed to lift Texas from economic starvation.

Richardson recognized the need for two steps essential to Texas economic growth. First, he saw that more population was necessary to vitalize Texas' great soil and other natural resources. Second, he saw the necessity for an efficient transportation system (railroads) to permit flow of the excess volume of new-found wealth to Gulf ports and from there to markets in the United States and Europe.

The *Galveston News* was soon recognized as a leading newspaper of Texas for the *News* had Richardson's able leadership and direction. The paper developed a strong reputation for journalistic honesty.

Trying times were to come. Outbreak of the war between the states was a severe blow even to the strongest newspaper in the frontier state. Richardson, then sixty, obeyed the order to evacuate when the capture of Galveston by federal troops was imminent. He loaded presses, type cases, paper stock, and office records on flatcars and moved to Houston. A few days after he set up shop in Houston a fire destroyed everything he had. Richardson bought a press and some type from a local publisher who had succumbed to wartime conditions. Richardson began to publish the *News* again. During the black years he continued to issue the *News* and returned in 1866 to Galveston.

ARIZONA'S WILD WEST JOURNALISM

An interesting story is told of the first paper in Arizona, the *Weekly Arizonian,* pulled from the press in March, 1859. The press on which the weekly was printed came around Cape Horn in 1858 and was brought by wagon to Tumac, Arizona. A year after publication was begun there the paper was moved to Tucson. Its publishers did some moonlighting. After the paper was printed they put their guns in their holsters and mounted horses for a little night riding. They held up a stage, and later, resisting arrest, one of the publishers was shot and killed. The *Weekly Arizonian,* appropriately, suspended.

NEW MEXICAN PRESS BEGINS

The first newspaper in New Mexico *El Crepusculo* (*The Dawn*) was printed in Taos in November, 1835. Only four issues came from the press. Twelve years later the first regular weekly, the *Santa Fe Republican,* appeared in September, 1847, with two pages in Spanish and two in English. Santa Fe got its first all-English weekly in 1849 when the *New Mexican* appeared.

MOUNTAIN AREA PAPERS COLORFUL

Newspaper Rivalry in Denver

The Rocky Mountain area was the most sparsely settled section of the nation, extending from Montana to New Mexico. In this region one of the most exciting incidents in frontier journalism occurred when two rivals sought to establish the first weekly in Colorado.

Word of discovery of gold in Pikes Peak region spread to the east. Two groups started out to launch a newspaper in the new territory. One of these groups, led by William N. Byers, started from Omaha, Nebraska. He was in the real estate business when he heard news of the gold strike. He then decided to move to Denver and publish a weekly. With several partners he traveled across plains and rivers. The partners transported a handpress with two pages of type already set up and locked in forms.

Meanwhile, a rival, John L. Merrick, got the same idea for a Colorado publication. He left St. Joseph, Missouri with his printing equipment. Merrick was first to arrive at Cherry Creek in the territory where gold had been discovered. Merrick prepared to issue the *Cherry Creek Pioneer,* but, knowing that Byers was on his way, took his time about publishing.

The Byers group from Omaha arrived ten days later, and the fight was on. Miners at the settlement offered a suitable prize to the group which issued the first newspaper. On April 23, 1859, at 10:30 P.M., the Byers team pulled the first copy of the *Rocky Mountain News* from the Washington handpress. Twenty minutes later the *Pioneer* appeared; Merrick, disgusted, sold his equipment to Byers and went prospecting for gold.

Byers' subscribers were few, his advertisers limited, and with paper hard to obtain, the editor just managed to keep his weekly going. Regional-minded and civic-minded, the publisher was in the forefront of all movements to build the area. He reported mining successes, advanced agriculture and fought for better mail service and the building of a railroad line to the town.

The *Rocky Mountain News* battled the town gamblers and murderers. Henchmen of one of them kidnapped the editor but didn't harm him. The gambler-killer later let Byers return to his newspaper shop. The killers then laid siege to the building. One gambler-killer was shot fatally before the fight ended. Often, on other occasions, guards had to stand outside the shop while printers were at work.

The *Rocky Mountain News* sometimes had to use wrapping paper for publishing its edition. In obtaining the latest news for his subscribers, the editor-publisher felt that regular mails were too slow so he established an overland pony express to bring news from the nearest express station. At the beginning the *News* sold for $1.25 per copy and forty-four dollars a year.

The paper, pressed by a new competition, became a daily within a year after it first appeared, but the weekly edition continued to be published and distributed to miners in the surrounding region. On the side, Byers bought mining claims and engaged in real estate, interests which led to his retirement after the Civil War.

Deseret News, Mormon Mountain Voice

An angry mob drove Mormons from Illinois, and after many hardships they reached the Great Salt Lake in Utah in September, 1848. Knowing the value of a printing press even in the wilderness, President Brigham Young ordered the press of this religious group brought west. After a thousand mile journey by ox-drawn wagon, the printing equipment reached Salt Lake Valley in August, 1849. Church literature was produced first on the little press.

Mormons, however, wanted news of the churchmen who began to settle in other parts of the Utah territory, news of activities in Washington, news of Mormons in other parts of the world. Young and his council finally made the decision in May, 1850, to publish the weekly *Deseret News, deseret* meaning "honeycomb."

Willard Richards, clerk of the Mormon Assembly, wrote the prospectus for the first newspaper in the mountains. The prospectus declared that the paper would be dedicated to "truth and liberty" and would cover the arts and sciences. Richards sought three hundred subscribers for the weekly. A small publication, 7 1/2 by 13 3/4 inches, the *Deseret News* had three columns of type on each of its four pages. It was the first newspaper in that vast mountain wilderness reaching between the Santa Fe and the Pacific Coast.

Different from other papers issued later in the mountain region, the *Deseret News* was not filled with stories of mining and of violence. The *News* was the organ of a well-organized, peaceful, agricultural people who had settled in the mountains for religious freedom. Their leader, Brigham Young, continually counseled them to till the soil and to stay away from the mines, where there was speculation and sin. The *Deseret News* was not a political booster. It was the voice of a people struggling in a desolate desert for their lives and for their church.

The *Deseret News* had a journalistic monopoly for eight years. Then events began to happen which led to new publications. In 1857 various charges were brought against the Mormons, including accusation of disloyalty. The Mormon territorial courts were punishing non-Mormons and setting Mormons free. The United States government, as a result, clamped down on the Mormons. A new territorial governor was appointed; troops were dispatched to the region.

With the troops came Kirk Anderson, a newsman who once worked for the *St. Louis Missourian.* Within two months after arriving, Anderson set up a printing shop and issued the first number of *Kirk Anderson Valley Tan Weekly* on November 6, 1858. This was the first opposition the *Deseret News* had. The *Tan* editor said he came not to make war on Mormons but to correct administration abuses and errors. In later numbers of the paper, Anderson poured out his venom on the church and its leaders, meanwhile extolling General Johnston, in charge of the camp of soldiers.

In the midst of the turbulent times, a third newspaper entered the journalistic arena. The *Mountaineer,* issued by three Mormon lawyers, was twice the size of the *Deseret News.* Although no organ of the church, the *Mountaineer* defended Mormons and their court practices. The *Valley Tan* succumbed when the troops withdrew.

Nevada's Gold Fields Get Written Papers

Launching and successfully publishing a newspaper in a mining region were as difficult tasks as finding gold. Nevada, which had only a scattering of population in this era, obtained its first newspaper, a written one, when Joseph Webb, an unsuccessful prospector, wrote by hand the *Golden Switch* in 1854 and sold the paper. He obtained news items as best he could and wrote them on sheets of paper for news-hungry miners. They paid him in gold dust at the Carson River crossing, where Dayton, Nevada now stands.

A rival sheet, the *Scorpion,* was also issued at Genoa at the eastern foot of the Sierra Nevada mountains. It was there that the *Territorial*

Enterprise, the first printed paper, was issued in November, 1858. When the paper was sold it was moved to Carson City, capital of the territory, and later transferred to Virginia City. The *Territorial Enterprise* prospered when the miners did; it suffered when gold panned out. Mark Twain worked on the paper. Carson City was not without its newspapers. When the *Enterprise* moved out the *Silver Age* was launched. A daily was attempted in 1863 but conditions were not suitable, and it lasted only a year.

Chapter 14

Pacific Coast Acquires First Weeklies, Dailies

Weeklies, and later dailies, were launched as pioneers, attracted by rich farmlands, fishing and gold prospects as well as fur and timber resources, moved into the Washington, Oregon and California territories.

OREGON'S FIRST PRESS

In the vast region which now embraces Oregon, Washington, Idaho and part of Montana lived perhaps twelve thousand white persons. With the symbolic subtitle "Westward the Star of Empire Takes Its Way," the *Oregon Spectator* was issued in Oregon City in August, 1846, by the Oregon Printing Association. Its first editor, Colonel William G. T'Vault, was also postmaster general of the provisional government. A succession of editors followed him. The paper pleaded the cause of the Whig Party.

George L. Curry, one of the editors, refused to be dominated by the Oregon Printing Association. Consequently, he resigned his editorship to start a rival paper, the *Free Press* in 1848. Having no press, he constructed one of wood and scrap iron, and bought about forty pounds of type from Catholic missionaries. The *Free Press,* however, continued only for a few months; most of its subscribers rushed to mines in the territory when precious mineral was found.

The *Portland Oregonian,* later one of the region's strongest papers, was founded in 1850 when Portland was one of the many little frontier communities strung along the river where land claims were being bought and town lots were being plotted for sale. Portland claimed a population of seven hundred. Business houses were all on Front Street. Drivers using the street had to guide their horses or oxen carefully to miss tree stumps. Houses were built of rough, whipsaw lumber or planks.

Two originators of the Portland townsite were determined that their community should have a weekly to sing its praises and to uphold the Whig cause. The opposing Democratic Party was then dominant in Oregon. These businessmen went to San Francisco where they persuaded Thomas J. Dryer, a printer, to return with them to Portland and open a printshop and publish a weekly. Formerly of New York, Dryer was a Whig, had a handpress and some time on his hands. He was looking for a place to set up a printshop. Portland looked like the opportunity he was waiting for.

Leading citizens of Portland stayed up all night on December 3, 1850 to help publisher-editor Dryer get his paper out, and in the early morning they hailed the paper's birth with shouting and bonfires.

During the *Oregonian's* first decade publishers of this and rival papers sought to increase their prestige and circulation by engaging in bitter, often libelous, word battles. Dryer was a forceful writer and contributed his full share to this form of controversy. He jousted editorially with the publisher of the Salem *Oregon Statesman.*

Dryer took an important step when he hired Henry L. Pittock as printer and young man-of-all-work. An able and vigorous speaker, Dryer now devoted more and more attention to politics. Young Pittock gradually assumed management of the *Oregonian.* Dryer gave up newspaper work entirely when Lincoln was nominated. By this time Dryer owed Pittock so much in back wages, which the publisher was unable to pay, that Pittock just accepted the paper in settlement, assuming its debts.

Pittock set the course for the *Oregonian* that was to guide it from this point forward. He sought to publish news of Oregon expansion and of the slavery conflict. In 1860 the *Oregonian* left its competitors behind when it obtained from San Francisco a Hoe one-cylinder, power-driven press that threw off 1220 sheets printed on one side or 600 complete four-page papers per hour.

With this new equipment the *Oregonian* went into daily publication on February 4, 1861. The *Oregonian's* circulation and prestige mounted as readers sought war news. The *Oregonian* declared itself prounion and found its sympathies shared by the great majority of Oregon citizens.

WASHINGTON'S EARLY WEEKLY

Meanwhile to the north, in what is now Washington State, the *Olympia Columbian* appeared in 1852. The publisher strongly advocated the separation of his territory from Oregon and changed the weekly's name to *Washington Pioneer* to emphasize his point of view.

CALIFORNIA'S PIONEER JOURNALISM

Prior to 1840 California, a vast area enormously rich in natural resources (soil, timber and minerals) was a land of romance. The choice regions were occupied by Catholic Spanish laymen, dreamy, pleasure loving and easygoing. They didn't want to work too hard. They tilled the soil in primitive fashion, had no manufactures and carried on little trade.

Although the number of American settlers, including Yankee traders, whalers and deserters from the ships, increased yearly, in 1840 there were less than four hundred Americans in a total population of five to six thousand. Tales of wandering trappers and newspaper accounts of California's wonderful climate and fertile soil, however, appealed to the imagination of every discontented frontiersman and those restless, hopeful residents in eastern cities. The migrants pushed west.

Conflict between Mexico and the United States over the right to annex Texas became sharp and led to war. When Mexico lost, a peace treaty was signed in February, 1848. By its terms Mexico ceded New Mexico and California to the United States. Less than two weeks before the treaty was signed, James Marshall, while engaged in building a sawmill for Captain Sutter in the Sacramento Valley, discovered that the region was rich in gold. Despite Sutter's efforts to keep the matter secret the news spread quickly. California's population boomed, and places like Stockton and Sacramento, which did not exist in 1848, were thriving towns by 1850. Population of San Francisco in a few years mounted from a few hundred to thirty-five thousand.

Of the thousands who rushed to California mines, only a comparatively small number reaped fortunes. Total output of gold rose from five million in 1848 to sixty-five million in 1853. Then the tide began to ebb.

Meanwhile, other economic developments were noted. Cattle-raising expanded to meet the needs of the growing population, and California soil and climate proved most congenial for wheat production. Grape culture offered strong economic possibilities for the state because a strong demand for table grapes and the derivatives, wine and brandy, existed. But most promising of all was citrus growing. By 1860 the state had four thousand orange trees and melon-bearing vines, practically all being grown in southern California.

The first newspaper in California was published by a minister and a former Philadelphia editor. In summer of 1846 the United States frigate *Congress* sailed into Monterey harbor after a long trip from the East Coast. Reverend Colton, chaplain of the ship, was tired of preaching to sailors and wanted to publish a weekly journal, for none was being issued in Monterey. In the town he met Robert Semple, formerly editor of the *Philadelphia North American,* who had migrated first to Kentucky, then to California. He dressed in buckskin and wore a fox-skin cap, and according to his partner was "true with his rifle, ready with his pen, and quick at the typecase."

Reverend Colton and Semple found beneath the rubbish in an old shed an old Ramage press built in Boston many years before. The press had been used to print the California governor's proclamations, and later fell into the hands of Catholic missionaries who printed religious tracts. Mice had burrowed in the deerskin balls used to ink the type. There were no rules, no leads and the type was rusty and all in pi. It was only by scouring that the letters could be made to show their faces, Colton later wrote. For rules and leads they found a sheet of tin and with a jack-knife cut it into usable material. Luckily they found a keg of ink with the press.

The two partners had workable equipment, but an essential was lacking for newspaper publication: paper. A current situation fortunately helped them. Native Californians were heavy smokers of cigars, rolling their own in a heavy form of wrapping paper. The sheets were large enough to print a small paper. "Why not use this paper for a weekly?" thought the future publishers.

They issued the *Californian* on August 15, 1846. One half of the paper was printed in English, the other in Spanish. Single copies sold for 12 1/2 cents, considered inexpensive. The first issue contained a declaration of war between the United States and Mexico, with an account of a debate in the Senate.

After six months Reverend Colton went back to his first love, preaching, and returned East. Semple, now sole proprietor, decided to take his paper to Yerba Buena, later called San Francisco. In May, 1847, he hauled his equipment to that growing town and sold out there to B. R. Buckelew, a jeweler with an interest in journalism.

San Francisco Journalism

In San Francisco a weekly had been launched in January of the same year. Sam Brannan, a Mormon leader, had brought a small hand-press on a ship from New York, and with the equipment published on January 9, 1847 the *California Star.* The weekly was four pages, 13 by 18 inches, with three columns on a page. The first edition came off the press in a grist mill. Brannan hired E. P. Jones as editor.

Thus two weeklies, the *California Star* and the *Californian,* were issued in a town which had only three hundred seventy-five residents. Eighty-nine of these couldn't read. A circulation war began. Editor Jones, of the *California Star,* told his readers that his paper "was the only independent paper and the only paper of respectable size in the whole of the Pacific Coast from the boundary of Mexico to the frozen regions of the north." He priced his weekly at a *real,* Mexican coin worth about 12 1/2 cents. Buckelew, publisher of the *Californian,* charged five dollars a year, or about 9 1/2 cents a copy, claiming his newspaper was the first in California.

The *Star* was used extensively to boom California, and extra editions were printed to circulate in other states. In 1848 the paper startled its readers with an innovation, a progress edition. Its new editor, Edward Kemble, from New York, issued two thousand copies and sent them overland by mule and express to the East.

It was difficult to check on facts, and with news scarce the *Star* printed whatever news it could get. The editor published a dispatch from one correspondent who described cannibalistic actions of migrants in wagon trains bogged down while attempting to cross snowy Sierra Mountains.

The rival editors missed the greatest news story of the period, the discovery of gold. News about gold did not break in any newspaper until March 15, almost two months after the discovery. Then editor Buckelew, of the *Californian,* placed the story on page two, bottom of column three. He used a half-column run-in head for the story:

> GOLD MINE FOUND—In the newly made raceway of the Saw Mill recently erected by Captain Sutter, on the American Fork, gold had been found in considerable quantities. One person brought thirty dollars worth to New Helvetia, gathered there in a short time. California, no doubt is rich in mineral wealth, great chances here for scientific capitalists. Gold has been found in almost every part of the country.

The *Star* took ten days to catch up to the scoop of the *Californian* and even then gave the news only a few lines. The Gold Rush was on. The April 1, 1848 issue of the *Star* finally reached the East, where the *New York Herald* printed the gold news in its August 19 issue. The news told the world for the first time that gold was in the Far West. In October, 1848, the first gold steamer went out of New York harbor.

Editor Kemble of the *Star* went to the gold field to see for himself what the facts were. He came back to pronounce the mines "all a sham, as supurb (sic) a take-in as ever was got up to guzzle the gullible."

Few persons listened to the editor. Strong rumors continued that the strike was real and rich. Gold was brought back and an exhibit was placed in a store window.

San Franciscans got gold fever. Carpenters left their jobs, shop clerks and even shopkeepers left their stores. San Francisco almost became a ghost city. This meant, too, that newspaper subscribers were leaving. In May, 1848, the *Californian* published a fly-sheet saying it was suspending. "The whole country, from San Francisco to Los Angeles, and from the seashore to the base of the Sierra Nevada, resounds with the sordid cry of gold! Gold! GOLD! while the field is left unplanted, the house half builded and everything neglected but the manufacture of shovels and picks."

Buckelew took one last flyer before he folded his paper. He cranked his press to get out a small slip of newspaper. He then sold his equipment and the *Californian* to three partners for its debts.

Meanwhile, the rival *Star* continued to publish but gasped its last on June 14. All of California was now without a newspaper.

As other Californians, Kemble headed for the fields. At the diggings he was disappointed. He didn't discover the golden dust or nuggets he came to find. He was sure he could never be a miner but might make a newspaperman. He returned to San Francisco, footsore and with a worn-out back. Kemble bought the *California Star* from Brannan for eight hundred dollars and wanted to begin publication again. The new editor-publisher had no money for newsprint and could not issue the weekly. He went to see the partners who owned the *Californian*, explaining that the town could hardly support one newspaper, much less two. He suggested a merger. No agreement was reached. Then suddenly Kemble found that he owned both papers. The *Californian*'s partners had walked out of town, left a note that Kemble could have the *Californian*, debts, equipment and goodwill—free.

For several months Kemble was not able to get the needed newsprint. Finally in November he issued the combined *Star* & *Californian*. He found it difficult to keep publishing and to pay his bills; however, his job shop added to his income. Soon two other partners joined his enterprise. One was Edward C. Gilbert, Mexican War veteran who had learned the printing trade in Albany, New York and had drifted to California. Kemble also discovered another printer, George C. Hubbard, who had some ready cash for a one-fourth interest in the Kemble enterprise.

The new weekly, the *Alta California*, came out on January 4, 1849. It began to make money because San Francisco was being repopulated. Within four months after the discovery of gold, $850,000 in gold dust poured into the city. The laborer who had received two dollars a day before the gold strike now got thirty dollars a day. Rents skyrocketed. Criminal gangs formed; many of the criminals were ex-convicts from England's penal colonies. Hundreds of gambling spots were prospering. It was monte, faro, roulette, rondo, rouge et noir and twenty-one. Professional gamblers were the most influential men in town. Bets of $20,000 were made on the turn of a card. San Francisco was a colorful town and drew people from all parts of the world. Down the 'Frisco streets among the miners walked Negroes, Chinese, Malayans, New Zealanders, Figi Islanders, Russians and Spaniards.

Circulation of the *Alta California* jumped and so did profits. The paper's partners even considered installing a steam press. Before the end of 1849 a number of weeklies appeared, rivals to the *Alta California*. The *Pacific News* publishers were enterprising for they started their publication as a triweekly. But they did not have the finances, and their publication died after a year. The *Journal of Commerce* was to appear as a daily, so the rumor flew. In 1850 the partners of the *Alta California* saw this as genuine competition and brought out their daily edition, the first in California, a day ahead of the rival. In that year John Nugent issued a *Daily Herald* that was to prove the biggest competitor of the *Alta California* and the longest lived.

Kemble by 1858 was able to write that one hundred thirty-two periodicals of various kinds had been started in San Francisco. Their owners, editors and reporters numbered more than one thousand, he said. He wrote:

> No city in the world can boast of a newspaper press as great in its development, so singular in its character, so wonderful in its fortunes. The papers have been reprinted in six different languages. Different nationalities have devoted themselves to the interest of religion, agriculture, news, and slander; have preached eight different forms of religion, and have been organs of seven distinct political parties.

They had such names as *The Hombre, Daily Whig, Satan's Bassoon, Curiosity Shop, Temperance Journal, Present and Future, Bon Ton Critic, Young American of the Pacific.*

"Wee" Willie Walker, pugnatious publisher of the *Daily Herald*, wrote a stinging editorial about the crime wave and mentioned the definite laxness of the courts. Judge Levi Parsons believed the finger had been pointed his way. He hauled Walker before him on contempt of court charges and fined the publisher five hundred dollars. Walker refused to pay and went to jail instead. A crowd, believing in the free press, marched around the jail and through the streets. The protest marchers shouted for Judge Parsons to resign. They even wanted to visit Walker in his cell, but the jail doors were too strong. The crowd returned to hear more speeches in the Plaza. A lawyer took out a writ of habeas corpus for the publisher; as a result, Walker was freed. The crowd then dispersed for drinks, and Judge Parsons closed the case.

Newspapermaking reflected the moods of the community which permitted dueling, Edward C. Gilbert, senior editor of the *Alta California* and a Mexican War veteran, became one of the state's first congressmen. He became embroiled with General J. W. Denver over a news story. This led to a duel. On the second firing the editor was killed. When his body was brought to San Francisco, flags were flown at half-mast and newspaper column rules were turned upside down to print a heavy black, used for mourning. John Nugent, while editor of the *Herald,* fought two duels, both with aldermen.

James King of William Begins the Bulletin

Several newspapers were begun during the 1850s and rose to influence and power. James King of William launched the *Evening Bulletin* on October 5, 1855. A banker, he became a millionaire during the Gold Rush but lost everything later. He was thirty-four years old, had a wife and six small children. King knew that much of the money missing from the city treasurer's office had disappeared into the pockets of politicians, led by Judge Ned McGowan. James P. Casey, editor of the *Sunday Times,* was connected with the gang, for he was a member of the board of election supervisors which rigged elections and stuffed ballot boxes.

James King of William decided to start a newspaper which would crusade against the political knavery. If profitable the publication might feed his family, he said. He borrowed money from a few friends and issued the *Evening Bulletin.* He had a furious hatred for moneyed interests. He blamed dishonesty of larger bankers for the loss of his fortune, declaring that their financial manipulations had caused a run on all San Francisco banks.

The *Evening Bulletin* printed a table showing the number of crimes committed in 1855: the total persons killed, four hundred eighty-seven; hung by the sheriff, six; hung by mobs, forty-six. King of William charged that his newspaper competitors failed to join him in a campaign to clean up the city. He attacked lawyer Alfred A. Cohen and city auctioneer Abia A. Selover, who were made receivers for the big Adams bank which had failed to open. Upon appointment, Cohen's first action was to back up a wagon to the bank and cart away $600,000 in gold slugs. When Cohen was brought to court in the bankruptcy proceedings, the judge asked him what happened to the money. He remained silent. Cohen was then jailed. The *Evening Bulletin* warned that Cohen would escape. He did—twice—but was captured each time. The lawyer was finally freed after an absconding banker in Australia said he had taken the money with him. The exciting story and the *Evening Bulletin*'s stand combined to drive the daily's circulation up to sixty-two hundred copies, far more than any of its rivals' circulations.

A running battle broke out between James King of William and editor Casey of the *Sunday Times*, an organ of the entrenched politicians. Following a minor quarrel over publication of some information, the *Evening Bulletin* disclosed that Casey would be exposed as an ex-convict from Sing Sing in New York, where he spent eighteen months for robbing his mistress. Casey had admitted, orally, his past when he was a witness in a San Francisco trial. Now Casey came to the *Evening Bulletin* office on May 4, 1856, demanding that the information not be printed. King refused. After Casey left, he consulted with Judge McGowan, who warned him to be careful because King of William was known to be armed.

King left his office that day after the *Bulletin* went to press. Casey waited for him along the Montgomery Block, nearby. A crowd, hearing of the trouble, gathered to watch. Casey walked across the street to meet King of William and fired. King of William staggered and groped his way to an express company. Several physicians came to help. They disagreed as to the course of treatment. The *Evening Bulletin* issued hourly bulletins as the editor went slowly to his death during the next few days. Casey was taken to jail. Judge McGowan and others were charged with being accessories to the attempted murder. When a mob gathered outside the jail, Casey was transferred to the stronger county jail. On May 20, James King of William died. More than one thousand persons marched with the body to the cemetery. Vigilantes tried Casey and decreed death by hanging. When Judge McGowan was tried as an accessory, doctors disagreed on cause of death of King of William. Some said his death was caused because of a dirty sponge being used on the wound. McGowan was freed.

Thomas King, New Publisher

Thomas King, who managed the *Evening Bulletin* when his brother died, whipped up the vigilante movement. He also carried on an exposé of the frightful conditions in San Quentin prison. He found that James M. Estell, state assemblyman who had contracted to feed and clothe

San Quentin prisoners for $10,000 a month, had sublet the job for $5,000 a month. King declared that, as a result, the prisoners were half starved, half naked and eaten by vermin.

Assemblyman Estell replied in the state assembly, calling this news libelous. He retaliated by asserting that King had deserted his wife who became a prostitute. The politician declared that King shared her profits and received enough money to come to California. King printed every word that Assemblyman Estell delivered.

The editor then had his investigators check into the assemblyman's past. King accused the legislator of taking two Negro boys from San Quentin and sending them to New Orleans to be sold back into slavery. He intimated that Assemblyman Estell had helped convicts escape from prison. The effects of the newspaper stories can be guessed: Estell went into political eclipse.

The *Evening Bulletin* prospered. Forty printers were employed, King boasted; besides, twenty-one carriers delivered the paper in the city and ninety-three in country districts. Expenses were from $2,000 to $2,300 per week. Circulation of the daily *Evening Bulletin* reached 6,500; the weekly edition had 10,000 readers.

Suddenly on January 17, 1859, King announced that he was giving up in San Francisco, selling his paper to C. O. Gerberding. King returned East. Within two months the new proprietor of the *Evening Bulletin* was joined in partnership by James W. Simonton, Washington correspondent of the *New York Times.* Simonton remained only a short time, then sold half of his interest to George K. Fitch, an experienced newsman.

Fitch had come to San Francisco to start a newspaper, but after looking over the competition decided to go on to Sacramento, where he established a newspaper. Later he returned to San Francisco, and with Loring Pickering began the *Times & Transcript.* When the Democrats offered the partners $30,000 for the paper, they accepted. Following a trip to Europe Fitch returned to San Francisco and bought into the *Evening Bulletin.* The political *Times & Transcript,* meanwhile, lasted only a few more years, then expired.

Daily Morning Call Begins

The *Daily Morning Call* began under odd circumstances. Its origin was typical of carefree San Francisco of the middle fifties. The city was suffering from a depression and printers were unemployed. Five of these gathered at their favorite saloon, the Blue Wing, in November, 1856. They had six hundred fifty dollars in the office of the saloon, money

TABLE 19

First Papers in Midwest, Southwest, Far West (1830-1865)

State	Paper	Date
North Central		
	Green Bay Intelligencer (Weekly)	1836
Wisconsin	Milwaukee Advertiser	1833
Minnesota	Minnesota Pioneer	1849
Iowa	Dubuque Visitor	1836
Nebraska	Nebraska Palladium	1854
Kansas	Shawnee Sun (Indian)	1835
	Kansas Weekly Herald (English)	1854
Southwest		
Texas	Telegraph and Texas Register	1835
Oklahoma	Cherokee Messenger	1844
New Mexico	El Crepusculo	1834
Arizona	Weekly Arizonian	1859
Pacific Coast		
Oregon	Oregon Spectator	1846
	(Oregonian—First Daily)	1861
Washington	Columbian	1852
California	Californian Monterey	1846
Far West		
Utah	Deseret News	1850
Nevada	Territorial Enterprise	1858
Colorado	Rocky Mountain News	1859
South Dakota	Dakota Democrat	1858
Idaho	Golden Age	1862
Montana	Montana Post	1864

set aside for newspaper publication one day. Now was the time. The unemployed printers sat in the saloon to decide on the name of the paper and to determine the kind of equipment they needed. To think more clearly they moved outside. Then one of the printers saw a bill poster across the street being pasted up to advertise an evening program of the Metropolitan Theatre. The name of the play was "The Morning Call." The printer shouted, "That's it. I've got it! 'The Morning Call.' "

The first *Morning Call* came off the press on December 1, 1856. The price was 12 1/2 cents. Few other papers were priced this low. The *Morning Call* appealed to the working man. The partners had a rough journalistic road to travel. A fire destroyed their printshop, but they started again. Several of the partners sold out by the opening of the Civil War; the *Morning Call,* however, survived the conflict, being purchased in 1868 by Loring Pickering.

Los Angeles Journalism

Just as northern California problems were reflected in San Francisco papers, the southern part of the state was mirrored in Los Angeles papers. In 1851 Los Angeles was a frontier community with a population of fifteen hundred, composed of whites and Mexicans. It had three or four two-story buildings but mostly adobe huts. The town was a combination of Spanish and Anglo-American culture. Newsmen who established journalism in Los Angeles had traveled west with the gold seekers. Reporters and editors tried mining for a period but soon abandoned mining equipment for typecases.

John E. Lewis and E. Gould Buffum saw possibilities in the future of Los Angeles and launched the *Los Angeles Star* in 1851. Buffum had worked on the *New York Herald* and had been city editor of the *Alta California* in San Francisco. Financial troubles beset the efforts of a succession of early publishers, but with the coming of an Englishman, Henry Hamilton, this situation changed. Hamilton had arrived in this country in 1848. After spending a year at the mines he turned to newspaper work in San Francisco. Soon after arriving in Los Angeles and joining the *Los Angeles Star,* Hamilton made the paper into a thriving, small-town paper, aided by economic expansion of the region and the development of Los Angeles.

Chapter 15

Civil War Press

The Civil War provided a severe test for newspapers. Even in northern states people were not unified in their attitudes toward the questions of slavery and southern secession. Newspapers reflected these feelings of bitterness of groups in the North and South.

NORTH-SOUTH SECTIONALISM GROWS

The North

In previous chapters growing differences between the northern and southern regions of the United States have been mentioned. Commercial and industrial interests of the North, whose views were reflected in the Whig and Republican press such as the *New York Tribune, New York Times* and *Chicago Tribune,* desired certain economic and political measures which would aid their sectional growth. Political and newspaper spokesmen for expanding textile and iron businesses wanted a high tariff. Other commercial interests sought federal aid in the form of subsidies for building a transcontinental railroad and for developing the shipping business. Big city bankers wanted a strong centralized system of banks for better credit control. Others in the North desired free farms in the West to be settled by small farmers and their families.

Meanwhile, in the North, a group of abolitionists opposed slavery on moral grounds. Although a small band at first and subject to many abuses, they eventually, under the spur of William Lloyd Garrison and his *Liberator,* persuaded others of the immorality of slavery. Abolitionists multiplied.

In border states other abolition publishers were at work. Cassius Marcellus Clay published the *True American* in 1845 in Lexington,

Kentucky, but the short-lived paper was legally seized as a result of a court injunction. When a legislative bill to muzzle the press failed, J. C. Vaugham, one of Clay's former employees, founded the *Examiner* in Louisville to continue Clay's efforts.

In Cincinnati, Ohio free territory, James G. Birney began the *Philanthropist* in 1836, and it was wrecked several times by proslavery mobs. Editors, even those not closely involved, began to feel that the constitutional guarantee of free speech was being jeopardized. One such was Elijah Lovejoy, who first issued the *Alton Telegraph* in July, 1836, saying he was not an abolitionist but was concerned with freedom to speak, write and publish whatever he wanted to on any subject. Three times mobs wrecked the *Telegraph,* but each time Lovejoy started his presses again. Then the mob once more attacked and Lovejoy was killed in the clash. The abolition movement had its first martyr, a newspaperman.

Lovejoy's death aroused sympathy for abolitionists in both North and South. Abolitionists became identified as defenders of traditional American rights, and men and women, severe and uncompromising, rallied around abolitionist editors. Local antislavery societies were formed and federated into national organizations. Petitions denouncing human bondage were circulated by the thousands.

Though their number grew, when the abolitionists entered the political arena they failed. Their Liberty Party in 1844 received only 65,000 votes of 2.5 million ballots cast. But the abolitionists had a powerful influence on the public, consolidating all wavering forces in the South against slavery. And with their small but powerful weeklies, abolitionists influenced such northern daily editors as Horace Greeley.

The South

In the South the planting economy developed. Although other crops were raised, cotton was indeed king. The slave system was used to operate the plantations. Southerners, whose views were reflected in their press, were opposed to high tariffs on imports, for they believed such legislation would raise the cost of imported commodities and the price of domestic manufactured goods as well.

The South objected to federal subsidies for a transcontinental railroad based in Chicago. The southerners intended to build a railroad from New Orleans, but this project did not develop. The South did not want the Midwest settled by small farmers because this meant the institution of slavery would not be extended. Southern leaders defended the system of slavery on Biblical grounds and indicated that the Negroes had benefited by their removal from Africa to a more advanced civilization: the United States. They argued that slaves on the southern plantations were treated better than wage earners in the northern factories.

Editors of southern papers voiced the fears of many who saw rapid population, economic and cultural growth of the region above the Mason-Dixon Line. Immigrants came and settled in the trans-Allegheny and Mississippi valley regions, swelling the census figures. In industrial cities population also increased rapidly. Southern banks were indebted to northern financial institutions. Southern cotton and other products were shipped to foreign ports by northern shipping companies who profited by this freight business. Merchants from northern cities moved to the South and took some of the trade opportunities away. Southerners feared they were becoming an economic colony of the North which was exploiting them.

Culturally the North moved ahead; southern young men went to northern schools. Magazine centers of the nation were in Philadelphia and New York.

Although the balance of political power remained in southern hands, the North and Northeast gained steadily each decade. Southern newspapers expressed the fear that the balance would be upset and would lean in favor of northern industrial and commercial interests. They objected to efforts being made to block the admission of new territory in the West as slave states, states which would help the South keep its congressional power and hence control over legislation and federal jobs. They objected also to the continuous agitation for abolition of slavery by the "fanatics," the abolitionists.

As more territory was added to the United States, the question of whether to admit the new regions as slave states recurred. Compromises were worked out for these sectional differences to keep the country from splitting in two and to retain a balance of power. The Compromise of 1830 admitted Maine as a free state and Missouri as a slave state. The Compromise of 1850 admitted California as a free state and abolished slave trade in the District of Columbia.

With admission of New Mexico and Utah into the Union, allowing settlers to choose free or slave state status for themselves, it was believed that the slavery controversy was finally settled.

The Kansas-Nebraska Bill of 1854 also allowed settlers to make their own decisions about slavery, but the results of this compromise were anything but peaceful. After the law was passed slavery and antislavery groups, each backed by commercial interests in the North and South, pushed into these territories to gain control. News of the bloody civil war which broke out in Kansas shook the nation, splitting northern and southern editors again.

In deciding the Dred Scott case in 1857, the United States Supreme Court contributed to the conflict. Scott, a slave from Missouri, was taken into Illinois and Minnesota, free states. Was Scott free? The Supreme Court said, "No." The court ruled he was not even a citizen; consequently, he could not sue for freedom in the courts. But the judges went further and declared the Compromise of 1850 unconstitutional. Congress had no power to bar slavery from states. This decision aggravated the troubles. Northern editors denounced the decision. Southern editors applauded.

LINCOLN RECOGNIZES VALUE OF PRESS

One politician who watched these events with interest was Abraham Lincoln. Early in his career in Illinois, Lincoln recognized the value of the press and what it might do for an ambitious politician. Secretly, he was part owner of a small German newspaper, the *Illinois Staats-Zeitung* in Springfield. When he ran for the Illinois legislature in 1836, he contributed articles to the *Sangamo* (Illinois) *Journal,* and even after he was elected he served as the *Journal's* correspondent. Lincoln also read a wide variety of newspapers published in Chicago, New York, Washington and even those in Richmond and Charleston. Originally a Whig, Lincoln joined the Republican Party.

When Senator Stephen A. Douglas, a nominee of the Democratic Party, ran for the Senate to succeed himself in 1858, his opponent was Lincoln, the Republican candidate. Lincoln followed Douglas throughout Illinois and then debated with him from the same platform. Newspapers featured these debates. The spectacle of a formal debate captured the public's attention. Texts of the speeches were carried in the press, and newspapers quarreled with one another as to which had the most accurate accounts. Printed speeches were not given by the debaters to the press before orations were made so correspondents had to take notes amidst the crowd. The Lincoln-Douglas debates published in the press of the nation pointed up the central issues of the slavery-extension problem.

Although Senator Douglas won the senatorial election, the effect of the newspaper publicity was to start a boom for Lincoln for President. In spite of the fact that Democratic papers, such as the *New York Herald,* favored Douglas, they printed news of the Lincoln boom. At the Republican presidential convention in Chicago in July, 1860, it appeared that

Figure 34. (Top) Lincoln Appreciates Press. Long before he became President, Abe Lincoln knew the value of the newspaper. He was an avid reader of Illinois weeklies when he clerked in the general store. Secretly, he was part owner of a small German newspaper, the *Illinois Staats-Zeitung* in Springfield. Later, he contributed articles to the *Sangamo* (Illinois) *Journal.* (Bottom) *Lincoln-Douglas Debates Reported.* When Abraham Lincoln debated the slavery issue with the formidable fighter, Senator Stephen A. Douglas, in 1856, reporters took down every word and spread the debates for all to see. While Lincoln lost, the publicity stemming from the debates launched him into the national political spotlight, leading to his nomination for presidency on the Republican ticket.

Governor William H. Seward of New York would be nominated. Journalists were active and influential in the proceedings. Joseph Medill of the *Chicago Tribune* worked hard for Lincoln, but it was Horace Greeley, editor of the *New York Tribune,* sitting as a substitute delegate from Oregon, who headed Seward off. Greeley was not in favor of Lincoln but supported Edward Bates, another candidate. The editor rushed about from delegation to delegation, persuading members not to vote for Seward. On the third ballot Lincoln votes jumped ahead. Then he won the nomination. This was sensational news; it was contrary to what had been expected.

Republican papers in the eastern states generally supported Lincoln's nomination. Some Democratic dailies indulged in ridicule. The New York *Journal of Commerce* declared Lincoln did not have the qualifications for the office. The Albany *Atlas and Argus* pointed out that Lincoln was a "slam-whanging stump speaker of which all parties are ashamed." The story of Greeley's role at the convention was spread on the pages of the *New York Times* and the *New York Tribune* for all to see.

Newspapers, meanwhile, reported the splitting of the Democratic Party into three groups, each group nominating a different candidate for president. During the campaign which followed the conventions, northern Republican editors, corresponding with Lincoln, advised him how to run his campaign and supported him.

Southern newspaper editors were in a ferment. They wrote that election of Lincoln would mean dismemberment of the Union. They reported that South Carolina's Governor William Gist urged his state to secede from the Union if Abe Lincoln won. Because of the split in the Democratic Party, Lincoln won.

TABLE 20

The Presidential Vote in 1860

Lincoln	1,857,610
Douglas	1,365,976
Breckenridge	857,953
Bell	590,631

Newspaper editors reacted with stunned surprise at the results. In border states and the deeper South, some newspapers were violent, others were cautious, still others urged secession. The *Richmond* (Virginia) *Enquirer* called the results a "sectional conflict," while the *Dispatch,* in the same city, cried out "The country is in peril." The *New Orleans Crescent* emphasized that the northern people had perpetrated a cold-blooded insult, while the *Atlanta* (Georgia) *Confederacy,* screamed "Every member of Congress representing a southern constituency should resign at once." In border states, reflecting the division of citizens, some newspapers took a secession stand, while other publishers were opposed to withdrawing from the Union.

In December, 1860, South Carolina passed an ordinance of secession and withdrew from the Union. South Carolina was followed by other states. In February, 1861, the Confederate States of America was formed; it elected Jefferson Davis, president, and Alexander Stephens, vice president. Extremists saw "the inevitability of the conflict." The leading exponent of secession was the *Charleston* (South Carolina) *Mercury.*

President Lincoln ordered relief for Fort Sumter. A mortar shell from a Confederate battery burst over the Fort on April 12, 1861. The Civil War began. Three days later Lincoln called for seventy-five thousand troops. The Confederate government moved to Richmond, and the *Richmond Examiner* called for the capture of Washington, where Lincoln "the beast of Illinois ape lived." The *Richmond Whig* vowed "vengeance on the tyrants."

NORTHERN PAPERS REPORT THE WAR

Editorial Criticism of the War

Lincoln and his administration did not have the solid support of Republican papers, and the President was also opposed by Democratic newspapers in the North. Most large cities had both Republican and Democratic papers representing various views and groups. It was difficult to tell who was loyal and who wasn't, under such circumstances. Lincoln was not the favorite of the powerful *New York Times* nor of the *New York Tribune* at the national Republican convention. The *Times* had favored Seward; the *Tribune,* Bates. Thus, although they supported Lincoln in the election of 1860, these papers had no hesitancy in criticizing him when he took office. They found fault with his indecision and they were unmerciful when his generals lost battles.

New York had close connections commercially with the South, therefore, New York merchants favored the South. This was reflected in the Democratic newspapers and the *Sun, Herald, World, Journal of Commerce, Day Book* and the *Daily News.* Before and during the Civil War the *Sun* was in a difficult position. It had always supported the Democratic Party, but its readers were confined to New York City, and it made no bid for a southern circulation as did the *Herald*. Although opposed to secession the *Sun* did not believe in military coercion. Once the war on the South was declared the *Sun* vigorously advocated fighting the plantation owners.

The *Herald* sided with the South in the conflict over slavery and was severe on abolitionists. Still, the *Herald*'s loyalty was doubted, and a crowd marched to the publishing office to demand that "old man Bennett" show his colors, meaning the Stars and Stripes. Bennett procured a banner and made his bow to the mob beneath its flaunting folds. However, as a precaution, he bought a supply of the best rifles and stored them in the *Herald* office.

Forced by the Unionist element in New York to shift his policy, Bennett sent his promise to Lincoln, via his Washington correspondent, Henry Villard, that the *Herald* would thereafter be unconditionally for radical suppression of rebellion by force of arms and would support any necessary war measures. From then on the *Herald* backed Lincoln, even attacking English papers pro-southern in their views.

As election day 1864 approached, Lincoln had only one New York paper entirely with him: Raymond's *New York Times*. Knowing how important it was to have the support of the *Herald*, Lincoln wrote Bennett that he proposed at some convenient and not distant day to nominate the publisher to the United States Senate as Minister to France. Bennett declined the foreign post; gradually, however, he moved toward Lincoln's renomination.

In New York, as in other cities, the Copperhead press, representing the Peace Democrats, was hostile from the beginning of the war.

Reporting the War

The Civil War was the first large-scale war covered by the American press. More than one hundred fifty reporters watched the battles and reported them for their newspapers. These correspondents were not officially recognized by the military, and they obtained their information in any way they could. Large big city newspapers had newsmen in Washington as well as on battlefields where they were attached to officers' staffs as aides or served as dispatch carriers and signal officers.

For the first time the telegraph could be used to transmit war news, but a telegraph censorship system had not been decided upon.

Battlefront Reporting

On the battlefronts, the *Boston Journal*, the *New York World*, the *New York Evening Post*, the *Philadelphia Press* and the *Inquirer* had their own correspondents. The *Chicago Tribune* sent out its own newsmen as did the *Cincinnati Gazette* and the *Cincinnati Commercial.*

So clearly had Bennett of the *New York Herald* envisaged the coming conflict that he was better prepared than any of his contemporaries to meet the war emergencies. He gathered a force of forty men and sent them splendidly equipped to various fronts. This force later grew to sixty men, and special dispatches were paid for liberally, a few exclusive lines bringing as much as twenty-five dollars for the sender. Thus, the *Herald* was always first choice among men on the spot as a market for their news. During the four-year conflict the paper spent $520,000 covering the rebellion. Five *Herald* correspondents were imprisoned. One *Herald* "special" was killed in battle, and three others died from illness and exposure during the war. Seventy-five of the *Herald* horses correspondents rode were killed.

One exploit that astonished the War Department both at Richmond and at Washington was the *Herald's* publication of an almost correct roster of the Confederate Army. Richmond thought it had been done by

Figure 35. Field Headquarters, *New York Herald.* The *New York Herald* covered the Civil War with the newspaper's usual thorough news. James Gordon Bennett even had a field headquarters which followed the northern army. This photo was made at Culpepper Court House, Virginia where General U. S. Grant established his headquarters. (A Mathew S. Brady photo)

some traitor to the cause, and Washington felt that the *Herald* had improper relations with the South. Actually, however, the achievement was the result of close calculations and the compiling of carefully gathered facts.

Correspondents on the battlefront had an unusually good opportunity to pick up news of what was occurring inside enemy lines. A regular exchange of newspapers kept the North and South informed about current news. Southern papers carried full reports on Jeff Davis' message to the Confederate Congress and the report of the southern Secretary of the Treasury. Papers came through the line at Petersburg, Virginia, and also through Alexandria, Virginia. Soldiers had their own codes, and pickets of both armies were allowed to exchange newspapers. Ex-general Roger A. Pryor, a Confederate, however, was caught while exchanging papers and put in prison in November, 1864.

A number of correspondents distinguished themselves for their abilities to get the news under difficult circumstances and write vividly about the din of battle and the charge of the footsoldiers and cavalry so the thousands of readers back home could visualize the war scenes. The "specials" obtained their information from first-hand observations and from talking to soldiers and commanding officers. Then the specials had to get this information back to their newspaper offices—a heroic effort in many areas.

A number of these correspondents made names for themselves and became top reporters, news executives and even editors after the war. Henry J. Raymond left his desk as editor to write vivid dispatches for the *New York Times.* Albert D. Richardson represented the *New York Tribune,* and while covering the Battle of Vicksburg with Junius H. Browne was captured by the Confederates and imprisoned. The two newsmen escaped and finally reached the Union lines. Another *Tribune* reporter, George W. Smalley wrote one of the great battle stories of the war at Antietam, but his dispatch was delayed in telegraphic transmission. Finally Smalley boarded a train and carried his story to New York, where the *Tribune* editor filled six columns with the battle news.

Writing under the penname of "Agate", Whitelaw Reid was the only correspondent to witness the battle of Shiloh; somehow he managed to get his dispatch to the *Cincinnati Gazette,* where the editor used ten columns of his battle story. Another newsman from Cincinnati, Murat Halstead represented the *Commercial,* of which he later became editor. Starting off as a special for the *New York Herald,* Henry Villard later became chief war correspondent for the *Tribune.* Charles Carleton Coffin, who wrote under "Carleton" for the *Boston Journal,* was the only "special" who served throughout the entire war.

STAGES OF NEWS CENSORSHIP

Censorship of Civil War news was not clear-cut but the enactment of federal regulations and the actions and responses of newsmen over a four-year period seem to indicate three stages of censorship development.

First Stage, 1861-1862

This first stage was a period of uncertainty and groping by the government for some workable solution. It was characterized also by voluntary self-censorship of the press.

At the beginning of the war the government had no guidelines for controlling the publication of military news which would help the enemy, nor did officials know how to get responsible newspapermen to do their own censoring and exercise restraint. Publishers were independent and strongly competitive and wanted to beat their rivals in getting the news for readers. During peace times this was a satisfactory situation, but what about during a war? Would this rivalry in news publication, result in revealing to the enemy information about troop strength and movements and plans of generals?

During the first phase of war censorship, which lasted from the opening of the war to the spring of 1862, the government by trial and error sought to find a way to deal with the press problem. Under the law of 1801 the federal officials could deny anyone the right to send messages to enemy lines. The government realized that messages from private individuals and newspapers might reveal military secrets.

On May 20, 1861 the first step was made to block the sending of such messages. Federal officials in New York and Washington pounced down on local telegraph offices and picked up telegrams being sent to the South. About six weeks later a more drastic and specific restriction was imposed. General Winfield Scott issued an order, dated July 8, 1861, which forbade telegraph companies to send any military information. This was backed up by Secretary of War Edwin M. Stanton.

Newsmen complained that their dispatches about frontline battles were interfered with. General George B. McClelland, therefore, on August 2, 1861, called a press conference at which two actions were taken. First, he got the newsmen to sign an agreement binding them to transmit no information of value to the enemy. Secondly, the general agreed to facilitate the gathering and transmission of news to newspaper offices.

This seemed to be a satisfactory answer, but the plan did not work out. Who was to be the censor and determine what was information of value to the enemy? At the time a rivalry existed between the Department of War and the Secretary of State. H. E. Thayer, of the Secretary of State's office, was placed in charge of press regulations. Many violations occurred. In three months McClellan's press plan broke down.

Then on October 22, 1861 the Secretary of State prohibited telegraph companies from sending any dispatches about the military *or* civilian operations of the government. Newspaper correspondents found this regulation too much of an interference. They abandoned their voluntary agreement and sought and published whatever news they could get.

Again complaints mounted. The government reacted. A congressional investigation of federal censorship problems began on December 5, 1861.

Second Stage, 1862-1864

During this second period, both further clarification of censorship regulations and a better understanding of the problem by government and the correspondents were achieved.

In February, 1862 all telegraph lines were placed under United States supervision. Secretary of War Stanton went into action to improve press-government relations, for President Lincoln transferred to him the responsibility for carrying out and perhaps improving the old newspaper agreement which had broken down. Stanton clarified the restrictions of the previous voluntary pact so that better guidelines were available for newsmen. The correspondents agreed to submit their copy to the provost marshall in the area for approval. He was to make no deletions of nonmilitary matters. More than before, newsmen knew how far they could go. Soon the congressional committee on press censorship made its report. In March, 1862 the committee recommended an end of restrictions on nonmilitary dispatches.

While the Stanton press plan was satisfactory on paper and worked fairly well in practice, it had its faults. The plan was poorly and not uniformly enforced. Carrying out the censorship was not an easy task because it meant that someone had to determine what was publishable. This determination depended on personal interpretation. The military commandant in the field could thus abuse the power. Ambitious military leaders could harass a correspondent who criticized him and could block the sending of dispatches, or trim them. General Grant got rid of General John A. McClerand because he abused his power.

General Sherman felt that newspaper leaks were enabling the South to win a number of battles. He had arrested Thomas E. Knox, of the *Herald,* accusing him of being a spy, as Knox sent dispatches violating regulations. Knox could have been shot, but this was not the intention of General Sherman; he wanted to make the Knox incident a test case. President Lincoln intervened in the case and Knox was freed. The test case, however, set a precedent that all correspondents should be accredited or recognized and that they also be acceptable to the commandant in whose area they worked.

Third Stage, 1864-1865

In this last period, the correspondents cooperated more fully with the federal government. The trouble arose when local area military commanders undertook to exert pressure on publishers whom the military felt were traitors.

Most of the problems arose from the Copperhead press. Wilbur S. Storey, publisher of the *Chicago Times,* was a strong-minded and militant newsman who printed violent attacks on President Lincoln. General Ambrose Burnside, in charge of the War Department in Ohio and the military district in Illinois, decided to suspend the *Chicago Times,* leader of the Copperheads in the area. As military commander, General Burnside said his power enabled him to silence expression of ideas and information harmful to the military. After Storey was given warnings, General Burnside had the *Chicago Times* padlocked. After three days President Lincoln rescinded the military order. The President, a patient and lenient man, wanted to back up his generals, but he also believed that the press should be free and unrestricted and that the public needed information about the war.

PUBLISHERS SUPPRESSED

Edited by Manton Marble, the *New York World* was owned by August Belmont, banker, and Fernando Wood, mayor. The *World* breathed hostility to Lincoln and his cabinet. This daily became the leading spokesman for the Peace Democrats. General John A. Dix suppressed the *World* and the *Journal of Commerce* for two days in May, 1864. The editors had printed a forged proclamation ordering the draft of four hundred thousand men. The forging was the work of Joseph Howard, Jr., city editor of the *Brooklyn Eagle.* He wrote the news on the regular onion-skin sheet of the Associated Press and had the news delivered late at night to various New York papers. Most of them suspected the forgery, but editors in charge of the *World* and the *Journal of Commerce* printed the news as truth. Howard was confined to a military prison for three months, then discharged. The *New Orleans*

Picayune copied the news and was suspended for two weeks by northern military occupying New Orleans. Some other Democratic papers were denied mailing privileges.

A New York federal grand jury offered a peculiar document, inquiring "whether certain newspapers such as the *Daily News, Journal of Commerce,* the *Day Book, Freeman's Journal,* and *Brooklyn Eagle,* were not guilty of disloyalty and subject to presentment, for encouraging the enemy?" No indictment was returned, but the postmaster general ordered the New York postmaster not to accept these papers for mailing. Loss of its mailing privileges did not deter the *Brooklyn Eagle* from continuing to oppose Lincoln. More drastic action was taken against the *Freeman's Journal,* a Presbyterian newspaper. The post office suspended it for eight months, and its editor, James A. McMaster, was confined to Fort Lafayette prison.

In other cities and states the press was equally divided over the war issue. Lincoln had staunch editorial friends as well as severe opposition critics. Military commanders in various parts of the country suppressed anti-Lincoln newspapers, sending their editors to prison. Often they languished there without formal charges being brought against them, only to be released after months of confinement. Irresponsible soldiers, aroused by editorials which ridiculed the administration or the military, wrecked newspaper offices and threatened to hang the editors. Civilian mobs, also aroused by editorials of their local newspapers, entered and damaged newspaper offices.

While many dailies cooperated and avoided publication of military news and secrets, many northern newspapers throughout the war printed news which was helpful to the South and caused battles to be lost and men to be killed. Even Republican papers favoring Lincoln published unfavorable news. Cincinnati newspapers printed information which delayed or thwarted the Union forces, and General Sherman thought the papers were doing infinite harm.

Although reprimanded strenuously for printing military information valuable to the Confederates, the *New York Evening Post* broke the news that the 11th and 12th corps were being sent to reenforce Major General W. S. Rosencrans, despite the fact that papers had been requested not to use the information. As a result of the news leakage, General Rosencrans suffered heavy losses. President Lincoln and Secretary of War Stanton became angry.

One of the best naval reporters of the war, C. S. Osbon, of the *New York World,* wrote that the northern fleet was ready to attack at Wilmington, North Carolina. This news got back to the southern forces so they were prepared to repel Union attackers. Secretary of War Stanton expected to prosecute Osbon for revealing the plan, but the War and Navy Departments could not agree on the course to pursue. Although Osbon was finally arrested, no charges were preferred, and he was released on parole, July, 1865.

Once William Swinton, representing the *New York Times,* was reprimanded by General Grant for his dispatches. Later General Burnside ordered Swinton arrested and shot, but Grant interceded and expelled him from camp with an order never to return.

SOUTHERN NEWSPAPERS FACE NEW PROBLEMS IN WAR

Until 1830 the slavery question could be debated freely in southern states. Antislavery societies were organized there. Proposals were made for gradual emancipation and colonization of the slaves. Restrictive laws were not enacted.

After 1830, however, the southern journalist faced a different problem. Repressive laws, aimed at restricting freedom of speech and of the press, began to appear on state books, motivated almost wholly by fear of the "black terror." By 1836 the press in the lower South was almost completely muzzled by law if slavery was to be discussed. Penalties ranged from fines, lashes and jail sentences to death.

Actually the laws were aimed at northern abolitionists rather than southern journalists. The courts' interpretations were uniformly lenient in the case of southern editors. However, public opinion usually discouraged the editor with reform ideas before his utterances had reached the prosecution stage. When public opinion failed, the abolitionist editor was run out of town. The statutes governing the press, however, did not solve the problem of abolition literature printed in the North, literature which found its way in the mails to slave states.

Southern press publishers had twice as many troubles as their northern contemporaries in publishing during the war. Southern printers and reporters enlisted in the Confederate Army; consequently, publishers were handicapped. A paper shortage soon occurred, as only 5 per cent of the mills were in the South; publishers, therefore, restricted the size of their sheets, sometimes issuing only a single sheet with a resumé of the news. Some publishers resorted to printing on wallpaper, as did the *Vicksburg* (Mississippi) *Daily Citizen.* The *Macon* (Georgia) *Daily Confederate* suspended when it could not get newsprint.

When actual fighting began news became scarce. Northern papers at first were sent in exchange, following the usual courtesies, but feelings were aroused and this supply was cut off. Southern papers were not wealthy enough to have correspondents in the battlefields, and often the editors would copy news from the New York papers when they were obtained.

Southern newspaper correspondents used pseudonyms in their reports. These included "Personne," "Bohemian," "Adsum," and also initials such as "D. G. D." and "O. K."

The southern press was not represented at many of the battles. On the eve of the first Battle of Manassas General Beauregard ordered all civilians except residents to vacate the area. Some exceptions were allowed for press correspondents. Although restricted as to what they were permitted to see and describe, correspondents were not excluded from Confederate lines until May, 1862, when General Bragg ousted them from his headquarters in Mississippi, a policy quickly initiated in other war theatres. Thus, the war news in the southern press suffered.

Correspondents of the southern papers often saw only brief service. Gustave Meyer represented the *Richmond Daily Dispatch;* P. W. Alexander, of the *Savannah Republican,* won frequent praise for his battle descriptions. F. G. de Fontaine, editor of the *Charleston Daily Courier,* wrote dispatches under his pseudonym, "Personne."

As the war interrupted the flow of news from the North and from other sections and as the rebellion stopped the news obtained before through the New York Associated Press, southern papers were presented with another obstacle. When the Civil War began, no system of preparing and transmitting news of public interest existed in the Confederacy. Southern publishers, therefore, began to think of filling this journalistic and public need.

Confederate Press Association Begins

In January, 1862, editors from six newspapers met in Atlanta to improve their news-gathering services. They formed their own Confederate Associated Press, establishing correspondence and some lines of communication and serving three-fourths of the southern dailies. Although various meetings were held, it was not until February 4, 1863, that a significant conference was arranged in Augusta, Georgia, where action was taken to establish definitely the Press Association of the Confederate States of America. A superintendent, J. S. Thrasher, was hired at three thousand dollars a year. The editors demanded a free press in the Confederacy and adopted a constitution which stated the importance of the Press Association in obtaining early, full and reliable intelligence by telegraph.

Military censorship became an immediate problem of the association's new superintendent. Thrasher learned how commanders and Confederate authorities took steps to prevent transmission of press reports over the telegraph.

Correspondents were instructed to dispatch no opinion or comment on events and to be careful to sift reports. Do not send rumors as news, they were told. To obtain objectivity of stories sent by the Confederate Press Association meant a complete revolution in the habits of writers for the southern press. Strenuous resistance developed in many quarters. In spite of Thrasher's efforts, correspondents encountered trouble in telegraphing military information.

A move was made in the Confederate Congress to transfer control of telegraph lines from the War Department to the post office. This was blocked. Then the South-Western Telegraph Company sought to become publishers of press association reports. The company charged heavily for news transmission and tried to limit circulation of the news to newspapers. At the same time, the telegraph company began distributing the news to numerous private clubs. The company tapped the wires; it sold the information to groups of men for sixty dollars. Thus a private group might obtain news as quickly as newspapers. Thrasher then copyrighted the PA news. The telegraph company now attempted to get the Confederate Congress to amend the copyright laws to exclude the press from the benefits of the laws. The attempt failed.

In January, 1864, the superintendent again fought for a free press when an effort was made in Congress to draft newspaper workers for the army. He saw this as new danger to the free press in the South. He feared the editors would be drafted because they dared to criticize. Again Thrasher succeeded. Whenever federal troops occupied a town and took over the southern newspaper, the PA service was necessarily suspended.

When federal troops moved into border towns and communities in the Deep South, the soldiers arrested some publishers, pushed others out of their offices, and in some instances had northern soldiers or northern correspondents run the newspapers, now changed to the pro-federal side.

When the war ended the South was crippled and the newspapers were similarly affected. For some time Republican newspapers were issued in some of the cities, depending on federal patronage to keep them alive. With the end of reconstruction days, the papers folded and left a Democratic press.

WAR NEWS PRINTED ON FRONT PAGE

The Civil War broke the advertiser's monopoly of front page space. Publishers learned that battle reports or any exciting event stimulated general reader interest. By raising the price of this front page space, as it assumed greater value, or by eliminating some of the ads, publishers decreased the amount of advertising matter on page one. Ads on the front page were thus eliminated, or reduced to a few lines.

Headlines began to develop vertically, with an increasing number of decks, or subheads being printed down the length of the column. Some subheads consisted of one or two cross lines; other subheads had three or four lines set in inverted pyramid style for variety.

EFFECTS OF CIVIL WAR ON NEWSPAPERS

Wars have always left their marks on journalism. The Civil War was no exception. The war gave readers a taste of lively, quickly transmitted news. The conflict quickened the public's interest in obtaining significant news and in purchasing newspapers.

The Civil War showed the value of the telegraph for rapid news transmission. Civil War news rang the death knell for long-winded essays and editorials. The 5-w summary lead for news articles began to appear more frequently.

HANG OUT YOUR BANNERS

UNION

VICTORY!

PEACE!

Surrender of General Lee and His Whole Army.

THE WORK OF PALM SUNDAY.

Final Triumph of the Army of the Potomac.

The Strategy and Diplomacy of Lieut.-Gen. Grant.

Terms and Conditions of the Surrender.

The Rebel Arms, Artillery, and Public Property Surrendered.

Rebel Officers Retain Their Side Arms and Private Property.

Figure 36. Civil War Headlines. One-column vertical headlines were used by editors to tell the story of battles. This was how the *New York Times* editors told their readers about the end of the war. Note the air of jubilation in the top crossline "Hang Out Your Banners."

One column, multiple-deck headlines made their appearance, and although editors reduced the number of decks after the war, they were destined to reappear when news became exciting and violent. Vertical, multiple-deck headlines became a part of the makeup of the American newspaper.

Emergence of the reporter as the dominant person on the staff was accelerated by the news sent in by reporters on the warfront and by Washington correspondents. The reporter's importance was observed in the printing of his initials at the end of stories; the initials were requested by the War Department for identification purposes. The policy of attaching the reporter's initials, however, forecast the later by-lined stories of outstanding newsmen.

Sensational war news stirred the appetite of the public also for more sensations and more exploits of reporters. This appetite was to be fulfilled in various ways by publishers and editors after the Civil War was over.

Chapter 16

Magazines Popularized

MAGAZINE WORLD CHANGES

In the Jacksonian era there was a surge of magazine publication. The magazine was affected by the same population expansion and commercial development which influenced daily and weekly newspapers. Similar educational and democratizing forces influenced all periodicals. They were part of the same social pattern. In some respects the magazine was more responsive to social changes than the daily press.

Like the newspaper publisher the magazine entrepreneur at this time did not need much capital to launch his periodical.

One of the distinguishing features of the magazine world in this period was the great variety of publications. Literary and political magazines had been issued before, and they continued. New women's magazines and sports magazines were now established to cater to specialized requirements of these readers. Scientific, dramatic, musical and artistic magazines appeared, as activities in these areas multiplied and as persons with specialized interests increased. All economic, educational and social levels of society found publications suited to them. Prices were decreased in an attempt to secure a mass market.

Although New York, Boston and Philadelphia continued to be centers of the magazine industry, other cities produced magazines, drawing on regional writers for regional themes. In Baltimore, Richmond, Charleston, New Orleans and Cincinnati, enterprising editors started monthly or weekly literary periodicals.

Circulations of magazines increased phenomenally with the expansion of the reading market. Thousands of new readers were attracted by changes in the contents and the improvements in typography and illustrations of periodicals.

GENERAL MONTHLY MAGAZINES VARIED

Some of the old magazines such as the *Port Folio* died, but others, for example the *North American,* continued into the new era. To these were added fresh publications. Just as New England had its *North American,* so New York produced the *Knickerbocker* in 1833. The *Knickerbocker* was peculiarly New York, featuring such writers as Washington Irving. Its most famous editor was Lewis Gaylord Clark. The scope of the *Knickerbocker* was widened to appeal to a larger audience in the 1840s when it published serially Francis Parkman's *The Oregon Trail* and other stories of the West.

One of the most successful of the new publications, *Graham's,* illustrates some new tendencies of the period. When George R. Graham was twenty-six years old, he combined the *Casket,* which was an offshoot of the established *Saturday Evening Post,* with *Burton's Gentleman's Magazine,* forming *Graham's* magazine in 1840.

Intended to be a monthly record of current events, *Harper's New Monthly Magazine* was established in 1850 by the book publishing firm. Edited by Henry J. Raymond, *Harper's* aimed to cater to the newly awakened interests of the literate public and to bring an immense amount of useful and entertaining information "within the reach of the great mass of people." One of the purposes was to bring news and advertising about the books being issued by *Harper's* publishing company. A kind of magazine digest of its day, *Harper's* reprinted from many American and foreign magazines, but it republished more fully than later magazines and weeklies. *Harper's* sought to cover such subjects as exploration, travel, science, art, poetry and fiction.

Seven years after *Harper's* magazine was issued, another distinguished periodical, the *Atlantic Monthly,* made its appearance in Boston. With James Russell Lowell as its first editor and Oliver Wendell Holmes, its chief contributor, the *Atlantic* published the work of the New England writers. Holmes' "Autocrat of the Breakfast Table" appeared in the first issue.

Another regional magazine that gained attention beyond its area was the *Southern Literary Messenger,* published in Richmond, Virginia, and edited by Edgar Allan Poe between 1835 and 1837.

WOMEN'S MAGAZINES CATCH FEMININE INTEREST

Appealing to the host of women readers were newly established women's magazines. They not only developed and appealed to the feminine market, but their competition forced some of the more general magazines such as *Graham's* to cater to their public with fashion articles, stories and illustrations. One of the earliest to recognize the women's market was Sarah Josepha Hale, who founded the *Ladies' Magazine* in Boston in 1828. She published sentimental reading matter and advocated more educational opportunities for women. Although she continued publication for nine years, the faster pace set by Louis A. Godey in Philadelphia with his *Godey's Lady's Book,* established in 1830, led her to join forces with him.

Godey's Lady's Book, although it may have been rated inferior to others of the more general type, had a strong influence on American life. It set the tone for manners and morals. It established styles for clothes, furniture and homes. Although it had no dealings with political matters or intellectual subjects, *Godey's* did publish some of Hawthorne, Longfellow and Poe, whose literary criticisms were printed and caused a stir. Godey hired the most popular women writers including Harriet Beecher Stowe, whose *Uncle Tom's Cabin* made a tremendous success. *Godey's* emphasized sentimental stories, elegant and moral tales and moral verse.

POPULAR WEEKLIES

A new type of periodical, something of a cross between a general magazine and a newspaper, made its appearance in the 1850s. *Bonner's Ledger,* established in 1855, made the most spectacular success. Robert Bonner aimed at a vast audience and issued a sensational magazine. He hired the most popular writers of the day, featured dramatic serials by Sylvanus Coff, Jr., and sprightly essays by a well-known woman writer, Fanny Fern.

Emphasizing current news and pictures, another group of weeklies appeared in this decade. Although *Gleason's Pictorial* was the first in 1851, it was followed five years later by *Frank Leslie's Illustrated Newspaper,* similar in content. Founded by Henry Carter, an English-born engraver who changed his name to Frank Leslie and who had been editor of *Gleason's,* this eight page tabloid was filled with murders, fires, railroad accidents, disasters and lynchings. *Leslie's* chief feature, however, was the illustrations made on woodblocks. The editor distributed the woodblocks among a force of engravers and then assembled the parts of the illustrations quickly. *Leslie's* object was to bring illustrated events quickly to its readers. The Civil War provided an extraordinary opportunity for *Leslie's* and other illustrated magazines.

Third periodical of this type, *Harper's Weekly,* was founded in 1857, and it is considered a forerunner of the weekly news and pictorial magazines of the twentieth century. *Harper's Weekly* had outstanding news coverage, well-written feature articles and effective editorials. It carried short stories and serials, essays and poetry, but its outstanding feature was its vivid pictures. *Harper's* printed a full page of them. During the Civil War *Harper's Weekly* writers and photographers, especially Mathew Brady, were on all battlefronts. The artists made pen and ink sketches which were sent to New York and converted into engravings of war scenes.

SPORTS MAGAZINES APPEAL

Magazines catering to special interests made their appearance. John S. Skinner established the *American Turf Register* in 1829 in Baltimore; three years later, William B. Porter launched the *Spirit of the Times* in New York.

KNOWLEDGE MAGAZINES REFLECT THIRST FOR INFORMATION

Reflecting the awakening of public interest and the expansion of public education was another group of magazines. The aim of these periodicals was to bring educational and useful knowledge to the masses. While other magazines catered to the interest in sentimental stories and literature, these publications, cheap in price, were aimed at enlightenment. Similar types appeared first in England and France. In 1830 the *U. S. Magazine of Useful and Entertaining Knowledge* was issued in this country. In the next decade a number of similar ventures were established with such titles as the *Penny Magazine,* the *American Magazine of Useful and Entertaining Knowledge* and the *American Penny Magazine.*

ANTISLAVERY MAGAZINE, NEWSPAPERS

Mention has been made of the influential antislavery newspapers which had characteristics of magazines. The most famous and powerful of these, William Lloyd Garrison's *The Liberator,* lasted from 1831 until he folded the publication in December, 1865.

References

NEWSPAPERS

New York Journalism

The Sun

O'Brien, Frank M., *Story of the Sun,* New York: Appleton-Century-Crofts, 1928. (The standard history of the *Sun*; tells origins and development plus personalities.)

Bennett's New York Herald

Carlson, Oliver, *The Man Who Made News: James Gordon Bennett,* New York: Duell, Sloan and Pearce, 1942. (A top job, gives details, philosophy and development of Bennett and his paper. Contains quotations from *Herald.*)

Hudson, Frederic, *Journalism in the United States from 1690 to 1872,* New York: Harper & Row, Publishers, 1873. (Managing editor Hudson gives inside details on the *New York Herald.*)

Seitz, Don, *The James Gordon Bennetts,* Indianapolis: The Bobbs-Merrill Co., Inc., 1928. (An earlier but readable volume.)

Horace Greeley and New York Tribune

Borden, Morton, "Some Notes on Horace Greeley, Charles Dana, and Karl Marx," *Journalism Quarterly* 34:457-465, fall, 1957. (Useful bit of research which throws light on Marx and Greeley.)

Greeley, Horace, *Recollections of A Busy Life,* New York: J. B. Ford and Company. 1868. (A lively autobiography.)

Stoddard, Henry L., *Horace Greeley: Printer, Editor, Crusader,* New York: G. P. Putnam's Sons, 1946. (Very readable book, covers main points, written by an admirer.)

Van Deusen, Glyndon G., *Horace Greeley: Nineteenth Century Crusader,* Philadelphia: University of Pennsylvania Press, 1953. (A thorough, workman-like book written by a historian with a strong interest in journalism and journalists.)

See Civil War Journalism: Harlan H. Horner, *Lincoln and Greeley.*

New York Times and H. J. Raymond

Berger, Meyer, *Story of the New York Times,* New York: Simon and Schuster, Inc., 1951. (Has useful information on this early period. Written by a *Times* reporter. Should be read in conjunction with Elmer Davis' and Ernest Francis Brown's volumes below.)

Brown, Ernest Francis, *Raymond of the Times,* New York: W. W. Norton & Company, Inc., 1951. (Thoroughly researched. Tells story of the *Times* and its editor during this period.)

DAVIS, ELMER, *History of the New York Times, 1851-1921,* New York: New York Times, 1921. (The first history, but competently and fairly written by a *Times*man.)
See also under Young Nation's Newspapers section, lives of Tappan and Hallock.

New York Evening Post

GLICKSBURG, CHARLES I., "William Leggett, Neglected Figure of American Literary History," *Journalism Quarterly* 25:52, March, 1948. (See also Arthur M. Schlesinger, Jr., *Age of Jackson,* Boston: Little, Brown and Company, 1945, for additional interpretation.)
NEVINS, ALLAN, *Evening Post, A Century of Journalism,* New York: Boni & Liveright, 1922. (One of the best histories of an individual paper written.)
RUBIN, JOSEPH J., and CHARLES W. BROWN, *Walt Whitman of the New York Aurora: Editor at Twenty-two,* State College, Penn.: Pennsylvania State College, 1950.
VAN DEUSEN, GLYNDON G., *Thurlow Weed, Wizard of the Lobby,* Boston: Little, Brown and Company, 1947. (A thoroughly researched volume on the Albany editor and New York politician.)
WHITE, WILLIAM, "Walt Whitman: Journalist," *Journalism Quarterly* 39:3, summer, 1962.
See also biographies of William Cullen Bryant.

New England Press

CHAMBERLIN, JOSEPH E., *Boston Transcript: A History of Its First Hundred Years,* Boston: Houghton Mifflin Company, 1930. (A weak volume but the best available.)
HOOKER, RICHARD, *The Story of an Independent Newspaper,* New York: The Macmillan Company, 1924. (History of the *Springfield* (Mass.) *Republican* and its founder.)
MERRIAM, GEORGE S., *The Life and Times of Samuel Bowles,* New York: Century, 1885. (A detailed study written in nineteenth-century style.)
SMITH, JAMES E., *One Hundred Years of Hartford's Courant,* New Haven, Conn.: Yale University Press, 1949. (An outstanding history of an important paper.)

Southern Regions

AMBLER, CHARLES H., *Thomas Ritchie,* Richmond, Va.: Bell Book Co., 1913. (A study of the Virginia editor.)
COPELAND, FAYETTE, *Kendall of the Picayune,* Norman: University of Oklahoma Press, 1943. (Capable biography of New Orleans editor. See Thomas E. Dabney.)
DABNEY, THOMAS E., *One Hundred Great Years: The Story of the Times-Picayune,* Baton Rouge: Louisiana State University Press, 1944. (Gives account of the beginnings of the New Orleans paper and its subsequent development.)
JOHNSON, GERALD W. et al., *The Sunpapers of Baltimore,* New York: Alfred A. Knopf, Inc., 1937. (The early chapters, dealing with the beginnings of the *Sun,* are the most adequate.)

SASS, HERBERT E., *Outspoken, 150 Years of the News and Courier,* Columbia: University of South Carolina Press, 1953. (Sketchy but presents beginnings and development of paper.)

TALLEY, ROBERT, *One Hundred Years of the Commercial Appeal,* Memphis: *Commercial Appeal,* 1940.

WHITE, LAURA, *Robert Barnwell Rhett: Father of Secession,* New York: Century, 1931. (Only biography of this influential southern editor.)

North Central States

Chicago

KINSLEY, PHILIP, *Chicago Tribune* vol. I, New York: Alfred A. Knopf, Inc., 1943. (A day-by-day account with considerable detail.)

MCPHAUL, JOHN J., *Deadlines and Monkeyshines, Fabled World of Chicago Journalism,* Englewood Cliffs, N.J.: Prentice-Hall, Inc., 1962. (Many useful facts, anecdotal in approach.)

MONAGHAN, JAY, *Charles H. Ray, The Man Who Nominated Lincoln,* Indianapolis: The Bobbs-Merrill Co., Inc., 1956. (Tells about life and journalistic activities of one of the publishers of the *Chicago Tribune.*)

TEBBEL, JOHN, *An American Dynasty,* Garden City, N.Y.: Doubleday & Company, Inc., 1947. (Gives facts and analysis of the McCormick-Patterson families and their newspapers.)

Cleveland, Pittsburgh

ANDREWS, J. CUTLER, *Pittsburgh's Post-Gazette,* Boston: Chapman and Grimes, 1936. (Continues account of paper begun in previous period.)

SHAW, ARCHER H., *The Plain Dealer, One Hundred Years in Cleveland,* New York: Alfred A. Knopf, Inc., 1942. (A thorough-going study, based on research into files of the paper.)

Minnesota

EIDE, RICHARD B., *North Star Editor: A Brief Sketch of Joseph A. Wheelock and His Policies as Editor of the St. Paul Pioneer-Press,* New York: King's Crown Press, Columbia University, 1944. (Considers this midwestern editor in his environment.)

Missouri, St. Louis

HART, JIM ALLEE, *A History of the St. Louis Globe-Democrat,* Columbia: University of Missouri Press, 1961. (A top study, detailed, readable.)

LYON, WILLIAM H., *Pioneer Editor in Missouri, 1808-1860,* Columbia: University of Missouri Press, 1965. (Well-researched; has considerable detail on battles of editors and contents of papers.)

TAFT, WILLIAM H., *Missouri Newspapers,* Columbia: University of Missouri Press, 1964. (Pieces together the complex history of the papers in this period.)

Southwest and Rocky Mountain

ACHESON, SAM, *35,000 Days in Texas: A History of the Dallas News and Its Forebears,* New York: The Macmillan Company, 1938.

Ashton, Wendell J., *Voice in the West,* New York: Duell, Sloan & Pearce, 1950. (Deals with *Deseret* (Utah) *News* and its competitors; written by a member of *News* staff.)

Perkin, Robert L., *The First Hundred Years, An Informal History of the Rocky Mountain News,* Garden City, N.Y.: Doubleday & Company, Inc., 1955. (A competently written account of the Denver paper and its rivals.)

Pacific Coast Journalism

California

Bruce, John R., *Gaudy Century,* New York: Random House, Inc., 1949. (Deals with California papers. Has rich material, is anecdotal, seeks to recapture flavor of papers and editors; sometimes hard to follow.)

Weigle, Clifford E., "San Francisco, Journalism, 1849-51," *Journalism Quarterly* 14:151, June, 1937. (Excellent but short account of papers.)

Young, John P., *Journalism in California,* San Francisco: Chronicle Publishing Co., 1915. (Has some worthwhile facts but written in old-fashioned style. Needs to be interpreted.)

Oregon

Turnbull, George S., *History of Oregon Newspapers,* Portland, Ore.: Binfords and Mort, 1939. (Has many useful details of early publishers and editors.)

CIVIL WAR PRESS

Andrews, J. Cutler, *The North Reports the Civil War,* Pittsburgh: University of Pittsburgh Press, 1955. (Most recent and thorough volume on subject.)

Angle, Paul M., ed., *Created Equal? The Complete Lincoln-Douglas Debates,* Chicago: University of Chicago Press, 1958.

Babcock, Havillah, "Press and the Civil War," *Journalism Quarterly* 6:1, March, 1929. (Facts plus interpretation.)

Crozier, Emmet, *Yankee Reporters, 1861-65,* New York: Oxford University Press, Inc., 1956.

Dillon, Merton L., *Elijah P. Lovejoy, Abolitionist Editor,* Urbana: University of Illinois Press, 1961. (A thoroughly researched and readable biography of this leader.)

Goldsmith, Adolph O., "Reporting The Civil War: Union Army Press Relations," *Journalism Quarterly* 23:478ff, fall, 1956.

Harper, Robert L., *Lincoln and the Press,* New York: McGraw-Hill Book Company, 1951. (A thorough and interesting study.)

Horner, Harlan Hoyt, *Lincoln and Greeley,* Urbana: University of Illinois Press, 1953. (Has considerable information on the war period.)

Nye, Joseph B., "Freedom of the Press and the Anti-Slavery Controversy," *Journalism Quarterly* 22:1, March, 1945. (Tells hitherto unknown facts about the slavery issue and the press; interprets material.)

Mathews, Joseph J., *Reporting the Wars,* Minneapolis: University of Minnesota Press, 1957. (First full-scale account of all war correspondents; has excellent chapter on Civil War reporting.)

Starr, Louis M., *Bohemian Brigade: Civil War Newsmen in Action,* New York: Alfred A. Knopf, Inc., 1954. (Well-researched volume, written in lively, feature style; gives much detail about newsmen and problems of coverage and censorship.)

Weisberger, Bernard A., *Reporters for the Union,* Boston: Little, Brown and Company, 1953. (Has some useful facts and stories about reporters. See Andrews, Mathews and Starr entries above for rounded history.)

Wilson, Quintus C., "The Confederate Press Association, A Pioneer News Agency," *Journalism Quarterly* 26:160, June, 1949. (An original contribution to a neglected subject. Needs more extended, book treatment.)

See previously cited books on newspapers and editors of this period, especially the biographies of Horace Greeley, James Gordon Bennett, Henry J. Raymond, William Cullen Bryant and histories of their newspapers, which were involved with the Civil War issues.

MAGAZINES

Horan, James D., *Mathew Brady: Historian With a Camera,* New York: Crown Publishers Inc., 1955. (Has new material about Brady and his associates; extensive photo section.)

Meredith, Roy, *Mr. Lincoln's Camera Man, Mathew B. Brady,* New York: Charles Scribner's Sons, 1946. (Gives biography; reproduces Brady photos, many of Civil War.)

Mott, Frank L., *A History of American Magazines,* Cambridge, Mass.: Harvard University Press, 1938-1957. (Thoroughly researched, full details of magazine content and development.)

Wood, James Playsted, *Magazines in the United States* rev. ed., New York: The Ronald Press Company, 1956. (A briefer account than Mott, but useful for quick, overall picture.)

PRESS ASSOCIATIONS

Gramling, Oliver, *AP: The Story of News,* New York: Farrar and Rinehart, 1940. (Gives early development of the *Associated Press,* its problems, and how they were solved; highly readable.)

Rosewater, Victor, *History of Co-operative News-Gathering in the United States,* New York: Appleton-Century-Crofts, 1930. (Has much detail, extremely valuable for further study.)

See volumes on James Gordon Bennett and the *Herald; New York Sun;* general histories, such as Lee, Emery [and Smith], Mott.

PRESS AND OTHER MECHANICAL DEVELOPMENTS

See previous entries at end of Colonial Period: Olson, Sutton, Alfred McClung Lee.

SPECIAL STUDIES

Hughes, Helen MacGill, *News and the Human Interest Story,* Chicago, University of Chicago Press, 1940. (Gives origins of human interest story and its appeal; traces development of features.)

MAHIN, HELEN O., *Development of Newspaper Headlines,* Ann Arbor, Mich.: George Wahr, 1924. (Gives facts and interpretation of headline development; many examples presented.)

SMITH, HENRY LADD and JAMES KNOX, "The Needlers: Our Journalistic Satirists," *Journalism Quarterly* 39:309-16, summer, 1962.

TAFT, WILLIAM H., "David Ross Locke, 'Forgotten Editor,'" *Journalism Quarterly* 34:202, spring, 1957. (Tells about Petroleum V. Nasby, editor of the *Toledo* (Ohio) *Blade.*)

WITTKE, CARL, *The German-Language Press in America,* Louisville: University of Kentucky Press, 1959. (A thorough study and a first-rate contribution to the understanding of total press history.)

Part Four

Gilded Age Journalism (1865-1900)

The World.
CONCLUSIVE FIGURES.
SUNDAY, APRIL 26, 1885.—TWENTY-FOUR PAGES.
PRICE THREE CENTS.
WHY HE SENT A CHALLENGE.
A FEVER-STRICKEN TOWN.
MRS. WRITING NO. 1 AND 2.

Joseph Pulitzer, publisher-editor of the *St. Louis Post-Dispatch* and *New York World*, who introduced many innovations in journalism, developed crusading, sensational methods and influenced other publishers and the American people.

Chapter 17

Industrial, Urban America and Its Press

NEWSPAPERS UNDERGO DEEP, DRAMATIC CHANGES

Gilded Age journalism was born of Gilded Age America, an America where population increased dramatically. In a few decades after the Civil War the United States became industrially mature, producing many factories and trusts, and creating large middle and working classes; America moved toward the cities, developing an urban culture and serious urban problems. These significant trends exerted a deep influence on the press.

By 1875 founders of the popular penny press of the pre-Civil War days died and their papers became respectable and sober. They had laid the foundation stones for the new journalism. Now, a new generation of dynamic editors came to the front to reenergize the press. They revamped the old penny press appeals by launching new journals with original and striking patterns or by giving to old dailies new stimulation and direction. America was irresistibly changing and so were its dynamic newspapers.

Thousands of new readers flocked to buy a morning, evening or Sunday issue, filled with exciting, dramatic or significant news. No wonder circulations were boosted and new papers were launched! Other factors were responsible too. They provided the solid base for the newspaper boom.

POPULATION DOUBLES IN THREE DECADES

High birth rate and heavy immigration between 1870 and 1900 combined to double the nation's population, which rose to seventy-five million. A steady influx of Europeans poured in; more than sixteen million of these newcomers peopled cities and farming regions.

These newcomers, largely from southern Europe, were especially attracted to newspapers with editorial programs favorable to them and appreciative of their problems and difficulties. Immigrants influenced particularly the press in eastern metropolitan areas, with some newspapers printing large headlines, primer-like texts and many pictures.

Partially as a result of population expansion, daily newspapers increased sixfold, from 387 to 2,326. Additional newspapers sprang up in older eastern, midwestern and far western cities where journals had been established before the Civil War. New towns in the East and West now also became thriving hubs of manufacturing, commercial, agricultural or mining regions, and in the process they acquired one or more dailies. Subscribers to dailies multiplied proportionately to the increase in newspapers, rising from 3.5 million to 15 million circulation.

Although the drift toward cities was marked, America, for most of the period, was still predominantly rural. Here, the weeklies continued to flourish.

ECONOMIC EXPANSION IS UNPRECEDENTED

Following the Civil War, the economic system, fortified with larger agricultural areas and with thousands of new factories to depend on, bounded ahead, although the national income was not distributed evenly.

Great agricultural regions in the Ohio and Mississippi valleys, producing grain, wheat, corn, enriched the tables of city dwellers. Farmers shipped an increasing volume of produce abroad. In the decade following the end of the Civil War millions of new acres of rich land were opened. Inventors, too, contributed new and improved farm machinery. The mining of coal and iron on a large scale contributed to the industrial economy.

The American industrial system moved into high gear. A greater variety of products, formerly produced at home, were manufactured now by thousands of companies. Manufacturing was changed into an automatic or semiautomatic process, enabling goods to be turned out faster, cheaper and in greater quantities. Inventors also turned their attention to the construction of faster and more efficient newspaper machinery, improving existing presses and substituting other machinery for manual operation. The electrical age was just beginning.

Improvement and extension of the railroad system helped both the farmer and manufacturer. Eastern railroad lines, pushing beyond the Mississippi, were met by tracks being extended from the Pacific Coast.

Telegraph lines were likewise extended into remote sections, stretching from Maine to California. The Atlantic cable was laid in 1866, further accelerating news transmission. The telegraph led to rapid development of the evening newspaper and to nationwide and sectional press associations. Midwest and Pacific Coast evening papers, because of time changes, could publish eastern news the same day it happened. Postal service continued as an additional aid to business, growing from thirty thousand to seventy-six thousand post offices in 1901.

Many industries—oil, steel, meat packing, railroads—were welded into large trusts to obtain the economies of large-scale operations and to eliminate competition and control markets and prices. By 1904 about three hundred eighteen trusts were organized from consolidation of over five thousand separate plants.

Expanding purchasing power of the American economy increased the sales market for the newspaper. Advertising, especially in newspapers, was needed to bring manufacturers' products to the attention of potential buyers. Both in large cities and in rural villages and towns, newspapers were used more than ever before as advertising media. In this period large city department stores, Lord and Taylor in New York, John Wanamaker in Philadelphia, Marshall Field in Chicago and many others who advertised regularly and took large amounts of advertising space, expanded. The women's market increased greatly at this time.

Advertising revenue in newspapers leaped. In 1870 advertising totaled about sixteen million dollars. This revenue expanded four times, topping ninety-five million dollars by the end of the century. This was not the only income rolling into the publishers' accounting offices. Rising circulations added a considerable amount. Subscriptions brought in more than forty-nine million dollars in 1880, but this figure nearly doubled in 1899 when it reached above seventy-nine million dollars.

The publishing business was becoming, in big cities, a large-scale enterprise, producing for successful owners considerable profits. With the additional revenue publishers hired skilled editors and reporters to write news and editorials and employed artists to draw cartoons and illustrations. Capital investment went into larger, faster presses, new linecasting machines and engraving apparatus. Some publishers purchased or built imposing buildings. These structures served to advertise the company's stability and solidity.

With their newspapers becoming large business enterprises, some publishers, with great capital investment themselves, became sympathetic to the views of large corporations. These were mostly owners of Republican papers. Other publishers seeing greater circulation possibilities among the masses, and in most instances being sympathetic with their

O'NEILL'S

SPECIAL SALES THIS WEEK.

STRAW GOODS.

Laces. Kid Gloves.

WE WILL OFFER ON MONDAY THE BARGAINS FOUND IN THIS COLUMN.

MISSES AND CHILDREN'S CLOAKS AND SUITS LADIES' UNDERWEAR AT REDUCED PRICES.

INFANTS' WEAR.

DRESS GOODS — SPECIAL SALE AT LOW PRICES.

DRESS SILKS.

WHITE GOODS.

SPECIAL SALE WASH FABRICS.

LACE CURTAINS AND UPHOLSTERY.

CRETONNES.

3,000 DOZEN HOSIERY.

H. O'NEILL & CO., H. O'NEILL & CO., H. O'NEILL & CO., H. O'NEILL & CO., H. O'NEILL & CO.,

JOHN SIMPSON, 725 and 727 6th Ave.

PARASOLS.

JERSEYS.

HOSIERY.

GLOVES.

ARNHEIM'S, Bowery, corner Spring St.

ARNHEIM'S

L. SHAW.

HOW TO BE BEAUTIFUL.

L. SHAW.

GEO. C BRYANT'S

LONG BRANCH.

SPECIAL!

J.&S. Baumann,

JACKSON'S 777 BROADWAY.

JACKSON'S

CARPETS.

MATTINGS.

SHEPPARD KNAPP

A. Lowentein's Sons,

FURNITURE, 39 and 41 West 23d st.

DA-TIL-MA.

IMPENDING WAR.

Figure 37. Women Buyers. Women became a greater market for merchandise in the Gilded Age. Many women continued to buy the materials and make their own dresses, but others began to purchase ready-made dresses, hosiery, gloves, shoes and parasols, as the advertisements indicate. They bought children's clothes and furniture. Housewives shopped the newspaper advertisements for bargains and sales. Advertising expanded. Some of the larger stores, such as H. O'Neill & Co., in New York, bought a half page to tell about their merchandise.

problems, advocated programs to tax the rich. They fought against trusts and monopolies and for unions. These owners were generally standard-bearers for the Democratic Party.

LABOR ORGANIZES NATIONALLY

While captains of industry organized into nationwide trusts, workers amalgamated into unions for their own protection. Wage earners increased from 1.3 million to 5.3 million. Employees now organized on a national scale to seek better wages, shorter hours and improved working conditions.

W. H. Silvis formed the National Labor Union in 1866, bringing together for the first time many groups of workers into one federation. For a variety of reasons his organization declined after six years. The American Federation of Labor was left in indisputable possession of the field. Its membership grew from about one hundred thousand in 1890 to a half million in 1900.

Newspapers reported to the news-hungry public the titanic struggles which erupted on railroads, in iron and steel mills and in coal mines during these decades. Between 1881 and 1900 about twenty-three thousand strikes involving six million workers were called. Union officials were usually fighting for recognition for their unions and the right to bargain collectively for the employees. Economists have pointed out that management perfected a series of weapons to fight labor organizations: the lockout, the blacklist of employees and the refusal to arbitrate and negotiate.

Two of the bloodiest labor uprisings were the Haymarket Riot in Chicago in 1886, when a policeman was killed and seven rioters were injured fatally, and the Homestead strike near Pittsburgh, Pennsylvania in 1892. Here, ten persons were killed following a strike to prevent reduction of wages and after the steel company's refusal to recognize the union.

Newspapers not only reported news of these economic struggles but commented on them editorially. On one side were conservative publishers who aligned themselves with captains of industry and attacked labor. On the employees' side were a number of publishers whose editorial slant was aimed at workers.

POLITICS OF THE PERIOD REFLECTS INDUSTRIAL TRENDS

Politics reflected the underlying economic trends of the industrial age. As in earlier periods, newspapers, following along tradition, gave much attention to political issues. With the exception of two Cleveland administrations (1884-88, 1892-96), Republicans won all the presidential elections between the Civil War and the end of the century. The Republican Party consisted of captains of industry, farmers of the Middle West, new immigrants, federal jobholders and pensioners, freed Negroes and many thousand small businessmen. Industrial magnates were heavy contributors to the party fund because they had a great stake in government.

The Democratic Party became a minority party, composed of the rank and file of farmers and mechanics who could not produce great leaders. Southern planters who had supplied Democratic leadership before were wiped out or disqualified from holding office. The party turned to industrial eastern cities for leadership among lawyers, merchants, financiers and officeholders.

In the Reconstruction Period, sometimes called the Tragic Era, immediately following the Civil War, the radical wing of the Republican Party gained control of Congress. This group sought to dominate the South as a conquered territory. These politicians' ultimate objective was to render the southern agrarians economically and politically unimportant so this group would not oppose the Republicans' plans.

While industrialists organized and sought to control the traditional Republican and Democratic parties, farmers formed their own organization to improve their lot. Farmers complained of excessive freight rates, high interest charges and exorbitant taxes. The declining price of the farmer's grain or livestock was his chief grievance. A complex set of causes contributed to this situation, but the man of the soil often lumped them together under "inadequate money supply."

During the 1880s powerful agrarian organizations, such as the Farmer's Union, the Agricultural Wheel, the Northwestern Alliance, grew up in the West and South. In 1892 these groups joined to organize the People's Party. The platform demanded unlimited coinage of silver and enactment of graduated income taxes, and it urged government ownership of railroads and telegraph. The People's Party made a bid also for industrial workers.

In 1896 the People's Party endorsed William Jennings Bryan, Democratic candidate, advocate of free coinage of silver. The Republican standard-bearer was William McKinley, who had been selected by Mark Hanna, Cleveland industrialist. The ensuing battle was the most dramatic and important in the post-Civil War era. It was the industrial East pitted against the agricultural West and South. Emotions ran high. Word was spread that Bryan's election would bring swift disaster. Farmers were informed that their mortgages would not be renewed. Workingmen were told that factory gates would be shut. Hanna spent three million dollars collected from various interests. McKinley won, receiving 7,107,000 votes to Bryan's 6,533,000.

Political corruption was notorious in Washington in the post-Civil War era. President Ulysses S. Grant had been a military man, not a politician, and corruption flourished right under his presidential nose. Outstanding party leaders of the era were accused of misusing the powers of their offices.

Corruption extended to political parties in large and small cities and towns of the United States in this period. New York City was typical. The Tweed ring, headed by William M. Tweed, controlled New York City. By 1860 Tweed's power extended to the Albany legislature and the governor. Construction of a New York county courthouse netted about $200 million to Tweed and his cohorts.

Similar conditions produced corrupt political rings in other cities such as Philadelphia, Baltimore, Chicago, Cincinnati, St. Louis and Kansas City. Even the far western city, San Francisco, had its political gang.

Newspapers reacted in various ways to the story of political corruption. A number of the publishers were complacent for various reasons, including party loyalty, fear of reprisal and stockholder influence. Other publishers and editors, freed from party fund dependence and relying on advertising and subscription revenue which had become large enough, met corruption head-on, exposing the unsavory alliance between business and politics.

In New York, Philadelphia, Kansas City and St. Louis, newspapers advocated civil service reform as a specific means of eliminating spoils system politics. Action was not taken immediately, but both state and federal laws were passed eventually.

The trend toward journalistic political independence, begun in the penny press era, accelerated in these post-Civil War decades, especially in larger cities. It was made feasible by the stronger financial structure of newspapers.

EDUCATION ADVANCES ON MANY FRONTS

The growing reading market for newspapers was also a result of the great advancement of the educational system. More children than ever before attended elementary schools and even high schools and colleges. By 1900 all states and territories in the north and west had compulsory school attendance laws. Between 1870 and 1900 the number of pupils in public schools increased from 6.9 million to 15 million. High school attendance climbed, and colleges and universities expanded.

CITY LIFE REFLECTED IN PRESS

Newspapers of this period reflected the urban trends of American life and the various classes in the city. The press became less rural and more a product of the metropolis. Newspapers gave a variety of news reflecting cosmopolitan interests of readers. Upper-income groups had huge mansions and country showplaces. They were the best educated and had many cultural interests reflected in their newspapers. Newspapers catered to this group with political and economic news, serious editorial pages, book reviews and financial sections. The middle group lived in less expensive brownstone-front homes and apartments. They purchased newspapers which catered to their economic and psychological interests.

Thousands of low-paid workers and families on relief occupied cheerless tenements, with little air and poor facilities, in the slums. Responding to the needs of society, many publishers, editors and reporters developed a keen social consciousness, a feeling of responsibility for the unfortunates of American democracy. In newspaper campaigns editors sought to establish funds for the poor, free medical service for the sick, free milk for the children and many other humane helps and aids.

Certain psychological changes, resulting from city life, affected the press. Farm and small-town life was essentially different from urban living. In rural areas the pace was slow; residents engaged in considerable outdoor life. The city dweller, on the other hand, working all day at a fast pace in factory or office, was eager for an escape from his humdrum factory work. He looked for something novel, something new, some change.

Some publishers recognized this need. Instead of selecting and emphasizing news for its intellectual appeal, its political and economic significance, these publishers looked for stories of the passing pageant which had excitement, humor and entertainment.

Cities bred crime. Children growing up in slum districts lacked normal outlets, had no parks and playgrounds. Many children became delinquents. It was a short step from petty thievery to robbery to murder. Adult gangs grew and crimes mushroomed. In 1881 there were twenty-five murders per million population in the United States; in 1898 the number of murders jumped to one hundred and seven per million people. Pulitzer and Hearst recognized this type of news as a circulation builder, and these editors became known for their exploitation of crime news. Because of corruption and inefficiency of police departments, reporters turned detectives to solve many crimes.

In the postwar period many companies were established to serve the cities with gas, water and transportation services. Cabs and horsecars dominated the street until the 1870s. New York adopted the elevated, and San Francisco, cable cars. They gave way to electric railways in the 1880s. Some newspapers fought political corruption growing out of franchises needed by utility operators.

BASEBALL, NEW STAGE PLAYS, VAUDEVILLE POPULAR

In the metropolis it was inevitable that mass commercial entertainment and recreation would develop. This period marked the rise of organized spectator sports. Baseball was the most popular, with national leagues being formed by the end of the century. Publishers and editors recognized mounting interest in this form of recreation and began to cater to it to win wide circulations. Sports news developed more rapidly toward the end of the century and became a mainstay of the popular yellow journals.

The theatre, a form of recreation, reflected various classes in American society, mirroring the problems of urban life. Expansion of the theatre revealed the quickened tempo of American people and showed their need for relaxation and their desire for excitement. Reflecting the restlessness and rapid tempo was the new form of entertainment, vaudeville, with each act lasting five or ten minutes. Vaudeville accounted for half the theatregoers in the 1890s; Keith's entertained five million annually. Actors and actresses always made good newspaper copy, and now they became subjects for Sunday features. Departments devoted to such amusements grew. Advertising derived from play producers and vaudeville entrepreneurs contributed to the newspaper's revenue.

MORE WOMEN READ THE NEWS

Associated closely with development of urban living and industrialization of America was the increase of women as purchasers of factory-made, store-bought merchandise and also their development as newspaper readers. Women achieved a new legal and economic status in this period. Thousands of women went to work in factories and stores. Immigrant girls and women were employed as servants and cooks, and earning their own money, purchased ready-made clothing. Hundreds of other women, whose husbands were successful businessmen or industrialists, bought elegant hats, dresses and household furniture from large department stores. Many women became rich through the inheritance of fortunes. More leisure for reading came to women in the upper and middle-class families whose household duties were lightened by new inventions and by purchase of articles formerly made in the home but now produced in factories.

Meanwhile, women's educational level was raised when they attended the public schools each morning, and for the first time, many women became newspaper readers. As a result, publishers and editors began to cater specifically to this feminine audience with news, features and pictures. As women's economic power grew and they purchased more goods from stores, retailers began to aim advertising at this group, to the profit of the press.

In addition to printing news and features in morning papers, publishers issued evening papers, catering largely to women readers. On Sunday the editions swelled with women's features and departmental news. Women in all classes became more style conscious and aware of the world of fashion than before. It was during this period that magazines such as *The Ladies' Home Journal, McCall's and Woman's Home Companion* appeared to capture a vast market.

EVENING EDITIONS OUTDISTANCE MORNING ISSUES

Evening editions of newspapers developed rapidly in this period partly because of expansion of the woman's market but also as a result of other factors. As in other phases of the newspaper there was a gradual change before the first form of evening newspaper evolved.

At first, when morning papers in the pre-Civil War era received late news by telegraph, publishers issued a second and third edition with the late news. During the Civil War when readers were anxious to get results of battles, such afternoon editions became more prevalent. Some publishers in the late 1860s decided to issue separate evening papers. These publishers thought people would be more apt to buy a separate paper with a new name rather than a morning paper marked "later edition." In some instances less daring morning paper publishers of the *Morning Journal* or *Morning Herald* called their afternoon editions, the *Evening Journal* or the *Evening Herald.*

In the 1870s evening editions steadily increased in importance. Businessmen had less time to read the morning paper before going to

Figure 38a. Early Female Typist. Thousands of women left home every morning to work in offices. The invention of the typewriter spurred this trend. These workingwomen bought their clothes in stores, especially those which saw the value of advertising regularly.

Figure 38b. Upper Class Socials. Women in the upper economic class belonging to the growing high society enjoyed formal affairs where they could show their beautiful dresses in the latest fashion. They were influenced by the news about clothes and the advertisements in the daily press.

work or after arriving at their stores or factories. Evening papers catered to the shopping crowds, homeward-bound workers and theatre fans. Department store owners, enlarging their stores and increasing their advertising, began to recognize afternoon papers as good advertising media, especially for the new group of women readers.

News of an event, sent by telegraph, could be published shortly after being received by means of improved presses, linecasting machines and stereotyping facilities. Newspapers then could be on the street soon after the event happened. Prior to this publishers were handicapped in issuing evening editions in competition with morning papers.

By 1880 there were more evening than morning papers. Publishers issued 533 afternoon editions and 438 morning papers. By the end of the century about two-thirds of the dailies were afternoon papers, with 1,631 newspapers published in the afternoon and 595 in the morning. Morning papers generally remained more influential editorially.

SUNDAY EDITIONS BECOME VERY POPULAR

Sunday editions developed during the postwar period, growing out of the changing conditions. If the family attended church in the morning the long Sunday afternoon and evening hung heavily. Sunday was the one complete day of relaxation from work in the roaring factories, whirring sweatshops and busy offices. The religious code was not as strong as it had been; reading of secular matter was permitted in many homes on Sunday. Other families, especially the non-Christians, did not attend church services on Sunday. Filling a gap, the Sunday papers furnished leisure-time reading matter for the entire family: father, mother and children.

Department stores recognized Sunday as a strategic day for advertising. The family had a chance to look over the paper and the advertisements leisurely, picking the purchases the family would make during the coming week. The department stores, growing in size, could afford large advertisements. They had many items about which to tell the public, and they wished to do so in large type. The stores needed more advertising space. Recognizing this situation as well as the profit opportunity, publishers of dailies added more pages of news, features and short fiction to balance the advertising load on Sunday. Sunday editions soon far out-classed dailies, both in circulation and in the number of pages per issue. The Sunday papers were revenue producers. In 1880 publishers issued 252 Sunday editions, more than 50 per cent being published by independents. By the end of the century 639 Sunday papers were coming from the presses, with 567 being issued by owners of regular dailies and only 72 by independents, for it was more economical for owners of dailies to produce Sunday editions.

CULTURAL DEVELOPMENT MARKED; NEW WRITERS ON SCENE

Great socio-economic problems of the Gilded Age were examined by novelists and writers. Mark Twain and Charles Dudley Warner described the social structure from bottom to top in a novel called *The Gilded Age,* in which they revealed the character of the new captains of industry. Regional novelists depicted the special color of various sections of the nation. Samuel Clemens, a newsman, who used the penname, Mark Twain, wrote *The Adventures of Huckleberry Finn,* which became a classic of boys' life on the Mississippi.

This was serious literature, but most of the public read dime novels. Men and boys consumed thousands of copies of *Buffalo Bill* and *Diamond Dick's Desperate Deeds.* Horatio Alger wrote a series about boys who succeeded in spite of many obstacles and dealt with immigrant boys on the streets of New York. To relieve the tensions of the Machine Age, America produced a number of wits and humorists. Chief among these were Peter Finley Dunne, Artemus Ward, Petroleum V. Nasby and Eugene Field, all displayed satirical wit and made people laugh at themselves. These four humorists were also newspapermen.

SCIENTIFIC PROGRESS IS NOTABLE

In every science, biology, chemistry, physics, geology, myriad research workers contributed to the advance of science in the era. Scientists were aided by the millions of dollars given by the captains of industry. Not only were laboratories better equipped than ever before, but schools and advanced institutes, dedicated to science and technology, were founded. Influencing both physical and social sciences was the Darwinian theory of evolution, which was applied to man's cultural institutions.

Most Americans saw benefits of the scientific revolution in the medical progress being made. Science provided fresh safeguards against disease and increased chances for recovery from illness. Newspapers began to tell the story of science, with more bizarre aspects of science being dramatized in Sunday supplements.

NEWSPAPER PERSONNEL EXPANDS

To cover this kaliedoscope of news, publishers expanded their personnel. With more money derived from increased subscriptions and expanding advertising, many publishers were able to increase their news and managerial staffs. The cycle was familiar. Social conditions produced certain news interests; the newspaper responded with more emphasis and attention to this kind of news. Specialized personnel was then added to carry out the job.

As city staffs were developed and local news coverage expanded, the city editor became more important. On the larger metropolitan dailies the managing editor took over the duties of the editor and directed the overall news operations.

This was the era of the reporter. Washington corps of correspondents were built up by more aggressive papers. In addition, the Mexican War and then the Civil War produced the war correspondent. The Civil War established the reputation of many newspapermen. Although they did not sign their names, their initials or pennames identified them. Special correspondents in the Gilded Age were sent to cover the Indian Wars in the West and the Spanish-American War in Cuba. Some of the larger newspapers, even in the Midwest, began to build up their foreign news service.

At home the rapid development of cities turned newspaper editors to a more intensive coverage of urban affairs. Reporters were given the city hall or police court beat, while others were kept on general assignment.

As more emphasis was placed on news as a commodity to be sold (to inform, entertain and persuade) the reporter grew in importance. Reporters with ability to get news under difficult circumstances and to write it interestingly became recognized and were in demand. Publishers who wanted to build up their enterprises quickly were willing to lure them with increased salaries.

With development of evening papers, extension of the use of the telephone and spreading of cities, personnel was further subdivided into legmen, who gathered news and phoned it in; and rewritemen, who remained in the office and wrote facts into acceptable stories. Although, at first, editors and reporters wrote headlines, eventually copyreaders who edited copy and wrote headlines became part of the city room scene.

As Sunday editions became more profitable, reporters with a flair for human interest writing became Sunday staffmen and editors. When pictures were recognized as attention getters, illustrators were added to staffs. Development of sports and women's news led to hiring of sportswriters and women reporters and editors. The telegraph editor emerged with the increased use of that means of news transmission.

Newspaper work became romantic, and newspapermen were known as romantic people. As keymen on newspapers, they went everywhere, met public officials, crooks, police, firemen. The newsmen attended big events of the day. The reporters knew what was happening in the world. They obtained information before anybody else. What gave newsmen a special thrill was that they knew their articles would be read the next day, or the next Sunday, by thousands of persons.

With the development of news and the rise of reporter to greater importance, the attention previously centered on the publisher and editor began to decline. Although this was still the era of personal journalism and readers of newspapers knew the publishers of the organization, an impersonal press institution was evolving. Many publishers and editors promoted this, with the accompanying anonymity of themselves.

The publisher had to be an efficient businessman to make a success. Thus, strong, aggressive and skilled managers with a knowledge of advertising, printing and labor costs and other corporate financial stock matters came to the front. Generally self-effacing, these publishers sought no personal publicity. They were concerned with making the institution a profitable success. They saw themselves as sellers of an important, needed commodity: news and advertising space. They had news for the consumer, and they had political and economic opinions. These were expressed through editors and editorial writers and through city editors who selected the news. While some publisher-editors held political office, they did not find this activity of great interest. The general rule was that politics and newspaper ownership do not mix.

Next subject of discussion is individual publishers and their newspapers, how they responded to the changing American scene and the journalistic forces.

Chapter 18

New York Press: The Innovators

NEW YORK IS STILL LEADING AMERICAN CITY

New York City continued as the leading American city, and its newspapers, reflecting the city's economic prosperity and cultural advancement, set the pace for journals in hundreds of other communities.

New York's great seaport, at the mouth of the Hudson River, provided the underpinning for the city's economic growth. Ships from all over the world docked at New York wharves. The Hudson River connected New York with the Erie Canal. In the post-Civil War period new railroads linked New York with the East, West and South. The city became an industrial workshop.

A financial center, New York, through Wall Street bankers, brokers and the stock exchanges, floated necessary money for expansion of American industry, railroads and steamboat lines. Retail business multiplied, with department stores, such as R. H. Macy, A. T. Stewart, Lord and Taylor, becoming large-scale enterprises.

Culturally, New York advanced, profiting by fortunes made by daring businessmen. It boasted Columbia University, City College of New York and Hunter College, as well as one of the great libraries of the world, the New York Public Library. New Yorkers sought diversions, and many theatres, including vaudeville houses, sprang up. Coney Island attracted thousands, although it was a considerable distance from the city.

New York's population was ever-expanding, with millionaires, the white collar class, factory workers and the poverty-stricken being jammed together. After many fruitless attempts, Greater New York was incorporated by 1898, so that, at the turn of the century, more than 3.4

Figure 39. Printing House Square. Newspaper buildings centered around Printing House Square in Lower Manhattan. Each publisher sought to outdo his rivals by building a taller, bigger, more impressive structure. The imposing newspaper plants testified to the growth of the news-communication business.

million lived in this metropolitan area. To meet the needs of these millions, the elevated lines with steam locomotives pulling cars were built in the 1870s, and Brooklyn Bridge was opened in 1883, connecting Manhattan and Brooklyn.

New York faced many problems because of its rapid expansion. Thousands of Italian immigrants and Jews from Poland, Germany and Russia poured into the city along with Chinese. While some immigrants moved to farms and smaller inland cities, thousands remained in New York. They settled in ghettoes, Chinatown and rotting slums. Criminals and prostitutes found the tenements good hideouts to ply their trade, producing much crime news. Health problems were acute in tenements. Political organizations, such as Tammany Hall, taking advantage of social disorganization and poverty, organized to win votes, to deal in franchises for city railways and gas utilities and to steal millions of dollars.

New York was a lively, varied and colorful city, and it produced a variety of newspapers which responded to these changes and in turn also influenced them. New newspapers were established and old ones revitalized with new ideas to meet psychological, cultural and economic needs of the various levels or classes in the metropolis.

NEW YORK SUN REFLECTS CHANGING CITY

Many aspects of the changing New York City and American scene were reflected in the *New York Sun,* revitalized by Charles A. Dana in 1868. Somehow Dana caught the hurrying, bustling spirit of post-Civil War people who desired to be amused and entertained. With emphasis on the human interest angle, he appealed to emotions and feelings of the public, stressing humor and pathos in the news. In this he laid the foundations for the sensationalists who came later.

Dana was peculiarly equipped to weld the literary and journalistic fields. Born in New Hampshire on August 8, 1819, he spent his youth and adolescence in western New York. Dana became a clerk in his uncle's store, gaining a business training which later proved to be of great value to him. In his spare time he studied Latin and Greek. This deep interest in languages gives a clue to his later journalistic work. Dana entered Harvard in 1839. Poor eyesight and weak finances prevented completion of his degree.

Finally Brook Farm beckoned; there he could teach, continue his studies and build this health. Dana joined the utopian community. He lectured in the school and helped edit the group's newspaper, *The Harbinger,* his first newspaper experience. One valuable contact Dana made at the Farm was with Horace Greeley.

After working on the *Boston Daily Chronotype,* Dana obtained a job on the *New York Tribune* and became city editor in 1847. Dana resigned to travel in Europe to study the revolutionary spirit in France and Germany. He sent dispatches to the Greeley paper and others. In 1850 Dana returned from Europe and rejoined the *New York Tribune.* He set out to elucidate Proudhon's proposal that all the ills of the laboring man could be eliminated by abolishing rent and interest and that a bank of the people was necessary. His ideas were later incorporated into a book.

In 1851, when Greeley was in Europe, and from 1855 to 1856, when Greeley was on the political front in Washington, Dana had almost complete charge of the *Tribune.* He had already been made managing editor, perhaps the first on an American newspaper. This was the beginning of absentee editorial control and ownership. Dana's sly humor, which was beginning to develop, caused friction between him and Greeley. Dana did not have the same point of view toward unpopular causes and creeds as Greeley had; Dana printed material that irritated the old editor.

When the Civil War issues became more acute the rift between Greeley and Dana deepened. Finally Greeley asked for Dana's resignation in 1862. Dana sold his *Tribune* stock for twenty thousand dollars. This departure from the *Tribune* was a disillusioning experience in Dana's life. Extremely sensitive, he took all events as highly personal insults. Sardonic, impish humor and cynicism toward all human improvements now became part of Dana's stock-in-trade.

The Sun.

THIRTY-NINTH YEAR. NEW YORK, FRIDAY, JULY 5, 1872. PRICE TWO CENTS.

FREEDOM'S 96TH BIRTHDAY.

THE FORRID HEAT.

THE WRECKED MENAGERIE.

THE SEVENTH IN SARATOGA

BRILLIANT MILITARY SPECTACLE AT CAMP SHERMAN.

Figure 40. Charles A. Dana and the *Sun*. Charles A. Dana, editor of the *New York Sun*, broke new journalistic paths with his daily, for he introduced sparkling writing into the news, the headlines and the editorials. He influenced many other publishers.

Dana soon joined the staff of the United States War Department, becoming in 1864 an assistant secretary of war under Stanton. Dana served as official government reporter at the warfront.

Afterward, Dana resigned from the War Department and became editor of the *Chicago Republican*. This job lasted only a short time. With a group of backers, Dana then purchased the *New York Sun* for $175,000 from Moses Beach in 1868. The *Sun* had already built up a reputation and won fifty thousand readers. The company was capitalized at $350,000, and besides purchasing the *Sun*, the publishing corporation also bought a building known as Tammany Hall to house the newspaper plant.

In his prospectus, Dana announced certain revolutionary principles which distinguished the *Sun* for many decades. In addition to reemphasizing the paper's independence, the new editor declared:

> It will study condensation, clearness, point and will endeavor to present its daily photograph of the whole world's doings in the most luminous and lively manner. It will not take as long to read the *Sun* as to read the *London Times* or Webster's dictionary; but when you have read it you will know all that has happened in both hemispheres.

Dana believed that the paper should be kept to four pages so he could sell it for two cents while other papers were selling for three and four cents. Brevity of the *Sun*'s news made the stories pointed; they told the essence of an event in a few words.

Dana formulated his theory of journalism in this fashion: "The first thing which an editor must look for is news. By news I mean everything that occurs, everything which is of human interest. I have always felt that whatever the divine Providence permitted to occur I was not too proud to report."

Besides colorful detail, the *Sun*'s reporters applied the storyteller's art, the fiction form, to journalism. Instead of summarizing facts in the lead, the reporter started from the beginning of the current happening, sometimes leading back twenty years or more.

To carry out his ideas, Dana employed men with unusual ability to staff his newspaper. The reporters constituted a galaxy of stars who could extract dramatic, tragic, humorous and, above all, human elements from an event. Julian Ralph, David Graham Phillips, Will Irwin, Samuel Hopkins Adams, all enlivened the pages of the *Sun*. The *Sun* training they received led them later into the writing of novels and plays and of articles for magazines. A number of them, like Arthur Brisbane, became stars for Pulitzer and Hearst.

Dana's editorial writers used humor, wit and satire to give a lively and interesting style to the *Sun*'s editorial page. They wrote with the same color and cleverness as the *Sun*'s able reporters. In connection with political campaigns they coined slogans and phrases such as, "To the victor belongs the spoils" and "No king, no clown to rule this town." They sought brevity in their editorials because they realized many persons did not have time to read and did not want long, thoughtful editorial essays. In addition to serious topics the editorialists chose lighter events in the passing news parade on which to comment.

The *Sun* conducted a series of exposés and campaigns which established a pattern in American journalism, a pattern followed by others who came later. The *Sun* exposed the Credit Mobilier of America, a company organized to build the Union Pacific Railroad. The *Sun* created a national sensation when it showed how the company had given stock to senators and representatives to influence their votes.

Dana was one of the first to recognize the need for news and features appealing to the new woman. The daily *Sun* published little stories of tragedy and comedy, having a sentimental appeal underneath literary polish. When the *Sunday Sun* was launched, a department devoted to women made its appearance. Sports coverage became a regular *Sun* feature. The *Sun*'s sports pages were a product of the new Machine Age era, but at the same time they were a force further stimulating interest in sports.

With this pattern of smart newspapermaking, Dana trebled the *Sun*'s circulation by 1884. The paper's readership increased from fifty thousand to one hundred fifty thousand. Dana's *Sun* ran closely with Bennett's *Herald* for top circulation position until Joseph Pulitzer entered the scene. Then the *Sun* dropped in the late 1880s to eighty thousand.

Evening Sun Successful

In March, 1887, Dana launched the cheaply priced *Evening Sun*. This evening edition had four pages and cost only one cent. The publisher secured for his staff able newspapermen, such as Amos J. Cummings, Arthur Brisbane, Richard Harding Davis and Jacob A. Riis, the outstanding police reporter of the day. The *Evening Sun* set a precedent that was soon followed by its competitors, the publisher of the *New York World* establishing the *Evening World* five months later.

In both the morning and evening *Suns*, Jacob Riis fought ceaselessly for humanitarian reforms, such as reduction of poverty, better housing, more playgrounds and the opening of schools for truant children. Riis found the camera a useful tool to illustrate his slum features. Discovery of flashlight powder in Germany enabled him to take pictures in dark dwellings and alleys.

The reporter began to write articles about his experiences for *Scribner's* magazine. These articles later led him to write a book called, *How the Other Half Lives,* which brought him considerable fame and aroused the attention of New York Police Commissioner Theodore Roosevelt who was able to help Riis with his local crusades. Riis joined the *Evening Sun* staff in 1890 although he continued to write for the morning *Sun* and for other newspapers on special assignment. On the *Evening Sun* Riis continued his police reporting and his crusades against poverty and firetrap tenements. He paved the way for the later magazine muckrakers.

Sunday Sun Founded

Beginning with four pages in 1875 the Sunday *Sun* evolved into a bulky twenty-four sheet newspaper by 1890. The Sunday formula of the seventies expanded gradually into the more elaborate product of 1900. At first the Sunday paper was merely an extension of the daily. Then, Sunday special features of human interest stories were added.

In its initial announcement to the public, the *Sun* had said it would wear the livery of no party, and the paper adhered to this policy. It fought, however, consistently for its set of economic principles to which parties had to conform. As a spokesman for upper-economic level groups, Dana's paper advocated high protective tariffs, sound money and business freedom from any governmental interference. It was in favor of a weak central government. The *Sun* was opposed to all attacks on trusts and fought income taxes. Regarding the rising labor movement, the paper objected strongly to unions and all strikes. The *Sun* was cynical about reform and reformers and called such movements as civil service "goo-gooism." In New York it supported some notorious Tammany candidates. Regarding foreign policy, the *Sun* was an exponent of annexation of Canada, Cuba and Santo Domingo.

In the campaign of 1884 Dana was in a peculiar situation. Though he was a Democrat, Dana did not favor Cleveland because of Cleveland's low tariff view, nor did he favor the Republican candidate, James G. Blaine, because of his connection with national scandals. Faced with this, the *Sun* supported General Ben Butler, independent candidate, who was considered by many as unstable as well as dishonest. It was an unfortunate choice for it characterized Dana as an inconsistent editor. The *Sun* lost many subscribers. The *New York World* supported Cleveland wholeheartedly and thereby won much of the *Sun's* circulation.

In summarizing Dana's contribution it may be said that he was perhaps the first editor to recognize the value of the human interest story and to emphasize the need of telling all news interestingly. Importance was not the criterion for news. In many departments of journalism he anticipated the two great editors of the Gilded Age, Joseph Pulitzer and William R. Hearst. They adopted many of Dana's methods and developed them further, creating a new and striking form of journalism.

DAILY GRAPHIC, FIRST ILLUSTRATED TABLOID

David Croly launched the *Daily Graphic,* the world's first tabloid illustrated newspaper, on March 4, 1873. Experimenting and developing picture techniques, Croly set the pictorial pace for other powerful daily newspapers which watched the improvements he made and imitated him.

Croly had predecessors in the weekly field who proved the attention-getting value of news pictures. *Frank Leslie's Weekly* and *Harper's Weekly* had already won large circulations with their striking pictures, but no one had attempted an illustrated daily.

Croly's *Daily Graphic* consisted of eight pages, of which three and a half were devoted to newsy illustrations, and the remainder to news items, editorial articles and entertaining reading matter, set forth in little doses. The process of making halftone reproductions of pictures had not been invented. Although the most modern photographic equipment was used by this enterprising sheet, its photos could not be reproduced as such pictures are today in newspapers.

The *Graphic*'s cameraman snapped a picture, brought it to the office, developed it, and from the photograph an artist made a drawing. This drawing could be reproduced on a special zinc plate, and the result, a zincograph, was superior to woodblocks used before. The zincograph was made possible by the recent advance in the engraver's art.

In 1859 a Parisian lithographer, Firmin Gillot, had made engravings by drawing on a metal plate and etching away by acid all except the lines of the drawing. In 1872 a son of Gillot linked the then new art of photography with his father's etching process and made it possible to enlarge or reduce the size of the drawing. These drawings could be reproduced because they consisted only of black lines on a white surface. These were full tones of black and white.

But photographs, in contrast to drawings, contained many intermediate gray tones. If a reproduction were made from a photograph, it

THE DAILY GRAPHIC
An Illustrated Evening Newspaper
39 & 41 Park Place
VOL. XIV NEW YORK, FRIDAY JULY 20, 1877 NO. 1354

THE DAILY GRAPHIC
An Illustrated Evening Newspaper
39 & 41 Park Place
VOL. XIII

Figure 41. First Illustrated Tabloid. David Croly made a fresh contribution to journalism with his *Daily Graphic,* the first-illustrated daily newspaper in the United States. The short-sleeved long-pants bathing suit of the girl on page one must have been a shocker then. On his front page, Croly featured murders and fires, as in the illustration on the right.

would print as a solid black. So pictures which appeared in the *Daily Graphic* were reproductions, or zinc linecuts of drawings made by the artist, copying from the photograph in front of him. The *Daily Graphic* abounded in carefully drawn portraits of statesmen and scientists as well as assassins. Croly published even a few action shots, such as pictures of horse-drawn fire engines dashing through New York.

The *Daily Graphic* celebrated its seventh anniversary on March 4, 1880, by announcing an innovation which paved the way for the modern halftone picture. It printed a picture of Shantytown, a ragged section of upper Fifth Avenue, not redrawn in the old manner but reproduced directly from the photographic plate through a screen having seventy-two vertical lines to the inch.

Croly admitted the process was in an experimental stage, but he expressed confidence that pictures would eventually be regularly printed in his pages "direct from photographs without the intervention of drawing."

The publisher was able to announce the innovation because in the *Graphic* office was a young photographer, Stephen H. Horgan, who had set to work to make use of a process for reproducing a photograph directly without redrawing it first. Others directed themselves to this problem. Among these was Frederic E. Ives, the official photographer at Cornell University, who developed a similar halftone process. Popular magazines, such as *Harper's Monthly* and the *Century* used the Ives method.

If Horgan alone did not discover the halftone process, he was the first to apply it to newspaper printing, especially to the rotary press.

The publisher of the *Daily Graphic* printed both linecuts and halftones. He was not in a great hurry about publishing news pictures. He declared it was his intention to deal honestly with the public in the matter of illustrations—no fakes!

The *Daily Graphic* was not squeamish about crime. When William Foster, convicted of murder, met death at the gallows, the *Graphic* artists displayed the same ingenuity and interest which later tabloids showed in their handling of the Judd Gray-Ruth Snyder murder case in the 1920s.

"It is a marvelous paper," wrote Mark Twain, after he had read the initial number of the *Graphic*. "I hope you will be able to keep it growing all the time, for I don't care much about reading . . . but I do like to look at pictures, and the illustrated weeklies do not come as often as I need them."

For sixteen years the *Graphic* lived. Circulation rose to ten thousand, and at this figure seemed to have reached its saturation point. In 1889 the paper lost its foothold and ceased publication. The process of producing zinc cuts and halftones ceased to be exclusive. The *New York World* had sprung into the field by 1884. For five years competition continued until the *Graphic* yielded the victory to the *World*. Failure of the *Graphic* was hastened also by financial mismanagement, unwise expenditures and investments.

The *Daily Graphic*, as the first illustrated daily newspaper, demonstrated the popularity of pictures as a supplement to the appeal of news. While the *Graphic* lost its fight for survival to a superior rival, Joseph Pulitzer and his *New York World*, the *Graphic* was an important link in journalistic development, proving the circulation value of pictures to make a news event graphic and vivid for daily readers and demonstrating the practicality of the linecut and halftone.

Because of technical printing difficulties, halftones were not used regularly by newspapers printed by high-speed web presses until 1897 when the *New York Tribune* began to print illustrations made by this process. By 1900 the halftone was in common use in newspapers. Because of conservative attitudes, some publishers held back for a long time.

PULITZER BECOMES PEOPLE'S CHAMPION

If the era of roaring business enterprise developed a keen spokesman in Charles A. Dana and his *New York Sun*, the period created an equally severe and articulate critic in Joseph Pulitzer, who came from the Midwest to blast monopolists in their own citadel of New York.

Possessed with dynamic energy, extraordinary originality and journalistic ability, Pulitzer came to New York in 1883 and revitalized the *New York World*, bringing under its banner the largest group of readers for any journal until that time. Methods and techniques which Pulitzer worked out for his daily and Sunday papers were so popular that they revolutionized journalism once more, as Day and Bennett had done in the 1830s.

Background of Pulitzer

No one can say exactly why Joseph Pulitzer ran away from his well-to-do home in Hungary when only seventeen, but it is known that young Joseph had already been noted for his tempestuous disposition. He was born on April 10, 1847, in Budapest, where his father was an invalid. Perhaps from him Joseph inherited his weak physical condition. Although young Pulitzer's constitutional defects were to provoke him for the remainder of his life, they served also to spur him on, whipping up his great energies, lashing him into larger enterprises.

When he left his Hungarian home in 1864, he was "recruited" by one of the many agents swarming Europe seeking recruits for the Union Army. In New York he joined the Lincoln Cavalry. The rough troopers were without mercy, and the high-spirited youth had a hard time. From this experience he developed a lasting antipathy toward militarism. After the war Pulitzer returned to New York where he sought work without success.

He became discouraged with New York and headed for St. Louis. There he worked as a mule holsterer, stevedore and riverboat hand. Between odd jobs Pulitzer haunted the Mercantile Library, reading omnivorously all day learning the English language. The young immigrant obtained an appointment as secretary of a German organization active in looking out for the welfare of the newcomers. An immigrant himself, he understood immigrant psychology. He drew on these experiences later in developing the *New York World.*

The *Westliche Post,* a German language paper, in 1868 needed a reporter, and Pulitzer was picked for the job. His working day was from 10 A.M. to 2 A.M. the next morning. His eagerness in the search of news, his still imperfect English and his gaunt figure topped by a bulbous head with its small, pointed chin, tufted with a few strands of red hair, often made him a laughing stock. He was guyed and misled, but his good humor and persistence soon turned his tormenters' attitude into one of respect, emphasized somewhat when his stories took the form of frequent "beats" on important local and political matters.

In Missouri and St. Louis Pulitzer found the corruption in the state and local governments that prevailed throughout the United States. Pulitzer, finding sympathy on the *Post,* attacked the Missouri orgy of corruption with intense zeal.

The *Westliche Post* supported the Liberal Republican Party in 1872, and Pulitzer campaigned for it. The party lost the election.

Pulitzer was able to buy an interest in the *Post* after the election when the editors felt it was ruined. Unable to stand the fast pace which Pulitzer soon set, the proprietors soon bought back their interest for $30,000, giving Pulitzer a substantial profit.

After two trips to Europe Pulitzer returned to St. Louis, and for the first time became a part owner of a broken down English-language newspaper, the *St. Louis Dispatch,* on December 9, 1878. He purchased it at an auction for $2,500, with a $30,000 lien on it. He had $2,700 left as working capital. Having a valuable Associated Press franchise, however, he combined the *Dispatch* three days later with the *Post,* owned by John A. Dillon, who needed an AP franchise. The newspaper was known as the *Post and Dispatch,* jointly owned by the two partners. Afterward the daily was called the *Post-Dispatch.*

Pulitzer continued to expose political corruption as he had on the *Westliche Post.* The public recognized the *Post-Dispatch* as a great public service organ and supported it. A little later Pulitzer bought Dillon's interest. Pulitzer began to gather around him men of talent, and the newspaper continued to advance. Profits ran from $40,000 to $80,000 a year.

The *Post-Dispatch* became the leading evening newspaper in St. Louis. The young publisher had an able lieutenant in John A. Cockerill who had hard newspaper experience in Cincinnati, Columbus and Washington. Pulitzer found him on the *Baltimore* (Maryland) *Gazette* and brought him to St. Louis as managing editor of the *Post-Dispatch.* Cockerill was a perfect complement for Pulitzer.

By means of exposés of city and state corruption, persistent campaigns against local monopolies in St. Louis, sensational crime and other news, plus a strong editorial page, the Pulitzer team built up the daily. The *Post-Dispatch* became the spokesman for small businessmen and the middle class against the powerful and wealthy. St. Louis was the newspaper laboratory where Pulitzer worked out his formula, or pattern for the new journalism. His income was about $40,000 to $50,000 annually. He was later offered $1.6 million for the daily but did not sell.

Pulitzer was now able to gratify his desire to travel. Although he was only thirty-five years old, his health was not good; therefore, he began to seek relief from office work and the climate. He went to New York. Meanwhile, his brother, Albert Pulitzer, who had followed him to America, had been on the *New York Herald*'s staff and then had established the *Morning Journal* on a working capital of $25,000. The paper, a one-cent sheet, succeeded from the start, and its success was not without its effects on Albert Pulitzer's older brother, Joseph.

Buys Run-down World

Financier Jay Gould, winding up his Wall Street affairs, had found the *New York World* a liability rather than an asset and was willing to sell the daily. Pulitzer bought the *World for* $346,000. Profits of the *Post-Dispatch* amply provided the first installment; after that, the *World* paid for itself. Here was a turning point in Pulitzer's career. The publisher now had a chain of two papers, one in St. Louis, the other in New York.

The *World* which Pulitzer bought had never been an outstanding success in the postwar period. The Pennsylvania Railroad purchased it because the railway president believed that a newspaper would be a useful organ for the pursuit of railroad privileges. The paper, however, continued to lose money and was turned over to Gould, another rail magnate. Gould lost $40,000 a year on the paper, which had slipped to about 15,000 to 20,000 readers.

Pulitzer believed there was a market in New York for a cheap newspaper which could appeal to the masses with a powerful psychological pattern and a liberal political and economic platform. Too, the Democratic Party had no journalistic spokesman of power in the city. The *News* and the *Star* had no standing. The *Times* and the *Tribune* were Republican; and the *Herald* and *Sun,* although claiming to be Democratic, were independent and not dependable. With the exception of the *News,* an afternoon paper, and Albert Pulitzer's *Morning Journal,* the dailies ranged in price from two cents to four cents, still persisting in wartime prices.

If Pulitzer could duplicate his success in St. Louis, he could cut a niche for himself in the New York newspaper market. Thousands of persons in the growing metropolis were not reading any newspaper. Besides, by making a superior newspaper, he might cut into the circulation of the standard dailies such as the *Sun.*

Pulitzer infused new ideas and energy into the moribund *World* A one man revolution shook the old office the first night. Pulitzer rewrote stories, gave assignments to reporters. He laid out the front page, dashed here and there, giving instructions to editors, and still had time to write the entire editorial page by press time that night.

Pulitzer's opening gunfire was dashed off in a few minutes on the repeated requests of a lieutenant in his editorial ranks. Pulitzer set forth on May 11, 1883, the principles which were for many years to guide the *World.*

> There is room in this great and growing city for a journal that is not only cheap but bright, not only bright but large; not only large but truly Democratic—dedicated to the cause of the people rather than that of the purse potentates—devoted more to the news of the new than the Old World—that will expose all fraud and sham, fight all public evils and abuses.

Pulitzer defined the new aristocracy of labor to which the *World* appealed, and he described the standards and virtue and honesty which the paper applauded. Here he was opposing Old World aristocracy and new wealthy aristocracy in America. Pulitzer wrote:

> Our aristocracy is the aristocracy of labor. The man who by honest earnest toil supports his family in respectability, who works with a strong heart and a strong hand, who fights his way through life courageously, maintains his good name through privacy and temptations, and winning

from his children in respect as well as love, is the proudest aristocrat in the American public. The new *World* is his organ.

Within a week, Pulitzer, influenced no doubt by his Midwest background, set forth an economic program which he offered to politicians as a substitute for their usual, long-winded pretentions. Pulitzer's objectives were on two levels: (1) economic reform, concerning corporations and wealthy persons, and (2) political reform, dealing with improvement of government and free voting. Pulitzer numbered his objectives, which we have grouped:

ECONOMIC	GOVERNMENT
1. Tax luxuries	7. Reform civil service
2. Tax inheritances	8. Punish court officeholders
3. Tax large incomes	9. Punish vote buying
4. Tax monopolies	10. Punish employers who coerce their employees in elections
5. Tax the privileged corporations	
6. [Impose] tariff for revenue	

The democracy which Pulitizer advocated was a new industrial democracy rather than a political democracy, which the mass of Americans had won earlier in the century with the aid of the press.

Pulitzer was the Horace Greeley of the Gilded Age. Like Greeley, Pulitzer wanted to reform bad conditions, advance the welfare of mankind and help the lower-economic class. He desired to use the newspaper to bring about social changes. In Pulitzer, Greeley's aims were continued or reborn in a new industrial age. Pulitzer, however, used new journalistic methods, such as newspaper crusades, and he employed the latest printing machinery and up-to-date picturemaking processes to appeal to the masses.

Pulitzer was a sincere believer in the new democracy; yet there was a business side to this idealism. While appealing to the urban masses of men and women, he could create a tremendous circulation for his paper, and hence the *World* could become an extraordinarily effective advertising medium for department and other stores. If the *World* could increase its reading public to seven hundred thousand, which it eventually did, for advertising purposes it could be a newspaper superior to other metropolitan journals. The publisher was a highly capable businessman.

He knew that reader interest and circulation came first, before advertising and profits. He turned his full attention, therefore, to the news department. The human interest story, mildly stimulating under Dana, burst into a new type of sensational journalism under Pulitzer. From his *Post-Dispatch* experience, he realized that the interest in crime and sex was universal; therefore, he filled the *World* soon with melodramatic headlines after he purchased the daily; he made the news stories breezier and more startling. Some of them reeked with melodrama: "School-Girl's Sad Fate. Decoyed Into a House of Ill-Fame at Coney Island." This was the lurid account of a very young girl "who had gone wrong." Many stories of this kind came from outside New York, the *World's* correspondents everywhere always being on the alert to send in similar news with an emotional appeal. When a murder was particularly gruesome, the *World's* front page was flooded with illustrations. Such pictures grew from one-column cuts to four- and five-column layouts toward the end of the century.

The response to the pathetic and sentimental was an age-old characteristic of human beings, and the new journalism found out that by weaving its stories around such themes, it could get thousands of readers to purchase papers. These stories often concerned children and animals. The insane mother who killed baby Jim while he slept so peacefully was treated fully in the columns of the *World.* Expert word-artists tried to pluck a heartstring or draw a tear, and they did.

Catastrophes received greater attention in the *New York World* than ever before. The St. Louis tornado news, on May 28, 1895, tore everything else off the front page of the *World,* and on the following Sunday, the illustrators, with the aid of their imaginations, had a Roman holiday. Exploding boat boilers, which sent hundreds of persons to their graves in Davy Jones' lockers, and scenes of burning buildings and of firemen rescuing women and children, drove other news of the day from page one. The art of displaying high-interest news, which had significance and sensational appeal to thousands of readers, was developed in this period.

The sports reporters of the *World,* when a big sports event occurred, came out to the games in full force, always accompanied now by illustrators. The dramatic spectacle of fifty thousand people attending a Yale-Princeton football game, with all the noise and color such a crowd produced, was interesting and as stirring as any news could be. Bennett's *Herald* had already opened the path to sports coverage. Pulitzer went further and exploited sports interest more fully, organizing a sports department when he purchased the *World.* While reporters and illustrators covered the outstanding sports events from every angle, the makeup editor gave the news and illustrations full space on page one. The results were eye openers that amazed and stunned thousands of readers. Three columns or more of space were devoted to regular sports events in the weekday edition of the *World,* and an entire page was given to sports on Sunday in a special department.

For its readers the daring reporters of the *World* were ready for any adventure or stunt. One newsman stayed in jail overnight to receive and store his impressions for a feature. Nellie Bly, daredevil girl reporter, faked insanity to expose conditions in an insane asylum. Stunt journalism, which had evolved from the *New York Herald*'s exploits, was developed in this period to counteract the sameness created by the identical news being sent to all papers by the Associated Press.

Pulitzer emphasized pictorial appeal in the *World.* At the beginning he made extensive use of linecuts. He explained later that he was not the father of illustrated journalism for which he had been given credit. The *Daily Graphic* led the way toward daily newspaper illustrations. The publisher of the *World* saw possibilities in pictures, too, for circulation-building purposes.

Pulitzer learned about a Russian artist in New York, Valerian Gribayedoff, and hired him. The artist drew likenesses from photographs, and Pulitzer printed in the upper right-hand section of the *World*'s front page a picture of a statesman, a fugitive absconder, a murderer in the news. Circulation leaped by thousands. It was the first time pictures were used so profusely in daily journalism. Later, when the halftone had been perfected, the *World* adopted this new process.

The *New York World* was the first morning paper to run a regular series of political cartoons. Bennett's *Evening Telegram* had published them before. Walt MacDougall, first *World* cartoonist, had contributed to *Puck*, the New York magazine of satire. MacDougall as well as Gribayedoff now drew for the *World* the series of cartoons on the Blaine-Cleveland presidential campaign, beginning August, 1884. The cartoons were graphic and effectively illustrated the editorial viewpoint and news in the *World.* THE FLESH POTS OF PLUNDER and THE REPUBLICAN PARTY'S LAST CHANCE were titles of two of these political cartoons that aroused attention in August, 1884. Cartoons were also used in national and local crusades of the *World.*

As in other techniques Pulitzer did not discover anything entirely new in his newspaper crusades. The *New York Times* had blasted away at the Tweed Ring before. The crusade in Pulitzer's hands, however, became an instrument of the middle and working classes. These were the groups to whom he appealed and of whom he became a champion; therefore, he readapted the journalistic crusade for their benefit.

Pulitzer had to overcome public inertia, indifference and work fatigue, and he was compelled to appeal to city dwellers' emotions by hammering away at their minds with news, features, cartoons, reprinted telegrams on page one, headlines and editorials. Conditions of urban living, in which there were many interests competing for readers' attention, called for this type of combined appeal. Many social, political and economic evils existed and needed to be corrected. The *New York World* sprang into action to act as the aggressive champion of those who had no voice to plead their cause against these evils. The Pulitzer paper responded to the needs of the age and, in turn, actively influenced the public.

Pulitzer eventually assailed all monopolies, but much of his attention at the beginning was directed toward Jacob Sharp, local city railway magnate who wanted a franchise along Broadway and was willing to pay each alderman $25,000 for his vote. Sharp had already paid a huge sum to the New York legislature for an act enabling the city council to grant the franchise. The *World* hammered away, arousing the public's interest and concern. The effect of the *World's* exposé and crusade was to indict Sharp and all but two councilmen. Sharp was jailed finally.

The New York Central Railroad came in for its share of Pulitzer's journalistic ire. William K. Vanderbilt, principal owner, was roasted continuously in the Pulitzer paper. When assailed for abusing Vanderbilt, the *World* replied that if it could attack a politician, it could likewise expose Vanderbilt, who was a public man, because of his vast economic interests which affected the public. Pulitzer laid the basis for attacks by magazine muckrakers after the turn of the century.

The *World's* outstanding crusade against J. P. Morgan & Company established the reputation of the paper more firmly as a daily representing the public interests. The United States government in February, 1895, floated a bond issue of sixty million dollars. These bonds were purchased by J. P. Morgan and resold on the market for a handsome profit. The *World*, in December, 1895, announced that another bond issue of one hundred million dollars was imminent. The *World* advised the Treasury Department not to sell any more bonds through Morgan because the public would buy them for more than the banker would offer. The publisher sent out ten thousand telegrams to banks around the country and found that the public would buy the bonds. His results were spectacular. On January 6, 1896, the *World* announced in a first page story, THE SYNDICATE SMASHED.

As a result of the agitation, though deeply indignant at the *World's* interference, Secretary of the Treasury John G. Carlisle, placed the loan before the public, and the loan was oversubscribed ten times. Seeking only to do a public service, Pulitzer made $50,000 on the transaction. This was typical of his newspaper career, in which he became a champion of the working and middle classes, and at the same time built up a fortune of many million dollars.

Pulitzer's fundamental theory behind all crusades was "PUBLICITY, PUBLICITY, PUBLICITY." One had only to expose facts about corruption in politics or about greedy monopolists. Then one passed a law eliminating the evils, checking the abuses and jailing the malefactors. The newspaper, because it reached hundreds of thousands of readers, was the great social agency to carry on the functions of investigation and exposure.

The *World* also fought for direct benefits to working class readers of its columns. It was strongly prounion and printed much labor news. In St. Louis Pulitzer had been a champion of the businessman as opposed to the large monopolist. In New York the editor aimed more directly at the laboring-man audience, perhaps because of the large industrial population and the strong unions in the big city. Pulitzer battled for the Saturday half holiday, the eight-hour day and payment of salaries by weekly check. In those days many workers were paid at the end of the month. They often had to borrow to pay for grocery bills until their wages were paid. Weekly paychecks would benefit thousands of employees. During the first year of the Pulitzer ownership of the *World,* the Brooklyn Bridge, connecting Manhattan and Brooklyn, was completed. The *World* successfully fought for abolition of bridge tolls. Among other benefits of eliminating tolls was the advantage to mothers of being able to roll their children in carriages across the bridge during the hot summers to get a fresh breeze.

Nationwide recognition was accorded the *World* when it campaigned for funds for the tremendous Bartholdi statue, now known as the Statue of Liberty. This statue was a gift of France to the American people, but the public or government here had not provided a pedestal on which "Liberty" could stand. Both Congress and a citizens' committee had failed to provide for enough funds, and in 1885 the *World* took up the cause, asking for the necessary $100,000. Pulitzer, an immigrant, understood the meaning of the statue to America and to his readers. The *World* got nickels and dimes and dollars from thousands of men, women and children. The campaign was a huge success, with the result that the Statue of Liberty was erected on the pedestal in New York harbor.

During this period the *World* became an arm of the police system and fought in behalf of justice. The paper attempted to investigate and rebuke corruption and inefficiency in the police department. Solving crime was an exploit which would be written up by a skilled reporter, and if he was successful his work could serve as an advertisement for the *World,* which called itself a "PUBLIC SERVICE NEWSPAPER." This became the "detective age" in American journalism. *World* reporters' stories sent to jail an astrologer who carried on a white slave business in girls who entered voluntarily or were forced into prostitution. The *World*'s detective-reporters also sent to the penitentiary a tenement housebuilder whose structure collapsed.

Glittering Sunday World Popularized

If Pulitzer proved to be a master journalist in appealing to emotions on weekdays, he demonstrated superabilities at these arts on Sundays in the *Sunday World.* One reason for spectacular development of the Sunday edition was that daily news was somewhat restricted; the editor was forced to depend on whatever the day's events brought forth. Sunday features, however, could be planned ahead and prepared with emotional appeal in mind. The *Sunday World* was new, and experimentation was required to find the right formula.

If the daily *World* ran to twenty-four pages, it was exceptional; but the Sunday edition expanded to fifty pages of news, features and pictures because increasing circulation produced more advertisements. About half the *Sunday World*'s content consisted of advertising. More than ever before, the editors had additional space for news and particularly for special features. The income from the advertising was huge. By 1900 the Sunday edition expanded some weeks to fifty-two pages.

In his advertisements Pulitzer declared that the *Sunday World* "contained more reading matter than four magazines." It was more than that; it was a vaudeville show and a shelf of dime novels combined into one newspaper. During the seventeen years from 1883, when the *World* was purchased by Pulitzer, to the end of the century, the *Sunday World* changed sharply in the direction of sensationalism. Pulitzer was aided by his Sunday editors, especially Morrill Goddard, who took over in 1895. Later Goddard was lured away by Hearst. Then Arthur Brisbane was made Sunday editor of the *World.*

The *Sunday World* reached its climactic development and its monster circulation in the nineties. As ninety-five thousand readers paid three cents to observe the antics of the *World* reporters in 1884, so six hundred thousand individuals in 1897 paid five cents to get a gaudier display and greater stimulation on Sunday.

In the *Sunday World,* as in the daily paper, romance and sex stories were surefire hits, and almost every week men and women found vicarious enjoyment in the highly wrought text and elaborate pictures.

Book reviews catering to the same sex sensations were turned into features and suggestive headlines were attached, for instance:

GRANT ALLEN'S LATEST NOVEL
A Story of Sin So Immoral
No Editor Would Publish it.

This feature on November 3, 1895 contained long, exciting quotations from the book but condemned the volume for its immorality.

The great controversial issue in the *World,* as in the *Sun,* was the "new woman," who had been emancipated and had entered business, professions and athletics. In other sections of the *World* she was satirized unmercifully. While riding the wave of women's emancipation, which began years before and which accelerated in the postwar era, the *World* reenforced and stimulated the trend. By the middle nineties the *Sunday World* carried a full page of news and features especially interesting to women.

Activities of the wealthy, no doubt appealing to slum dwellers, always made good Sunday features. So the *World* presented "How a Millionaire's Daughter Is Prepared for Marriage" in a half page with large illustrations. The purpose of such articles was not to expose or to attack the reigning wealthy families. Entertainment and vicarious thrills were stressed chiefly. Mansions on Fifth Avenue were described in words and pictures to achieve the same ends.

The *Sunday World* also used dime novel features. "Buffalo Bill's Wild Life" was presented to readers seeking adventure from the routine of New York life. Bret Harte's "Cessy," a story of the roaring West, ran serially.

The *World's* features on Sunday were international in scope. Articles on Egypt, Turkey, China, Africa and Alaska transported tired New Yorkers on magic carpets to foreign lands for ten minutes on Sunday, just as readers of serious upper-class newspapers and magazines were transported by sober travel articles. The Pulitzer articles helped broaden the horizon of tens of thosuands of native New Yorkers and the immigrants who began to read English and the *World.*

The freakish, the odd, the unique, the unusual in human and animal life were exploited, anticipating later features of "Believe It or Not" by Robert Ripley.

In an age when scientists and inventors were exploring new subjects and were becoming wonder workers, their laboratories and shops became the mecca for *World* reporters in search of startling and sometimes instructive material. The *Times* and the *Tribune* had a long-standing, sober interest in science. Pulitzer seized on this type of news and attempted to popularize science for the masses by emphasizing, whenever he could, the emotional element, the appeal to curiosity. A science column by Garrett P. Service, called "Wonders of Science," began on November 1, 1896.

American professional humorists in this period began to win popular attention. Mark Twain, originally a newspaperman, had his stories reprinted everywhere. Soon the *World* began to print Bill Nye's observations on the American scene. In the beginning this column consisted of jokes and short anecdotes; later, it was so successful that it was expanded into a full page containing illustrations of the jokes.

A special section, "Youth's Department," came in shortly and carried puzzles, stories and other juvenile reading matter. By the nineties this department had expanded to four pages and was in the form of a special supplement.

R. E. Outcault pictured child life in Hogan's Alley. This was more than a comic; it was a social satire on New York life, showing the kids holding an election campaign, a horse show and a fashion parade, as their elders did. Once again the newspaper mirrored the urban environment: tenement houses, back alleys and urchins who lived there.

The first attempt of any paper to use colored comics or colored features was made by the *World* in 1893. Outcault painted a bright yellow dress on the leader of the Hogan Alley gang, and this one-tooth ragamuffin, the "Yellow Kid," was such an outstanding success that it became the symbol of the Pulitzer-Hearst brand of sensational journalism. A magazine in England, *The Yellow Book,* filled with similar material, had become known in America, and Gilded Age journalism was stamped "yellow journalism" as a term of reproach. When Outcault was lured away by Hearst, George I. Luks continued to draw the "Yellow Kid" for Pulitzer.

A colored supplement containing Sunday features was also successfully tried by the *Sunday World* for the first time, November 19, 1893. These colored features and comic supplements, which fitted in with Pulitzer's fundamental pattern, were made possible by the advance in the printing art. In 1891 H. H. Kohlsaat, a Chicago publisher getting his ideas from France, used color printing on a small scale but not for fast newspaper printing. By 1893 the Walter Scott Company installed a new Hoe multicolored press which could print simultaneously eighteen pages. It was an expensive and troublesome process, but Pulitzer stopped at nothing to build circulation.

Strong Editorial Page

Pulitzer lavished loving care on the editorial page of the *World.* He felt that this was the heart of the newspaper. He admired Edwin L. Godkin's editorial style and would have published a paper like the *Evening Post,* but Pulitzer wanted a large audience. He put a great deal of force and power into the *World* editorials, and even after he remained away from the office for health reasons, he directed the editorial writers by mail or cable, stimulating them and criticizing them when they were weak in ideas or expression.

The *World* supported the Democratic Party fully. The paper came to exert a strong influence in elections in New York City. The *World* was a consistent backer of Grover Cleveland, and in 1884, when the *Sun* defected, Pulitzer was able to swing the city and the state, pivotal in importance, for Cleveland. The President appreciated and acknowledged Pulitzer's help.

Early in his career Pulitzer had written the hard money plank into his platform for the *St. Louis Post-Dispatch* when he established that paper. He continued to battle for the gold standard when the issue came

Figure 42. "Yellow Kid" and His New Phonograph. "The Yellow Kid," one of the first regular comic strips in the American newspaper, amused thousands of men, women and children on Sundays. The ragamuffin wore a bright yellow dress, and somehow the name *yellow* became attached to all sensational newspapers. Here, the kid is having a bout with the phonograph, then becoming popular.

up in the nineties. He therefore looked with disfavor on the nomination of William Jennings Bryan as the Democratic nominee in 1896. The *World* here departed from the midwestern influence and thought. Pulitzer, however, was as vigorously opposed to monopolies as Bryan. In the campaign of 1896 the publisher rejected the growing Populist movement. Aware of the sentiment of many persons, Hearst stepped in to fill the vacuum created by Pulitzer's move, and the Hearst journal picked up thousands of readers.

Pulitzer had owned the *World* for only four and a half years when his eyesight and shattered nerves forced him to leave active management of the paper. He thought his withdrawal would be temporary but it was permanent. Eventually he went practically blind. To a man with less drive and less mental capacity, this might have marked the end of his newspaper career and the beginning of retirement.

Instead, Pulitzer entered a new career and the *World* climbed to unprecedented heights. Pulitzer became the blind editor and absentee owner, sailing in his yacht over the Atlantic Ocean or staying at his various homes in America and Europe. He surrounded himself with highly intelligent and informed secretaries who read and discussed with him every column of the *World,* and whenever he touched port his criticism and policies were cabled to the *World* editors in New York. From his yacht he selected editors and editorial writers.

Pulitzer found, in 1888, that growth of the daily, evening and Sunday editions of the *World* necessitated larger quarters. He decided to erect a skyscraper which would be larger than any other building in New York. The building cost $2,500,000. The cornerstone of the structure was laid on October 10, 1889. From his sickbed in Germany, the *World* publisher dispatched an eloquent message in his characteristically vigorous and terse style.

When the building finally was opened, December 10, 1890, the *World* printed a special supplement. The building, said to be the largest in New York and a triumph of modern architecture, was in every sense a monument to Pulitzer's genius and the new formula of newspaper publishing. Appropriately enough, the structure was topped with a gilded dome and stood over other newspaper buildings in the area.

The *World* now had twelve hundred on its payroll. The paper had two hundred ten compositors and sixty stereotypers who could turn out a stereotype plate on Saturday night in six minutes. An art department produced five hundred and eight halftone engravings per week, the average time of each illustration being thirty-five minutes.

The *World's* circulation reflected the daily's increasing popularity. When Pulitzer took it over in 1883 the *World* attracted only fifteen thousand readers. At the opening of the Spanish-American War, the morning and evening editions of the *World* had about eight hundred thousand readers. The *Sunday World*, because of its features and comics, soon surpassed the morning or evening *World*. In 1896 the Sunday edition reached seven hundred thousand readers.

Pulitzer's part in bringing on the Spanish-American War in 1898 will be told in a later chapter devoted to that conflict.

Pulitzer's Contributions to Journalism

Pulitzer declared that he had effected a revolution in journalism and that other publishers were copying him. There were both immediate and gradual results on other newspapers in New York and in other cities of the United States.

Within four months Pulitzer forced competing publishers to drop the prices for their dailies from four to two cents, and for the Sunday edition from five to three cents. Keeping his daily price at two cents, Pulitzer gave readers of the newspaper the benefit of the diminishing price of woodpulp. The *World* became enormously profitable; the publisher made $500,000 a year from it.

For the press, Pulitzer revitalized the editorial page, while championing wholeheartedly the cause of workers and small businessmen. Pulitzer also developed the technique of the crusade, simultaneously carried on in both news and editorial columns.

He revived the sensationalism of the 1830s, stressing crime and sex and conflict of all types. To gain attention, Pulitzer developed "stunt journalism." He utilized pictures and cartoons as no daily paper ever before had done. He developed headlines and experimented with new types of makeup.

Pulitzer also popularized the Sunday edition with its feature section. He was the first to use colored comics and colored pictures in the *Sunday World*. Pulitzer likewise was the first to give readers a big newspaper bargain, a full newspaper at a low price. With his news, features and political and editorial program, Pulitzer reached hundreds of thousands of readers who had never purchased a daily or Sunday newspaper.

By his crusades he exposed political and business corruption and gave Americans an insight into the inner working of politics and business. Pulitzer also gave the middle and working classes a strong voice in American life. His campaigns led other publishers of dailies in New York and elsewhere to follow him. He provided the impetus for magazine muckrakers who protested on a national scale just as the blind publisher was doing locally.

Pulitzer's *World* stimulated an interest in sports and began to tear down the sex repressions of the Victorian era. Through his cartoonists he brought humor to the American newspaper and gave expression to this side of American life. Pulitzer tapped not only new levels of readers, but made women and children newspaper readers.

HEARST DEVELOPS DANA-PULITZER PATTERN

William R. Hearst learned Dana's and Pulitzer's methods and then went further than the older editors cared to go. Coming into the field toward the end of the century as Pulitzer's rival, Hearst, in the *New York Journal,* developed a more sensational newspaper pattern. A similar cycle was seen in the 1830s when James Gordon Bennett with his *New York Herald* stepped in to extend the ideas and methods of Benjamin Day's penny *Sun.*

Hearst's California Background

William Randolph Hearst was born in San Francisco on April 29, 1863. His mother, a refined, cultivated woman, urged him to become educated. His father, who made millions in mines, was a great gambler and great plunger, staking all on the turn of a card, the outcome of an investment. These daring qualities were displayed by William Randolph Hearst years later in the publishing business.

"Willie" spent his boyhood days in San Francisco, riding, hunting and fishing. After going to local grammar schools, young Hearst was sent East by his mother to St. Paul's School in Concord, New Hampshire. In the fall of 1882 he enrolled at Harvard, where he remained for almost four years. Hearst became business manager of the *Harvard Lampoon,* making an outstanding success of his job.

In the presidential campaign of 1884, Hearst had his first opportunity to put on a parade and show for the "boys," a technique which he utilized later on a larger scale, particularly in the Spanish-American War. When Grover Cleveland was elected President in 1884, Hearst raised such an all-night racket that he was suspended from school. About this time, his interest in journalism became more pronounced. Boston newspapers, across the river from Harvard, were his haunt. Hearst was finally ousted from Harvard in 1886 for a prank he played on the faculty. Hearst declared later that he determined definitely to go into journalism after his expulsion from college for the reason that newspapering appealed to him as "the most interesting pursuit he could take up."

Meanwhile, his father, George Hearst, had served a term in the lower house of the California legislature, contributed freely to party funds and advanced sizable sums for support of the *San Francisco Evening Examiner.* In 1880 the elder Heart took over this paper for debt. Later he became United States senator.

When William returned to San Francisco in 1887, he told his father that he wanted to publish the *San Francisco Examiner.* He began to pattern it after Pulitzer's *World.*

Hearst soon launched a series of crusades, campaigns and spectacular exploits. He attacked abuses and proclaimed radical democracy. He courted the applause of the crowd. The bitterest battle of his early activities was against the Southern Pacific Railroad, which had a stranglehold on the state.

With his enormous funds Hearst staffed the *Examiner* with the best reporters, editors and business executives he could find. Hearst carried this method of purchasing talent further than other publishers; he had larger capital, wanted quicker success. He was imitative rather than original in ideas. Within a year or two the *Examiner* had a first-rate staff of writers and artists.

With this able staff to back Hearst, the Pulitzer formula worked. *Examiner* circulation rose from about 25,000 to 80,000. Within five years he had built the *Examiner* into the greatest moneymaker on the coast

Figure 43. William Randolph Hearst. Hearst was a revitalizer of *San Francisco Examiner* and *New York Journal.*

and the second most profitable paper in the United States. At this time he conceived his project for a chain of newspapers. Pulling out a railroad map of the country, he drew rings around principal cities and remarked to his companion that some day his papers would be located in these cities.

Purchase of New York Journal

A double ring was drawn around New York, for Hearst had now definitely decided to transfer his operations to that metropolis. There was immediate need for funds for the New York experiment. His mother offered to advance the entire sum of $7,500,000. It required almost that amount to launch and keep the *Journal* issuing before it began to pay. He poured millions into salaries, equipment and promotions for the daily.

Driven on by this relentless ambition to succeed, Hearst, at thirty-two, turned to conquer New York with the *Morning Journal*. This one-cent paper had been established by Joseph Pulitzer's brother, Albert Pulitzer, who sold it to Hearst for $180,000 in 1895.

Shortly after he took over the *Journal* Hearst began to lure to his own staff the Pulitzer men who had built up the *World*. The duel of the two papers thus began. The *World's* staff was attracted to Hearst by outlandish salaries.

Morrill Goddard, the *World's* Sunday editor, came to the *Journal*. Arthur Brisbane, who wanted to write a daily comment on the news for the *World* but was refused permission, also joined Hearst. Brisbane soon furnished the intellectual power behind Hearst papers. Hearst brought his best talent from San Francisco to build the *New York Journal*.

When Hearst took over the *Journal* he strengthened each department. The transformation Hearst wrought was not sudden, but within a few months began to reveal itself. The Pulitzer formula was applied to the daily paper with an accented beat and also to the *Sunday Journal*. The balance which the old *Journal* had tried to keep between political and crime stories was soon overturned. Headlines showed an abundance of the following types of news, all stressing melodrama:

HAD FOUR WIVES

SHE JUMPED TO HER DEATH

SLAIN BY A SHELL

ALIVE IN A COFFIN

JOY AT THE BIER

LOYAL TO DEATH

Crime, preferably sexual, and criminal trials were now featured on the front page with all the power of the new typography and the new methods of illustration.

The *Journal*'s appeal to women required all the ingenuity of its editor. Every type of news and feature article, with lavish illustrations, appeared in the *Journal.* Women's pages also carried society events and gossip columns. Appealing to men, the *Journal* published columns on sports, foreign and national news. Large-scale disasters drew forth the best efforts of the *Journal* staff. The news was sensationalized, and illustrations were garish.

Expansion of Sunday Journal

It was in the Sunday *Journal* that Hearst developed the new Gilded Age journalism to a dazzling peak and produced a spectacle unheard of in any other country. He gave his readers a gorgeous, glittering show featuring articles on crime, sex, disasters, wars and popular science. Hearst filled a journalistic vacuum created by social conditions of the time. Schools and cities did not have a program for adult education and leisure-time activities. On Sundays, especially, time hung heavily.

By the spring of 1897 Hearst was offering an eighty-page Sunday *Journal,* with three supplements. He gave away the *American Magazine,* the *American Women's Home Journal* and the *American Humorist,* an eight-page comic section.

Biblical events, relating to excavations of ancient civilizations, were turned into fascinating features. Writers for the *Journal* drew on science and scientific laboratories for articles. Unusual and bizarre aspects of prehistoric American animals, being uncovered by scientists, made good copy. Popular science features, which described new devices for preventing snoring as well as others for demolishing tornados, found space in the Hearst supplement.

Following the Pulitzer pattern, Hearst became the crusading champion of the middle and working classes, fighting the "gorged trusts" and battling for other public service causes. He fought the New York Gas Trust and the national sugar combine. Campaigning for various labor measures, he helped the Brooklyn trolley employees get their daily working hours reduced. In the campaign of 1896 Hearst supported William Jennings Bryan for president and thus became the only New York publisher to favor the Democratic candidate.

The *Journal*'s role in arousing public opinion before the Spanish-American War will be told in a later chapter.

Debits and Credits

At this point, Hearst made certain contributions to American journalism and American life, and at the same time he left work for which he has been severely criticized.

On the Positive Side:

1. He made the morning, evening and Sunday editions more interesting.
2. He developed the human interest story.
3. He developed further the new headline technique, including the banner head, and he altered front page makeup.
4. He printed full-page Sunday features.
5. He embarked on crusades against corruption in government.
6. He exposed the trusts and set people thinking about the economic system.
7. He employed skilled writers and was the first to pay high salaries.
8. He popularized science for the masses.
9. He was a spokesman for lower economic classes.

On the Debit Side:

1. His reporters often exaggerated stories to make them sensational and appealing to large numbers of people.
2. He often twisted facts to gain effect, as in the Spanish-American War.
3. He emphasized crime and sex news.
4. He developed the newspaper as a medium of escape entertainment.
5. He aroused war spirit and goaded United States into Spanish-American War.

Chapter 19

New York's Standard Papers Forced to Change

SHREWD PLAYBOY GUIDES HERALD'S DESTINY

When James Gordon Bennett, retired from active management of the *New York Herald* in 1867, he left a well-established, highly successful middle-class newspaper to his son, James Gordon Bennett, Jr. The *Herald* throughout the last part of the nineteenth century was a mixture of impersonal, institutional elements (now becoming dominant in journalism) and the peculiar idiosyncracies of the younger Bennett.

Bennett was born in 1841 with "a silver spoon in his mouth." His father, embittered by his own life scars, lavished loving care on his son. Undoubtedly, the parents catered to the boy's slightest whim. This, with his enormous wealth, later had observable effects on the publisher. The young boy grew up on the Bennett estate in Washington Heights, then a suburb of New York City. Mrs. Bennett, to escape the everlasting stigma which had been impressed on her as a result of attacks on her husband and his *Herald*, retreated to France. There, Bennett received a scanty education by private tutors. Throughout his life he looked with disfavor on college training for newspapermen. Bennett's chief interest was in sports, and he developed into an expert boxer, swimmer and ballplayer. He became especially interested in yachting, and in 1866 he won a race from Sandy Hook to the Isle of Wight and was feted in Europe and America. Later, through the *Herald*, he popularized sports for millions of boys and men and awarded many athletic cups.

At twenty-five, Bennett took control of the *Herald*. How much actual personal direction of the paper he assumed is hard to tell, for he was still a New York playboy. Nevertheless, he did start, in 1869, the *New York Telegram* as an evening edition of the *Morning Herald* and developed his news coverage, obtaining worldwide beats. Inheritor of a vast fortune and possessor of a profitable paper, he drew from the *Herald* for the next forty years between $750,000 and $1,000,000 each year, one of the largest incomes derived by a single individual in the United States. Such were the financial possibilities of a well-established New York newspaper. The *Herald* was valued at $2,000,000 by eleven men who sought to purchase it in 1869.

The *Herald* continued to thrive, widening the scope of its circulation, increasing its income and meeting the lively competition of the new journalism. Pulitzer always considered the *Herald* his greatest rival, until Hearst's dramatic appearance in New York.

In the *Herald* office were a score of "sacred cows," members of the aristocratic Union Club, which reporters could not touch. If the *Herald* reporter forgot and joshed the members even mildly, Bennett immediately called the error to the writer's attention. The journalistic mirror of the *Herald* was thus distorted by Bennett's individualistic interests.

In 1876 he became engaged to a Miss Caroline May. Accused of insulting her while drunk on New Year's day, January 1, 1877, he fought a duel with her brother, but neither duelist was injured. The scandal broke in the New York papers; Bennett soon left for Paris. There he remained for the rest of his life except for rare visits to New York to check on his properties.

Now began a period of absentee ownership. Bennett kept in constant communication with the *Herald* by cable, directing its important moves and policies from his Paris office. In order to retain control, some magic practices were instituted. His office in the *Herald* building was in readiness for his sudden appearance. His chair in the editorial council room was left vacant, his presence being felt, if not in the flesh, in the spirit. He became an absentee owner who never wrote a line but decided policies and chose men who did the editing, writing and managing.

Hobnobbing with kings and other important European personages, Bennett continued to make the *Herald* the outstanding American newspaper in its foreign news coverage. In 1887 he started the *Paris Herald*, mainly for American visitors and residents in Europe. This paper was never successful financially until World War I. A similar venture in London was doomed to quick failure.

During the period between the Civil War and the turn of the century, the *New York Herald* went through various changes in its attempt to readjust to changing conditions. Like his father, Bennett, was able to sense what would interest people long before this interest was crystallized. He frequently dropped news stories and techniques when the public appeal in them waned slightly. The period between 1870 and 1882 was an energetic, enterprising and adventurous era in the *Herald*'s history. With the Civil War over Bennett realized that *Herald* readers needed some striking sensational news. Therefore, they were given unusual news gathered from international, national and local scenes. The *Herald* took the lead in this type of reporting and became one of the most distinguished newspapers in the United States, gaining an international reputation.

The *Herald* also embarked on a number of explorations which made news and made the paper famous. At this time the continent of Africa was being opened to exploration. In 1869 Dr. David Livingstone, a Scotch-Presbyterian missionary, who had kept Europe informed about his travels for thirty years, disappeared in darkest Africa. The belief spread that he was dead or helpless.

The *Herald* took on the job of finding Livingstone. The problem was first to find an explorer or reporter who could do the perilous job. Fortunately, the *Herald* had on its staff at this time the most courageous and capable reporter ever to become attached to the paper. He was Henry Morton Stanley.

After being given the assignment to "Find Livingstone" in Africa, Stanley set out on a trek through the jungle, a journey which lasted for more than two years. He overcame superhuman obstacles, such as sickness, death of his animals, desertion of his native porters. He finally found Dr. Livingstone. The news eventually reached the *New York Herald*, and Stanley's remarkable feat was told to the world. His venture dramatized the possibility that reporters might become explorers, adventurers, romantic fellows. It announced that the news reporter was about to take the spotlight from the old-time editorial writer.

Similar enterprise was shown by *Herald* reporters in covering national and local events. With his intensive interest in sports, Bennett saw that unusual coverage was given to all sporting events. In the early period sports were engaged in by wealthy readers, so the *Herald* emphasized yachting and international rowing matches. The *Herald* sports editor, who had been promoted from the pressroom, was an authority on horse racing and developed the technique of reporting by heats. Other outstanding features of the Bennett paper were the shipping news and the weather reports, the daily's owner having his own meteorology department.

The Sunday *Herald* during the seventies was a duplicate of the weekday edition. It was not until the eighties that the Sunday *Herald* began to stress entertainment features which became so popular. Under the influence of the *World,* the Sunday *Herald* blossomed with many new features. Like the *World's,* they were mild, one-column articles at the beginning, but they soon developed into full-page features on a variety of topics, decorated with larger and larger sketches.

The *Herald* received its greatest blow as well as its greatest stimulus from the dynamic *New York World* in 1883. From this time on the *Herald* aped the policies of the *World.* The tactics were highly successful. The *Herald* circulation figures revealed a steady increase which reached higher than it ever had during its entire history. Circulation increased from a low of 90,000 to 235,000 by 1892, and reached 500,000 in the Spanish-American War.

The *Herald* became strongly prolabor, antitrust in editorial policy and melodramatic, light, humorous, gossipy in news policy. Toward the end of the century the *Herald* was filled with pictures.

Managers of the *Herald* saw that great circulations could be secured in tenement districts among workingmen and women. The editors directed the paper's appeal there. If Pulitzer had no other influence, he made the *Herald* conscious of the workingmen's problems in New York. The *Herald* printed stories about "how the other half lived." During the winter months the *Herald* raised funds for the poor.

TRIBUNE, UNDER NEW PUBLISHER, CHANGES COURSE

In 1872 Horace Greeley, founder of the famous *New York Tribune,* died. Whitelaw Reid, his managing editor since 1869, gained control and reshaped the policies and course of the paper.

Reid was born in Xenia, Ohio, in 1838 of Scotch parents. He rounded out his preliminary education at the Xenia Academy and then entered Miami University at Oxford, Ohio when he was sixteen. He soon distinguished himself for his scholastic attainments. These scholarly interests continued throughout his life, even though he became a newsman concerned with day-to-day affairs. During the Civil War he became a distinguished correspondent for the *Cincinnati* (Ohio) *Gazette.*

When he met Horace Greeley, the two newspapermen became fast friends. Although Reid received several valuable newspaper offers after the Civil War, Greeley was able to lure him to the *Tribune.* Reid joined the paper in 1868, buying a share of its stock on Greeley's advice. Within a year Greeley made Reid his second-in-command.

Greeley ran for President as a Liberal Republican in 1872. He lost, but what was worse, the overexcitement of the campaign and the disappointment over the defeat by General Ulysses S. Grant contributed to Greeley's death. He was mourned by political leaders and editors alike, who reviewed his life and told about the contributions he made to America and to journalism.

Following Greeley's death in 1872, Reid formed a syndicate to acquire the *Tribune*'s options and a controlling interest, slightly more than a majority, for $500,000. This placed valuation of the *Tribune* at $1,000,000. Reid soon began to purchase the outstanding stock. By 1883 Reid, aided by his wealthy wife and father-in-law, obtained a majority of the stock and hence control of the *Tribune*. When Reid, then only thirty-five, took over publication of the *Tribune*, he pledged himself to a humanitarian program as had been championed by Greeley.

Reid's *Tribune* now became the Republican Party's most eloquent and powerful journalistic advocate. Greeley's paper had successfully appealed to labor, to the farmer and to the manufacturer, just as the Republican Party did. Now, however, economic lines were becoming sharper again. The Republican Party, more and more, became representative of industrial and commercial groups, and the *Tribune*, their spokesman.

Certain factors within the *Tribune* office influenced this decision. The *Weekly Tribune*'s circulation among farmers in the West began to drop. Reid had to concentrate more on the daily, appealing to upper-economic classes or to the laboring element. Daily circulation was about forty-two thousand. Another personal factor was important. By taste, by personal inclination, the new publisher chose to guide the *Tribune* along conservative lines. Within a few years he associated himself with leaders of industry in the nation and moved in their circle. He married the daughter of Darius Ogden Mills, wealthy Californian. Reid invested in the new Mergenthaler Linotype Company in the 1880s, and this helped swell his fortune.

Reid identified himself closely and consistently with the Republican Party, helping write campaign platforms. His editors wrote campaign literature. Reid was nominated for vice president on the Republican ticket in 1892, but the party was defeated. Reid held various diplomatic posts: minister to France, special ambassador to Great Britain several times, and finally ambassador to that country in 1908.

Especially interested in education, Reid was made a member of the Board of Regents of New York University and later became chancellor. He served on the Board of Leland Stanford University in California and on the Advisory Board of the School of Journalism of Columbia University.

Thus, the new publisher, because of his background and inclinations, directed the new course of the *Tribune* so that it would appeal to the wealthy and the educated. The *Tribune* was a reflection of their economic and political interests, their tastes and culture, just as the Pulitzer and Hearst papers mirrored the lower-income segments of the public. Unlike other Republican dailies, such as the *New York Times* and the *Evening Post,* the *Tribune* did not deviate throughout the remaining decades of the century from espousing Republican political and economic interests. The Republican Party, dominating the scene during this era, needed an effective medium in the commercial, industrial and banking center of the nation, and the *Tribune* answered this need.

Reid had no easy time rebuilding the old paper after Greeley died, but the new publisher's judgment about the course of the *Tribune* ought to take and about the moves he must make, was usually shrewd.

Reid, a superlative newsman and business administrator, recognized that the occasion required a spectacular stroke to reassure doubtful subscribers that the *Tribune* would continue. He decided to construct a large new newspaper building. The staff in 1875 thus moved into the finest home that any American journal could boast, the tallest commercial building in the city.

Reid improved various departments of the *Tribune.* He strengthened the city news, and appealing to the upper-economic class, offered a large amount of social news and men's club news. Coverage of yachting and horse racing appealed to many of his wealthy readers. Illustrations were slowly introduced.

In 1897 Reid, as indicated, introduced the halftone in the *Tribune,* the first daily to print regularly the illustrations made by this process. The *Tribune* used a number of photos in its Sunday magazine supplements.

Following the lead of the popular journalism, Reid revamped his headline schedule, using two-column headlines over important news. The *Tribune*'s front page, at this time, however, did not have the striking displays of the *World* and the *Journal.*

But it was in the literary, art, music and theatre departments that the *Tribune* shone brightly. Reid, an intellectual, was interested in keeping the *Tribune*'s reputation in these departments high, as they would appeal to educated and cultured clientele at which he was aiming.

Reid was able to push the *Tribune*'s daily circulation beyond that attained by Greeley. During the pre-Civil War period the daily *Tribune* had averaged about forty-five thousand. Following the election of 1872, when Greeley lost, subscribers dropped off, but under Reid the *Tribune* reached nearly eighty thousand subscribers by 1890.

Sunday Paper, Spectacular Development

Development of the Sunday *Tribune* was perhaps the most startling of the changes which occurred in the paper during the eighties and nineties. The *Tribune* had been issued occasionally on Sunday during the critical Civil War period when news could not be held over until Monday morning. Later, the Sunday paper was abandoned. Reid said he was praised by many for not violating the Sabbath day, but that he found these same persons reading other papers issued on Sunday. So the Sunday *Tribune* with ten pages, followed the trend, began regular publication in 1879. It was not until the 1890s that the *Tribune's* Sunday issue developed rapidly. By the beginning of that decade it reached twenty-two pages; at the end, about fifty pages. It was particularly strong on society news, and was distinguished by its music, art and literary features and reviews. Illustrated magazines were introduced. Personality sketches, embellished with portraits of the wealthy and their activities, were printed. The how-to-do feature, a type of popular science, appeared regularly.

In the eighties the Sunday edition reached between fifty thousand and seventy-five thousand subscribers. During the nineties it appealed to eighty thousand subscribers, about the same number as the daily.

Adolph S. Ochs, appearing on the scene in 1896, sought to modernize the old *New York Times* with a modified sensationalism. Faced with this competition the *Tribune* was due eventually for a modernization program also. During the nineties this could not very easily be made because the *Tribune* had strong traditions and connections. Its audience solidly supported it, and Reid himself was out of the *Tribune* office because of an asthmatic condition, and then he traveled in Europe on diplomatic missions. He could not realize the necessity for the changes; it was not until after the first decade of the new century that modifications were made which kept the *Tribune* afloat.

NEW YORK TIMES DECAYS BUT IS REGENERATED

Raymond, a Politician-Editor, Dies

Henry J. Raymond, after the Civil War, remained as editor of the *New York Times* for four years. As Chairman of the Republican National Committee, he made a speech in 1866 urging tolerance for the South, but his views were too liberal for the delegates. He lost his place as chairman, and, in turn, the *Times* lost thousands of readers.

Raymond's setback did not long affect the fortunes of the *New York Times*. Early in 1869 the owners refused an offer of a million dollars for the *Times,* established eighteen years before with $69,000 cash. Raymond died unexpectedly on June 19, 1869, two months before completing his eighteenth year as editor of the paper. His estate was valued at about $1,000,000. His thirty-four shares of the *Times* were worth $345,000.

When Raymond died, the *Times* had a succession of editors, but it was George Jones, business manager and partner, who supervised and guided the paper's policies.

The *Times* appealed to solid businessmen of New York, the class of readers who wanted information about the government and its economic policies which affected them: foreign news, market reports and financial affairs.

The *Times,* besides laying the basis for the daily and Sunday news and features of the *World,* also helped evolve one of the most important elements in the "yellow journal" formula: the crusading technique. This technique was developed in the *Times* as early as 1870 and 1871, before Pulitzer established the *St. Louis Post-Dispatch.* The *Times* by its crusade against, and its exposure of, the Tweed political ring, demonstrated the power of the newspaper in cleaning out political corruption.

During Grant's second term, the *Times* began to drift from strict Republicanism. Now awake to the need for reform, the *Times* called for a blockade of the political movement to nominate James G. Blaine as Republican presidential candidate in 1876. This insubordination by the paper led to an effort to grasp control of the *Times.* Jones, the largest stockholder, was not a majority stockholder; consequently, he had to fight the Republican politicians who attempted to get control of the *Times* to make it a thoroughly Republican party paper. Ten shares belonging to the estate of James B. Taylor, however, were on the market. Jones bought them, thus becoming owner of a majority of the shares, valued at $1,500,000.

Subscribing to a low tariff policy and opposed to political corruption, the *Times,* critical of the Republican administration, finally bolted the party in 1884. The *Times'* revolt both reflected and stimulated independent voting. This independent movement had accelerated after the Civil War, when national, state and local corruption demonstrated the necessity of independent voting. The *Times* still hoped the Republican Party would set itself right again, but the daily supported Cleveland, Democratic standard bearer, in 1884, 1888 and 1892. In 1896 however, the *Times,* like other Democratic papers, such as the *World,* the *Herald* and the *Sun,* found fault with the Democratic Party. The candidate, William Jennings Bryan, was characterized in the *Times* as a "Radical of Radicals" and ". . . an Untried Man, Leader of an Untried Policy."

The *New York Herald* meanwhile, delivered a mortal blow to Jones' paper. The *Times* failed to alter its journalistic pattern sufficiently to meet changing public desires. In the 1880s and 1890s, the *World*, a resurrected sheet itself, into which Pulitzer had poured his vitality, dug the ground from under the *Times*. The *World* was aided by the *Herald* and the *Tribune*, its imitators. The *Times'* circulation of thirty-six thousand began to drop.

The *Times* met the new competition in 1883 by reducing its price from three to two cents. Profits dropped off enormously, but the paper soon recovered. It earned between the years 1883 and 1888, a handsome profit, between $100,000 and $200,000 a year. Heavy expense was incurred in constructing a new building, begun in 1888, a building which Jones felt would be his monument. By the time the building was completed in 1889, profits had fallen to $15,000 a year.

Jones died in 1891. For two years his heirs ran the paper. Then, on April 3, 1893, the *Times* was sold to the New York Times Publishing Company. The new company, composed of *Times* workers, paid the Jones estate $950,000. Charles R. Miller, editor, was president. The presses were old and dilapidated, and the *Times* building was transferred to another company, controlled by Jones' heirs. The publishing company continued only as a tenant in the building.

Miller and his associates held on in this manner for three years. During this time the panic of 1893 hit the paper hard. Various ideas for making the *Times* popular and for following the new journalistic pattern of the period were tried. But the *Times* was doomed. Paid daily circulation had slipped to nine thousand.

Ochs: Capable Executive and Administrator

What the *Times* needed was a capable executive and administrator. The new journalistic age called for a newspaper manager. This man was Adolph S. Ochs, of Tennessee, who had a comprehensive understanding of the editorial department of a newspaper. With a thorough knowledge of the advertising and business departments, he also possessed an ability to get revenue.

Ochs was born on March 12, 1858, in Cincinnati, Ohio. His actual training in finance and newspaper work began early. At the age of eleven he was already at work in the office of the *Knoxville* (Tennessee) *Chronicle*. He became a printer's devil and later an apprentice. Afterwards on the *Tribune*, in Knoxville, he worked in the composing room, then transferred to the city room as a reporter. As assistant to the business manager, he received training in the business end. Meanwhile, the

The New-York Times.

THE SECRET ACCOUNTS.

Proofs of Undoubted Frauds Brought to Light.

THE ACCOUNT OF INGERSOLL & CO.

AFFAIRS IN EUROPE.

INGERSOLL & CO.

Figure 44. Raymond, Jennings, Jones and the *New York Times.* Able independent Henry J. Raymond (right) edited the *New York Times* for a few years after the Civil War, setting the independent course the daily was to pursue in the Gilded Age. He was followed by Louis J. Jennings, as editor, (left), but it was publisher George Jones (middle) who backed up his editors and reporters in their exposé of the Tweed Ring. The campaign against Tweed had appeared on various pages, but when the big story broke, it was given a three-column headline on page one. The *Times* campaign proved the value of the newspaper exposé.

Chattanooga (Tennessee) *Times,* though it held on in the face of competition, was tottering. Its manager offered to sell it to young Ochs for $800. Ochs was able to invest $250 for a half interest, which he stipulated should give him control.

With a working capital of $37.50, he became publisher of the *Chattanooga Times* on July 2, 1878. Ochs had a critical first year, but within two years was able to buy the other half interest. Under Ochs' leadership, his home town had a real estate boom, and he became a leader in the business, industrial and social life of the community. At thirty-eight, Ochs was a successful small-town publisher.

In 1896 a New York friend telegraphed Ochs that the *New York Times* needed a new publisher. Ochs went to New York to explore the possibilities in this position and was offered $50,000 yearly to become manager of the *Times,* but he declined, saying that he could not be successful unless he had control. Editor Miller and Edward Cary, another *Times* editorial writer, felt sure that Ochs could save the paper as an independent organization if given time.

The financial scheme which Ochs submitted to the *Times'* stockholders was similar in structure to that of the reorganization of any large company which had tottered. By investing $75,000 himself, Ochs, if he were successful, would be rewarded with a bonus and control of the $1,500,000 company. Just enough stock was held for him to make an absolute majority. When the paper had paid its way for three consecutive years, this stock was to be delivered to him. After the *Times'* stockholders agreed to this proposition, Ochs became publisher of the tottering but distinguished daily.

In 1895 sensational journalism, with many fruitful results of ten years of experimentation in the popularization of news and the Sunday paper, had broken the old ten commandments of journalism again. Yellow journalism was not respectable, however interesting. Ochs, at this juncture, stepped in to fill the vacuum: Publish a conservative paper with newer and livelier methods and appeals. Ochs utilized the new Pulitzer techniques, toned them down and made them respectable. Within a short time he spiced the news offered to *Times* readers; he employed headlines across the front page; he spread and displayed big stories in accord with the sensational formula; he looked for thrills in the news and even financed a polar expedition for romantic adventure news. He also cut the *Times'* price to one cent.

Ochs set forth his aims in taking over the *Times,* on August 18, 1896:

> It will be my earnest aim that the *New York Times* gives all the news, in concise and attractive form in language that is permissible in good society, and give it early . . . earlier than it can be learned through any other . . . to give the news regardless of party, sect, or interest involved, to make the columns of the *New York Times* a forum for the consideration of all questions of public importance, and to . . . invite intelligent discussion from all shades of opinion.

Since this was the beginning of the advertising slogan age, Ochs adopted the famous "All the news that's fit to print."

Ochs owed a debt to those popularizers of the Sunday paper, Pulitzer, Bennett and Hearst. These masters of sensationalism had put life into the Sunday edition. The Tennessee publisher utilized whatever methods his predecessors had worked out successfully but directed attention to more intellectual news. Pictures, full-page display and large headlines to lure readers certainly were borrowed from the journalistic pathbreakers.

The *Times* illustrated magazine supplement, issued first on Saturday, then with the Sunday edition, was informative, bright, typographically attractive. Its sixteen pages were filled with pictures and feature stories. The edition carried books and art news and reviews. The new *Times* reflected upper-class New York in a more up-to-date, flashy fashion than the older *Times* had.

The editorial page continued along in the same typographical and intellectual groove which it had followed for many years, Charles R. Miller and Edward Cary carrying the burden. The *Times,* as it opposed sensational journalistic news methods, also opposed trustbusting policies of new penny papers and their onslaughts against wealthy men. To meet competition from the yellow press, Ochs, as indicated, dropped the price of the *Times* from two cents to one cent. It was a bold, successful step.

The *Times* daily circulation reached 82,000 at the turn of the century, and the Sunday circulation mounted to 39,204.

NEW MANAGEMENT REVITALIZES POST, LIBERAL

Changing social conditions of the Gilded Age left deep marks on the *New York Evening Post,* which had been launched by Alexander Hamilton in 1801. Other such blanket-sheet contemporaries had either fallen by the wayside or had been absorbed by more progressive sheets. Continued prosperity of the *Evening Post* was a tribute to its lasting editorial vitality and the reinvigoration by new personalities: publishers, editors and reporters.

TABLE 21

Characteristics of Ochs' New York Times

What Ochs borrowed from Pulitzer and Hearst, showing diffusion and spread of newspaper methods

Makeup

1. Large headlines on front page
   2 or 3 column headlines
   4 column headlines
   Banner heads on front page
2. Inside page headlines
3. Front page boxes, calling attention to details
4. "Spread" of story over front and inside pages

Content

1. Emphasis on "big news"; building up story
2. Spice in news: melodrama, crime, sex, accident, disaster, sports (human interest stories)
3. Increased use of pictures
4. Promotion of thrilling adventure stunts
5. Exclusive stories by explorers
6. Science news

Sunday Edition

1. Headlines over features
2. Full-page features
3. Large pictures and sketches; art of display
4. Women's department
5. Types of features (1) science (2) big names (3) discussion topics
6. Pictorial section

Extra Journalistic Activities

1. Backs aviation, offers prizes
2. Backs exploration expeditions

A new period was opening, a period in which people began to turn, in larger numbers, to the afternoon paper. The trend placed the *Evening Post* in a strategic position. The daily had built up a good clientele, small but loyal, of twenty thousand circulation. A paper designed for Wall Street, the *Post* had an influence far beyond its actual circulation figures, particularly during the regime of Edwin L. Godkin after 1883. The *Evening Post* was sober, dignified, unemotional, even cold and severe in comparison with the lively *World* of Pulitzer; yet, Pulitzer said it was the ideal paper to publish for a limited audience. William Cullen Bryant, editor, died in 1868.

The *Evening Post*'s editors and traditions reached far into a previous journalistic age which called for men of culture and learning. When William Cullen Bryant became its editor, he gave the *Evening Post* dignity, tone and literary character. Bryant brought to the editorship a culture and background American journalism had not seen before.

Carl Schurz, Horace White and Henry Villard were searching for a daily into which they were prepared to put a considerable amount of capital. Bryant's family sold the *Post* to these three interested persons for $900,000. The daily earned about $50,000 annually.

While it was generally known that the real buyer was Henry Villard, this fact was concealed for some weeks. On July 1, a supplementary announcement appeared:

> Beginning with the next number, the *Nation* will be issued as the weekly edition of the *New York Evening Post.*

Why did Henry Villard purchase the *Evening Post* and combine it with the *Nation,* owned and edited by E. L. Godkin? Villard at this time was midway in his amazing career as a railway builder, although he had been a distinguished journalist during the Civil War. It was this journalistic interest which led him, while busiest with his great undertaking, to conceive the plan of buying a metropolitan paper and giving it the ablest editors procurable. Villard, with rare generosity, assumed financial responsibility for the paper but made the editors wholly independent by placing it in the hands of the three trustees.

In their fundamental viewpoints, the three editors, Carl Schurz, Horace White and Edwin Lawrence Godkin, were alike. Although they were one in wishing to make the *Post* champion of sound money, low tariff, civil service reform, clean and independent politics and international peace, they soon disagreed over labor issues. Godkin was antilabor; Schurz was sympathetic to unions. This quarrel led to Godkin's becoming editor-in-chief, with Horace White as assistant editor.

For the next sixteen years, between 1883 and 1899, until Godkin retired, Godkin definitely stamped his personality on the pages of the *Post.* He turned it into a sheet that was feared, respected and influential, far beyond its twenty thousand circulation.

Godkin contributed a powerful voice to the mainstream of American journalism. The *Nation* was the first weekly to have critical reviews by specialists, setting a new pace for American journalism. Godkin was also extraordinary in the sense that he was one of the few editors in America during the eighties and nineties who was almost exclusively concerned with the editorial page.

Godkin was born on October 2, 1831, at Moyne, in Ireland. Bored with the study of law as a youth, he found employment with a publishing house. At twenty-one, becoming interested in the people of Hungary and their struggles, he published his first book, *A History of Hungary.* He covered the Crimean War for the *London Daily News* between 1853 and 1855. Long interested in visiting the United States, he came to New York in November, 1856.

In 1858 he married a New Haven girl and decided to stay in the United States; also, he wanted a journal of his own. He felt that in the periodical press the educated men of America were not fairly represented.

The plan which he had meditated on so long came to fruition suddenly. James M. McKim, Philadelphia philanthropist and abolitionist, proposed joining forces with Godkin in starting this kind of journal. Forty stockholders provided capital of $100,000 for this new venture, the *Nation.* So great a number assured a wide interest but involved difficulties and misunderstandings about policy and control.

The *Nation* reached a circulation of ten thousand, chiefly among clergymen, editors, college professors and students.

When stockholders, being of varied beliefs, began to tell the editor, who was equally strong-minded, how to run the weekly, Godkin reorganized the company and the *Nation* continued on its way. For fifteen years Godkin with a few assistants published the paper, but it was too much for the editor. He was getting along in years, and he wanted some substantial income for his family. In 1881 he decided to sell the *Nation* to Henry Villard and make it a weekly edition of the *Evening Post,* of which Godkin became associate editor.

In taking over editorship of the *New York Evening Post,* Godkin secured a wider audience than he had before and continued his militant editorial campaigns. He was not especially interested in news, or in the new type of human interest stories. He rebuked the reporter who attempted to emphasize the sentimental account of a music teacher's death; Godkin said it smacked of sensationalism.

Godkin may be said to be the last of the great editors who relied so much on the editorial page. He brought a comprehensive and cosmopolitan knowledge of the world to his work. On the other hand, he was handicapped by knowing comparatively little of the great common people who made up the bulk of the large masses of newspaper readers, according to the *Post* historian, Allan Nevins.

Many persons considered Godkin a postwar Greeley in editorial output. Godkin brought the extremely cutting editorial style so characteristic of the *Nation* to the pages of the *Evening Post.* His exposition was constantly lightened by humor and often varied by irony or invective. It was the most natural thing in the world for him to compare the Tammany panic over the material which he published about its political leaders with introduction of a ferret into a rat cellar. He had an unequalled gift for compressing a homily into a humorous or ironical paragraph. But his most superb writing was that in which he delivered a straight-forward attack on some evil institution or person.

Godkin was reared in the doctrines of laissez-faire, advocating the least government interference with the economic system as the best. Godkin was long a believer in proportional representation, naming it in 1870 as one of the three great objectives of the *Nation* magazine. Another of these objectives, civil service reform, he took up after the Civil War. Not an economic reformer, but essentially a great political reformer, Godkin also advocated introduction of the Australian or short ballot, enactment of better election laws, reform of municipal government.

Godkin objected to demagogic attacks on capital, but he was more inclined to defend abuses by capital than abuses by labor. He was, however, more and more alarmed by the trusts, wanting evil combinations broken up, not regulated to prevent monopoly. Godkin had no sympathy for workingmen. He had a way of speaking of workmen, when they displeased him, as "ignorant," "idle," "reckless," indicting them *en masse.*

One of the *Post's* great reporters was Lincoln Steffens, who exposed the connection between crime, police and business interests. Born in a well-to-do family in San Francisco, Steffens attended the University of California in Berkeley and later traveled in Europe. On returning to New York he found a job on the *Evening Post* as a reporter and soon was assigned the Wall Street beat and later the police beat. He saw crime flourishing because the police department was so corrupt. Police took bribes from criminals and brothel owners as well as from saloon-keepers while claiming they were prosecuting those breaking the law. He found police with nightsticks breaking the heads of accused persons.

Dr. Charles H. Parkhurst, a clergyman-crusader, aroused Steffens to make a thorough investigation of Thomas F. Byrnes, a superintendent of police. The reporter found Byrnes knew all the pickpockets and crooks and where they operated, even allowing pickpockets to ply their trade in certain sections. Steffens discovered also that the Board of Police Commissioners consisted of machine politicians, who became wealthy from bribes. This led him to believe that bribery was the root of all evil, even prostitution.

The newsman agreed with Reverend Parkhurst's favorite slogan that good men should be substituted for the grafters in government. Steffens covered the Lexow investigating committee's hearings of the police department held in Albany, New York. These hearings will be described later.

Steffens left the *Evening Post* to become city editor of the old *Commercial Advertiser*. After a few years there he turned to writing magazine articles exposing corruption and graft in American cities. Always a great reporter, Steffens relied on his experiences and observations while on the *Evening Post* and the *Commercial Advertiser* to guide him in his investigations of other cities. He became known as one of the outstanding muckrakers of his time. Later Steffens wrote an autobiography which had an extensive influence. Magazine writers who exposed conditions in American cities will be discussed in the "Chain and Syndicate Era."

Some of Godkin's contemporaries believed his greatest reputation was won by his attacks on Tammany Hall in an attempt to eliminate corruption in New York City. As the election year of 1890 opened, Godkin resolved on a thorough-going exposure of the real character of the men who constituted Tammany, an exposé which would show how Tammany organizers reeked with slime.

On April 3, 1890, the *Evening Post* published nine columns of biographical sketches, exposing the twenty-seven members of the Tammany Executive Committee, including the big four of the so-called New Tammany: Mayor Grant, Thomas F. Gilroy, Bourke Cockran and Richard Croker. These sketches were published later in a pamphlet, of which thousands of copies were sold.

The sensation produced by the Tammany Hall exposé was profound. Within a few days the *Evening Post* reprinted delighted comments from

Figure 45. (Left) Lincoln Steffens, Able *Evening Post* Reporter; (Right) Edwin L. Godkin, Independent Editor of *New York Evening Post.* No one helped expose the corrupt Tammany Hall Ring and police corruption in New York as much as the *New York Evening Post.* Lincoln Steffens reported the climax of the story when Police Captain Schmittberger told of the payoffs to police by the owners of brothels and gambling houses.

half of the important newspapers of the East. From the public uproar grew the Lexow inquiry in the state legislature. Senator Clarence Lexow offered a resolution in the New York state legislature for an investigating committee. When the committee was appointed, he became chairman.

After a police captain "squealed," Inspector Byrnes resigned and other higher-ups confessed. Defeat of Tammany was assured; it was beaten in the next election. William M. Strong, a businessman, was picked by reform Democrats and reform Republicans for the position of mayor of New York City, and Theodore Roosevelt became police commissioner. Many believed that Mayor Strong's reform administration made many solid contributions and that his administration was one of the best New York ever had.

In competition with other evening papers, the *Post* began to stress sports news. In 1886 the daily employed a sports editor, and during the nineties it carried a regular sports page. The *Post* attempted to get sports news on the same afternoon the events occurred.

The *Evening Post*'s literature department was a chief attraction of the paper. As a result of amalgamation with the weekly *Nation*, the *Post* became the first American newspaper to publish book criticisms that were consistently excellent, discriminating and had a high literary quality. The *Evening Post* and the *Nation* did far more than all other periodicals combined to introduce the important Russian writers, Turgenev, Tolstoy, Gogol and Dostoevski, to the American public.

The financial section was another department of the *Post* which was most important for maintaining circulation among the group to whom the *Post* appealed. In 1891 Alexander Dana Noyes came from the *Commercial Advertiser* to serve as financial editor and give to the *Post*'s business pages a sense of authority.

Taking its editorial page, its financial department and its literary, music and drama criticism, the *Evening Post* was quite indispensable to New Yorkers of culture and, in most cases, wealth. Like Dana's *Evening Sun*, it represented the upper and middle class just as Pulitzer's *Evening World*, Bennett's *Telegram* and Hearst's *Evening Journal* appealed to the lower-middle class or working class. Godkin left the popularization of the evening edition to these new masters of journalism.

Godkin retired from journalism in 1899 and died in 1902. Afterward, the *Evening Post* began to feel the effects of the new journalism and adjusted to the competition in the twentieth century.

Through the publication of the *Evening Post* and the *Nation* Godkin had given an intellectual tone to American journalism and had sought to keep it on a high plane. His constant hammering in news columns on political corruption had its effects on other editors and led to reforms in city government, especially the introduction and spread of civil service as a means of filling municipal jobs.

His well-written editorial page inspired other editors to follow his lead in keeping editorial pages influential in a period when news was becoming dominant. The *Evening Post* and the *Nation* provided journalistic voices for educated, intellectual upper-class people concerned with American life, and Godkin publications stimulated their critical thinking.

Chapter 20

Atlantic Seaboard Journalism

NEW ENGLAND JOURNALISM SEES STRONG PAPERS APPEAR

Although the New York press boasted the largest, wealthiest and most influential journals, other sections of the nation saw strong papers develop. Some dailies had been established before the Civil War; others were launched now to reflect new public and journalistic trends. Dailies developed similarities as they responded to similar economic, political and urban conditions. They also acquired differences, growing out of local and regional situations. Journalistic personalities also influenced the direction the individual newspapers followed. Newspaper publication everywhere showed eventually the influence of the New York leaders, Dana, Pulitzer and Hearst.

New England had an historic American tradition of journalism. But even there, metropolitan influences were felt. Although with the sweep of people, commerce and industry to the West, New England lost somewhat her once dominant influence. The region remained highly industrialized and boasted some of the outstanding cultural and educational institutions in the nation.

Boston: Economic and Cultural Center

In spite of the fact that her supremacy was challenged nationally, Boston was still second to New York in commercial importance in the postwar period. Boston was the center of New England's manufacturing and foreign trade, and the city had banking facilities which financed enterprising factory owners and merchants throughout New England. With its strong educational and cultural traditions, Boston schools and higher educational institutions were well-known to many Americans.

Harvard University continued as one of the leading institutions of its kind; the university was joined by the Massachusetts Institute of Technology. Reflecting the interest in cultural activities, the Boston Symphony was organized in 1881. Boston pushed out its physical boundaries in all directions and added many acres. Population grew from 150,000 at the end of the Civil War to 560,000 in 1900.

Boston newspapers mirrored the economic, cultural and population growth and change. Boston papers varied. Traditional dailies, which were radical departures in the 1830s when the penny press era began, continued, solid and respectable now. New dailies developed to respond to changing wants and needs. Some of the old papers were reinvigorated to meet the new challenges of the era. Boston experienced patterns of journalism change similar to those which occurred in New York.

Boston Transcript

One of the older papers which remained vigorous was the *Boston Transcript*. Though the *Transcript* began as a Democratic paper, in the rising time of the slavery issue the daily shifted its views and opposed slavery, moving into the Republican side. The two owners, Henry W. Dutton and William H. Dutton, died in 1872 and the *Transcript* began to decline. A new company, the Boston Transcript Company, was formed with Samuel P. Mandell, a son-in-law of one of the Duttons, as president. Mandell began to rejuvenate the old daily.

The *Transcript* expanded its news and literary departments and acquired new editors. By 1880, when the daily reached its fiftieth anniversary, it was the largest paper in New England. Called "the bible of proper Bostonians," its appeal was to the old mercantile families, to the cultural residents. Although the *Transcript* had been Republican, it supported Samuel J. Tilden for president and Grover Cleveland four years later. It could not back William Jennings Bryan in 1896 because of his views on the silver question.

Feeling the competition from opposition papers (to be described) the *Transcript* began to alter its course at the end of the century. It expanded its editorial department, strengthened various other sections and introduced illustrations. Similarly, the *Transcript*'s advertising department was rejuvenated and became more aggressive.

Daily Advertiser

Another traditional newspaper continuing from the pre-Civil War era was the old *Daily Advertiser*. It was even older than the *Transcript*, as it was founded by the patriot Nathan Hale in 1813. A bible of the Bostonian moneyed interests, the *Advertiser* devoted much attention to literature, music and art. Its fine arts criticism was especially well known. The owners established the *Evening Record* in 1884 to meet the growing interest in afternoon papers. Now reaching a circulation of more than eighteen thousand the *Advertiser* was edited by Charles F. Dunbar, a Harvard political scientist.

Boston Globe Revived

Like Pulitzer and others who appeared in the 1880s to revamp the newspaper pattern and to broaden its appeal, Charles H. Taylor recognized the journalistic needs of Bostonians and satisfied them with the *Boston Globe.*

Colonel Taylor, a veteran of the Civil War, received his early newspaper experience on the *Boston Traveller* and had published the magazine *American Homes* until fire wiped it out. He was asked to take over the *Boston Globe* in 1873. The paper, only a year old, was hastening to join the great silent majority in the newspaper graveyard. The *Globe* was a four-cent eight-page paper. It had fifteen columns of poor advertising and eight thousand circulation. The daily was spending $180,000 a year and taking in only $120,000.

Taylor was only twenty-seven and times were bad. But Taylor began to apply what he knew about journalism. For more than four years the *Globe* was only one jump ahead of the sheriff. Taylor balanced the payroll at the tick of the clock, glad he got by another day. The *Globe* had no Associated Press franchise, and he used some makeshift arrangements, including swiping news from early editions of other Boston papers with the AP copy. From Eben Jordan, local merchant, Taylor borrowed $100,000 for the paper, and somehow managed to keep it afloat until he worked out a suitable pattern.

Because of the growth of Boston, increasing literacy and the multiplication of women readers, the *Globe* expanded. It sought to appeal to women readers whom other Boston publishers had neglected. With special articles the *Globe* likewise began to appeal to children. A father who voted Republican did not prefer the Democratic *Globe,* but he had to bring it home because the children and his wife wanted it. Competitive sports, athletic races and contests of all kinds were just being organized, and the *Globe* got the start on other papers in handling such sports news. Taylor had a gift for finding and publishing what was interesting to all sorts of people.

He also aimed to make the paper more human, and like Dana of the *New York Sun,* revamped the editorial formula. His cue was to print not what was traditionally important but what was interesting. He also eliminated much routine telegraph news. The *Globe* built up its own news service all over New England because the daily did not have the AP. The *Globe* became more individualistic than other dailies. Taylor used smashing headlines as Pulitzer did in New York.

Coming directly from the magazine field with his *American Homes*, which had been swept away in the fire, Taylor incorporated some of his magazine techniques into the daily *Globe* and *Sunday Globe*. He began to run serials. He also printed pictures, first woodcuts, then zinc plates. Realizing the value of humor, he added the American humorists, Bill Nye, Mr. Dooley and George Ade.

Taylor established the *Sunday Globe* in 1877. A Lord's day edition of a daily paper had been frowned on in Boston until eagerness for war news overcame puritanical scruples at the beginning of the Civil War. The competitive *Sunday Herald* had the jump, having the field to itself for fifteen years. The Sunday paper then was the poorest for advertising, but it later became the most profitable. The Sunday *Globe* gave the *Herald* strong competition.

Colonel Taylor began the *Evening Globe* in the spring of 1878. To acquire larger circulation, he reduced the price of the daily to two cents, a step other publications in other cities were also taking. The *Globe* thus had continuous publication, morning, evening and Sunday.

The *Globe* came out as an independent Democrat in politics. This met a long-felt want, as the old Boston *Post*, only Democratic paper in the city, had fallen asleep. The *Globe* stood by its political guns but did not abandon itself to blind partisanship that characterized other Boston papers. The *Globe* gave Republicans a fair deal in its news columns. Republicans swore at the daily but bought it since the reporters sought to give both sides of a political issue.

Taylor was able to infuse in his employees a high morale and was always on the lookout for talent and initiative. He allowed reporters to sign their names to articles. The employees had a strong tie to the paper, considering the *Globe* their home.

Taylor's journalistic reputation spread, and Joseph Pulitzer, whom he knew, offered him $100,000 a year if he would come to New York for only three days a week to manage the *World*. Taylor refused. In 1887 the *Globe* appeared to be rejuvenated, for it moved into a new building. By the end of the century the *Globe* reached 150,000 daily circulation for both morning and evening editions.

Boston Herald, Boston Post

Another Boston daily was able to survive journalistic changes and continued to appeal to a wide audience. The *Herald*, which was established in 1846 as a penny paper by some printers, had a morning, evening and Sunday edition by 1860. With one hundred thousand circulation by 1872, the *Herald* was considered a journalistic leader. It sought to cover news of New England thoroughly. The *Herald* was independent in politics, its editors seeking to appeal to both merchants and mechanics. While aiming at Boston circulation, the *Herald* was read throughout New England. It discarded the old journalistic formula and sought to meet the needs of the day. By the end of the era the publishers reached 140,000 families with their various editions.

Sensational methods became more pronounced in Boston in the 1890s. Edward A. Grozier, who had been private secretary to Joseph Pulitzer and an editor of the *New York World,* brought the Pulitzer type of journalism to Boston in 1891 when he began to publish the *Boston Post,* a readable paper, but then in a period of decline.

Other New England Dailies

In Springfield, Massachusetts the *Republican* continued in the Bowles family and remained an influential paper. Although published in a nonmetropolitan town, the *Springfield Republican* won a national reputation. In spite of bolting the Republican Party because of its reconstruction policies, the paper came back into the party later, but showing its independence finally shifted to the Democratic Party.

Another distinguished New England paper with a history extending back to the colonial period was the *Hartford* (Connecticut) *Courant.* In the Gilded Age it was edited by General Joseph R. Hawley who had been one of the founders of the Republican Party in Connecticut. He was later elected governor of the state and then United States senator. Some of the best literary material of Charles Dudley Warner, nationally known essayist and associate editor of the *Courant,* was published in the daily.

PHILADELPHIA'S NEWSPAPERS REINVIGORATED

Philadelphia's growth was particularly marked in the post-Civil War period. The city was the banking capital of Pennsylvania, furnishing capital for the western part of the state's rich coal and oil resources. Philadelphia's harbor shipping facilities rated along with New York's. Philadelphia's population rose from 565,000 in 1860 to 1,293,000 at the turn of the century.

With the continued growth of Philadelphia, vigorous journalism characterized the Quaker City. A wide variety of dailies appeared. Strong personalities rose to guide the leading journals. Most of the major psychological interests of the public and a variety of economic and political views found expression in the journals. With the changing public interests, new Philadelphia dailies were established to reflect those interests.

A half dozen or more of the papers established in the pre-Civil War era continued in Philadelphia. Some publishers and editors refused to change their styles and outlook to meet the new era; consequently, the papers went out of business or were absorbed by other papers. Other prewar dailies had won, however, a strong, loyal following and had built a favorable reputation. On the retirement or death of their publishers and editors, new owners or sons of the old publishers reinvigorated the newspapers. Because of the greater capital required, in some instances wealthy men such as Thomas Wanamaker, retail merchant, or Anthony Drexel, banker, supplied the funds. Newsmen from other cities saw journalistic and economic opportunities in thriving Philadelphia and entered the competitive journalistic arena.

In many respects Philadelphia paralleled New York; consequently, similar types of journalism flourished. As in New York and elsewhere, crusading journalism rose to do battle in Philadelphia, attacking political corruption and other current municipal evils, and fighting for a more attractive city. Typographical methods and other characteristics of the new journalism were introduced. With the shift to afternoon readership, publishers launched new evening dailies, and to supply news and reading matter on Sunday, also issued Sunday editions.

The North American, Vigorous, Influential

One of the more vigorous newspapers which was founded before the Civil War but continued to exert an influence was the *North American*. Owner Morton McMichael favored radical reconstruction policies and defended the Grant administration in its most embarrassing days. The publisher had no sympathy with newspapers which maintained political independence. McMichael colored the *North American* with his personality.

In many respects he was similar to Whitelaw Reid of the *New York Tribune*. If he had been able to accept the offer, McMichael would have been appointed minister to England. Ill health forced him to decline the permanent chairmanship of the Republican national convention in 1876.

McMichael retired from the *North American*'s management in December of that year and died three years later, in January, 1879.

In spite of the efforts of McMichael's sons and grandsons, the daily lost momentum. Ultraconservative and antireform, the publication became just another newspaper left from a bygone era. Finally its popularity all but vanished, and the time was at hand when it either would have to close or sell out. New journalistic competition was too strong.

The McMichaels chose to sell, and Thomas B. Wanamaker, elder son of John Wanamaker, the department store owner, purchased the paper in January, 1889, for $175,000. The new owner was a Princeton University graduate and had worked in his father's successful store. Thomas Wanamaker became one of the leading businessmen of the day. An ardent Republican, he watched his father defeated in his struggle with Matthew S. Quay for control of the Republican Party in Pennsylvania. Wanamaker was concerned about the extent of political corruption in the state and the vice which blighted Philadelphia.

Under the new regime, therefore, the *North American* suddenly stopped praising Boss Quay, its favorite Republican leader. The paper began to censor him. With precedents established by new Philadelphia journals, the *North American* became a forceful, crusading journal. Wanamaker recruited many of his editors and reporters from New York through the help of his friend, James Gordon Bennett, Jr.

So violent were the *North American*'s attacks on the city bosses that when Wanamaker moved the paper in 1901 to the North American building at 121 South Broad Street, the politicians did everything they could to have the structure condemned as unsafe.

Key figure at the *North American* was Editor Edwin A. Van Valkenburg. He had a background of practical political experience at Harrisburg as a Quay adherent before his break with the political boss to support John Wanamaker, who sought to win a seat in the United States Senate. Van Valkenburg was first assigned to the circulation department of the *North American* but soon took over management of the paper.

For twenty-five years he battled the Republican organization in Philadelphia and others in control of the state of Pennsylvania. In one crusade after another, Van Valkenburg fought doggedly, persistently and ably against the rule of political contractors. He slashed out at a Pennsylvania senator in a signed editorial in which Van Valkenburg wrote, "The stain of corruption is in our hands; the mark of corporate bribery is on your forehead."

Belligerency was the keynote of the *North American*. Hurling invective and denunciation, it followed every scent of corruption. The editor, for instance, embarrassed Mayor Samuel H. Ashbridge in 1901 by persuading John Wanamaker to offer $2,500,000 for street railway franchises that the mayor insisted on giving away to a group of political manipulators.

Van Valkenburg, in 1905, was able to block the "gas steal," a scheme to lease the city's gas works on unfavorable terms. The next year his wholesale exposure of the new state capitol in Harrisburg produced a scandal that almost wrecked the administration of Governor Samuel W. Pennypacker, who was personally an honest man but had Quay's backing.

For a quarter of a century, Van Valkenburg fought for such varied causes as direct primaries, popular election of United States senators, enfranchisement of women and prohibition. He battled for conservation of natural resources, rights of labor unions and a modern highway system. He was against excessive tariff rates and special privileges. Theodore Roosevelt became his idol.

Circulation of this Republican crusading newspaper rose to 160,000 in 1903.

Philadelphia Inquirer

The traditions of the *Philadelphia Inquirer* went back to the penny press era. Although the *Inquirer* started as a Democratic paper it shifted to the Whig and then the Republican Party. William Harding, son of the retired owner, came into control during the Civil War. Freed from parental ties, he quickly gave up old-fashion publication methods, changing the name from *Pennsylvania Inquirer* to *Philadelphia Inquirer*, showing the new focusing on city affairs. Such was Harding's success that he ran circulation up from seven thousand at the beginning of the war to seventy thousand at the end. The *Inquirer* won for itself a reputation for reliability, promptness and completeness.

In the postwar period the *Inquirer* continued to prosper, covering the news but remaining basically a conservative journal in its political opinions. In the 1880s the *Inquirer* appeared to slide downward. It became old-fashioned and outmoded when compared to new and up-and-coming journals. Harding underwent a long and wasting illness; the paper's financial condition went from bad to worse. With the situation at last precarious, circulation dropping below five thousand, Harding sold the *Inquirer* to James Elverson in 1889. There was little left of the once famous paper except for the good name.

Elverson, the new publisher, had been highly successful with his *Saturday Night*, a literary paper filled with stories and poetry, and with *Golden Days*, a weekly publication which reached three million boys and girls. Elverson now turned his attention to the daily *Inquirer*.

His astonishing business capacity and journalistic sense rejuvenated the *Inquirer.* Elverson expanded his editorial staff, bought new equipment and moved the papers into new quarters. He was the first Philadelphia publisher to operate his entire pressroom by electricity and to use long-distance telephones in gathering news.

In December, 1889, he started a Sunday edition of the *Inquirer.* To widen his circulation, the new publisher reduced the price of his weekday journal from two cents to one cent. Elverson sold a large newspaper for the low price, but many publishers thought his policy was suicidal. It will be recalled that New York publishers were reducing their price.

Elverson supported the various improvements for the beautification of Philadelphia, particularly the proposal to build an extensive municipal parkway. In politics, Elverson's *Inquirer* was strongly Republican, but he did not always follow the party in local government affairs.

Following the lead of James Gordon Bennett in New York, Elverson took pains to build up his classified advertising pages on the ground that such ads constituted news as well as revenue. He printed many help wanted and position wanted ads. The statement was made often that if you saw a man carrying an *Inquirer,* he was sure to be out of work.

With the steady increase in his circulation, Elverson again had to move the paper to new quarters, opening a six-story plant at 1109 Market Street in 1894. Before Elverson died in 1911 he had nursed the weak and failing *Inquirer* into a newspaper with one of the largest circulations in the nation.

Public Ledger

Another of the penny press era dailies, the *Public Ledger,* continued in this period as a leading Philadelphia newspaper. Of the three original owners, William M. Swain remained active on the paper. During the Civil War, Swain began to receive offers for the *Public Ledger* from George W. Childs who wanted to purchase the paper. Finally Swain and Arunah S. Abell, his partner, sold the *Public Ledger* to Childs for $154,000 in 1864. Neither Swain nor other Philadelphians knew that Childs' silent partner was Anthony L. Drexel, one of the richest bankers in the nation.

Under the new owner Childs, the *Public Ledger* was to prosper even more than it had before. The *Public Ledger* became the second largest daily in the country. Although his only experience was in book publishing, Childs was considered by many as the most famous Philadelphia editor since Benjamin Franklin. Operating according to an ethical code, the paper had a restrained, dignified tone. Much space was given to financial and business news, appealing to the businessmen. Despite competition from a dozen other Philadelphia papers, the *Public Ledger* reached one hundred thousand circulation in the 1880s and was regarded as one of the leading papers in the country.

Upon the death of Childs in 1894, his partner's son, George W. Childs Drexel, became publisher. His interests did not lie in newspaper work, however, and the *Public Ledger* failed to continue its prosperity and appeal. New Philadelphia competition began to exceed the *Ledger* in circulation. Before long Drexel said he was willing to sell if he could find a buyer; consequently, Adolph S. Ochs, publisher of the *New York Times,* bought the Philadelphia daily in 1902, consolidating it with the *Philadelphia Times.*

Public Record, Challenger

One of the papers which rose to challenge the *Public Ledger* was established in this period by William J. Swain, son of the *Ledger*'s founder. Young Swain launched his *Public Record* in 1870 as a two-cent morning paper. When the *Record* slipped into financial difficulties and circulation dropped to five thousand, it was bought by William M. Singerly in 1877. In metropolitan cities of America, it was beginning to cost more to establish dailies and to keep them operating successfully until they caught on in public favor. Singerly was a railroad and industrial owner.

Recognizing civic and journalistic value of exposés as Hearst did elsewhere, Singerly introduced civic campaigns and crusades, including one against the selling of medical diplomas to would-be doctors. He sought better parks and roads in Philadelphia. To get a large audience, Singerly reduced the price of the *Record* to one cent. He also improved news coverage and strengthened the financial and market pages to appeal to Philadelphia readers having stocks and bonds. Soon the *Public Record* passed the *Ledger,* reaching 120,000 circulation. By 1897 the *Record* found 170,000 readers, about half in Philadelphia and half in small towns of Pennsylvania. The Singerly interests crashed at the end of the century, and the paper was sold in 1902 to Thomas Wanamaker for $3,000,000.

Press, Times

Competing with the *Public Record* was the *Philadelphia Press,* which had been established before the Civil War. The *Press* was sold in 1877, and in a few years began to battle the *Record* in crusading for public welfare, reacting to the same conditions as Pulitzer and Hearst did in San Francisco, St. Louis and New York, and as Crozier did in Boston.

In the same group was the *Philadelphia Times.* Under Alexander K. McClure, a reformer in Pennsylvania state politics and a lawyer who had run for mayor, the *Times* found corruption at the Philadelphia City Hall and blasted away. McClure practiced the Philadelphia brand of aggressive, exposure journalism, and his paper benefited. He was the first to establish a Sunday edition. In 1889 the *Times* was sold to a local politician who could not maintain it in public favor. After the *Times* went into a decline, Ochs purchased it for $600,000, and, as indicated, merged the *Times* with the *Public Ledger.*

Three Evening Papers: Item, Bulletin and Telegraph

Reflecting increasing public interest in the afternoon field, the *Evening Item* gained considerable success in this period. Founded by Thomas Fitzgerald in 1847, the *Evening Item* developed into a lively newspaper, conducting a number of crusades. Its circulation topped 180,000 in the 1890s.

The *Evening Bulletin,* established before the Civil War, had slipped in circulation because of keen competition. The *Evening Bulletin* was finally sold at auction for $89,000, becoming the property of William L. McLean in 1895. McLean had previous journalism experience in Pittsburgh on both the *Leader* and the *Press.* He now bought the *Bulletin,* which had an Associated Press franchise. The paper had twelve thousand circulation among wealthy people. McLean felt that Philadelphia needed a high-grade afternoon daily sold at a popular price. He figured circulation potential would be high and advertising possibilities strong among the wealthy class. He made the *Bulletin* a penny paper, stressed local news, since he considered the suburban communities around Philadelphia just small towns. McLean added new equipment and produced three editions of his eight-page *Bulletin.* In a year he reached 33,000 readers daily. In five years he found 130,000 readers. Other dailies dropped by the wayside.

Philadelphia was not without other afternoon papers during the Gilded Age. The *Evening Telegraph* was established in 1864 and made some progress. Seeing the advantage of an afternoon paper in the city, Barton W. Warburton bought the *Evening Telegraph* in 1893, spending $175,000 on new presses and other improvements. He aimed at a quality circulation, solid business families. Warburton added a woman's page, an art page and devoted more attention to sports and theatricals than before. On Saturday he had a church page and gave attention to the secret and colonial societies of interest to older Philadelphians. His advertising reflected the group to whom he appealed, for the *Evening Telegraph* carried many carriage, bank and trust company advertisements. The daily was eventually absorbed into the *Evening Public Ledger.*

BALTIMORE'S ACTIVE JOURNALISM

Flattened by the Civil War, Baltimore felt the effects of it for decades afterward. When the South was crippled economically, Baltimore, tied closely to that section, was demoralized. Moreover, as Baltimore was divided in its loyalties, internal strife continued far into the postwar period. The city slipped from its position of third in population to sixth because of the rise of other cities, especially those in the midwest.

Baltimore eventually recovered much of its prosperity, and the city began to grow again. It was the largest city south of Philadelphia on the Atlantic seaboard. Baltimore had a deep harbor from which vessels sailed to and from all ports of call, both foreign and domestic. Baltimore's enterprising businessmen and bankers had foreseen the rich potential in transportation of foodstuffs raised in the Ohio Valley, across the Alleghenies. The Baltimorians' foresight in establishing the Baltimore & Ohio Railroad in 1828, paid off now, for the road brought to Baltimore farm products which were then transshipped on trains and boats heading for other cities. Manufactured goods sent west by the strategically located railroad increased.

The city's businessmen making their fortunes in Baltimore also made contributions to the welfare of its citizens. The Johns Hopkins Hospital and Johns Hopkins Medical School and University, the Enoch Pratt Free Public Library, the George Peabody Institute of Music and the Henry Walters Art Gallery were founded with money provided by these philanthropists.

Baltimore's population reflected the expanding commercial and industrial activity and the cultural advancement. In 1860 the city had 212,000 residents; they reached 508,000 by the end of the period.

Growth of the Sun

Newspapers in Baltimore reflected the paralysis and recovery. Established newspapers, as in New York, were challenged eventually by newcomers. The *Sun,* owned by the Abell family, and the first of the penny papers, built up the largest circulation. By the end of the

Civil War the *Sun* had established its grooves, was successful and did not intend to change much. The *Sun* printed a six page paper until the nineties. Advertising remained, as before, on the front page. Heads on news stories were small; no solicitation of advertising was permitted. Halftones were not used, though stereotyping had been introduced in the 1860s.

The *Sun* had always been Democratic in its leanings, but it adhered to one of its original tenets and eschewed partisan politics. Political corruption in Baltimore was as bad as in other large cities of the United States. Here was a situation which called for newspaper attention, but the newspaper ignored it until the 1880s.

Political bosses controlled the city, the state and the Maryland congressmen in the House of Representatives and Senate. Boss Arthur Pue Gorman represented the Pennsylvania Railroad and the sugar trust and was in favor of a high tariff, to which the Democratic *Sun* was opposed.

The political machine controlled appointments to the bench, and here the *Sun*'s first collision with the Democratic politicians occurred. One of its charges was failure of the judges to rotate from one court to another as prescribed by law. Both corruption and fixing of judges by politicians were inevitable, the paper said. The *Sun* opened its attack and supported an independent slate for the judiciary in 1882. The Independents won, and the courts were thus cleaned up. Instead of following this victory with other campaigns, the *Sun* returned to its previous apathy.

It remained for the up-and-coming newcomer to town, Charles H. Grasty who purchased the *Evening News,* to lead the assault on the machine. The *Sun* soon got into the political battle.

Sun reporters covered the regular Democratic conventions and parades, but its headlines and stories were loaded against Gormanism. The *Sun* made strenuous efforts to report the Republican Convention which was held in Cambridge, on the eastern shore of Maryland. When the *Sun* announced the results of the election, it was learned that for the first time a Republican city council, state legislature and the United States senator were elected. After the election the *Sun* returned to the Democratic fold in city and state elections. Nationally, the paper backed Cleveland in his campaign but opposed Bryan in 1896, though it supported him in 1900.

Meanwhile, in 1888, the founder of the *Sun* died, and his three sons, George W., Edwin and Walter R. Abell, inherited the business. The brothers, in 1892, decided to incorporate, and the A. S. Abell Company was capitalized at $300,000, with George Abell as president. When George died, Edwin Abell headed the company, and his son, as well as the sons of the other Abell brothers, became officers and directors. The paper continued to earn annually between 12 and 16 per cent, or about $54,000 above regular salaries and expenses.

The Abells did not let the business slump. They bought, in 1892, a new Hoe press capable of printing 96,000 eight-page newspapers per hour, and the number of pages in the daily jumped from six to eight. Ottmar Mergenthaler was working on his great printing invention, the Linotype, only a few blocks from the *Sun* office, but the machines were not used in the *Sun*'s composing room for some time after they were put on the market. Abell was afraid his printers might not be able to learn how to operate the machines, and the changeover might throw people out of work. Later, however, these fears were overcome, and the *Sun* bought ten of the new linecasting machines.

Enterprising Grasty and the News

The rising young publisher who began to challenge the traditional papers was Charles H. Grasty, who represented in Baltimore the new type of journalism coming into vogue in the West, Midwest and in New York City.

Grasty's story has never been told fully. He was a fighting, forceful and dynamic newsman. Charles was born in 1863, son of a Presbyterian minister living in Virginia. Charles cut his eye teeth in journalism on the *Mexico* (Missouri) *Intelligencer.* Although he wanted to study law his deeper interest was journalism. His real training began when he joined the staff of William R. Nelson's *Kansas City Star.* Grasty learned Nelson's methods of campaigning against corrupt politicians and he also observed Nelson's unbeatable combination: low subscription rate for morning, evening and Sunday newspapers. Within eighteen months Grasty became managing editor of the *Star.* Then he was attracted to Baltimore with an offer for a job as managing editor of the *Manufacturer's Record* and an opportunity to assist in development of Roland Park, a Baltimore suburb owned by English investors.

Grasty could not keep out of daily journalism long. In 1891 he had an opportunity to purchase the *Baltimore Evening News,* founded in 1872. He had backers among wealthy men of Baltimore who wanted someone to fight the political machine. Grasty fought it for sixteen years, forcing the *Sun* to align with him in 1895.

Baltimore American

The *Sun*'s chief Republican rival in Baltimore after the Civil War continued to be the *Baltimore American.* Charles Fulton, enterprising newsman, who had joined the paper in 1853, bought an interest in it.

During the war, in 1862, Fulton's partner, Robert A. Dobbin, died. Since his son, Joseph Dobbin, succeeded to the partnership, the firm's name continued to remain Dobbin and Fulton. Two years later Fulton bought the Dobbin interest, and Albert Fulton joined his father in operation of the *American.*

With this sound foundation and reputation already established, the *American* entered post-Civil War years as a strong Republican journal and continued to prosper. Fulton occupied a prominent position in state affairs, and for many years represented the party in the national conventions of the Republican Party. His background and experience paralleled that of Whitelaw Reid of the *New York Tribune.*

The *American,* meanwhile, sought to improve Baltimore and lent its support to projects to advance the city. The daily advocated purchase of the land for Druid Hill Park and the tax on passenger railways to meet the outlay.

On March 2, 1879, publication of the Sunday edition of the *American* was begun and met with a quick and favorable response. Desiring to house his growing newspaper in a larger building, Fulton constructed the first iron building for newspaper publication.

Felix Agnus Invigorates

General Felix Agnus, Fulton's son-in-law, added his vigor and ability to the *American* when he joined the staff. Born in Lyons, France, Agnus came to the United States, and after working in New York joined the northern army. Wounded, he was shipped to Baltimore where he was nursed by publisher Fulton's daughter, whom he later married. Following the war he joined the staff of the *Baltimore American.* Agnus served in the business department and then became business manager in July, 1869.

At the death of his father-in-law, the publisher, in June, 1883, Agnus became sole manager of the paper under the terms of the will. The new publisher of the *American* helped transform the old paper into a modern paper of the twentieth century. Agnus found the old Fulton machinery obsolete and ordered two new Hoe presses. Catching the afternoon trend, he established the *Star* in 1908. When the fire of 1904 destroyed the business district of Baltimore, Agnus found facilities for printing the *American* in Washington. Before the fire was out he started plans and soon constructed a sixteen-story building to house the morning and evening news operations. Locally, Agnus served on many commissions to improve Baltimore. In national politics he was an active Republican.

The publisher entertained United States presidents and other business leaders at his home in Greenspring Valley, near Baltimore.

Two other papers, the *Herald* and the *World* were established during this period but did not last far into the new century. Henry Louis Mencken obtained his first newspaper experience on the *Morning Herald.*

WASHINGTON: POLITICAL JOURNALISM DECLINES

Once Washington had been the center of national political journalism, but with decline of the political party press and the rise of independent journalism, capital newspapers lost their national influence. The movement was accelerated by development of strong local dailies in all sections of the country and by expansion of the telegraph which could transmit congressional news quickly. The Associated Press furnished political news to dailies, while some larger newspapers sent their own reporters to serve as their Washington correspondents. Washington papers no longer were spokesmen for political parties or represented the administration as they had done before. Washington's population continued to climb steadily in the Gilded Age, increasing from about 100,000 at the end of the Civil War to 278,000 at the turn of the century.

Washington Star

The *National Republican,* typical of old political papers, remained but eventually sold out. Two strong papers were published in this era. One, the *Washington Star,* was launched in 1852 by Joseph B. Tate. Tate conceived of a paper without political ties, a newspaper devoted to building up the beautiful capital city of Washington. A series of partners, in turn, owned the *Evening Star*. Samuel H. Kauffmann, who had been chief clerk of the United States Treasury and a former Ohio publisher; George W. Adams, a correspondent of the *New York World*; and Crosby S. Noyes, a Maine newspaperman who had come to Washington to act as correspondent for several New England dailies, eventually owned the paper.

At the end of the Civil War the *Evening Star* had four pages. The front page consisted of two columns of small advertisements and four columns of news. Small 14-point heads topped the stories. Communication with the South was reestablished, with news beginning to come in from Richmond and other southern communities. The telegraph also brought in bits of news from all over the world to acquaint readers of the *Star* with happenings elsewhere. The editor, however, continued the old policy of reprinting important or interesting news clipped from other American newspapers.

Crime and humorous court news was published regularly in the *Evening Star*. Foreign scandals and murders in other parts of the United States were covered, the articles usually being reprints from other newspapers. This was the type of news which Pulitzer later expanded and topped with strong headlines. The *Evening Star,* however, was largely a sober, serious daily newspaper, giving heavy emphasis to Washington and congressional political news.

The *Evening Star* directed its attention particularly to local Washington affairs, covering the city news thoroughly. The paper also reported news of nearby Georgetown. In the 1870s the *Star* actively campaigned for betterment of the nation's capital. With the commissioners heading the District of Columbia government in 1874, a new goal emerged; the federal government should pay a fair share to support the capital. A Committee of One Hundred, with Crosby S. Noyes as vice president, appeared before Congress with this proposal in November, 1877. As a result, Congress passed the Organic Act, creating a permanent commission form of government on June 11, 1878, pledging the federal government to pay 50 per cent of the District's operating costs.

Because it was published in the national capital, the *Evening Star* covered congressional news most thoroughly. This was in the tradition of Washington newspapers. The *Star* devoted columns to debates in the House and Senate when they were in session. A special reporter seemed to be assigned to the White House and to the President, because almost daily a story appeared about political and social activities of the chief executive.

In the 1870s the *Evening Star* was so successful that it expanded to eight pages. The paper published twelve pages in 1893, and following the journalistic trend of the times, dropped advertisements from the front page. Reflecting the growing interest in sports, the *Star* covered baseball, boating and bicycling in the column, "Outdoor Pastimes," in the 1880s. Attention was given also to football and boxing in general news columns. In the 1890s "Season's Sports" was the title heading a column of such news; small headlines were also used on other sports items.

Influence of the popular New York yellow press was shown in the pictorial coverage which changed and improved in the *Evening Star.* The daily hired, in 1890, a staff artist, William H. Chandler, who produced drawings for the *Evening Star;* twelve years later photographers replaced the artists, especially for illustrating disasters in the news, as the halftone was being used more extensively.

The *Evening Star,* in 1899, was offering a seven-column, sixteen-page newspaper for two cents. During the Christmas season some *Evening Star* issues expanded to twenty-six pages filled with news and advertisements. The front page carried one-column, 24-point headlines, with two crosslines serving as decks.

Because it had more space, the *Evening Star* printed more complete reports of congressional activities than before, giving columns to reports of department heads when these reports were made public. Reporters for the *Star* covered courts and local civic associations. A column was devoted to finance and trade, and a similar amount of space was given to sports news at the turn of the century.

The Saturday edition of the *Evening Star* served in place of a Sunday issue. This edition carried a variety of features, with animals and pets being given considerable attention. Some articles were illustrated with large halftones. As New York was the economic and social center of the country, the *Star* ran a regular column of Gotham news in the Saturday edition. Helping amuse its readers were short stories, requiring between three and four columns of type.

Beginning to emerge as a distinctive part of the *Evening Star* was the editorial page. At the end of the Civil War two columns of editorials were printed daily on a page, with three columns of advertising matter. The *Evening Star* promoted Washington interests. The editorial page urged removal of the Pennsylvania tracks from the Mall. The railroad company, a heavy advertiser, objected to the paper's attack and thought the company should be given special preference. The *Evening Star* stood its ground; the tracks were removed eventually, contributing to the beauty of the capital.

Advertising increased steadily. Not only did the number of advertisements increase, but size of the department store and jewelry store advertisements expanded. Half-page advertisements told about wares of S. Kann, King's Palace, Bon Marche, Palais Royal and the Galt Jewelry Company. Woodward and Lathrop's department store used three-column advertisements regularly.

The *Evening Star*'s circulation reflected the paper's energetic news coverage and growth of population in the capital. In the 1870s the paper's readers totalled about 12,000, reaching 32,175 in 1890 and stabilizing at this figure for the next ten years. About 1,500 to 2,000 of these subscribers lived outside the District of Columbia.

Owners modernized the *Evening Star*'s equipment. They installed the paper's first web presses and stereotyping plant in 1890, making larger-sized papers and faster printing possible. In 1893 the publishers moved to more modern quarters at 1335 E Street, where the *Star* continued publication for the next half century.

The *Evening Star* remained in the hands of the children of the Kauffmann, Adams and Noyes families, a situation which gave the daily stability and conservatism. The sons became reporters, city editors, managing editors and eventually editors of the publication. Some of the children entered the business department.

Washington Post

The militant *Post* was a success from the first day, December 6, 1877, when it slipped off the press. The *Post* was a success not because of its politics, but because it was a *news*paper, lively, interesting and aggressive. Its four pages were worth three cents. What gave the *Post* its peculiar slant and its interest was Stilson Hutchins. Born in New Hampshire in 1838, he started as a reporter in Boston at the age of twenty. Then he moved to Iowa to edit and publish papers in Osage and Des Moines. Hutchins founded, then sold, the *St. Louis Times* before coming to Washington in search of a larger journalistic opportunity. Some newsmen went West; he went East.

It took courage to start a newspaper in Washington in 1877, when the city had a population between 130,000 to 150,000. Hutchins had a lot of courage, and he was not dismayed by talk that his *Post* would become another tombstone in a city noted as a "newspaper graveyard."

The square-jawed newcomer had other attributes of a good publisher: boldness, a gift for choosing able lieutenants and sound business judgment. He sought to make the *Post* lively and interesting. When the *Washington Evening Star* predicted his newspaper's death, Hutchins asserted the *Star* was a dried-up mummy.

He asserted in an early editorial on December 9, 1877, that the rule in Washington journalism seemed to be "exalt respectability in management with the most dignified stupidity in utterance." The publishers, he said, seemed to have "a fond affection for the past with a contempt for the present." Hutchins declared he thought the 130,000 District residents, who had more spending power than those in other cities of Washington's size, could support at least "a live newspaper." The trouble with the old newspapers, he said, was "they suppressed everything that looked like good humor" and "excluded the big news of the day." Hutchins introduced metropolitan journalism to Washington, breaking away from the small-town political newspaper of the pre-Civil War era.

The publisher-editor improved the front page format, printing at least three large one-column heads with several crosslines. In a style reminiscent of Charles A. Dana's *New York Sun*, Hutchins wrote lively heads to attract attention to the news beneath. A few of these catchy heads were "Disastrous Fire," "Necktie Parties" (referring to lynchings), "Murdered for his Money," "Roasted Alive." Alliteration was used frequently as in "Howe's Horrid Howl" and "Diplomatic Dawdling."

Police and court news was reported regularly in the *Washington Post.* The daily gave robberies, murders and rapes in Washington prominent and detailed coverage. Here was a headline on a seduction in Washington:

POOR SOPHIE MAJOR
The Mournful Story of Her
Seduction and Shame
The Victim's Personal Appearance and
Position in Life—Driven Frantic by
Her Disgrace—Who the Seducer is—
The Church Trustees Deny The
Body Christian Burial—The Inquest

Editorially the *Post* editor commented on a wide variety of international and national topics in the news, as he promised in his early editorials. He also wrote on lighter subjects. The *Post* editor told about the long kisses actors used, commenting unfavorably on them. Hutchins opposed the woman suffragette who wanted equal voting rights, for he claimed the female was in back of all evil deeds in the world.

Hutchins increased the number of his editorials, expanding from a few editorials in the early period to several columns daily. Small 10- or 12-point heads were placed on each editorial, which the *Evening Star* did not do. *Post* editorials appeared on the same page with other news for many years. The publishers made little effort to make the editorial page attractive. Of all pages, the editorial page changed least.

On its first birthday in 1878, the *Post* circulation reached 11,875, and the paper blew its own horn. The editor said that the *Post*'s success was unparalleled in Washington journalism. The editor noted that Republicans as well as Democrats were *Post* subscribers.

"The secret of its success can be told in a few words. It has been independent and a newspaper," Hutchins asserted.

Other Editions Issued

The *Post* printed eight pages daily. On Sunday the *Post* jumped to twelve pages, offering many features. These ranged from international to national articles. The *Post* also offered short stories for Sunday readers. Some of these, such as "Joe, A Story of Frontier Life," dealt with the wild, wild West. In the Sunday *Post* Hutchins made a strong appeal to women.

The *Post* caught on in Washington. The Hutchins paper absorbed some of its rivals, while others fell by the wayside. Within a year after starting, the *Post* publisher bought the old *National Whig*, which had been the *Post's* only morning rival.

In 1888 Hutchins also purchased the *Critic*, an afternoon rival, and immediately launched the *Evening Post.* This was Hutchins first and only venture into afternoon publishing, for the last issue of the *Evening Post* was dated January 5, 1889. The evening journalism market in the capital was left to the *Evening Star.*

Growing pains had been felt in the small plant of the *Washington Post* at 914 Pennsylvania Avenue, N.W. During the next two years the publisher moved twice, each time to larger structures. Hutchins installed some of the first of the new Linotype machines, in which he became especially interested.

On January 5, 1889, Hutchins announced that he had sold the *Washington Post.* By this time he was intensely interested in the Mergenthaler linecasting machine. He brought the machine to the attention of Whitelaw Reid of the *New York Tribune*, W. C. Whitney and D. Ogden Mills. Hutchins played a major role in financing the invention which revolutionized printing. Invention of the Linotype and spread of the machine to other daily publication offices will be described later.

New owners of the *Post* were Frank Hatton, who had been United States Postmaster General, and Beriah Wilkins, a former congressman from Ohio. As Hatton was a Republican and Wilkins a Democrat, the *Post* became politically impartial. Hatton took the editor's chair, while Wilkins became business manager of the *Washington Post.*

As the twentieth century opened, the *Post* was prosperous and known favorably in the capital and throughout the country. Within a few years an important change of ownership was to occur. Frank Hatton died first, and the surviving owner, Beriah Wilkins, died in June, 1905. Four months later the *Washington Post* was taken over by John R. McLean, who already owned the *Cincinnati Enquirer.* The *Washington Post* was to remain in the McLean family for twenty-eight years.

Chapter 21

Southern Newspaper Leaders

SOUTH RECOVERS SLOWLY

The South was left economically broken and scarred by the Civil War and by Reconstruction. Whole sections of the southern countryside had been destroyed and laid bare by northern armies. One fourth of the white southern men had been slain, and the Negro had been left with no disposition for regular work. The South's dominance in political and economic spheres, held before the War of Brothers, was never to be regained. Cotton was no longer king, for wheat and meat products from the West supplanted the southern staple as the country's leading export.

Slowly the South began to recover from the devastating effects of the Civil War. The old historic plantations were dismembered and cut into small farms. Under the sharecropping system, cotton plantings began to grow again. Railroad building started up once more, and a line was soon running from Richmond to Atlanta, with branches reaching into South Carolina. New industrial activities began. Cotton mills were opened in increasing numbers. Lumber and furniture manufacturing companies were begun or expanded. Cultural life of the South was revived. Schools were improved and universities strengthened.

New groups arose on the southern political scene to try to gain control from conservatives. The small, independent, white farmers composed the movement, and by 1890 this group had captured the Democratic Party of South Carolina and elected Benjamin R. Tillman governor. Later they joined the ranks of the farmers of the West, forming the Populist Party.

Newspapers in the South were crippled after the Civil War. Yet certain newspapers, in spite of unhappy social conditions and general community disorganization, managed to be successful. They mirrored major national journalistic trends while reflecting their regions and cities and the individualism of their publishers.

JOSEPHUS DANIELS BECOMES NORTH CAROLINA CRUSADER

Josephus Daniels, young college student at the University of North Carolina, Chapel Hill, found it difficult to concentrate on his law studies after he had made arrangements to become editor of *Raleigh* (North Carolina) *State Chronicle,* a weekly. He had long dreamed of becoming editor of a newspaper in the state capital.

Born in 1862 in Washington, North Carolina, Josephus early wanted to become a newspaperman. He and his brother Frank had issued several amateur papers on an old handpress. Josephus eventually became local editor of the *Wilson Advance* and was keen to print every item of news of personal interest.

After graduation from law school, Daniels became editor of the *Raleigh State Chronicle* in 1885. The *Chronicle* had been operated by Walter Hines Page who later became famous as editor of the *Atlantic Monthly* magazine. Conducting a fight similar to that which Pulitzer and Hearst waged against railroads in the 1880s in other states, Daniels sought to curb railroad power in North Carolina and to make them pay taxes as other corporations. The railroads had been exempted when they were first established, but Daniels thought they were prosperous enough to bear their tax share.

Until this time, the *State Chronicle* spoke but once each week. Being published at the time in Raleigh were one morning daily, the *News and Observer,* and two afternoon papers, the *Visitor* and the *Evening Call.* Daniels had long wanted a daily. It seemed wise to consolidate the *Chronicle* and the *Call,* so in 1890 the two papers were merged under the name of the *State Chronicle.* The Daniels paper became a daily morning newspaper. Afternoon newspapers were not as popular in this section as in other regions. Daniels figured he had his position as state printer, bringing in yearly income of $2,500 to $3,000, and he earned $1,200 from the *State Chronicle.* He formed a company and sold stock to a number of prominent merchants and professional men to operate the daily.

In his new daily Daniels committed himself to an increased warfare on trusts and monopolies, the freeing of farmers and laborers from unjust taxation, and hostility to special privilege in all powers and forms. This was reminiscent of Pulitzer's platform in the *St. Louis Post-Dispatch* and the *New York World.* Daniels advocated industrial growth and development of water power and natural resources, expansion of railroads and universal education of people of North Carolina.

As did crusading editors elsewhere, Daniels opposed those monopolies which originated in North Carolina, showing regional variations of the national newspaper pattern. The American Tobacco Company of Durham, known to the *State Chronicle* as "The Tobacco Trust," came into existence on March 4, 1890. After the *State Chronicle* had become a daily paper and price of the farmers' tobacco had gone down following organization of the trust, Daniels spoke strongly against it. Washington Duke, a strong Republican, and his son, James (Buck) Duke, as president of the American Tobacco Company, presaged the world monopoly of tobacco manufacturers.

In spite of his editorial success in public welfare campaigns, Daniels was having financial troubles. He was unable to make the *State Chronicle* pay as a daily. In 1892 he sold it to Thomas R. Jernigan, a politically ambitious weekly publisher in Raleigh. Within a year the *Chronicle* was leased to the *News and Observer,* its former competitor.

Daniels did not give up his call to journalism. He saw an important political campaign coming and established in August, 1892, another weekly, the *North Carolinian.* The paper opposed what it called the return to Negro supremacy, and it fought for control by Democrats, opposing the Populists.

During this time Daniels was offered editorships by the *Atlanta* (Georgia) *Constitution* and by the *Birmingham* (Alabama) *Age-Herald,* but he declined both on the pretense that he did not want to leave North Carolina. But "the tar on his heels" did not stick. He went to Washington to join the Cleveland administration. He worked in the Department of the Interior, sending part of his salary back to Raleigh to keep the *North Carolinian* alive.

Buys News and Observer

His heart was in journalism. In 1894 Daniels had the opportunity to fulfill an old ambition, the chance to buy into the *Raleigh News and Observer,* which was floundering on financial rocks. It was sold finally to a representative of Daniels for $6,800. Daniels organized a corporation with stock valued at $10,000. Liquid capital was needed to buy machinery. Daniels wrote to one hundred North Carolinians, offering stock at $100 a share. More than seventy persons subscribed to furnish the money Daniels needed. The new editor was able to pay them off as the *News and Observer* grew and prospered.

Daniels made the Raleigh paper one of the outstanding liberal newspapers in the South. He continued his fights against the tobacco trust and railroad monopolies. When the state government fell into the hands of a coalition of Republicans, Populists and Negroes, Daniels backed a white supremacy movement. He advocated, however, equal educational opportunities for Negroes in a period when they were neglected. Prolabor in policy, he urged better wages and shorter hours for workers, and editorialized for abolition of child labor.

Daniels made mechanical improvements in the newspaper plant. The *Raleigh News and Observer* was first in the state to use Linotypes. Two were installed. The paper was also first in the state to use a political cartoonist, following the pattern set by New York crusading journalism.

CHARLESTON (SOUTH CAROLINA) COURIER PUBLISHED BY NEW OWNERS

The issue of February 18, 1865, was the last one of the *Charleston* (South Carolina) *Courier,* which bore in its dateline the words "Confederate States of America." That day the Federal forces marched into Charleston. The paper was taken over by the military, and two northern newspaper correspondents with the Federal Army were authorized to issue a loyal Union newspaper. The paper was enlarged, but a fire destroyed its building. On November 20, 1865, A. S. Wellington & Co. was permitted by the United States military to resume charge of the paper.

Days of the *Charleston Courier* were numbered; its three owners died, and it was judged necessary to sell the old paper at auction. The *Courier* was purchased in 1873 by Riordan, Dawson and Company. A new era now opened in the history of South Carolina journalism. Bartholomew R. Riordan had experience previously as a political correspondent for the *New Orleans Delta,* while Francis Dawson, the guiding editorial genius behind the *News and Courier,* was an Englishman of adventurous disposition and literary tastes. He had fought on the southern side and then the northern side during the war, and after the conflict worked alongside Riordan on the *Richmond* (Virginia) *Examiner.* Both newsmen reported for the *Charleston Mercury* before it was closed down. Then they established the *Charleston News* and within a short time built it up until it had the largest circulation in the Southeast. When they heard the *Courier* was for sale, they hastened to purchase the daily and combine it with their *News.*

As editor, Dawson opposed the Straightout movement which attempted to block Reconstruction measures. Dawson advocated cooperation with the Republicans. The opposition paper, the *Journal of Commerce,* increased in circulation; the *News and Courier* dropped. Eventually the new Radical Reconstruction changes were so outrageous and the Straightout movement so strong that Dawson reversed the paper's policy on that issue and opposed the Reconstruction Acts.

Dawson had a new conception of journalism, different from that of A. S. Wellington of the old *Courier.* The *Courier* had preferred the safe stand. Dawson believed the function of an editor was "to write for or against something; for or against an idea; for or against a party." Dawson threw himself into every political struggle and became a part of it.

While Dawson was carrying on slashing editorial campaigns, the business side was built up by Riordan. By 1881 the *News and Courier*'s income was nearly three times as large as that of the *News* of 1868.

In the decade after 1875 most important activity of the *News and Courier* was the crusade for law enforcement. During the Reconstruction most men had formed the habit of carrying pistols. This habit, with general lawlessness of the time, encouraged the tendency to settle quarrels outside the law. The *News and Courier* campaigned against dueling, homicides and lynchings. Dawson was aided by the paper's correspondent, N. G. Gonzales at Columbia, the capital.

The legislature in 1881 passed a law practically outlawing duelling. By an ironical twist, Dawson was shot and killed by a local doctor in March, 1889. Gonzales, who with his brothers had established the *Columbia* (South Carolina) *State,* was killed by Lieutenant Governor James Tillman in 1903 because the editor opposed Tillman who had sought to be governor.

Soon after Dawson's death, James Calvin Hemphill, then serving as city editor, was made editor. Hemphill came from a Scotch-Irish family long prominent in the South. Hemphill remained at the helm of the *Courier* throughout most of the paper's fight against the Tillman Revolution, a farmer's movement which had just begun to get underway at the time of Dawson's death. This represented a struggle of Conservatives against Reformers. Hemphill also took up and carried on an effort begun in the late 1870s by Captain Dawson to bring the mills to the cotton. The *News and Courier* helped make South Carolina rank as the largest cotton manufacturing state in the South, exceeded in the nation only by Massachusetts. Of great importance, too, was a campaign begun by the paper about 1890 to revive tobacco planting in the state. The paper distributed tobacco seed to farmers, gave instructions for planting and cultivating and published numerous articles by specialists. By 1890 tobacco had become one of South Carolina's chief sources of agricultural income.

The *News and Courier* also pressed for various other projects of economic benefit to the city and state. It continually advocated the construction of a U. S. Navy Yard at Charleston, and this improvement was eventually built. The editor urged also the construction of railroads from the coal fields to Charleston and the building of interurban electric car lines in the 1890s. The daily spent much time, effort and ink in the promotion of the South Carolina Interstate and West Indian Exposition of 1901.

HENRY W. GRADY BUILDS ATLANTA CONSTITUTION

Because of Henry W. Grady, its youthful managing editor, the *Atlanta Constitution* became one of the South's outstanding newspapers. Dynamic, energetic Grady, the spark behind the news and editorial departments, gave impetus to the paper's activities. A masterful writer and an eloquent speaker, Grady sought to promote reconciliation between the North and South, to develop better agricultural methods and to bring industry to the South.

Grady was born in 1850 into a middle-class southern family. His father operated a general store in Athens, Georgia. Grady's father died during the Civil War. Assisted by the money his father left, Grady enrolled in 1866 at the University of Georgia, where he became especially interested in oratory and debate. Later, while a graduate student at the University of Virginia, his reputation as an orator began to grow. However, a disappointment over an oratorical contest turned him from a career of public speaking to journalism in which he had always been interested. He had been a college correspondent for the *Atlanta Constitution.*

After experience in Rome, Georgia, as editor of a weekly and daily, Grady, in 1872, came to Atlanta where he became a partner in the *Atlanta Herald.* Atlanta's population was fourteen thousand in 1864; but by 1872 it had jumped to thirty thousand.

While working on the *Herald* Grady began to develop his ideas on the new South. As early as 1874 he began to advocate reconciliation with the North and industrialization and crop diversification for the South.

Just as Hearst, Pulitzer and other editors exposed railroad and political corruption elsewhere, so Grady revealed similar corruption in Georgia. The *Herald* demonstrated that former Governor Brown had spent $70,000 to have the legislature lease the Western and Atlantic Railroad, a state-built and operated line, to a company Brown headed. In retaliation, the Governor had the bank, which he controlled, call in the mortgage on the *Herald*. This led to a sheriff's sale which closed the paper.

Joins Atlanta Constitution

Grady joined the staff of the *Atlanta Constitution* in October, 1876. Within four years Grady was able to purchase an interest in the publishing company. Cyrus W. Field, millionaire northern capitalist, offered to lend Grady $20,000, and Grady purchased a fourth interest from Evan P. Howell, one of the owners, who no doubt recognized Grady's unusual ability. Thus, in 1880, Grady became a part owner and managing editor of the *Atlanta Constitution*, which had a daily circulation of 2,400 and a weekly circulation of 5,200. From that time on people came to identify the *Constitution* with Grady, and Grady with the *Constitution*.

Grady introduced a number of improvements in the paper, selecting the best methods for a particular need and welding these into a successful pattern for the locality. He utilized new journalistic devices; he changed the format of the paper to give it a brighter, livelier, newsier appearance; and he later increased the size. He obtained correspondents from every county in Georgia.

Grady became best known for his initiation of the Atlanta International Cotton Exposition in 1881. Attracting 250,000 persons, the exhibition helped draw attention to the possibility of building mills in the South near the cotton fields. Grady also became known as spokesman for the regenerated South as a result of a highly successful speech he was asked to make in New York in 1886. He pleaded for greater understanding between North and South, and indicated that the South, although it did not forget its prewar glories, was ready to move forward industrially.

Grady became a great behind-the-scenes power in Georgia politics in the eighties. He nominated and successfully backed governors, senators and representatives. In addition to being an enterprising newsman, Grady was an effective columnist and editorial writer. He seemed to have the knack of writing about news in which people were interested and, therefore, developed a wide following. Grady was also an outstanding promotion man for his own newspaper. He was especially interested in building up the weekly edition of the *Atlanta Constitution*.

As a result of all these activities, circulation of the *Constitution* increased from 5,200 daily in 1881 to 36,614 by 1915. The weekly grew faster, jumping from 10,500 to more than 100,000. Advertising in the paper expanded with growth of Atlanta's business. A new building was constructed at Forsyth and Alabama Streets for $100,000, and the latest machinery was installed. Profits of the company came in steadily. At this time the paper was valued at $400,000.

Following a speaking tour in the North, Grady died at the age of forty-nine from pneumonia. Many appraisals were made of his contribution to the growth of Atlanta, to Georgia and to newspapers. All seemed to agree that he was indeed a spokesman of the South and a symbol of Atlanta's progressive spirit.

MARSE HENRY WATTERSON AND THE LOUISVILLE COURIER-JOURNAL

Henry Watterson became one of the most colorful editors of the post-Civil War period. Watterson was a history maker affecting his times. He lived through the prewar days, Reconstruction, the smug eighties and the stormy nineties. He was a border-state editor in a nonmetropolitan but growing city; and, although outstanding, he typified the problems of such southern newsmen. He became known for his style, which was vituperative, bombastic, but always readable. Editors quoted his editorials and listened to him. Watterson was a handsome man. He was not tall, but his slimness gave him the impression of height. His hair was almost as long as Buffalo Bill's and was worn in the same fashion—long. The final touch was the goatee, giving him the appearance of a Kentucky colonel.

Watterson's father, Harvey M. Watterson, politician-journalist of Scotch ancestory, was an editor but became a congressman. At various times he edited the *Nashville Union* and the *Washington* (D.C.) *Union*, both political organs. Henry was born in Washington on February 16, 1840, during one of his father's terms in the House. His father had come from Tennessee, and the family, who had owned slaves, were people of wealth and prominence. Henry received instruction from private tutors and spent four years at a Philadelphia school. The boy aimed to be a writer, dramatist and musician, beginning the study of the piano at four. His broad interests were valuable later in newspaper work.

Because of his knowledge of music, Watterson obtained his first job as music critic on the *New York Times* in 1858, a position he held while the regular music critic was on leave. New York proved alien to him at this time, and he returned to Washington, where he went to work on the *Daily States,* a political sheet. There he came under the influence of Jane Casneau, a remarkable woman who was the editorial writer of the paper.

After the Civil War in which he served as a Confederate soldier and editor of an army organ, he went to Nashville, Tennessee, where, with the assistance of two army friends, he took over a broken-down newspaper, the *Nashville Banner,* and built it up. Then the owner of the *Louisville Journal* in 1867 offered Watterson a place as part owner and editor. At the same time Walter Haldeman, proprietor of the *Louisville Courier,* made a proposition to him to be editor and part owner of that daily.

Watterson accepted the job on the *Louisville Journal.* George Prentice had made the paper nationally known, but Prentice was an old man now and willing to relinquish editorial tasks to a younger man. The *Journal* had begun to slip; a vigorous editor was needed to revive it. Watterson, only twenty-eight but with plenty of newspaper experience, proved to be the right man. Soon Watterson looked over the situation and began a campaign to get the *Journal* and the *Courier* to merge. As he saw the newspaper situation, here were two rival Democratic sheets struggling for supremacy. Neither could succeed.

When Watterson's circulation began to rise, Haldeman saw advantages in the proposal. He merged the *Journal* and the *Courier.* He soon bought the *Democrat,* third daily in town. The combined papers became the *Louisville Courier-Journal;* the foundations were laid for one of the strongest newspapers west of the Alleghenies. Watterson received one third of the stock for editing the paper.

The *Courier-Journal* was never dull. The energetic new editor invariably had something to say in a style unmistakably Watterson. He spoke up for reconcilation between North and South, and he was listened to! He urged the North to bury the bloody shirt and forgive, and he wanted the South to bury its tattered shirt and forget the late war. He sounded the same note as Henry Grady on the *Atlanta Constitution.* Grady called his idea "The New South"; Watterson claimed his was "The New Departure."

Watterson spoke up for the Negro, for their being given citizenship and the opportunity to attend schools. He was a Confederate veteran, son of slaveowners and a Democrat. He was no Yankee. So he was given an attentive ear.

The paper built a strong national reputation and following, in large part because of its vigorous editorial page. Watterson considered it the heart and mind of the newspaper. He hired ten editorial writers, and it was said he had as many editorialists as news reporters.

As the paper grew, Watterson turned over many of his managerial duties to others. This enabled him to travel and make contacts. Haldeman handled the business side expertly. In a few years he was able to announce plans for a new five-story building costing $400,000. He put in electric lights and was the third publisher in the nation to adopt the Linotype. Haldeman and Watterson each drew $6,000 a year as salary, but soon this increased to $8,000. Circulation of the combined daily and weekly the company issued reached fifty thousand by 1880, largest circulation of any paper west of the Alleghenies. Over Watterson's objections Haldeman established the *Louisville Times,* an afternoon edition. The editor did not want to share glory of his morning paper with an upstart!

Watterson supported the Democratic Party although he did not always agree with everything the candidates said. He became one of the country's outstanding "political editors." He took an active part in politics, wrote publicity for campaigns in the New York office and spoke on the platform. He had two important political principles for which he fought: reduce the high tariff and expand the nation.

Watterson could not generate any sympathy for the Greenback movement in the South nor for William Jennings Bryan. He told the Free Silver people the United States would never stand for their program. Watterson was basically conservative on economic issues. He did not understand fully the rising protest of the farmer or the stirrings of labor in these decades. In Europe when Bryan was nominated, Watterson wrote a series of editorials which revealed that Free Silver was only one aspect of his opposition to Bryanism. He felt the Democratic platform was an appeal to class feelings. The editor saw revolution in the immediate future unless Bryan was crushed. When Republican McKinley won, the *Courier-Journal* rejoiced. The paper's readers did not follow the editor in this campaign, and the *Courier-Journal* lost half its circulation in a year. The afternoon edition, the *Louisville Times,* helped pull the company through the financial crisis.

Watterson had to hasten home from Europe to repair the damage. It required years to rehabilitate the paper. By 1900 Watterson was back in the party, supporting Bryan. "Bryan is four years older," was his admission. "He must have learned something."

Chapter 22

Midwestern Newspaper Voices

STRONG NEW DAILIES COMPETE WITH OLD PRESS IN CHICAGO

The Great Fire in 1871 marked the end of one era in Chicago's growth and the beginnings of a more vigorous period. Before the Civil War Chicago had gained control of commerce in the Middle West and had become the greatest corn market in the country and the greatest wheat center. This economic leadership continued in the postwar era. She also outranked her rival cities in the livestock business and its ally, meat packing. The city had an exceptional position as the terminal point of lake, canal and railroad traffic. Chicago was indeed the core city of the Mississippi Valley, a halfway point between East and West.

Chicago's manufacturing industries benefited by the growth of both the population of the city and the region it served. Chicago made everything from bread to soda water, from iron nails to hitching posts. Iron manufacturing grew because of extension of railroads. One of the most important industries was brewing because of the availability of grain.

With the commercial and industrial expansion came rapid growth of retail business. A number of merchants built large department stores. Every variety of merchandise was sold at Field, Leiter & Co. (later Marshall Field & Co.); John V. Farwell & Co.; Carson, Pirie & Co.; and Mandel Brothers. These stores bought an increasing volume of newspaper advertising.

Cultural advancements, meanwhile, were made in Chicago. The old University of Chicago was badly crippled after the Great Fire; the institution even closed down in 1886 but opened again six years later. In addition, Northwestern University and Lake Forest University, which had three professional schools associated with it, expanded.

Under this surge of commercial-industrial enterprise and cultural advancement, the population of Chicago doubled, reaching more than a million by the end of the century.

As Chicago emerged into national prominence during and after the Civil War, so did its newspapers. With its expanding commerce and growing population, the city supported a number of dailies which began to rival the New York journals. Enterprising newsmen launched new dailies. Altogether the Chicago papers reflected the various shades of the economic and political spectrum in the city.

Chicago Tribune

Chief among the city's newspapers was the *Chicago Tribune*. Owners of this already-influential journal, established in the previous era, were Joseph Medill, John L. Scripps, Alfred H. Cowles and William Bross. Horace White, who directed the editorial page, also had bought into the newspaper.

It was Medill who stamped his strong personality and editorial convictions on the daily *Tribune*. He lost control of the paper for a short time but was able to borrow funds from Marshall Field to regain possession, placing his own relatives in key positions. On various issues which arose, the daily took a conservative Republican viewpoint, opposing government regulation of business and imposition of the income tax. After flirting with the Liberal Republican movement in 1872, the *Tribune* returned to the regular Republican ticket. On labor issues, the *Tribune* was considered strongly antilabor. The paper fought against the eight-hour day, considering it "a foolish idea." In the violent language of the era, the editorial writer called strikers "scum and filth of the city" and characterized organizers for the unions as "lazy demagogues," while it denounced certain city councilmen as "communists." These charges first were made when railroad strikes, which began in the East in 1877, spread to Chicago.

Medill strengthened his foreign staff and his coverage of European news. A London bureau was set up in 1877. The publisher sent correspondents to each army in the Russo-Turkish War and directed one reporter to accompany Admiral Peary to Greenland to expore it in 1891. In the Spanish-American War the *Tribune* obtained the world news scoop on Admiral Dewey's victory at Manila before any other newspaper.

The *Tribune* gave full coverage to the World's Fair in 1893. Medill had fought hard to bring the fair to Chicago because the fair would mean considerable prestige for the city and about $10,000,000 in revenue; also Medill was a stockholder and director of the fair.

The *Tribune* began to report sports news, with championship boxing bouts being featured in several columns on page one. Special columns and illustrations were used to appeal to women. Cartoons were introduced in the 1870s and 1880s. Keeping up-to-date, the *Tribune* made use of the new halftone process and had a picture page.

The publisher sought to make the *Tribune* a strong businessman's paper because of the growth of Chicago's industrialists and others in the upper economic group to which the daily appealed. Because of the growing interest in music, the *Tribune* also employed George P. Uptmas as critic, writing under the pseudonym of "Peregrine Pickle."

Paralleling the situation in other metropolitan centers, the *Tribune* increased the number of its pages. Its Sunday edition waxed particularly fat. Price of the *Tribune* decreased from five cents to three cents in 1886. Following a decrease two years later to two cents, it sold for one cent in 1895; the *Tribune* was seeking wider circulation, perhaps spurred on by the *Chicago Morning Record,* the Lawson paper which recently had been established.

The boldness and independence, the strong editorial page and the effective news coverage of the *Chicago Tribune* were reflected in the increase in circulation. From 18,000 readers in the pre-Civil War period, daily circulation grew to 80,000 in the 1880s. Meanwhile, the Sunday edition grew even faster: Its circulation in 1887 was 67,000; by 1900 it reached 172,000. Advertising followed and profits were steady so that the *Tribune* was able to build a four-story marble plant at the cost of $225,000.

At Medill's death in 1899 Robert Patterson, his son-in-law, became publisher. Medill's 1,000 shares of *Tribune* stock were valued at $2,500,-000, reflecting the growth and prosperity under his management and the value of a successful metropolitan paper at the turn of the century.

Chicago Times, Democratic Daily

The *Tribune* spoke for many Republicans; the *Chicago Daily Times* reflected the interests of the Democrats in Chicago. The *Chicago Daily Times* was ably edited by Wilber F. Storey, a bold newsman who attracted much attention during his ownership. During the Civil War, the *Times* was a copperhead daily.

In the post-Civil War period the publisher drove the *Times* to greater heights. The paper's sensationalism paralleled that of Pulitzer's *New York World* and Hearst's *New York Journal,* showing that publishers of metropolitan papers were faced in the postwar period with similar environments. Storey did not use wide banner headlines and pictures as his New York counterparts, for these developments came later. His reporters, however, presented racy, word detail in their news stories. Storey's newsmen covered every divorce case, every murder, every seduction and robbery in Chicago. *Daily Times* also reported news of adultery. Many stories drew libel suits.

Storey was all for purity, however, and crusaded in favor of public morality. He blasted at the English burlesque queens who came to entertain in Chicago. He called them British barmaids and bawds. Retaliating, the entertainers printed a circular accusing him of gross and outrageous public insult. The publisher and his wife were attacked on the street by the leader of the troupe and some of her girls.

As Dana and Pulitzer, Storey sought to attract readers with colorful and sensational headlines. They stressed the alliterative and the striking. One of the most notorious headlines appeared on November 27, 1875:

JERKED TO JESUS

FOUR SENEGAMBIAN BUTCHERS WERE WAFTED TO HEAVEN ON YESTERDAY FROM SCAFFOLDS

TWO OF THEM, IN LOUISIANA, DIED WITH THE SWEET CONFIDENCE OF PIOUS PEOPLE

WHILE YET TWO OTHERS, IN MISSISSIPPI EXPIRED EXHORTING THE PUBLIC TO BEWARE OF SISTERS-IN-LAW

Other headlines, such as "Death's Darts" and "Fit for Flames," had similar catchy appeals.

Storey introduced the region's first Sunday newspapers devoted to entertainment journalism. He pioneered the Sunday feature story in Chicago, offering articles on scientific mysteries and social events. Franc B. Wilkie, Civil War correspondent of the *New York Times,* was lured to the *Chicago Times* and became Storey's first assistant. Wilkie later took charge of the *Times'* London bureau in 1881, hiring agents in principal cities. The Chicago paper thus was one of the first dailies west of the Alleghenies with its own foreign correspondent.

Storey appeared to his staff to be a vindictive man. He had a supreme contempt for mankind; he had no consideration for the feelings of others, his reporters thought. The publisher was favorable to labor, championing the right to strike and defending the eight-hour day, a point of view opposite that of the *Tribune.*

In his shop, however, Storey was opposed to a union. When he learned that the printers planned a strike in April, 1864, he declared in a style typical of the day, "I would rather go out of business than yield." He bought a building, where he installed complete composing room equipment. Then Storey hired forty young women to set type, which helped break the strike. The Chicago Typographical Union passed resolutions against him, but organized labor never got a foothold in the *Times* while Storey lived. The publisher died in 1884.

The *Chicago Times* then fell into the hands of James J. West. Finley Peter Dunne, a member of the editorial and reportorial staffs, made a considerable contribution toward rebuilding the *Times.*

In addition to political reporting, Dunne wrote political editorials. The *Chicago Daily Times* was a partisan Democratic organ. Dunne jabbed the *Tribune* as a "leap-year Republican." He charged that the daily was opposed to protection and lukewarm toward the Republican Party and the administration in all except election years. Dunne became the youngest city editor in Chicago.

Neither Dunne's abilities, nor West's management could save the *Times.* West had only a minority interest. The majority stock was owned by nonresidents of Chicago. Becoming suspicious of West's efforts to gain control, the owners ousted him, and with him went Dunne.

The *Times* deteriorated. Its force was gone. Carter Harrison bought it in 1891 when its circulation fell below eighteen thousand. Because it was the only Chicago paper representing effectively the Democratic Party, the *Daily Times* circulation grew, reaching about thirty-five thousand readers. By 1895 its impetus again had dissolved; the *Times* was consolidated with the *Herald,* the combined paper retaining only the *Herald* in its title.

Chicago Inter-Ocean

Another Republican newspaper, the *Inter-Ocean,* was established, frankly, as a partisan organ by J. Young Scammon in 1872. Its motto was "Republican in everything, Independent in nothing." It was reorganized as a stock company several times. William Penn Nixon, who became business manager, impressed his personality on the *Inter-Ocean.* He did not question the Republican Party's policies as the *Tribune* did on occasion. Nixon was protectionist on the tariff. The *Inter-Ocean* gained friends by supporting causes and organizations devoted to civic, religious and philanthropic activities. When the paper refused to accept advertising from gambling operators, it won approval of religious and other leaders.

The *Inter-Ocean* came, in 1891, into the hands of Herman H. Kohlsaat, a prominent and wealthy baker, restaurateur and real estate promoter. He introduced a number of ideas into the *Inter-Ocean,* using colored illustrations in the Sunday edition. Daily circulation reached sixty thousand in 1893, with Sunday sales of seventy-five thousand, many of which were made out-of-town. Kohlsaat had arguments with Nixon, and in 1894 Nixon regained control of the paper.

Chicago Daily News

Catching the trend toward the cheap, popular afternoon newspaper, the *Chicago Daily News* was founded in 1876 as the first one-cent paper in the Midwest by Melville E. Stone and two friends. Stone abandoned high school midway to become a cub reporter for the *Tribune.* He later joined the *Chicago Times* but switched to the *Inter-Ocean,* becoming its managing editor. A demotion to city editor and general dissatisfaction led Stone to resign and go to Washington where he became correspondent for several New York and St. Louis papers.

He returned to Chicago with an idea for establishing an afternoon paper. He joined with Percy Meggy, an Englishman who had $5,000, and William Dougherty, who had some newspaper experience. They launched the *Daily News* in a town which had six dailies already. These papers sold for five cents; Stone and his partners decided to sell for a penny. Issued as a four page newspaper, the *Daily News* caught on. It attracted nine thousand readers on the first day.

The *Chicago Daily News* soon had tough financial sledding. Stone's partners quit. Stone, however, was able to interest Victor Lawson, a former high school classmate, in his newspaper venture. Lawson was the son of the publisher of the *Scandinaven* and owner of the printing plant which produced the *Daily News.* Lawson assumed the debts of the company and furnished the capital. From then on Stone served as editor and Lawson as business manager. It was a happy and successful partnership.

Stone sought to give the *Daily News* character and reputation. In the Pulitzer pattern, Stone embarked on a series of exposés of public officials and engaged in detective journalism. He was successful in both. The *Daily News* brought to public attention the need for strict regulation of savings banks in which thousands of persons had invested millions of dollars. As a result, a law was passed by the Illinois legislature providing for rigorous inspection of banks.

Stone developed a strong editorial page. Following a policy established by John Walter of the *London Times*, he hired experts to write editorials on their specialties, drawing heavily on university faculties. On his editorial page Stone advocated civil service reform, and while usually Republican, he supported Cleveland but opposed Bryan. In the editorial columns, he derided the *Tribune*, calling it "The Daily Nuisance." Stone waged a mock campaign to nominate Medill for president of the United States, Alaska and Cuba, the inference being that the publisher would not be satisfied to run the United States alone. The *Daily News* gibed at Medill's eccentric beliefs. The *Tribune* publisher held the sunspots responsible for various misfortunes. When Chicagoans were stricken with influenza, the *Tribune* blamed it on the sun.

Stone engaged in some journalistic detective work. When D. D. Spencer, president of a Chicago bank, stole $2,000,000 and then left town, Stone trailed the banker to Germany. The newsman obtained Spencer's confession of the embezzlement and returned the banker to Chicago.

In the railroad strike of 1877 the *Chicago Daily News* condemned the railroads for their wage policy, and at the same time urged workers to refrain from violence. The daily gave full reports of the strike, and when businessmen sought to get Stone to suspend the paper, the owner declined. Editions could not be printed fast enough. Circulation before the conflict reached twenty-seven thousand; during the height of the story, the *News* distribution vaulted to sixty-eight thousand. The strike was settled by compromise, but the paper had given proof of its sympathy to wage earners. The *Daily News* had begun to establish itself in the public favor. The paper promoted humanitarian enterprises such as the Fresh Air Fund, a Sanitarium for Sick Babies, and sponsored clubrooms for newsboys.

Consolidation affected Chicago journalism. In 1877 the *News* bought out its competitor, the *Post and Mail*, for $15,000, acquiring the valuable Western Associated Press franchise.

The *Daily News* both drew to its staff and developed a strong battery of excellent writers. George Harvey worked for the paper, later going to New York where he joined Pulitzer's *World*. The *Daily News* also had George Ade and Bill Nye, humorists, and John T. McCutcheon, caricaturist. Eugene Field was also a member of the staff and won a wide audience with his column, "Sharps and Flats."

Finley Peter Dunne, mentioned in the section on the *Chicago Daily Times*, received eight dollars a week when he joined the *Daily News* staff. He started on general reporting but hated the routine. He liked to write special features. The editor assigned him not only features but also editorials. Managing editor White believed in short, pithy paragraphs for the editorial page. Not liking the physical exertion needed in reporting, Dunne soon had a desk of his own where he sat and wrote.

As Chicago was becoming baseball mad, the *News* decided in 1888 to print better baseball news. Before this the daily had been satisfied with publishing the results of yesterday's game without comment. Managing editor White selected Dunne to change this style. Cause of the great burst of interest in baseball news was the Chicago White Stockings, pride of the city. The team had a great pitcher in John Clarkson and some other colorful personalities such as Billy (William) R. Sunday, later a famous revivalist.

Dunne changed the formal, routine reporting style, so colorless and dull. He and Charles Seymour of the *Herald,* established a different type of sports story. Less concerned with formal recital of turns at bat, they wrote news stories that gave fans the kind of news they wanted. Dunne told about the high point of interest in the game, the crucial moment of the spectacular play, especially if the "Chicagos" made it. Eventually other papers followed the lead of the *News* and the *Herald* in sports news reporting. Dunne coined some baseball slang too. He used "southpaw" for a left-handed pitcher. Dunne traveled with the team to Detroit, New York, Boston and Washington in the old National League. The reporter, however, was more strongly interested in politics. He wrote political stories while on baseball trips. Dunne remained on the paper until he was lured to the *Daily Times.*

Chicago was as corrupt if not more so than New York, and the *Daily News* fought for better municipal government. It was a consistent opponent of Charles T. Yerkes, who controlled street railways and had obtained franchises by corrupting officials. Yerkes bought the *Chicago Inter-Ocean* in 1897 and his editorial writers attacked Lawson, who did not make any rejoinder. The *News* continued to oppose Yerkes, succeeding in preventing him from getting a fifty-year franchise on streets. Finally Yerkes sold out and left for London.

By 1885 the *Daily News* reached one hundred thousand circulation. The paper continued to expand its size, and a new building was built in 1890. Lawson's formula was be candid, comprehensive, concise, clear, cheap.

The *News* also laid the foundation for extensive foreign news service, which was to distinguish the Chicago paper later. Correspondents were first hired in London, Paris, Peking and Tokyo. After the Spanish-American War, Lawson realized that the United States had entered a new international era and that it must shoulder responsibilities and duties of a world power. He established his own correspondents in principal cities of the world and built up special news-gathering facilities to avoid domination of news by foreign governments. He had correspondents in Ireland, Paris, London; a reporter was also assigned to Washington, D. C.

In 1881 the morning *Daily News* was issued. It sold for one cent a copy and was intended to be livelier and more sparkling than competitive morning newspapers. Lawson forced other papers to reduce their price.

In 1888 Stone retired from the *Chicago Daily News,* selling to Lawson, who paid Stone $350,000 for his share, with the stipulation that Stone keep out of Chicago journalism for ten years. Stone later became head of the Associated Press.

In 1892 Lawson changed the name of the morning paper to the *Chicago Record.* Circulation of the afternoon and morning papers reached 243,000 by 1892. Charles H. Dennis became managing editor that same year.

Herald, Evening Post

The paper which absorbed the *Daily Times,* discussed before, was the *Chicago Herald.* The Democratic morning daily was owned by John R. Walsh and published by James W. Scott. Scott gathered a young and able staff, including Finley Peter Dunne. Dunne did all kinds of reporting for the *Herald* but was soon transferred to the afternoon edition, the *Evening Post,* where he was placed in charge of the editorial page. The *Post* was intellectual and literary in tone, with Norman Hapgood, lawyer-turned-journalist, and Cornelius McAuliff, as managing editor, on the staff.

McAuliff encouraged Dunne to write satirical editorials. Dunne made his daily editorial page widely read. Born of Irish parents and reared in an Irish neighborhood, he experimented with Irish dialect as a change from the regular style. The *Post* was generally independent in politics; therefore, Dunne was given considerable freedom. He opposed Charles T. Yerkes, municipal railway magnate. Dunne editorials were short and pithy, with two or three paragraphs becoming the standard length. More than half the editorials were witty and satirical. Lively and intelligent, the editorials, like those in Dana's *New York Sun,* could be read with pleasure. Some persons complained that the *Evening Post*'s editorials were too flippant and shouldn't be taken seriously.

When the *Post* planned a Sunday edition, the managing editor had sixteen pages instead of eight to fill, so McAuliff asked Dunne to do a piece for the Sunday paper at extra pay. Dunne wrote a dialect article, "Frank's visit to Grover." This was the beginning of the Mr. Dooley's essays. Dunne's characters were adapted from Chicago's Irish life.

When the Sunday *Post* was given up, Dooley articles were carried in the Saturday edition. Dunne changed the name of the leading character to "Mr. Dooley," altering also the location of the saloon. "Mr. Dooley" was put into a book and made Dunne nationally famous.

DETROIT HAS VIGOROUS PAPERS

A lake port, railroad center and farmer's market, Detroit made rapid strides in this era. The city tapped the vast lake region, with its thousands of miles of agricultural land and forest. Detroit also turned to manufacturing with the development of the Industrial Revolution. Detroit shifted particularly to metal manufacturing, including copper smelting. The city, however, eventually lost its iron and copper furnaces to communities near the mineheads. Energetic and enterprising, Detroiters then began to manufacture steam engines, carriages and wagons, providing the basis for the automobile industry. Charles King astonished residents in 1894 with his gasoline car, the first to appear in Detroit, while Henry Ford began to experiment in his wife's kitchen with a gasoline motor.

More than half the population of Detroit was foreign born, with Irish, English, Scotch and Welsh predominating. These immigrants, attracted by commercial and industrial opportunities in Detroit, went to work in the city's many factories and shops. Factory workers expressed their discontent with conditions in various ways; great strikes erupted on railroads.

Educationally, Detroit had shifted before the Civil War from private schools to low fee public schools, then eliminated tuition charges altogether. Wayne University was established in 1868; the University of Michigan was built at Ann Arbor. The Detroit Medical School was founded in 1870 and Detroit Teachers' College a decade later. During this era the Public Library was opened and the Detroit Opera House staged its first performance. A Park Commission was created, soon purchasing Belle Island, a lovely island park for the pleasure of residents. The horse-drawn street car system was extended in this period to all parts of the city; well-to-do citizens built large homes on the outskirts.

While businessmen controlled the city government, new political winds began to stir. The system of "mansion control" broke down. Detroit's rock-ribbed Republicans made changes and yielded to new men and ideas. Hazen S. Pingree, shoe manufacturer, became mayor and began to reform city government. Population of Detroit rose from 45,000 at the beginning of the Civil War to 79,000 by 1870. Commercial and industrial prosperity supported 285,000 by the end of the century.

Beginning of the Scripps Chain in Detroit

It was no accident that Joseph Pulitzer and Edward W. Scripps developed similar types of newspapers. Both were faced with similar urban conditions and political and industrial developments which called for their type of journalism. They saw political corruption, the workers' fight for better conditions and wages and the right to join a union. Both publishers were able to start on a financial shoestring in the post-Civil War period, but Pulitzer confined himself to St. Louis and New York, while Scripps forged a press chain in the smaller, growing towns of the Midwest and Far West.

Detroit Evening News

Detroit News traditions went back to the famous Scripps clan. The founder of the *Evening News* began his life as a farmer. He was one of the rugged pioneers who followed the westward trail. James Edmund Scripps was only nine when his father emigrated here from England, taking up a farm near Rushville, Illinois. After working on the *Chicago Tribune,* and afterward serving as business manager of the *Detroit Advertiser* and the *Tribune,* Scripps disposed of his stock and embarked on his long dreamed-of adventure.

Scripps founded the *Detroit Evening News* on August 23, 1873, setting forth a program in which he declared, "The wide diffusion of wholesome literature is a public good" and said it might be promoted by selling newspapers at two cents. He advocated condensed news because he said older papers were too big for people to read. Pointing out that the public wanted to make up its own mind on issues, he declared his paper would give facts and arguments on both sides.

In pursuing that formula the *Evening News* came to life, a small, compact newspaper of four pages, whose over-all dimensions were 19 inches long by less than 14 inches wide. Six columns were on a page. On the front page, half news and half advertising were printed. Scripps continued his concern with the common man to the end of his days.

James Scripps' younger half-brother, Edward W. Scripps, was born on a farm in Rushville, Illinois in 1854. By the time Edward was a teenager, James had become part owner of the *Detroit Tribune;* James often came to the Rushville farm where he discussed newspapers and current affairs. Farm chores did not seem glamorous nor important to Edward after that.

Edward wanted to be a newspaperman and to write. His first opportunity opened in Detroit but it was not in a newspaper office. With eighty dollars as his sole capital, he journeyed from the farm to the town to enter the pharmacy business. When this job did not materialize, Scripps followed his original bent and took a job as a floor-sweeper in his brother's newspaper, the *Detroit Tribune.* Ambitious, desirous of making money, he quit for a job as a window-shade salesman. On his brother's new newspaper, the *Detroit Evening News,* Edward became a collector, then a carrier. He devised a route system, hiring boys to work for him and deliver the papers all over Detroit. This was profitable for the boys and for Edward, who made forty dollars a week, more than other employees on the *Detroit News.*

But the desire to be a writer was strong. Edward withdrew his attention from the circulation department although his income continued, and he became an unpaid reporter. Soon he worked up to the city editor's job, and he was on his journalistic way. The *Detroit News* was a new publication and soon needed more capital. Persuasive Edward came to the rescue. He went back to the Rushville farm where he induced George, another half-brother, to invest $30,000 in the *Detroit News.* The first Scripps partnership was formed, James having majority interest, while George, Edward, Ellen, a half-sister, and John Scripps Sweeney, a cousin, owned minority interests.

Ellen Scripps, who was sixteen years older than her half-brother, played an important role in Edward's life. She gave him intellectual stimulus, backbone and financial help when he needed it most.

Detroit Free Press

Competitive with the Scripps paper was the *Detroit Free Press.* The paper had been established to fill a need in 1831 for a publication, as the *Detroit Gazette* had been burned out the previous year. In the years that followed there were several changes in management of the *Free Press.* Wilbur F. Storey, a fiery editor, purchased it in 1852. Storey introduced many journalistic innovations.

During this period the *Free Press* was a staunch organ of the Democratic Party. As events leading to the Civil War developed, Storey became unpopular because of his criticism of Union policy. Before the war was over he sold out and moved to Chicago where he established the *Chicago Times,* as indicated.

Storey's successor on the *Free Press* was William E. Quinby, under whose direction the paper prospered and attained great distinction in the region. Quinby hired top-flight writers: Charles B. Lewis (Mark Quad), Robert Barr (Luke Sharp), Henry Carey and others. These men won such attention that the *Free Press* published a special edition in London. It was while Quinby owned the paper that it ceased to speak for the Democratic Party. This break came when Quinby and other Michigan Democrats found they could not support William Jennings Bryan's Free Silver campaign in 1896.

CLEVELAND SCENE STRENGTHENED WITH NEW SCRIPPS PAPER

When Edward Scripps returned to Detroit from Europe in 1878, he looked for a likely spot for a new newspaper. He decided to locate in Cleveland, Ohio, which was not too far from Detroit. With $10,000 he established the *Cleveland Penny Press* in 1878. Scripps' idea for the *Penny Press* was similar to Dana's when he bought the *New York Sun.* He wanted to issue an inexpensive publication which would give in condensed form news of Cleveland, of Ohio, of other states and of the world, so that a person would read the *Press* and know what was happening everywhere.

The new Cleveland paper and all Scripps papers which were established later were aimed at the industrial and other working classes in the growing towns of the nation. Scripps saw men working twelve to fourteen hours a day, often a seven-day week. He observed that wages were low and that employees were laid off frequently. Child labor was widespread, and women worked under bad conditions at low wages. Unions grew slowly and in the face of much opposition. Scripps favored the workingmen and became their editorial spokesman. He advocated their unionizing, and he fought for a shorter workday, higher wages and better working conditions for them. He believed in raising their standards of living.

As the *New York World*, the *Cleveland Press* advocated other projects and measures of value to its particular segment of the public. The *Press* fought vigorously for a a bridge free from tolls, just as the *New York World* battled for a free Brooklyn Bridge.

Where other newspapers suppressed news when it involved prominent people, Scripps ordered his editors to print the news. When a well-known citizen committed suicide other Cleveland papers reported it as merely a death from natural causes, while the *Press* printed the death as a suicide. Scripps editors even reported the news that their publisher,

E. W. Scripps, was arrested and paid a fine for failing to provide his horse with shoes.

The *Cleveland Press,* after a slow start and many difficulties, finally caught hold. Edward now had a partnership in two papers, the *Detroit News* and the *Cleveland Press,* but once he got them running he was anxious to extend his chain. Now he learned that the *St. Louis* (Missouri) *Chronicle* could be purchased cheaply, and he persuaded his brothers to help him buy it. Here the Scripps brothers hit an unusual newspaper situation. They crossed paths with Pulitzer, who had just merged the *Post* with the *Dispatch,* and catered to the same section of the public with a similar platform to that of Scripps. The *Chronicle,* although its circulation increased, was eventually sold.

Cleveland Plain Dealer

Another Cleveland paper prominent at this time was the *Plain Dealer.* Founded by Joseph William Gray in 1842 as a weekly, it became a daily three years later. It was the only Democratic daily outside of Cincinnati. Greeley was one of its bitterest opponents, but when the New Yorker ran for the presidency in 1872, the *Plain Dealer* swallowed its bitterness and gave full support to him.

Charles Farrar Browne, a journeyman printer from Maine, joined the *Plain Dealer* staff, and under the pseudonym of Artemus Ward became one of the outstanding American humorists of this period, antedating Mark Twain.

After founder Gray died in 1862 the paper suffered many vicissitudes of fortune. It bought out the physical assets and advertising contracts of the old *Herald* and took over most of its morning and evening editions.

The year 1885 marked a new epoch in the story of the *Plain Dealer.* New capital, new energy and a new viewpoint were infused in the daily under the leadership of Liberty E. Holden. Holden had been a superintendent of public schools in Tiffin, Ohio. He came to Cleveland to complete his law studies and acquired a fortune in real estate and mining. The *Plain Dealer* was sold to Holden and a group of associates in December, 1884.

Name of the *Evening Plain Dealer* was changed to the *Evening Post* in 1893 specifically to give it a distinctiveness from the morning *Plain Dealer.* Always interested in outdoor recreation, Holden played an important part in getting for the city various parks. He was influential also in bringing into existence the Cleveland Museum of Art.

Recognizing that he needed expert help on the *Plain Dealer* to fight the competing paper, the *Leader,* Holden entered a contract with Charles

E. Kennedy and Elbert Hall Baker in 1898 to give them half control. It was a profit-sharing arrangement. Baker, who had been a drug clerk, a hardware store employee and later a bookkeeper in the *Cleveland Herald* office, had switched to advertising. He made a great success of the *Herald.* The opposition paper, the *Leader,* lured him away, and then Holden brought him to the *Plain Dealer.* Baker helped vitalize the paper to meet changing needs of the public and the competition being given by the *Press.*

CINCINNATI HAS DISTINGUISHED JOURNALS

Because of its strategic position on the Ohio River, Cincinnati had been a journalistic center since long before the Civil War. One of the best known of this city's papers was the *Cincinnati Enquirer.* It was established in April, 1841, as an afternoon newspaper by John and Charles H. Brough but became a morning paper two years later. Despite criticism from its contemporaries, the traditional Democratic *Enquirer* printed its first Sunday edition five years later. It was an instantaneous success.

A succession of owners published the *Enquirer,* but a new regime began in 1858 when James J. Faran and Washington McLean bought the daily. Faran had been mayor of Cincinnati and McLean was interested in steamboat building, among other enterprises. The two owners gathered a staff of newspaper workers of unusual ability. They also had an extensive printing business. When fire destroyed the entire printing plant in 1866, the *Enquirer* missed one edition only. A new site was acquired and a modern plant built.

Washington McLean acquired Faran's interest and succeeded in making the *Enquirer* the most prosperous and influential newspaper in that region. McLean decided to move to Washington and turned over part of the ownership in 1873 to his son, John R. McLean, who obtained full ownership eight years later.

Under his enterprising management, the *Enquirer* became undisputed leader in its territory. It was one of the most widely distributed and nationally influential organs of the day. Under McLean's direction, however, the *Enquirer* ceased to be a political organ and became primarily a newspaper. McLean advocated widespread news coverage and full use of all facilities of communication available for getting news quickly.

Taft Purchases Times-Star

Another vigorous paper in Cincinnati was the *Times-Star.* In 1879 Charles Phelps Taft purchased controlling interest in the *Times,* and in the following year consolidated it with the *Star,* established a few years before. Taft had been educated at Yale and Heidelberg for law. Admitted to the bar in 1866, Taft practiced law until he entered the newspaper business. The *Times-Star,* under Taft's vigorous leadership, became a strong, profitable enterprise.

Scripps Starts Cincinnati Post

Edward W. Scripps also moved into Cincinnati, for opportunity beckoned him. His brother James had expanded to Cincinnati where he invested $10,000 in the *Penny Post.* Edward Scripps bought out the paper's founders and thus got a 55 per cent interest in the enterprise. Scripps then changed the name of the newspaper to *Cincinnati Post* and transformed it into a militant newspaper.

Scripps often expressed his philosophy of militant journalism. He told his editors and business managers that no great combination of any sort of business interest can stand up against a fearless, fighting newspaper. He said that advertisers know this better than newspaper owners.

In order to buy the *Post,* Edward had to borrow $30,000 from his half-brother, James. James now thought it was time to call the loan, which would give him control of the Cincinnati paper. Edward was too shrewd and quick, however, and rushed to Ellen for financial aid. James owed her an equal amount, $30,000, which she now loaned or gave to Edward. James was stymied, and Edward had a majority ownership in the *Cincinnati Post.* Across the river from Cincinnati was Covington, Kentucky, and a paper was needed there, so Edward Scripps established the *Covington Post* in 1885, thus adding a fourth link, indicating the expanding journalistic opportunities in the United States.

During this time Edward was thrown more and more in contact with Milton McRae, a level-headed business manager of the *Cincinnati Post,* who also undertook the job of launching the Covington paper. Recognizing McRae's business acumen and his steadiness, Scripps formed with him a partnership, the Scripps-McRae League. By this arrangement Scripps was to get two thirds of the profits and be in charge of editorial and news policies, while McRae received one third of the profits and directed the business end. Scripps moved to California in 1890 for his health. He entered a new phase of his operations, long distance management. In California he started a West Coast chain.

NELSON OF KANSAS CITY STAR EXPRESSES MIDWEST

The *Kansas City Star* became the leading newspaper of the Missouri Valley and one of the most influential in the nation. The *Star* grew out of the development of the Missouri Valley and Kansas City. The *Star* helped transform Kansas City from a frontier mudhole to a thriving, attractive metropolis. The daily adopted crusading techniques as Pulitzer and Hearst had done.

Kansas City was strategically located on the Big Bend of the Missouri River. The town was the starting place for two great arteries of far western travel, the Santa Fe Trail and the Oregon Trail. Immigrants and commerce shifted in Kansas City from river transport to wagons. From Kansas City went great quantities of military supplies for conquest of New Mexico and California. Kansas City also became an important landing place and outfitting point for gold seekers and pioneers moving west. The city won out as the spot where a railroad bridge might be built across the Missouri. When the span was completed in 1869 four railroads on the east side of the river and three on the west were connected. During the postwar period thousands of immigrants came to Kansas City by rail and water. The town became a supply depot for settlers expecting to farm in Kansas and for miners burrowing the mountains of Colorado. Enterprising businessmen built stockyards and packing houses. The center of a rich agricultural area, Kansas City grew from 32,000 in 1870 to 163,000 by 1900.

William Rockhill Nelson, Publisher

Big-bodied, big-minded publisher of the *Kansas City Star*, William Rockhill Nelson, had made a fortune and lost it in the construction business before he became a newsman. His career had increased his sensitivity to homes, buildings and all types of construction work: roads, viaducts, bridges. Raw, frontier Kansas City benefited because Nelson, through the *Star*, carried on many successful campaigns to improve the community's facilities and its appearance.

Nelson was born in 1841 in Fort Wayne, Indiana, and early demonstrated his rebelliousness. His father sent him to Notre Dame, for the elder Nelson believed that instructors there would help "straighten out" his son. Instead, William was expelled. After the Civil War he entered the construction business. He built roads, bridges and buildings and made a fortune of $200,000. This money was lost, however, when he endorsed notes for his partner in Georgia, and the business there failed to materialize. Nelson, then almost broke, purchased an interest in the *Fort Wayne Sentinel*, which his father had once owned. Nelson operated the paper in conjunction with a partner, Samuel E. Morss. After a year Nelson came to the conclusion that Kansas City, a gateway to the West, held greater commercial promise.

On September 18, 1880, Nelson and Morss bought out the *Kansas City Star,* a four page sheet printed on an old flatbed press. The town in which the *Star* was issued called for a man of Nelson's talents and background. Built on high hills, the city had deep canyons. After the rains, water ran down the sides of hills like swollen rivers. Deep mud resulted. Sidewalks were wooden planks. Houses were jerrybuilt, thrown up to put a roof over the head rather than to provide comfort and beauty. Kansas City was also ridden with grafting political bosses. Elections were fraudulent, but the public did not care. The city was ripe for utility corporations seeking to secure long-term franchises from weak city councils.

Nelson, from the *Star's* first issue, believed strongly that anything which would improve Kansas City and the region it served should be championed by the *Star.* He was convinced, for example, that good transportation was the key to all progress. Noting the condition of the muddy streets in Kansas City, he advocated not only improved streets, but wide, beautiful boulevards connecting various parts of the city. Along with this street improvement, he advocated strong stone bridges to replace the tin structures, and he urged the building of viaducts. Joined to the street issue was the need for attractive parks. Nelson had to overcome intrenched opposition before Kansas City planned for and built lovely parks.

Nelson did not spare franchise grabbers. He found that an old horsecar company had a long-term franchise but provided only poor service. No regulation was imposed by the municipality on utilities at the time. Nelson backed the movement for establishment of regulatory bodies and later pointed out that the city would eventually own and operate its own utility services.

Nelson sought to help other communities and farmers in the rural western regions. He aided Kansas City, Kansas in securing a waterworks and in building a viaduct. He advocated through the *Star's* columns better protection for Missouri from floods. Out of the Midwest came governmental methods which aimed at keeping control of officials in the hands of the voters. Nelson thus advocated the initiative, referendum and recall. He also favored workmen's compensation laws.

In his first issue Nelson declared that he was going to be independent in politics. In 1884 and 1892 he supported Cleveland for the presidency, but was a lukewarm supporter of McKinley in 1896. Later he advocated formation of a progressive party and backed Theodore Roosevelt. Often the *Star* would support a Republican candidate for governor and a Democratic candidate for mayor, then would reverse itself in the following election.

Nelson gave his readers not only a strong editorial program but also a newspaper bargain. He purchased the *Kansas City Times,* a morning paper, in 1894 and seven years later began to issue a Sunday edition. He offered his readers the morning, the evening and the Sunday edition all for ten cents. This was about the biggest journalistic package for a dime in America. Subscribers got thirteen papers for ten cents, less than a cent a paper. Soon Nelson decided he could issue a weekly for twenty-five cents a year. Nobody had made such an offer before. The *Weekly Kansas City Star* began in 1890.

Typographically, Nelson followed a neat, conservative makeup. He used few illustrations and did not carry comics. By 1892 his daily paper exceeded fifty thousand circulation, and at the turn of the century, the *Star* had increased to eighty-seven thousand. By the end of the century the *Weekly Star* reached one hundred fifty thousand subscribers.

ST. LOUIS DEVELOPS FIGHTING EDITORS

Gateway to the West, St. Louis, after the Civil War, developed into an important commercial city on the Mississippi River. Many German immigrants mingled with native Americans to develop a lively commercial community with a strong interest in cultural activities. Political corruption, vice and gambling were widespread. Population grew to 575,238 by 1900. Several outstanding newspapers grew up in St. Louis, responding to these conditions.

Pulitzer's Post Dispatch

It will be recalled that in St. Louis Joseph Pulitzer began his journalistic career by merging two papers into the *St. Louis Post-Dispatch* in 1878. The *Post-Dispatch* developed into a crusading, liberal daily.

Globe-Democrat Merger Produces Strong Paper

Giving sharp competition was the *Globe-Democrat* which evolved from two separate papers. The *St. Louis Globe-Democrat* became a powerful and influential journal during this period. The daily was known for its enterprise in gathering the news and for representing conservative business interests. The paper laid the foundation for Pulitzer's new journalism and then was forced to absorb some of these new techniques to survive the competition.

Owners of the *Democrat* at the end of the Civil War were William McKee, originally a printer; Frank Blair, the first editor; and George W. Fishback, a lawyer who saw economic potential in the paper and bought an interest in it.

In the post-Civil War years, the *Democrat* rose to new heights in reputation and prosperity. Part of the daily's growth resulted from a sharp, able editorial policy and shrewd financial management. Part of this newspaper's success, too, was a result of the expansion of the nation; but more particularly, it resulted from the advancement of St. Louis and the Southwest, on which the city depended. St. Louisians dreamed of their city's becoming "The Great Future City of the World," and in this early era St. Louis actually surpassed Chicago. St. Louis made steady economic progress. The first of its kind, the Eads Steel Bridge across the Mississippi was built in 1874, providing a direct link with the East. Great department stores flourished in St. Louis.

Because of expansion in its operations, a new building was constructed for the *Democrat* in May, 1865, and new equipment was purchased. Changes were made in ownership when Blair sold his interest to Daniel M. Houser for four thousand dollars. Houser had been in the business office for a number of years and had learned much about newspaper management.

Still with heavy political leanings, the *Democrat* became nationally famous for its leadership in launching the Liberal Republican movement. The daily opposed Grant's political appointments and wanted removal of disenfranchisement from the southern states. Although the paper warred on Grant, it did not support Greeley in 1872 when he ran for the presidency.

Because of internal disagreement in the newspaper office and the feeling that he was not competent, William Grosvener was discharged as editor in 1871. With the appointment of Joseph B. McCullagh as editor, the *Democrat* moved into a new journalistic period. McCullagh had been a reporter on the *Cincinnati Gazette* during the Civil War and had won a national reputation for fairness and reliability. When the *Gazette* refused to print his report of a battle because he discredited Union soldiers, McCullagh resigned. He went to work for the *Cincinnati Commercial* at twice the salary. He served as Washington correspondent for the paper, and also as Senate reporter for the New York Associated Press.

McCullagh later edited the *Cincinnati Enquirer,* and then with a brother took over the *Chicago Republican.* That journal was destroyed by fire. The *St. Louis Democrat* was fortunate in getting the able and experienced McCullagh as editor. The proprietors offered him a small share in the paper to stay with them. With McCullagh, they believed they had a chance of beating their rival, the St. Louis *Missouri Republican.*

The new editor and the proprietors saw that the *Democrat* must function as a news medium if it was to succeed in the new post-Civil War period. The paper had much in its favor: a new building and new equipment. Most important, the publishers were willing to spend large sums of money for news.

The *Democrat* developed its news muscles, as James Gordon Bennett, Jr. did with his *New York Herald.* McCullagh increased the amount of foreign news because of the Atlantic cable. He printed more telegraph news, with reports coming from hot newsspots: Nashville; Chicago; St. Joseph, Missouri; Washington; and New York. McCullagh used the Western Associated Press services while he enlarged on state and area coverage, as he said "the paper must keep pace." Telegraph operators were appointed as correspondents in other states. The *Democrat* hired Henry Morton Stanley, ace reporter, who traveled through the West reporting whatever he saw. Stanley later became famous on the *New York Herald.* Big news events, the rise of the Ku Klux Klan in the South, Osage Indian frauds in the West, and Whiskey Fraud trials in St. Louis, were reported fully in the *Democrat.*

The *Democrat* expanded its local departments, reporting city and church news more elaborately. McCullagh stimulated interest in sports with his news of baseball, prizefights and steamboat races. Crude though they were, pictures were used more frequently. To take care of this news expansion, supplements to the *Democrat* were issued.

As a result, the paper gained a national reputation for fairness and reliability. The business department, meanwhile, made distinct advances through the efforts of business manager Houser. The *Democrat* proprietors thus made about $50,000 annual profit by 1870, and this increased steadily through the eighties.

Important changes in ownership occurred in the early 1870s. In May, 1872, Fishback bought out his partners for $304,066, as he already owned one third of the company. The new proprietor obtained the necessary funds by borrowing money from six local businessmen. They formed a corporation, capitalized at $500,000. The *Democrat* had been started on a shoestring in 1852. Fishback promised *Democrat* readers that he would publish a complete newspaper with a record of world news, appealing to commercial and manufacturing interests of St. Louis.

McKee and Houser Build St. Louis Globe

Meanwhile, former proprietors of the *Democrat,* Houser and McKee, made plans for establishing a new journal. They issued the *St. Louis Globe* within three months, on July 18, 1872. The new daily was more modern in appearance than the *Democrat.* The *Globe* had ten columns on a page, was 30 inches long. The publishers sold the daily for five cents a copy, or twelve dollars a year, a lower rate than the *Democrat* price. The *Globe* promised to carry all the news and to be "journal of western enterprise, Republican in principle and national in spirit." The *Globe* also lowered advertising rates to beat its chief competitors.

The *Globe,* however, was handicapped. It had no Associated Press wire service. At this time, Pulitzer bought the German-language newspaper, the *Staats-Zeitung,* which fortunately had an AP franchise. McKee and Houser now bought this paper from Pulitzer to obtain its wire service.

Fishback, publisher of the *Democrat,* attacked the new paper and its proprietors. He even exposed McKee's connection with the Whiskey Ring, which will be described later. Fishback, meanwhile, had internal newspaper troubles. He lost McCullagh because the latter would not work under the new editor Fishback had hired. Knowing McCullagh's value as a news executive, the *Globe* proprietors quickly employed him.

While Fishback broke in the *Democrat* the story of the whiskey scandals, McCullagh gave the news full and prominent treatment in the *Globe.* The Whiskey Ring included the district supervisor of Internal Revenue Services in St. Louis and others as well as publisher McKee. Federal taxes were not paid on the whiskey distilled in the area. Part of the money was kept by the distillers but part of it went to others in the Ring. It was charged that in fourteen months each member of the Ring received $45,000 to $60,000. Publisher McKee was caught up in the corruption of the period, moved by his strong desire for money. The trial of McKee began on May 10, 1875, before a crowded courtroom. McKee pleaded not guilty but was fined $10,000 and sentenced to two years in jail. He served six months of his sentence; however, during that time, he spent the nights at home. At the end of six months President Grant pardoned the publisher.

The *Democrat* began to slip. Faced with the new competition, Fishback wanted to sell his daily to McKee and Houser. After at first refusing, they decided to buy the *Democrat.* The merger of the *Globe* and the *Democrat* was announced on May 12, 1875, ending the three year rivalry. A new corporation, the St. Louis Globe-Democrat Printing

Company, was organized. Issued at first in blanket size, the *St. Louis Globe-Democrat* soon was reduced to the *Globe*'s smaller form. The Sunday paper reached sixteen pages. The *Globe-Democrat* grew steadily. Circulation of the daily was twenty-five thousand by 1876, and mounted another one thousand by the following year. Net revenue in 1878 was $100,000.

The daily's proprietors picked an able journalist when they hired McCullagh. It was he who developed the news and editorial arms of the *St. Louis Globe-Democrat* during the next two decades. He was aware of the spread of population to the Southwest and the growing literacy, all of which opened new readership possibilities for the paper. Like Bennett in New York, McCullagh hunted news and even created it when none existed. He developed religious controversies, and he made full use of the Texas correspondents to bring in crime news. The St. Louis paper gave so much competition to Texas dailies that editors there, claiming that McCullagh was distorting the news, initiated a boycott against the St. Louis paper.

While the paper was not a campaigner for the underdog, since it represented business groups, the daily did expose gambling rings in 1878 and 1879 and smashed the syndicate in the state. McCullagh agitated for a better St. Louis, now being surpassed by Chicago. The daily's proprietors paid well for news coverage, especially for information about disasters.

McCullagh looked for sensational news, news which was entertaining and dramatic. He thought his readers would like news about disaster, crime, sex, sports, religion and violence. Columns were given to the opening of the Union railroad station and the Southern Hotel fire. McCullagh illustrated these with large two- to four-column pictures. The editor built up the Saturday paper with features especially about cats and dogs. He expanded the news in the sports and society department too. Following the current journalistic trend, he published columns of features appealing to women.

Believing that readers would be more interested in short, pithy paragraphs, he built a reputation for concise editorials. In politics, the *Globe-Democrat* was more interested in building a controversy than being a party organ. This was the period when political organs declined and news media rose. McCullagh followed the Republican Party but was not enthusiastic about it. He tried to split the Democratic Party by using satire, as did Charles A. Dana in the *New York Sun*.

McCullagh's city room became a training ground for reporters and editors who became well known on other St. Louis papers and on dailies elsewhere. McCullagh initiated many yellow journalism trends which were developed by Pulitzer and Hearst.

The editor was able to carry out his effective news policies successfully because he was backed by publisher Houser. They worked together as a strong news team. Houser designed a functional ten-story newspaper building, constructed in 1891. He provided modern presses and a photoengraving department in 1897, at the same time furnishing money for extensive news-gathering operations of the paper.

Houser foresaw future growth of department stores and recognized the possibilities of increased advertising. As the paper increased in circulation, he raised advertising rates and modernized display advertising. In spite of the rise in rates, department stores took a larger amount of space, some managers using full-page advertisements. When newsprint dropped in price, Houser dropped the price of the *Globe-Democrat,* charging two cents for twenty pages, three cents for a twenty-one to twenty-four page paper. On Sundays, a flat five cents was the cost. By 1885 the Sunday edition of the *Globe-Democrat* reached forty-four pages.

When McCullagh died in 1897, Captain Henry King, who had been with the *Globe-Democrat* since 1883, took charge of the editorial department. St. Louis was now a metropolis of five hundred thousand, and King sought to modernize the paper to fit the city's metropolitan standing. He said his "chief object would be to print the news and to cooperate with business interests of St. Louis, as they were needed to advance the welfare and progress of the community."

King began to use the Pulitzer techniques. King had reporters cover a wider variety of crime stories and displayed them with larger headlines. He widened sports coverage and used larger illustrations than ever before. The editor developed real estate and railroad news, and he even printed a bicycle page to appeal to the growing cyclist public.

The Sunday paper took on the yellow hue to fight the popularity of the *Post-Dispatch.* Casper Yost was appointed Sunday editor of the *Globe-Democrat,* which carried sixty pages in five sections, devoted to news, editorials, classified advertisements and a magazine supplement. By 1900 the *Globe-Democrat* was on its way to great journalistic heights. With a circulation of about ninety thousand, the paper was valued at two million dollars.

Daily Competitors

Chief competition for the *Globe-Democrat* in the seventies and eighties was the *Missouri Republican.* It represented the large economic interests in the city. Internal changes weakened the *Republican.* Publisher Charles Knapp died, and a large interest in the daily was sold to an easterner, Charles H. Jones, who made it into a personal organ. Then Governor David R. Francis purchased an interest, and Charles Knapp, Jr., resumed editorship of the *Republican*.

The *Globe-Democrat* increased its circulation, so that by 1885 it had 37,000 readers, while the *Republican* could claim only 27,000. In the early 1880s the *Post-Dispatch* was behind with only 8,000 readers, but in the 1890s the Pulitzer paper became more competitive. The two papers came closer together by 1892 when the *Globe-Democrat* reached 53,000 and the *Post-Dispatch* 33,000. In 1893 Pulitzer lowered the price of his daily to two cents, and in the following year to one cent. Within four years the Pulitzer paper jumped ahead of its rival. By 1902 the *Republican* accelerated, reaching 100,000, while the *Globe-Democrat* fell 10,000 behind.

E. W. Scripps sized up St. Louis as a suitable newspaper town for his efforts. He established the *St. Louis Chronicle* in 1880, but he had to cross journalistic swords with Pulitzer. The *Chronicle* was eventually merged with the *Evening Star*, another afternoon daily established in 1895, to catch the interest in afternoon editions.

Chapter 23

Southwest and Mountain Press Mature

EXPANSION OF SOUTHWEST BRINGS MANY PROBLEMS

In the decades after the Civil War, the Southwest shed some of its pioneer characteristics. Texas, Oklahoma, New Mexico, Arizona and Colorado made steady economic strides. Indian wars in these areas were bitter and bloody, but the white man with his superior guns and supplies fought the natives and beat them. White men turned for their livelihood to cattle and later sheep raising, mining, lumbering and farming.

Stirring experiences and colorful events marked the growth of the range cattle industry. Much romantic fiction and folklore have grown up around the cowboy and the ranch life: thundering stampedes, roundups, lonely range riders and their long drives to market, hell raising at cow-towns and outlaws. But numerous historical sources substantiate the claims made concerning the unusual features of such life.

Main problem of cattlemen was driving the cattle to a northern market. Hundreds of thousands of cattle were driven to Abilene, Kansas, and to Wichita, Ellsworth, Dodge City, Caldwell and Hunnewell, Kansas. Railroad connections were made at some of the towns. With success of the cattle drives, ranching became a thriving industry in the Southwest.

Coming of home seekers and railways, however, brought to an end the long drives. Large ranches were fenced in to guard choice claims stretching along river courses and rich grazing areas. Small farmers also fenced in their holdings. After 1885 the range cattle industry declined. Growth of the sheep industry in mountain and plateau areas of the Southwest closely approached in economic importance the development of cattle raising on the plains.

Railroads brought an amazing transformation to the Southwest. They became arteries through which the lifeblood of the region flowed. As roads were projected into the plains area, towns and villages developed near the railroad station houses, established ten to fifteen miles apart. The Union Pacific and the Central Pacific, first transcontinental lines, joined near Ogden, Utah in 1869.

Even more significant was the development of agriculture. Thousands of farms and agricultural communities were established. Work of the farmer was not easy. Settlement was easy, but to conquer the forces of the plains required resourcefulness and patience. Droughts, electrical storms, tornados, lack of water, worms, all tended to discourage the would-be settler. But thousands of them persisted and overcame these adverse conditions. Transformation of the entire area of the southern plains constituted one of the most spectacular accomplishments of the nation. Irrigation and reclamation projects, sponsored by state and federal governments, helped farmers recover more than four million acres of arid land for productive use. Mineral deposits in New Mexico, Arizona and Colorado as well as in Idaho and Nevada led to further economic development in those areas.

Along with economic growth of the southwestern region came slow cultural development. Settlers brought to the frontier cultural traditions as well as wordly goods. Soon after the settlers had planted communities and towns, they built churches and schoolhouses.

Printing presses had been set up in some states and territories before the Civil War. Weeklies were issued. Now with economic, cultural and community expansion, more weeklies and even dailies were published. They were issued in the towns that developed, sometimes overnight.

Cow country, farmland, mining regions all produced towns, some of which grew into cities. Transportation facilities, particularly railroads, could make or break the towns. Although St. Louis and New Orleans were large cities by the time of the Civil War, most towns in the West had their greatest growth after that conflict and with the coming of the Iron Horse. Kansas City, Little Rock, Omaha, Dallas, Fort Worth, Oklahoma City, all recorded rapid increases during these decades.

TEXAS JOURNALISM IS REINVIGORATED

Of all the Southwest states, Texas exhibited the most rapid and solid development. Hundreds of thousands of catttle were raised on vast stretches of open range. As the state turned to agriculture, cotton was the principal crop. Two railroads were started to serve the settlers. Old towns, such as Galveston, expanded, and new ones in the interior, such as Dallas, Fort Worth and Houston, developed rapidly.

Willard Richardson returned to Galveston with the *Galveston News* in 1866, having been chased out by Federal troops in the Civil War. He began to improve his plant, being the first to install a steam-powered press and stereotyping machinery. Now the second publisher to impress his character on the mold of the *News* entered. Alfred H. Belo was born in Salem, North Carolina of a wealthy family. He entered the Confederate Army and rose to the rank of colonel. Colonel Belo was seriously wounded in the struggle in Virginia. Upon the surrender of General Lee, Belo moved to Texas, a land of hope for many southerners. After a job as tutor on a plantation, Belo obtained a position as bookkeeper on the *Galveston News*. Within a few months the publisher made Belo a junior partner. The *News* was one of the dailies forming the Texas Press Association in 1866. The organization began to use the newly strung wires of the Western Union for its news. When Belo saw Alexander Graham Bell's telephone at the Philadelphia exhibition in 1876, he was very impressed, recognizing its practical value to newspapers. Within a year he installed the first telephone in Texas, running the wire from the *News* office to his home.

Richardson, meanwhile, had been fighting the evils of the Reconstruction era, seeking to end the reign of the carpetbaggers. Texas was returned to the Texans shortly before Richardson's death in 1875. The *Galveston News* avowed it would follow "Democratic principles in a wide and general sense, holding free to combat the use of power wherever found."

In 1873 an event of great economic importance to Texas occurred. The hitherto isolated railroad network of Texas was connected with that of the United States. The great day of the development of the boundless interior had arrived. The *News* adjusted to the new conditions, at first by making an effort to serve the great expanding interior, facilitating delivery of papers from the home base in Galveston. A special motorcar was built and put on rails between Galveston and Houston. The motorcar was soon supplemented by a special train, on daily schedule. The newspaper installed its first modern rotary press, being able to print 12,000 eight-page papers per hour.

Dallas Morning News Established

Colonel Belo and his associates decided to establish a companion paper in north Texas, but where? A young man, George Bannerman Dealey, was selected to make the survey and to recommend a home for an inland edition. Young Dealey had been employed as an office boy at the *Galveston News.* Born in Manchester, England in 1850, he was brought to Galveston when he was eleven years old. Soon after being employed at the *News,* he was promoted to higher positions in the business office. He was placed in charge of the Houston office of the paper when the special train service was inaugurated.

Young Dealey's study of Texas potentialities led him to the belief that Dallas was the best location for the new upland home of the *News.* After several years of careful preparation, the *Dallas Morning News* came from the press October 1, 1885. The two newspapers, at Galveston and Dallas, issued duplicate editions. The 315 miles between the Texas cities were spanned by leased wire service. Simultaneous publication of the two newspapers drew nationwide comment.

Following a conservative Democratic line, the *News* fought Governor James Stephen Hogg because it seemed to the publisher and editors that candidate Hogg had adopted the tenets of the agrarian Populist Party and outside capital was being discouraged from coming to Texas. The *News* fought for good roads for farmers in this period.

ROCKY MOUNTAIN PRESS HAS ITS OWN COLORATION

During this period the Rocky Mountain region, settled sparsely by miners seeking gold dust, experienced more rapid growth. Gold, then silver mines, produced a steady flow of revenue, with a number of shrewd and lucky men getting fabulously wealthy. Some agriculture developed, and even tourists began to trickle in to see the wonders of the West. Railroads helped develop the area. The transcontinental railroad came through by the end of the 1860s, with feeder lines being built to spread a network for transporting goods and people. Population increased.

Towns which struggled to survive before the Civil War reflected this economic underpinning and grew rapidly; some towns became metropolises. Combining with its sister community, Auraria, across the creek, Denver City, Colorado, became the mining, retail-commercial and banking center of the Rocky Mountain region. Fighting and winning the privilege of being the capital of Colorado, the town was a hotbed of politics. Millionaire miners, railroad operators and real estate speculators invested some of their gains in cultural institutions and theatres. Residents totaling 3,000, at the time of the North-South conflict, grew to 35,000 by the 1880s. At the end of the century more than 100,000 persons were living in Denver.

The city's journalism reflected transformation of the mining town into a metropolis. While some papers had strong footholds, with reputations established before the Civil War, new weeklies and dailies appeared. They sought to cash in on expanding commerce, on increased number of people or on the need for a political organ to represent a faction or an ambitious man. In the 1890s Hearst-Pulitzer metropolitan journalism moved to Denver through the reactivated *Denver Post.* Its new publishers added a few special yellow hues of their own, which gave extra distinction and upset the traditional journalism of the mining community.

As in other cities, a number of mergers occurred. The financial base of the daily newspaper widened. The day of the weekly and the small daily of one thousand to three thousand circulation was soon gone. Circulations increased, more personnel and more equipment were needed. Larger buildings were required. Publishers had to have more money than before to launch and operate successfully a daily newspaper.

Even in Denver, the old-time printer with a shirtful of type and plenty of ambition gave way to a group of partners, or to a wealthy businessman who had made a fortune in other activities, yet had a yearning for newspaper publication, or sized it up as a profitable venture. Some Denverites, as indicated, used the newspaper as an aid in their political careers.

ROCKY MOUNTAIN NEWS

By the end of the Civil War, William N. Byers had built the *Rocky Mountain News* into a valuable, respected daily newspaper. It appeared that he would remain in journalism and benefit by the foundations he had laid and that he would profit by the increasing population and commercial prosperity of Denver. He built the News Block, consisting of a large brick building housing his own newspaper operations and an express company. Byers tried to publish a morning edition of the *Rocky Mountain News* in 1870. His commercial job printing was profitable.

Byers Sells Out

Byers, however, decided to sell his *Rocky Mountain News* in May, 1878. His decision was partly based on the scandal in which he had become involved. Although Byers was married and had several children, he became enamoured with a divorcee. After several years of the affair, she shot at him in a Denver street. The *Rocky Mountain News* told about the incident frankly, treating it in straight news fashion. The case eventually was dismissed in court. Although the event had little effect on the *Rocky Mountain News,* the incident did affect Byers' commercial job-printing business. Byers also thought that his real estate business, in which he had invested heavily, would produce in the next decades a greater income than his journalistic enterprise; consequently, he decided to sell the daily.

The new owner, William H. Loveland and his partners paid $30,000 for the *Rocky Mountain News,* exclusive of the News Block, which Byers continued to rent to the new owner of the daily. A local industrialist and railroad owner, Loveland was interested in using the *Rocky Mountain News* to help the Democratic Party, still a minority party in Colorado. He desired also to employ the paper to aid him with his own career, for he craved to be governor of Colorado. Because of his association with Jay Gould, crafty railroad financier, Loveland's name was passed over by party leaders. To buy the *Rocky Mountain News,* Loveland paid $5,000; other Democrats contributed an equal amount, with a mortgage for $20,000 being held by banker David A. Moffat, Jr.

Now publisher Loveland brought in a new editor, John M. Barret, to build up *Rocky Mountain News* circulation, then only 2,500. An experienced newspaperman, Barret had been editor of New Orleans and St. Louis dailies. Barret modernized the *Rocky Mountain News,* giving it the first news thrust since the Civil War. Improving news coverage, the editor also printed news on the front page and issued a ten page newspaper. Barret expanded old departments and added new ones. He also printed more features and sports and literary material in the Sunday edition. A book review column was introduced in the Saturday edition. The *Rocky Mountain News* sports page was the first in Denver. Special editions added to the prestige and revenue of the daily. To improve news coverage, the editor arranged for a leased wire for telegraph news in the nineties. Editorially, the editor attacked the saloons in town and claimed the *News* was not a corporation journal.

Now John Arkins, a small-town paper owner, with his brother, Maurice, purchased a majority interest in the *Rocky Mountain News,* valued at about $150,000. Arkins once had been a printer, working in the composing room of the *Denver Tribune.* He established the *Chronicle* in Leadville, Colorado. Returning to Denver, he became general manager of the *Rocky Mountain News,* of which he now bought the controlling stock. Loveland, at this time a minority stockholder, sold his interest to a third party.

Death of Maurice Arkins in 1887 led to the sale of the *Rocky Mountain News* to Thomas Patterson, a strong Democrat and lawyer by profession. After he was elected city attorney, he went on to become territorial delegate to the United States Congress. He helped win statehood for Colorado. Later Patterson became Colorado's first Democratic congressman. Remaining in politics all his life, Patterson used the *News* as his political weapon. Eventually he bought John Arkins' share in the *Rocky Mountain News* when Arkins died.

By this time the *News* circulation reached 23,000 daily and 31,000 on Sunday, in spite of competition with the other six Denver dailies. Patterson later bought complete control of the paper. Value of the daily was set at $400,000 in 1892. When Republicans tried to buy the *Rocky Mountain News,* they were unable to do so.

In the Silver State the *Rocky Mountain News* had favored the coinage of silver for years, but in 1892 could not go along with Democrats who were favorable to this issue. The paper bolted the party and supported the Populist ticket. Colorado voted strongly for the Populist presidential candidate that year. In 1896 the *Rocky Mountain News* was glad to get back into the Democratic Party.

Meanwhile, other dramatic changes were occurring in Denver journalism, changes which were to affect the *Rocky Mountain News.*

Yellow Journalism in the Rockies

The *Denver Evening Post* was the Rocky Mountain outcropping of the Hearst type of journalism. Two partner-publishers, Fred G. Bonfils and Harry H. Tammen, brought the crusading type of journalism to the mountain region, and in certain instances went beyond the master sen-

Figure 46. (Left) Harry H. Tammen, Co-Publisher *Denver Evening Post*; (Right) Fred G. Bonfils, Tammen's Partner in the *Denver Evening Post.* Using the sensational, crusading techniques of the "new journalism," Bonfils and Tammen developed the near-failing *Denver Evening Post* into a powerful newspaper. The daily was distrusted and disagreed with by many but was read by thousands.

sationalist of San Francisco and New York. The Denver publishers gave the yellow hue their own coloration. In buying the *Evening Post* in 1895 they upset the enterprising but conservative dailies of Denver and started a press revolution similar to that observed in other parts of the country.

The *Denver Evening Post* had been established in 1892 but could make little headway. Its circulation fell off to about six thousand, and the paper was put up for sale. Harry H. Tammen, a local curio shop owner, saw possibilities in it. Born in Baltimore, he had drifted west and became a bartender at the famous Palmer House. When he acquired enough money, he embarked on a venture of his own. He opened a curio shop in Denver. When the panic of 1893 hit him he was practically wiped out. The publication of the *Denver Evening Post* appealed to Tammen because he "saw everyone reading the paper."

On a trip to Chicago, he learned about Bonfils, who engaged in the real estate business and ran lotteries in Kansas City. Tammen approached Bonfils at the right time with a proposition to publish a Denver newspaper. The two partners purchased the broken-down *Post* for $12,500 in November, 1895.

The *Denver Evening Post* soon became the Rocky Mountain journalistic crusader. The daily immediately began a series of sensational attacks, aimed mostly at local corporations and vested interests. The *Post* publishers believed that the local press was concealing information from the public and that the *Post*'s job was to expose conditions. Tammen wrote a daily editorial, "So the People May Know," which he published in two-column wide style on the front page. He realized that any attempt to disturb the comfortable status quo enjoyed by some old-time residents would be resented. There would be efforts to cripple the *Post*. This danger did not stop him. Perhaps he balanced increased circulation against temporary advertising losses. Decision made, he attacked with fury, putting the opposition on the defensive.

He shelled particularly the Denver Union Water Company, a privately owned corporation. When the water company said it would cut off water from all those who did not pay its rates, the *Post* called the charges extortionate and told all readers to call the paper if their water was cut off. The editors declared the water was filled with sewage from other towns, from ranches and from slaughterhouses. As a result of the *Post*'s campaign the people of Denver decided to buy the water company and operate the facility. The paper also attacked the local trolley company and fought for better service as well as fairer rates.

The *Post* launched a systematic attack on Patterson, publisher of the *Rocky Mountain News*, as well as on David Moffat, owner of the *Denver Times*. Moffat was a power in banking, mining and other enterprises. The *Post* charged that big department stores were boycotting it and that the store owners were even sending emissaries to all the independent advertisers who continued to patronize the *Post.* These advertisers were discouraged from placing ads in the *Post.* This, Tammen said, showed the department store-owners' venom and hatred.

In retaliation the *Post* campaigned against child labor in local stores. An affidavit of a shopgirl was printed with this headline:

ARROGANT AND OUTRAGEOUS TREATMENT OF A SHOPGIRL

The campaign went on for months in that strain. Afterward the state legislature passed laws banning the labor of children.

The advertising campaign against the *Post* continued, but it was not as effective as it had been. One day Bonfils became so angry at the blasts and charges of blackmail made by publisher Moffat of the *Times* that the *Post* partner beat up his rival. Charges of assault were then brought against Bonfils.

At the trial all accusations against the *Post* publishers were brought out by the attorneys. On the witness stand, Moffat claimed that the *Post* owners had systematically blackmailed merchants into advertising. He said this was common knowledge but could not prove his assertions. The case was dropped.

The *Denver Post* was filled with human interest news and feature articles, particularly on local or Colorado happenings. The news staff was led, or driven by Josiah Ward, who had worked as city editor for Hearst in San Francisco, and had been employed also at the *Denver Times.* Tammen hired hard-driving Ward away from that daily.

"Let's make 'em sit up," Tammen said. "Half the town is good and half is bad. The good ones will read the *Post* to congratulate themselves on being so holy; the bad ones to see what we've found out about them."

On another occasion he declared, "We're yellow, but we're read and we're true blue." He formulated other slogans that caught the popular approval. He called the *Post,* "Young Big Brother" and "The Paper with a Heart and a Soul."

Tammen knew little or nothing about writing headlines from a technical standpoint, but he has been called one of the greatest "natural" composers of sensational and arresting headlines. He once criticized a lifeless banner headline and wrote instead:

JEALOUS GUN-GAL PLUGS HER LOVER LOW

The copyreader said the headline did not fit the space count in the page. Tammen replied, "Make it fit—get some advertising type—but make it fit." When the deskman complained that the line was grammatically wrong, Tammen answered, "That's the trouble with this paper—too God-damned much grammar. Let's can the grammar and get out a live sheet!"

Denver was lacking in commercial, industrial and transportation facilities, usually needed for municipal growth. No trunk line of a major railway served the state capital. Denver was blessed with being in the middle of a region of great natural wealth.

Bonfils decided to make the whole region a family, with the *Post* as patriarch. He would bind together with his paper the people of Colorado, Wyoming, Utah, northern New Mexico, Arizona and as much as he could of Nebraska and Kansas. He began to address the citizens of these states as "The Great Post Family." He told them, day after day, the *Post* was their big brother, and he clamored for better roads, and during the drought, relief funds for farmers. In his bid for reader interest in these neighboring states, Bonfils covered their local news thoroughly.

On one occasion, a famous girls' wrestling and boxing act appeared in Denver. The *Post* offered prizes to local girls who could make a good showing against the pros. One local aspirant was strapping Marie Soslusky, who with one fist could knock out most men. Marie and the other girls, dressed in tights, appeared to battle the pros. The pros agreed to go easy. Marie was in one of the bouts when a seam came loose. The audience howled, showering the girl with coins. The town talked about the *Post*'s stunt for days.

Tammen was enamoured with circuses and animals. He loved clowns and acrobats. Tammen started out by owning a dog and pony show, which he named after his sports editor, Floto, because Tammen thought the name so beautiful. Tammen added to his menagerie and eventually built up a good-sized circus which ran into competition with Ringling Bros., whom the *Post* accused of organizing a trust.

Post publishers built up an unusually strong writing staff, giving reporters enough leeway to develop original writing styles. Damon Runyon developed his storytelling skill on the *Post,* later becoming a magazine writer. Courtney Riley Cooper was a star for the *Post* and afterward wrote circus and western stories for an eager national audience. The paper's sports editor, Otto Floto, became an expert on boxing. Julian Hawthorne was hired at two hundred fifty dollars a week, but only a few of his stories, with his byline, ever appeared. Women writers brought talent and skill to the *Post,* being able to draw thousands of readers. Mrs. Leonard Ross O'Bryan, under the name of Polly Pry, was a favorite writer.

The paper also developed political as well as humorous cartoonists. One day Wilbur Steele, cartoonist for the opposition Republican paper, satirized Tammen and Bonfils. Tammen, who had a strong sense of humor, laughed at the cartoon. Recognizing ability even when it was directed against him, Tammen hired Steele for the *Post.* Paul Greg's western paintings, featured on the front page of the *Post*'s Sunday supplement, were treasured in remote mining cabins for years.

Seeking to draw attention and to be different, the *Post* used red ink on its banner headlines and a hodgepodge of various kinds of type in all sizes on the front page.

Addition of a Sunday edition in May, 1898, containing many new features, stimulated interest in the *Post,* contributing to its growth. Comic strips appeared in 1901, following the New York trend.

Post Meets Need: Circulation Rises

Somehow people of Denver felt that notwithstanding all the accusations against the *Post* it met their psychological needs and was a journalistic friend and champion. They began to buy the *Post* to read what Tammen and Bonfils had to say. Circulation rose rapidly from a dubious 6,000, when the partners bought the *Post,* to 27,333 two years later. Despite this circulation boost, the paper was not profitable immediately. The year's income was $122,000, the expenses, $117,000, the net earnings, $5,000. The *Post* employed sixty-nine, with twelve on the editorial staff, twelve in the business office, eighteen in circulation and twenty-seven in the mechanical department.

Soon after the turn of the century (February, 1901) the *Post* reached 30,000, passing the *Rocky Mountain News,* oldest paper in the city.

Chapter 24

Pacific Coast Crusaders

CALIFORNIA'S ECONOMIC DEVELOPMENT IS RAPID

Although built originally on gold, California's economic base widened in the decades after the Civil War. Mining still employed more of the state's workers than any other pursuit. Average annual output at the time of the war was about fifty million dollars. After 1865 gold production displayed a remarkable stability, leveling off at fifteen million dollars yearly.

Cattle raising expanded to meet the needs of the growing population. With miners providing a market for mutton, sheep raising revived. The wool industry improved and California soil and climate proved most congenial for wheat. Through its associated industry of winemaking, grape culture offered strong economic possibilities for the state. In the seventies and eighties orange growing forged to the front. A significant advance took place in irrigation.

Railroads contributed greatly to the rapid economic development of California. Theodore D. Judah was primarily responsible for the idea of building a transcontinental railroad. This engineer met with many discouragements but persisted in his idea. Eventually he was able to persuade Leland Stanford, wholesale grocer; Charles Crocker, dry goods merchant; Mark Hopkins; and Collis P. Huntington of the practicality of his plans, and they launched the Central Pacific of California.

Meanwhile, the Union Pacific was building from the East. The two railroads were built parallel, but an alarmed Congress designated Promontory, Utah as the place where they should meet. It was an epochal development in western history. The Pacific railroad heralded the transformation of California and the West; the Sierra mountain barrier had been overcome. The Pacific railroad, nevertheless, drew much criticism and was named the Octopus. The Big Four founders saw that their success hinged on establishment of a monopoly of California rails.

California's institutions of higher learning were developed during this period. Colleges and universities, including the state university, the College of the Pacific, were enrolling students during the 1870s. Now a dozen or more sister institutions were added. The University of Southern California was founded in 1879. Others included Occidental College and Pomona College. Amos G. Throop's school at Pasadena became the California Institute of Technology. Announcement that Leland Stanford would give the bulk of his fortune to found Leland Stanford University was electrifying news. By the end of the century one thousand students were enrolled in this institution which exerted a profound influence on the state.

California produced a number of writers: poets and novelists who reflected the California environment. Helen Hunt Jackson wrote a *Century of Dishonor;* Frank Norris wrote the *Octopus, McTeague* and the *Pit.* Jack London's works were produced at the beginning of the next century.

SAN FRANCISCO PAPERS VIGOROUS, COMPETITIVE

San Francisco profited by economic expansion of the state and the coming of railroads. Fortunes of the railroad builders and the millionaires who made their money in gold and silver mining, particularly from the Comstock lode, contributed to the city's wealth when the miners invested in real estate, hotels, theatres, mills. Farmers and ranchers also helped make San Francisco the richest and largest city on the West Coast. When mining declined and agriculture rose, San Francisco continued as the trade center, with wheat, wines and fruit becoming the commercial articles of sale. Here the Southern Pacific Railroad was born.

San Francisco had an extraordinary port, one of the best natural harbors in the world, still unchallenged by any on the Pacific. Ocean-going commerce brought freight from China. San Francisco was a colorful place. Here travelers going to and from all parts of the world changed from boats to railroads, or railway cars to steamships. In San Francisco political corruption was accepted as normal by many citizens. Wealthy residents lived on Nob Hill and in hotels, such as the six million dollar Palace Hotel. Chinatown had a mysterious reputation. Excellence of San Francisco's restaurants attracted many, offering French and Chinese food. San Franciscans could go to Morosco's Grand Opera

House, specializing in melodrama, later opera; the Tivoli, with its light and grand opera; the Alcazar, which had an excellent stock company; and the Orpheum, where vaudeville was shown. Artists came from all over the world to play in these theatres. From a population of 56,000 before the Civil War, San Francisco jumped to 342,782 by the turn of the century.

An account of William Randolph Hearst's crusading *San Francisco Examiner* has been told in the previous section.

San Francisco Chronicle Struggles

In 1865, two young men, with a borrowed twenty dollar gold piece between them, started a newspaper in the brash and bawdy town of San Francisco. It was a most unusual newspaper as it was devoted to theatrical business.

Charles and Michael de Young were still in their teens when they started their newspaper, the *Dramatic Chronicle,* on January 16, 1865. They borrowed twenty dollars, purchased two stands of worn type, an imposing stone to put type on, a battered redwood desk and some odd ends of newsprint. The *Dramatic Chronicle* was a tabloid-size giveaway, filled principally with theatrical news and advertisements and was distributed among hotels, saloons and the audience of Worrell's Olympic Theatre.

Three months after its first issue the *Dramatic Chronicle* scooped every newspaper in the city with its story on the assassination of President Lincoln. The inexplicable lethargy of other editors in town, all of whom failed to put out an extra, made the *Dramatic Chronicle*'s circulation increase until within a few months it had become San Francisco's leading newspaper, exceeding the *Call, Bulletin* and *Herald.*

Three years later, in step with its new affluence, the paper dropped the name *Dramatic* and emerged as a full-fledged, standard-size newspaper called the *Daily Morning Chronicle.* The editors even had the temerity to charge five cents a copy and announced in a lead editorial that they proposed to publish a truly independent newspaper—"independent on all things, neutral in nothing." In keeping with their stated editorial policy, the *Daily Morning Chronicle* was vigorous in exposing political scandals and land-grant frauds. Libel suits were frequent, but the paper proved its charges in case after case.

The paper developed a reputation for discovering writers and for its lively style. Writers like Bret Harte and Mark Twain were steady contributors, and their sharp pens punctured the dignities of the pompous and pointed out the sins of the iniquitous to a delighted and growing audience. By 1875 the *Chronicle* had the biggest circulation of any paper west of the Mississippi.

In 1880, just a year after moving into a new building at Kearny and Bush, Charles de Young, older of the paper's two founding brothers, was assassinated by the son of a man whom the paper had attacked during the course of a red-hot mayoralty campaign. Michael de Young carried on, continuing the *Chronicle*'s fearless, aggressive brand of journalism, increasing the paper's circulation. In 1890 he moved into the new ten-story *Chronicle* building at Market, Geary and Kearny Streets.

San Francisco Bulletin Gets New Editor

The *San Francisco Bulletin* was owned by Deacon Fitch, Loring Pickering and James W. Simonton. Fitch was a straight-laced Puritan. He was opposed generally to all city improvements on the ground that they increased taxes. He was also opposed to bosses and political machines which controlled city and state. When Simonton and Pickering died, the *Evening Bulletin* was purchased for six thousand dollars by Robert Alexander Crothers, brother of Pickering's widow. Crothers, a Montreal lawyer, had come to San Francisco previously. Crothers persuaded Fremont Older to leave a rival paper and come to the *Bulletin* as managing editor. The *Bulletin* had prestige but not much more. Circulation had dropped to nine thousand. There were many taboos: Professional sports, for instance, were never mentioned.

Fremont Older, managing editor and guiding genius of the *San Francisco Bulletin,* was an unusual newspaperman, the type the Midwest and the West seemed to spawn during this time. He was hated and loved by his readers for his editorial stands, which he often reversed. Born in 1856 in a log cabin in Wisconsin, he drifted to the Pacific coast. There he was variously a printer, ranch hand, legislative correspondent in both Nevada and California. He served in every newspaper capacity and acquired a complete knowledge of the business. Older was a tremendous force in California journalism. His influence was eventually felt throughout the nation. Tall, he was six feet two, with fierce handlebar mustache, Older was in most respects an extraordinary personality. He responded to the rough, tough San Francisco environment and sought to root out evil by publicity and by punishing the criminals.

When Older, who had worked on a number of newspapers in the West, became editor of the *San Francisco Bulletin,* he declared it was necessary to become successful quickly and to win attention and, hence, circulation before the paper went under. The physical facilities disheartened Older. The *Bulletin* was housed near the waterfront in a building with unstable walls. Cobwebs and dirt darkened the rooms. The solitary and indequate press could not produce more papers if circulation should increase. Type was still set by hand. There was no money to buy another press or hire a reportorial staff. The *Bulletin* was not dying without reason. It was a dreary sheet printed in small, close type, with single column heads and no illustrations. Older was managing editor in title but also city editor and reporter as well.

Under his leadership the *Bulletin* steadily brightened. News story heads were written in the form of questions to stimulate reader interest: "What Is the Railroad Saying to the Assembly in Sacramento?" "What Is President Grover Cleveland Planning in Washington?" Older tried contests to stir readers and build circulation.

Older was indefatigable in covering the news and displaying it in the most sensational fashion. The Durant murder case broke at this time and also aided Older in his search for circulation. Durant was a good-looking, mild young man from a respected family. He was studying medicine and was assistant superintendent of a church Sunday School. Then it was learned that Blanche Lamont, a twenty-year old church member, had disappeared. A search began. Then Minnie Williams, nineteen, her friend and also of the same church, disappeared. Minnie's body was found in the library of the church. She had been strangled and violated after death.

Older detailed men to run down every angle and clue on the Durant case. Reporter Baggerly covered the story for the *Bulletin,* and when Blanche's body was discovered, he rushed to Older's hotel with the news. Although it was on Sunday a crew was hastily called together, and Older brought out a Sunday edition. Suspicion pointed to Durant, but police hesitated for a time to arrest him. Urged on by the *Bulletin,* they finally made the arrest. The Durant trial lasted many weeks, and the *Bulletin* ran every word of testimony.

When the case went to the jury Older had three stories written, put in type, made up in page form, stereotyped and ready to be printed. One story was headed "Guilty," another, "Jury Couldn't Agree," and a third, "Acquitted." When the foreman of the jury said, "Guilty," the reporter for the *Bulletin* rushed for the door and got out just as the court door closed. All other reporters were locked in; the *Bulletin* beat the town. Circulation jumped to twenty thousand, and the *Bulletin* was in the lead.

Although news was important and helped zoom circulation, Older's crusades against political corruption won the *Bulletin* its reputation. Railroads, at the time, controlled the entire state and shaped public opinion by paying off publishers and editors. The *Bulletin,* for instance, received a monthly check for $125 as a goodwill offering. Older knew the evils of this arrangement and fought publisher Crothers on the issue.

In 1896 Older had a chance to help elect as mayor an honest man, James D. Phelan. Phelan's administration was progressive, and he helped turn out the grafters and defied the railroads. Then in 1901, when Phelan did not want to run again, the progressive trend was reversed.

The city now began to be graft ridden. Older exposed all these grafts except the railroad issue. The crusades demonstrated that he was a daring editor and that the *Bulletin* was a courageous newspaper. Crothers and Older were arrested seventeen or eighteen times on some civil or criminal action. The publisher was slugged, and a plot was hatched to kill the editor, but Older discovered it. He smashed time and again at political bosses for the next ten years. Boss Abe Reuf was eventually sent to jail and the police chief forced to resign.

Older created a western school of journalism. He was an inspiring, creative editor and listened to others' ideas, and in discussion gave them back more fully developed than they had been originally. Many of his reporters became world famous. They included John Francis Neylan, Willaim O. McGeehan, Sinclair Lewis, Robert L. Duffus, Lemuel F. Parton and Bruce Bliven. Although these men broke away from Older and went to wider fields, they continued to reveal the Older influence.

SCRIPPS EXTENDS CHAIN TO CALIFORNIA

When Edward W. Scripps moved to California in 1890 for his health, he entered a new phase of his operations, long-distance management, and began establishment of a West Coast chain. He loaned two young newsmen $3,000 to buy the *San Diego Sun,* and although Scripps sank $18,000 into the venture, the operators were not able to make it pay. Scripps' next selection of an executive was better, for he sold the daily to W. H. Porterfield, a former *Sun* reporter, who was able to put it on a sustaining basis. Porterfield later sold 51 per cent of the stock to Scripps, who began to evolve a practical pattern of chain journalism.

He believed strongly in economic opportunity for all rather than doles and charity. He sought to provide journalistic opportunity for smart young reporters and advertising men. He loaned them a few thousand dollars, enough to get a start on back streets with small, fighting newspapers; advertising men handled the advertising and business end. If they succeeded, Scripps retained 51 per cent of the stock of the corporation, and the young executives, the remainder.

Other newspapers were started in a similar fashion. The *Los Angeles Record* and the *Seattle Star* were purchased and daily publications in

Fresno, Berkeley and Oakland, California, were launched but were abandoned.

SACRAMENTO'S FIGHTING PAPER BATTLES RAILROAD OCTOPUS

The *Sacramento Union*, which had been established before the war and had become "the miners' bible" in this period, rose to great popularity in its fight on the monopoly and political corruption of the Central Pacific railroad.

Under editorial leadership of Samuel Seabough, the *Union* was convinced that California was about to be delivered into the hands of the railroad corporation. Impact of the battle between newspaper and railroad split California's ruling party. In the governor's campaign of 1867 the Union Party nominated railroad lobbyist George Gorham. The *Sacramento Union* bolted and helped swing the election to the Democrats.

The antirailroad campaign initiated by the *Union* in 1867 proved effective. Editor Seabough marshalled facts and figures. He challenged the company's practices. The *Union* had the support of the *San Francisco Bulletin* in its fight. Some political battles were won. In 1873, with major parties dominated by the Central Pacific, the *Union* spearheaded the Independent Party movement which got Newton Booth, its candidate, a seat in the United States Senate.

The *Union*'s activities were known to railroad magnates. A. P. Huntington wrote, "The *Union* hurts us very much. . . . If I owned the paper, I would control it or burn it. . . ." The Big Four railroads closed in. The Central Pacific banned the *Union* from its cars and boats. The railroad owned all lines of communication from Sacramento in all directions. The newspaper was bottled up in the heart of California's great inland valley. Dependent on its weekly edition, the *Union* could not compete with strong 'Frisco dailies distributed over a wide area by the railroad. Another factor causing the paper's decline was the changing California economy. In 1874 the *Union* was sold at public auction and merged with the *Record* a year later. The pioneer *Union* was a product of California's early isolated period.

LOS ANGELES SEES STRONG PAPERS LAUNCHED

Los Angeles had certain basic assets for growth, climate and geographical situation. Discovery of gold at Sutter's Mill made Los Angeles a way station and trading place for gold seekers. If they found gold they left it in Los Angeles later. Nearby vineyards produced grapes, wine and brandy shipped to miners in northern California. Southern California ranches also contributed beef for the miners' tables.

Los Angeles recognized that it needed a good harbor, so citizens dredged the shallow waters nearby to form a harbor. Colonel P. T. Banning promoted the building of a railroad, opened in 1869. Residents hoped to connect it with the transcontinental line. Arrival of the Southern Pacific in 1876 started a new era for Los Angeles. The Santa Fe railroad arrived in the next decade, bringing additional prosperity to the city.

Climate of Los Angeles was something that could be sold, and railroads and residents began to advertise the healthful region. The navel orange also brought new wealth to southern California and to Los Angeles. The city which had 5,000 residents at the end of the Civil War reached 102,000 by 1900.

Los Angeles Times Begins

The important paper which started after the end of the Civil War was the *Weekly Mirror,* the first issue coming out in 1873. It hardly deserved the name of newspaper at all and indeed was intended more as an advertisement of a single business than as a general circulation newspaper. Its publishers were Jesse Yarnell and T. Y. Caystill. They had begun a commercial printing company and the *Mirror* was issued to boost their business.

Los Angeles was overwhelmingly Democratic in those early years. It was in this sort of presumably hostile town that the *Los Angeles Times,* a Republican newspaper defying the jinx of many defunct predecessors, made its appearance December 4, 1881. It was issued from the same plant as the *Mirror.*

Nathan Cole, Jr., son of a rich St. Louis man, was one participant in the new venture. With him as a partner was a middle-aged English gentleman, Thomas Gardiner, who created a sensation wherever he went with his high black top hat, frock coat, spats and mutton chop whiskers. He and Cole were both good newspapermen.

The Cole and Gardiner combination did not last long. They put out a breezy little newspaper, but they also were paying their bills with breeze. After only a few weeks their slim credit came to an end.

The printing company which produced the paper decided to become publishers. The strain, however, was very great and the partners were happy to see Colonel Harrison Gray Otis come in on that hot July day in 1882 when the paper was only eight months old. Colonel Otis, who previously operated the *Santa Barbara Press,* became editor at a salary of fifteen dollars a week. He immediately began to strengthen the *Los Angeles Times.* A born fighter, he had a compelling style of writing and a keen sense of news.

The Republican *Times* found plenty of subjects on which to pick fights with its longer-established rivals, the *Express* and the *Herald.* The community began to talk about the scrappy newcomer. Otis was joined in partnership by Colonel H. H. Boyce, a flashy character from the East with money in his pocket. The company was incorporated for sixty thousand dollars.

Differences between Colonel Boyce and Otis became so acute in March, 1886 that the two men agreed to sever their business relations. Colonel Boyce said he would sell or buy a half interest for $27,000 (some say it was $18,000). Otis greatly astonished Colonel Boyce by agreeing to buy, and paid the purchase price, in escrow. The money, Colonel Otis later on let it be known privately, had been supplied by a good friend, a local banker.

In a few years Colonel Otis came into sole control of the *Times.* In 1885 a new circulation man joined the staff. Harry Chandler, like so many others, had been attracted to California by the sunshine and the promise of renewed health which the climate afforded.

Harry Chandler, New Force

At twenty-one, Chandler obtained a job as clerk in the circulation department of the *Times.* From the moment he joined the *Times* staff Chandler displayed a vitality and an ability to get things done which attracted the notice of Colonel Otis. Chandler had the faculty of inspiring loyalty and allegiance among employees and soon became circulation manager.

As the boom progressed, facilities of the *Times* became overtaxed and a new building was constructed. In 1887 the paper began to appear seven days a week; until this time there had been no Monday edition.

The land boom was continuing and there seemed to be no possibility of it ending. Then, almost overnight, the bottom dropped out of the real estate market. Railroads were deluged by disillusioned speculators trying to return to their former homes. The *Times* in its imposing new home, with a depleted revenue and a staggering burden of debt, had plenty to consider.

Los Angeles, during the next few decades, began to stagnate. Poverty was so extreme that many persons who had been wiped out during the speculative fever actually did not know where to get their next meal. Advertisers began to cut their budgets and the *Times* suffered. The four Los Angeles newspapers had been paying boom wages nearly double comparative rates paid in eastern cities. The publishers asked the Los Angeles Typographical Union to approve a moderate wage reduction. The union refused and called a strike.

First effect of the strike was to cut the size of the *Times* in half, from eight to four pages. Colonel Otis, a practical printer and member of the union, worked alongside the few men who did not strike. He believed he was fighting in the interest of the men as well as for the economic life of the city and the newspapers. He refused to give up.

Nonunion printers helped fill in the ranks. Then the union called a boycott against the advertisers. The *Times* lost a number of subscribers and for a time saw a falling away of its advertisers, but circulation later gained. Success of the *Times* in combatting the strike likewise had the effect of focusing national attention on Los Angeles as the home of the open shop. The American Federation of Labor then instituted a nationwide boycott against the national advertisers in the *Times*. But the boycott did not prove to be effective. In retaliation, Otis organized an aggressive Merchants and Manufacturers Association.

PACIFIC NORTHWEST NEWSPAPERS STRENGTHENED WITH NEW DAILIES

The Pacific Northwest, consisting of the states of Washington, Oregon, northern Idaho and western Montana, formed a geographical and economic unity, centering around the Columbia River and its tributaries. Natural boundaries contributed toward this oneness. The Pacific Ocean lay on the west; Rocky Mountains and Continental Divide formed the eastern barrier. Slowly, population increased in the post-Civil War era, as more people recognized the potential economic future.

Great basic wealth of the area came from farming, fishing, lumbering and mining. Extensive plains drew the eye of farmers and city folk migrating from the East, the South and the Midwest. With irrigation they raised a variety of crops, especially wheat. Because of the acres of forests one of the most important industries was lumbering. Sawmills were beginning to cut wood for many purposes. Salmon fishing along the coast had been engaged in from the early period, and this and other fishing provided a livelihood for many. In the mountains gold and silver mines were worked, and new discoveries were made, adding to the wealth of the section. Steamboat companies were established to provide freight and passenger transportation, and railroad lines coming from the East were linked.

Portland Oregonian

During the Gilded Age the *Portland Orgeonian,* which had been started when the Civil War broke out, became one of the strongest dailies in the Northwest. Henry Pittock, who had joined the paper in its early years and had become owner, hired Harvey Scott in 1865 as editor. Scott began an association with the *Oregonian* that endured, except for a short interval, until Scott's death in 1910. Scott was reared in Illinois, tramped over much of the Northwest as a boy and became a lawyer and city librarian. He wrote articles for the *Oregonian* and then joined the staff.

From 1877 on he shared in ownership of the paper. A scholar, he read widely and had a forceful writing style. He was opposed to the splinter Populist movements. Although he believed in states' rights, he did not think states should defy the national government or the national viewpoint.

As Portland grew and prospered, so did the *Oregonian.* In the panic of 1892 circulation fell off, but the paper recovered again. The first Sunday *Oregonian* was issued in December, 1881. First publication of a regular daily edition of more than four pages occurred in 1882, showing the growth of business and advertising. The *Oregonian*'s first continuous web press was installed in 1884 and turned out twelve thousand papers an hour, ten times the capacity of its first power press. Advertising disappeared from the front page of the Sunday edition in 1889 and from the front page of the daily in 1904. In 1894 the *Oregonian* installed Linotypes, ten years after Mergenthaler invented the machine. In 1900 the first halftone engraving appeared in the *Oregonian* on the back page. The daily moved into its new building in 1892, and again a new press went in. The *Oregonian* reached fifteen thousand circulation at the end of the century.

Seattle Newspapers

First newspaper to carry a Seattle dateline was published in Olympia by James R. Watson on August 15, 1863. His *Seattle Gazette,* first paper printed in that community, made its appearance on December 10, 1863, a few weeks after Lincoln delivered his Gettysburg address.

The same old Ramage press published the first edition of the *Weekly Intelligencer* on August 5, 1867. Seattle had less than one thousand residents. In 1887 the *Intelligencer* absorbed the *Puget Sound Dispatch* and the *Pacific Tribune.* The *Seattle Post* began publication on October 1, 1881, and then was combined with the *Intelligencer,* assuming the name, *Post-Intelligencer.* The great Seattle fire in June, 1889, destroyed the building and the home of owner Leigh Hunt. With arrival of the Klondike gold rush, Seattle changed overnight into a metropolis of eighty thousand, and the *Post-Intelligencer* became a power in its development.

Spokane Spokesman-Review Beginnings

On the morning that the first issue of the *Spokane Falls* (Washington) *Review* was issued, Frank Dallam, publisher, sought the seclusion of his office and waited the verdict of the town. At last there was a footstep. The door opened. Dr. J. M. Morgan entered. Throwing two silver dollars on the imposing stone, he exclaimed, "You've made a hit and the *Review* will prove a winner." Similar words came from others.

A California printer, Dallam had looked over the region around Spokane Falls and saw unlimited possibilities in it. Unable to buy out established papers in town, he issued the *Weekly Review* on May 19, 1883. During the boom resulting from the gold strike in nearby Coeur d'Alene Mountains, the next year he converted the *Spokane Falls Review* to a daily. Dallam purchased a Hoe drum-cylinder press, operated by steam, and he acquired a valuable Associated Press franchise for five thousand dollars. Disagreements with his partners led Dallam to sell the paper, and in a few years four businessmen bought it for twenty thousand dollars.

The Spokane paper had the AP franchise, coveted by Harvey Scott and H. L. Pittock, owners of the *Portland Oregonian.* Control of the *Spokane Falls Review* would give the publishers of the *Oregonian* additional stock representation in the AP. With this in mind they bought the *Review* stock. Nelson W. Durham was sent from Portland to be managing editor.

Others also recognized economic and journalistic potentialities in the region. Horace T. Brown launched the *Spokesman* on March 8, 1889, as an eight-page, standard-size newspaper. The *Spokesman* emphasized that the men who edited the paper, owned it. Competition between the *Review* and the *Spokesman* became very fierce and very costly. The *Spokesman* needed funds to survive.

Now William Hutchinson Cowles, of Chicago, learned about the situation. Cowles' father was Alfred H. Cowles, secretary-treasurer of the *Chicago Tribune.* Born in Evanston, Illinois, in 1866, William studied with tutors. In Chicago while attempting to climb the side ladder on a freight car of a moving train, he fell under the wheels and lost his left leg below the knee. William enrolled at Yale University and was selected chairman of the board of the *Yale Daily News* in his senior year. The *News* made money. Receiving his A.B. degree in 1887, young Cowles won his LL.B. degree two years later. Deciding on journalism rather than law, he got a position on the *Chicago Tribune,* working as a police reporter. As his health was not up to par, he thought a change of climate might be beneficial. Learning about the Spokane *Spokesman,* he came west and bought an interest in the paper.

When competition with the *Review* became too burdensome, Cowles effected a merger in February, 1893, calling the consolidated papers the *Spokane Review*. The name *Spokesman* was dropped. Scott and Pittock became his partners. When an economic depression came in the following year, Scott and Pittock were glad to sell out to Cowles.

On January 2, 1894, the day after the contract was signed, a new name, the *Spokesman-Review,* appeared on the masthead. Influencing the change was the fact that the name *Review* had become unpopular through being identified with control of the paper from Portland by Scott and Pittock.

Cowles officially became business manager and publisher. Although he never took the title of editorial director, he might as well have done so. From the first, he influenced, guided and controlled every phase of the editorial policy of the daily, improving it greatly. Features were added: a half-page book review, a social section, a department for news of fraternal orders. "Best Fun of the Week" became popular.

The presidential campaign of 1896 was marked with great excitement in silver-producing states. As one of the great silver-producing areas, the region shared in that excitement. Reflecting the viewpoint of the people there, the *Spokesman-Review* strongly supported William Jennings Bryan in his campaign for free coinage of silver.

In May, 1897, J. J. Browne, owner of the *Spokane Daily Chronicle,* a competitor with a circulation of eight thousand, wanted to sell. Cowles believed he could print the *Chronicle* on his presses more cheaply than Browne. The sale of the *Chronicle* to Cowles was completed in August. Cowles kept the entire editorial staff and let the newsmen run the *Chronicle* as a competitor.

Under the able guidance of Cowles, the *Spokesman-Review* grew faster than the population expansion in the city and the region. The *Spokesman-Review* circulation tripled, jumping from 3,388 daily to 10,418 copies at the turn of the century. The Sunday paper showed a similar rise, increasing from 4,537 (1894) to 12,881 copies.

Chapter 25

Press Fights a War (Spanish-American)

BACKGROUND OF WAR

The Spanish-American conflict was the climax of Gilded Age sensational journalism. The *New York World* and the *Journal* whipped up sentiment against the Spanish government and hurried America into conflict with Spain.

Spain, once a powerful nation, had slowly been declining. Cuba sought her independence and revolted several times in the 1860s and 1870s. American businessmen had heavy investments in sugar plantations there. The Cuban population faced an era of depression when the United States tariff on sugar was raised in 1894. Cubans revolted against the oppressive conditions, as thousands of families were starved and stricken by disease. A group of Cuban loyalists, called a Junta, set up in New York and supplied insurrectionists on the island with money and guns. Spanish officials sought by every means to quell the revolt. General Martinez Campos was sent to Cuba from Spain to carry out the orders.

Meanwhile, newspapers in the United States became interested and concerned about conditions in Cuba. Such conservative dailies as the *New York Sun* and the *Chicago Tribune* had for decades been imperialistic, calling for annexation of Canada as well as Cuba. Sympathy for the underdog also had become a part of the psychological tradition in this country, and this attitude was now extended to other nations seeking to be free of domination of mother countries, just as the American colonies had in 1776. Cuba was being oppressed by the ancient Spanish government.

It was in such a climate of opinion that the great Hearst-Pulitzer battle for circulation and supremacy occurred. Soon after outbreak of rebellion of the Cubans in 1895, Spanish authorities placed a strict censorship on news from Cuba. Correspondents had a difficult time getting news of the revolt. The Spanish government, in attempting to censor news of the insurrection, not only antagonized correspondents but encouraged inaccuracy. The fact that the New York press continued to receive accounts of the Cuban rebellion after correspondents had been expelled from the island, showed that journalists were not obtaining their news from first-hand investigation.

WEYLER'S BRUTALITY SENSATIONALIZED BY PRESS

In 1896 Valeriano Weyler was named Captain-General of Spanish armies. He had gained a reputation for his brutality, and it was predicted that blood would flow in Cuba. General Weyler issued orders requiring the people of Cuba to concentrate in camps around military headquarters, which put the population under complete control of the military.

By the time General Weyler began his program four New York papers, the *World, Sun, Journal, Herald,* had correspondents on the island. *World* and *Journal* artists accompanied their correspondents to make sketches illustrating the day's news. From this corps of newsmen a continual stream of atrocity stories flowed.

Hospitals were invaded, and inmates were lined up and shot while helpless women and children looked on, news articles reported. Men, women and children were found dead in heaps by the roadside, victims of famine and disease. Each news account was illustrated with pen sketches made by an artist from the impression obtained from the news report.

The *World* carried news stories telling also about atrocities perpetrated on Americans. Victims were mutilated after being shot down. In daily editorials dealing with Spanish atrocities, the *World* urged the President to intervene to put a stop "to the slaughter of innocent women and children. . . . ".

WORLD'S PART

General Weyler charged that the *World*'s reporter, James Creelman, was misrepresenting facts in Cuba, and the official sent a commission to investigate conditions in the camps. Following its reports, General Weyler issued an order banishing Creelman from the island. Creelman charged that his offense was that he refused to print false news issued by the general staff of the Spanish army in Cuba.

During this period the *World* carried many illustrations, most of them pen sketches with some photographic reproductions intending to show the results of General Weyler's policy and Spanish cruelties. Many *World* Sunday supplements printed dramatic pictures of Cuban conditions. One large illustration on November 18, 1896, depicted a Cuban soldier with forty-two body wounds, said to have been caused by Spanish machetes.

Cartoons dealing with the Cuban situation were used frequently. One of the cartoons on November 9, 1897, showed "famine" in the form of a hungry lion devouring an emaciated woman and child. The cartoon carried the title, "And Spain Calls This War."

HEARST'S ROLE IN CONFLICT SIGNIFICANT

Hearst's *Journal,* meanwhile, played an important part in inflaming the American public against Spain. Hearst came into New York in the fall of 1895, but it was not until 1896 that he began a determined campaign for the Cubans. By 1897 the *Journal* began to outdo the Pulitzer paper in obtaining sensational news. Richard Harding Davis, already a well-known correspondent, and Frederic Remington, one of the most celebrated newspaper "artists" of the time, were sent by the *Journal* to Cuba in January, 1897, with a vessel at their disposal.

Reports Spanish Atrocities

One of Davis' outstanding dispatches concerned the Olivette affair. Davis wrote of a refined, young American woman being stripped and searched on the U. S. S. *Olivette* by the brutal Spaniards. The illustrations were risqué. The political effect was immediate. A dispatch said that Senator Cameron would introduce a resolution in Congress dealing with the matter of Spain's searching women. The *World* was so provoked by the *Journal*'s scoop that it attempted show up the fake by producing the girl, who denied the story. Reporter Davis then explained to *Journal* readers that the girl was disrobed by the police matron in the privacy of a stateroom. Reporters said the picture was a fiction of artist Remington's imagination.

Remington, the *Journal* artist, informed Hearst that he could find no more atrocities to sketch in Cuba. Remington added that he would like to return to New York. Hearst replied: "Please remain. You furnish the pictures. I'll furnish the war."

The Hearst paper increased its circulation rapidly during this period. The *Evening Journal* was started September 28, 1896, as an evening edition of the *Morning Journal,* which claimed a circulation of 407,000. In November, 1896, the *Journal* stated its combined circulation was 1,506,634. This figure included circulation of the Sunday *Journal* which exceeded 500,000.

With regard to recognizing Cuban belligerency, the *Journal* was even more vigorous in its prosecution of this cause than the *World.* By means of striking display of news stories, editorials and cartoons, the Hearst paper kept the Cuban question before the public, arguing persistently for recognition of independence of the island and for intervention of the United States. War with Spain would have been welcomed by the *Journal.*

The *Journal's* special correspondent in Madrid sent out dispatches dealing with Spain's alleged activity in war preparations. After Creelman went to Spain, news articles telling about the feeling in Spain toward the United States appeared frequently. One of these dispatches was displayed with a front-page headline:

CRISIS IN SPAIN ALMOST AT HAND, WHOLE
NATION IS THRILLED WITH OVERPOWERING
SENSE OF IMPENDING DISASTER

News Events Exploited

The *Journal* exploited, during 1897 and early 1898, a series of news events which aroused public feeling against Spain. These were the Ruiz affair, the Cisneros rescue and the De Lôme letter. Hearst made the most of each event to antagonize the public against Spain and to develop sympathy for the Cubans.

The *Journal* found in the incident of Ricardo Ruiz, a Cuban dentist, an unusual opportunity to steer feelings of hostility against Spain. Ruiz had participated in the Cuban revolt of 1868 to 1878, then had come to the United States where he had taken out naturalization papers. Ruiz then returned to Cuba, married, reared a family and practiced dentistry. He was arrested on the charge of participating in a train robbery about the time of the rising interest in Cuba. Ruiz was found dead in his prison cell. When Hearst reporters found out about Ruiz, immediately the *Journal* blazoned on February 20, 1897:

AMERICAN SLAIN IN A SPANISH JAIL

For days the daily carried Ruiz news dispatches prominently displayed. Hearst said there was strong evidence to show that Ruiz was murdered in his cell by a Spanish policeman.

The Cisneros case had even greater emotional appeal. Evangelina Cisneros was a niece of Cuba President Cisneros Betancourt, who headed the civil government of the rebels. She was charged with having lured Colonel Berris, military governor of the Isle of Pines, to her house where hidden men killed him. The *Journal,* however, contended on August 17, 1897, that Miss Cisneros was the most beautiful girl in all Cuba and that her innocence and beauty had "excited the lust" of the governor, a nephew of the prime minister of Spain. Colonel Berris, according to the *Journal* account, offered protection to the girl's father "at the price of her honor." Miss Cisneros, the *Journal* related, turned from the brute in horror and told her friends, who planned his death.

She was convicted of sedition by a Spanish court martial. The Hearst paper reported that she was in imminent danger of being sent to Spain's African penal settlement for twenty years, but she was sent to a Cuban jail. The daily secured the aid of hundreds of prominent women throughout the country to protest her sentence.

After Miss Cisneros had spent many months in jail and innumerable articles had been published about her, the most thrilling incident of all occurred. The *Journal* hinted that a reporter was secretly sent from New York with orders to secure her escape. On October 10, the *Journal* announced that Miss Cisneros, the Cuban girl martyr, had been rescued by the *Journal's* Karl Decker. The paper proclaimed, "An American Newspaper Accomplishes at a Single Stroke What the Best Efforts of Diplomacy Failed Utterly to Bring About in Many Months."

Most of the front page of the paper was filled by two drawings, showing "Miss Cisneros Before and After Fifteen Months of Incarceration." On one side of the page was a beautiful girl; on the other, a worn-looking woman. Decker had rescued her by climbing to the roof of a building adjoining the jail. He recounted how he leaned over the broken and ancient rusted window bar. Miss Cisneros leaned out of her cell and Decker pulled. She was thus rescued, smuggled off the island and then brought to New York.

Hearst ordered a gigantic celebration for the Cuban girl in Madison Square Garden, followed by a reception at Delmonico's famous restaurant. Hearst's staff then arranged to have Miss Cisneros taken to the White House, where she was introduced to President McKinley, who gave the exploit his unofficial blessing. In a large front-page picture, the *Journal* showed Miss Cisneros shaking hands with the President.

Newspapers all over the United States used Associated Press dispatches telling of the *Journal's* rescue of Miss Cisneros. The event and news and pictorial coverage helped arouse emotional feelings of the public against Spain.

The De Lôme incident directly affected diplomatic relations between the United States and Spain and probably contributed more than any single event, prior to the sinking of the Battleship *Maine,* toward causing opposition to Spain. A member of the Cuban Junta, or a Hearst agent had "abstracted" from the Havana post office a letter written by Ambassador Dupuy de Lôme, Spain's ambassador to Washington. It was a personal letter, which the Ambassador could have, but had not, entrusted to his diplomatic pouch. It was addressed to Jose Canalijas y Mendez, editor of the *El Heraldo de Madrid.* The Spanish minister called McKinley a "low politician catering to the rabble." The passage:

> Besides the natural and inevitable coarseness with which he (McKinley) repeats all that the press and public opinion has said of Weyler, it shows once more that McKinley is weak and catering to the rabble, and besides, a low politician, who desires to leave a door open to me and to stand well with the jingoes of his party.

The contents of the De Lôme letter were sent by the Associated Press to member papers, which featured the incident. Several news services brought additional information to these papers. Various papers after publishing the news articles printed editorials demanding that De Lôme resign. The *Indianapolis* (Indiana) *Journal* commented that "it is not probable that the De Lôme incident will lead to war with Spain but it is possible."

The De Lôme incident created a sensation in Washington and Chicago. De Lôme was not sent back to Spain by the government of the United States, but he resigned two days after the letter was published. His resignation was accepted by the Spanish government.

EXPLOSION OF BATTLESHIP MAINE PROVIDES SPARK

The U. S. S. *Maine* was ordered to Havana on January 24, 1898, on a friendly visit, as there had been riots in the city, and United States citizens and their property were endangered. Most New York papers were jubilant. The *World* said the day of Cuban deliverance was near and war was close at hand.

In the Havana harbor on the night of February 15, 1898, the *Maine* exploded. Two hundred and sixty seamen were killed. This was the biggest news event since the assassination of President Garfield in 1881. Although the *World* and the *Journal* had used striking headlines for months, the sinking of the *Maine* may be said to have fixed definitely

$50,000 REWARD.—WHO DESTROYED THE MAINE?—$50,000 REWARD.

EDITION FOR GREATER NEW YORK

NEW YORK JOURNAL

AND ADVERTISER.

NEW YORK, THURSDAY, FEBRUARY 17, 1898.—16 PAGES. PRICE ONE CENT

DESTRUCTION OF THE WAR SHIP MAINE WAS THE WORK OF AN ENEMY.

$50,000!

$50,000 REWARD!

For the Detection of the Perpetrator of the Maine Outrage!

Assistant Secretary Roosevelt Convinced the Explosion of the War Ship Was Not an Accident.

The Journal Offers $50,000 Reward for the Conviction of the Criminals Who Sent 258 American Sailors to Their Death. Naval Officers Unanimous That the Ship Was Destroyed on Purpose.

$50,000!

$50,000 REWARD!

For the Detection of the Perpetrator of the Maine Outrage!

NAVAL OFFICERS THINK THE MAINE WAS DESTROYED BY A SPANISH MINE.

Hidden Mine or a Sunken Torpedo Believed to Have Been the Weapon Used Against the American Man-of-War---Officers and Men Tell Thrilling Stories of Being Blown Into the Air Amid a Mass of Shattered Steel and Exploding Shells---Survivors Brought to Key West Scout the Idea of Accident---Spanish Officials Protest Too Much---Our Cabinet Orders a Searching Inquiry---Journal Sends Divers to Havana to Report Upon the Condition of the Wreck.

Was the Vessel Anchored Over a Mine?

BY CAPTAIN E. L. ZALINSKI, U. S. A.

(Captain Zalinski is the inventor of the famous dynamite gun, which would be the principal factor in our coast defence in case of war.)

Assistant Secretary of the Navy Theodore Roosevelt says he is convinced that the destruction of the Maine in Havana Harbor was not an accident.

The Journal offers a reward of $50,000 for exclusive evidence that will convict the person, persons or Government criminally responsible for the destruction of the American battle ship and the death of 258 of its crew.

The suspicion that the Maine was deliberately blown up grows stronger every hour. Not a single fact to the contrary has been produced.

Captain Sigsbee, of the Maine, and Consul-General Lee both urge that public opinion be suspended until they have completed their investigation. They are taking the course of tactful men who are convinced that there has been treachery.

Washington reports very late that Captain Sigsbee had feared some such event as a hidden mine. The English cipher code was used all day yesterday by the naval officers in cabling instead of the usual American code.

Figure 47. The *New York Journal* Featured the Destruction of the *U. S. S. Maine* with Startling Makeup. A banner head across the entire page of the paper topped the news. Note the "skyrocket" head across the top of the page announcing the $50,000 reward. Hearst editors centered the secondary head in the middle of the page and flanked it with two boxes. The eight-column picture of the *Maine* also shows the location of the possible mine. The news story begins at the bottom of the page. The new, daring makeup set in motion a typographical trend, which, while not followed immediately, later influenced American journalism extensively.

the beginning of the practice by most American newspapers of utilizing heavy type across several columns in displaying significant news.

Immediately following destruction of the warship, the United States government appointed a Court of Inquiry to investigate the disaster and to determine its cause. The court's report, however, was not made public until late in March, six weeks after the catastrophe.

Meanwhile, during this period the *World*, the *Journal* and other papers continued to exploit the event, carrying news accounts daily of reported preparation for war and of expected findings of the court of inquiry. The *World* emphasized the work of its own "special investigators" and announced that their discoveries proved that a submarine mine caused the warship's destruction. One heading, February 26, cried out:

WAR SPIRIT RISING FROM THE WORLD'S EVIDENCE

Editorially, the *World* did not advocate war even if the explosion proved to be an act of an irresponsible Spaniard but said it would hold Spain to account. The only atonement adequate for such a deed would be liberation of Cuba. If Spain refused, war must follow, the *World* declared on February 27 and March 2 and 3. The Spanish warship *Vizcaya* was sent on a friendly visit to the New York harbor, but the *World* pointed to possible danger to homes in Brooklyn. In other Sunday feature articles, *World* reporters described elaborate preparations of the government to improve coastal defenses for a war.

After the *Maine* disaster the *Journal* reached greater heights than ever before. Following the explosion the *Journal* published a suppressed cable message from Captain Sigsbee, of the *Maine*, to the Secretary of the Navy, a message which said the vessel was "not blown up by accident." There is no evidence for the dispatch, historians say. The *Journal* also asserted that United States divers had uncovered evidence showing proofs of treachery. Actually, divers had sought for victims, but it was not until several weeks later that inspection of the wreckage was begun. The *Journal*'s fake news articles were carried by the Associated Press. The *Journal* offered fifty thousand dollars for detection of the perpetrators of the deed and began to raise funds to build a monument in memory of the *Maine* victims.

The Hearst paper now started the war scare in earnest. One of Hearst's boldest strokes was to send a congressional committee, composed of a number of Senators and Representatives, aboard his yacht to get firsthand information in Cuba. Each member contributed articles to the *Journal*, describing suffering and privations of people on the island. Following the inspection trips to Cuba, the "commissioners" reported in speeches before Congress the terrible conditions on the island, asserting that newspaper accounts were not exaggerated.

Long before the Court of Inquiry made its report, the *Journal* announced the court's verdict was that "Spain is Guilty."

The Court of Inquiry finally made its report. It said the disaster resulted from external causes, but the court did not fix responsibility. Disappointed over the decision, the *World* reiterated that Spain planted the mine. It declared: "If Spain will not punish the miscreants, we must punish Spain. The explosion was an Act of War." The *Journal* emphasized that "Suppressed testimony shows Spain is guilty of blowing up the Maine."

Though destruction of the *Maine* did not plunge the nation into an immediate war, it created a situation from which escape was well-nigh impossible. President McKinley had been attempting a solution through diplomatic pressure but that suffered a serious blow. The public was aroused to a high pitch of excitement. Interventionists were stimulated to renewed activity by the event.

The emotional press did not get by without scalding criticism from other editors. E. L. Godkin, of the New York *Evening Post* and the *Nation,* said that "during the present war crisis, the newspapers' lying with a view of promoting the outbreak of war, has excited the disgust and reprobation of all intelligent people." But the *World* did not care. Its circulation jumped from eight hundred thousand to one million for both morning and evening editions during the controversy leading up to the war.

MCKINLEY'S ATTITUDE

McKinley's attitude toward Spain had been conciliatory until his message to Congress in April. He had instructed, on March 27, 1898, the United States Minister to Spain, S. L. Woodford, to tell Madrid that the United States did not seek acquisition of Cuba but immediate peace. President McKinley urged establishment of an armistice on the island until October 1 and immediate revocation of the Concentration Order. The Spanish government replied that it would submit to arbitration differences arising over the sinking of the *Maine* and that the reconcentration order relating to camps had already been revoked. An armistice would be granted only if the insurgents asked for it.

On April 9, Minister Woodford was able to cable that an armistice had been granted to take place at once. The next day he cabled the

President that peace could be secured by negotiations, and the Spanish government would give autonomy to the insurgents, or recognition of independence of the island, or cession of the island to the United States. He related that the President could "win the fight on your own lines." This indicated a complete surrender by Spain.

But the record shows that President McKinley ignored the cable. He gave into those who were pressuring for war. Public opinion had been aroused too far. The next day, April 11, McKinley went to Congress to place the facts before the representatives. He made only passing mention of the Woodford cable of the day before. He said nothing of what was, in effect, Spain's complete surrender. Perhaps he had no faith in the Spanish government's sincerity, or in Spain's ability to carry out its program in view of hostile Spanish public opinion. President McKinley was also tired of fighting the American jingoes, the sensational press and some of his fellow Republicans. Patriotism, economics and journalism had combined to produce a war. Now the tide was too strong, it could not be checked.

The *World*, on April 17, 1898, bannered the congressional resolution:

DECLARATION OF WAR

The paper's circulation jumped to 1,300,000.

Three New York papers had demanded war, the *World*, the *Journal* and the *Sun*. They were not alone. Also strongly interventionist were the *Chicago Tribune*, *New Orleans Times-Democrat*, *Atlanta Constitution* and *Indianapolis Journal*. Oustanding newspapers such as the *New York Times*, *Chicago Daily News* and *Boston Transcript* were opposed to an open conflict.

PRESS COVERAGE OF WAR EXPENSIVE

Publishers and editors recognized the news value and public interest in the Spanish War. According to biographer Don Seitz, Pulitzer said he "rather liked the idea of the war, not a big one, but one that would arouse interest and give him a chance to gauge the reflex of his circulation figures." This was the first war which had been fought since the Civil War. Editors of New York and other dailies sent their best reporters, photographers and artists to tell about land and naval battles. Richard Harding Davis, Creelman and Scovel, already mentioned, and Frank Norris and Stephen Crane, novelists, also were sent as correspondents.

While other publishers did not get into the battle as did Hearst, their reporters covered the news thoroughly. Correspondents had to get

WORLD CIRCULATION, 1,043,829

The World.

"Circulation Books Open to All."

THE WORLD'S WANT GROWTH. 8,300 More In March Than Last Year.

NEW YORK, SUNDAY, APRIL 17, 1898.

PRICE FIVE CENTS.

DECLARATION OF WAR!

Both Houses of Congress Have Said that Spain Must Get Off This Continent AT ONCE!

McKinley Takes No Stock in the Cuban Republic and Also Thinks Congress Cannot Declare in Its Favor.

THE PRESIDENT ALONE, HE BELIEVES, HAS THE RIGHT TO RECOGNIZE IT.

He Holds that the Entire People of the Island, Not a Faction, Should Decide Their Form of Government.

The Republic of Cuba Is Recognized by a Vote of the Senate of the United States.

ADOPTION OF TURPIE RESOLUTION CLEARS UP THE ATMOSPHERE.

Hope of Peace Has Been Abandoned by the President—House Will Take Speedy Action.

SENATE RESOLUTIONS TO RECOGNIZE CUBAN INDEPENDENCE AND EXPEL SPANISH GOVERNMENT FROM THE ISLAND.

RESOLVED,

That the people of the island of Cuba are and of right ought to be free and independent, and that the Government of the United States hereby recognizes the Republic of Cuba as the true and lawful Government of that island.

Second, That it is the duty of the United States to demand, and that the Government of the United States does hereby demand, that the Government of Spain at once relinquish its authority and government in the island of Cuba and withdraw its land and naval forces from Cuba and Cuban waters.

Third, That the President of the United States be, and he hereby is, DIRECTED AND EMPOWERED TO USE THE ENTIRE LAND AND NAVAL FORCES OF THE UNITED STATES and to call into the actual service of the United States the militia of the several States to such extent as may be necessary to carry these resolutions into effect.

"Fourth, That the United States hereby disclaims any disposition or intention to exercise sovereignty, jurisdiction or control over said island, except for the pacification thereof, and asserts its determination when that is accomplished to leave the government and the control of the island to the people."

SENATORS DISCUSSING THE CUBAN RESOLUTIONS.

IS INEVITABLE, AND WE WANT IT NOW."

SPANISH FLOTILLA SPIED IN ENGLISH CHANNEL.

Figure 48. Spanish-American War Front Page. The Spanish-American War introduced large horizontal headlines and remade the front page of the American newspaper. The front page was never the same again. The journalistic duel between Joseph Pulitzer of the *New York World* and William Randolph Hearst of the *New York Journal* forced each of these rivals to produce a more powerful front page than his competitor. The largest type in the composing room was brought out to tell the story of the Spanish-American War. Banner headlines were employed for maximum appeal. Column rules were broken to introduce the two- and three-column headline. Large illustrations gave the page greater impact. In bold headlines the *New York World* told its readers about the declaration of war.

the news to Key West, Florida from where the stories were transmitted by cable to New York. Reporters were also with the Navy, as they accompanied Admiral Dewey to Manila and Admiral Schley to Havana.

Costs of reporting and transmitting news were high for publishers, but most of them thought the expenditure worth it. The *Journal* spent $500,000 on the war. People waited eagerly for Hearst dailies as well as for other papers in every part of the country. Some metropolitan publishers issued many editions every day; Hearst's *Journals*, morning and evening, produced forty editions daily.

The war lasted four months. Pulitzer was sorry he had gotten into the fight with Hearst and that the war had come. Cable expenses were great; circulation was wasteful because the readership was not held.

HEADLINES WIDENED

Another misery for the owner that grew out of the war was the headline in huge type. These headlines were invented by Foster Coates, managing editor of the *Evening World* during this period. They made a great hit with the public but not with Mr. Pulitzer. Coates used them in a conflict of extras with Hearst's *Evening Journal* which Arthur Brisbane now edited. Coates improved the big block letters by ornamenting them with stars and stripes.

Headlines in the Spanish-American War were the climax of a trend toward larger and bolder headlines which began at the end of the 1880s. On extraordinary occasions two-column headlines had been used before. Now in the sensational press more striking effects were desired. Pulitzer used banners first in his Sunday paper to attract attention to sensational features. The Spanish-American War produced the first regularly used "banner," a headline stretching across the entire top of the page. For weeks during the crisis preceding actual outbreak of the war, the *World* flamed with its attention-arousing, interest-provoking headlines that propagandized for war. Banner headlines grew from a half inch high to one and a half inches.

The *World* shouted:

SPAIN MUST CHOOSE BETWEEN PEACE AND WAR!
PRESIDENT AND CONGRESS NOW UNITED FOR WAR

Pulitzer endured the screaming typography until the end of the fighting, then he ordered his foreman to collect all large letters and melt them. This the foreman did, but they refused to stay dead. The rival sheet, the *Journal,* continued their use with profit, and after a short subsidence they reappeared to stay not only in the *Evening World* but in afternoon papers generally.

Although large headlines and banners were first used regularly by the *World,* Hearst's *Journal* displayed a more bizarre makeup and produced more striking displays than his rival. Inside banners were used frequently, giving a powerful effect. On February 25, 1898, the fourth and fifth pages consisted of a double spread in colors, with the headline, "One United Country." The *Journal* editors experimented with a great many kinds of large heavy headlines each day, seeking to get variety, something new. On April 17, the *Journal* used three-inch type, probably the largest in history up to that time:

SENATE DECLARES FOR
REPUBLIC'S RECOGNITION
BY A TWO THIRD'S VOTE

CUBA FREE!

The Spanish-American War experience proved the value of the headline as a selling feature of the paper.

But newspaper promotion of the Spanish-American War went down in history, with later historians placing the entire blame on yellow press publishers. Pulitzer and Hearst led the press, but Dana's *Sun,* Bennett's *Herald,* Medill's *Chicago Tribune* and many other powerful papers in all parts of the nation contributed their share. Pulitzer originally set the pace in exploiting the Cuban rebellion, only to be outstripped by Hearst and beaten at his own practices.

Chapter 26

Struggles of Expanding News Associations

Feeding a steady stream of news into newspaper offices in all the states were news-gathering agencies. Wire services enabled daily papers in all parts of the far-flung country to get international and national news quickly. This tended to stimulate the appetite for news and contributed no little to the growth of the newspapers. It helped keep Americans informed about current events. Wire services were depended on by most newspapers for information about events beyond their communities since only relatively few large journals could afford their own correspondents. Control of the wire service meant that someone might shape the thinking of newspaper readers everywhere.

ASSOCIATED PRESS EXPANDS RAPIDLY

By Atlantic cable, by Cuban telegraph, by ship from South America, by clipper from China and by American telegraph, news flowed into the New York office of the Associated Press in the early decades after the Civil War. About thirty-five thousand words came in daily from London, Paris, Washington and San Francisco.

At AP headquarters on Broadway, news was hastily copied on thin manifold sheets. One of these was given to each New York member of the AP, and then the news either was sent over the wires or given to New York agents of client newspapers in all parts of the country. A fifteen hundred-word report of the world events was moved to larger papers, while smaller ones received a condensed report. The AP service went to about two hundred papers in the 1870s; others used the stereotyped plates of the American Press Association, which forwarded the news by train.

Desiring to speed up service by making its reportorial copy more readable to telegraphers, the AP began installation of typewriters in 1884. It put part-time men on as stringers to get more adequate and faster coverage, and it began to develop the summary factual lead of news stories to give the busy reader the nub of the events. The condensation also saved telegraph tolls.

Stories sent over the AP circuits were not always easy to get. Often reports of the association demonstrated extraordinary courage and persistence in securing the news. In May, 1889, information reached the AP offices that a dam had broken and that waters were flooding Johnstown, Pennsylvania. Telegraph and telephone lines were crippled. In Pittsburgh, the nearest large city, William Connolly and a telegrapher prepared to go to Johnstown. They inquired about train service but learned that no trains were going through. The AP men then hired a special engine and car to take them to Johnstown.

Accompanied by Pittsburgh newspapermen and Clarence Wetmore, a *New York World* special correspondent, the AP men started out. The train roared down the tracks; as it approached the stricken city, water began to mount. Soon water reached the driving wheels, and the engineer said he could go no farther. This failed to stop Connolly. He set out in the water to find other means of transportation and succeeded finally in employing for fifty dollars a farmer with a wagon to take him and other reporters miles across the mountains. After many hours of slow traveling, the little brigade of newsmen came to within three miles of the city. No wagon could go farther. The newspapermen now struggled through mud and debris to reach the town. They found it completely destroyed; 2,200 were killed. Buildings were torn from their foundations.

Connolly scribbled his story, but how was he to get it out? A short distance from town the *New York World* reporter found a telegraph lineman on a pole sending railroad messages on a hand telegraph set to his home office. He refused to send the AP story, but Wetmore persuaded him to check with his office for permission. This was done, and the telegraph company allowed the AP stories and other dispatches to go through.

Meanwhile, internal problems of the AP became critical. Since organization of the New York Associated Press in the 1840s by six New York city publishers, control had remained in their hands, for then the New York newspapers were the largest and most powerful, dominating American journalism. The trans-Atlantic cable was successfully completed in 1866 after a number of failures, but cablegram costs for news transmission from Europe were heavy. The telegraph was increasingly used in the United States for news, especially from Washington, and this proved expensive. To carry on the work of the AP, New York papers paid one-third the costs, the dailies outside of that city, the remaining two-thirds.

Loose federations of newspapers, it will be recalled, had grown up in various regions of the United States to promote their interests. The Philadelphia Associated Press, the Western Associated Press, the Southern Associated Press, the New England and the New York State groups and others were formed before, during and after the Civil War. Of these groups, most vigorous was the Western Associated Press which developed because of multiplication of journals in the western region and rapid growth of its metropolitan papers.

After the Civil War, western publishers felt it was a psychological moment to come to New York where they would seek further concessions and more voice in the AP wire service at its source. They objected to having a New York angle put on all news reports. Western publishers felt that commercial news about shipping and boat disasters was not especially interesting or important for inland readers. They also resented the New Yorkers' encouragement of new papers in the West while discouraging other publishers from starting journals in New York.

Meanwhile, Daniel H. Craig, chief agent of the New York Associated Press, made plans for the establishment of his own United States and European News Association. He was encouraged to do so by the Western Union telegraph company officials. When AP members learned of Craig's plans, the directors fired him. Craig proceeded to found his own news agency and to get a monopoly of the Atlantic cable and the national telegraph lines. He offered lower rates and better reports and solicited clients everywhere. The Western Associated Press considered aligning with Craig and they used the new agency as a threat to the New York Associated Press.

Battle for better news service and greater equality in the voice of the New York Associated Press began. Both New York and Western AP groups lined up for the conflict and marshalled their forces. Finding too burdensome the problem of supplying Craig's agency and the New York Press Association with telegraph services, Western Union forced peace on the New York and the Western Press Associations.

A compromise was worked out in 1867, whereby the western papers received some concessions. They obtained a better news report and received permission to continue a news representative in the New York AP office but was to furnish western news to the New York AP agent in Cleveland or Pittsburgh. The Western AP was to control franchises west of the Alleghenies and north of the Ohio River. New York publishers, however, still retained control over the foreign and domestic news report. The AP withdrew from Craig's news service which soon collapsed.

Some years passed. Western publishers again asked for full partnership. An agreement was reached for a five-man board. It was ratified in 1883. A five-year contract was signed, and the New York AP named Charles A. Dana, editor of the *Sun*, as chairman of the Joint Executive Committee. Dana thus held the control and the veto power for the entire organization. Peace came to the AP again.

Throughout these decades suspicion was aroused regarding: (1) the AP's connection with the Western Union Telegraph Company in an attempt to build up a monopoly similar to those developing in industry and commerce; (2) the AP's being controlled by the telegraph company, or its own managers to manipulate public opinion on elections and in other controversial issues.

General agent Simonton answered some of these charges in 1879 before a Senate committee investigating the AP. Simonton declared that the AP was a private business, carried on under the same legal and constitutional rights which permit any one paper to collect or publish its local news. It operated under no franchise from the government, he said, and no congressional power could take away its tools.

Committee hearings produced no results, nor was any action taken. But the charges did not die. During the 1880s the public sensed some unsavory relationships. Jay Gould, president of Western Union, was accused of manipulating returns in the election of 1884, when Republican Blaine, whom he favored, ran against Democrat Cleveland. Oliver Gramling, historian of the AP, in his *AP, The Story of News,* asserted that "a handful of men in charge of the monopoly" continued to take liberties with the news whenever it dealt with politics, economics or other controversial issues.

(FIRST) UNITED PRESS ORGANIZED

Organization of the first *United Press* in 1882 eventually had important effects on the established New York AP which had already weathered many storms. To service many newspapers which did not take the New York AP wire, Walter Polk Phillips with Francis X. Schoonmaker as general agent organized the United Press. Phillips made every effort to improve the service of this private news company and recruited a number of new and powerful clients. He organized the Cable News Company to get foreign dispatches. Although he had to depend on Western Union, he made considerable progress. His backers, it was known, were John R. Walsh, part owner of the *Chicago Herald,* and

William Laffan, business manager of the *New York Sun.* At this time it will be recalled, Charles A. Dana, editor of the *Sun,* was chairman of the AP Joint Executive Committee, operating both the New York AP and the Western AP.

BATTLE OF THE AP VS. FIRST UP

In the latter 1880s some publishers of the Western AP became suspicious of connections between the United Press and AP's own Joint Executive Committee. These western publishers believed that some mysterious and unhealthy arrangements were being made between the UP and the AP Executive Committee. Victor Lawson, of the *Chicago Daily News,* saw that financial news was being phrased or delayed so that interested persons were profiting in the millions.

The Western AP decided on an official inquiry in 1890. Lawson headed the investigating committee. His report, made in August, 1891, stunned the other publishers. Lawson presented evidence which pointed to the fact that Walsh, Laffan and Phillips were in control of the country's news-gathering agencies, both the AP and the UP.

This control had been accomplished by a trust agreement between the United Press and members of the Joint Committee of the AP. Officials of the United Press gave stock valued at $367,000 as a gift to AP committee members. Dana of the *Sun,* Whitelaw Reid of the *Tribune* and Laffan of the *Sun* received $72,500 each; while the general manager of the AP and two representatives of the Western AP received $50,000 each.

When the investigating committee of the Western AP discovered the facts about the secret agreement, a fight to the finish for control of the nation's dominant news-gathering facilities began. The United Press eventually lost the fight and then filed a petition in bankruptcy. It sent out the last dispatch in March, 1897. Dana rejected an invitation to bring his *Sun* into the AP and began his own costly Laffan News Service.

The Associated Press had won the battle of the news association giants.

MONOPOLY SUIT AGAINST AP WON

After this successful struggle the AP was faced with another serious problem. The *Chicago Inter-Ocean* had used the New York AP's dispatches, violating the rule of the new Associated Press of Illinois which prohibited this. The AP of Illinois consequently desired to expel the

Chicago paper from membership. Not wanting to lose its valuable franchise, the *Inter-Ocean* fought back. It secured an injunction in January, 1898, to restrain the AP of Illinois from interrupting the *Inter-Ocean*'s reception and use of the news from the AP of Illinois. The first court decided in favor of the AP of Illinois and the news association canceled the paper's membership. The *Inter-Ocean* appealed the case to higher courts.

In February, 1900, the Supreme Court of Illinois reversed the lower court. The judge declared the AP was a public utility. The Chicago paper was given back its membership in the AP and was awarded $40,500 for damages.

Under the ruling the AP of Illinois had to admit to membership any paper that desired it, providing the publisher could pay the costs. This created a difficult situation, for the AP franchises were valuable, but under this ruling would become worthless from the viewpoint of the current AP members.

The AP lawyers searched for an answer to this problem and found it in New York laws. New York enabled stock exchanges, social clubs, charities and other organizations not organized for profit, to incorporate. Such groups controlled the rules and regulations admitting persons to membership. This seemed to be what the AP, a nonprofit organization, needed. A new Associated Press of New York was incorporated, and it purchased the property and business of the AP of Illinois. The old AP organization wired its last dispatch on September 30, 1900. Each member of the new AP could purchase one to forty bonds of the organization at twenty-five dollars each.

GROWTH OF THE ASSOCIATED PRESS MARKED

Growth of the AP is seen in the following figures. In 1880 the AP had 355 members: 228 morning and 127 evening. By 1900 its membership had increased to 690. Its first leased wire, 264 miles, was started in 1884. By the turn of the century it had about 30,000 miles of leased wire for its dispatches. It sent out 35,000 words daily in the 1870s; at the end of the era they reached 50,000. Cost of the AP service amounted to $1,900,000 at the end of the century.

HASSON'S AGENCY STRUGGLES FOR PLACE

The AP was not without competitors during the decades after the Civil War. We have already traced the beginnings of Craig's United States and European News Association, which lasted only a short time.

That there was some basis for the charge that the telegraph company had a monopoly and had close connections with the AP is seen in the history of the news agency John Hasson formed. This newsman organized the Hasson News Association in 1869 to service afternoon papers dissatisfied with the New York AP, which favored the morning sheets. Hasson's agency became the American Press Association in 1870 and soon had eighty-four clients. It reorganized as the National Associated Press in 1877. Its chief trouble was poor telegraphic service from an independent wire company, the Atlantic and Pacific Telegraph Company, on which it depended.

When the Western Union Telegraph Company absorbed the Atlantic and Pacific Telegraph Company, Western Union officials raised the rates sky high. This action adversely affected the National Associated Press. This press service was able to keep going until it was absorbed a few years later by a new and powerful rival, the United Press.

It will be noted that all these associations had the word *national* or *united* or *American* in their titles, indicating close integration of the country as well as journalism, and its development on a national scale.

SCRIPPS ORGANIZES OWN SERVICE

Meanwhile, Scripps developed his own news association to furnish news to Scripps papers. When the dispute between the Associated Press and the United Press, a rival news service, broke out, Scripps did not want to participate in the fight and saw advantages of an independent news-gathering organization. At this time, J. B. Shale, another enterprising newsman, also saw possibilities in such an organization, so he formed the Publishers' Press Association. Scripps went to meet Shale in New York where Shale had his headquarters. The two men entered an agreement for exchange of news, with the Scripps-McRae papers gathering western news and the Publishers' Press Association eastern news. They were to cooperate with the *New York Sun* in getting cable news from abroad. Scripps later consolidated the Scripps-McRae news services with Publishers' Press Association to form a new United Press.

Chapter 27

Newspaper Syndicates and Chains Begin

PIONEER SYNDICATES LAUNCHED

In a period when newspapers were increasing the number of pages of their daily issues and the Sunday paper was becoming popular, it was natural that organizations would develop to syndicate news, features, photographs and cartoons to editors. Syndicates had become established already in England and France and were needed in America. They were economical and popular writers could be employed to build reader interest.

Early Attempts

Individual editors and publishers recognized this need before regular syndicates were organized. The *New York Sun* sold ready print or printed sheets of its attacks on politicians. The *New York Sun* later sold, to a selected list of newspapers, stories by such outstanding authors as Bret Harte and Henry James. Some New York newspapermen picked up extra money by writing weekly letters to out-of-town newspapers.

The first successful specialized company for supplying features to large dailies was Irving Bacheller's. In 1883 he dealt in short stories by prominent authors and correspondents. When publishers found this material successful in Sunday issues, they used more and more of it in their daily editions.

McClure's Syndicate Extends Idea

The man who made the syndicate successful and spread it to many more newspapers was Samuel S. McClure. A great merchandiser of fiction and nonfiction to the press, he bought literary products for reasonable prices and sold them to many newspapers at a profit. An expert in analyzing what would appeal to the public, he also had a keen business sense. McClure's life parallels the Horatio Alger legend and is similar to the story of other poor, immigrant boys who, seeing possibilities in providing a product or service, built large businesses from nothing. McClure's business happened to be literature, or reading matter. McClure came in when the reading market was expanding, with women especially proving to be a booming new class of readers. He found newspapers multiplying, their circulations increasing and the physical size of each edition expanding, especially the Sunday edition. Publishers needed additional readable material.

With his wife, McClure began a small syndicate business in their apartment in New York. In 1884, McClure had twenty-five dollars in the bank, but he had a big idea. He managed to secure contracts from some of the most popular authors and to uncover writers who were unknown except in out-of-the-way magazines. Jack London was one of these writers. McClure hopped the train and peddled the literary wares to newspapers along the coast. Short of funds, he borrowed even from his own writers.

These authors were impressed with McClure's great flow of words and his enthusiasm. Besides, he opened new markets for them. At the time book publishers provided the only solid outlets. *Harper's*, *Scribner's* and the *Century* magazine took a select few novels and paid poorly. McClure sized up the new reader market and concluded that the public wanted more realistic reading matter; consequently, he obtained stories of western life, of Pennsylvania coal fields, of factory workers in big cities.

McClure was always on the lookout for ideas for fiction and nonfiction. He read between twenty and thirty newspapers daily and about ten to twelve books a week. He was perpetually inquisitive, perpetually learning. He clipped newspapers, recognizing in various items of news, possibilities for fuller-length treatment for his syndicate.

McClure went to England to secure such famous writers as Rudyard Kipling, Robert Louis Stevenson, Conan Doyle and George Meredith. He made eight round trips to Europe and crisscrossed the country as many times to talk to writers and sell the syndicate to editors. When editors asked for women's features, he furnished feature articles and even wrote cooking recipes himself. He also began a "Youth Department."

At first he sent out five thousand words weekly; by 1887 he furnished fifty thousand words—short stories, serialized novels and special features—to editors. When he came to their offices, editors welcomed him because of the yawning empty columns they had to fill daily and on Sunday. McClure's idea was to get a brilliant smash each month and a blockbuster in November, the opening of the season.

McClure found that he had to pay heavily for good writers and that his income from newspapers was too small to earn him a large profit. By 1891 he grossed $100,000 but his expenses were almost that much. He decided to establish *McClure's Magazine,* which would print the best of the syndicated articles. The syndicate would thus supply material for the magazine which could become a thriving, profitable business. He therefore launched *McClure's* in 1892, a publication which will be discussed in the section on this type of periodical.

Newspapers Organize Own

Between 1895 and 1900 the *New York Herald,* the *World* and the *Journal* organized their own syndicates and supplied publishers with Sunday comics and features. The New York Herald Syndicate began in 1895 with a news bureau. Three years later the *World* began syndicating R. F. Outcault's comic cartoon, "Yellow Kid," when a number of papers asked for him. Soon Hearst organized his syndicate service and offered the popular cartoon, "Katzenjammer Kids" as well as articles by Dorothy Dix.

Syndicates made for a uniformity and standardization of all newspapers. A publisher could buy enough syndicated material, such as editorials, cartoons, features, add a few local stories and produce an interesting paper. The newspaper thus tended to become a tailor-made affair; the parts were made in New York and assembled locally.

Ready Print for Weeklies

Another influence contributing to standardization was the patent insides, or ready print. This had been used by the *New York Sun* before the Civil War. The *Sun* sold to newspapers printed sheets of its material, such as presidential messages. The method was used previously in England.

When a labor shortage developed in shops of several weeklies published near Milwaukee after the Civil War, their publishers appealed to the job office of the *Milwaukee Evening Wisconsin* to aid in getting out their sheets. The *Evening Wisconsin* filled two pages with reading matter from its own columns, printed these pages on one side of the sheet and shipped them to the country towns. There editors set enough local items and advertisements to fill the outside pages. The plan was successful. A. J. Aikens, part owner of the *Evening Wisconsin,* circularized other country papers, asking if they needed similar help. A number of country publishers responded favorably. Aikens also secured advertising from Milwaukee department stores for these patent insides, for the papers were near enough to Milwaukee to make them profitable advertising media.

CHAIN JOURNALISM EXTENDS

Chain journalism was one of the new and outstanding trends in Gilded Age journalism. If Standard Oil and railroads could combine to affect operating economies, so could an enterprising and ambitious newspaper publisher. He might command large capital, or he could build slowly, adding newspaper links to form a nationwide chain. Paper and machinery supplies, successful editorial features, news correspondence and cartoons could be bought in wholesale quantities with resultant savings not open to independent newspaper operators. Profits could be pooled to launch new ventures.

Before the turn of the century several publishers owned two papers, in some instances loosely connected, in other instances, more closely linked. Pulitzer thus operated two papers: the *St. Louis Post-Dispatch* and the *New York World;* Hearst had the *San Francisco Examiner* and the *New York Journal.* Ochs also owned two: the *Chattanooga Times* and the *New York Times.* Edward W. Scripps developed chain journalism further. By 1900 he owned nine dailies, the first extensive newspaper chain.

Chain journalism was to grow into a mighty force in the next period, but its foundations were laid at this time.

Chapter 28

Advertising Sells American Products

PRESSURE TO SELL INCREASES

During the decades following the Civil War, advertising developed more rapidly than before because American manufacturers faced a selling problem, especially in the 1880s and 1890s. Quantity production and invention of specialized machinery made manufacture of various products easy. Development of railroads and expresses speeded distribution. Shipping goods across the nation and even into small remote towns was no longer a problem. The greater income of thousands of families enabled them to purchase personal and household necessities and luxuries.

The great need was to get people to buy articles which they had not been habitually buying, either because their families had made the merchandise at home or because the goods had not been available in stores. Housewives who made their own dresses and household articles had to be told that factory-made merchandise purchased at the local store was just as good as, perhaps better than, the homemade variety. Advertising in journalistic media played an important role in that process.

The 300 per cent growth of press advertising showed the greater use being made of this selling media. It should be remembered that this was not an overnight growth. Advertising's general trend, in spite of setbacks, was upward and showed greater recognition of its value as a force in selling goods. Advertising revenue which amounted to more than $39 million in 1880, jumped to $145 million by 1904.

ADVERTISING CHANGES ARE MANY

In the decades between the Civil War and the end of the century, advertising changed immensely, and these changes made a greater appeal to the public and accelerated advertising growth. Typography was improved; content and style of advertising was altered, and use of slogans, jingles and pictures gave it more appeal. The amount of space employed was also increased to give advertisements greater effect.

Dark ages of typographical display, the period of the agate-size type and the single-column width in advertisements, ended in the late sixties and early seventies. Popular dailies then awoke to the necessity for greater freedom for advertisers in their efforts to get attention in the twelve-page papers.

Large, bold display had been used in France since the early 1850s. Advertisers there had used two and three columns and even the entire width of the page. At times the type ran 3 inches high. Paris stores were the first to use full-page space to tell about their offerings. American retailers followed this lead, another example of the diffusion of methods of journalism.

TABLE 22

Revenues of American Newspapers: Subscription, Advertising

	Total Amount of Advertising	Subscriptions	Percentage Advertising	Percentage Subscriptions
1880	$39,136,306	$49,872,768	44.0	56.0
1890	$71,243,361	$72,343,987	49.6	51.4
1899	$95,861,127	$70,298,691	54.6	45.4
1904	$145,514,591	$135,063,043	56.6	43.4

In New York, R. H. Macy, and Lord and Taylor, department stores, were pioneers in display soon after the close of the Civil War. They led the breakaway from agate type and the single-column ads to large type and double-column space.

In the 1890s was born the slogan style of advertising in newspapers and magazines. Drawn from billboards, where only a short phrase was possible, the slogan technique was adapted to regular newspaper and magazine advertising. One of the first and most famous was that of the Eastman Kodak Company. "You Press the Button—We Do the Rest." Another popular one of the period was Ivory Soap's "It Floats" and "99 44/100 per cent pure."

Human interest advertising copy was also evolved, with children being featured. Manufacturers of wool soap were consistent users of this appeal. Pictures to illustrate advertising made their way slowly. Patent medicine advertisers developed the copy and mechanics of advertising so that advertising was ready for the larger and more legitimate use by manufacturers. Toward the end of the period some magazines and newspapers began to ban quack medical ads from their columns.

NEW NATIONAL ADVERTISERS APPEAR

In the 1880s, in addition to patent medicinemakers, those who advertised on a national scale regularly were manufacturers of Sapolio Soap, $400,000; Royal Baking Powder with $500,000; Pears' Soap; and Ivory Soap. Kodak spent $750,000. By the end of the century a tabulation in *Press and Printer* showed the kinds of advertisers who were using periodicals of general circulation regularly. The total was 2,583. The roster of advertisers indicated the extent of industrialization of the United States. Medicines and remedies sold in drugstores topped the list with 425; 216 furniture and household manufacturers came next; followed by 193 wearing-apparel makers and 152 food and drink dealers. An annual appropriation of $25,000 could conduct a national advertising campaign at that time. In the larger class, individual annual expenditures of $100,000 could be counted by the score.

ADVERTISING AGENCIES MULTIPLY

Chief among the forces which began to build up advertising in this period was the steady growth of advertising agents. At the end of the Civil War there were about thirty agents in New York and half that number elsewhere who placed ads in newspapers for advertisers. By 1880 this number had increased considerably.

Agents continued to place advertising in newspapers and magazines on a hit-or-miss basis since no accurate list of newspapers existed. In 1869 George P. Rowell, an advertising agent, published the first continuously issued American newspaper directory, listing 5,411 publications with their circulations, calculated by systematic methods. Manufacturers could now have confidence in placing their advertisements, and so advertising grew. Rowell also inaugurated the plan of buying space in bulk on on an annual contract and retailing it to advertisers at a profit to himself. Aiding the newspaper broker was further development of the thin stereotype plates which enabled the advertiser to see his advertisement before it was printed. The plates were sent to many papers simultaneously.

RATIO OF ADVERTISING TO SUBSCRIPTION INCOME INCREASES

So great was the growth of advertising that each decade saw it creeping up on subscriptions as a source of revenue. By 1880 it reached 44 per cent of the total revenue; by 1899 it exceeded the income from subscriptions, for it was recorded at 54 per cent. In short, the balance between the two sources had shifted. More money was to be made from advertising than from subscriptions. The foresighted publisher could see that a large circulation was a necessity if big returns were to be derived. Eventually money would not be made from circulation directly, but from advertising which would follow the increased number of readers.

Chapter 29

Presses Turn Faster

MORE MECHANIZATION APPLIED TO NEWSPAPER PLANTS

As in previous eras, newspaper publishers utilized every new invention and every improvement in existing machinery that fertile brains of inventors could design. As in factories of the nation, mechanization of newspaper plants reached greater heights than ever before. Better, faster and more productive printing presses were made, and new auxiliary machinery to speed up and to cheapen the printing processes was introduced.

PRESS TECHNOLOGY ADVANCES RAPIDLY

Before the end of the Civil War, William Bullock had installed a press for the *Philadelphia Inquirer* that could print, or "perfect" both sides of a sheet of paper at once. For the first time a roll of paper, instead of single sheets, was fed into the press. It cut this roll into sheets *before* printing.

Following development of an English press that cut paper *after* printing, R. Hoe & Company in the United States patented a mechanism that would feed, print and cut the papers. By 1875 this Hoe press attained an average production capacity of twelve thousand to fourteen thousand newspapers an hour, but it had no folding device. Various newspaper printers now built folders, and while these hastened production, they were not perfected and lagged behind press development, retarding output for many years.

As advertising increased, newspapers increased the number of their pages. Now the publishers needed presses that would print an eight- or sixteen-page issue rapidly. In 1874 the Hoe Company turned its attention to manufacturing a "double-perfecting press" that delivered 10,000 sixteen-page papers per hour. If a smaller edition were needed the press could produce 20,000 eight-page papers per hour.

Demand for larger presses, however, was insatiable as circulation continued to expand, boosted by increasing population and rising commercial activity. Soon Hoe built a double supplement press which, by means of various devices, harnessed two presses together, placing one at right angles to the other in tandem style. This machine could deliver 20,000 ten-page papers per hour, or if advertising increased and more pages were required, 10,000 twenty-four-page papers an hour.

Also, when this double-equipment press fell far short of publishers' needs, especially for Sunday editions, larger and larger presses were developed. Presses were manufactured now in decks, one on top of the other, to save space. After the quadruple press and octuple presses also failed to meet mounting press needs, Hoe manufactured double presses. These enabled a publisher to issue an eighty, eighty-six or even one hundred twenty-eight-page daily. Prices of presses now ran from $40,000 to $80,000 each, which increased the capital required for large newspapers.

Instead of steam, electricity was now harnessed to drive the presses. But generators and motors in the 1880s were too small to produce power for the bigger presses. Hearst encouraged George Pancoast, his mechanical engineer, to experiment with electricity and, in 1896, had an effective motor.

Color presses were also added in the last decade of the century to make Sunday comics and supplements more appealing. The *New York Journal,* on April 27, 1897, was the first daily printed in two colors.

TYPESETTING MACHINES INTRODUCED

With increasing size of newspapers and development of presses, setting type by hand was laborious and relatively slow. More than forty patents for mechanisms that would set type were granted in 1880. These typesetters could be used in book printshops but not newspaper offices. Ottmar Mergenthaler, Baltimore signal device inventor, produced a working model which cast a line of type at a time. These lines could then be assembled for a column of type.

It was a historic day in the *New York Tribune* office when, in July, 1886, the first line of type was cast on the Mergenthaler Linotype machine. The Linotype revolutionized printing. It was comparable in importance to the first rotary press, for the Linotype transformed a hand operation to a mechanical one, and thereby speeded the printing process tremendously. The machine was adopted rapidly. By 1905, 8,018 Linotypes were casting type in newspaper offices. The machine could cast type six times faster than a compositer could set type.

Figure 49. Ottmar Mergenthaler and the Blower Linotype. Mergenthaler found the answer to the bottleneck in the composing room with his Linotype. Mergenthaler's first linecasting machine was used in 1884. It was crude, but it worked. By 1886, he had developed the bigger, more elaborate blower linotype machine, to be used regularly in the *New York Tribune* and other newspaper plants. (Used with permission of the Mergenthaler Linotype Company.)

Another machine which contributed to the printing process was the monotype. Patented by Tolbert Lanston in 1887, this machine supplemented the Linotype. The monotype cast type for hand-setting headlines, advertisements and other special work.

PICTURE-ENGRAVING PROCESS IMPROVED

Woodcuts had been used to great advantage by some illustrated weeklies, but woodcuts were crude as well as expensive, and they could not be produced fast enough for daily production. An etching or engraving process to reproduce on plates directly the drawings of artists was

TABLE 23

Newspaper Advances (1865-1900)

1. Editorial Department

    News
    - Local news coverage widens
    - Human interest features introduced
    - Washington correspondents increase
    - Press associations expand
    - Foreign correspondents employed

    Editorial Page
    - Revitalized in some papers
    - Weak in others

    Crusades developed
    - Based on (a) news, (b) editorials, (c) cartoons

    Pictures used more extensively (linecuts, halftones)
    - News pictures introduced
    - Cartoons used

    Makeup
    - Headlines made more interesting, varied, larger
    - General makeup is more varied, stimulating

2. Advertising

    Break made from old typographical traditions
    Larger advertisements used by department stores
    Many new sources for advertising tapped
    Classified ads expanded
    Increase in total volume of advertising noted

3. Circulation

    Subscriptions
    - Reached new heights

    Newspapers
    - Reached new readers
    - Costs reduced for consumer

4. New Editions

    Evening editions multiplied
    Sunday editions expanded
    - Features, supplements, comics added

    Syndicates developed to supply features

5. Business side

    More systematic business methods introduced
    More profits from operations ($500,000 year, N.Y. World)

TABLE 23 (continued)

Newspapers moved into large plants
More capital required for launching, operating in larger cities

6. Mechanical Facilities

Printing
- Perfection of old machines
  - Stereotyping, improved, spreads to many papers
  - Presses improved, with
    - greater volume, speed attained
  - Color presses introduced
- New machines introduced
  - Linecasting machines developed, speeding up composition
  - "Fudge" device introduced for late news
  - Halftone engraving developed
  - Woodpulp used: cheapening cost of production

News-transmission
- Telegraph extended to all parts of United States
- Trans-Atlantic cable is used
- Telephone introduced and extended
- Railroads span nation

7. General Characteristics

Greater variety in newspapers

Newspapers developed to appeal to all classes

introduced. While superior to the old woodblocks, the picture which resulted was black and white. There were no grays. Then several men working independently directed their attention to this problem. They aimed to reproduce photos snapped by a camera rather than those drawn first by an artist. As indicated, Stephen H. Horgan, working in the *New York Graphic office,* and Frederic Eugene Ives, a photographer, experimenting at Cornell about the same time in the 1870s, developed the halftone engraving process, which gave gray tones as well as black and white. The new engraving method speeded reproduction and improved the appearance of photographs when they were published. The halftone was found practical for daily newspapers printed on web presses in 1897 and this engraving method spread.

STEREOTYPING SPEEDS PRODUCTION

Stereotyping machines, invented before the Civil War and used for the first time during the 1860s for newspaper work, were now employed more widely. The stereotyping process helped speed and cheapen production. Duplicate stereotyped plates could be made from the same type and fitted onto several presses. These could be operated simultaneously.

The newspaper plant by the end of the century became a huge factory filled with machines for the efficient and quick production of newspapers in great quantities. More editions with last minute news were published, especially by evening newspapers. Cost of establishing and operating a newspaper increased rapidly. In addition to cost of machinery, labor necessary to operate the various devices increased, adding to the expenses. By the 1890s some metropolitan papers employed 1,000 to 1,200 persons for their printing, editorial and advertising staffs.

WOODPULP PAPER CHEAPENS PRICE

Just as the penny press in the 1830s was made possible by introduction of the Fourdrinier machine for making newsprint, so utilization of woodpulp as a raw material for papermaking decreased the price of print paper in the 1870s and 1880s. For a number of years a cheaper material than rags was sought by papermill owners. Then in 1866 the Pagenstecher brothers imported from Germany two practical machines for grinding woodpulp. Mills were soon started in various parts of this country. Eight woodpulp plants in 1870 grew to one hundred sixty-eight in 1900. The price of newsprint was reduced from about eight cents per pound in 1870 to one cent at the end of the century. This enabled publishers, seeking mass circulation, to decrease the price of their dailies.

Chapter 30

Magazines Widen Their Appeal

NEW TYPES OF MAGAZINES APPEAR

The same population, economic and educational factors shaping the daily and Sunday newspapers also influenced development of magazines in this period. Great industrial advances, increasing wealth and the march of thousands of sons and daughters of the working and middle classes to schools resulted in a widening of magazine markets. Hundreds of thousands who had not been magazine subscribers before now began to read weekly and monthly periodicals.

Publishers, alert to the possible mass market for their magazines, dropped the price from 35 cents to 15 cents and even to 10 cents. The introduction of cheap woodpulp to make glazed paper for periodicals made this possible. Some magazines reached three hundred thousand readers. The greatest circulation advances, however, were recorded in the women's group. One periodical devoted to serials, fashions and cooking, reached nearly a million subscribers.

Unlike the individual newspaper, magazines sought a national market. Unrestricted by local pressures and prejudices, the magazine could deal with controversial subjects. Nationalization was made possible now by the extensive railroad system which could distribute publications quickly to every hamlet in the nation. More manufacturers, too, seeking a national market for their products, found, in part, that these magazines were effective advertising media. Manufacturers could use magazines in addition to the local newspapers. Invention of the halftone engraving process enabled magazine publishers to improve the pictorial attractiveness of their periodical and to use many more pictures at lower cost.

Total figures reflect the awakening interest in magazines. About 700 periodicals were being issued in 1865; this reached 3,300 by 1885.

SERIOUS LITERARY REVIEWS STILL PUBLISHED

Serious monthly magazines, such as the *Atlantic Monthly, Harper's* and the *North American Review,* firmly established in the previous period, continued to appeal to a select educated and upper-class audience. They published essays, poetry, travel articles and reviews of literature. While their circulations increased steadily, their appeal was limited.

McCLURE'S MAGAZINE SETS FAST PACE

McClure's, established in 1892, was one of the most successful of the popular magazines. Samuel S. McClure, whose biography and an account of his establishment of the McClure newspaper syndicate was recounted in a previous section, had decided that the syndicate was not profitable enough. McClure believed that a magazine might be successful, for he could use the best fiction from his syndicate and add current nonfiction articles. William D. Howells, novelist, had proposed such a magazine with McClure as publisher, but the periodical required $97,000 to launch.

McClure leafed through *Scribner's, Harper's* and the *Century* concluding that his fiction and articles were as good if not better. He therefore established *McClure's Magazine* in June, 1893, with a capitalization of $7,800. John S. Phillips, his business manager and partner in the McClure newspaper syndicate, invested $4,500; a son, Robert McClure, had $500; and McClure put in $2,800. McClure was editor-in-chief. His chief assets were his abilities, his experience in publishing and his safe full of literary properties.

Within a short time McClure was publishing Kipling's *Jungle Stories* and Anthony Hope's sequel to the popular *Prisoner of Zenda.* He began to publish nonfiction articles on current affairs. He discovered that what he needed was his own writers who could research a subject and write in an interesting, readable style. He learned about Ida M. Tarbell, who was free lancing for his and other magazines. On one of his trips to Europe, he found her in France writing articles. He hired her for his staff. Later he added Lincoln Steffens; Ray Stannard Baker, a Chicago reporter who had contributed special articles; and William Allen White. McClure published Booth Tarkington's *A Gentleman From Indiana* and short stories by O. Henry.

McClure set Miss Tarbell to work writing a biography of Napoleon. This interesting, lively series was illustrated with unusual photographs. Circulation jumped from 35,000 to 100,000. Later he assigned her a series on Lincoln. While other magazines published serious, heavy articles on the Civil War President, Miss Tarbell wrote in a brisk style. Her articles were illustrated with a number of rare photos which McClure and Miss Tarbell were able to secure.

McClure's Magazine began to hum with fresh ideas and newness. Readers looked forward to the surprises the publisher had for them. The articles were written in sprightly fashion and were more readable than those in other publications. McClure used many illustrations. His scientific articles were thoroughly researched and quickly published after the discoveries became news. Newspapermen were cynical or satirical about the scientists. McClure's writers took the scientists seriously. He published an extensive article on Dr. William Roentgen's X-ray together with sixteen photos.

Frank Munsey pioneered when he dropped the price of his magazine and proved this was a strategic move. McClure followed, cutting his magazine's price from 35 cents to 12 cents to 10 cents.

As a result of McClure's shrewdness in selecting the right fiction and nonfiction, in using illustrations and in hiring the best writers, *McClure's* circulation rose steadily. This circulation rise was aided by his policy of cutting the magazine's price. From an initial 35,000, the magazine moved up to 190,000 in November, 1895; 150,000 in December, 1896. A war issue in 1898 produced 400,000 sales.

His circulation rose so fast that his advertising rates were always behind. His business manager raised the rates as fast as he could. Income from the magazine was $60,000 in 1897; rose to $80,000 in 1898. The three months of 1899 showed an income of $40,000.

With increased revenue, ambitious McClure established a book publishing business, making Frank Doubleday the manager of this enterprise. The McClure syndicate, magazine and book publishing businesses were valued at one million dollars.

WOMEN'S MAGAZINES MORE POPULAR

Godey's Lady's Book continued to hold its own for a decade after the Civil War, but it was then outstripped by the older *Petersen's Magazine* as well as new women's magazines which rose to meet new demands of readers. Among these were *Woman's Home Companion* (1873),

Ladies' Home Journal (1883), *Good Housekeeping* (1885), *Vogue* (1892) and *McCall's* (1897).

Ladies' Home Journal

Most successful of these, the *Ladies' Home Journal,* expressed the new magazine tendencies effectively. Its beginnings were largely accidental. Cyrus H. K. Curtis, a Portland, Maine publisher, had transferred his ambitious operations to Philadelphia, and there issued the *Tribune and Farmer* in 1879. A department for women was edited by his wife. It was so successful that this section was issued in 1883 as a separate magazine for women, containing illustrated serials, articles on flowers, fashion notes and advice on the care of children. It also had other appeals for the housewife, such as articles on cooking, needlework and handicrafts. The formula was popular, for within a year, circulation increased to twenty-five thousand. Curtis spent lavishly for popular women writers and for advertising his magazines.

In 1889 he made one of his best moves by employing Edward Bok as editor. Projecting his personality through the magazine, an innovation in magazine publication, Bok sought to enliven the writing which appeared in the *Ladies' Home Journal.* By the end of the century Bok's *Ladies' Home Journal,* now forty-eight pages, reached a national audience of 800,000 subscribers. This large circulation drew many advertisers, and Bok gave credit to advertising for the success of the magazine and its low price to subscribers.

The *Journal* and other women's magazines carried many short stories and serials. Some of this fiction was of a sentimental kind with slick plots, unreal and unrelated to life, with impossibly beautiful women and handsome men. Other magazines carried the best writers of the day: Dorothy Canfield Fisher, Zona Gale, Willa Cather and Edna Ferber.

WEEKLY NEWS AND PICTORIAL MAGAZINES STRONGER

Weekly news magazines continued to hold the public's interest. Some faded out in the post-Civil War period, others continued and grew in strength, while new magazines sprang up to meet the changing needs. All sought a national audience now.

Although *Leslie's Illustrated Weekly* had initiated a strong campaign against the dairy industry in the pre-Civil War period, it was *Harper's Weekly* in the 1870s which developed the crusading formula, copied by other magazines and newspapers. *Harper's* attack, as indicated, was on the Tweed Ring, operating in New York City and New York State. The

Tweed political ring, already referred to, was composed of William M. Tweed and three others. They controlled the city and robbed it of $200,000,000. *Harper's Weekly* hit the ring editorially, being aided by the cartoons of Thomas Nast. Inside information about the political corruption leaked out, and was published by *Harper's* and the *New York Times*. Mayor A. Oakley Hall forbade the sale of *Harper's Weekly* on newsstands, and Tweed offered Nast $200,000, which later was raised to $500,000, to go to Europe to study art. Nast refused. The circulation of *Harper's* trebled, reaching 160,000. The ring was smashed.

Harper's received national attention. The magazine and the crusade method had proved its value and its strength in political battles. These lessons were not lost on other magazine and newspaper publishers.

Saturday Evening Post, established in the previous era, went into a period of decline in this period, for although its size was doubled and it printed low-type serials, it could not gain the approval of a large public. Its revival in 1897 by Cyrus H. K. Curtis belongs more properly to the next era.

Chapter 31

Professional Advances Made

PRESS CLUBS ARE FORMED

Following the spread of organizations of other groups in America, newspapermen bound themselves together at first for social purposes. Three reporters, in 1862, formed the Bohemian Club in New York; membership grew to twenty-five, but the organization did not last long. The first New York Press Club was active about 1869 and gave dinners at Delmonico's Restaurant. The second New York Press Club, started in 1872, was long-lived and served as an example for other cities to follow. The chief purposes were social and benevolent, taking care of members who were sick and needy and burying the dead. With New York as a precedent, the press club movement spread. These organizations were largely formed for their members to have a good time.

NEWSPAPER UNIONS MEET LITTLE RESPONSE

Although the newspaper reporters' magazine, the *Journalist,* had advocated a union or brotherhood of reporters as early as 1886, it met with little response. Pittsburgh reporters decided to organize in 1891. Altogether, thirteen groups had started newswriters' unions by 1900, but these lasted only a year or so.

PUBLISHERS' ASSOCIATION FOUNDED

A number of state editorial groups, composed of both editors and publishers, appeared in the 1850s and 1860s. Since the positions of editor and publisher had not differentiated until after the Civil War, separate associations did not appear at first.

In February, 1885, the International Editorial Association was organized. The following year the name was altered to the National Editorial Association.

W. H. Brearly, advertising manager of the *Detroit Evening News*, recommended a convention of business managers. In February, 1887, the first session of the American Newspaper Publishers' Association was held in Rochester, New York. The value of the group came to be understood later, and its membership gradually and steadily increased. In 1892 it had one hundred thirty-nine members; by the turn of of the century membership had increased to two hundred. The Association was incorporated in 1897.

The organization dealt with advertising agency relations, postal service and newsprint and labor problems. At the annual convention mechanical problems, advertising problems and proposed laws which would affect the newspaper as an industry were discussed. One of the more important achievements of the publishers' association was compilation of a list of responsible advertising agents in 1888.

FIRST EFFORTS MADE TO ESTABLISH JOURNALISM SCHOOLS

This period marked the first faint beginnings of journalism schools. The South deserves the credit of doing pioneer work in journalism instruction. After the Civil War General Robert E. Lee became president of Washington College, now known as Washington and Lee in Virginia. He believed that one of the chief essentials in restoration of peace was the training of educated and responsible editors. Accordingly, on March 30, 1869, he recommended to the trustees of his college that they provide for sixty scholarships for young men proposing to make printing and journalism their life work and profession. Mayor John J. Lafferty, editor of the *Virginia Gazette*, joined the small faculty. The school lasted from 1869 to 1878, when journalism courses were dropped from the catalogue.

On all sides, General Lee's school had met opposition, ridicule and scorn from newspapermen. Henry Watterson, of the *Louisville* (Kentucky) *Courier-Journal*, James Gordon Bennett, Jr. and others laughed at the idea. Cultured Whitelaw Reid of the *New York Tribune*, in 1872, however, advocated formal instruction in history, law, politics, modern languages, logic and economics be given at a school of journalism.

About this time Joseph Pulitzer, publisher of the *New York World*, desired to raise newspaper standards and, in spite of sneers of other editors, offered to supply funds to Columbia University to found a school. This was in 1892. But President Seth Low refused the offer at the time.

However, other universities saw the need for systematic journalism instruction and offered courses or established small departments of journalism. These included the University of Pennsylvania; Cornell, where the department lasted only one year; and the University of Missouri.

JOURNALISM LITERATURE APPEARS

Not many books on technique of journalism were issued, but several histories made their appearance. Frederic Hudson, *New York Herald* managing editor, wrote in 1873 *Journalism in the United States,* and S. N. D. North, *History and Present Condition of the Newspaper and Periodical Press of the United States in 1884.* Biographies of Greeley, Bennett, Bryant, Thomas Paine and Samuel Adams were issued. The great burst of biographies was to come in the next century.

JOURNALISM TRADE MAGAZINES ARE LAUNCHED

As other professions and industries, journalism itself needed publications which would report the spot news of current happenings and trends in newspapers and which would take editorial stands for and against journalism practices. Such publications, too, could express their views on national and state legislation affecting newspapers.

The *Journalist,* launched in March, 1894, was the pioneer in the field of journalism magazines. This newspaperman's paper was not too successful, and a year later Allan Forman became one of the co-owners, and later sole proprietor. He announced that he would make the *Journalist* bright without being nasty, aggressive and yet not scurrilous, dignified but not "tame."

In the next few years, newspapermen issued three similar publications. Charles S. Patterson saw the possibilities in the trade publication field and launched *Newspaperdom* in March, 1892. Patterson's was a neat monthly with little news but had technical articles on the mechanical department of the newspaper, editorial techniques and business office methods. Two years later Ernest F. Birmingham, publisher, and Frank L. Lancaster, editor, issued the *Fourth Estate.* This was a twelve-page paper, strictly interested in news about journalism and containing line-cuts and halftones. For a quarter of a century *Fourth Estate* had a notable career. The *Newspaper Maker,* which began in 1895, lasted only six years.

Publishers and advertisers had other publications. G. P. Rowell & Company started the *Advertiser's Gazette* in 1867 to send to its cus-

TABLE 24

Press Plays Important Role in Democracy (1865-1900)

1. Press Gives News, Information and Current Events of the Era
   a. Political events presented
   b. Economic affairs told
   c. Crime described
   d. International news; state and local news related
   Result: made many readers news conscious, alert

2. Press Gives Expression to Contending Groups
   a. Variety of newspapers were published
   b. Workers' problems related and championed in some papers
   c. Middle-class problems reported in all papers
   d. Upper economic groups, manufacturers and bankers, have voice in conservative dailies
   e. Farmers' views championed in some papers
   f. Women's emancipation sought by some groups, backed by press

3. Press Crusades Against Social Evils
   a. Political corruption exposed in many papers
   b. Trust development fought by some dailies
   c. Crime exposed by many dailies
   d. Basis laid for magazine muckrakers
   e. Foundations laid for progressive era after 1900

4. Press Serves as Cultural Organ
   a. Some papers publish science news
   b. Book reviews printed by larger dailies
   c. Some publish art, music, theatre news and criticism

5. Press Acts as Recreational Medium
   a. News of recreational activities given
   b. Stimulated sports activities
   c. Articles of entertainment value published
   d. Comics with entertainment value given

TABLE 24 (continued)

6. Press Serves as Advertising Media of Machine Age, Economic System
   a. Brought buyers and sellers together
   b. Stimulated sales
   c. Introduced many new products to public
   d. Made mass production, mass distribution possible

tomers. This developed into the *American Newspaper Directory* in 1869; and two years later the *Gazette* became the *American Newspaper Reporter and Advertisers' Gazette.* Although its main object was to boom Rowell's advertising business and printer's supply house, it was of benefit to the newspaper world. A monthly publication, the *Proof Sheet,* issued by a type founders company in 1867, carried trade information and advertising for the company. *Printer's Ink,* a weekly trade journal for advertisers, was launched by Rowell in 1888.

References

Many of the penny press papers continued beyond the Civil War, hence histories of these newspapers and the biographies of their editors may be used for background in this period. New publishers and editors came to the front, and new papers were established, however. Previously cited general histories may be used.

NEW YORK JOURNALISM

New York Sun

MITCHELL, EDWARD P., *Memoirs of an Editor,* New York: Charles Scribner's Sons, 1924. (Mitchell, one of Dana's editors, tells the philosophy of the human interest story in lively style.)

O'BRIEN, FRANK M., *Story of The Sun,* New York: Appleton, 1928.

STONE, CANDACE, *Dana and the Sun,* New York: Dodd, Mead & Co., 1938. (A detailed study, particularly effective in dealing with economic and political views of Dana.)

See also below biographies of Richard Harding Davis and Jacob Riis.

Graphic

BESSIE, SIMON, *Jazz Journalism,* New York: E. P. Dutton & Co., Inc., 1938. (Has chapter on the *Graphic.*)

Joseph Pulitzer

BARRETT, JAMES W., *Joseph Pulitzer and His World,* New York: Vanguard Press, Inc., 1941. (A factual and interpretive biography of the publisher and the *World.*)

JUERGENS, GEORGE, *Joseph Pulitzer and the New York World,* Princeton: Princeton University Press, 1966. (An analytic study; has much detail of contents of *World,* news, features, campaigns.)

KING, HOMER W., *Pulitzer's Prize Editor: A Biography of John A. Cockerill,* Durham, N. C.: Duke University Press, 1965.

RAMMELKAMP, JULIAN, *Pulitzer's Post-Dispatch 1878-1883,* Princeton: Princeton University Press, 1967. (Discusses content of daily; gives excellent picture of St. Louis and other papers in competition.)

SEITZ, DON C., *Joseph Pulitzer: His Life and Letters,* New York: Simon and Schuster, Inc., 1924. (First biography; has extended quotations.)

SWANBERG, W. A., *Joseph Pulitzer,* New York: Charles Scribner's Sons, 1967. (The latest study of this genius.)

See *Seventy-Fifth Anniversary of the St. Louis Post-Dispatch,* Dec. 13, 1954 for excellent material on that paper and early days of Pulitzer. Issued by the *Post-Dispatch.*

William Randolph Hearst

CARLSON, OLIVER and E. S. BATES, *Hearst, Lord of San Simeon,* New York: The Viking Press, Inc., 1936. (A thorough, critical study.)

LUNDBERG, FERDINAND, *Imperial Hearst,* New York: Equinox Cooperative, 1936. (A severe study, but documented.)

OLDER, MRS. FREMONT, *William Randolph Hearst,* New York: Appleton-Century-Crofts, 1936. (Gives the constructive side of the publisher; has details on his crusades.)

SWANBERG, WILLIAM, *Citizen Hearst,* New York: Charles Scribner's Sons, 1961. (A full-scale portrait. Thoroughly researched. Reprinted as Bantam Book, 1963.)

TEBBEL, JOHN, *Life and Good Times of William Randolph Hearst,* New York: E. P. Dutton & Co., Inc., 1952. (Seeks a fair appraisal of publisher; written in highly readable style.)

New York Evening Post

OGDEN, ROLLO, ed., *Life and Letters of Edwin Lawrence Godkin,* New York: The Macmillan Company, 1907. (Useful biography of editor; written in older style.)

PRINGLE, HENRY F., "Great American Editors: Godkin of the Post," *Scribner's,* 96:327-334, December, 1934. (Is an interpretative account.)

See previous entry, Allan Nevins, *New York Evening Post,* in Part II, Part III.

James Gordon Bennett

CLARKE, JOSEPH I. C., *My Life and Memoirs,* New York: Dodd, Mead & Co., 1926.

COLEMAN, ALBERT E., "New and Authentic History of the *Herald* of the Bennetts," *Editor and Publisher,* Vol. 56, March 24, 1924, to Vol. 58, June 13, 1925. (Significant detail given.)

HUDSON, FREDERIC, *Journalism in the United States from 1690 to 1872,* New York: Harper & Row, Publishers, 1872. (Has useful inside facts on *Herald* since book was written by the paper's managing editor.)

O'CONNOR, RICHARD, *The Scandalous Mr. Bennett,* Garden City, N.Y.: Doubleday & Company, Inc., 1962. (Has new material on the publisher.)

See previous entries on Bennett: Seitz, Carlson in Penny Press era.

New York Times

JOHNSON, GERALD W., *An Honorable Titan,* New York: Harper & Row, Publishers, 1946. (Only biography of Adolph S. Ochs.)

See also previous entries, Berger, Davis, Brown.

New York Tribune

BAEHR, HARRY, JR., *New York Tribune Since the Civil War,* New York: Dodd, Mead & Co., 1936. (An intensive, scholarly work; heavy on political views.)

CORTISSOZ, ROYAL, *Life of Whitelaw Reid* 2 vols., New York: Charles Scribner's Sons, 1921. (In the old style of biography, but has the facts; written by member of *Tribune* staff.)

See previous entries on Greeley for end of his life.

Other New York Reporters, Editors

CARLSON, OLIVER, *Arthur Brisbane: A Candid Biography,* Harrisburg, Pa.: Stackpole Books, 1937. (Gives detailed background of Brisbane, a Pulitzer and Hearst editor, and tells about Brisbane's liberal father.)

CHAMBERS, HENRY KELLETT, "A Park Row Interlude: Memoir of Albert Pulitzer," *Journalism Quarterly* 40:539, autumn, 1963. (Important piece on Joseph Pulitzer's little-known brother.)

CHURCHILL, ALLEN, *Park Row,* New York: Holt, Rinehart & Winston, Inc., 1958. (Seeks to recreate New York newspaper scenes; has colorful material on publishers and their papers.)

DAVIS, RICHARD HARDING, *Adventures and Letters of Richard Harding Davis,* New York: Charles Scribner's Sons, 1918. (The story of the swashbuckling reporter written by himself. See Downey entry.)

DOWNEY, FAIRFAX, *Richard Harding Davis,* New York: Charles Scribner's Sons, 1933. (Lively written biography of romantic reporter.)

NOBLE, IRIS, *Nelly Bly—First Woman Reporter,* New York: Julian Messner, 1956. (Well-written, lively account of the *New York World's* star woman reporter.)

PARKMAN, M. R., "Modern Viking: Jacob Riis," *Heroes of Today,* New York: Century, 1917. (First biography of great reporter.)

WARE, LOUISE, *Jacob Riis, Police Reporter, Reformer, Useful Citizen,* New York: Appleton-Century-Crofts, 1939. (The best study of the crusading reporter.)

ATLANTIC SEABOARD JOURNALISM

New England Press

MORGAN, JAMES, *Charles H. Taylor,* Boston, 1923, privately printed by Globe newspaper company. (Tells about *Boston Globe* and its publisher's background and problems.)

See previous entries in Popular Penny Press era, Chamberlin, Merriam, Hooker, Smith.

Philadelphia

SCHARF, J. THOMAS and THOMPSON WESTCOTT, "The Press of Philadelphia," *History of Philadelphia* Vol. III, Philadelphia: L. H. Everts & Co., 1884, pp. 1958-2062.

WAINRIGHT, NICHOLAS B., *The History of the Philadelphia Inquirer,* supplement to *Philadelphia Inquirer,* Sept. 16, 1962. (An excellent, short history of the press in Philadelphia.)

Baltimore

SCHARF, J. THOMAS, *The Chronicles of Baltimore: Being a Complete History of the Baltimore Town and Baltimore City from the Earliest Period to the Present Times,* Baltimore: Turnbull, 1874. (Has some sections on the city's newspapers.)

See previous entry for Popular Penny Press era, Johnson.

Washington

Washington Post, Special Edition, January 23, 1951 and December 7, 1952.

SOUTHERN NEWSPAPER LEADERS

Josephus Daniels

DANIELS, JOSEPHUS, *Tar Heel Editor,* Chapel Hill: University of North Carolina Press, 1939. (A colorful account of Daniels' early journalistic days in North Carolina; tells of his crusades in the state.)

MORRISON, JOSEPH L., *Josephus Daniels Says . . . ,* Chapel Hill: University of North Carolina Press, 1962. (An unusually good biography of the North Carolina crusading editor.)

Henry Watterson

DREWRY, JOHN, *Post Biographies,* Athens: University of Georgia Press, 1942. (Tom Wallace, "There Were Giants in Those Days." A useful, briefer study of Henry Watterson.)

KROCK, ARTHUR, *Editorials of Henry Watterson,* Louisville: *Courier-Journal,* 1923. (A useful collection which captures the editor's style.)

MARCOSSON, ISAAC, *Marse Henry, A Biography of Henry Watterson,* New York: Dodd, Mead & Co., 1951. (An earlier account of the Louisville editor.)

WALL, JOSEPH FRAZIER, *Henry Watterson, Reconstructed Rebel,* New York: Oxford University Press, 1956. (A top biography with excellent detail on Watterson's personality and journalism.)

Georgia

GRIFFITH, LOUIS T. and JOHN E. TALMADGE, *Georgia Journalism, 1793-1950,* Athens: University of Georgia Press, 1951. (Has main outlines of state's developing newspapers.)

HARRIS, JOEL CHANDLER, *Life of Henry W. Grady,* New York: Cassell, 1890. (First study of the editor of the *Atlanta Constitution* by an associate of Grady.)

NIXON, RAYMOND B., *Henry W. Grady, Spokesman of the New South,* New York: Alfred A. Knopf, Inc., 1943. (A thorough and interesting biography of the Georgia editor.)

Louisiana

DABNEY, THOMAS, *One Hundred Great Years: Story of the Times-Picayune,* Baton Rouge: Louisiana State University Press, 1944. (A detailed, but readable study of the *Times-Picayune* and its changing environment.)

MIDWESTERN NEWSPAPERS

Chicago Journalism

DENNIS, CHARLES H., *Victor Lawson, His Time and His Work,* Chicago: University of Chicago Press, 1935. (A highly readable biography of the *Chicago Daily News* founder.)

Ellis, Elmer, *Mr. Dooley's America, A Life of Finley Peter Dunne,* New York: Alfred A. Knopf, Inc., 1941. (Recreates the times and the life of an all-around newsman.)

Kinsley, Philip, *Chicago Tribune* Vol. II, 1865-1880; Vol. III, 1880-1900. Chicago: *Chicago Tribune,* 1947. (The official history, with a day-by-day account of the paper's content.)

McPhaul, John J., *Deadlines and Monkeyshines; Fabled World of Chicago Journalism,* Englewood Cliffs, N. J.: Prentice-Hall, Inc., 1962. (Has considerable content from newspapers, gives details of strikes; stresses anecdotes and humor in press.)

Stone, Melville E., *Fifty Years a Journalist,* Garden City, N.Y.: Doubleday & Company, Inc., 1921. (Tells about beginnings of the *Daily News.*)

Tebbel, John, *An American Dynasty,* Garden City, N.Y.: Doubleday & Company, Inc., 1947. (Continues critical account of McCormick-Medill families and their paper.)

Walsh, John E., "To Print the News and Raise Hell—Wilbur F. Storey's Chicago Times," *Journalism Quarterly* 40:497, autumn, 1963.

Detroit

White, Lee A., *Detroit News, 1873-1917, A Record of Progress,* Detroit News Association, 1918. (Not very detailed, but the only account available.)

Ohio

Cochran, Negley D., *E. W. Scripps,* New York: Harcourt, Brace & World, Inc., 1933. (Adds much to portrait of the publisher.)

Gardner, Gilson, *Lusty Scripps,* New York: Vanguard Press, Inc., 1932. (First of biographies of liberal publisher; still useful.)

Harrison, John M., "David Ross Locke and the Fight on Reconstruction," *Journalism Quarterly* 39:491, autumn, 1962. (Has fresh interpretation of Locke's views.)

Hooper, Osman C., *History of Ohio Journalism,* New York: The Macmillan Company, 1924. (Gives some useful chronological information.)

Knight, Oliver, *I Protest, Selected Disquisitions of E. W. Scripps,* Madison, University of Wisconsin Press, 1966. (Latest book on publisher, gives views and philosophy in own words.)

McCabe, Charles R., *Damned Old Crank,* New York: Harper & Row, Publishers, 1951. (Useful account of Scripps; has many personal details of publisher, his philosophy, methods.)

McRae, Milton A., *Forty Years in Newspaperdom,* New York: Brentano's, 1924. (A useful autobiography of the Scripps' partner and business manager.)

Shaw, Archer H., *The Plain Dealer, One Hundred Years in Cleveland,* New York: Alfred A. Knopf, Inc., 1942. (An extended history of the *Plain Dealer,* but also includes much on its competition.)

Smith, Henry Ladd and James Knox, "The Needlers: Our Journalistic Satirists," *Journalism Quarterly* 39:309-316, summer, 1962.

Taft, William H., "David Ross Locke, 'Forgotten Editor,'" *Journalism Quarterly* 34:202-207, spring, 1957. (Tells about Petroleum V. Nasby, editor of the *Toledo* (Ohio) *Blade.*)

———, *The Toledo Blade, Its First One Hundred Years,* Ph.D. dissertation, Western Reserve University, 1951. (Only study made of this Ohio paper.)

Minneapolis

MORRISON, BRADLEY L., *Sunlight on Your Doorstep,* Minneapolis: Rose & Haines, 1966. (First study of the beginnings of the *Minneapolis Tribune.*)

St. Paul

EIDE, RICHARD B., *North Star Editor; A Brief Sketch of Joseph A. Wheelock and His Policies as Editor of St. Paul Pioneer-Press,* New York: King's Crown Press, Columbia University, 1944.

———, *Influences of Editorship and Other Forces on the Growth of the St. Paul Pioneer-Press, 1849-1909,* Columbia: University of Missouri Press, 1939. (An excellent study showing effects of social environment on press.)

St. Louis Press

BRYAN, CARTER R., "Carl Schurz; Journalist and Liberal Propagandist," *Journalism Quarterly* 40:207-212, spring, 1963. (A worthwhile contribution to the study of a liberal editor; traces his origins in Europe.)

HART, JIM ALEE, *A History of the St. Louis Globe-Democrat,* Columbia: University of Missouri Press, 1961. (Hart continues excellent history of the paper, showing changes in it.)

KING, HOMER W., *Pulitzer's Prize Editor, A Biography of John A. Cockerill,* Durham, N.C.: Duke University Press, 1965.

WITTKE, CARL, *German Language Press in America,* Lexington: University of Kentucky Press, 1957. (A valuable contribution.)

See Pulitzer entries under New York, especially those relating to St. Louis *Post-Dispatch* (Rammelkamp).

William E. Nelson and Kansas City Star

BRANDENBURG, GEORGE F., "Kansas City Star Retains Independent Traditions," *Editor & Publisher* 79:11, July 27, 1946.

JOHNSON, ICIE F., *William Rockhill Nelson and the Kansas City Star,* Kansas City, Mo.: Burton, 1935. (A detailed, highly valuable study.)

Kansas City Star Staff, *William Rockhill Nelson, The Story of a Man, A Newspaper, and a City,* Cambridge: Riverside Press, 1915. (An early but pertinent study.)

ROGERS, CHARLES E., "William Rockhill Nelson and His Editors of the Star," *Journalism Quarterly* 26:15, March, 1949. (Throws more light on the Kansas editor.)

William Allen White

HINSHAW, DAVID, *Man From Kansas,* New York: G. P. Putnam's Sons, 1945. (Has some useful information on White's early days in Kansas.)

JOHNSON, WALTER, *William Allen White's America,* New York: Holt, Rinehart & Winston, Inc., 1947. (An interpretive volume, telling about the publisher and giving background of the era, state and nation.)

RICH, EVERETT, *William Allen White, Man From Emporia,* New York: Farrar and Rinehart, 1941. (Contributes to portrait of White, but Johnson's volume still the best.)

WHITE, WILLIAM ALLEN, *Autobiography,* New York: The Macmillan Company, 1946. (Adds to picture of publisher; still need Johnson and other biographers for full story.)

SOUTHWEST AND ROCKY MOUNTAIN PRESS

ACHESON, SAM, *35,000 Days in Texas,* New York: The Macmillan Company, 1938. (Acheson continues account of development of *Dallas News* in postwar period.)

ASHTON, WENDELL J., *Voice in the Wilderness, Biography of a Pioneer Newspaper,* New York: Duell, Sloan & Pearce, 1950. (A thorough history of the *Mormon Deseret News* of Salt Lake City. Other papers fitted into the account.)

BEEBE, LUCIUS, *Comstock Commotion, The Story of the Territorial Enterprise and Virginia City News,* Stanford, Calif.: Stanford University Press, 1954. (A lively tale of a pioneer paper.)

KAROLEVITZ, ROBERT F., *Newspapering in the Old West. A Pictorial History of Journalism and Printing on the Frontier,* Seattle, Washington: Superior Publishing Co., 1965. (Has excellent pictures and some flavorful history.)

Denver Journalism

FOWLER, GENE, *Timber Line: A Story of Bonfils and Tammen,* New York: Covici-Friede, 1933. (A rousing story of the *Denver Post* and its founders.)

MARTIN, LAURENCE, "So the People May Know," *Denver Post,* 1950. (Special issue of the *Denver Post* contains very useful material, favorable points on Tammen and Bonfils.)

PERKIN, ROBERT L., *The First Hundred Years, An Informal History of Denver and the Rocky Mountain News,* Garden City, N. Y.: Doubleday & Company, Inc., 1959. (The well-written, detailed account of the Denver paper and its competitors.)

PACIFIC COAST NEWSPAPERS

Northwest

DYAR, RALPH E., *News for an Empire,* Caldwell, Idaho: The Caxton Printers, Ltd., 1952. (Tells vividly about the *Spokane Spokesman Review* in great detail. An outstanding study of a paper and its locale.)

TURNBULL, GEORGE S., *History of Oregon Newspapers,* Portland: Binfords & Mort, 1939.

California

BRUCE, JOHN, *Gaudy Century: The Story of San Francisco's Hundred Years of Robust Journalism,* New York: Random House, Inc., 1948. (Bruce continues account of city's newspapers; lively, anecdotal.)

FIREBAUGH, DOROTHY G., "Sacramento Union: Voice of California, 1871-1875," *Journalism Quarterly* 30:321ff., summer, 1933. (A valuable study of a crusading newspaper and its problems of survival.)

History of the Los Angeles Times. (Issued in booklet form by that newspaper. No date. Has some worthwhile detail.)

McWilliams, Carey, *Ambrose Bierce, A Biography,* New York: Albert and Charles Boni, 1929. (An interesting study of a Hearst writer.)

Older, Fremont, *My Own Story,* San Francisco: Call Publishing Company, 1919. (Can be used to supplement Wells' better book about the crusading editor.)

Wells, Evelyn, *Fremont Older,* New York: Appleton-Century-Crofts, 1936. (A thorough account of the editor.)

Young, John P., *Journalism in California,* San Francisco: Chronicle Publishing Co., 1915. (An old work but has chronological detail of some value, details which have to be extracted.)

SPANISH-AMERICAN WAR

Brown, Charles H., *The Correspondents' War,* New York: Charles Scribner's Sons, 1967. (Most recent study of Spanish-American War; emphasizes reporting activities; contains dispatches.)

Creelman, James, *On the Great Highway,* Boston: Lathrop, 1901. (A war correspondent's version of the war.)

Godkin, Edwin L., "Growth and Expansion of Public Opinion," *Atlantic Monthly* 81:1, January, 1898. (Tells conservative editor's views on the conflict; gives general condemnation of other papers and publishers.)

Millis, Walter, *Martial Spirit: A Study of Our War with Spain,* Boston: Houghton Mifflin Company, 1931. (Has background of war, causes, battles and press treatment.)

Wilkerson, Marcus, *Public Opinion and the Spanish-American War,* Baton Rouge: Louisiana State University Press, 1932. (The first full-length study of the subject, dealing with newspapers all over the United States. See Wisan's book.)

Wisan, Joseph, *Cuban Crisis As Reflected in New York Press,* New York: Columbia University Press, 1934. (An excellent, authoritative study, concentrating on New York papers. See Wilkerson's volume.)

See biographies of Joseph Pulitzer, William Randolph Hearst, Edwin Lawrence Godkin, as they were involved in the war.

PRESS ASSOCIATIONS

Knights, Peter R., *The Press Association War of 1866-67,* Journalism Monograph, No. 6 of Association for Education in Journalism, Madison, University of Wisconsin, December, 1967. (Thoroughly researched study of important episode in AP history.)

Morris, Joe Alex, *Deadline Every Minute, The Story of the United Press,* Garden City, N.Y., Doubleday & Company, Inc., 1957. (A full-length story of the wire service, with important facts on its beginnings.)

See previous entries, Gramling, Rosewater, Alfred McClung Lee in Popular Penny Press era, dealing with news associations. Also biographies of Hearst, Scripps.

NEWSPAPER SYNDICATES AND CHAINS

Lee, Alfred McClung, *Daily Newspaper in America,* New York: The Macmillan Company, 1937, pp. 576-602.

LYON, P., *Success Story,* New York: Charles Scribner's Sons, 1963. (Tells about the life and journalistic activities of S. S. McClure.)
MCCLURE, S. S., *My Autobiography,* New York: Stokes, 1941.
WATSON, E. S., *A History of Newspaper Syndicates in the United States, 1865-1935.* (Issued as a supplement to *Publisher's Auxiliary,* Chicago, November 16, 1935.)

ADVERTISING

HOWER, RALPH M., *History of an Advertising Agency, N.W. Ayer & Son at Work, 1869-1939,* Cambridge: Harvard University Press, 1939.
LEE, ALFRED MCCLUNG, *Daily Newspaper in America,* New York: The Macmillan Company, 1937, pp. 314-376.
PRESBREY, FRANK, *History and Development of Advertising,* Garden City, N.Y.: Doubleday & Company, Inc., 1929, chapters 29-47. (A thorough, pioneering job of telling the advertising story. Useful for all periods.)

MAGAZINES

BAKER, RAY STANNARD, *American Chronicle,* New York: Charles Scribner's Sons, 1945. (Adventures of a muckraking reporter.)
———, *Native American,* New York: Charles Scribner's Sons, 1941. (More about Baker.)
BOK, EDWARD A., *A Man From Maine,* New York: Charles Scribner's Sons, 1923. Autobiography of the magazine publisher with original ideas.)
———, *The Americanization of Edward Bok,* New York: Charles Scribner's Sons, 1924.
DAVENPORT, WALTER, and JAMES DERIEUX, *Ladies, Gentlemen, and Editors.* Garden City, N.Y.: Doubleday & Company, Inc., 1960.
FILLER, LOUIS, *Crusaders for American Liberalism,* New York: Harcourt, Brace & World, Inc., 1939. (Tells story of the muckrakers, with many examples.)
LYON, P., *Success Story,* New York: Charles Scribner's Sons, 1963. (Excellent biography of muckraking magazine publisher, S. S. McClure.)
MCCLURE, S. S., *My Autobiography,* New York: Stokes, 1941. (Gives McClure's account of his magazine venture.)
MOTT, FRANK LUTHER, *A History of American Magazines,* Cambridge, Harvard University Press, 1957, Vol. I, II, III. (Contains much content.)
NOEL, MARY, *Villains Galore, The Heyday of the Popular Story Weekly,* New York: The Macmillan Company, 1934.
PETERSON, THEODORE, *Magazines in the Twentieth Century* rev., Urbana: University of Illinois, 1964. (Has excellent background material on the magazines.)
POLLACK, GUSTAV, *Fifty Years of American Idealism,* Boston: Houghton Mifflin Company, 1915. (An account of the beginnings and development of *The Nation,* liberal, powerful weekly, edited by Edwin L. Godkin. See New York papers, Godkin, also Nevins, *Evening Post.*)
STERN, MADELINE B., *Purple Passage, Life of Mrs. Frank Leslie,* Norman: University of Oklahoma, 1953.

Wolseley, Roland E., *The Magazine World,* Englewood Cliffs, N.J.: Prentice-Hall, Inc., 1951. (Has useful material on history of magazines.)

Wood, James P., *Magazines in the United States,* New York: The Ronald Press Company, 1956.

PRESSES AND OTHER PRINTING MACHINERY

Mengel, William, *Ottmar Mergenthaler and the Printing Revolution,* Mergenthaler Linotype Company, 1954.

See previous entries on Alfred McClung Lee, Olson, Hoe, Sutton in Popular Penny Press.

PHOTOGRAPHY

Taft, Robert, *Photography and the American Scene,* New York: Dover Publications, Inc., 1938. (Has an account of rise of photography and a section on newspaper and magazine illustrations.)

McDougall, Walt, "Old Days on the World," *American Mercury* 4:21, January, 1925. (Tells about his experiences as an artist for the Pulitzer *World.*) See also George Juergens, *Joseph Pulitzer and the New York World, op. cit.,* Chapter 3, "Illustrations."

PROFESSIONAL ADVANCES

Editor & Publisher, "Golden Jubilee Edition, 1934." (Covers many phases of journalistic history of the period. Also daily trade magazine changes.)

———, "75th Anniversary Edition, 1959," June, 1959. (Has useful information on nineteenth-century press.)

ASSOCIATIONS

Baker, Elizabeth Faulkner, *Printers and Technology, A History of the International Pressmen and Assistants' Union,* New York: Columbia University Press, 1957.

Emery, Edwin, *History of American Newspaper Publishers' Association,* Minneapolis: University of Minnesota Press, 1950. (An authoritative, comprehensive treatment of the publishers' association.)

Lee, Alfred McClung, *Daily Newspapers in America,* New York: The Macmillan Company, 1937, p. 226ff. (Has account of publishers' and other newsmen's associations.)

EDUCATION

O'Dell, DeForest, *History of Journalism Education in the United States,* New York: Columbia University Press, 1935. (Has some useful facts about important developments.)

Sutton, Albert A., *Education for Journalism in the United States from its Beginning to 1940,* Evanston, Ill.: Northwestern University Press, 1945. (Thorough, well-presented study, giving many phases of education.)

COMICS

Becker, Stephen, *The Comic Art in America,* New York: Simon and Schuster, Inc., 1959. (An interpretive study.)

"Funny Papers," *Fortune* Vol. VII, April, 1953. (Has worthwhile material but deals chiefly with later era of the comics.)
MURRELL, WILLIAM, *A History of American Graphic Humor* Vol. I, Whitney Museum, 1934; Vol. II, New York: The Macmillan Company, 1938.
WAUGH, COULTON, *The Comics,* New York: The Macmillan Company, 1949.
WHITE, DAVID MANNING and ROBERT H. ABEL, *The Funnies,* Glencoe, Ill.: Free Press of Glencoe, 1963. (A well-researched and unusually interesting sociological interpretation of an American phenomenon.)

HEADLINES

See Helen O. Mahin's previous entry in earlier periods.

"NEEDLERS": NEWSPAPER SATIRISTS

CLEMENS, CYRIL, *Petroleum V. Nasby,* Webster Groves, Mo., International Mark Twain Society, 1936. (A useful study of this early needler and newsman.)
PAINE, ALBERT BIGELOW, *Th. Nast, His Period and His Pictures,* New York: The Macmillan Company, 1904. (An early study of this famous political cartoonist.)
SEITZ, DON C., *Artemus Ward,* New York: Harper & Row, Publishers, 1919. (A lively study of this famous satirist.)
See also Henry Ladd Smith, under Ohio journalism.

Part Five

Chain and Syndicate Journalism (Since 1900)

Adolph S. Ochs with his *New York Times* set the newspaper pace in the twentieth century with his abundant news coverage and his freedom from sensation.

Chapter 32

Journalism in the Age of Mass Production

GIANT FORCES TRANSFORM AMERICA

Gigantic forces have transformed America and its mass communication agencies during the twentieth century. The first half of the century proved to be an exciting period packed with many stirring events. Population increased and industrialization accelerated, with larger factories, housing thousands of workers, dotting the land. Labor grew and organized on an unprecedented scale, extending into the semiskilled and unskilled workers. Picketing, strikes, factory sit-ins and some violence accompanied this struggle.

During this period the United States emerged as a world power on the international scene and fought two global wars. This nation sparred with Soviet Russia in an undeclared Cold War in the 1940s and 1950s. The nation has faced new opponents, Communist North Koreans in Korea in 1949 and Communist North Vietnamese in Vietnam in the 1960s.

On the national scene, one of the most striking developments has been urbanization. Huge metropolitan areas with satellite suburbs can be found in every section of the country, producing a multitude of new municipal problems. Recreational activities have expanded and changed. Before losing patrons to television in the 1950s, movies attracted as many as fifty million people weekly. Spectator sports have become more popular, with baseball, football, basketball and horse racing leading.

The newspaper has mirrored the dramatic events and helped shape the national and social destiny. The press has continued many of the traditions forged in the previous century. To the traditional newspapers and magazines have been added newsmagazines and picture magazines.

Radio and television, newcomers to the family of news communication media, have proved to be sharp competitors and have widened the news horizons of the public.

POPULATION DOUBLES, CIRCULATION EXPANDS

Many social forces have contributed to shaping the characteristics of these media, which in turn have exerted strong influence on the changing American scene.

The American continent having filled up steadily, has now been almost completely settled except for some poor land and the mountain districts. Although the birth rate generally has begun to decline and immigration has been practically cut off since the 1920s, the number of people has doubled, jumping from seventy-five million to one hundred fifty million during the first five decades of the new century. Population reached 200 million by 1968.

The increased number of people who have become better educated plus those whose leisure time has been extended because of the shortened workweek, have given newspaper circulation an added impetus and sent subscriptions soaring, from twenty million to fifty-three million by mid-century. Labor-saving devices in the home have given women additional free time to read. They have become interested in local, state and national affairs. By 1965 circulation had reached sixty million. While population had been rising to one hundred ninety million, circulation had mounted faster.

Although more readers have bought the dailies, the number of newspapers published has decreased during this period. According to the figures, 2,226 dailies were issued at the beginning of the century. They reached their greatest peak in 1916 when 2,600 papers rolled from the presses. By 1968 the dailies had dropped to 1,817.

Another trend has occurred. Popularity of the afternoon edition has increased, accounting for 82 per cent of the nation's dailies and nearly 60 per cent of the total circulation. Evening editions had reached 1,463 with a circulation of 35.8 million. Reasons have been varied. Readers have had more time in the evening. More women read dailies. Extension of the telegraph and telephone have permitted news breaking in the morning or afternoon to be transmitted quickly and published the same day. Development of linecasting machines for composing rooms, and of faster presses for the pressroom have contributed to the speed of production. Daily sports results and stock market quotations have been wanted quickly; mechanical facilities have made quicker delivery of this news possible.

There were 354 morning newspapers issued in 1968, with a circulation of 24.4 million. A story of increasing circulation and decreasing papers similar to the dailies can be told of the weeklies.

ECONOMY, WITH SOME SETBACKS, MOVES AHEAD

Development of journalism has been profoundly affected by the changing economic forces. Total wealth of the United States has leaped ahead during these decades. Setbacks, though severe, have been only temporary. National wealth based on farms, mines, factories and real estate has jumped five times, from $8 billion to $40 billion. Vast segments of the population still have been living on a low-income level, but the standard of living for many, nevertheless, has been steadily raised. Many factors have contributed to the expanding national wealth and income.

Increasing mechanization has stimulated farm production. Scientists have studied soils and plants and have produced hardier crops and livestock. The farmers' living standards, in spite of setbacks during the depressions, have been generally improved. These agricultural advances have had multiple effects on the journalism of the nation. Manufacturers as well as retailers have aimed advertising at the farmers.

In the twentieth century America's industries have become the marvel of the other countries of the world. Inventors have been busy designing and introducing new machines and new products; new materials, such as plastics and nylons, have been put on the market. The electrical power industry has been expanded, while the electric appliance, auto, motion picture, radio, television, plastics and other industries have boomed. Food processing, including freezing, canning and packaging, has become one of America's great industries. The value of manufactured products between 1900 and 1950 had increased from $11.5 billion to $74 billion. In the next ten years the value of these products reached $163 billion. Manufacturers have sought more aggressively than in the previous years to capture national markets by advertising.

EFFECTS ON JOURNALISM

Economic development of the country together with the expansion of population has had important influences on the development of journalistic media. Newspaper circulation revenue jumped from $84 million to $275 million between 1900 and 1929. After the slump, because of the depression, the subscription income pulled up again and in 1963 totaled $1,231,000,000. Total advertising in all media rose from $490 million at the beginning of the century to $14 billion by 1964, with the newspapers getting about a third of this.

The bulk of newspaper revenue, as before, has come from local advertisers, who have multiplied and grown larger in ever-expanding cities. To downtown stores have been added suburban stores. Chain stores also have affected the retail department store competition. These chains, depending on mass newspaper appeal to bring in customers, not only have been able to afford to advertise more regularly, but have also been able to expand daily and Sunday advertising space. Local advertising had reached about $2 billion in 1957 and $3 billion in 1965. Classified advertising had also helped swell newspaper revenue during this period.

To make the newspaper profitable in many cities, larger economic or manufacturing units have been needed. Growth of press chains, there-

TABLE 25

Indices of Circulation and Adult Population (1946-1964)

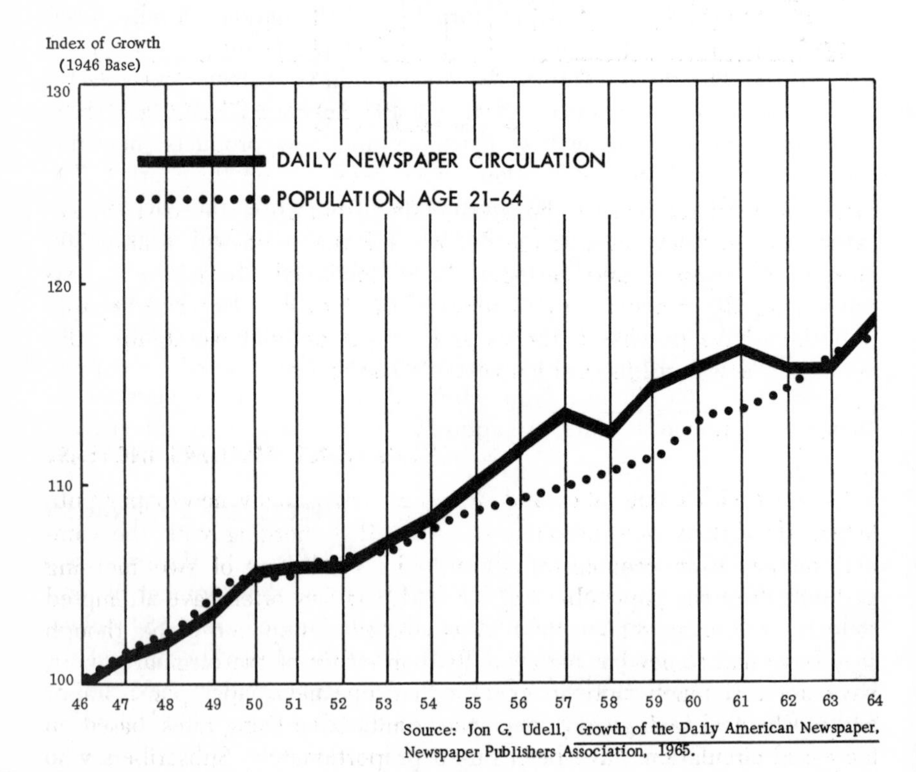

Source: Jon G. Udell, Growth of the Daily American Newspaper, Newspaper Publishers Association, 1965.

TABLE 26

Indices of the Growth of Newspaper Advertising and the U. S. Economy (1946-1964)

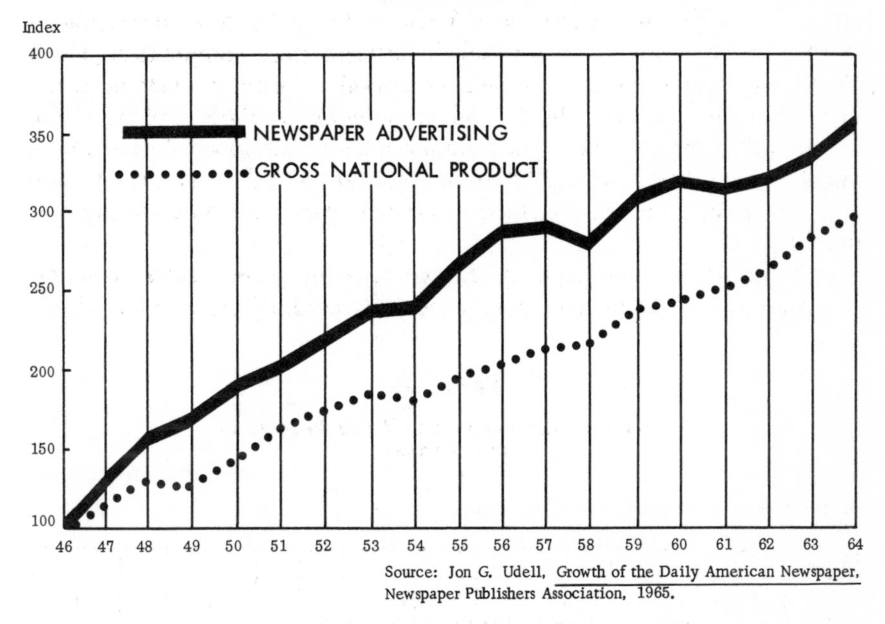

Source: Jon G. Udell, Growth of the Daily American Newspaper, Newspaper Publishers Association, 1965.

fore, has accelerated, their links stretching from coast to coast. Syndicates, because they have reduced costs for the publisher, selling him inexpensive features and cartoons, have flourished. To insure a continuous supply of paper, raw material of the industry, larger newspaper publishers have purchased forests and bought or built woodpulp mills, perfecting a vertical integration in their enterprises.

CONSOLIDATIONS, MERGERS INCREASE

Faced with rising labor and newsprint costs, many newspaper publishers throughout the nation have found that merging with the competition has been economically profitable. Publishers of two morning and two afternoon papers have discovered that they often have attempted to cover the same reader field. A combined newspaper plant, though they have had somewhat higher costs than either of the original papers, have not cost much more to operate than one newspaper plant. Labor and mechanical savings have been the result. Advertising rates, based on increased circulation, have been raised proportionately. Subscribers who have wanted the news of one journal and the excellent features or departmental news of another newspaper, now have had to subscribe only to one publication. By midcentury, three hundred local combinations had been organized in various cities. The merger trend has been accelerated by the further development of chain journalism.

CHAIN JOURNALISM GROWS

Economic factors which have caused development of chain grocery, drug and cigar stores also have led to development of more and larger newspaper chains. Newspaper chains have saved money by supplying the same news, editorials, photos to all links in the organization. Talented managerial, editorial, reportorial specialists have been employed to work for the chain. Wholesale buying of materials also has proven economical.

Chain ownership, as a result of these economies and advantages, has spread rapidly in the new century. In 1900 ten chains controlled thirty-two American dailies. By 1960 the trade magazine *Editor & Publisher* listed 114 groups publishing 563 morning and evening dailies, almost a third of all newspapers.

Leaders in chain journalism have been Hearst, with twenty-six dailies and the Scripps-Howard interests which owned twenty-five newspapers at their peak, but dropped down later. Other large chains have included the Patterson-McCormick; the Speidel; the Paul Block; the Rider, Howe, Frentress-Marsh; and the Lee Syndicate and Thompson chains. The newest chain, the Newhouse group, rose rapidly in the 1940s.

SYNDICATES MULTIPLY, FLOURISH

The increasing number of feature syndicates which have been established to meet the needs of editors have provided a wide variety of editorial matter at low cost. The syndicate trend has been one of the most significant developments in the twentieth century. The number of syndicates rose from 100 in 1926 to 212 by 1960. More than five thousand persons—executives, artists, writers and clerks—were employed in the industry, which had an estimated payroll of $15 million, by midcentury. Gross sales boomed to $50 million annually.

The editorial page has felt the effects of standardization; "canned" editorials, columnists, cartoons and advice columns have made many pages look alike and read alike. Editors have not had to think about or express views on international and national issues. The publishers often have let the burden fall on the syndicated columnists. The variety of syndicated matter has been great and the quality often unusually high.

Without syndication, many small-town newspapers would have been duller and their readers far less informed.

COMICS CHANGE

Stock offering of syndicates has been the comics, developed at the end of the last century. Types of comics have changed during the period under examination. In the early part of the twentieth century, "Mutt and Jeff," "Maude the Mule," "Maggie and Jiggs," "Abe Kibbible," "Buster Brown" were popular. "Barney Google" attracted millions of children and their parents. Each cartoon had a sequence of pictures, with a joke at the climax. The characters got into and out of funny situations. One-panel cartoons, such as "The Toonerville Trolley That Meets All the Trains," appealed to thousands. Then in the 1930s the trend toward adventure, crime and melodrama became definite. "Buck Rogers," "Flash Gordon," "Superman," "Terry and the Pirates," "Steve Canyon," all had many adventures and millions of followers.

Severe criticism has been made of many of the comics on the grounds that they have emphasized the gory and the subhuman. Some editors have felt they have had a right to cut out suggestive cartoons. Others have charged that "Little Orphan Annie" has had a Republican slant.

Publishers of comic sections have recognized the great advertising pull of such characters as "Blondie and Dagwood," "Popeye," "Toots and Casper," "Barney Google," "Tillie the Toiler" and "Little Annie Rooney."

SUNDAY PAPERS BECOME MORE POPULAR

Syndicates have been a contributing factor to the extraordinary expansion of the Sunday edition of American newspapers in the twentieth century. At the end of the nineteenth century Pulitzer and Hearst discovered methods for making the Sunday issue of their New York papers popular.

Other publishers in New York and throughout the United States began to introduce features similar to those of Pulitzer and Hearst and to expand their own Sunday editions. Although Sunday baseball games were held, and the ban on motion pictures lifted after the First World War, plenty of time for consuming the Sunday edition was still available. Sunday newspapers have flourished, and in many instances have pulled much of the seven-day week newspapers' income, balancing the lean days of Monday and Saturday. A number of metropolitan newspapers have developed their own tabloid feature sections.

Figure 50. The Older Funnies. Millions of readers followed the adventures of their favorite comic strip characters—from "Maggie and Jiggs" to "Andy Gump" to "Little Orphan Annie" and "Polly and Her Pals." (Maggie and Jiggs, reprinted by permission of King Features syndicate; Andy Gump and Little Orphan Annie, courtesy of the Chicago Tribune-New York News Syndicate; Polly and Her Pals, King Features Syndicate.)

Figure 51. New Type of Comic. The daily comic strip, "Alley Oop," by T. V. Hamlin, became widely popular. In less than a year, the likeable, impulsive, free-swinging caveman, his pet dinosaur and his prehistoric pals built up a strong following in five hundred daily newspapers. (From an advertisement in *Editor & Publisher,* July 21, 1934, a year after this cartoon began)

Syndicated tabloid magazines have come to the aid of many publishers of smaller newspapers. These magazines have been printed at a central plant, with the individual client's newspaper name printed on the front page. Metropolitan paper owners also have obtained the rights to distribute one or two of these magazines to their readers.

By 1958 the four dominant syndicated Sunday tabloids, *This Week, Parade, American Weekly* and *Family Weekly,* reached 310 distributing newspapers with a circulation of six million. (Hearst corporation dropped the *American Weekly* when the newspaper chain was shrunk.) Concentrating heavily on pictures, these tabloids have added color, creating attractive sections. In addition, groups of large newspapers, organized under the name of Metropolitan Sunday Newspapers, have edited their own tabloids. Metro has been selling group advertising.

Newspapers and magazines, then radio from the 1920s and television from the 1940s have carried out the necessary role of salesman. Advertising has hastened acceptance of new goods and useful appliances, a result which formerly would have required decades to accomplish.

TRANSPORTATION MOVES IN NEW DIRECTIONS

Closely integrated with the nation's industrial and commercial development have been expanding transportation facilities. To the railroads have been added passenger automobiles, trucks, and airplanes.

The auto has helped the reporter get to the fire more quickly than the old horse and carriage method. The taxicab has become essential in metropolitan cities. Similarly, the truck and bus have supplanted distribution of newspapers by horse and wagon. Vast and complicated distribution systems, depending on bus, truck, railroad and airplane, have been worked out by astute publishers and circulation men to cover entire states with their papers. The auto industry has invested millions of dollars in newspaper advertising annually.

The airplane experiments carried on by the Wright brothers on the lonely sand dunes of North Carolina in 1903 also have had repercussions on journalism. Man's conquest of the air has accelerated the speed of the reporter. He has been able to get to distant scenes of important news events more quickly than by any other means. Airplanes have also been used to distribute daily newspapers to distant communities quickly.

URBANIZATION ACCELERATES, PRODUCES NEW PROBLEMS

As a result of the various economic and transportation improvements, urbanization has increased in the twentieth century. More than half the United States population lived in urban areas at midcentury.

Enormous growth in the city population, together with economic developments, has produced a tremendous expansion in newspapers. These factors have increased the number of advertisements, the circu-

TABLE 27

Growth of Largest Cities (1900-1960)

	1900	1960
New York	3,437,202	7,781,980
Chicago	1,698,575	3,550,404
Philadelphia	1,293,697	2,002,512
Los Angeles	102,489	2,479,015
Detroit	285,754	1,670,144
Boston	560,000	697,197
St. Louis	575,238	750,026
Baltimore	308,957	939,424
Cleveland	381,768	876,050

U. S. Bureau of Census

lation and the revenue of newspapers in many towns and cities. The size of editions, especially evening and Sunday papers, has been enlarged.

Cities have faced many serious problems of social welfare—the poor, housing, slums—and newspapers have directed their readers' attention to these questions. Most of the large cities have had growing pains, and the suburban trend has produced a number of transportation, utility and taxation problems, which newspapers have reported and commented upon.

The migration of Negroes from the South to large cities in the North, Midwest and West after the Second World War has caused additional problems. With the tremendous influx of Negroes has come the shift of white residents to the suburbs and adjoining towns. Negro ghettoes have appeared in the cities. Newspapers have reported the abject poverty, unemployment, overcrowding and dismal slum conditions in which the Negro, unused to urban life, has found himself. These conditions have led to disenchantment in waiting for civil rights legislation to improve the situation. The call by Negro militants and the upsurge of Black Power have stirred a rash of discontent, resulting in riots, lootings and burnings in low-income areas. Many persons, black and white, have lost their lives. Millions of dollars in property damage have also resulted.

Multiplication of city activities and increasing revenue from advertisements have enabled publishers to increase their reporting staffs and their personnel to specialize. The expanding city has also presented distribution problems for publishers in reaching readers in outlying sections.

Community Newspapers

With expansion of the city, enterprising newsmen have established neighborhood and district weeklies. They have covered the news of their areas which large-circulation newspapers have not had room for. The community press reporters have written about local school events, Parent-Teacher Association meetings and playground activities.

District weeklies have carried on campaigns for health centers, recreational facilities and cleaner streets, and they have supported school improvement loans. When the district issues have reached the city council level, metropolitan papers have reported the news. Crime has not been emphasized in these weeklies.

A new principle, free distribution, has been instituted and has become popular in many cities. Circulations of 5,000, 10,000 or 50,000 can be guaranteed the advertiser. The small merchant has had a low-priced advertising medium which has reached the particular market in which he has been interested and from which he has drawn his customers. His advertisement has not been buried among hundreds of others in a metropolitan daily.

Suburban Publications

Similar weekly publications have been launched in suburban communities adjoining metropolitan cities. Even dailies have been established to meet local needs. Surburban reporters have covered local news intensely, developed special features appealing to women and used local pictures to attract readers. Many of the weeklies have paid circulations. Recognizing that they had interests in common, the publishers founded the Suburban Press Foundation, obtaining Dr. Curtis D. MacDougall, of Medill School of Journalism of Northwestern University, as consultant.

ORGANIZED LABOR STRUGGLES FOR RECOGNITION

Manning the machines in factories, digging coal in the mines have been the workers. At the turn of the century the American Federation of Labor was left in undisputed possession of the field. The union membership grew from 550,000 to 2,000,000 by 1914, with every important skilled labor group affiliated, except the railroad brotherhoods.

With coming of the depression in 1930, all the gains which had been made by labor were in danger of slipping away. Wages were cut. The openshop was employed in many industries, and the injunction was invoked. In the 1930s various acts were passed by Congress to assist labor in getting on its feet again to establish protections against the hazards of industrial life, and to guarantee the rights of collective bargaining. The Fair Labor Standards Act, the Social Security measure and the National Labor Relations Act, all were designed to accomplish these ends.

With this protection, the union movement was revitalized. A group broke from the A. F. of L. and organized the Congress of Industrial Organizations in 1935. The aim of the C.I.O. was to bring into the union the unskilled and semiskilled employees in mass production industries. The A.F.L. and the C.I.O. merged in 1955.

As organized labor has grown in membership and influence, most newspapers have recognized union activities as news. Some editors also have seen labor's growing influence as a menace. When strikes have been called, they have been reported as before, but the industrial struggle has now moved to congressional halls and courtrooms. It has required experts in labor law to report intelligently the various legal moves which have been made and the actions of the various government labor boards. Editors have assigned reporters to "the labor beat." Although preceded by others, Louis Stark, of the *New York Times,* became the first labor reporter to make a national reputation. He won the confidence of both sides and became an expert in industrial reporting. He has been followed by other labor reporters, knowledgeable and competent.

Development of unions in new industries and the protection afforded by federal laws led to formation of the American Newspaper Guild under the leadership of Heywood Broun, columnist for the *New York World-Telegram,* a movement which will be discussed in a later chapter.

POLITICAL WINDS SHIFT

Regardless of which party was in power during the first sixteen years of the new century, this period has been called by historians the Progressive Era. A loud, ever-growing protest began to make itself heard and eventually swept the whole country, affecting both Republicans and Democrats. This reform movement resulted in both economic and political changes.

It will be recalled that, before the turn of the century, Pulitzer and Hearst, Scripps, Older and others carried on campaigns exposing local government graft and enlargement of the trusts. A number of magazine journalists, called muckrakers, exposed on a national scale these conditions. People read these articles and were shocked by the exposures. The voters demanded, through their leaders, reform of politics and industry.

The new reform movement then moved to the national scene. Populists and Democrats under William Jennings Bryan were not able to win the national election in 1896, but their discussions and protest against basic economic injustices, created by railroads and trusts, stirred public interest. The voters elected Theodore Roosevelt, who became a trustbuster. As a result of a split in Republican ranks, Democrat Woodrow Wilson, with the slogan "the New Freedom," came into office in 1912 to continue the reform movement.

In the post-World War I reaction of 1920, the newspapers reported how the country swept Republican Warren G. Harding into office, and later Calvin Coolidge, governor of Massachusetts. He was followed by Herbert Hoover in 1928.

Hoover had not been in office more than a few months, however, when the front page proclaimed the stock market collapse, and very shortly, news of a widespread agricultural, industrial and banking depression. With a New Deal slogan of reform, Franklin D. Roosevelt, nominee of the Democratic Party, won the election in 1932. Roosevelt initiated a number of measures to help the faltering economic system.

While nearly all the Democratic press supported Roosevelt in his first term, his social and economic reforms did not find favor with publishers when he ran again in 1936, 1940 and 1944. Many editors charged he was about to wreck the country. A number of editors who supported Roosevelt when he ran for the first time opposed his proposal to expand the United States Supreme Court, adding liberal members to it so that New Deal measures would be declared constitutional. Editors called this a court-packing scheme. President Roosevelt labeled such publishers "economic royalists," and the battle raged.

In each succeeding presidential campaign, more Democratic newspapers shifted to the Republican column. In 1944 Republican candidate Thomas E. Dewey had the support of 60 per cent of the dailies but lost to President Roosevelt. This trend toward the Republican column continued when Roosevelt died in 1945 and Harry S. Truman, Vice President, filled the unexpired term and sought the presidency in 1948. In that year Dewey was favored by a majority of the dailies. Truman, however, won.

When the voters elected the Democrats to office while the dailies supported the Republican candidates, considerable controversy arose as to the waning editorial power of the press. It was pointed out, however, that President Roosevelt had an extraordinary news sense and made news which was reported on the front pages, thereby holding greater influence than many editorial pages. President Roosevelt likewise used radio for his fireside chats, which kept newspapermen on their toes. They had to report the speeches or get "scooped."

Various surveys showed that newspapers generally gave fair *news coverage* to Democratic presidential candidate Adlai E. Stevenson in his contest with Republican Dwight D. Eisenhower in 1952, although most of the editors, with 80 per cent of the nation's circulation, supported Eisenhower on their editorial pages. There were many individual papers showing a strong news bias for the Republican Party.

During the 1956 campaign President Eisenhower's popularity with the editors dropped some, but in the presidential race that year he had the support of 67 per cent of the editors.

In the 1960 election Republican candidate Richard C. Nixon, without Eisenhower's strong appeal, won 57 per cent of the daily support, or 70 per cent of the total daily circulation. Democratic candidate John F. Kennedy secured the backing of 16.4 per cent of the dailies with a circulation of 30 per cent. In the final vote Kennedy won the presidency with a little better than 49.7 per cent of the votes.

The 1964 election, in which Lyndon B. Johnson was standard bearer for the Democratic Party, and Barry Goldwater, the Republican candidate, showed reversal of the newspaper pattern of support. President Johnson, who had taken office when President Kennedy was assassinated, had more newspaper endorsements than his Republican opponent. Many publishers and editors could not agree with what they called the "extreme views" of Senator Goldwater. His apparent commitment to the abolition of the social security system and to carrying on a nuclear war antagonized many editors. Large-city newspapers with huge circulation, therefore, gave strong support to Johnson.

Surveys showed that Johnson had the endorsement also of a number of chain newspapers which had followed the Republican banner in previous elections. Johnson was supported by the Hearst, Scripps-Howard, Knight, Cowles, Ridder groups, and most of the Newhouse and Gannett chain-linked dailies.

INTERPRETATIVE TREND GROWS

The economic depression of the 1930s had an effect on the development of the interpretative trend in journalism. The editorial page had been the source of the interpretation of current affairs for a century, but readers were becoming more educated and wary of any editorial writer's opinion. Readers now wanted to learn the facts for themselves. The spot news story, giving the who, the what, the where, the when, the why and the how, was objective but bare. Spot news told only the surface facts about current happenings.

Newspaper readers now desired to learn especially the why of the news. They wanted to know why the country's economic system had skidded and had come to a slowdown in a land of such great scientific and technological advancement. As a result of this need city editors directed their reporters to dig into the happenings of the day and bring back the news behind the news. News features were written by investigative reporters seeking to explain the happenings on page one.

In Washington, reporters such as Raymond Clapper became writers of special columns. Paul Mallon even called his column, "News behind the News." Marquis Childs, the Alsop Brothers, David Lawrence, Westbrook Pegler and Drew Pearson became syndicated columnists with wide followings. The Newspaper Enterprise Association, a division of Scripps-Howard, supplied its clientele with special news features giving background. The Associated Press, reluctant to depart from the objective, impartial traditions it had established, moved slowly toward the explanatory features, as the AP called its background articles.

In a similar attempt to give news more meaning, some newspapers instituted weekly pages reviewing the news of the week and presenting historical information about the news, as *Time* magazine had led the way already. The *New York Times* and the *New York Herald Tribune* produced some of the best sections of this kind. A number of journalism texts have been written, reflecting this background trend.

WOMEN'S ECONOMIC IMPORTANCE INCREASES

The twentieth-century's industrial age has had deep effects on the women of the nation. A marked growth in the number of women wage earners has occurred. In addition to industrial and white collar jobs they held before, women practically took over teaching in public schools in the early part of the century. Many women have broken down the barriers in other professions, trying cases in courts as lawyers, and tending the sick as physicians. Some women have become scientists, working in laboratories, where they have explored the unknown in chemistry and biology. Thousands of women have now become members of the leisure class. Women have played an important role in the economy for they shape the styling of goods; it has been estimated that women buy more than 80 per cent of the manufactured commodities.

Responding to these developments, newspapers have expanded their special pages to cover women's club meetings and social activities. News and features about food, clothes and household decorations and about family relations and children have filled these pages. Radio and television, likewise, have made their appeal to the housewife, especially in the morning and afternoon hours, with entertainment, news comment and sentimental plays, which have acquired the name "soap operas" because of their frequent sponsorship by the soap manufacturers.

EDUCATION EXPANDS

Public education, which had become entrenched in the American scheme by the end of the nineteenth century, has made steady progress, and by widening the market for readers has contributed to the rapid expansion of the newspaper. Education also has affected the newspaper contents.

School attendance laws spread through the states and raised the compulsory school-going age. When the century turned, more than fifteen million children were enrolled in the elementary grades. By 1960 more than twice as many boys and girls marched to school every morning. More spectacular jumps were noted in the higher grades. A half-million students attended high schools in the nation at the turn of the century; but the total reached 9.24 million in 1960.

In the twentieth century, particularly during the post-World War I period, a college diploma became a requisite for success, according to Americans. In 1900 only a quarter of a million young men and women were enrolled at colleges and universities. This number reached 3.5 million by 1960.

The results on the newspaper of these educational advancements have been many. Almost the entire population has become literate, although some segments, such as the low-income Negro class, white persons in backward rural areas and newly arrived immigrants, still have not learned to read. Their numbers have been estimated at two million. Illiteracy has decreased from 10 per cent of the population to 2 per cent during these decades. As population has grown and the attack on illiteracy has made headway, the newspaper reading market has enlarged.

When the population went beyond the high school level, cultural interests developed. Larger newspapers recognized this in their special book, art and musical columns and sections. As science was introduced into the high school and college curricula, and when chemistry, biology and physics became more popular and important for work in medicine and industrial research, a broader interest in scientific affairs resulted. Newspapers and syndicates, as indicated, responded with science news and features.

College courses in psychology and sociology led to a demand for a better understanding of the backgrounds of the news. Studies in propaganda have made students alert to the detection of influences in controversial issues and to the problem of coloration and bias in the news.

Many newspapers have seen the value in school news and have assigned reporters to the "school beat," while other dailies have helped inform voters on the need for school loans. Still other publications have engaged in attacks on the progressive school methods and liberal college instructors.

SPORTS NEWS COMMERCIALIZED

American people have become more and more sports conscious. Sports have become a big business in the new era. Shrewd promotion abetted by newspaper and radio, and later, television reporters have aroused the American public to an extraordinary interest in athletic events, mostly professional. Baseball has continued to attract large crowds. College football has made great headway, and the public has followed avidly the players. Newspapers have contributed greatly to the buildup of this sport, with thousands of stories having been printed about Red Grange, of Illinois, and Knute Rockne, of Notre Dame.

Sports promoter Tex Rickard promoted boxing more successfully than anyone before him. Fans followed enthusiastically each of the bouts in the press and read gravely the comments of the sports writers on Jess Willard, Georges Carpentier, Jack Dempsey and other heavyweights such as Gene Tunney, the boxer-Shakespearean scholar, and Joe Louis, who held the title longer than anyone else.

As important as all other sports combined, especially with bets considered, horse racing has been built into a huge industry. New tracks have been opened in cities, the stakes higher than ever. Newspapers have supplied information on the races, with bets being placed on the basis of this information. Some editions of metropolitan papers have been filled with late racing news, as many street sales have depended on it.

With the development of sports departments, the sports staff has expanded. On many newspapers a sports editor has presided over a group of subeditors and reporters who have covered every phase of professional, school and sandlot athletics. Frequently newspapers have developed sports departments with their own photographers, copyeditors and special desks for handling sports copy. Sports writers have developed a sports language and coined many words which have slipped into the American language. Sports columnists have also made their appearance. Makeup of the sports pages often has been livelier and has shown more originality than news or editorial pages.

MOVIES, SILENT AND TALKIES, PROVIDE ENTERTAINMENT

Various kinds of entertainment have been introduced during this period, with widespread effects on journalism. The first new type of entertainment was the motion picture. Thomas A. Edison developed the kinetoscope by 1890, when crude animated pictures were thrown on a screen. Short subjects, resorted to at first, were used as filler on live vaudeville programs. By 1903 the first full-length story, "The Great Train Robbery," was shown. Thousands of pictures were produced in the movie studios, located originally in New York then in California. With the "Jazz Singer" in 1927, a new era began, for sound was synchronized with pictures which began to talk. Movie-going in these decades became an ingrained American habit.

The effects of motion pictures on the press have been many. News about the movie stars and films have been eagerly sought by the movie-going public. Newspapers have filled these potential wants by publishing news, features, interviews and pictures of the players. Entertainment sections have expanded. Hollywood columns were born to tell the inside gossip of filmland's glamorous queens and dashing actors. When television developed as an entertainment medium, newspapers responded in like fashion, with news, features and pictures of the television programs and personalities.

LITERATURE BECOMES NEWS

Newspaper publishers have been aware of the steadily rising interest in literature by the more educated group in the population. More book publishers have entered the business and thousands of new titles have been issued yearly. This has led newspaper publishers to print weekly literary supplements in their Sunday editions and even daily columns on new books. Syndicated book reviews were introduced in the daily press.

SCIENTIFIC ADVANCES REPORTED

Science has played a larger part in the daily life of society than ever before. The time lag between research and popularization, however, was long in the early decades of the new century. Newspapers covered science as they did other matters; sometimes well, sometimes badly. Much pseudoscience of a sensational kind fitted into the newspaper pattern. There was a running feud between reporter and scientist: The scientist did not trust the reporter, the reporter could not understand the scientist.

Out of these experiences Science Service was organized in 1921 with trustees nominated by three scientific associations, by the journalism profession and by the E. W. Scripps estate.

It was not until the 1930s that science writing became a specialty on various papers. Many of the first science writers were radio editors of the 1920s, who told readers how to build crystal sets. When this boom died, as factories turned out inexpensive radio products, the radio editors turned to science writing. These practitioners banded together into the National Association of Science Writers. Numerous syndicates besides Science Service have supplied "March of Science," "Science Briefs," or "Science News Reports." The time lag between research and popularization of the findings has been reduced considerably. More of the American public have become better informed on advances made in science than ever before.

The developments of individual newspapers in various sections of America are next examined to see how they responded to the changing American scene and to local problems. The various chapters will point up also the transformations in journalism.

Chapter 33

New York's Dynamic Newspapers

NEW YORK, METROPOLIS, FACES TWENTIETH-CENTURY CHALLENGES

New York, which had won leadership among American cities in the nineteenth century, has continued to shine as the outstanding metropolis of the twentieth century. Although challenged by other industrial cities, New York has remained the center of banking and shipping. Headquarters of the garment industry and book and magazine publishing activities, New York has some of the largest retail department stores in the world.

A center of education and other cultural activities, such as music and art, New York boasted one of the oldest of America's great universities, Columbia, followed closely by New York University. But city residents have been able to attend other local colleges and universities, such as City College and Fordham University. Many other specialized institutions such as the Julliard School of Music have become well known nationally. The New York Philharmonic Orchestra has been rated among the top musical organizations in the country. With their priceless collections, the Metropolitan Museum of Art and the American Museum of Natural History have attracted hundreds of thousands of visitors each year. The United States theatre was centered on Broadway between 42nd and 59th streets. In the first quarter of the century, before the era of sound motion pictures and television, vaudeville's top performers considered the Palace Theatre their Mecca.

New York City's population grew from 3.4 million at the turn of the century to 7.6 million in 1960. More than ten million residents were living in the trading zone by this time.

New York newspapers have mirrored this prosperity, this vitality and these changes. Because of the large concentration of population in the metropolitan area, experiments in journalism could be, and have been tried. A large and sufficient market could be found to support almost any type of journalism which might be evolved. Extensive groups of people in every class—the low-economic, the industrial workers, the middle-class and the upper high-bracket class—lived in the area. All levels wanted the news and the features that journalism provided for information and for entertainment. The heavy, informative *New York Times* and the breezy, entertaining tabloid, the *New York Daily News,* have succeeded.

Since the 1940s New York publishers have had to meet the challenge of the exodus to suburbs, where residents bought local dailies for local news. Instead of buying two Manhattan-published newspapers, one in the morning, another in the evening, commuters and suburbanites have cut down to one Manhattan paper plus a local journal or have eliminated the Manhattan issue altogether. Publishers also had to face new rivals in the communication industry: radio and television. Rising costs of publication have plagued publishers with a constant threat to their survival.

NEW YORK WORLD'S SENSATIONALISM MODIFIED

In the Machine Age, the *New York World,* founded by the dynamic Joseph Pulitzer, continued its nineteenth-century traditions of sensational, crusading journalism, but with modifications. These grew out of the *World's* own internal changes and the alterations in the journalistic and social environment just described.

The *World* became respectable in the 1900s. The moral war which had been waged against the *World* and the *Journal* before the turn of the century was one of the reasons for the decline of sensationalism. In the new era, New Yorkers lost their mid-Victorian viewpoint; and the *World's* sex sensationalism, so amazing and startling, now appeared conventional. Melodrama went out the door as smart sophistication came in.

A section of the *World's* readers, drawn from the middle class and the immigrants, became better educated, more informed. This was especially true of their sons and daughters, who graduated from high school or college and read more widely. At its audience changed, the *World* began to make an appeal on more serious grounds: well-written national and international news. The paper also added columnists with an intellectual appeal.

Decline of sensationalism was gradual but was accelerated toward the outbreak of the World War in 1914. Faced by the European conflict, the interests of American people pushed sentimental, crime and sex news from the front page. When the United States plunged into the war for democracy, the attention of the *World's* million readers was centered on this supreme life-or-death issue.

Crusading against big business and the irresponsible wealthy class, the *World*, during the eighties and nineties, helped set in motion the forces which produced between 1900 and 1914 the march toward social and economic democracy. Pulitzer was the first of the muckrakers. Many magazines dedicated to the new social crusade developed *after* 1900.

Figure 52. Joseph Pulitzer, Editor-Owner of the *New York World*. (Courtesy of the *St. Louis Post-Dispatch*)

Besides being under the guidance of the powerful, crusading Pulitzer, the *World* benefited by the newcomer to its ranks: Frank I. Cobb. Cobb's background was filled with little schooling and a lot of hard knocks. At twenty-one, Cobb became a reporter on the *Grand Rapids* (Michigan) *Herald* at eight dollars a week and later became editorial writer for the *Detroit Free Press*. While Cobb was working on this job, a Pulitzer scout discovered him. Thirty-four years old when he joined the staff of the Pulitzer paper as editorial writer, Cobb led most of the crusades of the *World* in the twentieth century, including the campaign for America's participation in World War I on the side of the Allies, the climax of the great crusades in this era.

Most spectacular and perhaps most successful of the *World's* fights was the insurance scandal exposé of 1905. Young James Hazen Hyde, who had inherited a majority of the Equitable Life Insurance Company's stock, was charged with misuse of the funds to carry on his playboy activities. Permanent results occurred from the *World* crusade. The New York legislature in 1906 passed the Armstrong Insurance Code based on a report of an investigating committee.

Fearlessness of the *New York World's* crusades was demonstrated again in December, 1908, when it demanded that Congress investigate the "Panama Canal Scandal." The *World* declared the government had paid $40,000,000 for property on which the canal was built. The land could have been bought for $4,000,000. As this information was reprinted in the *Indianapolis* (Indiana) *News* and circulated in West Point, which was government property, the government brought libel suit against both the *World* and the Indianapolis paper. The cases against these papers were dismissed in a federal court.

In the Machine Age, the *Sunday World*, building on popularity already created, flourished and grew larger with its specialized departments. Gaudy blood-and-thunder melodramatic features became modified; serious articles, discussing contemporary problems, were introduced. New features were added. Prominent news personalities wrote pieces on their specialities. Pulitzer also added a "Metropolitan Section," giving a humorous twist to the news.

Politically, the *World* in the new century did not deviate from its democratic allegiance. The daily was lukewarm toward Bryan who had attached himself with bulldog tenacity to the party and led it to defeat in 1896, 1900 and 1908.

The *World* found a number of President Theodore Roosevelt's big stick policies in accord with its own views and sometimes praised him, particularly for his prosecution of the Northern Securities case, involving the merger of railroads. But essentially the *World* and Roosevelt were natural antagonists. Pulitzer was responsible for this conflict. Criticism of the President became the order of the day in the *World* office. President Roosevelt's prosecution of the *World* for libel in the Panama Canal case alienated Pulitzer still more. In Woodrow Wilson's campaign in 1912, the *World* took up the fight against plutocracy again.

Long before he died, Pulitzer wanted to do something constructive to build up his profession. He became interested in journalism schools and made arrangements to endow one. He originally intended to give the funds to Columbia University, but a quarrel arose over the board of directors for the new school. In his will he gave $2,000,000 to Columbia University, where the cornerstone for the journalism school was laid July 2, 1912.

Pulitzer also established a fund for annual prizes in the interest of letters, drama, music and good newspaper work, since known as the Pulitzer prizes. The newspaper awards provided considerable incentive for civic campaigns by newspapers. Other organizations followed the Pulitzer lead, offering awards for effective journalistic reporting and crusading.

The World in World War I

On June 29, 1914, out of clear sky, the *World* told on its front page a story that was to last for more than four years:

Heir to Austrian Throne and His Wife Assassinated in Bosnia; Second Attack Succeeds After He Wards Off Bombs

From the beginning, the *World* was pro-Ally. The *World* used the same appeals to influence its readers as it had in previous crusades. It stressed human rights, idealism and altruism. It fought the autocracy of the Kaiser. The man immediately responsible for the *World's* attitude was Cobb, chief editorial writer.

The English cut the cables between Germany and the United States in August, 1914. This left only the English cables, heavily censored, available. Although German officials pointed this out, their protest was lost in the flow of war news. The *World* subscribed to the news service of the pro-Ally *London Daily Telegraph.*

German press agents in America were not as adept at propaganda as the English. The Germans openly backed certain peace societies and were caught red-handed when they purchased a daily newspaper and sought to interfere with munition production.

Soon after the European war began in 1914, American correspondents were rushed to Europe. The invasion of Belgium and the atrocity stories helped sway the American press and its readers against Germany. Historians believe that extent of damage to Belgium was exaggerated and that the atrocity stories were fakes.

President Woodrow Wilson declared United States' neutrality in August, 1914, but isolation was impossible. The State Department asked the belligerents if the Declaration of London of 1909, regulating the sea rights of belligerents and neutrals, would be observed. The code provided that blockades would not extend beyond the borders of the enemy and prohibited the capturing of ships destined for nonblockaded ports.

On May 8, 1915, the *World* reported across its front page:

Two Torpedoes Sink Lusitania, Twelve Hundred May Be Lost; President, Stunned, In Seclusion

Sinking of this British liner, on which were traveling many Americans, proved to be one of the most sensational war stories in the period 1914 to 1917. The event contributed a great deal to the shaping of public opinion in this country against Germany. About 1,100 passengers and crew were lost; 124 Americans were among these.

The *World* printed the answer of Captain Von Papen, who asserted that Germany was entirely within her rights in sinking the ship after warning had been given, as a newspaper advertisement to this effect had been published prior to the sailing of the Lusitania. Von Papen regretted that American lives were lost.

An opposite view was argued in another story: "Rights of the United States Violated, Law Expert Tells the World." The *World* editorially declared that the time called for self-restraint. It combated the notion that Americans had been warned. On following days the *World* charged Germany with a cowardly and infamous deed. American citizens, it said, were murdered in cold blood by a deliberate act of the German government.

Clouds began to lift in 1915 as the United States began to supply Allied needs. These included raw materials, foodstuffs and munitions. Moreover, merchants here reached into new markets formerly supplied by warring nations. An unprecedented economic prosperity was experienced in the United States. Meanwhile, J. P. Morgan & Company became the central purchasing agent for the Allies. Exports in munitions in 1916 reached 1.29 billion. The financial company also floated about $1 billion in loans for the Allies. Germany made fewer purchases, about $25 million.

By the middle of 1916, English and French credit had reached the limit. The Federal Reserve Board pointed out that too much money was being tied up in foreign loans, not leaving enough liquid capital for American commercial and manufacturing purposes. Many believed that if England and France fell, Germany's next victim would be the United States. Many societies developed urging American preparedness.

Herbert Bayard Swope went abroad for the *World* in 1916 and made his way into Germany, where he wrote a series of articles for the Pulitzer paper. These articles won the Pulitzer reportorial prize in 1917.

The *World*, on August 15, 1915, was able to publish what became known as the Dumba German correspondence. The United States had put the Secret Service on the trail of violators of American neutrality. Frank Burke, one of the agents, trailed Dr. Heinrich Albert, of the German staff in New York, and sat near him on an elevated train on July 24. The German got off at a street corner and left his bag. Burke grabbed it and turned it over to the Secretary of the Treasury, William G. McAdoo. McAdoo turned the most telling of the documents over to Cobb for publication on condition that the source be kept an absolute secret. The *World* blazed the story of the document on page one, creating a national sensation. Letters in the bag revealed the workings of the German propaganda bureau, the subsidies to writers and speakers. The letters also told of plans to buy into American munition factories. These documents tended to discredit the German cause, making the Germans' subsequent statements suspect.

On April 7, 1917, the *World* told its readers:

> **President Proclaims War With Germany;**
> **Plans Rushed to Co-Operate With Allies:**
> **96 Ships Seized: Giant Vaterland Injured**

About forty American press writers covered the activities of the American Expeditionary Forces, making up a small fraction of the total newsmen on various fronts. It is estimated that more than five hundred correspondents represented newspapers, magazines, news and feature agencies. Among the correspondents were a few women. Peggy Hill, representing the Newspaper Enterprise Association, was the only accredited woman correspondent. Censorship of all cables and mails was conducted by the Military Intelligence Service.

War Censorship

In the United States various censorship regulations and laws were passed. President Wilson issued a proclamation ten days after this country entered the war. He announced that publication of any statement or information giving "aid or comfort" to the enemy was liable to prosecution for treason.

Figure 53. Rollin Kirby, Forceful Cartoonist. With a bold, broad stroke, Rollin Kirby, famous cartoonist for the *New York World*, interpreted the passing political and social scene. He translated the forceful editorials of the *New York World* into forceful cartoons. "The Death Grapple," published on April 4, 1917, represented the battle between autocracy (Germany) and democracy (United States) of World War I.

The Espionage Act of 1917 implemented this proclamation. Passed in June, 1917, the law provided for heavy fines and imprisonment for causing disloyalty or obstructing recruiting. Publications guilty of violating the act were subject to being deprived of mailing privileges, a blow to most periodicals. The measure was fought in Congress bitterly, but the bill finally passed both houses of Congress and was approved by the President. The Espionage Act was followed by the passing of the Trading with the Enemy Act in October, 1917, which provided for censorship of messages abroad. Foreign language newspapers had to file sworn statements with local postmasters.

The final censorship act invoked severe penalties. The Sedition Act, approved May, 1918, amended the Espionage Act, imposing heavy fines and imprisonment for the writing or publication of disloyal statements about the United States, its military, its government or its flag. The act's language was very broad, and while enforcement was up to the Department of Justice, the Post Office Department, under Postmaster General Albert S. Burleson, was active in enforcing the Sedition Act. He could deny mailing privileges to any publication he believed was guilty of disloyalty. The courts, to which appeal was made, upheld his broad powers. About seventy-five papers, many of them German-language newspapers, felt the postmaster's hand.

Realizing the nation must be unified behind the war effort, President Wilson set up the Committee on Public Information within a week after the war began. A liberal newspaperman and crusader, George Creel, was appointed chairman. A code for suppression of news of aid to the enemy was established for newspapers. Even the Associated Press objected to some of the rulings, refusing to kill news of the landing of United States troops in Europe. Hearst newspapers were in frequent trouble. The Creel Committee issued about six thousand news releases. Creel had great power, but exercised great restraint in a trying job.

The *World* published much war news about civilian activities. To mobilize (a word which seemed to fit any situation involving war preparations) the nation's industrial forces, President Wilson took over the railroads. The *World* featured the news in this fashion:

WILSON TO SEIZE RAILROADS TOMORROW;
McADOO DIRECTOR; PROFITS GUARANTEED
ON BASIS OF LAST THREE YEARS

War Ends

But all things have to end, and the *World* told on November 7, 1918, of the end of the war:

German's White Flag Crosses Allies Line;
Sudan is Fired As Americans Draw Near;
Senate Race Close; House Republican
Smith's Lead 12,952; Election Seen Sure

Roy W. Howard, representing Scripps-Howard newspapers and the United Press, was in Europe when World War I was coming to an end. Through an American intelligence officer, he learned that the armistice had been signed but no official announcement had been made. Without waiting for further official confirmation, Howard sent a report of this significant end-of-the-war news to his New York office. He stated that the war was over and that Germany and the Allies had signed an armistice at 11 A.M., November 7, 1918. UP newspaper clients published the news in huge headlines on the front page. Citizens all over the country began to celebrate the end of the war. The war, however, was not quite over. When Howard learned officially that the signing of the armistice was unconfirmable, he sent a second dispatch, but it did not reach New York headquarters until the next day. Some minor censorship official in Washington had held up the message.

The Associated Press, meanwhile, carried a bulletin from Washington stating that the State Department had not announced that the Germans had signed an armistice. Many inquiries from editors then came to the UP office asking about its armistice report. W. W. Hawkins, UP general manager in New York, answered the inquiries by saying that "the dispatch came from the President of the United Press and it is all we know. Roy Howard is not a faker." The UP officials feared that the armistice release would injure the prestige of the wire news service. Howard now had Admiral Wilson issue a statement relating that the United Press had acted in good faith with its premature announcement and that it was the result of an error for which the agency was in no way responsible. Howard and the United Press rode out the storm of recriminations and denunciations. The tumult diminished. The wire service lost only one client because of the unintentional, false story.

In the postwar period the *World* fought valiantly for the League of Nations as a means of preventing future wars. Cobb raised an eloquent voice against the spirit of revenge, and he wrote many strong editorials against the failure of the war aims.

Postwar Period (1918–1931)

The *World* in the last decade of its life, following World War I, became more and more conservative in its economic views and news policies. Nevertheless, the *World* was still known as a liberal newspaper which defended the rights of minorities, fought for free speech and was always ready to battle against political and legal injustices. It stood as a beacon light for thousands of liberals in New York and in the nation. Republicans continued in power from 1921 to 1931 and social reform was out. The *World* reflected this newer viewpoint.

Its founder died in 1911, and his sons now published the papers with the aid of executives. Internally, the staff of the *World* changed. The famous Cobb died in 1923. In charge were others: Ralph Pulitzer, who had been connected with the paper for almost two decades, was president of the Press Publishing Company; Herbert Bayard Swope, was executive editor. Later, Herbert Pulitzer, the youngest son, took command. Instead of the fighting Cobb, the *World* now had scholarly Walter Lippmann, Harvard graduate and writer on politics, as chief editorial writer. Stress was placed on civil rights. The *World* was pro-League of Nations, antiprohibition, and anti-Ku Klux Klan.

The *World* was still Democratic and continued to oppose conservatives and the Republican Party.

News policies of the *World,* like its economic doctrines, were modified. Its old sentimentalism practically disappeared.

The *World,* in the 1920s, exemplified as well as led important trends toward columnists and special magazine features, which American journalism produced in the twentieth century. Prominent newspapermen were given a column to themselves where they could comment on the news, tell anecdotes, print poetry, relate the antics of their children and their dogs and give vent to their personal likes and dislikes.

Swope is credited with building up the "page-opposite-editorial" in the morning *World,* where the columnists congregated. This became a distinguished page and even rivaled the *World's* editorial page for distinctive flavor and literary touch.

Crusades of the *World* in the postwar era proved that the Pulitzer paper still had great power and force. Significant and influential campaigns were those concerned with worldwide disarmament, exposure of the revival of the Ku Klux Klan in the South, and defense of Sacco and Vanzetti, charged with murder in Massachusetts.

After 1923, when Cobb died, the paper began a period of decline. Competition which the *World* faced in the postwar period became exceedingly keen, and profits dropped. Since before the war the *New York Times,* under management of Adolph S. Ochs, had built up a large circulation among serious news readers at the top. Moreover, the *Herald Tribune,* under new leadership of Ogden Reid who became editor in 1912, began to ape the policies of the *Times,* cutting into the upper-level circulation. From beneath, the tabloids—the *Daily News,* the *Mirror* and the *Graphic*—were cutting into the class to whom the *World* had once appealed.

Then came the depression. Caught without reserves and faced with keen competition, the *World* had no strong, powerful hand to guide it. Swope had resigned on January 2, 1929, before the economic crash came in the fall. Ralph Pulitzer also left the paper at the end of the year. Herbert Pulitzer, who had worked for the *World* for a few years, but had spent most of his time on the continent, came to take charge at this time.

By the end of 1930 the Pulitzer brothers were negotiating for the sale of the *World.* The papers lost one million dollars during that year. The Pulitzers made arrangements to sell the papers to Scripps-Howard, which already owned the *New York Telegram.* The news concerning the possible sale was a blow to liberals and conservatives everywhere.

In a last-minute effort to keep the *World* alive, the newspaper's staff formed an organization under the leadership of James W. Barrett, city editor, to raise enough money to buy the paper from the Pulitzer estate. The organization was able to get $2,000,000, pledged by former staff members, and perhaps would have been able to accumulate more, but time was short. An offer of $5,000,000 had been made by the liberal Scripps-Howard newspapers, which had agreed with the *World* on many issues. In the end, Roy W. Howard won control of the *World* and merged it with his *New York Telegram* in February, 1931. To many readers the death of the *World,* an important institution was like the death of a good friend.

As a result of the merger, the morning and *Sunday World* went out of existence. The *Evening World,* however, continued as a part of the *Telegram,* which became the *World-Telegram.* The Pulitzer papers had been unable to change and thereby became victims of the merger process of the twentieth century. The *St. Louis Post-Dispatch,* under Joseph Pulitzer, Jr., continued vigorous and strong.

HEARST'S CHAIN JOURNALISM GROWS

William R. Hearst, in the new century, became a powerful force in American journalism and American life, and was an opponent to be reckoned with. Hearst continued to be the arch showman and master psychologist. Personal factors in Hearst's life must be integrated with general movements in journalism and changing economic and social conditions in American life for an adequate, comprehensive picture of his chain.

American conditions gave rise to Hearst, and they perpetuated him. Hearst sought to fill a newspaper and social vacuum and became the

TABLE 28

Spread of Modern Journalistic Techniques

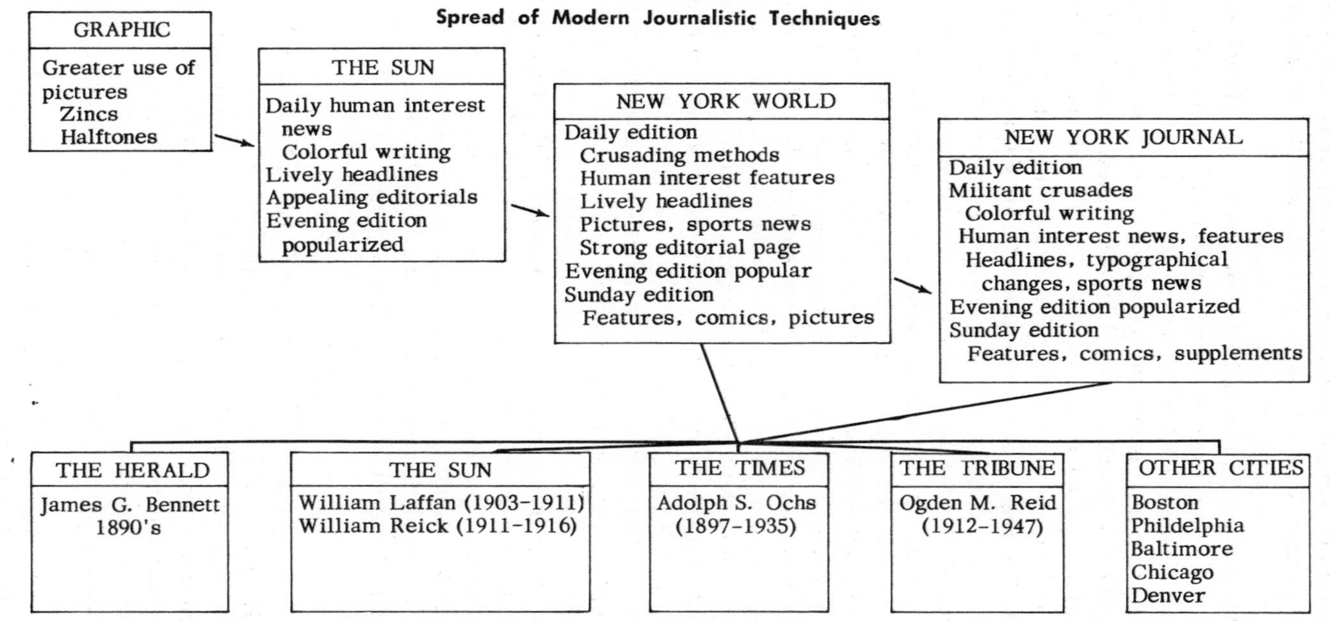

The chart, Spread of Modern Journalistic Techniques, shows how the modern techniques of journalism spread. The New York Graphic contributed pictures to the mainstream of journalism, while the New York Sun developed the human interest story and colorful writing of news and features as well as lively headlines. These techniques passed on to the New York World, which added the militant crusading technique and the strong editorial page. In the duel with the Journal, the modern large headline extending across the page was developed. The World set the pace for the Hearst Journal, and both of these, while called sensational and yellow at first, were copied by the standard papers in New York and elsewhere. It required, very often, a new publisher or editor before the transition was made, as was seen in the Sun, Times and Tribune.

champion of the working classes by giving them melodrama, sex, crime, entertainment, sports and an economic program of trustbusting. Not only did he become the outstanding American newspaper chain owner, but his compelling ambitions led him to become one of the wealthiest men in the United States. He possessed in 1935 the second largest fortune in the United States: $220 million.

While Pulitzer receded at the turn of the century from the more sensational aspects of Gilded Age journalism, Hearst continued to carry this banner aloft.

Throughout this period the *Evening Journal* and the morning *American* continued to use the news, headlines and cartoons to bark, snarl and even bite at the trusts. Locally, the two main fights were against the Ice Trust and Gas Trust. The fight against the latter company lasted ten years but resulted in a $10 million refund to consumers.

The *American* also supported the municipal ownership movement with effective news and editorials. Hearst was practically the sole owner of the Municipal Ownership League and argued that, since the city created the need for gas and electricity, the municipality should own the utilities. He further fought for such improvements as fireproof buildings, increased pay for letter carriers and aid to indigent, sick mothers. Striking, effective cartoons flaming with the cause of labor reinforced Hearst editorials.

His papers carried the slogan, "An American Paper for Americans," arousing patriotic feelings of his vast audience. He was a strong nationalist and was called the superimperialist of them all. He urged intervention and annexation of Mexico, and raised the cry of the yellow peril in Japan. Hearst papers were belligerent toward England early in the century, fearing English trading abilities.

Two outstanding changes were made in the *Journal* and the *American* in this first decade of the new century. The first was popularization of the editorial page, and the second was development of the "star system," or "big name system," as regular staff writers or contributors to the Hearst papers.

While previous attempts had been made by Hearst to enliven the editorial page, he was still in the experimental stage when the new century dawned. He now shifted the editorial page contents around. Hearst tried new and large type for editorials, and he also used headlines on editorials, as he had used headlines to draw attention to the news. Hearst also spread the editorial over several columns, and he varied his writers. Editorial cartoons supporting the editorials gave a graphic, lively appearance to the editorial page.

Hearst developed the "star system" many other publishers later found profitable. Realizing papers had become more and more standardized as press associations sent the same dispatches to all papers, Hearst wanted some distinctive features, some exclusive writers or cartoonists who had built up a following, or who could attract thousands of readers.

Hearst's Sunday *Journal*, the name of which had been changed to the *American*, soon reached with its many departments and features, a circulation of more than 700,000 and constantly increased in the first decade of the new period. The Sunday edition exceeded by far the average daily morning circulation which hovered between 200,000 and 300,000. The Sunday *American* was a swollen newspaper, running almost to a hundred pages, crammed with features, humor, pictures, cartoons, color and advertisements galore. While there was a news section or two, this department seemed crowded out in the flood of other stirring material and special feature sections.

Some Changes, Explanation

About 1910, Hearst's *American* began to lose its violent antipathy for trusts and its strong sympathy for the working classes. Correlated with this was a diminution of its garish appeal. The trust campaigns left page one. B. C. Forbes strengthened the financial department, which had often been an index of the audience of a newspaper.

In explaining the causes of the recession from old-time sensational journalism and the prolabor views the *American* once held, biographers of Hearst's career have combined the personal factors of Hearst's life with the economic and sociological changes of the period.

Newspaperman Will Irwin, in an article, "The Spread and Decline of Yellow Journalism" (*Collier's Magazine*, March 4, 1911) pointed out that a number of reasons existed for the shift in policy. Hearst, Irwin said, had become interested in politics and found it necessary to compromise with large interests to which he had been inimical. The publisher had married Millicent Wilson and was a family man by now, which made for conservatism. Thirdly, Hearst found it was now profit-taking time: He had circulation, now he needed advertising and began to cater to advertisers. Also, externally the public began to be fed up with old-fashioned sensationalism and lost confidence in Hearst. Becoming better educated, other readers abandoned the Hearst papers.

Later biographers, who had access to more material and could study Hearst's career over a period of years, emphasized political defeats as the principal cause for the shift in Hearst's economic views. Curiously enough, this Hearst change of viewpoint coincided with the general decline of trustbusting and muckraker magazines. Other students of Hearst pointed to the enormous growth of his fortune as influencing his beliefs. Thus Hearst, for a variety of personal and environmental reasons, gradually shifted his position. In the post-World War I period, this was revealed more clearly and openly.

In 1900, William Jennings Bryan, needing a party newspaper in Chicago, called on Hearst to supply one. The Hearst *Chicago American* came out the same day Bryan was nominated, and it blew his trumpet in the midwestern city. In exchange for this service Hearst was made president of the National Association of Democratic Clubs. This marked the personal entrance of Hearst into practical politics.

Hearst realized that he must make a beginning as an active office-holder in the arena of national politics. He was elected to Congress with the help of Boss Charles Murphy of New York's Tammany Hall. It was the shortcut, the publisher believed, to the presidency of the United States. In 1905, Hearst ran for Mayor of New York City. He resolved on a program of attacking Tammany Hall and offering a reform program, as Grover Cleveland had done. He lost by less than four thousand votes. In 1906 Hearst decided to run for governor of New York on an independent ticket. He lost by fifty thousand votes. Students of Hearst psychology have said that this defeat and his previous political defeats were terrible blows to the publisher's ego. Because he felt that the public had rejected him for public office, his deep concern for the average man's welfare diminished, it was claimed.

In view of Hearst's consistent shouting for more than twenty years for bigger navies and armies and the general chip-on-the-shoulder belligerency of his papers, his decided neutrality and stand-off policy toward World War I seem a reversal of policy.

Hearst, however, believed he had little to gain from this World War, for, unlike the Spanish-American War, this international conflict was not of his own making. As later evidence revealed, he did not have a foreign staff and had been faking the news. At home, Hearst's circulation was spread heavily among the Irish and Germans, and the Irish antagonism toward England was deep and profound.

Hearst, always the representative of an aggressive America in foreign affairs, saw in England a strong commercial rival of America. Moreover, he argued, in the scrap between the foreign powers, there was a splendid chance for United States manufacturers to step in and capture the trade, while England, France and Germany were busy clawing each other.

Here was a complex of causes, personal, historical, commercial, that kept Hearst a neutral, that made him oppose violently the entrance of the United States into the war, especially on the side of the Allies. His analysis of the motives of both Allies and Central powers has been borne out in large measure by many postwar historians. His predictions about the grab for territory after the war were extraordinarily prophetic.

Once the United States entered the war, the *American* supported the Allied cause. Hundreds of his columns were devoted to Red Cross and Liberty Loan campaigns. Yet the editorials teemed with the old policy. "Let us keep our men, money, and supplies on this side of the water." On July 27, three and one-half months after war began, Hearst called for "immediate peace rather than sending a million of our splendid young Americans to be offered up in bloody sacrifice."

Hearst papers were bitterly attacked. The *New York Tribune,* in the spring of 1918, ran a series of militant and venomous attacks entitled, "Coiled in the Flag, Hears-S-S-T," articles which were reprinted and broadcast. As a result, Hearst papers were burned in a number of communities. Many clubs, patriotic organizations, war associations and religious societies boycotted the papers. The Hearst counterattack was swift.

Postwar Hearst: The New and the Old

Hearst, in the period following World War I, was a curious combination of the old and the new in journalism. In the postwar decade, Hearst papers reflected newspaper techniques of an immediate past. Critics charged that the war, Gilded Age characteristics—violence of utterance and action, unscientific sentimentality and rugged individuality—all continued in his newspapers.

In the period immediately following the war, sex was relegated to a minor position, frequently on inside pages in the *American.* World War I drove sex headlines from the front page. Now, after peace was declared, the nation's thoughts turned to significant problems rising out of the war. The tabloid *Daily News* starting in 1919 revived, however, the newspaper interest in the sex theme, and the paper was such a success that pressure on Hearst's *American* became strong. Hearst himself launched the *Mirror,* a tabloid, in 1924.

Because of competition and current social and psychological conditions to be described, the *American* now blossomed with front page banners about sex and crime, and the editors soon covered the inside pages with scandal stories of actresses and actors.

When World War I was over, Hearst, returning to his old nationalistic campaigns, battered away at the Treaty of Versailles and organized a nationwide campaign in support of Henry Cabot Lodge, the "irreconcilable Massachusetts senator" who blocked adherence to the League of Nations.

Hearst vigorously supported Franklin D. Roosevelt in 1932 and called his program humane. The National Industrial Recovery Act, Hearst declared, embodied basic principles long advocated by Hearst newspapers. But Hearst soon became one of the most violent opponents of the New Deal, arguing that Roosevelt polices were leading America to communism and dictatorship. All phases of the New Deal were pilloried in bold editorials and striking cartoons such as "The Raw Deal."

Realizing the trend toward afternoon papers, Hearst closed down his morning *American* and combined it with the *Evening Journal,* calling the merged paper the *Journal-American.* Competition of the tabloid *Daily News* and his own *Mirror,* which had appealed to the same market as his old *American,* was too strong, consequently he eliminated his morning edition. In 1960 the *Journal-American* found 571,765 subscribers on weekdays, and 778,562 on Sundays. The amalgamation of the *Journal-American* with other New York dailies in 1966 will be described in a later section.

In other parts of the country, Hearst, according to plan, added to his chain, buying, selling and merging as local conditions required. At his peak in 1933, Hearst, as indicated before in more detail, had twenty-six dailies. His seventeen Sunday editions reached an even greater audience. Hearst likewise controlled the International News Service, furnishing news to his own papers as well as to other editors. He was also proprietor of King Features Service. Hearst branched out into the magazine and movie industry, controlling thirteen magazines and two motion picture companies. He also entered radio and built or purchased eight stations, some of which were sold later.

Hearst died in August, 1951, at the age of eighty-eight. Although still the largest chain, his newspaper empire had shrunk to eighteen papers. This represented 5,265,420 subscribers or 9.8 per cent of United States daily circulation.

Average annual profit for the period 1935 to 1939 was nearly $5 million. Hearst's sons, who took over after he died, sought to revitalize the Hearst chain. They revamped the traditional *American Weekly,* the Sunday supplement, later eliminating it. They sold a number of the less profitable dailies. The *Pittsburgh Sun-Telegram* was sold to William Block who merged it with his *Post-Gazette.* In Chicago the *Tribune* bought Hearst's *American.*

NEW YORK TIMES SELLS NEWS

The true genius of Adolph S. Ochs, who took over the tottering *New York Times* in 1895, was demonstrated in the twentieth century.

An unrivaled newspaper manager, an extraordinary business and financial expert, Ochs built up to great heights the bankrupt *New York Times.* Today it has taken its place among the world's greatest newspapers, and in its own field of gathering and disseminating news on a wide variety of topics, it has become a master. Many consider the *Times* the one United States national newspaper that has exerted a profound and deep influence on American journalism. The *Times'* standards have become the goals toward which many other newspaper publishers have aimed. United States editors read it daily or on Sunday to keep informed about national news and happenings and trends throughout the world.

Ochs: News Merchandiser

During the first decades of the twentieth century, Adolph S. Ochs and his managers developed an extraordinary news-gathering machine. The *Times* represented the climax of the development of the news department and the relative subordination of the editorial page.

The *Times'* news and makeup policy was predominately conservative. However, when its managers considered an event of sufficient importance, or when forced on by its sensational rivals, the Ochs paper printed its full share of crime, disaster, sports and sex. Its readers might have been more educated and might have represented the upper intellectual strata, but they could stand a shock and thrill; they too were interested in murder, fire and scandal.

Exploration, aviation, radio and science became specialties of the *Times.* The daily developed, created and stimulated news and general interest in these subjects. Out of the exploration and aviation news, the *Times* made news thrillers, full of suspense, adventure and romance, tingling the tired nerves of even the educated and intellectual readers. In its news of exploration, the *Times* was akin to the *Herald* of James Gordon Bennett, Jr., just as it had been related to both senior and junior Bennett in the merchandising of news and the lack of stress on a powerful editorial page.

From the turn of the century the *Times* began to build up its foreign news service, as the interest of many Americans expanded to worldwide horizons. As American business stretched its arms to all parts of the earth for markets and as increasing numbers of American travelers visited European capitals, the *Times* responded to this change in public interest and within a short time dominated the foreign news field.

In the new era, the *Times* continued to strengthen its various departments in the daily edition, but the financial and business section received the major share of attention. The *Times* became the indispensable organ to the up-and-coming businessman, who did not care to read such a highly specialized paper as the *Wall Street Journal,* but wanted business and financial news along with current political, sports and cultural information.

While the *Times* covered sports events in the daily, the Sunday paper carried a wider variety of such news. It was not until after World War I that the sports department of the *Times* developed rapidly. Then, bylines were given to writers, and sports columnists appeared. John Kieran was perhaps the most imaginative of the sportswriters.

Appealing to its upper-class, educated audience, the *Times* issued on Saturday a book review, like the financial review, in tabloid form. This tabloid was transferred to the Sunday edition before World War I. Ochs rode the wave of a growing interest in books. Eventually, book publishers began to advertise heavily in this section.

It was in the Sunday edition of the *New York Times* that the hand of Ochs was most clearly shown and that contributions to the art of newspapermaking were made. After a period of experimentation, the Sunday *Times* became the leader in its field. It was bold in trying new types of features.

Ochs did not fail to borrow methods and techniques from the great popularizers of the Sunday paper: Pulitzer, Hearst and Bennett. Styling of the article and the artistic display distinguished the new journalism from the old. *Times'* Sunday features were informative but not critical. The writers accepted the economic world as it was and gave information about it.

In 1915 managing editor Carr Van Anda learned about the German rotogravure press, and on instructions from Ochs, Van Anda examined it when he visited Germany. The *Times* soon had a rotogravure press installed in New York, introducing the brown and white process in this country, the *Pictorial Section* of the *Times,* emerging from the old magazine tabloid into a division of its own, covered a wide range of events.

Ochs did not change the editorial policy of the *Times* nor alter the general economic and political views which had prevailed in the office under the direction of editor Charles R. Miller. Just as the *Times* had been established in 1851 to counteract, in part, the "ism" of the radical Whig, Horace Greeley, so in the new century, the same paper, under Ochs, championed the cause of the industrial entrepreneurs and defended them from the encroachment of legislation and attacks of critics. The editorial page followed the plain dignified format it had inherited from the nineteenth century. Headlines were small; editorials were printed in regular size type, one column wide. No political cartoons appeared on the page.

Politically, the *Times* in the new century could not tolerate the economic heresies of the "revolutionary" from the Midwest, William Jennings Bryan. The Ochs paper, therefore, jumped party lines whenever Bryan presented himself as a candidate. The *Times* discovered in Woodrow Wilson a leader it could support in the Democratic Party.

In many respects, the *Times*' reaction to World War I was similar to that exhibited by the *World*. The *Times*' editorial writers from the very beginning seized on the explanation for the war that Germany was wrong and that autocracy and militarism were the basis of the trouble.

While anti-German emphasis prevailed in the *Times*, the paper also presented the German viewpoint by means of features and pictures. The *Times* was handicapped indeed by the fact that the news cable from Germany was cut and the *Times* correspondent, Frederick W. Wile, was compelled to leave Germany. The daily published objections of local German groups who raised the issue of the *Times*' unfairness; the editor, however, printed their objections on page two.

Postwar Period

In the post-World War I period, the *New York Times*' vast organization was ready to tackle any happening on the universal stage, including the celestial spheres. The *Times*' faith in its formula of giving news in great quantities was fully justified. Muckraking, attacking the current system and criticizing it, did not pay—permanently. Ochs did not develop columnists or give his readers comics. News, a variety of it and in great quantities, was the key to the *Times*' prosperity, he believed. Many people wanted to know the facts about the world. They could make up their own minds about the meaning and what attitudes they should take toward the events, he believed. An appetite for solid news could be cultivated and stimulated.

By the middle of the 1920s, the *Times* was forced by tabloids to sensationalize its crime and scandal news. The competitive process had compelled many staid newspapers in American history to emphasize such news. The *Times*, though leaning on the serious side of the news, did break its uniformity at intervals, and a humorous story made its appearance in the columns of the paper occasionally.

The aviation seed which the *Times* planted in the early part of the century came to full flower after the war. This was the period of trans-Atlantic and round-the-world endurance flights. The *Times*, by its early promotion and encouragement, helped arouse interest in this new airplane era.

The *Times*' enterprise in getting exclusive story rights from explorers, scientists and pioneer fliers surpassed anything in history. The daily gave the world the most gripping adventure stories: William Beebe from the floor of the tropical seas; August Piccard from the stratosphere; stories from scientific explorations in jungles or polar regions. It was Jules Verne stuff, but true. The new wireless helped transmit such news immediately from all parts of the world.

The Sunday issue became one of the most voluminous in the United States in the post-World War I period. Each of the older sections of the edition expanded, and new sections were added. Ochs issued on Sunday a magazine tabloid which sought to give background to political and economic events and also to discuss social characteristics of the nation. Stimulated by the newsmagazines' success, the *Times*' editors launched a News-of-the-Week-in-Review section in January, 1935. This section reviewed in lively style the significant events of the week and also carried extensive discussion of current issues. The Sunday edition reached 1,254,635 by 1960.

Selling news in large quantities, the *New York Times* avoided all appearances of being a crusading newspaper. The *Times* followed the Democratic Party in the 1920s. It supported Franklin D. Roosevelt in 1932 and 1936, but because of his proposal to enlarge the Supreme Court and because he had already had two terms in office, the *Times* broke with him and backed Republican Wendell Wilkie in 1940. Then World War II came, and the *Times*, believing in the foreign policy of Roosevelt and his conduct of the war, returned again to the Democratic Party. In 1948, however, the paper threw its weight behind Republican Thomas E. Dewey; and in the 1950s it backed Republican Dwight D. Eisenhower. The *Times* shifted back to Democrat John F. Kennedy in 1960 and supported Lyndon B. Johnson in 1964.

How much weight the editorial page carried, no one knew; however, the learned, thoughtful and well-reasoned editorials were read by thoughtful, influential persons and government officials. Makeup of the editorial page was about the same as it had been in Raymond's *Times*. Some changes in content and makeup of the editorial page were made toward midcentury: Columnists were added, and in 1958 editorials were set two columns wide. The editorial page seemed to be overshadowed by the overwhelming amount of objective news in the daily edition and by the background articles in the Sunday editorial section and the Sunday magazine. Breaking its tradition to avoid crusading, the *Times* conducted a constant attack against Senator Joseph McCarthy, who carried on a campaign against Communists in government and who was charged with smearing the reputation of many innocent persons in the 1950s.

Adolph S. Ochs died in April, 1935. He had built a great newspaper institution, and when it had become profitable, ploughed two-thirds of the profits back into the business to expand it. If Pulitzer and Hearst influenced American journalism along certain directions, Ochs' influence was equally as powerful. Both streams of journalism, with rivulets in the past, sprang out of the end of the nineteenth century. Both influenced each other.

Coverage of World War II

As early as 1921, Anne O'Hare McCormick, then a free-lancer, had written about the rising Benito Mussolini, founder and leader of the new Fascist in Italy, and she made the flat assertion that in this swashbuckling newcomer, Italy had probably found her master. This was prophesy with a deadly accuracy.

Meanwhile, the *Times* correspondents chronicled every step in Adolf Hitler's rise to power in Germany as the leader of the new Nazi Party. The *Times* recorded Hitler's march into Austria in March, 1938 and related how he moved into Czechoslovakia.

When German planes were dropping bombs on England, especially on London, to create confusion and destroy morale, correspondent Raymond Daniell wrote news about these air raids while bombs were bursting around him. The *Times* correspondents were jailed and then expelled from Rome and Berlin when Germany and Italy declared war on the United States on December 11, 1941. In order to understand the problems of the soldiers as well as his correspondents in the field, publisher Sulzberger took a 28,000 mile journey to Moscow in June, 1943.

The Allied forces pushed on and liberated Paris. The *Times* was happy to tell its readers on May 8, 1945:

WAR IN EUROPE IS ENDED!

Meanwhile, William L. Laurence, *Times* science reporter, vanished from his office a month before. Laurence was taken to Oak Ridge, Tennessee, where scientists were experimenting on the making of an atomic bomb. Later he was taken to New Mexico where the first actual test of the bomb was made. All the reporter's copy was put in a safe. Laurence's stories, providing background for newsmen, were released when the bomb was dropped on Hiroshima, Japan. The *Times* trumpeted the news in this fashion on August 7, 1945:

First Atomic Bomb Dropped on Japan;
Missile is Equal to 20,000 Tons of TNT:
Truman Warns Foe of 'Rain of Ruin'

Aware of the implications of the atomic bomb and future possibilities of atomic energy, the *Times* devoted ten of its thirty-eight pages to the story that day. Two days later the paper told of the dropping of the bomb on Nagasaki, Japan. On August 15 the front page of the *Times* shouted the good news:

Japan Surrenders, End of War!
Emperor Accepts Allied Rule

The *Times* local reporters in New York City described how the city "let go" after five days of waiting, rumor, intimation of fact and distortion. The reporters related that more than two million persons jammed Times Square in celebration of the end of the war.

But it was not to be the end of wars. The *Times* has continued to report fully the Cold War: the Korean War in the 1950s, the Vietnam War in the 1960s. The *Times'* reporters have given in detail the reaction of huge numbers of Americans to the United States's involvement in the Vietnam conflict.

Other big stories have concerned the race between the United States and Russia to put a man on the moon. The *Times* has reported in great detail the United States's efforts to launch satellites and to send astronauts circling around the earth.

On the domestic scene, the struggle of the Negro to gain civil rights has been reported by the *Times'* correspondents in all sections of the country. The Timesmen have dispatched stories of the effort to integrate the schools in both the North and South, to open all eating places to Negroes and to eliminate all discrimination in housing. The *Times* has given full coverage to the riots in Harlem as well as other Negro ghettoes in metropolitan cities.

When Ochs died in 1935, the controlling stock was left in trust to his widow and his daughter (Mrs. Arthur Hays Sulzberger). The executors and trustees in 1958 were Mrs. Ochs' daughter, Iphegene; her husband, Mr. Sulzberger; and their son-in-law, Orvil E. Dryfoos, president of the company.

In 1961 Mr. Sulzberger retired, with Mr. Dryfoos becoming chairman of the board. John B. Oakes replaced Charles Merz as editor of the editorial page. Two years later, in May, 1963, Mr. Dryfoos died. His successor was Arthur Ochs Sulzberger, thirty-seven, son of Arthur Hays Sulzberger and grandson of the rebuilder of the *Times*. The young man, as president and publisher of the *Times* company, instituted a number of changes in the *Times'* staff, placing Turner Catledge as executive editor in charge of news and Sunday departments. Lester Markel, who had built the Sunday edition and was an exponent of backgrounding the news, became an associate editor, as did James Reston, Washington correspondent.

The *Times* was hit hard by the newspaper strike which began in December, 1962 and lasted into April, 1963. The staff, still working, went on a four-day week. Those with salaries below $15,000 were cut 20 per cent; executives who received more than that were cut 50 per cent. Disagreement of the International Typographic Union No. 6 with New

Figure 54. (Left), Arthur Hays Sulzberger; (Right), Arthur Ochs Sulzberger. The older Sulzberger succeeded Adolph S. Ochs in 1935 as publisher of the *New York Times.* Later he became chairman of the board. Arthur Ochs Sulzberger, son of Arthur Hays, became publisher and president of the *New York Times* in 1963. (Courtesy of the *New York Times*)

York newspapers caused the trouble. New York publishers stood solidly together. No agreement could be reached day after day. The *New York Post* eventually resigned from the publishers' association and began publication on March 1. The strike continued until April 1, when a settlement was reached. It was estimated that New York's business, labor and government lost between $190 million and $250 million. Newspapers lost $108 million in revenue; their employes about $50 million.

New York Times circulation in 1968 reached 840,495 readers; on Sunday this nearly doubled, with 1,494,704 buying the paper for its many news specialities and supplements.

In building this great newspaper, conditions of the journalistic and economic age required that the Ochs' family erect a highly complex institution, costing millions of dollars to operate. The *New York Times* employed more than six thousand persons, who received more than $63 million million in 1967. The daily had assets of $91 million and did a gross business of $194 million. Its net profit was $11 million.

MUNSEY'S MULTIPLE MERGERS

When Charles A. Dana, who developed the human interest story, died in 1897, he left two established newspapers, the morning *Sun* and the *Evening Sun,* along with a strong set of traditions, to his son, Paul Dana. The *Sun,* in 1900 presented the appearance of a sober, respectable newspaper with one-column headlines on the front page, no political cartoons or comics on the inside. The *Sun* catered to and represented the conservative businessmen of New York.

The *Sun* was sold to William Laffan in 1903. A friend of banker J. P. Morgan, who aided him financially, Laffan began the *Sun*'s transformation into twentieth-century journalism. Laffan had money to spend. The *Sun* adopted some of the methods that had made the *World,* the *Journal* and the *Times* popular. Larger headlines were introduced; sketches and some halftones were used to illustrate features; and human interest news was supplied to round out the variety.

Now with the aid of some wealthy friends, who, the *New York Tribune* intimated, were Clarence MacKay of the Western Union Telegraph Company, and James Stillman, banker, William Reick bought the *Sun* from the Laffan estate for about $2,500,000 when the publisher died. Such was the value of a metropolitan newspaper at this time. Reick was an experienced newspaperman, having been an executive on the *New York Herald* and on the *New York Times*

It was during Reick's regime, beginning in December 1, 1911, that transformation of the *Sun* to a modern newspaper was accelerated, and it began to shed its nineteenth-century format and style. The old cluster of brilliant *Sun* reporters and executives had transferred to other dailies by this time.

When World War I began, the *Sun* became even more up-to-date. Ochs had already transformed the *Times;* the old rivals, the *Sun* and *Tribune,* changed soon after. While young Ogden Reid assumed management of the *Tribune,* Reick bought control of the *Sun.* Thus, new regimes with new viewpoints were now in charge of the old nineteenth-century newspapers. Reick purchased new equipment and began to popularize the *Sun,* particularly the *Sunday Sun* and the *Evening Sun.*

In spite of all the modernization, Reick operated under a severe financial handicap, with the *Sun News Agency* instead of an Associated Press franchise. The *Sun* slipped in circulation, particularly the morning *Sun.* In 1912 the *Sun* had 90,000 circulation; in two years it dropped to 62,000. Although the interest in World War I news stimulated sales, the *Sun* was only up to 66,000 in 1916. Meanwhile, costs of publication mounted steadily. Externally, the competition the *Sun* faced was severe. Lack of an AP franchise was felt keenly.

Reick decided to sell in 1916, and his purchaser was entrepreneur, Frank A. Munsey. Like his predecessors who owned the *Sun,* Munsey was a New Englander, having been born on a farm near Mercer, Maine, in August, 1854. He had made money in a grocery chain and published *Munsey's* Magazine.

At the time he bought the *Sun,* Munsey owned the *Press* which he had purchased in 1912 for $1,000,000 to help Colonel Theodore Roosevelt with the presidency. Munsey paid $2,468,000 for the *Sun* properties, the morning and evening editions. He amalgamated the *Press* and the *Sun,* stating that the *Sun* would get the Associated Press franchise of the *Press,* its good will and its sizable circulation. By virtue of the consolidation, the *Sun* secured $50,000 worth of advertising it had never carried before, and it also acquired some of the best men on the *Press.* The morning *Sun,* after a spurt, sank back and remained at the tail end of New York papers.

The *Evening Sun* bounded forward however, and was prosperous. Munsey, faced with a losing morning newspaper, looked over the morning field again. In January, 1923 he purchased the *Herald* and *Telegram* for $2,488,000.

Herald and Sun Combined

Munsey startled New York by announcing consolidation of the prestige-laden *Herald* and the long-traditioned morning *Sun.* The *New York Times,* in commenting on the purchase and merger, said: "It was in line with modern ideas of business efficiency in cutting down expenses." Eight months later Munsey announced that he would change the name of the *Sun* and *Herald,* the morning paper, to the *Herald.* The *Evening Sun,* however, would retain the traditional name of the *Sun.*

But the morning *Sun,* in effect, was dead. In its place was an amalgamation of the *Herald* and the *Sun.* Whatever remained of the Dana spirit and newspaper philosophy was scattered to the four corners of the United States and incorporated in other papers.

Munsey began to look around again. He had consolidated the morning competitors, the *Herald* and the *Sun.* What about the *Globe* and the *Evening Sun?* The *Globe* held a brilliant position as a paper with no political axes to grind, with a fresh and independent style and a liberal viewpoint. Furthermore, it was a sound business institution. For a quarter of a century its editor had been Henry J. Wright, a man of distinguished mind who enjoyed amazing freedom in management. The owner was Edward D. Searles, an aged recluse who made his home at distant Methuen, Massachusetts, and while conservative in his views did not bother to interfere with the *Globe's* policies. The *Globe* had found a liberal audience and was profitable.

Searles died in 1920, and the executors and wrangling heirs were not long in seeking a buyer for the paper. There were various bids from persons who wished to continue publication of the *Globe,* but Munsey topped them all with an offer of $2 million. On June 4, 1923, a week after the purchase, the *Globe* and the *Sun* were consolidated. The *Globe*'s AP franchise and its features moved over to the *Sun.*

The *Globe-Sun* merger, however, was one of the most profitable consolidations in newspaper history. It took the curse off Munsey ownership and broke his procession of failures. The Munsey paper gained in both circulation and advertising.

When Munsey died in 1926, he left his papers to the Metropolitan Museum of Art. His estate, including his newspapers, grocery chain and real estate, was valued at $13 million. William T. Dewart, who started as office boy and became business manager of the *Sun,* formed a company to purchase the Munsey papers. Dewart sold stock to the employees, but retained control of a majority interest. The Metropolitan sold the *Sun* and the *Telegram* to the new corporation for $3 million. Within a year Dewart, in turn, sold the *Telegram* to the Scripps-Howard interests.

With amalgamation of the Pulitzer *World* and the *Telegram* in 1931 and its shift to a more conservative political position, the *Sun* faced stiff competition in its own afternoon field. The *Sun* was aimed at the same block of newspaper subscribers as the *World-Telegram* in the 1940s. The *Sun*'s circulation reached a high-water mark by 1947. Then it began to drop off, slipping to 277,530 in 1949.

The *Sun* failed to keep its public and to increase its circulation, according to Irving Kolodin, its music critic, because it had hardening of the arteries. It had become too bound to its tradition, and its views remained fixed in a changing world, this former *Sun*man said. Other explanations were offered. William T. Dewart, Jr., *Sun* publisher and son of William T. Dewart, who had been in charge after Munsey's death, attributed the *Sun*'s failures to rising costs and decreasing advertising revenue. Whatever the reasons for the *Sun*'s failure to keep pace, the 116 year old *Sun,* as other nineteenth-century rivals, had succumbed to the merger trend.

The *Sun* was sold to Scripps-Howard in January 1950. Roy Howard said that the *World-Telegram* had inherited the Pulitzer and Scripps tradition, and now through the *Sun,* it was adding Dana's. Amalgamation of the papers produced the *World-Telegram and Sun,* which stood as sole representative of the Republican Party in the afternoon field. Circulation reached 596,936 during the first year of the merger. The Saturday edition had 326,543 subscribers. It was topped only by Hearst's *Journal-American* which appealed to a different audience.

TRIBUNE, STAUNCHLY REPUBLICAN, REJUVENATED

After the death of publisher Whitelaw Reid in 1912, his son, Ogden Mills Reid, a Yale graduate with a law degree, became managing editor of the *New York Tribune*. He made sharp changes in the old nineteenth-century Republican paper, for Reid was faced with the change in public interest and the competition from the modernized *New York Times,* which represented the Democratic Party.

Young Reid, with his new, enterprising and humane spirit, instituted a number of reforms: News pages and sports pages were expanded; editorials were shortened; the Sunday edition was improved.

Mrs. Whitelaw Reid, who had survived her husband, the ambassador, and was deeply interested in humanitarian work, particularly hospitals and health, took part in the affairs of the *Tribune.*

Young Ogden Reid married Helen Rogers of Racine, Wisconsin, who had received her A.B. degree at Barnard College. A strong personality, she joined the *Tribune* staff in 1918 and later became vice president and director of advertising. She was responsible for many progressive projects, such as the Herald Tribune Forum, where outstanding people discussed current affairs.

During World War I, the *Tribune* was pro-English and violently anti-German. The Reid paper used many techniques borrowed from Hearst and Pulitzer to arouse interest in the war. They ranged from war benefits to the raising of battleship funds. The Reid paper was especially susceptible to atrocity stories because of the great amount of news it received through British sources and because of the pro-Ally sympathies of Richard Harding Davis and of staff member Wilbur Forrest.

After the war the *Tribune* was in favor of drastic punishment of Germany, and the daily reacted strongly when Germany complained of the truce terms as being severe. Editorially as well as in special feature articles and cartoons, the *Tribune* hammered away at Hearst's war record.

Prosperity of the gay twenties, enjoyed by those in the upper strata of the population, was naturally felt by the newspaper which most nearly catered to them. The *Tribune* rode the high tide of the building, auto and stock booms. By 1921 the *Tribune* reached 140,000 subscribers. In 1924 it merged with the *Herald* and formed, at the time, one of the most successful consolidations in American journalism, after the Reid family paid Munsey $5 million for the *Herald.* The Reid paper made a special drive for the financial clientele, and the daily's promotion department proclaimed that 75 per cent of the brokers and Wall Street men bought and read the *Herald Tribune.*

Gradually, the *Herald Tribune* completely changed its typographical display. By 1950 the paper's typography had such excellence that the publisher won many prizes. He now added columnists, cartoonists, comics and more special writers, such as the liberal Reverend S. Parkes Cadman and Mark Sullivan. In 1931, when the *World* closed its doors, not only did Walter Lippmann come over to the *Herald Tribune,* but Franklin P. Adams, who had gone to the *World,* returned to the *Herald Tribune.* The *New York Times* and its morning rival, the *Herald Tribune,* fell into the same general journalistic class, but the *Tribune* was more experimental typographically and tended to emphasize better writing in its news columns. Politically, the two dailies were in opposing camps, giving New Yorkers a choice of standard-sized morning papers.

When Ogden Mills Reid died in 1947, his elder son, Whitelaw Reid, moved up to direct the paper, and in 1953 was named president of the corporation. His mother, Mrs. Helen Rogers Reid, long active in the operations of the paper, became chairman of the board. In training also on the *Herald Tribune* staff was a younger son, Ogden Rogers Reid, who became chief executive officer, directing the editorial and other departments in April, 1955. A further revamping of editorial content was announced in October, 1957.

In 1958 the *Herald Tribune*'s circulation on weekdays was 325,478; on Sunday it reached 529,715.

Reid Paper Sold to J. H. Whitney

Then in August, 1958, control of the *New York Herald Tribune* and its European edition, published in Paris, was acquired by John Hay Whitney, United States Ambassador to the Court of St. James. The Reid family, which held a controlling interest for eighty-five years, retained a substantial stock interest.

Explaining the sale, Whitelaw Reid said that since World War II the *Herald Tribune* had not done well financially. Change in ownership would insure its future, he pointed out. The *Herald Tribune* at the time of the sale had more than nineteen hundred employees. Ogden Reid declined comment when a reporter asked if a rumor that Mr. Whitney paid $15 million for controlling interest was correct.

Whitney was a senior partner of J. H. Whitney & Company, industrial financiers. He was chairman of the board of the Freeport Sulphur Company and director of Great Northern Paper Company. J. H. Whitney Company owned the Corinthian Broadcasting Company, operators of four stations. Earlier in the month the company had purchased *Parade,* syndicated newspaper magazine, from Field Enterprises for $7 million. In July, 1959, Whitney selected a Democrat, Robert White, II, of the *Mexico* (Missouri) *Ledger* to become editor of the Republican *Herald*

Tribune. He left later. Whitney then brought in other news executives to find the right news, advertising and business formula for the century-old *Herald Tribune.*

A later section will tell about the efforts to merge the *Herald Tribune* with the *World-Telegram* and the *Journal* in 1966.

EVENING POST CHANGES HANDS, POLICY

The *Evening Post* changed ownership six times in the new century: Oswald Garrison Villard published the *Post* between 1900 and 1918; Thomas Lamont, 1918 to 1922; Edwin Gay Syndicate, 1922 to 1924; Cyrus H. K. Curtis, 1924 to 1933; J. David Stern, 1933 to 1939; Dorothy Schiff, 1939–.

Edwin L. Godkin, who had brought national fame to the *Post* in the nineteenth century, retired, somewhat disillusioned and in poor health at the turn of the century. His spirit, in the form of powerful traditions, lingered on. After his death, Horace White, who had been his associate editor, took over the paper, but the general policy and viewpoint of the *Post* remained fixed.

Because of rising costs of operating a newspaper, Villard sold the *Evening Post* to Thomas Lamont in 1918. Lamont was a member of the firm of J. P. Morgan and Company and a director in many other business enterprises. Between $1 million and $1.5 million was paid for the paper. After losing $1 million, the *Evening Post* was sold to Cyrus H. K. Curtis of Philadelphia for $1.8 million in 1921. More information about this publisher will be given in the section on Philadelphia newspapers.

Following the Pulitzer-Hearst techniques of popularization, Curtis began to brighten the *Post* with larger headlines, banner headlines, byline columns and a feature page. Editorials became short comments on the news instead of extended essays. Heads over the editorials were snappy summaries of the editorials' contents.

Curtis died in June, 1933. His newspapers were left in charge of John Martin, his son-in-law, who had been general manager before. The *Evening Post,* in spite of all the funds poured into it by the Curtis-Martin organization, lost money steadily. In one last drastic experiment to revive the *Post,* it was made into a conservative tabloid in September, 1933.

Militant pro-New Dealer of Philadelphia, J. David Stern, owned the *Camden* (New Jersey) *Courier* and the *Philadelphia Record.* When Stern purchased the *New York Evening Post* in 1933, the paper shifted from the Republican to the Democratic side. The shift seemed to coincide with the changing temper of the times. Stern's first announcement indicated that the paper would become a standard-size sheet again. The publisher declared:

> The *New York Evening Post* appears today not merely in its old form, but in its old traditions. It has been a fighting, independent, liberal newspaper in the past, and it will be so again in the future.
>
> The *Post* will support the New Deal as long as that New Deal offers hope of alleviating maldistribution of wealth, which is our fundamental ill, and of restoring economic health and social justice.

Stern published the *Post* for six years until 1939, but then he believed he should concentrate on his Camden and Philadelphia newspapers. He sold the *Post* to Dorothy Schiff who also had liberal economic and political views, although she had been born into a wealthy family. She later bought the *Bronx Home News,* a suburban daily, and combined it with the *Post.* With James Wechsler as editor, the *Post* represented Roosevelt and the New Deal in New York. *PM* was the other consistent Roosevelt supporter, but it folded, leaving the Schiff paper to the liberal Democratic field.

Wechsler used all the techniques of the tabloids to gain public attention. News and makeup policy was in the tabloid tradition. A variety of liberal columnists, including Arthur Schlesinger, Jr., Harvard historian, wrote for the *Post.* Wechsler's persistent attacks on the illiberalism of Senator Joseph McCarthy of Wisconsin led to the senator's investigation of the editor. Senator McCarthy had conducted an extensive investigation of Communist activities in the United States. Because of the type of questions asked and the general tone of the senator at the hearing, Wechsler considered the senator's investigation an inquisition. The senator said he wanted to find out if the editor and the *Post* were communistic. Wechsler pointed out that he conducted campaigns for a long time against Communists. Thus the McCarthy-Wechsler debate ended. Senator McCarthy was later censored by his colleagues in the Senate for his irresponsible attacks on many innocent people.

The daily subscribers of the *Post* in 1964 totaled 317,137, while the Sunday *Post* found 250,207 buyers. As a result of the merger of the *World-Telegram, Journal* and *Herald Tribune* and their death in 1966, the *Post* boomed. The *Post*'s daily circulation in 1968 reached 628,146, with a Saturday circulation of 354,497.

SCRIPPS-HOWARD FORGES A CHAIN

In 1927 when the Scripps-Howard newspaper chain entered New York with the purchase of the *Telegram,* the chain already possessed a liberal newspaper tradition and philosophy. Although founder Edward

W. Scripps remained in control for several decades, two new personalities came up in the Scripps organization to take charge: Robert P. Scripps and Roy W. Howard.

Robert P. Scripps, son of the founder of the chain, was born in 1895 in California, and was privately educated until he was sixteen. He worked for a short time with the Scripps-McRae *News Post* in Philadelphia but resigned to travel in foreign countries.

In Honolulu, young Scripps met novelist Jack London, and they became friends. Later Robert worked for a newspaper in Australia. Returning home in 1916, he became a staffer on the *Daily News,* Scripps paper in Washington, where his family had moved. At the end of his first year, at the age of twenty-one, he had become editor-in-chief of the Scripps papers. He had the liberal and humane views of his father.

Background of Roy Wilson Howard was in sharp contrast to that of young Scripps. Howard was born in Ohio in 1883 to poor, uneducated parents. His father, a railroad laborer, dreamed of the day his son would be a white-collar worker. When the *St. Louis Post-Dispatch,* for which young Howard worked, refused to give him a raise, he quit and took a job with the *Cincinnati Post,* a Scripps-McRae paper. There he convinced his editors that they should send him as a correspondent to New York, and they did. He later became manager of Scripps-McRae's news agency, the Publishers' Service.

When several press associations merged into what is now the United Press, Howard was named president. His enthusiasm, initiative and driving force built the organization into a world-girdling service. In 1920 Howard gave up his position with United Press to become business manager and chairman of the board of the Scripps chain. On this occasion, he said to a magazine reporter, "Bob Scripps and I are as different as it is possible for two men to be. Ours is a most fortunate combination. Our faults seem to checkmate each other and our abilities, to supplement each other."

When Edward W. Scripps died on March 12, 1926, management of the Scripps chain was left in the hands of his son and Howard.

In 1927, as indicated, the Scripps-Howard chain purchased the *Telegram.* Upon assuming ownership, Howard said: "In all ways and to the limit of our ability, the *Telegram* will be a New York newspaper. In conformity with the policy of the Scripps-Howard Company, it will be independent in thought and action. It will be a NEWS paper. It will furnish its readers with information on which they may form their own opinions."

Four years after the Scripps-Howard organization began publication of the *Telegram,* it purchased the *New York World* (morning, evening and Sunday) for $5 million, using stock in other Scripps-Howard papers as collateral. It is interesting to note that one of the reasons given by the Pulitzer brothers for selling the *World* to Scripps-Howard, regardless of higher bidders, was the belief that the aims and goals of both organizations were similar.

In the merger operation, the *Evening World,* the morning *World* and the Sunday *World* were eliminated from competition. In actual, tangible things, the chain merely bought the circulation list, the advertising contracts and clipping "morgue"; but, above all, Scripps-Howard was strengthened by the *Worlds*' goodwill, reader confidence, reputation and tradition.

Speaking for the Scripps-Howard management, Howard promised a "rebirth of the *World.*" The *New York Telegram* and later the *World-Telegram* developed, in the first years of ownership by Scripps-Howard, a trigger sensitivity to problems of the Machine Age and newer viewpoints toward dealing with those problems. The daily, in turn, had an effect on its readers, stimulating them to think about current problems from a liberal standpoint.

During this time the Scripps-Howard newspaper advocated the newer "liberal" viewpoint in economics and the daily faced realistically the issues of the Machine Age. The editors sought to build a humane, intelligent, industrial democracy and advocated an enlightened capitalism which would abolish unemployment, spread education and improve social health. Scripps editors, therefore, fully endorsed Franklin D. Roosevelt's candidacy in 1932 and his reform programs.

One of the distinctive and strong points of the *World-Telegram* was its light, human-interest personality sketches. The second strong plank in the *World-Telegram* platform was the special background features that ran in series. Published daily, the articles ranged the whole field of life. They dealt with social and economic problems and delved into literature, art, architecture and the theatre. They featured women as well as men, when personalities were sketched. These features represented an attempt on the part of the *World-Telegram* to link antecedent events to the day's news for the reader, to give some continuity to the flow of news.

Third strong pillar of the *World-Telegram* was its staff of feature columnists. While there were certain regular standbys, such as Dr. Harry Elmer Barnes, Heywood Broun, Westbrook Pegler and Harry Hansen, at least a dozen columnists found space in the daily at one time or another. The *World-Telegram* also printed David Deitz's column issued by Science Service, a Scripps project.

Perhaps the most striking and original contributions made to the art of columning were the "ABC columns" which explained the intricate page-one news. When utility rates were being discussed, William O. Trapp was called on to write a series on "The ABC of Public Utility Rates." These articles were of a primer-like character, drawing together many facts and explaining them in simple, every-day language.

In 1950 the Scripps-Howard chain, as indicated, bought the *Sun*, a Republican paper. Circulation of the *Sun* and the *World-Telegram* overlapped, and its political and economic views by this time were similar. Reported price for the *Sun* was $2 million. The amalgamated papers became the *World-Telegram and Sun*. Circulation high in 1949 of the *World-Telegram* was 365,854. After merger with the *Sun*, the Scripps-Howard paper found 596,000 subscribers the first year. By 1964 the *World-Telegram and Sun* had dropped to 373,849 purchasers due to growth of suburbs and suburban papers, as indicated.

Consolidation of Three Historic Papers

The *World-Telegram and Sun* became a part of an extensive merger of New York daily newspapers in 1966. The original plan, as announced in April, called for consolidation of the Scripps-Howard *World-Telegram and Sun* and Hearst's *New York Journal*, both afternoon papers, with Whitney's *New York Herald Tribune*, morning daily with a Sunday edition. A strike by the American Newspaper Guild prevented publication of the new paper, to be known as *New York World Journal Tribune*. The strike continued through the summer, and Whitney decided to fold up the *Herald Tribune*. On September 12, the one hundred forty-day strike came to an end, and the new paper appeared as an afternoon daily with a Sunday edition. The morning edition had dropped by the wayside.

The *World Journal Tribune* tried to appeal to nearly all segments of the public. The daily seemed to be an amalgamation of a number of journalistic patterns. The editors carried a wide variety of columnists. The *World Journal Tribune*'s publishers sought to find a journalistic pattern which would appeal to between 800,000 and 1,000,000 New Yorkers and enable the paper to survive and be successful as the only standard-size afternoon daily with extensive international, national and local coverage of the news. Its only afternoon rival was the tabloid *New York Post*, short on local coverage. Manhattan, Bronx and Brooklyn had no afternoon newspapers of their own.

The *World Journal Tribune* did not get a chance to find a suitable formula. It closed down in eight months, in May, 1967. A dispute with the typographical union over wages led management to stop publication suddenly. The closing stunned the public and the newspaper world. Publisher Matthew Meyer said the daily was losing about $700,000 a month, or an estimated $8.4 million yearly, and that the contract demanded by the typographical union would cause even greater losses which could not be made up. Advertising revenue in the *World Journal Tribune* was insufficient so far. Many advertisers had been lost during the previous strike, and after it was over the experienced staff had obtained jobs elsewhere. Editor Frank Conniff said the *World Journal Tribune* had never developed a distinct identity, and Madison Avenue advertising agencies were looking for a specific market profile: Who was buying the paper? Where did they live? How much income did they have? The paper had made progress in developing this kind of information but did not have time to complete the necessary task, Conniff confessed.

Bertram S. Powers, union representative, claimed the three owners, John H. Whitney, Jack Howard and William R. Hearst, could not agree on policies, nor would any of them buy the paper. Powers said the union would have given the paper special consideration if officials had come to him and asked for it.

Thus, New York has been left with the *New York Times* and the tabloid *Daily News* in the morning, and the *New York Post* tabloid in the afternoon. From fifteen dailies in Manhattan in the beginning of the century, three have remained. Newspaper readers commuting to New York read their hometown community newspapers, as these have grown in circulation and advertising.

Chapter 34

Tabloids: Kisses, Bullets and Liberals

ILLUSTRATED DAILY NEWS IS LAUNCHED

When the *New York Illustrated Daily News* was ushered into the world in 1919, few of its readers realized that the tabloid would soon become the daily spokesman and organ of the strap-hanging stenographer in the subway, the taxicab driver and the Broadway habitué. This tabloid has proved to be the most spectacular journalistic success of the era, influencing deeply and widely the course of American newspapers.

Other publishers also had considered launching tabloids; the state of journalistic development, it appeared, was ripe for the tabloid innovation in this country.

The *New York Illustrated Daily News* was established by the *Chicago Tribune,* controlled by Robert R. McCormick and his cousin, Joseph M. Patterson. The *Tribune* showed enormous profits; some of these were used to experiment with a tabloid. Over $1 million was borrowed from the Chicago Tribune Company for the launching of the New York publication.

Patterson, who was to be in charge of the New York paper, was born in 1879 into a wealthy home but was caught up in the new reform movements of the early twentieth century. He enrolled at Yale University but took time off to become the *Tribune* correspondent in China, covering the Boxer Rebellion. Returning to the United States, he was graduated from Yale in 1901. Patterson turned to reporting for the family newspaper and developed a strong interest in reform politics and the problems of the average man. Patterson campaigned against boss rule and won a seat in the Illinois legislature. This was the period when socialism was making forward strides in Chicago and the Midwest. Patterson helped organize the Muncipial Ownership League and was appointed Public Works Commissioner. Working as a reporter and editorial writer on the *Tribune,* he could not agree with its conservative Republican policies and left the daily. He retired to write books and plays on an Illinois farm. On his return to the *Tribune* he served as co-editor with his cousin.

Before America entered World War I, Patterson became a European war correspondent for the paper. When the United States entered World War I, he went overseas as a lieutenant and later was promoted to captain.

While in England, Patterson observed the success of Lord Northcliffe's *London Daily Mirror,* the picture tabloid which reached one million readers daily and two million on Sunday. Patterson met his cousin, Robert R. McCormick, also an officer, in France and discussed the possibilities of issuing a similar tabloid in the United States at the end of the war.

When the armistice was signed, Patterson returned to this country and made plans for publishing the *New York Illustrated Daily News.* Patterson and McCormick obtained, as indicated, a million dollar loan from the Chicago Tribune Company with which to launch the New York City tabloid. On June 26, 1919, Patterson printed the *New York Illustrated Daily News* in the plant of the *Evening Mail,* the presses of which were idle at night. Patterson decided on a morning issue because the paper could be sold all day and would get a better position on newsstands. All New York papers appeared to him to be alike; none had strong picture display. He intended to give the public something which other papers did not have: pictures. He saw the Hearst *American* as chief competitor.

The serious sixteen-page *Illustrated Daily News* tabloid with the blurred, hazy pictures was a newspaper baby, born in the midst of a strife-torn world, and it showed its birthmarks. Although soberminded, the *Illustrated News,* like its big brother newspapers, published sex and crime news, but it did not emphasize them at first. Appeal to women was strong in the *Illustrated Daily News.* The *News* also made a special appeal to men with its sports pages. The tabloid gave up-to-the-minute pictures of boxing, baseball and other sports events. These photos were published on the back page, an innovation in journalism.

By March, 1921, the *News* had undergone by degrees a startling transformation from its original purpose of being a small-size newspaper, giving news of the world in concise text and pictures. It became, many charged, "a daily erotica for the masses." The *Daily News* began to serve in regular and big doses crime and illicit sex relations to thrill vicariously its rapidly increasing readers.

Actually, the tabloid publishers and editors merely rediscovered the old Pulitzer formula. The *Daily News* publishers were driving for circulation and, ultimately, profits. But why at this time, 1921 to 1928, did the bullets and love-nest formula, as interpreted by the tabloid, catch on in popular favor?

With the return of two million men from battle in France, a demand for excitement was created. A larger group who had stayed at home were worked up to a fever pitch by local war activities and war news. Standards of old-time morality had taken a sharp decline for both men and women. Revolt against the shackles of the prohibition law became a sport in the 1920s and the rebellion spread to other activities. Sensing this change in viewpoint between 1919 and 1921, the publishers and editors of the *Daily News*, as newspapermen had done in the past, began to cater to it. The *Daily News*, too, found prosperity in the previously built interest in sports. The tabloid, therefore, expanded its sports department to meet this postwar interest.

All writers who have dealt with the tabloid repeat: The function of the tabloid has been to give vicarious enjoyment and thrills to its readers. The *News* early established a reputation for obtaining pictures and love letters written by the principals in scandals and divorce proceedings. Since this type of news was the basis for its appeal, the *News* spent an unbelievable amount of effort and ingenuity and, of course, money to acquire such material. The tabloid became identified during this period with the love-nest story. In addition, the tabloid served strong doses of horror stories and murder news.

One of the outstanding news events of the era was Charles A. Lindbergh's solo flight across the Atlantic Ocean in May, 1927. The *Daily News* greeted the flyer upon his return to New York with this chummy headline:

HELLO, LINDY!

Specializing in photos, the *Daily News* gave a great impetus to photography in the American newspaper. Patterson encouraged the development of the photographic department, deciding to print pictures on the front page, inside pages and back page. The paper became widely known for its picture scoops. In 1955 the *Daily News* won a Pulitzer prize for the general excellence of its photos. Photographers of the paper pioneered in aerial photography. The *News* had used airplanes to speed the transmission of pictures; as early as 1925 it began to use pictures transmitted by wire.

Beginning with the "Most Beautiful Girl Contest," the *Daily News* conducted more than one hundred contests during the next few years.

The competitions became a steady feature of the tabloid, gaining considerable drawing power. The *Daily News* in its early period printed serials for its readers. E. Phillips Oppenheim, Zane Grey, Luke Short and Agatha Christie were featured.

The *Daily News* also developed columnists of its own, writers who captured a following of hundreds of thousands and became pillars of the paper's success. With experience on the *Chicago Tribune,* Patterson developed a number of highly successful comics for the New York tabloid. Comic strips which had proved successful in the *Chicago Tribune* were printed also in the *Daily News.* Readers were intensely interested in the doings of Old Doc York, who became Andy Gump.

Guiding policies from the very beginning was Patterson, a square-jawed, brown-eyed man, compactly built into a 5-foot, 11-inch frame. He cared little for dress or show. At first he operated the paper by remote control, telephoning and writing from Chicago because he did not know whether the paper would be a success or not. It was decided finally that he would leave cousin McCormick in charge of the *Chicago Tribune,* while Patterson would move to New York to direct the *Daily News.* In 1926, after the tabloid had proved itself, Patterson came to New York permanently. A student of the public taste and interest, he haunted the subways and stood alongside newstands to watch what people read. If they picked up the *Daily News,* he went up to them and bluntly asked why they liked the paper and what they read. He was a movie fan and attended motion picture theatres regularly. He sought to learn the interests of the masses so he could shape his paper accordingly. His able group of editors translated his ideas into news, features, headlines and photos as well as editorials.

Editorials were written in a casual fashion, appealing to the reader in his own language and making an effort to talk directly to him. The *Daily News* gave tentative approval of Franklin D. Roosevelt as Democratic candidate for the presidency in May, 1932. Roosevelt's views seemed to parallel Patterson's earlier youthful ideas. After FDR won, the *Daily News* gave vigorous support to the New Deal. Closely allied to its Chicago sister paper, the Republican *Tribune,* the *Daily News* began to disagree with the President on foreign policies.

The *Daily News* did not continue in the 1940s as a daily erotica for the masses, with emphasis on the lighter side of life. As the public's problems and interests changed, so did the tabloid. It began to use more national news on pages two and three. The White House became more important on certain days than New York City Hall. International problems became acute. The *Daily News* won plaques for public service and was given Ayer Typographical awards. In a series of articles the editor campaigned against east-side firetraps. Reuben Maury, editorial writer

The Washington Daily News

CITY EDITION

FRIDAY, OCTOBER 26, 1951

TORIES WIN

And Here Comes Winnie!

Britain's Tory Party, led by 76-year-old Winston Churchill, was returned to power today in the General Election.

Left, the familiar, bulky figure of Britain's wartime leader who now becomes prime minister again at a time in Britain's history when her fortunes around the world are in as grave a state as when Mr. Churchill was first called to head the government in 1940.

Right, a facsimile of the front page of The News of July 26, 1945, when the voters of Britain cast him out in favor of Clement Attlee's Labor Party.

(Story on Page 3.)

The News

THERE GOES WINNIE

Attlee Slated to Take Over Premiership

Figure 55. Tabloid Front Page. The tabloid front page was the essence of simplicity: a headline or two and a large picture. This front page was typical of those of the *New York Daily News*. The *News* headlines were often chummy: "Here Comes Winnie!" referring to Winston Churchill, October 26, 1951. (Courtesy of the *New York Daily News*)

for the *Daily News,* won a Pulitzer Prize for editorial writing in 1940. In 1958 the Pulitzer Prize was given to the reporting team of Joseph Martin and Phil Sentera, who wrote a series on the Cuban revolutionary buildup of Fidel Castro.

Recognizing new trends toward electronic journalism, Patterson explored the possibilities of radio news. The *Daily News* began to broadcast over WNEW in February, 1942. Patterson laid plans for entering television news broadcasting; his station WPIX went on the air June, 1948.

Advertising came into the *News* slowly. The revenue for July, 1919, the first month, was $1,530. When circulation began to increase, advertisers came to recognize the value of the *Daily News'* increasing readership. By September, 1923 circulation passed 633,000, exceeding Hearst's *New York Journal.*

Publisher Patterson died May 26, 1946, leaving a net estate of more than $9 million. Management of the paper was left in the hands of Patterson's executives, Richard W. Clarke and F. M. Flynn. Circulation of the *News* topped by far any other newspaper in the United States. By midcentury the *Daily News* circulation reached 2,887,337 on weekdays and 4,329,560 on Sundays. In 1968, 2,074,004 subscribers purchased the *News,* while 3,099,658 bought it on Sundays.

HEARST LAUNCHES THE MIRROR

Faced with competition from the *Daily News* in 1921 and 1922, the Hearst organization experimented with a New York tabloid, calling it the *American Pictorial,* publishing it as a supplement to the regular morning *New York American.* Hearst's tabloid paper featured sex stories, following the *Daily News* pattern.

Soon, however, the Hearst organization launched the *Daily Mirror* in 1924 as a rival of the successful *Daily News.* In many respects, the Hearst paper duplicated the *News.* The *Mirror* won a large daily audience of 847,979 with 1,275,193 buying the tabloid on Sunday in 1960. On October 16, 1963, the Hearst corporation closed down the paper although its circulation ran about 800,000. Officials said the tabloid had become unprofitable. Lack of advertising and rising costs aggravated by a strike caused the owners to kill off the *Mirror.* Only the *Daily News* remained as the comparable morning tabloid in the city.

THE GRAPHIC BECOMES PORNOGRAPHIC

Five years after the *Daily News* was begun, Bernarr MacFadden established the *Evening Graphic* on September 15, 1924. It was the same year Hearst issued the first edition of the *Mirror,* showing that both publishers were reacting in similar fashion to new conditions and potential public wants.

MacFadden's experience in publications had been confined to publishing *Physical Culture,* a magazine which had attained four hundred thousand circulation, and *True Story* magazine, which acquired two million readers.

The day's big contest was a forerunner of many the *Graphic* used to build reader interest and circulation. The first contest grew out of MacFadden's interest in physical culture and genetics. The publisher declared he would give $10,000 for the ideal marriage consummated by the male and female winner.

Emile Gauvreau, the editor, developed composographs, a faked photograph of a real scene which the cameraman was unable to shoot. The composograph grew out of the desire of the *Graphic* to photograph the courtroom scene in the Kip Rhinelander divorce case. Rhinelander, a wealthy playboy, was suing his wife for annulment of their marriage on the grounds that she had not told him that Negro blood ran in her veins. She contended that it had always been perfectly obvious to him that she was not white. In an effort to prove this, she undressed to her waist in court. What a picture for the tabloid! However, before the disrobing occurred, the court was cleared by the judge, and photographers were expelled. The *Graphic* realized what a good picture for its purposes this would make, so a chorus girl stripped to the waist and was posed in a fake courtroom scene with other persons in the background. The picture was then retouched, and faces of the courtroom characters were pasted on the photo. It was then reshot. A tiny note at the bottom of the picture told the reader it was not genuine. But the composograph had accomplished its purpose. The *Graphic* used composograph frequently after this initial experiment.

By means of its many sensations, the *Graphic* reached seven hundred thousand readers at one time. But, because of its methods, it became known as the *Porno-Graphic,* and it was banned from many homes on the grounds that it was "the worst form of debauchery."

Advertisers who might possibly have come into the paper to support it were extremely hesitant about it. In the meantime, there were heavy yearly losses, made up by MacFadden's profitable *True Story* magazine. For a number of years the *Graphic*'s gay abandon attracted a large number of readers, but collapse was inevitable. Circulation itself began to decline after 1930. The economic depression affected all newspapers. In May, 1932, MacFadden withdrew his financial support and the *Evening Graphic* closed down.

Significance of the Tabloid

In summarizing results and influences exerted on other papers by the *Graphic*, historian Simon Bessie pointed out in *Jazz Journalism* that the *Graphic*'s despised sensationalism forced competing papers to adopt a louder tone. Tabloids compelled newspapers to use more pictures than they did before and to re-examine their makeup styles.

Within the next decade about fifty tabloids were established in cities, varying in size and character from New York City to Mount Pleasant, Texas. The tabloid passed through the same cycle as other institutions. The extremely sensational type disappeared, and tabloids increasingly turned to serious matters. They represented a strong trend in the twentieth century. Some, of course, shifted back to the standard-size format, especially when they were merged with standard papers. The tabloid *Chicago Times* became the *Sun-Times;* the *Baltimore Post* emerged as the standard-size *News-Post.*

INGERSOLL STARTS PM, JOURNALISTIC EXPERIMENT

Establishment of *PM* by Ralph Ingersoll in 1940 reflected the need for a liberal newspaper in tabloid form with plenty of pictures. *PM* was the brainchild of Ralph Ingersoll, trained in the new weekly newsmagazines, *Time* and *Life; PM* seemed to inherit a number of the techniques of these publications.

Ingersoll persuaded a number of wealthy people to invest in *PM*, but the largest block of stock was taken by Marshall Field, III, who provided $2 million. As Field eventually bought the stock of the other original investors, *PM* came to be known as the Marshall Field paper. Field believed earnestly in the publication. He wished to make a financial investment in a liberal newspaper but not to edit it. He believed such a paper was necessary to equalize the public's problem of getting liberal views and to offset the standard papers.

On June 18, 1940, *PM* appeared. *PM* was a square tabloid, beautifully printed with a special ink, and stapled so that the pages would not fly apart. It had thirty-two pages, with a front page consisting of headlines and pictures, a style it followed for the first few years. *PM* was more readable than other papers, as it was printed in 9-point type as compared with the 7- or 8-point of other newspapers. The publication was departmentalized. A column of excellent analysis of current radio was offered. Instead of paid advertisements, *PM* carried a resumé of advertisements appearing in other papers. Artist-reporters wrote stories and drew pictures.

PM expected to carry no editorial page. If the assistant managing editor or reporters in a department had comments to make of the news breaking in their areas, they could write editorials for their own pages. Ingersoll, however, did define the general goals of his new publication. *PM* stood for social justice and the rights of small businessmen against monopolies, and consumers against manufacturers and retailers. *PM* also opposed racial intolerance. It used many background stories written in feature style. *PM* made no pretense at full coverage. It selected what its editors thought were the most important aspects of world, national and local events and shot its full force on them.

PM embarked on a number of exposures. One of these was a campaign against bad conditions existing in the New York poultry market. Pictures of dead chickens accompanied the articles. *PM* proceeded against the credit installment houses which, it charged, were cheating the public. Opposing intolerance of all kinds, *PM* aroused its readers against Father Coughlin's radio broadcasts, with the result that officials of *PM* received thousands of letters of protest against the radio speaker. One of the most skillful of *PM*'s specialists, Albert Deutsch, focused on health and other sociological subjects, seeking to give the background of the surface social problems in the news.

Photographs by Weegee, who won prizes, and by Mary Morris and Margaret Bourke-White became one of the paper's strong appeals. *PM* also had a section on modern living edited by Elizabeth Hawes, who was concerned with food, health, clothes and household affairs. Her pages were consumer centered and advocated legislation which would protect the buyer's interest. Other strong appeals of the paper included its theatre column, conducted by Louis Kronenberg.

In spite of the appeals of the tabloid, Ingersoll and his staff could not develop the broad, popular support the paper needed. Lack of full news coverage in a competitive New York situation made *PM* a specialty paper. The middle class and intellectual working class to which it appealed were avid for news in great quantities. The usual tabloid readers were satisfied with less, but the paper did not appeal to them. As a result, the intellectual *PM* reader had to purchase another newspaper for his extensive news, to which he had become accustomed. This was too expensive for many New Yorkers. This situation likewise applied to *PM*'s Sunday edition which could not compete in size and coverage with the *New York Times* and the *Herald Tribune*.

Persuasive, able and earnest, Ingersoll was a strong-minded man. Some reporters objected to his being a prima donna, and they could not get along with him. He was confronted, too, with internal factional fights. After a brief army service, Ingersoll returned to *PM*. His stay was short; an argument over the advisability of including paid advertising caused him to resign from the publication.

John Lewis, who had been editor during Ingersoll's absence, was placed in charge. In the face of increasing costs, he sought to make the tabloid profitable by reducing the number of pages to twenty-four and, at the same time, securing better news coverage. Originally *PM* had no comics; five were now developed, with "Barnaby" acquiring the most appeal. Billy Rose's column was added for sophisticated entertainment. Advertising now brought in $600,000; although this cut the losses, Field still had to contribute $500,000 to the budget that year. Altogether, Field spent $5 million on the paper during its eight years of existence.

Believing that he had given the experiment enough time to prove its value, Field decided to sell *PM*. Joseph Barnes, liberal foreign editor of the *Herald Tribune,* and Bartley Crum, California lawyer, paid $300,000 for it. It was reported that Field loaned them, afterward, $500,000 to keep the daily going.

The Star

In order to eliminate prejudices and bad tastes still lingering over the paper, the new owners changed its name to *The Star* when they began publication in May, 1948. The *Star* lasted only eight months.

NEWSDAY, SUBURBAN TABLOID, GAINS SUCCESS

Some newspapers in suburban New York demonstrated their value and survived the fierce competition of metropolitan dailies just described. Problems faced by the *Long Island Newsday* were typical of suburban papers in the United States. *Newsday* was one of the few dailies to start in the twentieth century and make a roaring success in spite of many obstacles.

Newsday could not be separated from its publisher-editor, Alicia Patterson Guggenheim. Some referred to the Long Island success as just another manifestation of the famous "Patterson touch." Her father, Joseph Patterson, co-founded and developed the *New York Daily News* and helped build the Patterson-McCormick chain. Miss Patterson worked for the *American Magazine* and wrote a series on how to get a job without experience. She did promotional work and book reviews on the *New York Daily News,* disagreeing with her father's opposition to President Roosevelt. She married Harry Guggenheim, copper magnate, in 1939. Her father discouraged her from publishing a tabloid *Newsday* in Long

Island, but Mrs. Guggenheim went ahead anyway. Her husband bought the Long Island paper for $70,000; it had eleven thousand subscribers.

Latest world news appeared in *Newsday,* but often this was published alongside bold headlines announcing the visit of some celebrity to Long Island. The local angle was featured. This daily stressed pictures strongly also, with the centerfold of two pages devoted to a local picture spread.

Newsday also carried on crusades against illegal gambling, high school immorality, water pollution. Most dramatic of all *Newsday* crusades was the one in which a reporter, Don Kellerman, changed identity in the fall of 1952, committed a minor crime, spent seven weeks in jail —all to expose substandard conditions in Suffolk County jail. In a series of six stories, Kellerman described brutality of prison guards, unsanitary conditions, near-poisonous food and the open traffic in narcotics. Kellerman's ordeal resulted in some needed reforms in the Suffolk County prison system.

Newsday cost the Guggenheims more than $700,000 before the daily began to break even and then make a profit. Mr. Guggenheim owned 51 per cent of *Newsday* stock. Publisher Alicia Patterson Guggenheim owned the other 49 per cent. *Newsday*'s editions ran between sixty-eight and one hundred twenty-eight tabloid pages in 1958; some days *Newsday* carried more advertising than any other metropolitan New York paper. When Mrs. Guggenheim died in July, 1963, her husband took charge. He appointed Mark F. Ethridge, of the *Louisville Courier,* as editor. *Newsday* in 1968 reached 421,356 subscribers.

Chapter 35

Atlantic Seaboard Dailies

BOSTON'S VARIED NEWSPAPERS

Boston has remained the commercial, industrial, wholesale and financial hub of Massachusetts, perhaps of New England. Boston reached a population of 800,000 by midcentury, but, like New York, its residents began to fill up the adjacent suburbs, so that in the metropolitan area lived more than one million persons. A cultural center since colonial days, Boston has been able to boast Harvard University, Radcliffe College, Massachusetts Institute of Technology, Boston University, Northeastern University and others of high caliber. Boston's public library has more than thirty branches. The city has many outstanding museums, and its Boston Symphony Orchestra and popular Pops Symphony have been recognized nationally.

Boston's journalism went through a process of change, reflecting the trends observed on the national scene and in New York. Mergers and consolidations reduced some of the established journals, while the Hearst and Munsey chains made their inroads. In 1900 Boston issued eleven daily newspapers with seven ownerships. In 1960 seven dailies were published with three ownerships. Both the *Boston Post* and the *Boston Transcript* were eliminated in the new century.

Hearst's Mergers

Hearst established the *Boston American* in 1904 as part of his plan to expand his chain in New England. Using techniques he had devised in New York to win readers, he began to build up the *American*. He combined into his organization several papers; in 1917 he bought the *Advertiser*, established in the previous century, and the *Record*, founded in 1884, so that eventually he issued the *American* in the evening, the

Record in the morning and the *Advertiser* on Sunday. Hearst transformed the *Advertiser* into a tabloid in the 1920s and 1930s.

In the early 1960s the Hearst organization, in its economy drive, combined the *Record* and the *American* into a profitable morning paper, reaching 455,873 readers by 1968.

Boston Globe

Another paper which survived and was still in the race was the *Boston Globe,* published by Charles H. Taylor. He felt the best office for him was the *Globe* office. He avoided sacred cows or excessive praise for persons in whom he was personally interested. After trying subscription-building contests in the 1890s, Taylor found that substantial news was the only surefire way to permanent newspaper ownership.

General Taylor died on June 21, 1921, and control of the paper passed into the hands of his son, William O. Taylor, who continued as publisher until 1955. Grandson William D. Taylor became president-publisher; John T. Taylor, treasurer; and Charles H. Taylor, assistant treasurer.

The *Boston Globe* at midcentury sought to cover the news of the metropolitan Boston region and New England. The *Globe*'s front page was striking and bold with inch or inch and one-half high headlines and pictures which attempted to attract attention. On big, spectacular human interest news, the editors gave the events everything they had in headlines and photos.

In seeking to cover the region for news, the *Globe* printed regularly a strong human-interest feature, "Calling on the Neighbors." A typical feature of this type was headed, "Clock Maker, 92, Starts Work on His 120-Foot Masterpiece." The clockmaker lived in Waltham, a nearby community. A two-column picture accompanied the feature. The *Globe* ran special news features in series; A. Forman, for example, wrote on "Why Johnny Can't Read," an educational problem of wide interest in the 1950s.

The editorial page followed a somewhat modernized style, featuring "Uncle Dudley's" as a leading editorial writer. This long editorial was written in a chatty style, sometimes dealing with the lighter side of the news, but most often was concerned with serious problems of the day. A women's page, sports section, business page and radio-television page completed the *Globe*'s edition. The morning *Globe* reached 241,712 readers; the evening *Globe* had 196,923 by 1968.

Thirty departments were represented in the *Sunday Globe,* with news, features, photographs, all topped with large, powerful headlines to catch the eye. The editors presented art, auto, boating, books, camera and chess departments. Readers could also keep up with homes and gardens, music, mystic organizations. Those interested in finance, and real estate had pages of reading matter. For hobbyists concerned with stamps and sports cars, the *Sunday Globe* had solid news and informative features for them. Women's pages were filled with household information, cooking recipes and articles about rearing children. For the large Jewish population in Boston, two full columns on their activities were found in the Sunday editions.

Reporters and political writers contributed to the Sunday edition news features which backgrounded current affairs. The writers were concerned with international and national news and trends. They covered New England regional news and Massachusetts as well as Boston events. Features spread across the top of the inside pages of the news sections and were headed with striking headlines.

The *Sunday Globe* reached 555,905 in 1968. Published on newspaper row for a half century, the *Globe* moved into a $12 million modern plant in Dorchester, a nearby suburban community, in 1958.

Herald—Traveler

The *Herald,* a morning paper also originating in the nineteenth century, had been taken over by some New England financiers and industrialists and was managed by John W. Holmes. They added, in 1912, the *Traveler,* as the evening edition. Five years later, the company absorbed Frank Munsey's *Journal,* which Munsey purchased in 1902. The *Herald* obtained 175,483 subscribers; the *Traveler,* 161,453 by 1964. On Sundays the *Herald* appealed to 281,586 subscribers. As a result of the merger of the papers, the *Herald-Traveler* reached 230,817 morning subscribers. On Sundays the paper had a circulation of 302,436 by 1968.

Christian Science Monitor Nationally Known

Best known nationally of the Boston papers, however, has been the *Christian Science Monitor.* Growing out of a revulsion against Pulitzer-Hearst sensationalism, the *Christian Science Monitor* was launched on November 24, 1908, by Mary Baker Eddy, founder of the Christian Science Church. A journalistic sport in the evolutionary sense, the *Christian Science Monitor* had no profit motive to drive it. The object of the paper was to publish constructive news with a religious tone. It sought to avoid emphasis on crime, sex and disaster news being featured in the daily press in Boston and elsewhere. The editorial board had many restrictions on publication of news. In the early years of the *Monitor,* whose slogan was "to injure no man, but to bless all mankind," the editors ignored news involving death, scandals, crime and disasters.

Following Christian Science doctrine, even the word *death* was not mentioned; public officials "passed on." When ordinary persons died, the event was omitted in the *Monitor*. The *Titanic* ship disaster was ignored, and in World War I, the paper spoke of "terrific casualties" not deaths. The *Monitor* was consistent with the church's teachings, for the daily lost thousands of dollars in declining to accept liquor, shotgun or tombstone advertisements.

Erwin D. Canham, who later became the distinguished editor of the *Monitor,* joined the staff as a cub reporter. Born in 1904, Erwin worked as an office boy for the *Lewiston* (Maine) *Sun,* where his father was agricultural editor. Canham went to Bates College in Lewiston. There he continued his interest in journalism by editing a weekly and serving as correspondent for big-city papers.

After attending Oxford University as a Rhodes scholar, Canham began to work for the *Monitor* as a reporter. His ability was soon recognized, and he won foreign assignments, covering the League of Nations in Geneva and the London Naval Conference. He was made head of the *Monitor's* Washington Bureau; then, in 1939, he was recalled to Boston where he became news editor, then managing editor of the paper. At the age of forty-one, Canham was appointed editor.

Although he said that "ideals of the paper were more important than any individual," Canham was responsible for many improvements. He sought to revitalize the columns of the *Monitor* and win for it a large audience. It became less and less an organ of the Christian Science Church and more like a newspaper. Canham had a particularly difficult problem to solve. Although he had to compete with Boston daily papers, most of the circulation of the *Monitor* was spread through the United States and in ninety-six foreign countries. Thus, the bulk of his readers got the *Monitor* with news they had read in their daily papers. To offset this, the *Monitor* printed regional editions and a foreign edition. Canham printed the spot news but also advocated and developed background, interpretative articles on national and international events.

The *Monitor* built up its foreign and domestic coverage, and for some time did not subscribe to the AP or the UP. Finally, the *Monitor* added the AP service to its own correspondence. The *Monitor* specialized in regional news developments. The social aims of the New Deal found a favorable response in the paper, but the *Monitor* did not fail to criticize corruption in relief activities and to attack court programs of President Franklin D. Roosevelt. The *Monitor* was friendly to the worker and the farmer as inseparable links in the American economy.

Canham denied that the *Monitor* avoided crime news, but said that such news was not overemphasized, and he declared the causes of crime and the means of eliminating it were presented in the daily. The *Monitor,* thus, sought to publish constructive news. Its circulation was 156,267 in 1960, but it climbed to 201,145 by 1968.

CONSOLIDATED PHILADELPHIA DAILIES GROW LARGER

Conservatism characterized the thinking of Philadelphia's leaders, while the Republican Party dominated its City Hall. At the turn of the century, Philadelphia numbered 1,243,000 residents; during the next decades this population multiplied, forced expansion of the city limits and extended into many suburban communities. Population of Philadelphia by 1964 reached more than 2,200,000. Within its closely packed trading area, the metropolitan area had 4,285,000 people.

Philadelphia newspapers reflected this growth and the commercial and industrial prosperity. For the most part the press mirrored, too, the conservative views of the Philadelphia leaders, although the liberal *Record,* in the 1930s and during part of the 1940s, represented a challenge to the status quo. As in other communities, total circulation of the Philadelphia newspapers continued to mount, but because of economic factors the number of dailies decreased. At one time, Philadelphia could claim sixteen dailies, representing all shades of political and economic opinion. By 1965 the number of newspapers had been reduced to three dailies, one of which was a tabloid.

Evening Bulletin: Big Small-Town Daily

One of the dailies which survived, the *Evening Bulletin,* reached new heights of circulation and financial prosperity. The *Bulletin* was a family-owned newspaper and had been for more than a half century. Its strong, conservative traditions and its successful newspaper formula were set and fixed by William Luppard McLean back at the end of the nineteenth century.

McLean purchased the *Bulletin* in 1895 in the face of stiff competition. The paper then had less than 7,000 circulation in a city where thirteen papers were being issued with a combined circulation above 850,000. With his experience as a spectacular circulation hustler in Pittsburgh and seventeen years as business and circulation manager of the old *Philadelphia Press,* McLean began to build up the tottering *Bulletin.* He catered to local neighborhood or community interests within Philadelphia.

Although Philadelphians lived within one of the largest metropolises in the United States, they considered themselves residents of local sections: Kensington, West Philadelphia, Germantown, Frankford and others. These community distinctions were very real to residents, though no geographical boundaries existed. McLean filled his *Bulletin,* therefore, with community news and local items, no matter how small. He gave Philadelphia "the biggest and best small-town newspaper in the United States." He believed that what interested newspaper readers most was the haps and mishaps of their neighbors, the kind that could have happened to themselves. In a year McLean had increased the circulation to 33,000 daily. In five years the *Bulletin* reached 130,000. Other Philadelphia papers dropped by the wayside.

The *Evening Bulletin* at various times supported reform movements and opposed the corrupt City Hall gang. But McLean was not a crusader usually. When a managing editor put on page one an exposé of a gambling house running blast, McLean asked, "Do you think this is quite the sort of thing the *Bulletin* ought to do?" The executive caught the hint. If the police raided a place, the *Bulletin* printed the fact. The daily didn't stir up trouble. Plain, factual news stories were presented, while cleverness and sophisticated writing were not encouraged.

"The newspaper is a visitor in the home," the publisher of the *Bulletin* declared, "and so there should never be anything in it which conceivably could offend any member of the family." This policy extended to the comics. When Winnie Winkel was about to have her twins, the editors decided that the strips were too realistic for *Bulletin* readers. The *Bulletin* asked the syndicated cartoonist to draw for its readers another, more delicate set.

Politically, the *Bulletin* adhered closely to the Republican Party. A strong personality, Frank Fuller Shedd served as editorial writer on the *Bulletin* from 1911 to 1921, when he became editor-in-chief. As president of the American Society of Newspaper Editors, he did much to bring about a closer relationship between instructors and practitioners of journalism. He also sought to elevate standards of professional education for journalism and taught at Pennsylvania State College for several years. He died in 1937.

Meanwhile, Robert and William McLean took over management of the *Bulletin* when their father died in 1937. They followed his general publishing principles but sought to adapt them to the new age. New writing talent was brought in. In 1968 the *Bulletin* reached 671,525 readers on weekdays and 728,276 on Sundays.

Philadelphia Inquirer Rejuvenated

As many other well-established metropolitan dailies of the twentieth century, roots of the *Philadelphia Inquirer* go back more than a century. Before he died in 1911, James Elverson, Sr., had nursed the weak and impoverished *Inquirer* into one of the largest newspapers in the United States. His son, James Elverson, Jr., took it from there. Under his direction the *Inquirer* increased its prosperity and strengthened its impress on political thought in the predominately Republican state. The paper kept pace with the mechanical age, converting to motor trucks and color printing. Again, the *Inquirer* became too large for its building facilities. Colonel Elverson bought ground at Broad and Callowhill streets for a new building. The $10 million building was one of the most modern and completely equipped newspaper plants in the world when the first issue of the daily in its new building rolled out in 1925.

Curtis Regime

Following death of Col. Elverson, the majority interest in the *Inquirer* was sold to Curtis-Martin Newspapers, Inc. in 1930. Financial circles reported that negotiations were on the basis of $10.5 million for control. President of the purchasing company, Cyrus H. K. Curtis, was also president of the Curtis Publishing Company, which issued the *Saturday Evening Post.* After he built up the *Saturday Evening Post,* Curtis purchased the *Philadelphia Public Ledger* from Adolph S. Ochs in 1912.

Now he launched a bewildering series of mergers just as Munsey did in New York, and other publishers did elsewhere. Curtis bought the *Philadelphia Evening Telegram* in 1913, and after acquiring the *Philadelphia Press* combined the two papers. Five years later, in 1918, he bought the venerable *Philadelphia North American* and fused it with the *Public Ledger.* Upon purchasing the *Inquirer* he consolidated the *Public Ledger,* morning and evening editions, with his new daily. The century-old morning *Ledger* came to an end. In 1942 the evening edition went bankrupt. It will be recalled that, meanwhile, Curtis had purchased the *New York Evening Post.*

Curtis now decided to withdraw from newspaper publication, and the Elverson Corporation resumed control of the *Inquirer.* Again Mme. Patenotre, a daughter who inherited the *Inquirer,* sold the paper, this time to M. L. Annenberg, on August 6, 1936. The new publisher paid $13 million for the *Inquirer,* which had at the time, a circulation of 280,093 for the daily, while the Sunday edition reached 669,152.

Annenberg had fought his way up to become circulation manager for Hearst's *Chicago American.* Later he became a publisher of the *Milwaukee* (Wisconsin) *News.* But he became best known for his connection with horse-racing publications. He acquired the *Daily Racing Form* and the *New York Morning Telegraph* and also formed a nationwide racing news service, the AP of sports news. He owned the *Miami* (Florida) *Herald* for a period.

Annenberg sought to make the *Inquirer* a better paper and to surpass the *Philadelphia Record,* which had a larger circulation. Annenberg invested money to build a better news organization and to strengthen the paper's features. Its mechanical equipment also needed improvement.

The new publisher focused on women readers. Able experts were hired in home economics, fashion, interior decoration, women's clubs and child welfare. To appeal to men, the *Inquirer's* financial pages were strengthened and the sports section improved, giving more sports news and game results. The *Inquirer* also aimed its columns at young readers. Sports pages included school games. New quality comic pages appealed to children and adult readers.

The *Inquirer* conducted a number of campaigns for the benefit of its readers. In 1860, the Hardings, publishers of the *Inquirer*, had promised that the paper would protect domestic manufacturers and work for advancement of industry in Philadelphia and Pennsylvania. A similar campaign was undertaken by Annenberg in the twentieth century. Reporters were assigned to get the facts about the decline of the state's industry. *Inquirer* newsmen traveled thousands of miles, interviewed hundreds of people. What the reporters learned was offered readers in 1938 under the title, "The Migration of Industry from Pennsylvania." Widespread results followed. The state administration formulated a plan to relieve industry of a heavy tax burden, and other efforts were made to keep factory owners from moving out of Pennsylvania and to attract new industry.

Walter Annenberg, New Publisher

Following the elder Annenberg's death in July, 1942, his son, Walter, became publisher. He also became editor in December, 1944 when John T. Custer died. Walter Annenberg's creed was stated:

> The newspaper merits its franchise only by virtue of its public service. A newspaper's public service can comprise anything from supplying a baseball score to employing all its resources in behalf of a public principle.

Annenberg conceived of the *Inquirer's* "Delaware Valley, U.S.A." campaign in 1951. Piecing together news items emanating from all sections of the area, he and his editors recognized that the Philadelphia market was entering a boom era. Many new plants were moving in. "What can we do to publicize the expansion? How can we impress this 'Renaissance on the Delaware' upon the minds of America?" were some of the questions raised. A campaign was begun to publicize the name "Delaware Valley, U.S.A." and to tell the story of the expansion. The Chamber of Commerce soon joined the movement. The idea spread quickly. In 1953, the Chamber of Commerce gave Annenberg its commerce and industry award, and the same year he was given the Philadephia Public Relations award.

Philadelphia has been a great business, financial and industrial center, and the *Inquirer* has aimed to mirror the business and financial world in its business section. It has published complete stock, bond and curb market tables from the financial capital of the world. Circulation by 1968 was 516,640 daily and 936,135 on Sundays.

Philadelphia Record: Liberal Voice

Liberal voice in the conservative city, the *Philadelphia Record,* was reinvigorated with the personality of J. David Stern, who became publisher in 1928. Stern bought the *Record* from the Wanamaker department store interests.

Stern had forsaken law, his original profession, for journalism and had become a reporter for the *Philadelphia Ledger.* Stern was fired because he told the editor how to run the paper. In 1911 he borrowed $1,500 and invested in a newspaper in New Brunswick, New Jersey. He caused the defeat of a political candidate, favored by a local wealthy pharmaceutical company, which then paid Stern $25,000 for the paper to get rid of him.

Returning to New Jersey several years later, he purchased the *Camden Evening Courier* and eventually added the morning *Post* to it. In Camden he fought Senator David A. Baird, overthrew the Baird political despotism, and promoted a commission form of government. In 1928, as indicated, Stern purchased the *Philadelphia Record* and proceeded to strengthen its news coverage and editorial page.

An early New Dealer, Stern advocated the candidacy of Roosevelt and began to take an active role in Philadelphia Democratic politics. Stern carried his liberalism into his own newspaper plant and was the first to sign a contract with the American Newspaper Guild.

However, it was his conflict with the Guild in 1946 that led to his suspending publication, although the Guild claimed that this was not the real reason. In January, 1947, he announced that the paper had been suspended and that he was selling the assets to the *Bulletin.* He received $13 million for the *Record,* the *Camden Courier-Post,* and the radio station. But the liberal *Record* was no more. It left the Philadelphia field to the *Inquirer,* the *Bulletin* and the tabloid *News.*

BALTIMORE JOURNALISM

Baltimore, metropolis with an excellent harbor and location near Chesapeake Bay, has kept pace as a shipping, industrial and wholesale center during the new century. Thousands of workers have labored in its steel and copper mills and its oil and sugar refineries. Garmentworkers have turned out millions of men's suits a year in its nationally known clothing factories.

In the first decades of the new era, Baltimore continued to serve as the wholesale dry goods distribution point for merchants in the South, but the wholesale houses declined in the 1920s. Other industries, such as airplane manufacturing, arose near Baltimore to replace these establishments. The largest tidewater steel mill in the world was erected at Sparrows Point nearby.

Baltimore journalism slowly began to duplicate journalistic trends exhibited by its northern neighbors. Pulitzer-Hearst methods, merger process, chain journalism and mechanical improvements eventually left their mark on Baltimore journalism. But in certain respects it retained a peculiar local flavor which distinguished it from journalism elsewhere.

Sunpapers Dominate Scene

Dominating the scene during most of the time were the *Sun*papers. Changes and rejuvenation which occurred in these papers were typical of the evolution of many large American newspapers.

At the turn of the century the *Sun* had built a strong, enduring reputation for honesty and integrity and had won fame as a recent fighter against corrupt local and state political machines. It had followed many successful traditions of the founder, A. S. Abell. His formula worked; the business was successful; there was no need, his heirs thought, for significant departures.

The *Sun* emphasized politics and had strong convictions on all issues, national, state and local. It participated in all except primary campaigns. The heart of the *Sun* was its editorial page; here, distinguished writers turned out thoughtful, polished prose under small headlines.

Ownership of the paper was in the hands of the various grandsons of the founder. Some stock of the company, which had become a corporation by 1892, was controlled by the Safe Deposit and Trust Company, as trustee for other heirs. The grandsons on the board of directors were in conflict, however, and struggled for control. This trouble did not become serious until later.

The *Sun*'s owners and editors felt secure, believing that every white literate person in Baltimore and Maryland read the daily morning *Sun* or the weekly *Sun*. Competition of up-and-coming papers and the force of changing public wants, however, caused a number of gradual modifications to be made. A Sunday edition was started in 1901. Halftone photographs were used for the first time in this issue, later spreading to the morning *Sun,* although pictures did not appear on the front page.

When its rival, the *Herald,* collapsed in 1906, Henry Louis Mencken came over to become *Sunday Sun* editor, the beginning of his long association with the *Sun*papers. The first comic section was introduced in 1911, almost driving some readers to apoplexy. The first columnist of the *Sun,* Folger McKinsey was hired in 1900, but he was principally a poet.

Meanwhile, the *Sun* faced two issues. First was internal dissension between the owner-grandsons, a conflict becoming more acute. Second was external newspaper pressure. The vigorous *Evening News,* at first owned by Charles H. Grasty who had built it up and sold it to Munsey in 1908, was making advertising inroads. In addition, Grasty, a dynamic, aggressive publisher, was looking for a newspaper and might buy one which could prove disastrous to the *Sun.* Faced with these internal and external critical problems, James Nelligan, president of the Safe Deposit and Trust Company, representing certain of the Abell heirs, persuaded the Abell grandsons to sell to Grasty. They followed Nelligan's advice reluctantly.

Grasty's backers included a group of outstanding industrialists and bankers with whom he had become acquainted. Grasty did not have enough cash to buy the *Sun,* with its expensive building and machinery.

Evening Sun Establishment

One of Grasty's most important innovations was establishment of the *Evening Sun* in 1910. Grasty was aware of the trend toward the evening newspaper because of growth of department store advertising, development of women readers and the changed time for reading papers. Fearing Hearst's entrance on the scene, Grasty bought the *World,* an evening competitor, for $63,000, and he proceeded to take some of the *World*'s features and its personnel. He acquired the United Press franchise. Grasty issued twelve pages and aimed at the "family audience," which meant men and women. The *Evening Sun*'s headlines then were moderately large. Four columns of advertisements remained on the front page.

Editor of the *Evening Sun* was John Haslup Adams, a fighting liberal of the Godkin type and a great admirer of reformers. He had been an editorial writer on the old *News,* and Grasty sought him out. Adams started "Editorials by the People," a letters-to-the-editor column which became popular. He was a believer in free speech and fair play. The *Sun,* while Democratic, had not favored Bryan, but found in Woodrow Wilson an answer to the party's needs for 1912.

Building up the *Evening Sun* was no easy job. The company made money on its morning and Sunday editions, but the losses sustained by the new journalistic infant caused it to go into debt. Grasty backers were called on for more money. Some members of the board of directors believed that better business methods might be installed. The board then curtailed Grasty's control over the business departments, a move to which he acceded. Within a short time, however, he retired from active management and eventually sold his stock to his backers.

In 1914, when Grasty retired, the *Sun* directors composed of previous backers and trustees for the Abell estate, faced a problem of finding a replacement for the skipper. They decided to place Van-Lear Black, son of H. Crawford Black, a *Sun* director, in charge. The younger Black was an exceptionally able businessman. He had been an official of the Fidelity and Deposit Company and of the Black-Sheridan-Wilson Company, coal operators, of which his father was head. Mr. Black was also a director of some of the nation's largest industrial and banking companies in New York.

Sun Rejuvenation By Van-Lear Black

He now undertook further rejuvenation of the *Sun*papers and made an attempt to pay the debts which Grasty had acquired. It took ten years to do so. News and editorial staffs of the morning and evening *Sun* were separated, and efforts were made to build up the staffs of both papers. Salaries were raised; new personnel was hired. The *Sun*'s Washington and London bureaus were strengthened. The *Sun* retained its conservative makeup, and its editorial page continued to present carefully polished editorials on the day's news. The *Sun* was outdistanced by its afternoon sister, the *Evening Sun,* in both circulation and advertising.

The *Evening Sun,* under Hamilton Owens, editor, brightened up and adopted a modern style. It followed the new trend in makeup, running single, double and even triple banners on page one. Eventually all advertisements came off that page as they did later in the morning *Sun.* The editorial page of the evening edition developed a sophisticated style. Brief and bright, the editorials nipped at politicians and all reformers. Mencken contributed editorials and a Monday article on the Babbits and Buffoons, as he called the politicians and the mass of Americans. *Sun*papers during this period stood for many liberal causes, as the editor believed strongly in political and economic liberty. The papers were strong advocates of free speech.

With this impetus and stimulation, circulation of all the *Sun*papers climbed steadily ahead. Advertising followed, so that the *Sun*papers ranked among the top newspapers in volume of advertising. A blow was struck when Van-Lear Black disappeared from his yacht in 1931, but the *Sun*papers continued, reaching greater circulation. By 1968, the morning *Sun* reached 186,878 readers; the *Evening Sun* 213,289; the Sunday edition had 345,651 subscribers.

Baltimore American

One factor which aided the *Sun*'s growth was decline in local competition. The ancient *Baltimore American,* a morning paper, established in the last century, had become a part of the Munsey organization in 1920, while the *Evening Star* was merged with Munsey's *Evening News.* Then, three years later, Hearst bought out Munsey, publishing both the morning *American* and the *Evening News.* Eventually Hearst killed off the less profitable morning *American,* keeping only its Sunday edition.

Meanwhile, Scripps-Howard invaded Baltimore with a tabloid *Post* in 1930. Under the direction of an able editor, Harold D. Jacobs, it struggled to survive and give the *Evening Sun* and the *News* some sharp news competition. But the *Post* was bucking a strong conservative trend in Baltimore. A fire in its printing department did not help matters. Hearst eventually bought the *Post* and merged it with his evening edition into the *News-Post.* Some of the old *Post* writers were taken over and appeared soon on the Hearst pages. Name of the combined papers was changed to *News-American* and won the largest circulation in the city.

With the death of Hearst, one of his sons became affiliated directly with the daily. Its editorial viewpoint was liberalized and better coverage of the news was given. Heavy emphasis was placed on local affairs. The editorial page and page opposite were improved. Louis Azrael, local columnist, continued to write in a chatty, informal style. Formerly an executive on the *Evening Sun,* Neil Swanson joined the *News-American* staff as foreign editor and columnist, contributing to the raising of its intellectual appeal. He established the tabloid, *Young World* for young readers, publishing it as a part of the Sunday edition.

The *News-American* daily reached 221,738 readers, and on Sunday found 321,833 readers by 1968.

WASHINGTON'S CAPITAL PRESS GETS NEW SPURT

Although Washington, D. C., had long been the political capital and during the 1940s became increasingly influential in other areas—financial, legal, humanitarian—the city did not develop strong, outstanding, nationally scoped newspapers representing all shades of American controversy. The importance of Washington journalism in influencing senators and congressmen was recognized, however, by chain publishers such as Scripps and Hearst as well as McCormick. For, in addition to subscribing to their hometown newspapers, the congressmen, while in Washington, were apt to pick up a local daily with their coffee in the morning, or take home an afternoon paper to get the drift of public opinion.

A number of reasons existed for the lack of strong dailies. Washington was, until the 1930s and 1940s, not in the top metropolitan class, and extensive advertising was lacking, or drifted into one paper, the *Evening Star*.

Because of widespread use of the telegraph, large American newspapers in other cities could get the Washington news quickly from their correspondents. Wire services, the Associated Press, the United Press and the International News Service furnished out-of-town dailies with up-to-the-minute capital news. Thus, distinctive, nationally influential newspapers did not develop in the capital city. Washington, however, did become the center for more correspondents and syndicated political columnists than any other city in the nation.

With the coming of two wars and the New Deal, Washington's government bureaus and agencies expanded enormously, and the city rose to the metropolitan class among the large cities of the nation. New and beautiful government buildings made the city one of the most attractive in the country.

Population almost tripled, growing from 278,718 at the beginning of the century to 785,000 in 1965. In addition, more than 500,000 people lived in surrounding areas, placing Washington in the million-population metropolitan regions of the nation. Out of this activity, the newspapers which survived the merger process grew, presented the news, argued over controversial measures, gathered profits and constructed handsome new buildings in which to house their operations.

The Evening Star: Traditional

The *Evening Star* has been one of the largest, wealthiest and best known of the Washington papers. It has remained in the hands of the Noyes and Kauffmann families, which have been publishing it since 1867.

At one time the *Evening Star* was known for its conservative makeup and its thorough news coverage of every small incident which happened in Washington. It was consistently the leader in advertising linage in the city and among the top papers in the country. A modernization of its news concepts began in the 1940s. Samuel H. Kauffmann pointed out the need for interpreting the news and making it meaningful for readers. The news was a commodity like fresh air, he said, and belonged to all the people, who had the right of access to it at all times. The *Evening Star* had 309,245 readers in 1968, and its Sunday edition totaled 358,738.

Washington Post Rejuvenated

The *Washington Post* changed hands in 1905. The new owner was John R. McLean, publisher of the *Cincinnati Enquirer*. Under the new ownership, the *Post* began to lose some of its earlier zeal for advancing the city's welfare. McLean was attached to the Democratic Party, and the paper followed its line more closely. The *Post* continued to flourish for several more decades.

Then it went under a cloud in the late 1920s. By this time its owner was Edward B. McLean, ill-starred son of John R. McLean. McLean switched allegiance of the paper to the Republican Party. The publisher milked the paper's profits without attempting to reinvest some of the money in personnel and machinery. The paper went down and down. McLean suffered a crackup.

The *Post* then went into receivership and was sold at auction on the steps of the newspaper building on June 1, 1933. Although there were other bids, Eugene Meyer, California-born millionaire, bought it for $825,000. Meyer had come to Washington in 1917 to serve under President Woodrow Wilson in World War I. He served in executive posts under five Presidents. Meyer had been thinking of retirement, but he decided he could make himself useful and do a public service by publishing the *Post*. He was fifty-seven.

Battered though it was, the *Post* had a tradition and famous name. Many Washingtonians were devoted to this morning paper. Under Meyer's generalship, the newspaper began an exciting comeback. Within ten years, circulation trebled and advertising grew.

Meyer had brought a new ideal to the *Post*, that of public service. Indeed, he had gone back to the point of view of Stilson Hutchins, founder. Once again the *Post* asserted its independence and aimed at publishing the truth. Here were Meyer's principles:

> The newspaper's duty is to its readers and to the public at large and not to the private interests of its owners.
>
> In the pursuit of truth, the newspaper shall be prepared to make sacrifice of its material fortunes, if such a course be necessary for the public good.
>
> The newspaper shall not be the ally of any special interest, but shall be fair and free and wholesome in its outlook on public affairs and public men.

Meyer enlarged the staff and gave bylines. He utilized larger type and brightened the heads. Felix Morley, a distinguished Baltimore *Sun*-

paper man, was placed in charge of the editorial page, for it was Meyer's aim to make that page the heart of the paper. He added a number of columnists to make the page a genuine forum of discussion. The news department acquired Alexander (Casey) Jones as managing editor and engaged in a number of crusades which aimed at clearing slums, chasing gamblers from Washington and cleaning up the police department. Jones was succeeded by J. R. Wiggins, who believed "news ought to be handled only by dedicated men and women who understood each day's newspaper, giving not only a report of the past but a forecast of the future."

Wiggins fought a strong, tireless battle for bringing down the curtains of secrecy in government affairs. Editorial writer Alan Barth added distinction to the paper with his fight for protection of citizens against the government. Herbert Elliston, of the *Christian Science Monitor*, became chief editorial writer when Morley left. Herbert Block (Herblock) won a national reputation for the incisiveness of his editorial cartooning.

When Meyer decided to relinquish control, having been appointed president of the International Bank, he turned the paper over in 1946 to his son-in-law, Philip L. Graham. Graham had prepared himself for a law career. He was born in the mining town of Terry, South Dakota in 1915, but his family moved to Florida when he was six. After being graduated from the University of Florida, he went to Harvard Law School, where he was president of the *Harvard Law Review*. In 1939 he went to Washington to serve as law clerk, first to Supreme Court Justice Stanley Reed and then to Justice Felix Frankfurter.

Joining the *Post* as an associate publisher in 1946, later that year Graham was appointed publisher after his father-in-law became president of the World Bank. At that time Graham was thirty-one, one of the youngest metropolitan newspaper publishers in the country.

Graham pledged in 1948 that he would follow the course developed by his father-in-law and said:

> The Post is an independent paper, standing for programs rather than parties, for measures rather than men. It is grounded in its local community, wedded to the traditions of our country, fixed with a love of liberty, capable of indignation over injustice, and aware of the responsibility of America as a world leader. . . .

The *Post* developed one of the largest news staffs in Washington. News had become so specialized that a "world desk" had to be organized to handle global news, for Washington officials, government workers and the public had become concerned with international affairs. The *Post* Sunday paper grew as voluminous as the *New York Times*, with many departments appealing to special interests.

In 1950 the *Post* presses issued 184,502 daily copies and 190,360 on Sunday. When the merger with the *Times-Herald* occurred four years later, this circulation jumped immensely.

Graham expanded the *Post*'s holdings by acquiring a controlling interest in the Columbia Broadcasting System's radio station, WTOP-AM and FM. The *Post* also purchased a TV station which became WTOP-TV, an affiliate of the Columbia Broadcasting Company. Entering the newsmagazine business, owners of the *Washington Post* bought *Newsweek* in 1961.

In 1954, as indicated, the Graham-Meyer combination bought Robert R. McCormick's Washington outlet, the *Times-Herald.* Although both the *Post* and the *Times-Herald* had followed the Republican Party, the Meyer-Graham paper was believed to be an advocate of the more liberal wing of that party. Most of the popular features and writers of the *Times-Herald* were taken over by the *Post* to hold the readership. Full responsibility for the *Washington Post and Times-Herald* fell on the shoulders of Graham when Meyer died on July 17, 1959. Publisher Graham died in August, 1963, and his wife became president of the company. In 1968 the combined *Post* and the *Times-Herald* reached 467,505; on Sunday it had 600,357 subscribers.

Washington Daily News: Scripps Tabloid

Established in 1921 by E. W. Scripps as a part of the expansion of his chain, the *Washington Daily News,* a tabloid, followed the Scripps-Howard pattern in its editorial and news policies. The *Daily News* has been distinguished by its experimentation with front page tabloid make-up. It was edited for many years by liberal Lowell Mellett, and Ernie Pyle, famous Scripps-Howard war columnist, worked on the *News.* By 1968 the *News* had 200,000 readers on weekdays.

Chapter 36

Southern Newspapers

SOUTH INDUSTRIALIZES

In the twentieth century the South has turned from farming to industry. Not that the farmland was forgotten; cotton, tobacco and vegetables still provided considerable revenue. More and more, however, factories have been built and new industries begun. Many New England cotton manufacturers have established plants or moved nearer to the southern source of supplies. With introduction of nylon and other synthetics, some plants have converted from cotton manufacturing.

As a result of economic developments the trend toward urbanization has been marked in the South, but million-population metropolises have not developed. Large-size cities of the 100,000 to 500,000 level have dominated the scene in some states. Influential newspapers, most of which began in the last century, can be found in leading cities. These dailies have developed extensive circulations within their communities and have extended their range to outlying districts, sometimes as much as 150 to 250 miles away.

Southern consolidations have been characteristic of the newspaper industry as in other sections of the nation. Large communities with four to six dailies at the beginning of the century now have only one newspaper organization controlling the two remaining papers. Other towns have had only one daily left out of the merger process. Chains have made inroads in some southern states, especially in the larger cities. National chain owners may not have found the South a profitable area in the first part of the century, but they have moved in more rapidly since World War II.

RICHMOND, VIRGINIA PAPERS MERGE

Geographically well-situated, Richmond has become the industrial, commercial and financial hub of Virginia. Railroad lines have connected the city with all parts of the country. Richmond has become a tobacco, clothing and iron manufacturing community. It has also developed into an educational center with its University of Richmond. By 1960 the population had reached 240,000, with another 57,000 in the city's trading zone.

Greatest consolidation in the history of Virginia newspapers took place on January 23, 1903. This was the first appearance of the combined morning *Richmond Times-Dispatch* and the afternoon *News-Leader*. Four papers were consolidated into two, both issued by Joseph Bryan. Later, before he died in 1908, Bryan acquired complete ownership of the afternoon *News-Leader*. His son, John Stewart Bryan, decided in 1914 to concentrate all the organization's effort on the *News-Leader*, and so he sold the *Times-Dispatch*.

For the next twenty-six years, the two dailies went their separate ways. Then in 1940 the Richmond papers followed the merger trend and consolidated again under one Bryan ownership. Each newspaper had its own staff of editors and reporters, but the *Times-Dispatch* and the *News-Leader* had their offices in the same building and were printed in one large plant.

John Stewart Bryan always had a strong interest in education and became president of William and Mary College in Williamsburg, Virginia. One of the best-known editors in the South and perhaps the nation, Dr. Douglas Southall Freeman, was editor of the papers for many years. He wrote extensive biographies of General Robert E. Lee and his generals.

Bryan's son, David Tennant Bryan, became president of the publishing company and publisher in 1945. Educated at private schools and the University of Virginia, he went to work as a reporter for the *News-Leader* in 1928. John S. Bryan's duties as president of William and Mary kept him away from Richmond, so David assumed more newspaper responsibilities. During World War II he served aboard the battle cruiser *Alaska*. In 1944 his father died, but Bryan was not able to take over until he returned to inactive duty as Lieutenant Commander. As the large and strong newspapers in Virginia, the Richmond papers circulated in an area covering about two thirds of Virginia, reaching twenty-two counties and ten cities. Out of every one hundred families who read any daily newspaper in that area, seventy-nine read either the *Times-Dispatch* or *News-Leader*.

Times-Dispatch News, Editorial Policy

The morning Richmond *Times-Dispatch* presented a dignified display of international, national, state and local news on its front and inside pages. News came to the paper from the Associated Press and also from its own correspondents in Washington, in Williamsburg and other Virginia communities. The daily was particularly strong on state news, as it was the largest paper in the state and was looked to for current news of Virginia. Because of industrialization of the city, the editors presented two or three pages of business news and stock quotations daily.

Presided over by Virginius Dabney, the editorial page upheld the states' right doctrine and took strong prosegregation stands on the public school issue during the 1950s. The paper feared "the labor monopoly" and opposed the "liberals" in the Democratic Party. Syndicated columnist Westbrook Pegler discussed, from a conservative viewpoint, international as well as national problems of the day in his sock-'em style, while Robert Ruark gave a lighter touch to the day's news for Richmond readers.

The *Times-Dispatch* had its own editorial columnist, Ross Valentine who had a highly personal and appealing writing style. The Richmond *Times-Dispatch* reached 150,788 persons each morning in 1968.

Evening News-Leader Close Behind

The evening *News-Leader* followed close behind, with 125,938 subscribers. Considerable foreign news was printed, but when the school segregation news became prominent in the 1950s, it usually took precedence over all other types of news. The paper devoted much attention to area news, centering it on one page, but also scattering additional Virginia news throughout the paper. Also published was an unusually large number of features relating to men and women and children in the circulation area of the *News-Leader*, giving it a distinct flavor.

James Jackson (Jack) Kilpatrick, as editor, became known throughout the United States for his views on journalism and on segregation. The paper's editorial page carried extensive editorials, many, of course, dealing with the segregation issue. David Lawrence and Holmes Alexander, national conservative columnists, were featured, along with a letters-to-the-editor forum. The editor did not hesitate to use striking photographs and reproductions of paintings in large scale on the editorial page.

The Sunday *Times-Dispatch* was the largest of the newspapers issued from the plant, reaching 201,375 families. Each section of the regular daily *Times-Dispatch* was expanded, with the Sunday paper sometimes reaching 178 to 200 pages. With more space to spare, the editors increased foreign news so that a rounded view of the world was presented to Sunday readers.

The Sunday editorial page gained strength from the addition of the background news page, where a variety of writers sought to interpret the news and add additional facts. The Bryans acquired the morning *Tampa* (Florida) *Tribune,* later adding the afternoon *Tampa Times* as a part of their two-city chain.

NORTH CAROLINA HAS LIBERAL RALEIGH NEWS AND OBSERVER

Josephus Daniels and his sons made the *Raleigh* (North Carolina) *News and Observer* one of the outstanding liberal Democratic papers in the South and the nation.

Daniels and the *News and Observer* were among the early supporters of Woodrow Wilson. Even before Wilson became a candidate for presidency of the United States, he came to North Carolina to speak at the University of North Carolina in Chapel Hill, and the publisher was impressed by Wilson's fire and his leadership qualities. Wilson's views on monopolies and the need to curb trusts and punish industrial evildoers fitted in with the editor's approach to the great issues of the day.

As national committeeman, Daniels attended the Baltimore, Maryland convention of the Democratic Party and supported Wilson over Champ Clark for nomination for President. During the campaign the *News and Observer* helped swing North Carolina for Wilson. Daniels became chairman of the Democratic Party's Publicity and Literary Committee, working in the headquarters in New York.

When Wilson was elected President, he appointed Daniels Secretary of the Navy. During World War I, Daniels was a member of the War Cabinet, the Council of National Defense and the Committee of Public Information. Daniels had recommended the formation of the Committee On Information to President Wilson to provide news instead of censorship of war news. Daniels went to Paris with the President as adviser after the war was over, and the publisher supported the League of Nations later.

After Republicans won the presidency in 1920, Daniels retired from public life, returning to Raleigh where he turned to publishing and to writing editorials again. The New Deal of Franklin D. Roosevelt coincided with the publisher's liberal views, and he supported Roosevelt for the presidency. In 1933 Daniels was appointed Ambassador to Mexico, where he went to build up the Good Neighbor Policy.

During the time he was in Washington or on diplomatic missions, the *Raleigh News and Observer* was in charge of the publisher's sons, Josephus, Jr., Jonathan W. and Frank A. Daniels. When Josephus Daniels died in 1948, his sons assumed management of the daily.

In midtwentieth century, the inland *Raleigh News and Observer* sought to cover the news along the "Golden Belt," extending along the coast and southwest to Southern Pines and Pinehurst, North Carolina. Daily circulation reached 130,088, while Sunday subscribers totaled 146,216 by 1968. A large building was constructed in the fifties to house the expanding operations.

Raleigh Times Purchased

In June, 1955, the *Raleigh Times*, an afternoon paper, was bought by the Daniels Company. Circulation of the *Times* at the time was 14,783. The *Times* moved eventually into Daniels' new plant. Mechanical, advertising, circulation and photography departments of the *Times* were merged with those of the *News and Observer*.

Times reportorial staff was increased, and coverage of surrounding counties was intensified. Sports and women's pages were strengthened. Circulation in 1968 was 23,979, concentrated in Raleigh and five counties around the city. Josephus Daniels, Jr., became chairman of the board, Frank Daniels the publisher and Jonathan Daniels the editor-in-chief of both papers.

ATLANTA HAS DISTINGUISHED DAILIES

Atlanta, Georgia, in the twentieth century, has fulfilled the practical dream Henry W. Grady had during the previous century. Atlanta has become the New York of the South. In many of its characteristics, Atlanta resembled a northern metropolis. Although it still has retained its position as an agricultural marketplace, Atlanta, with the further industrialization of the South, has become the center of manufacturing and banking for the region.

Atlanta journalism has benefited by this commercial expansion. Newspapers reflected eventually the major trends as shown in the northern press. Sensationalism had been brought in at the end of the previous century, but this was accelerated when William Randolph Hearst came to the city in 1912 to link the *Atlanta Georgian* to his chain. Banner headlines, lively makeup, features and columnists became a part of the Atlanta press pattern. Mergers had occurred throughout Atlanta journalism history, but toward the middle of the century came to a climax with the reduction of the number of dailies to two, both owned by the same organization.

Atlanta Constitution: Notable Southern Paper

In Atlanta developed one of the notable newspapers of the South and the nation. The *Atlanta Constitution* was built on foundations constructed by Grady and the reputation he made before his death in 1889. Although it lost its leader and some of its spark, the *Constitution* was able to adjust to the new journalistic conditions and the public opinion in the new century. In spite of its acquiring characteristics of the new journalism and despite its merger, the *Constitution* retained much of its regional individuality.

The *Constitution* became known for its liberal views. It supported Franklin D. Roosevelt for presidency in 1932 and in each subsequent campaign. It had open conflicts with conservative Governor Eugene Talmadge who drew his support from rural areas, and the daily had to fight attacks on it by the legislature, which considered the question of imposing taxes on Atlanta newspapers circulated through the state.

The *Constitution* made an effort to build up a strong news department. It subscribed to the regular wire services as well as to the *Chicago Tribune*'s, the *New York Daily News*', the *New York Times*' and the *North American Newspaper Alliance's* special services. Many of the *Constitution*'s news features were staff written. The daily developed extensive society, sports, financial and business coverage. The *Constitution* retained much of its individuality and newspaper personality through its staff-written news articles as well as through its home-grown columnists. Even its executive editor, Ralph McGill, had his own column on page one.

Cox Buys Journal

Meanwhile, James M. Cox, owner of the Cox group of dailies, purchased the *Atlanta Journal* for $3 million in 1939, and then bought the *Georgian*, its Hearst competitor. Cox now merged the *Georgian* with the older paper. The *Journal* had had a distinguished career and was a lively evening newspaper, reaching an even larger audience than the morning *Constitution*. The *Journal's* makeup was more sensational, its banners larger, and it featured more crime and disaster. The *Journal* carried comic strips and special articles written by prominent persons on Sunday; its sports coverage was extensive. Like the *Constitution*, the *Journal* was one of the first newspapers in the South to promote autos, helping establish a national highway from New York to Florida. The daily had printed its own Sunday magazine since 1912. The *Journal* won numerous awards in the 1930s and 1940s.

In 1950 publisher Cox purchased the *Atlanta Constitution*. A company was formed to publish both the *Journal* and the *Constitution*, with the Sunday edition being combined into the *Atlanta Constitution and Journal.* The merged papers were the largest in the South. In 1968 the *Atlanta Constitution* reached 200,603 subscribers; the *Journal* had 251,203 evening subscribers, while the Sunday *Journal-Constitution* appealed to 523,581 readers. The circulations were spread through the entire state, particularly on Sunday.

The Sunday paper developed into a large edition, running between forty-eight and sixty pages. The edition carried sixteen pages of comics, the *American Weekly Magazine,* when it was being distributed, and *This Week,* as well as its own locally edited tabloid magazine. This was beautifully illustrated with pictures, some of which were in color.

Atlanta Times Starts and Stops

To oppose the liberalism of the Cox papers, a group of Atlanta businessmen invested between one and two million dollars to establish the *Atlanta Times* in June, 1964. The paper could not get a foothold. Many causes contributed to its failure. The *Times* sought to get statewide circulation before it became solid in Atlanta. Internal difficulties and poor management also contributed to its failure. A succession of editors and managers tried to keep it in operation, but they were unable to do so. A contribution of $100,000 from Lammot DuPont Copeland, of the Wilmington DuPonts, could not prevent the *Atlanta Times* from folding. More than $2.4 million was lost on the venture, which suspended August, 1965.

LOUISVILLE'S LIBERAL COURIER-JOURNAL EXPANDS WITH REGION

One of the South's outstanding liberal newspapers, the *Louisville* (Kentucky) *Courier-Journal,* was stamped in the twentieth century with the personality of its famous editor and part owner, Henry Watterson. A vigorous editor, he had a strong interest in national issues and national politics and possessed an individualistic writing style which made his editorials thunder. Although he didn't hold office, except once, Watterson was politically active in the Democratic Party for more than fifty years. He won nationwide attention for himself and for his newspaper.

Walter Haldeman, Watterson's partner, died in 1901, and thus began a series of events which Watterson did not anticipate. After much internal battling between Haldeman's sons over control of the *Courier-Journal,* Bruce Haldeman, one of the sons, withdrew. William Haldeman remained. Watterson was elected president of the publishing corporation.

Neither Watterson nor William Haldeman was qualified or trained for the business side of the newspaper, nor did they have children who might have taken over. Business responsibilities of the two newspapers proved too much for the aging Watterson. He and Haldeman sold their interests to Robert Worth Bingham, who had represented successfully the legal interest of William Haldeman. Bingham was a Louisville lawyer and former mayor of the city. He was a man of great wealth and the most likely prospective buyer in Louisville. On August 6, 1918, he purchased the controlling stock of both newspaper corporations and became editor of the *Courier-Journal.* The purchase price was not revealed, but Watterson on the same day deposited in a local bank $186,000, his half of the sale. This would make the two papers worth $372,000.

Watterson was given the title of editor emeritus, and, at an annual salary of $10,000, contributed editorials. He also received a $20,000 contract from the *Saturday Evening Post* to write his memoirs, which later were published in book form as *Marse Henry.*

Watterson soon came into conflict with the Democratic editorial policies of the Louisville *Courier-Journal.* In the postwar period, Watterson was opposed to President Wilson's idea of a League of Nations. Meanwhile, the *Courier-Journal* had come out openly for the world organization. Officials of the paper wrote Watterson asking him to "vary the subject matter of his editorials." Watterson, surprised that the request had not come sooner, resigned. He was seventy-nine. Watterson died in December, 1921.

Publisher Bingham established WHAS, first radio station in Kentucky in 1922. Bingham stated his family's policy toward the newspapers in this fashion, "I have always regarded the newspapers owned by me as a public trust and have endeavored so to conduct them as to render the greatest possible service." Judge Bingham became Ambassador to Great Britain. He died in 1937. His son, Barry Bingham, who had started to work on the papers in 1930 and became publisher six years later, now became president of the company. He also served as editor-in-chief of the two papers.

Associated with him in building up the papers was Mark Ethridge, formerly of the *Richmond* (Virginia) *Times-Dispatch.* Two others were added to the staff to make the *Courier-Journal* outstanding and nationally known. James S. Pope became executive editor, and Norman E. Isaacs, who had been on the *St. Louis* (Missouri) *Star-Times,* became managing editor. The *Courier-Journal* found 230,430 morning subscribers, and on Sunday reached 343,823. The afternoon *Times* had 171,477 subscribers in 1968.

Chapter 37

Midwestern Journalism Voices

In the twentieth century Chicago has begun to fulfill the promise and vision of its founders. It has leaped forward industrially and commercially and is second only to New York in size and financial strength. Chicago's meat-packing business has declined, while the city has become a center of large manufacturing industries, especially steel and steel products. Chicago's gigantic banks have extended the city's financial lines and control into many states.

A great variety of foreign countries was represented by Chicago citizens of foreign descent, giving the city a distinctive cosmopolitan atmosphere. The Poles were the largest, followed by the Germans, Italians, Russians, Scandinavians and Irish. Since World War I, Negro population has greatly increased. Population of Chicago reached 3,620,962 by 1950, but dropped to 3,520,000 fifteen years later. By contrast the population of the suburbs increased from 5,177,868 to 6,627,000.

Educationally, Chicago has become known throughout the world for its institutions of higher learning. A number of universities, colleges, medical schools and teachers colleges as well as theological seminaries are located in the city. The University of Chicago, founded at the end of the last century, has risen to greater heights and has become known all over the world for its graduate programs and research as well as its innovations in general education. Northwestern University, which has a large downtown branch in Chicago, has been a top-ranking institution. Many students attend the college of medicine, dentistry and pharmacy of the Chicago branch of the University of Illinois. The Illinois Institute of Technology and Science has continued its high level of science and engineering programs. The liberal Roosevelt College, with its downtown location, has attracted many students. DePaul and Loyola

Universities have been known for undergraduate, graduate and professional schools. One of the largest medical complexes in the country, the Medical Center of the Westside, has twenty public and private institutions, six hospitals and seven medical-teaching schools.

Chicago has experienced a vigorous and varied cultural life. It has had grand opera companies from the beginning of the century. The Chicago Civic Opera Company was organized in 1922. The Lyric Theatre of Chicago began to present opera in 1954. Orchestra Hall was completed under Theodore Thomas in 1904; its name was changed to the Chicago Symphony Orchestra later. The city has produced also civic, youth and businessmen's orchestras, while several community orchestras have been established. Goodwin Memorial, affiliated with the Art Institute, has presented plays for children as well as adults. An outgrowth of the Columbia Exposition of 1893, held in Chicago, the Field Museum was opened in 1921, furthering science education for children and adults.

Like other metropolises, Chicago experienced many social pains and acquired a number of urban problems after World War I. A large number of Negroes came up from the South to work in the factories. Between 1920 and 1960 the Negroes increased from 109,000 to 813,000, causing the usual problems of ghetto-living. Corruption also sprang up, particularly during the Prohibition Era. The city was called "wide open" for gang warfare, rackets and gang rule. Some of the newsmen were involved in these rackets.

Becoming aware of the need for renewal of the old city, Chicago has engaged in extensive slum-clearance and slum-prevention projects. To carry the heavy load of traffic from the suburbs and through the city, Chicago has constructed a multimillion dollar network of expressways.

Chicago journalism has reflected the growth of this metropolis and of the great midwestern region. The Chicago newspaper evolution has been similar to that which occurred in New York. Consolidations have reduced the number of dailies, yet sufficient papers could be supported in Chicago to represent the Democratic Party's and the Republican Party's viewpoint. In other characteristics, the city's journalism has had a stamp of its own. Many suburban residents have subscribed to the Chicago papers and thousands of readers have been found in the Midwest.

CHICAGO DAILY NEWS: REPUBLICAN, ISOLATIONIST

Under Victor Lawson, the *Chicago Daily News* continued its strong position in the forefront of journalism. Chief among its achievements was expansion of the foreign news service which became a distinguished feature of the paper, counteracting the *Tribune*'s nationalistic Midwest emphasis. Reputations of many of the *News* correspondents were made while sending dispatches from all corners of the world.

Politically, the *Daily News* preferred to be known as independent. It supported Woodrow Wilson in 1912 but opposed him in 1916 for backing the Adamson Railroad Act, providing for an eight-hour day for railroad workers. The *Daily News* followed the Republican banner in 1920 and in the presidential campaigns for the following years.

During the next few decades the *Daily News* passed successively through several ownerships. When Walter A. Strong died suddenly in 1931, the owners sought a new publisher. Frank Knox, manager for Hearst, became publisher of the *Daily News*. Later, President Franklin D. Roosevelt chose Knox as Secretary of Navy, although he was a Republican. When Knox died in 1944 his successor as publisher was John S. Knight, owner of a small but vigorous chain, the *Akron* (Ohio) *Beacon-Journal*, the *Miami* (Florida) *Herald* and the *Detroit* (Michigan) *Free Press*.

When Knight took over the *Chicago Daily News* in 1944, he "dedicated it to public service" and told reporters "to investigate everything and to frown on off-the-record conferences with officials." Under the astute direction of Basil Walters, managing editor, the *News* campaigned for a cleanup of crime conditions on Skid Row, where derelicts hung out, and called attention to the work of Alcoholics Anonymous. With the *St. Louis Post-Dispatch*, the *Chicago Daily News* exposed the attempt of the Illinois Republican machine to influence the press by putting the small-town editors on the payrolls of local governments. The *Chicago Daily News* won twenty awards in 1950, and both the *News* and the other Knight papers won Pulitzer awards. As president of the American Society of Newspaper Editors, Knight in 1944 set in motion a campaign against worldwide barriers to the free flow of information.

A capable businessman, Knight was able to pay off the $12 million mortgage on the *Chicago Daily News* in five years. By 1958 circulation totaled 584,911 on weekdays and 569,249 on Saturdays. Deciding to concentrate on his other newspapers, Knight sold the *Daily News* to Marshall Field, III, who combined it with his *Sun-Times* in 1958. Daily circulation dropped in 1968 to 462,916, with a few more on Saturday.

CHICAGO TRIBUNE

The *Chicago Tribune* became one of the storm centers of newspaper controversy in the present century. The *Tribune* developed into one of the largest newspapers in the United States, ranking high in circulation and income. The *Tribune*'s thundering voice could be heard from coast to coast. Before midcentury, the daily developed strong links in a chain which extended to New York, through the *Daily News* and to Washington, through the *Times-Herald*.

The *Chicago Tribune-New York News* features and comics appeared in many newspapers. Catching the new tide, the *Tribune* branched out into radio, developing a powerful station. The paper's control over its source of newsprint mills gave the corporation a vertical control "from trees to *Tribune*." The Tribune Company, through its able owners and managers, developed a well-knit journalistic empire. The *Chicago Tribune* had a history of strong Republicanism with many significant traditions stemming from Joseph Medill, the early builder.

Robert W. Patterson, son-in-law of Medill, was virtually in control of the paper before Medill died. He had worked his way up through minor jobs until he was made business manager. When Medill died, Patterson was made editor-in-chief. Patterson continued in the grooves which had been cut and had made the *Tribune* an outstanding exponent of industrialism and the Republican Party.

Patterson's health failed about 1905, and Medill McCormick, copublisher Joseph Medill's grandson, was made publisher. A graduate of Yale, young McCormick had been a reporter on the *Tribune*. His influence on the paper was negligible, as he was interested in politics. He did, however, lead the *Tribune* into the Progressive fold in 1912. The man who was in charge of the *Tribune* during this period and who was responsible for the progress it made was James Keeley. He had become city editor of the paper in 1895. Like Ochs and Bennett, he saw news as a salable commodity. Keeley recognized all angles of a news event at a glance and then proceeded to extract every drop of news from it. Keeley made the *Tribune* a top-notch newspaper, devoted to news and features. He saw, however, that Robert Rutherford McCormick and Joseph W. Patterson, grandsons of the pioneer Medill, were going to take over, so he left. But the *Tribune* he had built was strong.

The two cousins who came into control were quite different in political and economic beliefs at the time. Both soon demonstrated their editorial and business abilities, and eventually their views on foreign and domestic affairs coincided. The background of Joseph W. Patterson was told in the chapter on tabloids.

Robert R. McCormick who finally emerged to take over the whole empire in the 1950s was born in Chicago in 1880 and educated at Groton and Yale. He studied at Northwestern law school and later became an alderman and president of the Sanitary District, involving the construction of a $60 million sewage disposal plant. Although trained for the legal profession, McCormick's interest in journalism proved to have a stronger interest for him. He joined the *Tribune,* specialized in the business side.

Although the *Tribune* opposed America's entrance into World War I, the daily supported the war effort once the United States entered. McCormick served on Pershing's staff in 1917 and rose from major to colonel in the artillery. Col. McCormick received the distinguished service medal, and at the end of the war was commandant at Fort Sheridan, Illinois.

McCormick's cousin, Joseph Patterson, early expressed his liberal leanings, as indicated in a previous chapter on the *New York Daily News.* The two cousins, however, were able to work hand-in-hand, and the *Tribune* was strengthened, its circulation being doubled. The morning edition reached 499,725 and the Sunday issue climbed to 802,028 by 1921. Then the *New York Daily News* was established and Patterson left for New York; eventually, he established residence there and McCormick was left in control in Chicago.

Tribune's popularity was also built on the many effective promotions. It started the Golden Gloves tournament, when legislation prohibited such exhibitions.

Credit and Criticism

Although the *Tribune* was given credit for its features, comics and promotions, it was criticized for its slanting of the news and its attempt to fit information about events into its editorial pattern. The paper represented the Republican Party's views generally, but there were differences between its methods of expression and viewpoint and those of other Republican papers, such as the *New York Herald Tribune.* The *Chicago Tribune* fought against President Franklin D. Roosevelt and his New Deal measures with great vigor. The *Chicago Tribune* believed that President Roosevelt was seeking to become dictator and that the New Deal, if it succeeded, would disrupt American civilization and its institutions.

Colonel McCormick died in April, 1955. The Hearst *American* in 1956 was purchased by the Tribune Company and issued as a separate operation. In 1968 the *Tribune* was able to appeal to 805,851 persons in the morning and 1,124,946 on Sunday. The *American* had 446,945 evening subscribers and 486,643 on Sundays.

CHICAGO TIMES

The new *Chicago Times,* launched in 1929 by Samuel Emory Thomason, a general manager of the *Tribune,* became one of the McCormick's bitter political enemies. When McCormick began his operation of the *Chicago Tribune,* he brought his old classmate and law partner to the paper as business manager. Thomason rose to become vice president and general manager of the daily in the 1920s. His yearly salary and bonuses totaled about $250,000, perhaps one of the highest newspaper salaries in the country. When Thomason visited Europe he was impressed by Sweden's cooperative schemes for unemployment insurance and public housing. He returned to Chicago and related his views to the publisher of the *Tribune.* Colonel McCormick believed that his general manager was straying from conservative Republicanism. Thomason resigned in 1927.

Thomason, as publisher, and Richard L. Finnegan, as editor, launched the city's first tabloid, the *Daily Illustrated Times,* an evening newspaper. They thus revived a masthead which had been used earlier by Stephen A. Douglas, Cyrus H. McCormick and Wilbur Storey. The *Times* was Democratic, as its predecessors had been.

Format of the *Times* was derived from that of the *New York Illustrated News.* The Chicago *Times* appeared in September, 1929. It seemed to be a good time for the venture. The stock market was at an all-time high. The *Times* intended to be noncomformist, saucy, zestful, imaginative.

The *Times* was seven weeks old when Wall Street "laid its egg" and dumped sixteen million shares of stock. The *Times* took the opposite position to that of the *Tribune* in giving advice as to what should be done about the ensuing depression. McCormick urged President Hoover to cut back federal expenses. The *Times* recommended spending.

After Hearst turned against the Roosevelt New Deal, the *Times* was the only paper in Chicago to support the President. The *Times* used wit, satire and irony in spearing its opposition. The paper pinned its faith on the New Deal and pulled out of the red.

When Thomason died, Marshall Field bought the *Times,* paying $5,339,000 for the paper and an additional $2,500,000 to discharge its obligations. The merger resulted in a single paper, the morning tabloid *Sun-Times.*

CHICAGO SUN: DEMOCRAT, LIBERAL

At the meeting in 1941 which denounced the *Tribune,* speakers said that encouragement ought to be given to a newspaper which would offset the Republicanism of the *Tribune* in the morning field. The *Chicago Sun* was established to fill in that journalistic vacuum. With launching of the liberal *Sun* by Marshall Field on December 4, 1941, the battle of Chicago journalism broke out again.

Field, who had already backed *PM* in New York, wanted to counteract the isolationism advocated by McCormick, as well as to oppose the *Tribune's* anti-Roosevelt viewpoint. Field represented everything to which McCormick was opposed: the New Deal, an English background, an international viewpoint and a competitive paper.

On the editorial page the *Sun* boasted of a wide variety of columnists of all political opinions. The *Sun* published Walter Lippmann, representing liberal Republicanism, as well as Samuel Grafton, liberal Democrat. It offered also Mark Sullivan and Frank Kent, representing right-wing Republicanism.

The *Sun* expressed its belief in the Roosevelt administration and said that the paper would support the New Deal as long as it merited that trust. The *Sun* declared that it believed in the American system of private enterprise: "in fair and faithful labor unions and in all the legitimate rights and privileges they have won." The *Sun* expressed its faith "in human freedom, in the four freedoms of President Roosevelt."

The *Sun* had internal and other difficulties. All was not as smooth and as harmonious as it could be. Although publisher Field found that some of his associates were as strong for the New Deal as he, others on his staff were not. The general appearance of the standard-size paper and style of writing were good, but could not be called striking. The *Sun,* although liberal in outlook, seemed to be another conventional newspaper which would lack a popular appeal. Later, bolder appearance was achieved and was more in accord with the *Sun's* general editorial position. Eventually a successful book supplement was added and comics were developed in competition with the *Tribune's*.

Although he subscribed to the United Press and used photo services, Field was handicapped by lack of the Associated Press franchise. It cost the publisher about $405,000 yearly for a variety of news and photo services, which the *Sun* might have obtained for $50,000 through the AP. He, therefore, applied for admission into the AP, but the bylaws provided that no one could be admitted without consent of other papers. The case was taken before the Department of Justice which proceeded in 1942 to prosecute the AP for being in violation of the Sherman Anti-Trust Act.

The *Sun* won the case in the lower district court, but the AP appealed to the Supreme Court of the United States. The judges upheld the lower court. The majority decision said that the effect of changing the bylaws "will not be to restrict AP membership, but only to compel the organization to make the dispatches accessible to others." The Associated Press at its next meeting revised its rules and the *Sun* was allowed a membership in it.

By 1947 circulation of the *Sun* reached 362,299 daily and 421,585 on Sunday. Field needed the strength of the *Chicago Times*. The afternoon New Deal tabloid was established in 1929 by Samuel Emory Thomason, former business manager of the *Tribune*. The *Times*, a lively newspaper, had built up a strong following, and Field thought if he combined it with his *Sun* this would give him a morning as well as an afternoon paper. He bought the *Times* and amalgamated it with his *Sun*.

When Field died, his son took over. Marshall Field, as indicated, had purchased the *Chicago Daily News*, combining it with his *Sun-Times*. Chicago thus had two newspaper organizations left instead of four. By 1968 the *Sun-Times* had 552,155 readers with 717,814 on Sunday.

JOURNALISM FLOURISHES IN THE AUTO CAPITAL

In the twentieth century, Detroit, Michigan, has become the auto capital of the United States and the third largest manufacturing center in the country. The city's prosperity has reflected the widespread use of automobiles as a necessity in the United States.

As the industry was tied so closely to the up-and-down swings of consumer demand for autos, Detroit sought to diversify its economy. By 1965 more than 6,500 different manufacturers were producing machine tools, paint and varnish and other products.

While the intense industrial activity was said to have hindered Detroit's cultural development, the city's increasing wealth enabled a number of educational and cultural institutions to get their start, or to expand. Wayne State University in the city has established ten schools and colleges. The University of Detroit, a Jesuit school, started in the last century, has made rapid strides. Three engineering and technical schools, the Chrysler Institute of Engineering, the Detroit Institute of Technology and the Lawrence Institute of Technology, have supplied trained personnel for local and state industry. Meanwhile, the arts were not neglected: The Detroit Institute of Arts, the Detroit Symphony and the Detroit Historical Museum were founded.

Reflecting the economic prosperity, population climbed steadily during the first half of the century. Detroit increased from 285,705 to 1,840,000 by midcentury, but dropped back to 1,670,000 by 1967. Meanwhile, the metropolitan area showed a 24 per cent increase, with a total of 3,720,000 residents living in the region. More than a half-million Negroes were attracted by the employment opportunities in the area.

But they were crowded into slums and many of the men became unemployed. Racial disorders broke out, with the worst one a five-day riot in 1967, when local police were joined by the National Guard and United States Army troops to bring peace to the disturbed sections.

Detroit journalism has reflected the many trends observed in other large cities. Consolidations were effected, and chains added Detroit links. Circulations of the Detroit papers reached the 500,000 to 900,000 level.

Detroit News

Established in the last century, the *Detroit News* was the largest home-delivered evening newspaper in America. It reached a circulation of 700,321 daily readers and 947,155 Sunday readers in 1968.

Publisher James E. Scripps pioneered in radio, or wireless telegraph as it was then called. By his influence, encouragement and gift of money, Scripps helped the young inventor, Thomas Clark, continue his radio experiments. Although the founder died, his son, William Scripps, continued the interest in radio. On August 20, 1920, WWJ, established by the *Detroit News,* went on the air as the world's first broadcasting station. This Scripps interest in electronic journalism later led his company to establish station WWJ-TV, reaching an area where six million people lived.

Free Press

In the second decade of the twentieth century the *Detroit Free Press* was purchased by Edward D. Starr and Phillip McMilland. In 1916 Starr took over the majority control. He had the paper until it was bought by John S. Knight in April, 1940, being then operated as a part of the Knight chain, already referred to. The *Free Press* found 590,546 weekday morning readers with about 40,000 more on Sunday in 1968.

OHIO DEVELOPS THREE NEWSPAPER CENTERS

The *Cleveland Press,* under Scripps-Howard management, continued as a breezy, independent newspaper, known for its dedication to the workingman and for its crusading spirit. During the present century it began to be concerned more than ever before about world problems. Louis B. Seltzer, its editor, won a national reputation for his liberalism.

Locally the *Press* continued its fights for civic improvements. It carried on a constant war against gambling. There were all kinds of crusades for a better gas and light franchise, a decent street railway and municipal electric and water plants. The *Press* came out for a new city charter. The daily also crusaded against rent gougers, for lashes for food profiteers in the war, and made appeals to railroad workers in critical periods to stay on the job instead of striking. In 1940 the *Press* fought for adequate city planning, got extra powers and extra cash for a new commission. Decent housing was a continued interest of the paper.

The *Cleveland Press* had a unique Public Service Bureau, established to carry on the extra journalistic projects for the community. Every year, on the first Sunday after Thanksgiving, downtown Cleveland became a fairyland, dominated by the bright faces of children. They brought their parents to see the annual Press Christmas Parade. The press bureau also sponsored the Folks Festival, the Show Train to New York, low-cost trips to the West Coast. The *Press* backed a marbles tournament and a Camera Clinic. The press bureau also turned out books on a wide variety of subjects, tour guides, helpful hints for mothers, recipes, draft information.

The *Cleveland Press*'s opposition was the *Plain Dealer* and the *News*, both published by the Forest City Publishing Company. In 1960 the *Press*, however, absorbed both papers. In 1968 the *Press* reached 389,695 people.

Cincinnati, Columbus Mergers

In two other Ohio newspaper centers, Cincinnati and Columbus, a similar merger process occurred, leaving these cities, in the end, with one newspaper organization, or with all papers being issued from one plant.

Although the employees were able to purchase the old *Cincinnati Enquirer* in 1952, control passed to the publisher of the *Evening Post*, the E. W. Scripps Company, in 1956. Two years later the same company bought out the *Times-Star*, which had been built up by Hulburt Taft. Cincinnati was thus a Scripps-Howard town, the company owning the morning and Sunday *Enquirer* and the afternoon *Post* and *Times-Star*. The *Enquirer* had a weekday circulation of 190,169 with 302,042 purchasers on Sunday by 1968. The *Post* and *Times-Star* had 243,165 evening readers.

In Columbus, capital of the state, Robert F. Wolfe and Harry P. Wolfe, shoe manufacturers now venturing into other businesses, bought the well-established *Ohio State Journal* in the early part of the century, adding to it the *Columbus Dispatch* in 1905. Meanwhile, the afternoon *Columbus Citizen* was published by Scripps-Howard.

The *Ohio State Journal* reached 78,884 morning subscribers in 1958; while the *Dispatch* had 177,806 evening circulation weekdays and 238,275 on Sundays. The *Columbus Citizen*, issued by Scripps-Howard, had 89,520 evening subscribers, with 95,903 on Sundays.

In November, 1959, important switches were made in the Columbus newspaper situation. The journalistic mergers paralleled the experience of other cities. Scripps-Howard abandoned its afternoon *Columbus Citizen* and turned to the morning field, publishing the *Citizen-Journal,* which was bought by 115,215 subscribers in 1968. The *Ohio State Journal,* issued by Wolfe, made its last morning appearance. The remaining afternoon paper, the *Dispatch,* also published by Wolfe, continued as the only afternoon paper. The *Dispatch* reached 220,105 every evening and 310,335 on Sunday.

Chapter 38

Mississippi, Missouri Valley Press

COWLES BROTHERS PROVE KNOW-HOW

Two slogans or statements served as guiding lights for Gardner Cowles, Sr., founder of the small but effective midwestern Cowles chain. The first was "Things don't happen; somebody makes 'em happen," and the second, describing aptly the circular process of journalism, declared: "We must have more circulation to get more advertising to make a better newspaper, to get more circulation."

Cowles came up the hard way. Son of a Methodist minister, he worked his way through school by selling from door to door. Finally he became a school superintendent at Algona, Iowa. The attractions of journalism proved too strong, and he entered the business by becoming a partner in the *Algona Republican*. Meanwhile, he built up his fortune by dealing in land; it was an easy transition to becoming a banker. When, in 1903, he learned that the *Des Moines Register and Leader* was for sale, he supplied the $300,000 necessary to purchase it. Following the experience of other publishers, Cowles bought other Des Moines papers, consolidating them with his own. He purchased the *Tribune,* an evening paper, thereby being able to publish a morning and evening newspaper. Later he obtained the *Scripps News* and then the *Capital,* which he merged with his established papers.

Meanwhile, Cowles' sons, Gardner Cowles, Jr., and John Cowles, entered their father's newspaper, with Gardner concentrating on the editorial end, particularly news and pictures, and John on circulation and advertising. The Cowles brothers used the latest research methods in improving the paper. They employed George Gallup, an instructor then at the State University of Iowa, to make a survey of their paper's readership. The survey indicated that people like to look at related pictures, and, as a result, Cowles began to use more picture sequences to tell the news in the rotogravure. Sports coverage was also improved in the Des Moines paper. Making use, too, of new means of rapid transportation, Cowles brothers bought their first airplane in 1928 to rush news and pictures from all over the Middle West to Des Moines. Later, three planes, including an autogiro, were used.

Because of progressive methods, the *Des Moines Register and Tribune* circulation by midcentury reached 367,000, which was larger than the 196,000 population of the city in which the newspaper was issued. By 1968 the *Register* reached 242,371 morning subscribers; the *Tribune* found 116,120 evening readers; the Sunday *Register*, 512,401.

In 1936 the Cowles family began to spread its journalistic interests. Cowles purchased, for one million dollars, the *Minneapolis Evening Star*, a poor newspaper but well respected. Then began a repetition of what had happened in Des Moines and elsewhere. Under the leadership of Basil Walters, the *Star* adapted for its purposes Gallup ideas, considered radical for Des Moines. Within four years, Cowles purchased the opposition *Journal* for $2.5 million, and then the *Tribune*. These were consolidated with the *Star* into the *Star-Journal*. Minneapolis was a strategic city for newspaper building. It had a diversified industry. Employment in food processing reached 12,000 at midcentury. The city's flour production was third in the nation, for Minneapolis was headquarters for some of the largest flour processing companies in the United States. The city's chemical plants processed Minnesota's large flax crop for linseed oil and oil coke. In the city's factories were employed 259,000. Minneapolis' population reached more than half million by midcentury, growing steadily in the next decade.

The Cowles brothers used the same shrewd methods in building up the *Minneapolis Star-Journal* as they had employed in Des Moines. They developed new methods in news and feature writing and issued a strong editorial page under the leadership of Gideon Seymour, Carroll Binder, formerly of the *Chicago Daily News* and, later, W. P. Stevens. Liberal Republican, the paper struck an "intelligently conservative" note. The daily promoted the candidacy of Wendell Willkie and others who expressed broad international views.

Cowles had the only papers left in Minneapolis. By 1968 the evening *Star* had 282,219 subscribers; the *Tribune*, 238,776 morning subscribers; the *Tribune* Sunday readers totaled 668,941.

During World War II, Gardner Cowles, Jr., was domestic director of the Office of War Information. Having had some experience with pictures and recognizing the growing interest in them, Cowles brothers established *Look* magazine in 1937, and *Quick* in 1950, but the latter was abandoned.

MILWAUKEE JOURNAL, EMPLOYEE-OWNED, GROWS POWERFUL

As managing editor of the *Milwaukee* (Wisconsin) *Sentinel* Lucius Nieman felt it was time for a strong, aggressive paper to be published in Milwaukee. He managed to purchase the newborn *Journal* when it was only twenty-two days old in 1882, and so he was always considered the paper's founder. His motto was "Never care about the classes, but about people. Get all of the information you can about matters of importance, giving both sides of the question." When more than seventy people died in a hotel fire, other newspapers called it "an unavoidable tragedy." The *Journal* said the hotel was a known firetrap and denounced its owners for "greed" and "criminal negligence."

The publisher, from the very beginning, was fearless. In 1915 Nieman was describing Germany as an international menace, and he therefore urged preparation for war. In Milwaukee, where Germans were strong, his paper was denounced and threatened. Nieman stuck to his editorial guns and pointed to the pro-German propaganda to prove some Germans were more loyal to the Kaiser than to the United States.

Harry Grant, who was to become a great driving force behind the paper, arrived at the *Journal* in 1916 in the midst of the battle the *Journal* was having. Grant was a strong, dynamic personality. The son and grandson of stable owners in Ohio, Harry had to quit high school when his father died. The boy went to work as a five dollar a week railway messenger. He taught school and studied at night. By the time he was twenty-two, Grant had saved enough money to enter Harvard University. Although he made two tries at graduation, he never had enough money to finish his university education. Later Grant entered the advertising business, going to work for N. W. Ayer in New York, later switching to Milwaukee. Nieman hired him as business manager for the *Milwaukee Journal* at $250 a week, with a promise of stock in the paper "if things went well."

Grant began to build up the paper, which was second to the *Milwaukee Sentinel.* He believed the more successful a paper, the less susceptible it was to influence by advertisers. When an advertiser asked for special treatment in the news columns because of his $50,000 contract, Grant canceled the contract.

The *Journal* sought to serve the public by reporting virtually everything that happened in Milwaukee, down to the theft of a few chickens, and by covering national and world news thoroughly. The *Journal* relied on the wire services and the *New York Times* news service for national and international news. The paper had two correspondents of its own in New York and Washington. On its society page it printed pictures and stories about Negroes.

Readers got their entertainment in one neat, lively package: the daily four-page Green Sheet. It was filled with comics, pictures, a crossword puzzle and bridge columns as well as advice to the lovelorn. The publisher gave away a Peach Sheet every afternoon when important late news came in after edition time. The *Journal* ran one hundred pages weekday and up to four hundred pages on Sunday. It used color for advertising. Although it had a monopoly of the afternoon field, its ad rate was kept very low. The *Journal* owned the radio-television station WTMJ, a top moneymaker.

The paper's politics varied. In one election it supported a socialist, a Republican, a Democrat and a Wisconsin Progressive. The *Journal* backed Franklin D. Roosevelt in 1932 and 1936, and Wendell Willkie in 1940 because of the third-term issue. The paper supported Dewey in 1948 and Eisenhower four years later.

The *Milwaukee Journal* was one of the few papers in the country with employee-ownership. When Lucius Nieman, who owned 55 per cent of the stock, died, his wife set up the Nieman fellowships for newsmen at Harvard with a $1.4 million fund. She gave the remainder of his interest in the paper to Harvard to dispose of the stock to a group "most likely to carry out Nieman's ideals."

Grant persuaded Harvard to sell the Nieman stock to the employees for $3,850,000. Grant held 20 per cent of the stock at the time. He arranged for the employees to get a $250,000 cash bonus to pay for a quarter interest on 25 per cent more. He got a Milwaukee bank to lend the employees the balance at 3 per cent interest. The employees were able to pay their debts largely out of earnings. Grant reduced his holdings to 12 1/2 per cent of the stock. In 1952 he announced that the staff held 55 per cent and would own 67 1/2 per cent in five years.

The salary of each of the top executives of the *Journal* amounted to about $40,000. Each official owned 3 per cent of the stock, with a value of $250,000 to $500,000. Total value of the *Journal* stock was estimated at $8 million. Because of the employee ownership, the American Newspaper Guild did not make any headway in organizing the employees. Grant told his employees: "The time has come for you to choose between my management or the Guild—you can't have both." His speech ended the first drive of the Guild campaign. The *Journal* in 1968 reached 368,520 evening readers; the Sunday paper found 561,851 subscribers.

Meanwhile, William Randolph Hearst entered the Milwaukee journalistic competition in 1918 with the purchase of the *Evening Wisconsin*, the *Daily News* and the *Free Press*. All of these he merged into one daily, the *Wisconsin News*, an afternoon daily. In 1924 Hearst bought the *Sentinel*, with its morning and afternoon editions. Hearst killed off its afternoon edition, as he already had an evening paper. Hearst decided in 1939 to eliminate the evening *Wisconsin News* and merge it with the *Sentinel,* which was published as a morning and Sunday daily.

The American Newspaper Guild struck the *Sentinel* in May, 1962. Eight weeks later, in July, Hearst sold the *Sentinel* to the *Journal.* Hearst officials explained that the *Sentinel* had been losing money for a long time. The *Journal* company said it never wanted to acquire the *Sentinel,* but it felt it had an obligation to the people of the city and state. "Permanent passing of a morning newspaper in Milwaukee will result in serious loss of reader and advertising service."

The *Sentinel* continued as a six-day morning paper, with its Sunday edition having been eliminated. The *Sentinel's* editorial and news departments have been housed in the *Journal* annex. Thus, Milwaukee's two big newspapers have been operated and owned by one company. Hearst's radio and television stations, WISN and WISN-TV, have not been affected by the merger. The *Sentinel* appealed to 170,264 readers in 1968.

KANSAS CITY STAR REMAINS INFLUENTIAL

William Rockhill Nelson continued to make the *Kansas City Star* the dominant newspaper in his city. As headquarters for the second largest meat-packing and livestock center in the United States, Kansas City, Missouri has grown steadily. It is continguous with Kansas City, Kansas.

Part of Nelson's appeal was his intense local and regional coverage, his campaigns for civic improvement, and his low price. When he bought the *Kansas City Times* in 1901 to use it as a morning edition, he continued to give his subscribers thirteen issues a week for the same ten-cent price he had charged before. Competitors, therefore, were blocked in their efforts to gain foothold. His *Weekly Star,* a farm paper selling for twenty-five cents a year, reached 300,000 circulation by the opening of World War I.

A Democrat in his early career, Nelson could not support Bryan in his attempt at the presidency; the daily, therefore, shifted to the Republican Party. Nelson became a friend and admirer of Theodore Roosevelt and urged the building of a new Progressive Party in 1912. Nelson was active in the state and national campaigns of the Progressives. Roosevelt became a contributing editor of the *Kansas City Star* when he retired from the presidency.

When Nelson died in 1915, he left most of his fortune to found an art gallery for Kansas City. His wife became trustee of the two newspapers. They were transferred to a daughter on the death of Mrs. Nelson. Mrs. Irwin R. Kirkwood, his daughter, died in 1926. According to Nelson's will, the papers were to be sold and the funds given to the art gallery. Surviving his wife by a year, Mr. Kirkwood helped the employees of the *Star* and the *Times* organize a stock company. They raised $2.5 million to support a bid of $11 million total for the two papers. The bid was successful.

Driving force behind the paper, revitalized by the sale, was Henry J. Haskell. The *Star*'s campaign for lower gas rates resulted in a libel suit by Henry L. Doherty, utilities owner. Doherty sued for $12 million. The total suits amounted to $54 million, but all were eventually dropped.

During this time the *Star* did not change its old-fashioned typographical dress, still using the one-column heads with many decks. Foreign news, however, was increased and halftones and comics were used. Meanwhile, Roy A. Roberts, who had joined the staff in 1908, was promoted up the executive line. He served in various positions until he became head. Roberts was prominent in Republican Party circles. In 1968 circulation of the *Star* reached 327,623 evening readers; the *Times* found 334,746 subscribers in the morning and on Sunday had 396,260.

Journal Post

The *Star,* as indicated, continued to meet all opposition. Bonfils and Tammen, owners of the *Denver Post,* came to Kansas City in 1909 and bought the *Kansas City Post,* an evening paper, for $250,000. They applied the scarlet-hued journalism they developed in Denver to Kansas City, but the community was too conservative. Meanwhile, a wealthy industrialist, Walter S. Dickey, seeking political office, bought the *Kansas City Journal* in 1921. Dickey purchased the *Post,* the price being $1,250,000. Thus, the *Journal* appeared in the morning and the *Post* in the afternoon, both issued by the same organization. In 1928 they were merged under the name *Journal-Post.*

WILLIAM ALLEN WHITE BECOMES MIDDLE-CLASS SPOKESMAN

William Allen White, whose newspaper activity began in the Gilded Age, was most influential in the first four decades of the twentieth century. His story paralleled the growth of America from a rural-farming era to an urban-industrial one, from isolationism to internationalism. His change in viewpoint mirrored this change, for in his early newspaper period he upheld the Republican Party. He was alarmed over the Populists' demands for more democratic political government and for more regulation of the great industries and railroads. In his later days he shifted and advocated the Progressive Republican stand, calling for enactment of many of the very same Populist measures.

White was born in Emporia, Kansas, February 10, 1868, son of a frontier doctor and pharmacist. He worked as reporter and editorial writer for *Kansas City Star*. Then White decided to return to a small town and to engage in small-town journalism. He did not relish the fact that he received no credit for the editorials and other articles he wrote for the *Star*. After trying to persuade several other weekly publishers to sell, he finally obtained the *Emporia Gazette* in 1895. The three thousand dollars he needed to buy the little weekly was borrowed from the town banker, the governor of the state and the estate of a senator. Although White's mechanical equipment was poor, he had some effective ideas and was a hustler. He went after the church and school news and launched an Emporia street fair.

Following an argument with some Populists one day, White returned to his little office and dashed off an editorial, "What's the Matter With Kansas." This article, which ridiculed the Populists and Democrats in satirical fashion, catapulted White to national fame. The article was reprinted by Republican papers in Chicago and New York. Soon, such magazines as *McClure*'s, *Scribner*'s and the *Saturday Evening Post* were calling on him for short stories and articles.

Although circulation of the *Gazette*, which now became a daily, reached only three thousand, White's editorials in the *Gazette* were reprinted and commented on widely, for he represented the voice of rural and middle-class America. His sharp observations, his sparkling style and his original ways of expressing ideas made the outpourings of his typewriter interesting and influential. White continued to write regularly for magazines, such as the *American, Collier's* and the *Saturday Evening Post*, his subjects being the current American scene and the outstanding politicians. He also covered national conventions of both parties and wrote European articles for national news syndicates. His books on similar topics and his fiction portraying small-town life were widely read.

In the post-World War I period, White was appalled at the reaction sweeping the country. The attacks on liberal thinking were led by Attorney General A. Mitchell Palmer. White rose to the defense of liberals and defined his own brand of Americanism, as all his progressive ideals seemed to be in eclipse. He declared more bigotry and reaction were hiding under the term *Americanism* than ever before. Americanism, to him, meant freedom of speech, of thought and of press.

White's tolerant attitude toward Franklin D. Roosevelt's reform and his unwillingness to join in the general Republican abuse of the New Deal increased White's prestige with liberals throughout the nation. Although he supported a large share of the New Deal measures, he opposed Roosevelt in 1932, 1936 and 1940.

During this time White became "an American institution." White seemed to offer a sense of security to those whose values were in a state of flux. He appeared to be a rock of stability in an America and in a world that were undergoing epoch-making changes. Many people saw in this successful, mellow, small-town editor a justification for their type of civilization. White received thousands of letters each year from people who wrote to him asking for his advice. Such was the fame of the *Gazette* that White was offered $400,000 for it but never sold. It was his forum. The *Gazette* became the training school for a number of newsmen who came from everywhere to learn White's methods. Many later owned papers themselves.

Many honors were conferred upon White, including the presidency of the American Society of Newspaper Editors. He served, for a few years, as a member of the Board of Regents of the University of Kansas.

White died from cancer in January, 1944. President Roosevelt, whom he supported between elections and opposed every four years, summed up the views of many when he said White "expressed himself in characteristic colorful language. As a writer of terse, forcible, vigorous prose, he was unsurpassed. He ennobled the profession of journalism."

A group of citizens established a fund which provided the basis for the William Allen White School of Journalism at the University of Kansas. The William Allen White Emporia Memorial Foundation was also establised to perpetuate the memory of this great grassroots editor with the international viewpoint.

ST. LOUIS NEWSPAPERS CONTINUE CRUSADES

During the first half of the twentieth century St. Louis had three outstanding newspapers which had traditions derived from the nineteenth century when the journals were founded. The *Post-Dispatch* carried on the crusading, liberal spirit of Joseph Pulitzer who established it in 1878, and then went on to build the *New York World.* The *Post-Dispatch*'s two rivals were the *Star-Times* and the *Globe-Democrat.* St. Louis papers became nationally known because of their crusading campaigns and comprehensive news coverage for their areas.

St. Louis grew from 575,000 population at the turn of the century to 870,000 by 1960. Its metropolitan district included many towns in adjacent Missouri and southern Illinois.

St. Louis Post-Dispatch: National Newspaper

The *St. Louis Post-Dispatch* continued the traditions set by the founder. Joseph Pulitzer, Jr., whom his father had sent to St. Louis to operate the paper, built the *Post-Dispatch* into an outstanding institution.

The *Post-Dispatch* became a thoroughly national newspaper so that it was called by some of its readers, the *Manchester Guardian of America.* It received an increasing volume of news from press associations but also sent its own writers to every part of the world and particularly the hot newsspots in the United States to cover the big news of interest to St. Louis.

The *Post-Dispatch* continued to carry out its founder's policy "never be content with merely publishing the news." The paper sought to expose corruption in politics, in business and in the courts. By means of a hard-hitting type of subsurface reporting, it brought to the public attention news which other papers had overlooked. The paper likewise campaigned by means of news articles, editorials, pictures and cartoons for many civic improvements in the St. Louis and the Missouri region the *Post-Dispatch* served. Its editorial page and its "dignity page," carrying controversial articles on public questions, upheld the tradition of a strong editorial policy when other dailies had backed off from expressing strong views.

Carrying out the policy of aggressive journalism on the news side was Oliver K. Bovard, the *Post-Dispatch*'s managing editor. Bovard came to be recognized as one of the great managing editors in his ability to size up a news situation and develop its underlying causes. Bovard joined the *Post-Dispatch* in 1898, going there from the *St. Louis Star,* which wouldn't print his exposé of the traction company's corruption of city officials. After a few years on the *Post-Dispatch,* his ability was recognized, and he was promoted to city editor. Then in 1908 Bovard became managing editor.

Known as a whip-cracking taskmaster, he inspired great loyalties among his men and stood behind them when they were under fire. Austere and impersonal in his relations with reporters, he was master strategist in his planning and getting the news. He visualized news as a shield against corruption and a spear of progress. When he left the *Post-Dispatch* after some difference of opinion with the publisher in

1938, he was succeeded by Benjamin H. Reese. In 1951 the city editor, Raymond L. Crowley, became managing editor.

In 1922 the *Post-Dispatch* exposed the alliance between oil and politics. Senator Robert M. LaFollette demanded an investigation of the Teapot Dome naval oil leases. The St. Louis paper was one of the few which recognized the news. When the investigation finally got under way, this crusading journal was the only newspaper to maintain a staff correspondent at the hearings. Paul Y. Anderson was the reporter. The paper was criticized for trying to blacken the name of patriotic officials. Eventually the United States Supreme Court vindicated the *Post-Dispatch* and restored the naval reserves to the nation.

Acting on evidence gathered and presented to it by the *Post-Dispatch,* Congress in 1925 directed a special commitee to inquire into the official conduct of the United States District Judge George W. English of East St. Louis. The committee brought in a resolution recommending the impeachment of Judge English for abuse of his powers. He had played the part of tyrant, showing gross favoritism in bankruptcy cases. The House of Representatives voted 300 to 60 for impeachment. Judge English resigned in 1926, before the date set for his trial.

At the close of World War II in 1945, it became apparent that housing was a desperate need of all classes of people. Slum clearance and rehabilitation of older sections of the city were tied to this. The *Post-Dispatch* explored the problem intensively and informed its readers of the findings by news articles, editorials and pictures. The paper fostered the cause of housing and slum clearance locally and nationally.

Editorial page of the *Post-Dispatch* sought to express the paper's own opinions, frankly, fully and forcefully in attractive, readable literary style. The page did not pussyfoot on controversial issues of the day. The daily took vigorous stands seven days a week. The editor of the *Post-Dispatch,* until his death on March 30, 1955, was Joseph Pulitzer, II, son of the founder; his son, Joseph Pulitzer, Jr., grandson of the founder, was associate editor and became editor upon his father's death. In direct charge of the editorial page since 1928 were Clark McAdams, then Charles G. Ross who was followed by Ralph Coghlan. In 1949 Irving Dilliard, a newsman with a strong sense of professional responsibility, became editor of the page.

The editorial page carried strong cartoons by Daniel R. Fitzpatrick, nationally known for his vivid style and comment on the passing but significant events. "A Mirror of Public Opinion," one of the other features of the page, carried selected articles and editorials in a wide field, reprinted from other publications. Dilliard later became an editorial writer, while Robert Lasch became editor of the editorial page.

Purchase of Star-Times Assets

When the *St. Louis Star-Times* ceased publication on June 15, 1951, the *Post-Dispatch* purchased the assets of the company, including circulation lists and distribution facilities. This resulted in an increase of 100,000 in daily circulation of the *Post-Dispatch,* jumping the circulation of the daily paper to about 400,000. The Sunday circulation reached 475,000.

When Joseph Pulitzer, Jr., the grandson, succeeded his father as editor and publisher of the *Post-Dispatch,* on April 4, 1955, he had about twenty years of newspaper experience behind him. During many of these years he was trained under his father. St. Louis was the birthplace of Joseph Pulitzer, Jr., on May 13, 1913. He attended St. Mark's School, Southborough, Massachusetts, and received his A.B. Degree from Harvard University in 1936.

Joseph Pulitzer, Jr., was made a director of the company January, 1937, and was appointed vice president in October, 1939. He served as a lieutenant in the United States Naval Reserve, on destroyer duty, and later he worked in Navy Intelligence from 1942 to 1945. He returned to the *Post-Dispatch* and was named associate editor in October, 1948.

Taking over his new position as editor of the *Post-Dispatch,* Pulitzer pledged to continue the daily in accordance with the standards established by his father and grandfather and set forth in the newspaper's platform on the editorial page. He promised the newspaper would not only report the daily news but would also "illuminate dark places" and interpret the background of current events. "Editorial opinion will be strong for what is believed to be right and equally strong against which we construe to be wrong. The newspaper will also strive to entertain its readers," he said. In 1968 the *Post-Dispatch* reached 375,154 daily readers and 601,534 Sunday subscribers.

Globe-Democrat Survives Competition

After Joseph B. McCullagh died, the *Globe-Democrat*'s managing editor was Captain Henry King, who sought to develop a rounded paper in news and features, and in social and editorial pages. King made a special effort to build up the Sunday edition.

Great rivalry existed between the *Globe-Democrat* and the *Republic.* These morning dailies usually ended up on different sides of the political fence, and not where their names would indicate. The *Republic,* for the most part, favored the Democratic Party, while the *Globe-Democrat* was strongly Republican. The *Republic* during these years was owned by David R. Francis. In 1919 these two historic papers followed the merger trend. The *Globe-Democrat* bought out its political rival. St. Louis, however, still had Pulitzer's *Post-Dispatch,* favoring the Democratic Party, and the *Star-Times.*

E. Lansing Ray, a nephew of Simeon Ray, one of the partners in the previous century, became publisher of the *Globe-Democrat.* He had worked on the newspaper for many years. Through his editorial page editor, Casper Yost, Ray proclaimed the paper to be no longer politically partisan. He wrote:

> The *Globe-Democrat* is an independent newspaper, printing the news impartially, supporting what it believes to be right, and opposing what it believes to be wrong without regard to party politics.

The paper followed the Republican Party usually, but it surprised its readers sometimes. Although it opposed President Woodrow Wilson's candidacy, the paper backed his League of Nations. Ray became a member of the President's cabinet.

New Editors

On retirement of Captain King in 1915, publisher Ray sought to divorce still further the news from the editorial departments. Joseph McAuliffe was installed as managing editor. Casper Yost, the Sunday editor, became the first editor of the editorial page. He became the advocate of ethical practices in journalism. Yost was succeeded by Louis La Coss.

On the publishing side, continuity was achieved through the sons of the founders who held executive positions. But E. Lansing Ray, Jr., who was to succeed his father as publisher, was killed in World War II.

The *Globe-Democrat,* through its early managing editor, King, aided in the founding of the first school of journalism in the United States, established at the University of Missouri in 1908. The paper's publisher, Ray, had a strong civic interest and promoted many community projects. Because of its efforts in behalf of aviation, the *Globe-Democrat* was credited with keeping the city ahead in the aviation picture. The morning paper sponsored spelling bees and high school reviews through radio station KWK, in which it had a minority interest. The daily's annual Christmas Choral pageant and Missouri Soil Conservation Award programs developed wide public interest. In 1931 the paper moved into a large modern newspaper plant at 12th and Franklin streets.

Sold To Newhouse

The century-old *Globe-Democrat* was sold to Samuel Newhouse, eastern chain owner, in 1954. This left St. Louis with one family-owned newspaper, Pulitzer's *Post-Dispatch,* and a chain-owned daily, the *Globe-Democrat.* In April, 1959, following difficulties with the American Newspaper Guild, Newhouse closed down his mechanical department and printed on the *Post-Dispatch*'s presses. The *Globe-Democrat* had 327,594 daily subscribers and 356,929 Sunday readers in 1968.

Chapter 39

Southwestern and Mountain Regional Newspapers

TEXAS JOURNALISM FAR-FLUNG

Texas newspapers have reflected many of the characteristics of one of the largest states in the union, a state turning, to a marked extent, from agriculture and cattle raising to industry. Texas has developed large metropolitan centers and advanced educationally with rapid strides. The quickening prosperity of the Lone Star State during the twentieth century has been mirrored in the economic stability and corporate development of many of the newspapers.

Texans like to brag. But, humor aside, much of their boasting has had a solid foundation in economic fact. Oil refining has become the most important part of the state's economy, with meat packing second and cottonseed products third. The heart of the oil industry has been centered around Houston. Texas has led the nation in sulphur production and has developed a great chemical industry. The state has ranked eleventh in manufacturing in the nation.

Vastness of Texas, 760 miles long and 620 miles wide, led to publication of many newspapers scattered throughout the state, some with small circulations of one thousand to three thousand. Texas had more than one hundred dailies in 1958. A few of them, the *Houston Post* and the *Dallas News,* acquired circulations above the 200,000 level.

HOUSTON POST MIRRORS, SPURS CITY EXPANSION

Published in the largest city in Texas, the *Houston Post* mirrored the expansion and prosperity of Houston, contributing to its many-sided development. The *Houston Post* was, at midcentury, the oldest paper in the community. When it was established on April 5, 1885, it was called the *Houston Daily Post.* By 1900 it had a circulation of 12,000 and was printing a daily paper of twelve pages. In that same year W. P. Hobby acquired his first ten shares of stock. He had come to the paper in 1895, starting as a circulation clerk at eight dollars a week. In 1901 he transferred to the editorial department as commercial editor, subsequently being promoted to city editor and managing editor. In 1907 Hobby went to Beaumont, Texas, where he became editor and manager of the *Beaumont Enterprise,* building that paper into a strong daily. Hobby was elected lieutenant governor of Texas in 1914 and became governor when James E. Ferguson was impeached. Hobby was later elected to another term in the governor's office and retired from it undefeated.

The newsman returned to the *Houston Post* in 1924. The name had been changed to *Post-Dispatch.* Becoming publisher of the daily in 1932, one of Hobby's first official actions was to change the name back to the *Houston Post.* At this time the circulation was under 62,000, but with Hobby's leadership it grew to 80,000 in 1934 and to 100,000 by 1941.

Associated with her husband in publication of the *Post* was Oveta Culp Hobby. The daughter of state representative Ike Culp, she used to sit beside her father in the Texas House of Representatives when she was only fourteen years old. At twenty, she became parliamentarian for the House. When Congress created the Women's Auxiliary Corps, during World War II, she was appointed to organize it. She resigned in 1945 with the rank of Colonel. Interested in advertising progress, she served on the board of directors of the Advertising Federation of America, and in 1948 became president of Southern Newspaper Publishers Association. In President Eisenhower's administration, she was a member of his cabinet, holding the rank of Secretary of Health, Education and Welfare. She was publisher and editor of the *Post.*

The *Post* sought to give a thorough, timely coverage of international, national, state and local news in a dignified fashion. The daily tried no unusual typographical appeals, aiming at readers who wished thorough information about current affairs. On page two, the editor of the *Post* presented a double-column feature called "Newcasts," a one paragraph summary of the news at all levels, serving as an index to the entire issue that day.

On Sundays, the *Post* expanded in all directions, with each department adding pages to the usual daily budget. Expansion of the *Post* caused the publishers to build and move into a new $5 million structure in 1955. Daily circulation by 1968 reached 274,248; Sunday circulation, 304,238.

HOUSTON CHRONICLE GIVES STRONG COMPETITION

Competing closely with the *Houston Post* was the *Houston Chronicle,* an evening and Sunday paper. The *Chronicle* was started in 1901 by Marcellus E. Foster, editor of the morning *Houston Post,* and a group of associates, with a capital of $25,000. Foster, a legend known as "Mefo," from his initials, spent more than forty-two years in newspaper work in Houston, working at one time or another for the three newspapers there.

With an editorial department staff of two reporters, Foster and Charles Meyers, the new publishers, put the *Chronicle* on the streets for the first time on October 14, 1901. It was a sensational beginning; the *Chronicle* was Houston's first two-cent newspaper. The management made the most of it by displaying a keg of fifty-thousand pennies and letting the newspaper boys make the change when they sold a *Chronicle.* Houstonians carried few pennies then.

Two thousand copies of the *Chronicle* were sold on the streets the first day. By the end of the first month the *Chronicle* had a circulation of four thousand in a city with a population of forty-five thousand. In the tradition of the period, the *Chronicle* embarked on various kinds of crusades. It campaigned to run out of business the owners of the private water service if they did not raise water pressure. The paper fought for closing saloons on Sunday morning during church hours and for chasing gambling off the main street. The daily's fight against the Ku Klux Klan was vigorous. Less than a year after its birth, the *Chronicle* bought out the third paper in town, *Daily Herald,* for $6,000, also acquiring its Associated Press franchise.

In 1908 the *Chronicle* started to build its own home, a ten-story building at Texas and Travis streets, which it occupied two years later. Jesse H. Jones, rising financier and builder, constructed the building and went into partnership with Foster in *Chronicle* ownership. In 1926 Foster sold his interest in the paper to Jones and retired temporarily. Jones became a power in the Democratic Party.

The *Chronicle* by the 1960s used the wire services of the Associated Press, the United Press International, the *Chicago Daily News,* the *New York Times* and the *Chicago Tribune.* It also had available the Reuter's and New York News services. The paper also received its Washington news from its bureau, headed by Edward Jamieson. Flashy, bold headlines stretching across the page attracted the more than two hundred thousand afternoon readers. Large-scale catastrophes throughout the world, and murders and crime were featured in news, features and photographs. Reflecting local interest in the oil industry, the *Chronicle* devoted a considerable amount of space to this news. News features and pictures told of the many activities in this industry, not only locally but internationally as well. On Sunday the *Chronicle* blossomed with expanded departments and colorful tabloid magazines, appealing to 216,567 readers in 1960. The reader got a full paper of 266 or more pages from which he could select news and features relating to his every interest and hobby.

Houston boasted a third newspaper, the *Press*, published by the Scripps-Howard chain. An afternoon newspaper, in 1960, it reached 101,398 daily and 88,677 on Saturdays, but four years later sold out to the *Chronicle* for four million dollars.

When Jones died he left the *Chronicle* under control of the Houston Endowment, Inc., founded as a philanthropic organization. In December, 1965, the *Houston Chronicle* was purchased as a part of an $85 million package deal of John W. Mecom, one of the country's richest oil men. At the time of the sale, circulation of the morning edition of the *Houston Chronicle* was 267,620 and its Sunday edition sold 289,000 copies. Six months later the sale was canceled and the paper reverted to the endowment trust. The *Chronicle* found 280,472 daily readers in 1968. On Sunday 327,121 subscribers read its many sections.

DEALEY GUIDES INFLUENTIAL DALLAS NEWS

The twentieth century brought a period of transition for the *Dallas News*. When Colonel Alfred H. Belo, publisher, died in 1901, presidency of the company fell to his son, Alfred H. Belo, Jr., but he also died within five years. George B. Dealey now came to the front in the organization. With the death of young Belo, Dealey was named vice president and general manager of both the *Galveston News* and the *Dallas News*.

From this time on he was the actual head, although the titular presidency fell to young Belo's mother. Upon Mrs. Belo's death, in 1912, her brother-in-law, C. Lombardi, became president. Dealey became official head of the firm in 1926. Dealey then was able to buy controlling interest in the *Dallas News* from the Belo heirs.

Dealey stated the creed of the *News*:

> Build the news upon the rock of truth and righteousness. Conduct it upon the lines of fairness and integrity. Acknowledge the right of the people to get from a newspaper both sides of every important question.

These words were engraved on the new *Dallas News* building. Dealey devoted much of his personal energies to civic improvements. One of his earliest campaigns was aimed at cleaning up Dallas physically. He headed a movement to improve Dallas through formation of the Cleaner Dallas League. But his efforts ran into ward politics of the aldermanic form of city government.

Dealey's diplomacy reconciled the officials of two rival Dallas fairs and laid the basis for the present State Fair of Texas, valued at $35 million. The *News* was a leader of the movement to bring Southern Methodist University and a branch Federal Reserve Bank to Dallas.

In 1922 the newspaper company's first radio station was opened. Expansion was rapid. Power was increased from 500 to 5,000 to 50,000 watts. Radio station WFAA became the first superpower radio station in the South and the first of its size to be owned by an American newspaper. In 1950 the company entered into the new field of television with the establishment of station WFAA-TV.

G. B. Dealey resigned as president of the company in 1940, becoming chairman of the board, with Ted Dealey, his son, being made president of the company. When the elder Dealey died in 1946, responsibility then fell upon his son.

The *News* moved into a new six million dollar plant which the elder Dealey had planned. World War II had cut short building operations, consequently construction was delayed. The most advanced machinery and equipment which science and technology had made available were installed. Growth of circulation and daily size of the *News* later forced the purchase of new units, bringing the cost of the presses to two million dollars. During the 1950s and 1960s the *News* circulation increased steadily. Morning readers totaled 226,804 while Sunday readers were 264,344 in 1968.

DENVER POST FOUNDERS DIE; HOYT REVITALIZES PAPER

When Tammen died in 1924, and Bonfils followed in 1933, the *Denver Post*'s fire was gone, and circulation fell. A new publisher was sought. Palmer Hoyt, publisher of the *Portland Oregonian,* came in 1946 to occupy the publisher-editor's desk. Born in 1897 in Roseville, Illinois, Hoyt spent his boyhood in New England but later returned to the West, settling in Montana with his family. After serving in World War I, Hoyt enrolled at the University of Oregon. He became a copyreader on the *Portland Oregonian.* On this, the oldest paper in the state, his ability was soon demonstrated, and he moved up through various jobs to that of managing editor, then publisher. Hoyt proceeded to revamp the various departments, to emphasize pictures and to dress up the paper typographically.

When he came to the *Denver Post,* readers knew that a new personality had taken charge. He kept the vigor of the old *Post* but stamped it with his own vitality. Strongly motivated by ideals of Sigma Delta Chi, professional journalism fraternity, Hoyt improved the news coverage, dug into subsurface news. He toned down the *Post*'s flamboyant typography and engaged in a series of campaigns for local improvement.

The *Post* plunged in and helped solve health, housing and traffic problems. The paper exposed the difficulties minority groups faced. It sought reforms in state government: in the highway department, civil service, penal system, tax system and procedures of the state legislature. On the national level the *Post* became a state leader in the fight for civil liberties and for sound farm and medical care programs.

The *Post* jealously and zealously maintained the right of the press to get and print the news. In February, 1949, editorials condemned the "Star Chamber" sessions of the state legislature's legislative committee, the *Post* conceding the committee's legal right but questioning the propriety of its actions. The sessions came out into the open. The *Post* also objected strongly to Colorado's poor treatment of its Mexican-American citizens.

Hoyt also instituted increasing story-and-picture coverage of local and regional news. This was supplemented in the months following by devoting more space to schools, agriculture, motion pictures, music, theater, arts and books. News enterprise was shown in sending men on assignments throughout the nation and the world to write series of stories and gain editorial background. Hoyt established a Washington bureau as well as other local bureaus in Colorado. A variety of articles-in-series to background certain issues became a distinguishing feature of the *Post*. Articles covered the Public Service Company franchise and education in Colorado. Others concerned such questions as, "Your Tax Headache," "The Colorado: Whose River?"

The *Post* editorial page was reconstructed under the direction of Fred W. Colvig. He made the page "a meeting place for all shades of opinion." When he died in 1949, Edwin P. Hoyt, son of the publisher, was named editor of the page. He described the practices and philosophy of the page. "It was not to be afflicted with Afghanistanism—writing about remote subjects; was not out to get anybody; had no sacred cows; and would not use a lot of big words." The page worked for both short-range and long-term objectives. It offered a wide variety of columnists with different points of view, needed, it said, in a democracy. "The opinions of the columnists are their own, offered to stimulate the readers' thoughts, which is the purpose of any editorial page," the *Post* claimed.

Independence of the *Post's* editorial page extended to political parties. The daily declared it was nonpartisan, "calling the shots as the editors saw them." The *Post* followed the Republican banner in national elections, but it backed a Democrat for governor.

Hoyt streamlined the typography of all pages and sections. Early in 1947 Vogue headline faces replaced the slim, hard-to-read, condensed Gothic. Capital and lower-case headlines, set flush left, replaced the all-capital style, except for a banner. The pink cover of the first section of the home edition of the daily paper, long a tradition, was last used in 1948. Only a red overline or head was used on page one. A pink Ben Day background for the nameplate gave additional color to the first page. The Sunday edition continued to run one or more red headlines. The Sunday edition was departmentalized. Instead of separate *Rocky Mountain Empire* magazine and rotogravure sections, each consisting of eight pages, Hoyt started a tabloid magazine of thirty-two to forty pages in 1950.

To cover the news and pictures, the *Denver Post's* staff was increased from fifty-six to one hundred twenty-three. A beautiful six million dollar building was constructed to house the operations of the paper.

As a result of these accomplishments and of the new spirit infused into the *Denver Post,* its circulation, between 1946 and 1950, jumped 20 per cent, reaching 231,888 daily subscribers; while the Sunday edition jumped 15 per cent, being bought by 363,784 persons. Advertising increased 90 per cent.

Its historian, A. Gayle Waldrop, pointed out in the *Journalism Quarterly* (June, 1947; summer, 1951) that the *Post,* in exercising the power of leadership, encouraged attention of and evoked participation by the public in discussion of democracy's problems at all levels, and raised its own mature and much-quoted editorial voice to help create the conditions under which democracy can function successfully. The *Post* in 1968 reached 253,280 subscribers weekdays; the Sunday readers totaled 341,595.

Chapter 40

Pacific Coast's Booming Newspapers

PACIFIC NORTHWEST'S ECONOMIC DEVELOPMENT

Journalism in the Pacific Northwest has expanded with the growth of farming, fishing and lumbering, basic wealth of the Pacific Northwest. The stimulus of World War II spurred industry in the Northwest market. New towns developed, small towns became large cities. Irrigation brought into cultivation tens of thousands of new acres of farmland. Development of huge hydroelectric dams and plants made possible low-cost power for new and expanding industry. Natural gas also arrived via pipeline from New Mexico and Colorado.

Among the most important industries in the area have been those related to pulp and paper. Giant aluminum plants have been built in the region because of availability of ore and power supply. Perhaps the greatest boom has been experienced by the aircraft industry. The great atomic energy plant in Hanford has added new wealth to central Washington.

Seattle Post—Intelligencer

William Randolph Hearst, in his period of newspaper chain expansion, purchased the *Post-Intelligencer* in 1921. The editors of the *Post-Intelligencer* conceived that their job was to stress local news, as they were convinced people were most interested in news about the people who lived close to them. Each edition of the *Post-Intelligencer* was packed with local stories and hundreds of local news items.

The newspaper championed and won, often against open or covert newspaper opposition, a number of campaigns. The *Post-Intelligencer* fought for a floating bridge across Lake Washington. The paper also battled for the West Seattle viaduct. This great project eliminated a serious traffic bottleneck. The paper was especially concerned with communist inflitration into Seattle labor unions and educational institutions and sought to eliminate the communist influence.

The daily's editors believed that much of the news of midcentury, closely affecting people's lives, did not happen in the sense of a fire or an election. They thought that in the quiet laboratories, in population movements, in changes in collective thinking and customs was the news that most profoundly affected the public now and in the future. A series, "Our Disappearing Salmon," revealed to most people, for the first time, that one of America's greatest natural resources was in danger of extinction. Conservation measures swiftly followed publication of the articles.

Under editorship of Royal Brougham, nationally known sportswriter, the *Post-Intelligencer's* sport pages strove to reach a high quality. Attractive features on the sports section included Emmett Waton's daily column on baseball, Dick Sharpe's news of boxing, Cliff Harrison's column on "Out O'Doors" for fishing and hunting enthusiasts. Waton won the 1952 headline award for the best sports column of any paper in the nation. The paper sponsored a "Man of the Year" dinner, Golden Gloves amateur boxing tournaments and annual swim classes in which thousands participated. The *Post-Intelligencer* developed a lively business section, edited by Fergus Hoffman, "who talked the language of businessmen and financiers." The *Post-Intelligencer* also gave its women's pages particular attention. They were edited by Marion Stixrood, nationally known fashion writer. She had a large staff of reporters and writers who covered every interest of women and homemakers. She tried to make her pages attractive, bright and interesting. The daily edition of the *Post-Intelligencer* reached 205,859 in 1968. The Sunday readers totaled 256,930.

PORTLAND OREGONIAN REFLECTS REGIONAL GROWTH

In the new century the *Portland Oregonian* grew with the rapid development of the Northwest region and the expansion of the city of Portland. The *Oregonian* has served a territory which includes Oregon, a part of Washington and Idaho. Lumbering, fruit growing and shipbuilding have been the principal industries.

The *Oregonian* has served as spokesman for many of these economic groups. Harvey Scott, the scholarly, hard-hitting editor who helped the paper gain a solid reputation at the end of the last century, continued to head the paper until 1910 when he died. Henry Pittock, his partner, was left to publish the *Oregonian*. As Portland grew and prospered, so did the *Oregonian*. The *Evening Telegram* was started as an afternoon edition of the *Oregonian.* The *Telegram* was sold to the Wheeler brothers. After passing through several changes of ownership, the *Telegram* was sold to the *Portland News.* The merged *News-Telegram* perished several years later.

When in 1919, Pittock died, his will left his majority ownership of the *Oregonian* in trust for his heirs and set up a twenty-year trusteeship. At the end of that period, descendants of the Scott and Pittock families came into full control and elected a board of directors which operated the paper through the general manager. Under the new regime, typography and makeup were modernized. Spread-over of news stories from page one to an inside page was eliminated.

Radio became an adjunct of the *Oregonian* in 1922 when KGW broadcast its first program from a maze of wires and gadgets in an improvised studio in an old clock tower. The station became affiliated with the National Broadcasting Company network in 1927.

The *Oregonian* moved into a four million dollar building, designed for efficient newspaper production and radio operation. The new presses were able to roll out ninety thousand papers an hour, and with the addition of other units could take care of circulation up to one million.

Ambitious Newhouse Buys Oregonian

In 1950 Samuel Newhouse, an alert, ambitious eastern chain owner, purchased the *Oregonian* for five million dollars. Circulation reached 215,000. Newhouse had started his newspaper career as an office boy on the *Bayonne* (New Jersey) *Times* in 1918. He studied law at night and learned the newspaper business during the day. When the *Times* went bankrupt, Newhouse was able to persuade the creditors he could rebuild it. He did. From then on, his rise was steady. In New York he purchased the *Staten Island Advance,* then the *Long Island Press* and *Star Journal.* Soon he added the *Jamaica Press.* Newhouse then moved into New Jersey with the purchase of the *Newark Ledger* and the *Star-Eagle,* making a success of this venture. While other chain publishers had slowed down or stopped expanding in this period, Newhouse continued to add more links. He bought the *Syracuse* (New York) *Herald-Journal* and the *Harrisburg* (Pennsylvania) *Patriot.* Finally, he added the *Jersey City* (New Jersey) *Journal,* which was tied up for a long time in extensive litigation. He also bought, as indicated, the *St. Louis* (Missouri) *Globe-Democrat.* Newhouse had centered his attention on the East Coast before, so it was something of a surprise when he jumped to Oregon to purchase the *Oregonian.* By 1968 circulation of the daily reached 240,566, with the Sunday edition selling 401,946. A prolonged strike against the paper began, leading the former editorial staff to establish the *Reporter,* first as a weekly then as a daily.

COWLES BUILDS SPOKANE SPOKESMAN-REVIEW

The *Spokane* (Washington) *Spokesman-Review,* under ownership of William H. Cowles, had begun to show a profit at the turn of the century. Its infantile troubles were over. Cowles had bought out the *Chronicle,* an afternoon paper, and made it part of his operations. Although journalistic opposition arose to the *Spokesman-Review,* the attempted daily lasted only a brief time, so strongly was Cowles entrenched and so expensive was the economics of newspaper publishing in large cities. Contributing to growth of the *Spokesman-Review* were the boom times in the section of Pacific Northwest the paper served. Influx of settlers to the district was of tidal wave proportions. The region's growth was reflected in the expansion of the *Spokesman-Review.*

The Cowles paper, as indicated, was not without journalistic opposition, but it did not last long. The *Inland Herald* began in November, 1910 as an evening and Sunday paper. Because of financial difficulties, the paper died in May, 1911. Circulation of the *Spokesman-Review* continued upward. By 1911 it climbed to 30,000, with its Sunday edition reaching 50,000.

Publisher Cowles was especially interested in promoting economic advancement of the region. After 1904 the daily always had one employee concentrating on promotional activities. During the second ten years of Cowles' control, four publicity men were on the job. They publicized the Northwest to thousands of manufacturing companies and their advertising agencies throughout the United States. The *Spokesman-Review* promotion men mailed circulars, folders and booklets, extolling the value and the features of the Northwest. Elaborate market surveys of the region were made.

Cowles gave much attention to local problems and building up the community. Many articles on government and taxation were published in his daily. A notable series dealing with state, county and city finances appeared on the editorial page in March, 1914.

In November, 1920, the *Spokesman-Review* took the initiative in formation of the Pacific Northwest Newspaper Association. Throughout his career, Cowles joined hands with other publishers in advancing the interest of the newspaper industry.

Now, Cowles' sons joined the staff of the *Spokesman-Review.* William H. Cowles, Jr., elder of the publisher's two sons, after his graduation from Yale in 1924, began to work on the paper. A younger son, Cheney Cowles, also a Yale graduate, gained experience in various departments. The elder Cowles planned for Cheney to direct the editorial operations, while his brother would be in charge of the business and mechanical departments. Cheney Cowles was killed in World War II in a crash of a war plane, dashing his father's hopes.

The *Spokesman-Review* campaigned for parks and playgrounds and worked for a one million dollar park bond issue. Thirty-one miles of riverbank along the Spokane River were bought by the city through efforts of the daily's Civic Betterment Department, headed by Audrey L. White.

Publisher Cowles died on January 15, 1946. He left his entire estate, with the exception of personal effects, in trust for his eight grandchildren. Trustees of the estate were William H. Cowles, Jr., John McKinley, treasurer of the publishing companies, and Alfred Cowles, nephew, of Chicago. Upon the death of his father, William Cowles, Jr., became publisher of the *Spokesman-Review.* Circulation reached 86,673 weekdays and 128,778 on Sundays by 1968. The *Chronicle,* published in the same plant, had 70,955 afternoon readers.

CALIFORNIA METROPOLITAN PRESS VIGOROUS

California has experienced a phenomenal growth in the twentieth century and so has its journalism. To use a term employed most frequently in Hollywood, its movie capital, California's population, agricultural, industrial and cultural expansion has been *fabulous.* Rapid development of irrigation, intensive cultivation and increase of small farms in the twentieth century have made California a great agricultural region and fruit-producing area.

LOS ANGELES BECOMES WEST'S NUMBER ONE CITY

California cities have gone through the same revolutionary expansion and have developed into metropolitan areas as other cities in the East. In California, however, urban growth has been more rapid in recent years than in other sections, pushing its key city, Los Angeles, with its 2,448,000 residents, into a top position in 1960. The Los Angeles metropolitan area had 6,690,000, thus becoming the second largest urban region in the United States.

Los Angeles economy has shown extraordinary growth. In retail sales, it was second only to New York. Los Angeles sales volume reached annually 9.1 billion dollars. Los Angeles has been America's third manufacturing center. It has led other cities in the manufacture of transportation equipment. The city's many factories also have produced motor vehicles and equipment, air craft and parts, and ships and boats. Los Angeles has been third in the nation in apparel manufacturing for men, women, and children.

The *Los Angeles Times* entered on a new era of success in this era. In the twentieth century Colonel Harrison Gray Otis was still publisher, but his son-in-law, Harry Chandler, took a more active leadership in the expanding journal. Chandler was full of ideas and full of energy, devoting himself to building the *Times* and southern California.

Union labor's fight against the *Times* continued from the previous century. On October 1, 1910, someone set off eighty sticks of dynamite beneath the *Times'* building which caused a fire, killing twenty-one. The newspaper building was shattered. The *Times* was issued, however, in an auxiliary plant, as Colonel Otis had anticipated trouble and was ready for it. Following the incident the building contractors, in a labor quarrel with the International Union of Bridge and Structural Workers, hired the William J. Burns Detective Agency to find the perpetrators. In a sensational trial attracting national attention, the accused dynamiters, J. B. and J. J. McNamara, pleaded guilty through Clarence Darrow, defense attorney. The McNamaras were sentenced to San Quentin penitentiary. Two years after the dynamiting incident, the *Times* occupied its new home, built on the same site.

The *Times* now championed a colossal new community project. With backing of the *Times,* Los Angeles undertook the daring plan of bringing water from Owens Valley, a distance of 238 miles. Completion of this great engineering feat was followed by an unprecedented growth in population and new industries.

On July 30, 1917, the *Times* recorded the death of its publisher, Colonel Otis, who was eighty years old. Into his place stepped his son-in-law, Harry Chandler. The publisher had left detailed instructions to carry out the purposes and traditions of the paper. The *Times* grew in both circulation and advertising, so that by 1921 and for three years, it led all other newspapers in advertising. The *Times* also surpassed all other newspapers in classified advertising. The rotogravure, the *Times* Sunday magazines, and the Mid-winter Number added to the prestige of the paper throughout the United States.

The *Times* increased its efforts for a better city and state, advocating a greater system of auto highways and fostering community friendships. It boosted improved agricultural methods and helped achieve such objectives as the building of the Colorado River Aqueduct and the development of scientific centers such as the California Institute of Technology.

The *Times* on July 1, 1935, entered into the third phase of its existence. This was the date it occupied the new building at First and Springs streets. Management sought to provide ideal conditions for work and for newspaper production. The architectural style, monumental modern, was chosen to harmonize with the Civic Center which the building faced.

Chandler died on September 23, 1944, at the age of eighty. He had helped build the newspaper and the Southwest region as well. Long before his death, Chandler prepared his sons to carry on the *Times*, starting them like any beginners in various departments of the newspaper. One son, Norman Chandler, had been active in all departments since 1934. He became president and publisher, while his brother, Philip Chandler, became vice president and general manager of the Times-Mirror Company. Another brother, Harrison Chandler, also served as vice president of the Times-Mirror Company.

When Hitler's legions poured into Poland, the impact of the *Times*' half-century campaign to industrialize southern California was fully felt. At San Pedro, shipyards were ready to produce transports that would bring aid to beleagured countries. Orders poured in from purchasing commissions for aircraft. Southern California helped forge the materials of war. To give more news of the world, the *Times* expanded its war news coverage. In addition, a new magazine, *Home*, appearing in the Sunday *Times*, was edited expressly for "Southlanders."

As a result of successfully fighting a contempt of court case through to the Supreme Court, the *Times* was awarded the Pulitzer Prize in 1941 for the "Most Disinterested and Meritorious Service Rendered by an American Newspaper." Two other Pulitzer prizes subsequently were awarded to members of the *Times* staff. Cartoonist Bruce Russell received the Pulitzer editorial cartoon award in 1945 and photographer John Gaunt won the news photography award in 1955.

The *Times* built its own permanent staff of correspondents in key centers of the United States. The daily had sixty staff correspondents throughout southern California. It had its own European correspondents with headquarters in Paris, and it operated its own Washington bureau. A reporter was stationed in Sacramento when the state legislature was in session. The *Times* used the AP and UP-I, the *Chicago Tribune* Foreign Service and the Foreign Service of the *New York Times*.

On August 31, 1936, the *Los Angeles Times* pioneered in becoming America's first streamlined newspaper. This meant a complete new typographical makeup, including the largest body type used by any metropolitan newspaper. The dress of the *Times* was copied by scores of newspapers, and in 1936 the nation's highest award for typographical excellence, the Ayer cup given annually by N. W. Ayer & Son, was awarded the paper. Because of the great growth in area population, the *Times* almost doubled its circulation between 1960 and 1968. The morning *Times* reached 856,621 readers and the Sunday edition, 1,145,645 by 1968.

Mirror Launched

In September, 1946, construction was begun on a building at 2nd and Spruce streets, adjoining the *Times* building. For many months Los Angeles speculated on the reason for this new structure. It was not until two years later, August 3, 1948, that the answer became known. On that day President Norman Chandler called his co-workers together and announced that *Times-Mirror* would soon begin publication of an afternoon newspaper, the *Mirror*.

The *Mirror,* Chandler revealed, was to be a completely separate newspaper from the *Times,* housed in its own plant, and with its own staff and organization. Virgil Pinkley, an outstanding newsman, was named editor and publisher. The *Mirror* flourished and grew in circulation and advertising. In December, 1954, the owners purchased the name, certain features and assets of the *Los Angeles Daily News,* a tabloid.

Recognizing the importance of television as a medium of public information, the *Times* in 1944 petitioned the Federal Communications Commission for permission to erect and operate a television station. This permission was granted, with the *Times* being assigned a broadcasting channel and the call letters KTTV. The initial telecast was January 1, 1949, covering the Tournament of Roses parade and football game, the first time these events had been televised.

One of the hard lessons the *Los Angeles Times* learned from World War II was that newsprint was indeed the life blood of any newspaper. The *Times* was unable to secure as much newsprint as it needed. To insure at least a more dependable supply of newsprint in the future, the *Times,* with a few other western newspapers, purchased two paper mills, one at West Tacoma, Washington, the other at Oregon City, Oregon. The *Times* was the principal owner of the Oregon City mill which covered fifteen and one-half acres and had its own forest for timber supply.

Envisioning its broadened role in community life and betterment gained through war-born sponsoring of public events for charity, the company set up a nonprofit organization devoted to civic improvement. The aim was not only to furnish top entertainment but to provide sports activities. Golden Glove boxing matches and national football games were held. The funds were used for the Lincoln Heights Chapter Boys Club of America, since renamed Los Angeles Times Boys Club. The club had three thousand members who enjoyed the facilities of the half-million dollar clubhouse with its $80,000-a-year operation expenses.

Boddy's Supersalesman of Daily News

In the post-World War I period, Cornelius Vanderbilt, Jr., became interested in the newspaper business and sought to establish tabloid newspapers in strategic cities in the country. One place he selected for location for a newspaper of the new type was Los Angeles. There, he established the *Illustrated Daily News.* But the Vanderbilt chain did not last; for one reason, the Vanderbilt family, which had supplied $3 million, originally, refused to pump any more millions into the newspaper venture. The tabloid idea for Los Angeles was a sound one, however, as Manchester Boddy, who had worked his way up from a pots and pans salesman to book publisher, recognized. It remained for this supersalesman to make a success of the *News.*

When Boddy learned that the *Illustrated News* was about to fold, he persuaded the Vanderbilt family to sign over the paper to a receivership committee. Later he outbid a newspaper group which offered $150,000 and expected to eliminate the paper from the Los Angeles competition. Boddy organized a syndicate, and the old Commercial Board, whose house organ he had edited, loaned him money to operate the *News.* The Chandler interests purchased the *Illustrated News,* as indicated, in 1954.

Hearst Consolidates Examiner, Herald and Express

To counteract the antilabor reputation of the *Los Angeles Times,* W. R. Hearst entered into competition with the *Los Angeles Examiner,* a morning paper which he established in 1903. This became one of Hearst's most successful papers. In 1922 Hearst bought the *Los Angeles Herald,* issued as an afternoon paper. Nine years later he absorbed the old *Express,* combining it with the *Herald* as the *Herald and Express.* By 1960 the morning *Examiner* had 369,537 daily and 684,605 Sunday circulation. The *Herald and Express* reached 355,764 afternoon readers.

After the morning *Examiner* was eliminated, the *Herald-Express* appealed to 721,397 afternoon readers in 1968 and on Sunday, 708,047 subscribers.

SAN FRANCISCO AREA JOURNALISM VIGOROUS: CONSOLIDATIONS

Population and commercial expansion in the San Francisco area has been rapid. By 1960 San Francisco's population totaled 800,000. Substantial gains were recorded in Santa Clara, San Mateo and Marin counties, all in the Frisco area, the population of which climbed to 3.4 million people. Effective buying income of the San Francisco nine-county bay area amounted to $7.8 billion. Of this, San Francisco contributed more than $2 billion. The buying power has been in the suburbs.

Six dailies were vying for public favor and patronage at the turn of the century in San Francisco: the *Call*, the *Chronicle* and the *Examiner* in the morning field, with the *Globe, Post* and *Bulletin* addressing the afternoon audience. The *News* started publishing in 1903.

The *Examiner* was published by William Randolph Hearst. The *Chronicle* was ably conducted by M. H. de Young; the *Call* was owned by industrialist John D. Spreckles; while the *Bulletin* was owned by the Pickering estate and edited by militant Fremont Older. The *Post* and the *Globe* were both controlled by interests that were the targets of the municipal graft prosecution of 1906-1907.

A series of mergers reduced the number of dailies in San Francisco. The *Globe* was merged with the *Post,* becoming a Hearst property in 1913. The publisher bought the *Call* and combined the *Post* with it, as the *Post* had an Associated Press franchise. Having the *Examiner* already in the morning, Hearst transferred the *Call* to the afternoon field, selling it for a penny.

Bulletin Changes Hands

After the death of Mrs. Loring Pickering, owner of the *Bulletin,* Robert A. Crothers held title to the *Bulletin* as trustee for her son, Loring Pickering, Jr.

Loring, Jr., inherited other properties from his mother. He also had other interests and was away most of the time as an Army Air Force officer in World War I, later as founder and manager of the North American Newspaper Alliance. In 1924 an offer was received from Herbert Fleishhacker and his group to purchase the *Bulletin* at a price Crothers felt was satisfactory.

The *Bulletin* was sold to these men, but five years later, in 1929, Hearst, publisher of the *Examiner,* bought the *Bulletin.* He combined the *Bulletin* with the *Call,* making it the *Call-Bulletin,* with Fremont Older as editor. Hearst then issued the *Examiner* in the morning and the *Call-Bulletin* in the evening field. The *Call-Bulletin,* after a merger with the Scripps-Howard *News,* had a circulation of 210,903 in 1960. The *Examiner* sold 276,026 copies daily and 482,821 on Sundays.

Chronicle Individualism Continues

The *San Francisco Chronicle* continued in the de Young family. Becoming editor of the *San Francisco Chronicle* in 1935, and general manager two years later, Paul Clifford Smith made the paper one of the outstanding dailies on the West Coast. He experimented with news presentation, headlines and makeup techniques. Smith also fought for academic freedom. San Francisco was affected by the general strike of dockworkers on San Francisco Bay. Smith demanded that both sides make peace. Later he was appointed mediator and negotiated a satisfactory agreement.

Politically, Smith followed the Republican banner. He launched a campaign for Wendell L. Willkie for President in 1940. When World War II began, Smith became chief of the news bureau of the Office of War Information. Then he resigned and enlisted in the marines as a private. He won many war citations and rose to become a second lieutenant.

Other newspapers may have had more syndicated columnists in accordance with the twentieth-century journalistic trend, but no newspaper could boast a greater collection of home-based byliners than the *San Francisco Chronicle.* Each columnist was a top professional in his specialty, nationally known through excellence of his *Chronicle* writings. This was in the tradition of the paper, extending from the previous era, when its editors always sought to discover "coming writers."

Writing for the *Chronicle* was Herb Caen, sometimes called "Mr. San Francisco" because of his love for the city. He prowled the city and wrote human interest features for his column. Stanton Delaplane had a penchant for the unusual and was sent frequently on zoo stories. Delaplane, who wrote the feature "Postcards" daily, received a Pulitzer prize for brilliant coverage of the proposed secession of five northern California and Oregon counties from their states. The editorial page of the *Chronicle* also featured its own columnists.

In 1934 the *San Francisco Chronicle* pioneered a new idea in western newspapers when it added a scientist-journalist to its staff to cover developments in the medical and scientific world. The *Chronicle*'s science writer, Milton Silverman, with his Ph.D. in biochemistry, analyzed and reported science news in clear, readable newspaper style. William Leiser and Art Rosenblume were responsible for the *Chronicle*'s "Sporting Green," sports section of the paper, which drew five hundred inquiries from sports fans every week.

Because of industrial and commercial activity in San Francisco, the *Chronicle* built a strong business and financial section edited by Sidney P. Allen. The pages carried Sylvia Porter's syndicated column, "Your Money's Worth," and complete quotations of New York and San Francisco stock and of mining exchanges. The *Chronicle* had 491,809 morning readers and 701,185 subscribers bought the *Examiner and Chronicle* on Sunday in 1968.

Scripps-Howard issued the evening *News,* which had a circulation of 103,000 weekdays in 1958. In 1959 a merger of the Hearst *Call-Bulletin* with the *News,* as indicated, was negotiated.

Chapter 41

Covering Global War Proves Staggering Job

WORLD WAR II BECOMES A FIVE-CONTINENT WAR

World War II was the first global war newsmen had to cover. The fighting was not confined to this country, as in the Civil War, or to a few islands, as in the Spanish-American War, or to one section of the world, as in the First World War. The conflict was on five continents, seven seas and a dozen fronts, separated by tens of thousands of miles. Newsmen were with invasion forces as they crossed the English Channel. Reporters carried their typewriters on the North African campaign. Many suffered hardships of the Bataan campaign in the South Pacific to bring the news to millions of Americans.

Meanwhile, the home-front story of drafts, mobilization of industry and manpower for war, and rationing of food and other essentials had to be told. Both abroad and at home, newsmen battled the censors to give the war news, good and bad, without revealing military secrets to the enemy.

The American public was well acquainted with the rise of Adolph Hitler in Germany and his conquest of European countries between 1939 and 1941. News services and individual newspapers, aided by the radio, had on hand in Europe more than two hundred American newsmen, plus many others to tell the expansion of German Naziism and Italian Fascism.

TELLING THE PEARL HARBOR NEWS AND AFTERWARD

On December 7, 1941, a hundred Japanese planes dived down and, aided by midget submarines, struck unexpectedly at Pearl Harbor. The radio was first to tell the awful news that Sunday. United States battleships, destroyers, minesweepers and planes were destroyed. More than 2,300 army and navy officers were killed. Congress declared war on Japan the next day, and for the second time in a generation, the United States was in a worldwide war. Congress also declared, three days later, that a state of war existed with Germany and Italy. Newspapers, wire services, magazines and radio networks strengthened their coverage. Between four and five hundred newsmen covered the battles at any one time. During the three and a half years of fighting, the United States War Department accredited 1,646 correspondents.

Correspondents experienced many hardships of the soldier, the sailor, the marine and the airplane crew. They faced similar, perhaps greater, dangers than newsmen in previous wars. Difficulties of writing and getting copy transmitted back to home offices were severe.

Robert St. John of the AP, Russell Hill of the *New York Herald Tribune,* and Leigh White of the Overseas News Agency, were in Belgrade when the Germans made their attack on Yugoslavia in April, 1941. They traded their auto for a sardine boat. Making their way along the coast of Greece, they narrowly escaped destruction by mines. They boarded a troop train, which was machine gunned, and finally arrived at their destination.

One of the toughest assignments the American soldier had was the South Pacific, and it proved to be the most dangerous for the war correspondent. Clark Lee reported the Japanese invasion of the Philippines for the Associated Press. Then he escaped from Manila in a small boat. He had with him Melville Jacoby, of *Times Magazine,* and his bride. They shared the foxhole of the last defenders of Bataan. Later Jacoby was killed in an airplane accident.

Traveling in all sectors, trying to get the common soldier's view of the war, Ernie Pyle covered the conflict for the Scripps-Howard group. Even before the United States entered the war, Pyle, who had been on the *Washington* (D. C.) *News,* shipped to England where he described the German bombing of London. He continued his folksy coverage of the war when this country entered the worldwide conflict, winning a Pulitzer prize for his correspondence. Pyle was killed while reporting the war.

PHOTOGRAPHERS DON UNIFORMS

American journalism also covered the war by means of pictures. Cameramen faced a tremendous job of worldwide picture reporting. Because the war was not concentrated as in 1917-1918, it posed extensive problems of manpower, expense, transportation and communication.

The job of toting and preserving chemicals to develop and print pictures in the subzero Arctic or in tropical jungles had to be met. Interest in pictures reached a new high among United States readers when the war began. For the first time in any war, pictures were transmitted across the continent by wire, across oceans by radio waves. A machine was developed to send pictures over the air waves direct from a war front to the United States.

Responsibilities for the photography job fell primarily on three American picture-gathering agencies, the Associated Press, Acme News-pictures and the International News Photos. *Life* magazine had an equal stake in the task, as did the army and navy, which realized the importance of publicizing their war activities and still not revealing military information.

The wartime photographic pool, known among picture men as "The Pool," was developed. The three picture services and *Life* magazine, signed agreements in January, 1942, to pool their resources, to supply photographers from all four organizations for all fronts and to make their pictures available to all four participants. This eliminated scoops, but better coverage at less cost was obtained. The combined picture product was made available to all the daily and weekly newspapers of the country through the photo agencies.

Frank Prist, an Acme photographer, trudged with the Americans and British up from Port Moresy across the mountains and jungles to the sea at Buna. It was a hard trek for a man who had been covering the movie beat in Los Angeles, but Prist stood up under it. Once he lost his camera in a river covered with mangrove beds. The natives refused to retrieve it. Prist jumped in and managed to get his equipment. The natives then told him that the river was full of crocodiles! Sam Goldstein, of International, one of four Pool cameramen who landed with Americans in North Africa, went to work sooner than he planned. The ship carrying him from England was torpedoed. Goldstein took pictures of the sinking, the transfer of troops and their safe arrival in Africa.

RADIO REACHES NEW PEAKS IN WAR BROADCASTS

Between World War I and World War II, the country witnessed the birth and phenomenal growth of radio as a news medium. During the first World War American people got their news from extras, hawked on street corners. During the second conflict, sixty million radio sets were in use, informing Americans hourly of developments on the fighting fronts. H. V. Kaltenborn, of the Columbia Broadcasting System, was on the air continuously when Hitler moved into Czechoslovakia and when Mussolini marched into North Africa.

Later, when the United States entered the war, radio newscasters poured out the latest information from the various battlefronts. Wire recorders were used to give newscasts directly from war theaters. On D-Day, June 6, 1944, when the English and United States armies invaded Normandy, France, radio pooled its resources for the big newscasts. George Hicks, of the American Broadcasting Company, recorded the invasion aboard a landing craft moving toward the beach and under attack by the enemy.

Meanwhile, the home front still had to be covered. The typewriter battalion, working in Washington and in every town in the United States, faced tremendous problems of getting the news and printing it. Newsmen had to gather news not only of the military but of industries which produced materials of war. Effects of the war on the civilian population and the multiple campaigns conducted to get people to save scrap, to raise vegetables and to get both men and women into war-production jobs, all were important.

Newsmen were confronted with the same problems they had faced in previous wars: They wanted to tell the public news of what was going on. Yet they did not want to give information to the Germans and the Japanese. At the same time they resented any loss of their freedom to report the news.

OFFICE OF WAR CENSORSHIP CREATED

From experience of previous wars, the President established the Office of War Censorship and the Office of War Information. When President Franklin D. Roosevelt founded the censorship office in December, 1941, with Byron Price, AP executive news editor in charge, he declared that all Americans "abhor censorship as they abhor war, but the experience of this and other nations demonstrates that some degree of censorship was essential in war time." Price's job was to head a division which advised on censorship outside of military areas. A code was set up which banned improper publication of information dealing with planes, troops, fortifications, shipping, weather and production, until released by proper authorities. Radio was requested expressly to avoid mentioning of weather news which could be used by the enemy.

Elmer Davis, former *New York Times* editorial writer and later news commentator for the Columbia Broadcasting Company, headed the Office of War Information, established in June, 1942. This office was an outgrowth of four governmental agencies which had been set up previously to handle war news. President Roosevelt asked Davis to coordinate war information activities of all the federal departments and agencies so that news would be accurate and consistent, with duplication being avoided.

An important phase of the OWI work was explanation to the civilian population of why there were restrictions on many activities and food. This had to be understood if the government was to get cooperation and compliance. Campaigns and drives constituted an important part of the work of the Office of War Information. More than fifty campaigns were conducted with the help of the communications media. Newspapers, magazines and radio stations turned into great and influential social instruments to carry out civic and war objectives. These drives included food, victory gardens and fat salvage. Other campaigns aimed at reducing forest fires, getting people into war jobs and keeping them there, and recruiting for the various branches of the armed forces.

The results were amazing. More than fifteen million gardens were started in 1942, producing about half a ton of food on each plot of land. The next year, about twenty-three million were started, with nineteen to twenty million completed. Twenty thousand tons of scrap were collected each month for the steel production.

GI NEWSPAPERS PUBLISHED ON MANY FRONTS

Telling the story also of the war and the army, navy and air force activities were publications of the GI's. About one thousand camp papers were issued, ranging from four-page mimeographed sheets to tabloid and standard-sized newspapers. They were printed on duplicating machines, offset and regular flatbeds and rotaries. Newspaper plants near Army camps were used. Some papers had excellent news and features, cartoons and pictures; all reported the regular news and the gripes and groans of men in uniform. Newspapers were also issued on ships at sea.

As in World War I, overseas newspapers were produced under difficult circumstances. In April, 1942, *Stars and Stripes,* published first in World War I, was reissued. First appearing as a weekly in London, seven months later it became a daily. A tabloid of eight to sixteen pages, *Stars and Stripes* had editions which were printed in Africa, Italy and France, and later Germany. A beachhead edition in Normandy was begun, but a bomb destroyed it. *Stars and Stripes* obtained news from the wire services and featured Bill Mauldin's cartoons on the life of the GI. *Stars and Stripes* reached a circulation of one million.

Selling for five cents, *Yank,* a publication of a more literary type, was founded about the same time as *Stars and Stripes.* It had twenty-two editions which reached a circulation of 2.5 million. The marines had their own newspaper, *Leatherneck.* In remote installations, soldier newspapers were also issued, the *Kodiak Bear* appearing in Alaska, the *White Falcon* being published in Iceland.

FINAL WAR SCOOPS CREATE INTEREST, STIR DEBATE

At the end of the war, several incidents relating to coverage of the finish of the conflict created considerable controversy. The first of these has been dubbed "The Ed Kennedy Case." On May 7, 1945, sixteen newsmen representing newspapers, news services and radio networks, witnessed the signing of the peace in General Dwight D. Eisenhower's headquarters in Rheims. They had been told not to communicate facts about the conference until the news was released officially. The release was held up until the next day at 3 P.M.

Meanwhile, Edward Kennedy, Associated Press chief of the Western Front, listened over the radio to German announcements of the surrender broadcast in Denmark. The news was picked up in England and also reached armies in the field. Kennedy decided to file the story without waiting for official release. He dictated three hundred words out of fifteen hundred when the military's phone he was using faded out. But he had produced a great news beat.

News of the surrender and the victory was published in American newspapers and happy celebrations were begun. Newsmen then raised the question: Had Kennedy violated the pledge not to release the news? Had he been unethical? By military order he was suspended from serving as a correspondent in Europe. He and two assistants were discredited as war correspondents, but nothing further was done to punish them. The discrediting was penalty enough.

In his defense, Kennedy said that postponement of the announcement of the surrender was not a military matter but political, as Stalin had requested simultaneous announcement in all countries. Later, when the excitement died down, Kennedy was restored to his full rights as a correspondent. After various vacations, Kennedy left the AP, obtaining a job as managing editor of a California newspaper.

False UP Dispatch

Four months after the AP case, the United Press carried a false dispatch about a Japanese surrender. Two days before actual surrender on August 14, 1945, the UP carried on its wires the flash that the President had just announced that Japan had accepted the surrender terms of the Allies. The Washington Bureau checked, found the flash false. The news was ordered killed. But radio newscasters had already picked up the news and broadcast it. News editors on newspapers, however, were alerted by the flash but were waiting for a regular bulletin. They did not get caught. The UP management instituted a check to determine what hoaxer put the news on the wire. Although officials found the news had been sent from a southern relay point, the guilty person was never found.

Chapter 42

Press Associations Girdle Nation, World

The Associated Press, the United Press and the Hearst International News Service continued to expand, introducing new machinery for quicker, more economical transmission of news.

ASSOCIATED PRESS COVERS FAR-FLUNG NEWSFRONTS

The sweeping decision of the Supreme Court of Illinois in 1900 stunned members of the Associated Press. It will be recalled that the judge declared that AP was in the nature of a public utility, and in consequence, the organization was bound legally to supply, without distinction, or discrimination, any persons who wished to publish information and news. A new corporation was formed in New York also called the Associated Press. New York had a liberal law applying to cooperatives and nonprofit organizations. The provision of the law included one which stated that "no person who was not duly elected shall have any rights or interests in the corporation nor enjoy any of its assets."

Kent Cooper, traffic manager and later general manager of the Associated Press, carried on a twenty-year crusade to free the AP of the entangling and repressive international news service alliances which had been made in 1893 by general manager Melville E. Stone. The three dominant agencies, Reuter's of Great Britain, Havas of France and Wolff of Germany had divided among themselves coverage and distribution of world news. All news of foreign countries which the AP received in the United States came through these agencies; in like manner, all the AP news sent from the United States was distributed to newspapers throughout the world by these organizations. These associations were in close alliance with European governments. This made for distortion of foreign news arriving in this country and the selection of news about the United States which the foreign agencies transmitted. The foreign papers were filled with United States murders, lynchings, gang wars and accidents.

Cooper wanted the AP to have the right to get the news before its publication in the foreign press and to transmit it quickly. He desired to establish in other European countries press associations similar to the AP, free from private or government control. He recognized that Roy W. Howard, of the Scripps-Howard association of newspapers and manager of the United Press, already had freed his service from the foreign control. Although Cooper's efforts were first blocked by general manager Stone who thought it would be very expensive to set up independent bureaus in Europe, Cooper was later able to persuade Stone and the board of directors of the AP to let him explore this problem. On Stone's retirement in 1925, Cooper became general manager, and four years later proceeded to establish the Associated Press in Great Britain, Paris and Germany. He placed correspondents in these cities and opened AP bureaus. By 1934 the AP alliance with the old foreign news agencies was finished.

Cooper also made a number of improvements in domestic news coverage and transmission. He persuaded the telephone company to lower its rates, and also proved that a number of newspapers could be linked in a talking-news circuit. News was transmitted by telephone to all newspaper offices from a centrally located AP bureau. This method was used until the introduction of the Morkrum Telegraph Printer, or teletype circuit, in 1914. One of Cooper's greatest contributions to the AP service was his development of state bureaus as the basic unit of AP operations. Adjusting to the changing public interests and the sharp competition of the United Press, the Associated Press began to furnish an afternoon sports service, a financial service and a feature service.

News piracy proved to be a thorny problem for the AP, and it finally brought a suit all the way to the United States Supreme Court. The question was whether a newspaper had a legal and exclusive right to the news it covered, and whether this right prevented any individual, newspaper or wire agency from picking up the news and copying it after it had been printed.

Legal cases relating to news seemed to point to the fact that the organization which distributed the news as a service had a property right in the news. Although these decisions upholding the property right in the news were on the books, newspapers continued to steal the AP news. World War I stimulated the activities of news pirates. Without extensive news-gathering organizations abroad, various news agencies began to prey more and more on the reports of the Associated Press.

The British government barred in 1916 the Hearst International News Service because of what the British termed garbling of messages and breach of faith. Other European countries followed the British lead. Despite these actions, the Hearst news service continued to supply the news to American papers as though Hearst correspondents were receiving the information from original sources.

The pirating practices of INS were exposed by an employee, who reported that news was being bought from the AP. With written statements and affidavits, Cooper took the suit to the federal district court in New York in 1917. When the Hearst papers lost the suit, the case was moved to the United States appeal court in New York where Justice Pitney gave the majority opinion which upheld the AP. The court ruled that the literary copyright law did not apply to news because it was not a creation but a report of a public event. The decision turned on the question of unfair competition in business. News was costly to obtain and must be distributed while it was fresh; any unauthorized appropriation of news to be sold for profit was unfair competition. Justice Oliver Wendell Holmes dissented.

In the early 1940s the *Chicago Sun* sought to be admitted to membership in the Associated Press, as indicated in Chapter 37 on "Midwestern Journalism Voices." The *Sun* could not join the AP without the consent of other publishers in the service. Consent was refused and the Department of Justice prosecuted the AP for violation of the Sherman Anti-Trust Act. The lower federal district court found against the AP; later the United States Supreme Court upheld the decision. When the AP revised its rules at the next meeting, the *Chicago Sun* was admitted to membership. The decision had the effect of democratizing the news agency, allowing any publisher the opportunity to obtain the AP report if he joined the Associated Press.

UNITED PRESS—ENTERPRISING SERVICE

Chief rivals of the Associated Press were the United Press and the International News Service. When Edward W. Scripps, founder of the Scripps chain, did not want to join the AP when it was formed, he proceeded to organize his own news service on a national scale. He worked out a cooperative arrangement with Publishers' Press, and then combined the services of the Scripps-McRae and Scripps News Association, which had been serving each sectional group of his newspapers. He called his new service the United Press Associations.

The new general manager Roy W. Howard now began to set up a foreign service organization competitive with the Associated Press. The UP made contracts with independent news agencies in England,

Germany and Australia in 1909, while the AP was hamstrung by its alliances with Reuters', Wolff and Havas. Howard later built up strong news contacts in Japan and the Far East, and was able to send exact war communiqués of Germany to South American newspapers during World War I because he was not controlled by European agreements.

The UP began to humanize its news by stressing persons and outstanding personalities in the news. Routine news was eliminated. Activities of people who never had been covered before were reported.

Unlike the AP, which required membership and often a costly franchise in the early decades of the century, the United Press service was sold to anybody or any newspaper which could pay for it. Because of its open policy toward selling its service and because of its improved coverage and writing, the UP service grew. By 1928 the total membership, including European and other continental outlets, reached 1,650.

Coming up in the organization was Hugh Baillie, whose career reflected the growth of the UP from pigmy to giant, as he had been with the service for a number of years. Baillie was a strong, dynamic personality and had much impatience. Baillie preferred to work away from the desk in New York and he often flew into dangerous situations such as the war zones to get the news. When his superior, Karl Bickel, retired in 1935, Baillie was promoted to presidency of the UP.

By midcentury the UP supplied with dispatches thirty-five hundred newspapers, radio and television stations, spending $6 million annually for newsgathering and transmission.

HEARST NEWS SERVICES SERVE CHAIN

At the opening of the twentieth century Hearst began to see the need for a wire service which would supply his papers with timely news in San Francisco, New York, Chicago and Boston, where his dailies were published. In 1910 Hearst launched the International News Service for evening newspapers, with Richard A. Farrelly at the head of the wire services. During World War I, England denied the use of the British trans-Atlantic cables to Hearst; France and Japan gave the publisher the same treatment. A number of American editors felt that the Hearst news services had a taint of Hearstian propaganda in them. Even Hearst editors found the services "reliably unreliable," according to Moses Koenigsberg, one of the chief executives. It will also be recalled that Hearst lost the court suit charging his organization with news piracy.

When Koenigsberg had shown his ability to build up the King Features Syndicate, he was drafted to do the same type of job for the Hearst news services. He switched operations and made International

News Service supply news for evening newspapers and Universal Service news for morning papers. In 1927 Barry Farris became general news manager and five years later editorial manager of INS, contributing greatly to the solid development of the service. The number of clients doubled in eight years, with income increasing from $690,000 to $2 million. The Hearst slogan had been "Get it First." Koenigsberg improved on it with "Get It First, But Get It Right."

In the 1920s and 1930s INS began to establish bureaus in major cities. The Hearst service gave bylines to writers, building up reporters and special correspondents who could write interestingly and with popular appeal. In the foreign field, H. R. Knickerbocker and Floyd Gibbons became outstanding Hearst writers. Bob Considine, James L. Kilgallen and, later, Inez Robb received bylines for their national news stories. In sports, Paul Gallico, Damon Runyon and Arthur "Bugs" Baer had wide followings. Edwin C. Hill wrote about many events from a human interest angle. Washington and New York bureaus had equally famous bylined writers.

After a quarrel with Hearst in 1928, Koenigsberg resigned. International News Service marched on without him. Joseph V. Connolly was appointed head. In 1945 Seymour Berkson became general manager. Reduced to a supplementary special service in 1928, Universal Service was killed off.

By 1954 Hearst had 2,800 clients, including magazines, newspapers, radio and television stations. A photo service supplied pictures. About 325 newspapers, including those in the Hearst chain, subscribed to INS, in comparison with 711 AP subscribers and 434 UP clients. Some papers took all three services, others had a combination of two.

MERGER OF UP AND INS

In May, 1958, announcement was made of the merger of the historic International News Service and the United Press to create a single agency, United Press-International (UP-I). This consolidation followed the trend of daily newspaper mergers, with the wire agency consolidation effected for similar economic reasons. In explaining the reasons for the merger, Frank A. Bartholomew, president of the UP, said, "Economics was an important factor in the creation of the great news network. Costs of covering the world newsfront have risen steadily with the rapidly improving means of transmitting both news and pictures and electronic processes."

The wire service consolidation caused an investigation by the United States Senate Anti-Monopoly Subcommittee, whose chairman was Senator

Estes Kefauver (D. Tenn.). The committee was concerned with the possibility that the merger represented an antitrust violation. The senate hearings brought out that the Associated Press offered its services exclusively to its own membership. Witnesses testified to the extreme losses of both the INS and the UP. With this evidence before him, the Attorney General concluded that the formation of the UP-I fell easily within the purview of the antitrust laws exemption. The Act stated that no violation of the antitrust law existed where an acquired company had been losing money. This was the end of the International News Service. Many of its personnel, however, were absorbed into the new United Press International wire service.

UP-I Meets Challenge

Following the merger, the UP-I has sought to meet the challenge of the big stories in both domestic and foreign news coverage. Efforts of the scientists to probe into outer space have been reported by bureaus in Florida and California. UP-I correspondents dispatched news of the Vienam War as thousands of American troops were sent into the battle. On the national scene, the wire agency has reported the Negro struggle to gain political rights and economic advantages. Full coverage has been given the Negro ghetto uprisings in the city slums. The need to explain the news-behind-the-news has been met with additional explanatory material in both wire and UP-I news-feature departments.

With the opening of 1960, the UP-I reported world news for more readers and listeners than ever before. It delivered news and pictures to 6,208 clients. President Bartholomew reported the agency maintained 234 news and picture bureaus in fifty-seven countries. Of these bureaus, 140 offices were in the United States. More than 10,000 full- and part-time employees were involved in these worldwide operations.

Chapter 43

Newsmen Fight To Get and Publish News

GOVERNMENT TIGHTENS NEWS RESTRICTIONS

During the twentieth century, newspaper organizations and individual newsmen have continued to fight for the right to obtain news of their government and to publish these reports. Various types of censorship imposed by the government during World War II have been discussed. Newsmen went along with these restrictions on the ground that publication of the military secrets might endanger the security of the country.

But new and often unnecessary restrictions have been imposed during peace time and have been used to cover up the news. Newsmen have faced a tightening of regulations and an increasing number of barriers which have prevented them from obtaining and printing news which the public has had a right to know and which has not endangered national security.

STATES PASS RESTRICTING LAWS

A number of efforts were made by state legislatures to pass laws enabling administrators to suppress newspapers of the opposition. Some of these cases were appealed to the United States Supreme Court, and have become landmarks in free press history.

Minnesota enacted a "gag law" in 1925, permitting suppression of salacious and scandalous publications. The law was applied by a court to the *Saturday Press* of Minneapolis to stop the newspaper's smear attacks on public officials. Robert R. McCormick, publisher of the *Chicago Tribune* and chairman of the American Newspaper Publishers Association's Committee on Freedom of the Press, carried the case to the United States Supreme Court. Colonel McCormick thought that the attack on the *Saturday Press* might become a dangerous threat to all newspapers.

Chief Justice Charles E. Hughes, speaking for the majority of the court, declared the Minnesota law unconstitutional because it permitted restraints on publication. Suppression was a greater danger than the irresponsible attacks on public officials. The officials, the court said, had recourse to the newspaper's attack through a libel suit.

To crush opposition, Governor Huey Long of Louisiana was able to get the legislature in 1934 to pass a 2 per cent tax on gross advertising income of Louisiana newspapers. The law applied to newspapers with a circulation of twenty thousand or more, the big city press. It was shown that a dozen of the thirteen papers affected by the law were opposed to Governor Long and his political machine. Newspaper publishers appealed the case to the United States Supreme Court. The court declared this law unconstitutional. The justices held that the Long bill was a device to limit circulation of information to which the public was entitled.

FEDERAL BARRIERS TO NEWS INCREASE

Since World War II the United States has been involved in a Cold War with the Soviet Union, a period of undeclared conflict and tension. This has been an era in which extensive preparations have been made by all nations for a possible outbreak of an atomic war which could be devastating to the world. This situation has led to uncertainties and tensions in official government circles, tensions especially related to the release and publication of news directly affecting the war situation but often only remotely connected with it.

President Harry Truman, on September 24, 1951, issued a new restricting order relating to release of governmental news. The State and Defense departments already had orders to classify and withhold news endangering the security of the country. The Truman order extended the restrictions to other military and civilian departments. Although newsmen protested these restrictions, a Security Advisory Board was set up, setting the categories of classified information which, if published, would endanger the security of the United States. There was much misuse of classified categories. A recipe for upsidedown cherry cake was classified as "confidential" by the Department of Agriculture. Other similar incidents occurred. Sigma Delta Chi, the national professional newsmen's organization, and other journalistic groups protested. They took their case before President Eisenhower shortly after he was elected. Their appeal led to the withdrawal of classified information from twenty-nine strictly civilian agencies, and modifications of other areas of restricted news. This represented an advance in decreasing the barriers to news coverage.

Newsmen received a positive break when Representative John E. Moss, Democratic congressman from California, began his inquiries into barriers to the news. He found that officials were using the "Housekeeping Law" of 1798 to hold back the news. The law authorized department heads to set regulations relating to use and preservation of records and papers of their departments. When it was passed, the Moss amendment to the law made it clear that this historic regulation did not authorize the withholding of information from the public or limiting news availability. The Moss measure stated that department heads did not have the discretionary power to determine what was given out and what was withheld. President Eisenhower, in signing the bill, said that the history of the measure in Congress showed that Congress, however, did not intend to alter the existing power of *executive agencies* to keep information or papers confidential if officials felt it was in the public interest.

This seemed to exclude *executive agencies* from the meaning of the bill. President Eisenhower and other presidents used executive privilege to keep information confidential and reporters out. Newsmen have recognized the desirability of this on occasion.

One of the campaign issues of John F. Kennedy, when he ran for President in 1960, was that the Eisenhower administration had made excessive use of secrecy. Because of this the United States Information Agency had damaged United States prestige, candidate Kennedy said. He declared further that he wanted to be a President who would take the country into his confidence and that people are entitled to the fullest possible information.

Cuban Invasion News

In April, 1961, a number of former Cubans living in Miami, Florida decided on an invasion of Cuba to overthrow Premier Fidel Castro. They had men and ammunition. They sought to land on the island, but Castro was prepared for them and repulsed their forces. The invasion was unsuccessful.

President Kennedy denounced American newspapers for revealing the plans for the invasion. Managing editor Beebe of the *Miami* (Fla.) *Herald* said he had had the invasion story and requested guidance from the State Department and from the Central Intelligence Agency, where officials said they knew nothing about the invasion plan. Rumor began to spread that the CIA had trained the Cubans and helped them in their plans. This was denied. When protest against the United States was expressed at the United Nations, Ambassador Adlai E. Stevenson also continued to deny that the CIA was involved. Later it was disclosed that Stevenson had no knowledge of the CIA's activities. After the unsuccessful invasion, newsmen pieced together the whole story, showing the important part the CIA had played in the invasion preparations. Editorial writers protested that the public had not been permitted to know about the efforts of the CIA in helping ex-Cubans overthrow a government, all of which involved the United States.

During the fall and winter of 1962 to 1963 the country was shaken by a controversy over "news management." Arthur Sylvester, chief of the information for the Department of Defense, asserted that "It is the inherent right of the government to lie to save itself when it is going up in a nuclear war," according to reports in *Editor & Publisher,* December 15, 1962 and March 30, 1963. "We in the newspaper business have got to realize that we are living in a different world that has neither peace nor war. It is difficult for all, but newsmen have not lost any basic rights," Sylvester declared.

Sylvester's views aroused the deepest ire of editors, reporters and columnists. They interpreted the phrase "management of news" to mean that the government had a right to hold back the news, distort the truth and mislead the public. Reporters said they were irked particularly by failure of the government to release quickly information on the Soviet missile buildup in Cuba.

Sylvester appeared before the House of Representatives Subcommittee on Government Information on March 25, 1963. He had either modified his views or rephrased his language, for he said: "The government does not have a right to lie to the American people." He testified that if his original statement had not been taken out of context, his statement on news management would not have been misunderstood, nor would it have raised so many objections.

STATE AND LOCAL NEWS BARRIERS ERECTED

In various hearings before official agencies and in discussions, newsmen have made the point repeatedly that secrecy on the federal level led to secrecy on the state and local level. Governors, mayors, sheriffs, school superintendents and boards became tougher as a result of the federal example.

Drives were carried on by Sigma Delta Chi and other groups of newsmen to secure (1) open access to official records (2) open government meetings. To accomplish these goals, Sigma Delta Chi drew up model laws giving newsmen and the public access to the news. The open record model law compelled all state, county and municipal records to be open for examination to all citizens. Any official who refused the privilege would be subject to removal or impeachment, and, in addition, be guilty of a misdemeanor. The open meeting law required all meetings of governing bodies of municipalities, counties, bureaus, boards, supported by public funds or spending public funds, be public meetings and be open. Persons violating the law would be guilty of a misdemeanor.

Local chapters of the professional organization pushed these measures with considerable success. They recorded that, by 1962, thirty-five states had passed open record laws, while twenty-five states had approved open meeting laws.

Moss Bill Finally Passed

After extensive hearings, the "Freedom of Information" bill (S 1160), which was before Congress in various forms for a decade, and advocated by Representative Moss, was passed by the Senate October 13, 1965, by a voice vote. The House approved the measure by a 307-0 roll call on June 20, 1966. The law guaranteed that every agency should make available a variety of information hitherto bottled up and that officials should make records available promptly to any person. In event of noncompliance with a request for information, the person might seek an injunction against the withholding officer in a federal district court. The bill called for a prompt hearing, and the burden was on the agency to sustain its action. The whole concept of judicial review was new to federal information access statutes.

The bill also contained a number of exemptions covering security and foreign policy as well as the revealing of confidential regulations relating to internal personnel. The exemptions also included trade secrets, interagency or intraagency memorandums or letters not available by law to a private party in litigation with the agencies.

President Lyndon B. Johnson signed the bill on July 4, 1966, and it went into effect a year later. He said that he did not share the concern that the language of the bill might be construed in such a way as to impair government operations. It had sufficient exemptions, he indicated. "A democracy works best when the people have all the information that the security of the nation permits. No one should be able to pull curtains of secrecy around decisions which can be revealed without injury to the public interest," the President declared.

Chapter 44

Press Technology Makes Many Advances

Inventors and scientists, spurred by the needs of publishers, have made many notable improvements in the mechanical department of the newspaper in the twentieth century. In some instances revolutionary printing processes have been introduced to speed up production, to decrease per unit costs and to improve quality and appeal of the publications.

IMPROVED PRESSES ON MARKET

The press manufacturers continued to meet the demands of increased circulations and multipaged newspapers by building larger and faster presses with a greater capacity than ever before. The machines were able to print eighty to ninety and even 128-page papers by 1902. For some publications, the presses printed seventy-two thousand 32-page newspapers per hour. New types of folders, introduced by the Goss Printing Press Company in 1907 and by R. Hoe & Company a year later, doubled press deliveries.

Press manufacturers now turned to the perfection of units which might be linked into a series of larger presses, or used individually by small papers. Between 1898 and 1902, the modern unit-type printing press was put on the market. A new type of tubular plate press also was patented for use of publishers in small cities with populations between twenty thousand and fifty thousand.

Improvements in color printing for newspapers were also introduced. In 1912 the Duplex Company manufactured a unit type of color press for one comic supplement. Later, Hoe introduced a multicolored press with eight cylinders, giving impetus to the use of colored Sunday magazine sections. Advertisements could be printed in color, and increasingly in many newspapers, readers found their advertisements in colors. By 1950 printing colored daily comics and photographs promised to be the next important step; during the next decade a number of newspaper publishers used colored pictures on a regular schedule.

Newspapers also made use of the rotogravure printing process. This method had its beginnings in England in 1895, but it was not used until 1912 in this country when the *New York Sun* and the *Cleveland Press* began to print with the process. First to publish regularly a rotogravure section, however, was the *New York Times,* which began its Sunday rotogravure section in 1914. Soon rotogravure sections became regular weekly features in a number of newspapers. A daily gravure in the *New York Evening Post* was short lived. The first experiments with four-color rotogravure were carried on in the *Chicago Tribune*'s plant, the *Tribune* calling this process "colorato."

AUTOPLATE FOR STEREOTYPING

In the metropolitan cities where publishers required a number of stereotyped plates to produce newspapers efficiently and quickly, stereotyping seemed to be a slow operation. Prior to 1900 stereotyped plates had been made manually by pouring molten metal into a tight box containing a matrix, or positive impression of the type to be produced. It was hard, hot work, involving the lifting of more than fifty pounds of hot metal in a heavy ladle from the melting pot to the casting box for every page plate cast.

The shop which could cast thirty plates in a half hour was exceptional. In fact, so costly and cumbersome was the process that some New York daily newspapers in 1900 were still printing from type, locked in semicylindrical forms known as "turtles." Press manufacturer Henry A. Wise Wood worked on this problem and brought out the autoplate which made the stereotyping process automatic. It was used by the *New York Herald* in 1900, and soon after by the *New York World, Boston Post* and *Chicago Tribune,* becoming standard equipment later in newspaper plants everywhere.

OTHER DEVICES FOR SPEED INVENTED

Several automatic devices were introduced to speed newspaper production. Improved folding and stuffing devices were also built. Automatic inking pumps replaced hand operation. New impression cylinders were constructed that gave better printing effects and greater speed.

In the new century, electricity was substituted more widely for steam as the motive power for the presses.

TELETYPE DEVELOPED

Transmission of news and pictures was speeded up in this period. The old method of transmitting news by telegraph continued until introduction of the Morkrum Telegraph Printer in the early 1900s. Under the old system the sending telegraph operators translated news dispatches into the dot and dash code and transmitted about twenty-five to thirty-five words a minute.

Charles L. Krum, of Chicago, and his son, Howard, worked to perfect a machine that would send the printed word more speedily, without the translation into the dot and dash signals. Krum's invention, the teletypewriter, could transmit news hour after hour at the rate of sixty words a minute, double that of the old telegraph method. The press associations eventually placed teletypewriters in all offices of their members or clients. In 1939 a leased cable to Europe enabled the Associated Press to send messages to New York to be relayed to member papers.

TELETYPESETTER SPEEDS PRODUCTION

Automation made inroads into the composing rooms of newspaper plants in the 1920s when the teletypesetter was introduced. Early in 1926 Walter M. Morey suggested that equipment could be developed for automatic operation of linecasting machines from one or more remote points. The suggestion was discussed with Frank E. Gannett, head of the Gannett chain of newspapers in the eastern part of the country.

Later that year the idea was further explored with the owners of the Morkrum-Kleinschmidt Corporation, manufacturers of the teletype equipment described before. During 1927 engineers of the company developed a machine which perforated tape; they built an operating unit which would automatically control the linecasting machine. Several busy years of testing and refining the equipment were spent by engineers of the Teletype Corporation. A separate corporation was organized under the name of the Teletypesetter Corporation. Experimental equipment was placed in operation at the *Evanston* (Illinois) *News-Index* during 1929 and 1930.

In 1932 the teletypesetter equipment was considered satisfactory to place on the commercial market and the first commercial installation was made in the *Newburgh* (New York) *News* and the *Beacon* (New York) *News*. News was prepared in tape in justified line form at the

Beacon News, and by means of the teletype equipment, tape was simultaneously reproduced over a telegraph line at another location, where it was used for automatic typecasting. At the end of 1960 about twelve hundred daily newspapers, four hundred weekly newspapers and many commercial shops in the United States were using teletypesetter equipment.

Newspaper publishers, looking for means to decrease composing room costs, found the teletypesetter equipment economical. The usual linecasting machine operation required many time-consuming duties and distractions inherent in manual operation. Automatic tape operation eliminated peaks and valleys of stop-and-go operation. The machine ran continuously at its highest output level, four hundred or more lines per hour. Many publishers also found it practical to mechanize the handling of taped local news copy within the plant.

PICTURES SENT BY WIRE

Although photographs were being used in newspapers more and more after the turn of the century, the distribution of pictures to newspaper offices was a relatively slow process compared to transmission of news. News pictures were shipped by train, plane, auto, or, in some instances, by carrier pigeon.

In the 1920s laboratories of the American Telephone and Telegraph Company developed a limited commercial system for transmitting pictures over phone wires. The first picture was transmitted from Cleveland to New York in May, 1924. Sending and receiving stations were set up in only eight cities. Almost an hour was required to prepare a picture for sending; actual transmission was slow and the delivered picture was blurred and indistinct.

Bad as the system was, it was all that was available, and the AP and other wire agencies used it until June, 1933 when the American Telephone and Telegraph Company abandoned the project. Kent Cooper, then AP general manager, was still nursing an old dream that a nationwide network of leased wires could be set up to flash AP pictures to members all over the country.

Meanwhile, Bell laboratories, of the AT and T which had been experimenting along different scientific lines, announced in October, 1933 a new picture-sending apparatus, faster by far than the old telephoto and far more reliable. All picture services were invited to attend a demonstration. Cooper was excited about the device. It would be expensive, probably cost more than a million dollars a year. But he felt that the AP had to follow the new trail to a new pictorial journalism. He encountered much opposition by many members who felt the scheme was impractical. The fight reached its climax at the AP annual meeting in April, 1934. After a long and intense debate the question finally came to a vote. Wirephoto was approved by a heavy majority. AP Wirephoto transmitted its first picture in January, 1935.

Not to be outdone by the Associated Press, Hearst pushed Soundphoto, developed in 1935 by Walter Howie, one of his managing editors. By September of the following year, Hearst's International News Photos had twenty customers. On February 21, 1936, the *New York Times*, having developed Wide World Photos, boasted of portable photo transmitters.

Shortly after the AP and Hearst introduced their rapid photo transmission services, Scripps-Howard's N.E.A. Acme Photo Service, entered the field with Acme Telephoto, and in June, 1936, was sending pictures of the Republican National Convention. Acme claimed a sending time of three and a half minutes per picture.

Scanagraph Invented

To facilitate newspaper reproduction of photos, becoming so important to journalism, the Engravagraph was invented to etch plates on type metal in the 1920s. The Fairchild Company, taking over the experimental work, marketed the Scanagraph machine. This machine eliminated the somewhat elaborate engraving departments of newspapers by reproducing the photographs on thin plastic plates by an electronic process. It proved economical for smaller papers, freeing regular engravers for color work. The Scanagraph cut down on overtime work and extra pay.

COLD-TYPE PRODUCTION SPREADS

With rising costs of newspaper production and the threat of paralyzing strikes, publishers sought new methods of printing which would cut costs of typesetting and even of stereotyping. The result of this search was called "the revolution" in printing, the first major change since Gutenberg. The revolution consisted of making a photoengraving of typewritten copy instead of setting it on linecasting machines.

The *Literary Digest* magazine experimented with the method somewhat successfully in 1919 when newspapers and magazines were strikebound in New York City. Then, in 1946, John H. Perry, Sr., owner of the Western Newspaper Union, acquired a string of Florida weeklies. He put his sons, John H., Jr. and Farwell W. Perry, in charge. To them came William J. Higgins, an industrial engineer who thought the old printing machine and processes were obsolete. His idea was to adapt photo processes used in lithography to letterpress printing. In November,

1947, Higgins and the Perrys came to a parting of the ways. Higgins operated a pilot plant using his process for small dailies in the East. The Perrys continued their experiments in Florida.

Meanwhile, other newspapers, magazines, and to a lesser extent, book manufacturers, plus paper, ink, photographic and equipment manufacturers were engaged in a search for a combination of tools and processes which would enable periodicals to meet the threat of strikes and to counteract rising costs. Manufacturers worked on photo-composition machines. These machines permitted copy to be "composed" on page-size film. This film was applied directly to magnesium or other plates, which were then photoengraved and put on the press. The Intertype Corporation developed Fotosetter and Lumintype. Both reproduced type selected from a keyboard on the photographic film in many sizes and faces. More than twenty complete fonts of type could be selected at will. The Fotosetter was essentially a standard typesetting machine which substituted photo equipment for metal pots and molds. It produced printed type on film quickly. Mergenthaler Linotype Company developed a similar machine, the Linofilm.

A number of newspapers began to use these machines, especially for advertising reproduction. At the mechanical conference of the American Newspaper Publishers Association held in Chicago in June, 1955, color slides showed how the *South Bend* (Indiana) *Tribune; Milwaukee* (Wisconsin) *Journal; St. Petersburg* (Florida) *Times;* and the Perry Printing Process in Ocala, Florida were using the Fotosetter with satisfactory results.

Franklin D. Schurz, *South Bend* (Indiana) *Tribune* publisher, said that "at the present time in case of most ads the photo-composition method is not cheaper." This was because the method was so new, the economics of production were only partially realized. He thought that research would simplify operations, bringing about additional economics. The *Middletown* (New York) *Record*, which began as a new paper, used offset methods from the beginning and found it successful in the 1950s. Offset production of dailies and weeklies spread as the method was improved and costs were lowered. In the 1960s even large dailies began to use offset presses for printing their editions.

Computer Operation

In the 1960s newspaper production has been further automated with linking of the computer, used in many other business operations, to the newspaper. Although still in the early stages of development and use, the computer has promised to open new areas for efficient, economical printing department operations.

Chapter 45

New Communication Facilities: Radio, Television

NEW ELECTRONIC COMMUNICATIONS MAKE DEBUT

The twentieth century may be called the electronics communication age, for the new means of communication which have been introduced are based on the use of electricity. News had been transmitted by telegraph and telephone since the previous century. Now the telephone has extended rapidly, increasing from one million telephones at the beginning of the epoch, to thirty-eight million by the midperiod. This has made for greater news coverage and quicker transmission of the news. The telephone has contributed to the growth of evening newspapers and created the distinction between legmen who gathered the news and the rewrite men who are stationed in newspaper offices.

RADIO BRINGS NEW ERA OF ELECTRONIC JOURNALISM

Development of wireless and radio had the most widespread effect on the nation, and, ultimately, on newspapers. Again, inventions and discoveries of one era had a profound influence on journalism in the next epoch. Pioneers, such as Guglielmo Marconi, were working on wireless or radio telephone at the end of the nineteenth century. He founded the Marconi Telegraph Company in 1895. At the turn of the century (1901), Marconi sent messages across the Atlantic Ocean.

The *New York Times* and the *New York Herald* recognized possibilities in wireless for news transmission and were the first to print news received by wireless. Wireless news was in competition with cable news. Meanwhile, experimental efforts to improve wireless so that the human voice could be clearly and easily transmitted were carried on.

Technically, radio was soon ready to be born as a mass entertainment and news facility.

On November 2, 1920, Westinghouse broadcast from KDKA, Pittsburgh, Pennsylvania the Harding-Cox election returns. Interest in radio mounted as more persons purchased sets.

BROADCASTING GIANTS BUILD NETWORKS

Three large manufacturing and service companies, General Electric, Westinghouse and American Telephone, controlling the patents, entered the broadcasting industry. They developed national network broadcasting and acquired the largest radio stations. All three of the giants pooled their resources and bought out Marconi. In 1910 they formed the Radio Corporation of America, a parent company. The National Broadcasting Company was formed as a subsidiary in 1930.

Shortly after formation of NBC a rival network was organized. Known first as the United Independent Broadcasters, it later became the Columbia Broadcasting System. Two new broadcasting companies entered the radio industry, the Mutual Broadcasting Company and the American Broadcasting Company. Meanwhile, by 1927, some seven hundred radio stations were operating in communities across the nation. By midcentury, twelve thousand stations were broadcasting. Millions of families had radio sets.

RADIO OFFERS COMPETITION TO NEWSPAPERS

Radio proved a news as well as an advertising competitor of newspapers. At first, newspapers, considering radio only a novelty, used it to boost interest in news and newspapers. Foreseeing trouble ahead, the Associated Press in February, 1922, cautioned against use of AP news or local news over the air. But some newspapers owned radio stations by now and wanted to broadcast the news. They feared competitive stations might use the UP or INS news. Hearst announced in 1924 that he would establish a chain of four broadcasting stations from coast to coast at a cost of one million dollars.

In face of this mounting storm, AP relaxed its news regulation somewhat, permitting the broadcasting of baseball scores. Interest in radio news was so strong that many editors ignored the strict AP rules and broadcast the results of the Coolidge-Davis-La Follette presidential election in 1924. The trend toward radio news continued to mount, and in 1928 the AP joined the other wire services in supplying the National Broadcasting Company with news of the presidential fight between Herbert Hoover and Alfred E. Smith. Meanwhile, some radio stations decided they needed to develop their own staffs to gather the news. KMPC of Beverly Hills, California, in 1934, was the first to have its own reporters gather the news. They broadcast three times daily.

The economic depression, beginning in 1929, cut into newspaper revenues heavily, and publishers began to be concerned about the upstart radio, which garnered at the time about $5 million in advertising revenue. After a survey which indicated a majority of publishers did not want to cooperate with radio, the American Newspaper Publishers Association in 1933, defined the newspaper-radio policy more clearly. The association decided to bar the giving or selling of news to radio chains and to limit its own members with broadcasting stations to brief bulletins covering events of major local, national or international importance.

PRESS-RADIO PLAN PROVES UNSUCCESSFUL

Restrictions did not check the interest in radio news. To supply news each broadcasting company formed its own broadcasting news services. The daily publishers began to back down. An agreement called the Press-Radio Plan was worked out in March, 1934, whereby AP news was to be broadcast twice a day for five minutes, but not before 9:30 A.M. for the morning news and not earlier than 9 P.M. for the evening news.

The plan proved unsatisfactory. New, independent radio news service companies were established to provide news at other times. United Press and International News Service officials felt the necessity for selling their news to radio stations for longer and more frequent broadcasts. Commercial sponsors also were found for the current news. The Associated Press in 1940 succumbed to the inevitable tide and began to furnish a regular news report to radio stations.

IS RADIO NEWS COMPETITION OR SUPPLEMENT?

Newspaper publishers found that radio did not eliminate the news functions of journalism or kill interest in printed news. Dr. Paul Lazarsfeld, of Columbia University, discovered that when big news events were reported over the air, the broadcasts whetted the appetite of the public for more details than broadcasters had provided. Radio did eliminate, however, the necessity for newspaper extras.

Big news accelerated interest in radio. In World War II people sat by their radios for hours waiting anxiously for news of Hitler's march into Czechoslovakia and Mussolini's aggressive invasion of Addis Ababa in North Africa. The great news of the Japanese bombing of Pearl Harbor in 1941, which drew this country into the war, came over the air on a Sunday afternoon. The public read a fuller account in next morning's paper. In addition to election results, politicians took to the microphone with the introduction of radio into nearly every home. President Franklin D. Roosevelt recognized the value of speaking directly to voters, inaugurating his famous "Fireside Chats," when he informally discussed economic problems. This news was reported the next day in the columns of the press.

NEWSCASTERS DEVELOP VARIED STYLES

In addition to bulletins from the wire service read by reporters, radio also offered its own newscasters who developed special styles of their own. In the 1920s Graham McNamee and Floyd Gibbons pioneered the reporting of news events by radio. Lowell Thomas and Boake Carter established reputations as newscasters and won huge followings. By the 1930s their names had become household words. Later, as World War II approached, H. V. Kaltenborn, Elmer Davis and Raymond Gram Swing became the first news analysts to interpret the news on the air as columnists did on newspapers. All these radio news analysts had been newsmen and possessed a rare blend of talent and experience their new jobs demanded. All had literary or artistic interests beyond daily journalism.

Exception to the rule that the best radiomen came from newspapers was proved by Edward R. Murrow. He had no experience other than in radio. His knowledge of public affairs and European events was equally as broad as the other newscasters. Murrow first began visiting Europe in 1932 as president of the National Student Federation. He went later as assistant director of Carnegie Corporation's Institute of International Education. Recognizing his ability, Columbia Broadcasting System appointed him head of its department of talks and education. Three years later he returned to Europe as chief correspondent for CBS. Rated a good reporter and interpreter of world news, Murrow attracted the interest of millions of American listeners during the German air-raid blitz on London in 1940 and these and additional listeners heard his later coverage of the war. Newsmen elected him in 1945 president of the American Correspondents Association of London, an honor never before given a radioman.

Besides newscasting and news analyzing, radio developed special programs for discussing current problems. "Chicago Round Table of the Air," which appeared in the 1920s, and "Town Meeting" as well as

"American Forum" began to broadcast over the networks. One such program, "Fact Forum," was exposed as being organized and sponsored by a wealthy Texas oilman. Many communities had their own local forums discussing community problems in the news.

RADIO ADVERTISING GROWS SPECTACULARLY

While it appeared that radio would be a serious competitor for the advertising dollar, the fact is that radio seemed to stimulate the investment of more money in advertising. Although newspaper advertising continued to increase, as indicated, radio advertising jumped from $4 million in the 1920s to $658 million at midcentury, but the increase came in part from the greater industrial activity of the country.

After their first opposition to radio, newspaper owners began to realize the news and advertising potentialities of the new medium. The publishers of dailies purchased radio stations or established new ones. The stations were run in conjunction with their newspaper operations or as separate establishments. Affiliations between newspapers and radio and television stations increased from 95 in 1929 to 785 in 1949. About one third of the radio stations in the 1960s were owned by newspaper publishers.

TELEVISION IS SECOND NEWCOMER TO NEWS COMMUNICATION

Television made inroads into the family of mass communications in the 1940s and 1950s, getting its start in taverns by presenting boxing and wrestling shows; but, moving soon into millions of homes, television pushed out into news and entertainment. On an experimental basis, television broadcasting began in 1929, but the public had an opportunity to see it in 1939. From then on its development has been rapid. Television has had an impact on radio, forcing it to change considerably.

Television news programs adopted many techniques from newspapers, radio and newsreels. Following the radio newscasters' practices, telecasters, in the early years, ripped and read the radio news from the wire services' teletype news, news gathered by the vast army of newspaper reporters, correspondents and bureaus throughout the world. But the telecaster has had one advantage over the radio newscaster. The audience can *see* the telecaster as well as *hear* him. This sense of realism has been television's most important contribution to news communications.

Americans from forty-eight states saw Dwight David Eisenhower in 1952 raise his right hand and promise to defend the Constitution as President of the United States. More fellow citizens saw this thirty-fourth inauguration than had watched all thirty-three previous inaugurations, from George Washington to Harry S. Truman.

Broadcasters developed several types of news programs. The first, the spot news type, focused the viewer's attention on the hour-by-hour, day-by-day changes that occurred in his community. Newsreels were squeezed in the 15-minute, later 30 minute, broadcast pattern, taken from radio. As television caught on, networks began to go beyond the wire services they first used. Network television company officials developed their own reporters and bureaus in Washington and other centers of news in the United States and in foreign countries. These television newsmen had to report the news and supply still pictures and film to accompany their stories. Reporters pounded beats carrying video recorders and portable camera transmitters in hand, on trucks or in jeeps. By 1957 Columbia Broadcasting System gave five-minute broadcasts, five days a week. Some telecasters, such as Douglas Edwards, had an audience of six million homes.

More and more telecasters began to broadcast directly from the scene of the news. Elaborate preparations were made for these special events. Millions watched General Douglas MacArthur's triumphant entry into many American cities when he returned from the Far East. Television cameras were brought into the Senate committee along with radio microphones when Senator Estes Kefauver investigated crime in America.

Today, better coverage of national and international events has been achieved by television news staffs. The broadcasting companies have added more trained men and have constantly improved their picture transmission equipment. Full crews reported the Vietnam War as the United States sent officers and troops to aid the South Vietnamese. The telecasters, both news reporters and cameramen, stood in the middle of the battles in jungles, in rice paddies and in the streets of Saigon, the gunfire bursting all around them. They brought the horror of war right into the homes of millions of American viewers. A number of television and newspaper reporters and photographers were wounded and killed while on their jobs.

On the home scene similar realism has been projected on the screens. The telecasters were on the spot when President John F. Kennedy was assassinated in November, 1963 in Dallas, Texas. Television stations eliminated all other programs to bring viewers accounts of the funeral of the President. Similar coverage was given when civil rights leader

Dr. Martin Luther King, Jr. was felled by a bullet in Memphis, Tennessee, in April, 1968. The news of the slaying of Democratic Presidential candidate Robert F. Kennedy, brother of the so-recently slain President Kennedy, in June, 1968 in Los Angeles, California, was telecast, and the stations devoted themselves exclusively to the reporting of his funeral services in New York City and the burial in Arlington Cemetery outside Washington, D. C.

Events relating to the civil rights movement spurred by the favorable decision of the United States Supreme Court regarding equality of education in 1954 have been covered by the television cameras. They reported the efforts of the Negroes to achieve education, economic, housing and political advancement all over the nation. The burnings, lootings and general riots which broke out in New York's Harlem and Brooklyn, in Newark, N. J., Baltimore and Washington, D. C. on the East Coast; in Detroit and Chicago in the Midwest; and Los Angeles on the West Coast were telecast vividly and gave viewers a sense of being on the spot. Some critics said that telecasting these events spurred slum residents elsewhere to throw Molotov cocktails and to loot stores. Newsmen defended their reporting on the grounds that they did not make the events, they only reported what was happening, and that the public had the right to know what was happening. An extensive report by the Kerner Commission, appointed by President Lyndon B. Johnson, gave an entire section to the role of the mass media and what they might do to prevent the causes of the disturbances.

Cameramen have moved into the opening sessions of state legislatures. Many sports events, such as college football games and the World Series, have been telecast to millions of fans.

The problem in telecasting news events from the beginning was the gear which was necessary. But after the midcentury mark, cameras became more lightweight and portable and more sensitive, requiring fewer lights than originally. On-the-spot television was expected to become easier.

In addition to the straight newscast and the special events, television editors developed a background program which helped the viewer understand the meaning of the news. *Telementary* was coined to describe this kind of television documentary, comparable to the series of news-feature articles in newspapers.

CBS has maintained a staff of more than forty full-time correspondents scattered throughout key news areas of the world. London, Paris, Bonn, Berlin, Vienna, Rome have established bureaus. Similarly, CBS has had reporters and cameramen at Beirut, Cairo, New Delhi, Hong Kong and Tokyo. The full-time complement of CBS in foreign bureaus and in

Bishop Mardaga Installed In Wilmington—Page 20

WEATHER

Sunny, cool today, high in mid-50's; chilly tonight.

THE EVENING SUN 5STAR

Vol. 116—No. 146 BALTIMORE, SATURDAY, APRIL 6, 1968 ★ 20 Pages 10 Cents

19 DEAD IN WIDESPREAD RIOTING; PARATROOPS PATROL D.C. STREETS

Allied Patrols Push Outward At Khe Sanh

Chicago Regaining Measure Of Calm, Officials Report

(By the Associated Press)

KING'S ASSASSIN HUNTED; VIOLENCE FLARES IN CITIES

The News American

Baltimore, Friday, April 5, 1968

White and Bl...

THE SUN

Challenge On Convention To Be Dismissed: Page C20

48 Pages 10 Cents

BALTIMORE, WEDNESDAY, APRIL 10, 1968

The Weather

Partly cloudy, cooler; high, upper 40's today. Fair, cool tonight. Sunny tomorrow. Yesterday's high, 72; low, 58. (Details and Map, Page C8)

Vol. 262—No. 125—E

Backbone Of Riots Broken In City, Officials Say; Lootings, Fires Drop, But Some Sniping Continues

U.S., HANOI ARE CLOSER TO 'CONTACT'

Johnson Reveals New Feelers On Choosing Site For Talks

Lull Descends As Allies End 5 Viet Offensives

OPEN-HOUSING VOTE SET IN HOUSE TODAY

McCormack Optimistic As Rules Unit Clears Way For Action

BONN OFFERS PACT TO REDS

Talks On Renouncing Force Proposed To Soviet

Dr. King Is Laid To Rest In Atlanta

Mrs. Martin Luther King, Jr., comforts her daughter during funeral services in Atlanta

NEW BRITISH BILL CURBS MOST BIAS

Grievance Courts Would Be Set Up In Broad Measure

150,000 March Final Time With Slain Leader

DEATH TOLL RISES TO 6; 50 POLICE AMONG 600 HURT IN 4-DAY UNREST

Arrests Near 5,000 Mark; Banks To Open Doors Today; Guard Troops Told To Remove Bayonets From Rifles

RIOT LOSS PUT AT 10 MILLION

Insurance Group Compares City Cost To D.C., Chicago

Colder

Partly cloudy, windy and colder today, temperatures in 50s. Clear and much colder tonight, lows mid 30s. Chance of frost.

Figure 56. Riots in the Cities. Television and newspapers throughout the nation covered in great detail the uprisings in the urban Negro ghettoes. The assassination of civil rights' leader Dr. Martin Luther King, Jr., in Memphis, Tennessee, had repercussions in a number of cities. Here is how the Baltimore *News American* and evening *Sun* played the news on April 6, 1968. The Baltimore morning *Sun* on April 10 featured the end of the riots in that city on page one, usually reserved for national and international events. (Courtesy of the *News American* and *The Sun*)

the United States has totaled four hundred persons, with Walter Cronkite heading the New York operations. National Broadcasting Company (NBC) has developed a parallel organization, both being in competition with the American Broadcasting Company (ABC). Chet Huntley and David Brinkley have comprised the team of national newscasters for NBC, while Frank Reynolds held a similar position for ABC.

TELEVISION GROWTH REFLECTS PUBLIC INTEREST

Figures have reflected the interest of the public in television. The number of homes having television sets jumped from 4.2 million in 1950 to 66.4 million in 1967. The number of commercial stations increased in the same time from 104 to 608 stations.

Meanwhile, advertisers recognized, too, the pulling power of television's pictorial impact. They spent $200 million on television in 1950. This skyrocketed to $2.7 billion in 1966. Considering the total spent on advertising, television's annual expenditure increased from .35 per cent to 16.7 per cent during this period.

An average television program on a national network can expect to attract an audience of 7.5 million. The typical television viewer spends an incredible total of slightly over six hours a day watching television!

Though television crowded the radio set out of the front room in many homes, the number of radio sets has continued to increase. Radio has been mobile. It has retreated from the front room but has found a welcome dwelling in other parts of the house: the bedroom, the kitchen, the basement workshop, the den and the front porch. It has also moved out of the house into cars, boats, ballparks and beaches. Radio has been a personal companion, a constant provider of entertainment and information for people everywhere. Though television took a big bite out of radio's nighttime audience, chiefly during prime network hours, the great increase of radio sets in use has offset this loss with increased listening in the morning and afternoon hours. Eighty-two million sets have been in use in American homes, shops and offices, and another thirty-five million sets have been operating in cars, boats, tractors and other places outside the home.

Further analysis revealed that radio can more effectively reach certain groups or specialized audiences. Where advertisers deal with products consumed heavily by certain specialized groups, radio has been used by advertisers who have found that news and music have great appeal.

Chapter 46

Magazine Change and Expansion in the Twentieth Century

MAGAZINES REFLECT SOCIAL, ECONOMIC, CULTURAL CHANGE

Reflecting social changes, economic growth and educational advances of the country, the magazine market, like the newspaper market, has expanded. Old magazines have changed format, style and publishing pattern. When they have failed to meet public needs, they have expired or merged. New types of publications then have made their appearance.

A variety of magazines to suit nearly every taste has been published. Circulations of some with a mass appeal have reached into the millions, and national advertisers have found these publications effective media. Twelve to fifteen magazines by midcentury had circulations of two million or more; national advertising in such periodicals reached $442 million by 1947. By 1968 this volume totaled $1.2 billion. With increased revenue, publishers have been able to buy the best in art, in paper and in writing skill. Like newspaper chains, some magazine companies have become great industrial empires, ranking with other vast business enterprises.

Magazines and newspapers have competed, and through an interacting process, influenced each other deeply. In some instances, newspaper publishers have bought successful national magazines, just as they have radio and television broadcasting stations.

This section will focus on magazines concerned primarily with current affairs and those which comment on news events.

MUCKRAKERS EXPOSE EVILS

Between 1902 and 1912 muckraking magazines appeared. Writers in this new type of periodical sought to expose the evils in American life. They wanted to show that crime was related to politics, business and government. These writers also wished to demonstrate the connection between the evils of business and politics. They exposed the meat-packing industry, insurance company corruption, railroad rate fixing and discriminations. The magazinists also wrote about the exploitation of child labor and the prostitution industry involving young girls.

In the Gilded Age, while Pulitzer and Hearst crusaded in the large cities, Scripps used the exposé in the smaller towns, and other publishers followed the lead. The magazine which launched the exposure trend was *McClure's.* Samuel S. McClure was always sensitive to what the public would want and would read. He had built up a newspaper syndicate and established *McClure's* magazine, it will be recalled, at the end of the last century. The publisher recognized that the trusts were on people's minds; the public was concerned about the rapid growth of corporations and its practices.

Ida M. Tarbell's series, "The Rise of the Standard Oil Company," began in October, 1902 and ran for nineteen months in *McClure's.* She revealed the secret agreements between the oil company and the railroads, by which railroads gave lower rates to transport Standard oil than to carry the product of rival companies. The tumult raised by the articles caused the government to bring suit against the Standard Oil Company under the Sherman Anti-Trust Act, with the company later being fined $29 million and ordered to dissolve.

Lincoln Steffens, who had written exposé articles for the New York dailies, was sent by *McClure's* to report on the various conditions in large cities. His "Tweed Days in St. Louis," in the October, 1902 issue of *McClure's,* showed how business supported political bosses because businessmen wanted certain favors. Steffens demonstrated in other articles that similar situations existed in Minneapolis, Pittsburgh, Chicago and Philadelphia.

Other powerful writers and researchers on *McClure's* staff wrote articles which caused reform in various businesses and levels of government. Ray Stannard Baker's article on "Right to Work," which told about the labor-management problems in the railroads, described labor racketeering and told how unions prevented workers from getting jobs. Baker also revealed that employers boycotted workers. Both capital and labor worked with machine politicians and criminal elements in the community, Baker said. In "Railroads on Trial" this writer showed how railroads arbitrarily fixed rates, especially freight rates. These rates discriminated against smaller shippers and farmers. As a result of investigations and hearings, Congress passed in May, 1906 the Hepburn Act which tightened up on the railroads and authorized the Interstate Commerce Commission to fix reasonable rates for the carriers.

Because of Burton J. Hendrick's "The Story of Insurance," which also appeared in *McClure's* magazine, the New York legislature passed stringent laws governing the operations of insurance companies to prevent the fleecing of the public. Ten thousand girls, many of them young daughters of immigrant families, had been lured into prostitution by a well-organized prostitution industry. The annual income of the syndicate reached $20 million. As a result, George Kibbe Turner wrote a series on this problem for *McClure's*. "The City of Chicago" in the April, 1907 issue and "Daughters of the Poor" in the November, 1909 issue stirred investigations in New York City and led to the passage of the Mann White Slavery Act by Congress in 1910. The Act prohibited transportation of women across state lines for immoral purposes.

The magazine articles met with popular favor. People waited at the news stands to buy copies. Circulation of *McClure's* climbed amazingly, from 363,674 in 1900 to 414,000 six years later. President Theodore Roosevelt was aroused to get Congress to pass reform legislation. Eventually, however, he turned against the writers publicly and dubbed them "muckrakers," for like the muckraker in Bunyan's *Pilgrim's Progress,* Roosevelt said, they looked down at the mud and failed to see the positive side in American life.

The frauds of the patent medicine industry were exposed in *Collier's* by Samuel Hopkins Adams. Many patent medicines, he showed, contained syrups with 80 per cent alcohol; tonics had cocaine and morphine in them. The Adams articles led to the passage of the Pure Food and Drug Act in January, 1907.

After 1912 muckraking began to decline. Many poorly researched articles had begun to appear in various magazines, leading to a loss of public confidence in the exposé articles. The government, too, took care of many of the evils described in the articles by passing laws and by establishing agencies such as the Pure Food and Drug Administration. The public believed, therefore, that there was little need for additional exposés. In some instances, advertisers, whose companies had been attacked in the periodicals, withdrew their advertising. Banks, which had extended credit to some of the magazine publishers, now tightened up. Some magazines, as a result of these situations, went bankrupt and others were merged with different periodicals.

Public interest in the muckraking exposés also drained off into the Progressive Movement with the election of Woodrow Wilson as President in 1912. Then World War I broke out, with the attention of the country being directed toward the European conflict and on the role of the United States as a participant in the war.

The results of the magazine exposés had led to the passage of laws affecting railroads and the food, drug, banking, stock brokerage, insurance and prostitution business. The public also had been alerted to social, economic and political problems and to shortcomings of American society.

While the magazine muckraking had run its course, the pattern of exposure had become established as a technique of magazines and newspapers. From this time on, exposés have been used by courageous newsmen on many occasions as a means of calling attention to the shortcomings of municipal, state and national government, and alerting the public to the evils of other phases of American life.

MAGAZINES OF COMMENT AND OPINION

The *Nation,* the weekly which had offered critical comment on the American scene since Godkin founded it in 1865, continued with its traditional format and critical articles and comment. When Oswald Garrison Villard, son of Henry Villard who had endowed the *Nation,* took charge in 1917, the publication developed an even more critical and economically liberal slant. Villard fought many battles for civil liberty until he retired in favor of Freda Kirchwey, his managing editor, in 1933. Other editors succeeded in making the *Nation* a strong, liberal voice. The *Nation* was prolabor, a foe of radical discrimination and opposed to unrestrained economic laissez-faire. The weekly opposed the rising tide of fascism and was in favor of some form of world government.

Croly Founds New Republic

Meanwhile, Herbert Croly felt that another journal of opinion similar to the *Nation* was needed; consequently, he established the *New Republic* in 1914. Aided by Bruce Bliven, Walter Lippmann, Edmund Wilson, Malcolm Cowley and Robert Morss Lovett, the publisher sought to build up a strong journal of critical opinion for politics, economics, literature and the arts. For a short time, Henry Wallace, former Vice President of the United States and Progressive candidate for the presidency, edited the publication.

The *New Republic* was subsidized by the Willard Straight family, as the publication could get few ads from national or local advertisers. Circulations of both the *Nation* and the *New Republic* slowly expanded, however. By the midcentury the *Nation* reached about 39,000 and the *New Republic* 52,000. In view of the huge majorities voting for Roosevelt and Truman between 1932 and 1948, these circulations were quite limited. A mass magazine formula with a liberal appeal had not been developed successfully. Seeking to fill this magazine gap, the *Reporter* followed a liberal pattern but had longer in-depth articles than the *Nation* and *New Republic,* and was published on slick paper in magazine format. By 1965 the *Nation* dropped to 28,000, the *New Republic* reached 108,000, while the *Reporter* climbed to 204,000. In 1968 the publisher decided to close down the *Reporter.*

Harper's, Atlantic

Two monthly magazines of serious purpose and appeal for a limited intellectual audience, *Harper's* and *Atlantic,* became more news conscious than previously. Their articles have been less literary and more timely, providing information and background on current economic, political and social problems. Their literary sections have continued to have high standards.

Mencken's and Nathan's American Mercury

Another of the insurgent, critical magazines of the period, the *American Mercury,* grew out of previous publication, the *Smart Set,* established in 1890. It was edited for an exclusive group. Arthur Griscom and Charles H. Towne transformed the *Smart Set* into a witty journal, calling it a "magazine of cleverness." Beginning about 1912, George Jean Nathan conducted a column of theatrical criticism for the *Smart Set,* while Henry L. Mencken, Baltimore journalist, reviewed books. Two years later they became co-editors. The two editors launched the *American Mercury* in 1924, catching the postwar cynicism and desire to reassess American life. Editing the publication alone after the first year, Mencken determined the general policy. He obtained as contributors a variety of effective writers, including many journalists, all of whom proceeded to take apart American institutions and reexamine them critically.

NEWSMAGAZINES AND DIGESTS

Some magazines have attempted since colonial times to give a coherent resumé of the news or opinions on the news. The *Literary Digest,* which had been founded in 1890, continued into the early decades of the new century to fill the newsmagazine gap. The editors offered both sides of controversies in the world and gave developments in art, literature, science and religion. The reader was supposed to make up his own mind on the information given him. Because it gave the comment impartially, the *Literary Digest* was used in high school and college English, history and civics classes.

With the development of straw votes, the *Digest* was one of the first to use them to predict political events. The *Digest* was written somewhat in heavy style, and readers' interest began to wane in the thirties. Its straw vote, giving a wrong prediction of the outcome of the election in 1936, was said to be a factor in its demise.

Luce, Hadden Establish Time

Actually, some of its public had been captured already by a new rival in the magazine field. This was *Time,* founded by Henry Luce and Briton Hadden in 1923. Luce, born in China of missionary parents, went to school in England. Back in the United States, he met Hadden at Hotchkiss Prep School, where they conceived the idea of a new newsmagazine. They developed the idea further at Yale University. Dissatisfied with existing newspapers and magazines for presenting news in disorganized, chaotic fashion, and for giving inadequate coverage to world events, they worked out a new formula.

The two young university men intended to organize the world's news of the week into a coherent and orderly account, giving the news in narrative form and telling what it meant. Luce and Hadden desired to describe in greater detail the people who made the news.

Luce and Hadden intended to have departments as the *Literary Digest* had. After five years and considerable difficulty getting financial backing, Luce and Hadden launched *Time.*

Time, whose slogan was "curt, clear, complete," met certain needs of the public and by 1928 reached 200,000 subscribers. *Time*'s success was marked, and by 1948 circulated to 1,690,000 readers. The newsmagazine developed a distinct style which became known as the *Time* style. This was characterized by inverted sentences, slick nicknames and other mannerisms. Most of these stylistic tricks were modified or dropped later. The magazine employed a staff of researchers to give background to the news and perspective to each important event. The *Time* staff engaged in group journalism, with reporters, researchers and editors combining knowledge and talent to produce copy. No bylines were used. Hadden died of an infection in 1929, leaving Luce to carry on. By 1968 *Time* reached 3,710,574 subscribers and issued a number of foreign editions. In national affairs, Luce followed the Republican banner. He developed something of a magazine chain, establishing *Fortune,* the magazine of business in 1928, and *Life,* a pictorial magazine in 1936, which will be mentioned later.

Newsweek Successful

When *Time* proved the value of the newsmagazine formula, other publishers entered the field. About ten years after *Time* was launched,

Newsweek entered the market to compete with it. *Newsweek,* some readers felt, depended less on stylistic methods and more on substantial, factual news. It published sections such as "Periscope," "Washington Trends," and departmentalized the news as had *Time.* Henry Hazlitt, conservative economist, wrote a special column. Although *Newsweek* did not achieve as great a circulation as the Luce publication, it did manage to win a substantial audience by 1959 of more than 1,200,000 subscribers. *Newsweek* was sold in 1961 to the *Washington* (D. C.) *Post and Herald,* indicating a new trend of publishers to diversify their operations. In 1968 *Newsweek* appealed to 2,090,563 subscribers.

U. S. News & World Report

The same year *Newsweek* was issued, David Lawrence, who had been a Washington correspondent, launched the *United States News* in the capital. This was a weekly in newspaper format devoted to a resumé of governmental activities, giving the background of spot news, economic and political stories. Pictorial graphs were used to illustrate serious reading matter.

Later Lawrence combined this publication with *World Report,* which dealt with international affairs. The format transformed to a small slick magazine. *U. S. News* & *World Report* sought to compete with newspapers and its rival newsmagazines by having its news backgrounded inside and headlined on its cover. The Lawrence magazine specialized in economic news and covered government with top businessmen in mind. *U. S. News* & *World Report* found 1,580,536 subscribers by 1968.

Effects on Daily Press

These newsmagazines arose in response to the need for more complete and more timely knowledge of world events than the old magazines could provide. The newsmagazines filled a publication gap which newspapers left open. The magazine editors and reporters improved styles of news stories, emphasizing color and personality. They attempted to background and place the news in context. *Time* and *Newsweek* began to affect the daily press. Newsmen became more conscious of their own stereotyped writing style and their lack of coherence in presenting world and national events. News-of-the-Week-in-Review pages were included in Sunday editions, although eventually most of these sections died out. More background feature stories on current happenings, too, were printed in daily and Sunday papers as a result of the newsmagazine competition.

Critics have risen to challenge the objectivity of *Time, Newsweek* and *U. S. News* & *World Report,* charging them with bias toward the

Republican Party in their news accounts. A series of such critical articles appeared in February, 1959, in the *New Republic.* Aware of these charges, many readers, however, have continued to subscribe to the newsmagazines because of their colorful humanizing of the news and their writing style. The magazines have also been bought because they give coherence to the news of the world and because of their special departments devoted to science, literature, education and finance and other particular interests.

PICTORIAL MAGAZINES STRIKE POPULAR RESPONSE

Luce, as noted, launched *Life* in 1936, purchasing the humor magazine with the same title for $85,000 to get its name. *Life,* like *Time,* was a brief, one-syllable word which symbolized what the editors sought to do, tell about life. Pictorial weeklies had been produced successfully before, but *Harper's Weekly* and *Frank Leslie's Illustrated Newspaper,* the two most popular, had expired. Since the *New York Times Mid-Weekly Pictorial* had failed more recently, gloomy predictions were made about Luce's venture.

Life, however, hit the right appeal in pictures in an America which had become photo-minded. "*Life*'s purpose is to see life and see it whole, to eyewitness great events . . . to watch the faces of the poor and proud . . . to see and be amazed . . . to see and be instructed."

The editors packed each issue with many photos of current important events as well as less important but more popular human events. *Life* found 7,407,712 home subscribers and newsstand purchasers in 1968.

Life magazine was followed by *Look,* issued by the Cowles Brothers. Devoting itself frequently to one big event or trend in news, *Look* won 8,212,303 readers by 1968. Other pictorial magazines, such as *Peek,* made their appearance but did not win wide markets. These picture publications compelled the dailies to examine the public and its interests more clearly. Pictures in greater profusion were used in daily and Sunday newspapers as a result of the pictorial magazine competition. The pictorial trend in both newspapers and magazines grew out of the improvements in cameras, lenses, flash and electronic equipment as well as the increased quality and speed of films. Illustrations were made possible, too, by the advances in printing technology for printing both black and white and color photographs. In the background also was the competition of the news communication media of television.

Chapter 47

Press Clubs, Unions and Associations

In the twentieth century, all newsmen (publishers, editors and reporters) have been affected by the industrial and political tides which shape the nation. The Bohemianism of the previous era continued into the first decade of the new era. Reporters felt they were professionals and white collar workers who needed no organization to advance their economic interests and to protect them. In this respect, they were like millions of employees in other industries and commercial establishments. The young newsmen hoped to become star reporters or better-paid editors.

They had valid reasons for their hope during the first decades of the period. Newspapers were expanding, for the merger process had not become widespread. New journals were launched, and older papers increased their staffs. The syndicates had made some headway but not enough to decrease local opportunities. As this situation changed in the 1920s and 1930s, accompanied by severe economic upsets, some of the newsmen's attitudes changed toward the need for organization.

EARLY PRESS CLUBS WERE SOCIAL ORGANIZATIONS

The International League of Press Clubs made considerable headway during the first decade of the twentieth century. The league held a convention in Denver in 1906 and planned to build a home for aged and invalid newspapermen. John Simon Guggenheim, copper tycoon, gave $2,500 as a nucleus for the building fund. Many press clubs in the United States had as many nonwriters as writers among their members. The chief purpose of the press clubs became social.

The National Press Club was a more substantial organization. Thirty-two Washington correspondents joined together and formed an organization in 1908, a group which is still flourishing. An office building was constructed in the heart of downtown Washington, where press associations and out-of-town correspondents had headquarters.

NEWSMEN'S UNIONS MAKE SLOW PROGRESS

During the first two decades of the era, the American Federation of Labor made slow headway in organizing workers in industries and crafts. Reporters' organizations reflected this same indifference and apathy among newsmen. The International Typographical Union, however, gave about forty-four charters to newswriters, but, as in the previous period, the locals were of short duration. Only six unions retained charters for more than five years. One of these which lasted longer was the Scranton News Writers Union.

In 1919 the St. Louis Association of Journalists was formed to improve the lot of reporters, not by affiliation with a trade union but by securing economic benefits in a dignified, professional fashion. This became known as the St. Louis Plan and had the cordial support of publishers. The St. Louis association included among its membership managing editors, but it rejected those who did not write for newspapers, as it did not want to become "another press club." The St. Louis group sponsored the American Journalists Association, which received favorable publicity in *Editor and Publisher* and had the backing of journalism schools, where chapters could be organized.

Meanwhile, a number of new newsmen's locals, chartered by the International Typographical Union in 1919, collapsed within a year after they were established. Hard times following World War I contributed to their failures. The Typographical Union withdrew from the newswriters area entirely in 1932, as reporters' unions complicated the printers' negotiations with publishers. Meanwhile, the St. Louis group granted nine charters between 1923 and 1925. Five of these locals continued and later affiliated with the American Newspaper Guild.

DEPRESSION AND RECOVERY SPUR UNIONIZATION

In 1929 the industrial depression affected all business, including newspapers. As the enormous economic disaster spread in the next few years, journals everywhere were hard hit. Newspaper advertising dropped 45 per cent. Some newspapers were forced to close; those dailies which survived, retrenched their staffs. Many newspapermen lost their jobs. In an attempt to stabilize the economy, Congress passed the National Industrial Recovery Act in June, 1933. The Act called for the shortening of working hours and the raising of wages to certain minimums. One clause, 7a, guaranteed the right of collective bargaining, thus protecting all employees who wanted to form unions.

The government was to assume leadership and supervision but industry was expected to cooperate voluntarily and submit its own codes. Companies which cooperated could fly the "Blue Eagle," a symbol adopted by Hugh S. Johnson, former army general who became administrator of the National Industrial Recovery Act. A license for all business was required; if a company failed to have a license, the officers could be prosecuted.

Through its counsel, Elisha Hanson, the American Newspaper Publishers' Association, representing the newspaper industry, objected strenuously to the National Industrial Recovery Act's application to newspapers. Hanson found especially unsavory the licensing provision of the Act, arguing that it violated the free press principle. He also objected to Section 7a, relating to collective bargaining.

The publishers' group advocated in its temporary code of August 8, 1933, an open shop principle, by which employers were free to bargain individually with their employees. The association also proposed that reporters and other editorial workers be exempt from the provision regarding hours of work. The newspaper counsel also requested exemption for carrier boys. What aroused much controversy was the statement regarding a free press which Hanson wanted included in the newspaper code. Publishers desired a statement that adoption of the code would not be construed as waiving or modifying any rights secured under the constitution. Government officials thought this statement entirely unnecessary because protection of press freedom was already in the constitution.

The important question of whether there should be two codes, one for larger metropolitan papers and one for smaller dailies and weeklies, which had different problems and less income, was critical. The final settlement provided for two codes, the smaller papers being able to take their choice. President Roosevelt signed the code in February, 1934, and it became effective in March.

Provisions of Code

The newspaper code clarified the term *professional worker* so that most news and editorial workers came under the provisions of the Act. It permitted collective bargaining. The code also provided for a forty-hour week for employees of newspapers published in cities of more than 50,000 population. Minimum wage scale was fifteen dollars a week for those larger dailies in cities of 500,000 or more. This minimum wage scaled down, depending on the size of the city. In small cities of less than 25,000, employees were to receive at least eleven dollars a week. Mechanical employees got forty cents an hour. The minimum age for carrier boys was twelve, but those under sixteen could work only during the day.

Newsmen thought that the minimum wage provisions were particularly low and that they did not provide for a decent standard of living. New York reporters considered forty dollars a week a proper minimum, but under the code, they could expect only fifteen dollars.

A Newspaper Industrial Board of four publishers and four employee members was set up to hear appeals over all labor disputes arising under provision of the code. The newspaper code was administered by the Code Authority, consisting of ten members. In six weeks after the code began, 1,000 publishers assented; the total number of publishers reached 1,223 by March, 1935.

Then in May, 1935, the United States Supreme Court declared the N.I.R.A. unconstitutional, and the Blue Eagles were taken off the newspaper front pages. By June 16, the press codes were inoperative. From that time on the question of wages and hours was thrown back into the area of collective and individual bargaining, with no recourse to governmental action. As a substitute for the N.I.R.A., Congress soon passed the Wagner National Labor Relations Act in 1935, a measure which included an article protecting the right of employees to bargain collectively. The act covered all types of business engaged in interstate commerce; no dailies were included.

Broun Spurs Formation of Guilds

Meanwhile, Heywood Broun, columnist for the *New York World-Telegram,* who had sought to organize newsmen in 1923, believed the code wage provisions were too low and that reporters should have a union of their own. He spearheaded the movement for formation of a newspaper guild. In his column in August, 1933, he pointed to the need and said that on October 1 he was going to do his best to "get up" a newspapers' union. His views were shared by many other reporters and copyreaders in other parts of the country. Even before October, a local was formed in Cleveland. The Cleveland Editorial Employees Association was followed by the establishment of similar organizations in various cities. A number of newsmen hesitated to join, fearing the wrath of publishers. Some news workers believed that reporters were professional workers and should not join a trade union such as the printers in the backshop had.

Broun, nevertheless, organized a permanent Guild of New York Newspaper Men and Women. The Guild favored a forty-hour, five-day week, a minimum wage scale of thirty-five dollars for men with one year's experience. The first number of the *Guild Reporter,* organ of the group, was issued on November 23, 1933. Other guilds were now formed in Boston, Buffalo, Cincinnati, Duluth. Newsmen also established similar organizations in St. Paul, Minneapolis and Tulsa.

It Seems to Me
by
HEYWOOD BROUN

"YOU may have heard," writes Reporter Unemployed, "that, although the newspapers are carrying the bulk of NRA publicity, a number of the publishers themselves are planning to cheat NRA re-employment aims.

"The newspaper publishers are toying with the idea of classifying their editorial staffs as 'professional men.' Since NRA regulations do not co[illegible]fessionals, newspaper [illegible] ye[illegible]fore, would co[illegible]rtedly the [illegible] instances to work [illegible] his wage s[illegible] and a[illegible] many bosses have [illegible] week. [illegible] not a single Legree [illegible]. Concerning every one o[illegible] it was possible to say, "Oh, well, after all, he used to be a newspaper man once himself."

But the fact that newspaper editors and owners are genial folk should hardly stand in the way of the organization of a newspaper writers' union. There should be one. Beginning at 9 o'clock on the morning of October 1 I am going to do the best I can to help in getting one up. I think I could die happy on the opening day of the general strike if I had the privilege of watching Walter Lippmann heave half a brick through a Tribune window at a non-union operative who had been called in to write the current "Today and Tomorrow" column on the gold standard.

Figure 57. What Started the Guild. This was Heywood Broun's first column to suggest the organization of newspapermen, which later became the American Newspaper Guild. He became the first president of the organization.

Broun called for a national convention in Washington on December 15, 1933. Delegates from thirty cities and proxies from twenty-one more met and supported the organization of the American Newspaper Guild, with Broun being selected president and Jonathan Eddy, the first executive secretary. Purposes of the organization, officials said, were to preserve the vocational interests of its members, improve conditions of work through collective bargaining and raise the standards of journalism.

Several newspapers, the *New York Daily News,* the *Philadelphia Record,* the *Milwaukee Journal* and the *Chicago Tribune* had already instituted the five-day week in all nonunion departments and found the plan practical and beneficial. Publisher Joseph M. Patterson, of the *New*

York Daily News, said, "We couldn't blame the reporters and rewrite men for organizing."

The first annual convention of the American Newspaper Guild was held in St. Paul in June, 1934, and boasted of seventy guilds with an active membership of 3,665. A number of strikes to secure contracts in subsequent years were held. The Guild charged that a number of employees were discharged for union activities. D. S. Jennings was discharged by Hearst's *San Francisco Call-Bulletin* for guild activities, the Guild claimed. The National Labor Relations Board, after a hearing, ordered his reinstatement.

Strikes were called between 1936 and 1938 against some large papers as well as the four Hearst papers, the *Milwaukee* (Wisconsin) *News,* and the *Seattle Post-Intelligencer,* the *Chicago American* and the *Chicago Herald and Examiner.* Meantime, the Guild extended its scope to cover advertising and commercial office employees, a move to which some reporters objected.

By 1938 the Guild had seventy-five newspaper contracts, and signed with the United Press. But the battle with the Associated Press was not so easy. In 1935 Morris Watson was discharged by the AP, he claimed, because of his guild activities. Such a discharge was illegal under provisions of the National Labor Relations Act which had replaced the National Recovery Act. The National Labor Relations Board upheld Watson and the AP appealed the case to the United States Supreme Court.

In the meantime, Elisha Hanson, counsel for the American Newspaper Publishers Association, urged publishers not to comply, as he said the National Labor Relations Board had no power to interfere with the press. Publishers were requested not to bargain with the Guild on the guild shop principle, as it restricted publishers' rights. Many newspaper owners refused to go along with this view. J. David Stern, of the *Philadelphia Record,* resigned from the association, while other publishers signed contracts and granted higher salaries.

In April, 1937, the Supreme Court decided the Watson versus AP case and upheld Watson again. Five justices said the writer had been discharged illegally; four declared with the AP that freedom of the press would be endangered if the Wagner Act applied to the newspapers. The favorable decision strengthened the Guild.

In the next few years the Guild developed left-wing elements, strongest in the New York City local. Fight for control of the national organization broke out. The first president, Heywood Broun, died, and leadership fell to President Milton M. Murray, and then Harry Martin. They were backed up by Sam Eubanks and Ralph B. Novak, executive vice president. The Communist Party group was beaten down.

Meanwhile, salary minimums were constantly raised. By World War II, weekly salaries rose to $55 for larger papers and $40 to $45 for smaller dailies. With great inflation of all prices in the postwar period, the Guild aimed at a $100 goal. By 1954 this had been reached by 90 per cent of the papers with contracts. Scales for top reporters in cities like New York and in the AP and UP reached $135 per week. With the increasing cost of living, goals were set at $150 for experienced reporters. This objective was achieved on a number of metropolitan dailies. By 1965 the Guild aimed at a $200 week minimum for experienced newsmen.

By 1950 the Guild in its ninety-three locals enrolled 23,740 as members, with 21,000 paying dues. Ten years later more than 31,000 were in the Guild. The Guild sponsored an annual $500 Broun memorial award, given for the most outstanding newspaper job of the year.

PUBLISHERS' ASSOCIATION BECOMES POWERFUL

In the twentieth century the American Newspaper Publishers' Association has gained in strength and has developed an aggressive ability to promote the cause of its members and to defend them against attacks of critics and hostile legislators. After 1913 the organization merged with other similar but smaller bodies. The Bureau of Advertising was established by publishers for the purpose of general promotion of newspaper advertising.

As early as the 1880s the publishers' group had expanded from the promotion of advertising into the area of labor relations, labor becoming a more pressing problem at this time. It was not until 1900 that a special standing committee on union labor was appointed and bulletins issued. An open shop committee was added in 1922.

The first great struggle over the free press issue occurred in 1912. The Postal Act was passed on August 24, requiring the filing and publication twice a year of sworn statements of ownership and management. It required also that publishers give the average circulation of daily newspapers. Publishers also had to label as advertising all reading and editorial matter for which payment was made.

When the law began to be rigidly enforced in 1913, the ANPA went to the Supreme Court for relief, but the court upheld the postal laws. The ANPA from that time on supported the law wholeheartedly. The Audit Bureau of Circulations was organized as a result of this law. The bureau required publishers to give honest circulation reports and checked their figures.

The publishers' organization, as indicated, played a prominent part in proposing and having established the Newspaper Code as part of the National Industrial Recovery Act of 1933. The ANPA fought other New

Deal legislation largely on the grounds that such measures would endanger press freedom because of various restrictions.

Meanwhile, the publishers' association had achieved a reasonable relationship with the mechancial unions. A system of voluntary arbitration of disputes was developed. Eventually, however, the ANPA could not come to terms with the International Typographical Union on the contract. Publishers objected to featherbedding practices by which newspapers were compelled to reset all matter received in stereotyped or matrix form from other shops or agencies. An open shop department was established and furnished nonunion printers to strikebound plants.

In 1947 Congress eliminated the National Labor Relations Act and passed instead the Taft-Hartley Labor-Management Relations Act. The new measure forbade the closed shop. The ANPA brought suit against the International Typographical Union that year on the closed shop provisions of their contract and the featherbedding issue. It was not until 1949 that the National Labor Relations Board rendered a decision. The Board declared that the ANPA was right in its contention that union practices are subject to arbitration and that the union had a closed shop but upheld the featherbedding as a standard practice of the union. The United States Supreme Court in 1953 confirmed this. The relations between publishers and the ITU continued to be strained. Effort of the Typographical Union to establish competitive papers in various cities did not prove successful.

EDITORS FORM AN ASSOCIATION

American newspaper editors had discussed organizing a group while attending various get-togethers. They had talked about newspaper problems at the Press Congress of the World in San Francisco in 1915 and at a similar meeting later. It was not until 1922 that Casper Yost, editor of the *St. Louis Globe-Democrat,* and author of the high-minded *Principles of Journalism,* spurred the organization of the American Society of Newspaper Editors. The original membership of one hundred and seven adopted a constitution which declared the aims of the organization were to develop a strong *esprit de corps* and to maintain the dignity and rights of the profession. The society, too, aimed to establish ethical standards of conduct and to exchange ideas for the advancement of professional ideals. Although originally aimed at admitting editors of dailies of cities of 100,000 population, the constitution of the editor's society was amended to reduce this minimum to 50,000.

At its 1923 meeting the editors adopted seven "canons of journalism." These canons set forth ethical standards which should govern newspapers and they emphasized freedom, fair play, responsibility. The editors also stressed impartiality and sincerity in newspaper work.

EDITORIAL WRITERS ORGANIZE GROUP

As each group within journalism had specialized interests, they formed separate organizations. In 1947 a few editorial writers attending the American Press Institute at Columbia University proposed establishment of a group which should be concerned only with editorial page problems. They formed the National Conference of Editorial Writers, met annually and issued *Masthead,* a publication devoted to the problems of editorial writers and directors of editorial pages: how to improve editorials, stimulate letters to the editor, arouse interest of readers in the editorial page.

SIGMA DELTA CHI POINTS TO HIGH GOALS

Newsmen during this period also developed a professional greek-letter fraternity at De Pauw University, Greencastle, Indiana. This organization parallels the professional fraternities in law and education. Sigma Delta Chi was formed in April, 1909, and the idea caught on; by the time the fraternity held its first annual convention three years later, it had twelve chapters. Sigma Delta Chi has sought to promote a spirit of professionalism among members and has made annual awards for good newspaper work. It has served as another link between practicing newsmen and journalism educators. Theta Sigma Phi for newswomen was also organized, at the University of Washington, in the same year as the fraternity was formed.

One of the most persistent battles Sigma Delta Chi and the American Society of Newspaper Editors together with the Associated Press Managing Editors Association carried on in the 1950s, as indicated, was the effort to tear down the curtains of secrecy imposed in government offices. The association was opposed to officials at all levels—national, state, county and city—keeping legitimate information about government business from the public, including reporters. With the cry "The people have a right to know," representatives of the association made speeches about this evil, and, as indicated in Chapter 43, some newsmen even brought suit to compel government officials to open their books for reportorial scrutiny.

Chapter 48

Professionalism Grows

JOURNALISM INSTRUCTION EXPANDS

Professional instruction in journalism has advanced in several directions in the twentieth century. At first courses were offered at a number of universities, then some departments and later schools of journalism were established. Some schools toward the midcentury gave graduate instruction in journalism. To the technical reporting, feature writing, editorial writing, editing and photography courses were added those which gave emphasis to the social approach in journalism. With the growing use of electronic journalism, radio and television divisions have been incorporated into the instruction of many schools. Some have become schools of communication and journalism.

Joseph Pulitzer, of the *New York World,* first proposed a school of journalism for Columbia University in 1892, as indicated, but the plan was not put into effect at the time. The first four-year integrated program for journalism, developed at the University of Illinois in 1904, and the first School of Journalism became a reality in 1908 at the University of Missouri. The difficulties at Columbia University were resolved, and in 1912 the Pulitzer School of Journalism was established with the 2 million dollars the publisher left in his will for this purpose.

Journalism instruction spread. Professor Willard G. Bleyer began to teach at the University of Wisconsin in 1905 and was responsible for a number of textbooks on reporting and one on the history of journalism. At this institution, a School of Journalism was organized twenty-two years later. Meanwhile, William J. Murphy, publisher of the *Minneapolis Tribune,* left in 1918 a large sum of money to the University of Minnesota for journalism instruction. A strong school was organized there. In a similar fashion, publishers Robert R. McCormick and Joseph Medill Patterson, of the *Chicago Tribune,* contributed money for the founding of the Medill School of Journalism at Northwestern University in 1921.

In other sections of the United States a similar pattern was followed. M. Lyle Spencer directed the studies at Syracuse University, and James Melvin Lee at New York University. Both of these men contributed to the literature of the press. In the West, Eric W. Allen developed the School of Journalism at the University of Orgeon, while Merle Thorpe built the school at the University of Washington. A strong school was organized at the University of Kansas by Leon Nelson Flint, who wrote one of the first texts on editorial writing, and another school was developed at the Kansas State College by Nelson Antrim Crawford.

By 1950 one hundred schools and departments were listed in *Editor & Publisher*'s annual directory, while sixty-nine other departments were tabulated elsewhere. About five hundred institutions were giving some instruction in journalism; some of the offerings consisted of one or two courses. Journalism instruction has been given in a number of two-year junior and community colleges, growing so rapidly in the nation. Graduate work, leading to the master's and doctor's degrees, has been offered in some of the large schools of journalism, where the emphasis has increasingly been on research in mass communications.

The influence of the journalism schools has been widespread. Although when journalism courses were first suggested, many practicing newsmen gave violent opposition, this attitude has been gradually changing as the century has progressed. Editors have begun to recognize that journalism graduates have gained not only a liberal arts education but have learned something about gathering news, writing leads and even composing headlines and making up front pages. Publishers also have been turning to schools for research studies on their newspapers.

With the growth and interest in better trained personnel has come workshops for editors, reporters and circulation men at schools of journalism. The American Press Institute set up a workshop at Columbia University, and newsmen with experience on either large or small dailies have been given the opportunity to study under Nieman fellowships at Harvard University. At Syracuse University special training has been given in news coverage and interpretation of mental health. In Washington, D. C., Director Ray E. Hiebert of American University set up with the aid of various foundations the Washington Journalism Center, where newsmen can learn firsthand more about indepth reporting of national and international news. Professor Hiebert has since become head of the Department of Journalism, University of Maryland.

JOURNALISM TRADE MAGAZINES SPREAD

Journalism periodicals have reflected developments in the newspaper, both on the professional and business sides. To the trade magazines giving the spot news of journalism have been added research publications which emphasize history, scientific research and social responsibility.

Within the trade magazine groups, consolidations have characterized the business. Jacob B. Shale, president of Publishers' Press Association, first issued *Editor & Publisher* in June, 1901. The publication was to dominate eventually the newspaper trade periodicals, as it purchased most of its competitors. Besides giving top news of developments in editorial, press technology, advertising, circulation, and financial phases of journalism, *Editor & Publisher* campaigned for statements of verified circulations of newspapers and backed the establishment of the Audit Bureau of Circulation. The periodical has fought regularly through the years for a free press and clobbered those who would erect barriers to news on any governmental level.

To answer the needs of publishers of weeklies and small-town dailies, *Publishers' Auxiliary* in newspaper format was founded in 1865 by the Western Newspaper Union, a printers' supply and ready-print company. The publication was merged in 1905 with the *Western Publisher,* the house organ for this company. John H. Perry obtained control of the Western Newspaper Union in 1938 and issued both the *Publishers' Auxiliary* and the *American Press,* the latter printed in magazine form. These two publications were later operated under different ownerships. *Publishers' Auxiliary* shifted, in accord with the new trends, to tabloid format and to offset printing, producing an attractive publication with many clear, well-reproduced photos.

PROFESSIONAL PUBLICATIONS MULTIPLY

Desiring to have a publication which would discuss teaching problems and trends in journalism, journalism educators decided in 1924 to issue the *Journalism Bulletin* to be edited by Professor Lawrence Murphy, of the University of Illinois. Six years later Professor Frank L. Mott, then of the University of Iowa, became editor, adding many articles on research. The name of the *Bulletin* was changed to *Journalism Quarterly* in accordance with its increased status and changing purposes.

In 1935, Director Ralph D. Casey, of the University of Minnesota, became editor. The publication began to reflect the new emphasis on the integration of the social sciences and the newspaper. With the development of radio, research articles on this communication facility appeared. Professor Raymond D. Nixon, then of Emory University, and later of the University of Minnesota, contributed further to the progress of the *Journalism Quarterly* when he headed the magazine in 1945. Dr. Edwin Emery, of the University of Minnesota, succeeding Prof. Nixon as editor, further strengthened the magazine.

The *Journalism Educator,* presenting articles on professional education of newsmen, has been issued by the American Society of Journalism Administrators, and the *Nieman Reports,* edited by Louis M. Lyons at Harvard University, has published penetrating articles of general interest to newsmen and teachers of journalism. Published by the American Newspaper Guild, the *Guild Reporter* has dealt with wages and working conditions for newsmen and often has contained articles on journalism trends. In addition to these publications, newsmen and students have had the opportunity to read stimulating articles about their profession in the *Quill,* issued by Sigma Delta Chi, and in the *Masthead,* published by the National Conference of Editorial Writers, dealing with editorial writing and editorial page problems.

Meanwhile, the University of Montana's School of Journalism brought out a general interest magazine for newsmen. This was followed by the analytical *Columbia Journalism Review,* produced by Columbia University, carrying searching articles on the strength and shortcomings of the profession. Of particular interest has been the *News Workshop,* produced by students at New York University and carrying well-researched and lively written articles on current New York City newspapers and general journalism trends.

References

This is the journalistic period during which many books on newspapers and newsmen were issued, and many magazine articles were published. See general histories of American journalism, *Dictionary of American Biographies* and *More Post Biographies* (University of Georgia Press) (1943-1947). Extensive references may be found, in addition to those mentioned, in *Readers' Guide to Periodical Literature, Journalism Quarterly Index, New York Times Index* and *Industrial Arts Index*. Check newspapers and magazines at the time of editors' or publishers' deaths and when papers merged or changed ownership.

NEW YORK JOURNALISM

New York World

ADAMS, SAMUEL H., *A. Woollcott, His Life and His World*, New York: Reynal & Company, Inc., 1945. (Biography of New York reporter and theatre critic.)

CHILDS, MARQUIS and JAMES RESTON, *Walter Lippmann and His Times*, New York: Harcourt, Brace & World, Inc., 1959. (Excellent essays on the editor-columnist.)

HEATON, JOHN L., *Story of a Page*, New York: Harper & Row, Publishers, 1913. (Deals with the *World*'s editorial views.)

KRAMER, DALE, *Heywood Broun*, New York: Current Books, 1949. (Only biography of *World*'s columnist and founder of American Newspaper Guild.)

WEINGAST, DAVID E., *Walter Lippmann*, New Brunswick, N.J.: Rutgers University Press, 1949. (An informative biography of the editor.)

See previous entries about *World* by Barrett, Juergens, Rammelkamp, Seitz, Swanberg in section on Gilded Age Journalism.

William Randolph Hearst

"Portrait," *Fortune Magazine* 12:109, November, 1935. (Shows Hearst in detail from the Henry Luce-*Time* point of view.)

Editor & Publisher vol. 84, April 21, August 18, September 1, 1941.

Notice previous entries on Hearst by Carlson and Bates, Lundberg, Swanberg and Tebbel in Gilded Age Journalism. Tebbel and Swanberg bring the account of Hearst up to date. Both are excellent.

Adolph Ochs, Sulzberger, and New York Times

FINE, BARNETT, *A Giant of the Press*, New York: Editor & Publisher Library, 1933. (Biography of Carr Van Anda, *Times*' managing editor.)

KAHN, ROGER, "House of Adolph Ochs," *Saturday Evening Post* 238:32-38, October 9, 1965. (The latest study of the *New York Times,* with changes being made in operations and personnel.)

"Without Fear or Favor," *Time Magazine* 55:68-74, May 8, 1950. (An extensive account of the *New York Times.* See other magazines during this week, the one hundredth anniversary of the founding of the daily.)

See previous entries on *Times* and Ochs by Berger, Davis, Johnson, in Gilded Age Journalism.

New York Herald Tribune

BRITT, GEORGE, *Forty Years—Forty Millions,* New York: Farrar and Rinehart, 1935. (A full and critical biography of Frank Munsey and his chain.)

Editor & Publisher, July, 1959, had articles on new publisher, J. H. Whitney, and new editor, Robert White, II.

GARDNER, MONA, "Queen Helen," in Drewry's *More Post Biographies.* (Deals with Mrs. Ogden Reid.)

ROOSEVELT, NICHOLAS, *A Front Row Seat,* Norman: University of Oklahoma Press, 1953. (A *Tribune* editorial writer gives his biography.)

SHAPLEN, ROBERT, "Denson's Revolution at the Herald Tribune," *Saturday Review* 44:36, July 8, 1961.)

For news and editorial reaction to the closing of the *World Journal Tribune* see *Editor & Publisher,* May 13, 1967, and other magazines and newspapers during this period.

See previous entries, Baehr, Seitz, in Part Four.

E. W. Scripps, Roy Howard

DAVIS, FORREST, "Press Lord," *Saturday Evening Post,* March 12, 1938. (Reprinted in Drewry's *Post Biographies.*)

LIEBLING, A. J., "Publisher," *New Yorker* vol. 17, August 9, 16, 23, 1941. (Story of Roy W. Howard.)

See biographies of Scripps in preceding era.

New York Evening Post

STERN, J. DAVID, *Memoirs of a Maverick Publisher,* New York: Simon and Schuster, Inc., 1962. (Excellent inside story of liberal Camden, N.J. and Philadelphia publisher.)

WECHSLER, JAMES A., *Reflections of an Angry Middle-Age Editor,* New York: Random House, Inc., 1960. (Biography and views of *New York Post* editor) Nevin's history of paper brings the story up to the 1920s.

See Richard Strouse entry under Middle Atlantic Press, Philadelphia.

Tabloids

ALEXANDER, JACK, "Vox Populi," *New Yorker* vol. 14, August 6-20, 1938. (Is extensive account of Joseph Patterson, *New York Daily News.* See also obituary, *Editor & Publisher,* June 1, 1946.)

BESSIE, SIMON M., *Jazz Journalism,* op. cit. (The most complete volume dealing with tabloids.)

CHAPMAN, JOHN, *Tell It to Sweeney,* Garden City, N.Y.: Doubleday & Company, Inc., 1961. (Has wealth of material on *Daily News,* first successful tabloid.)

COHEN, LESTER, *New York Graphic: The World's Zaniest Newspaper*, Philadelphia: Chilton Books, 1964. (The latest attempt to describe the antics of this tabloid.)

DANILOV, VICTOR, "Fifty Tabloids Give Lie to Their Critics," *Editor & Publisher*, January 9, 1960. (Tells new conservative trends in compact papers.)

GAUVREAU, EMILE, *My Last Million Readers*, New York: E. P. Dutton & Co., Inc., 1941. (The *Graphic* editor tells his story.)

HUGHES, HELEN M., *News and the Human Interest Story*, Chicago: University of Chicago Press, 1940. (Contains excellent material on the tabloids.)

MALLEN, FRANK, *Sauce for the Gander*, White Plains, N.Y.: Baldwin Books, 1954. (An account of *Evening Graphic* by staff member.)

OURSLER, FULTON, *True Story of Bernarr MacFadden*, Bernarr MacFadden Foundation, 1935. (An account of the publisher's life.)

SCHNEIDER, WALTER E., "Fabulous Rise of *New York Daily News*," *Editor & Publisher* 62:5ff., June 24, 1939.

SPIVAK, JOHN, "Rise and Fall of a Tabloid," *American Mercury* 32:306ff., July, 1934. (Deals with *Graphic*.)

STEWART, KENNETH and JOHN TEBBEL, *Makers of Modern Journalism*, Chapter 14, "Medill McCormick and the *Chicago Tribune*." (Deals with background of *Daily News* owners.) *op. cit.*

"This Is the Life I Love," *Saturday Evening Post* 231:19ff., February 21, 1959. (Concerns Mrs. Harry Guggenheim and *News Day*. Also "Alicia in Wonderland," *Time Magazine* vol. 64, September 13, 1954.)

PM Newspaper

BECKER, STEPHEN, *Marshall Field, III*, New York: Simon and Schuster, Inc., 1964. (Analytical study of *PM* backer.)

DONOHEW, LEWIS, "*PM*: An Anniversary Assessment," *Columbia Journalism Review* vol. 4, summer, 1965. (A competent summary of the beginnings and development of *PM*.)

FIELD, MARSHALL, *Freedom Is More than a Word*, Chicago: University of Chicago Press, 1945. (Has an account of Field's connections with *PM* in Chapter 6. See also Becker and Tebbel.)

GIBBS, WOLCOTT, "A Very Active-Type Man," *New Yorker* vol. 18, May 2, 9, 1949.

INGERSOLL, RALPH M., *Point of Departure: An Adventure in Autobiography*, New York: Harcourt, Brace & World, Inc., 1961. (The editor of *PM* tells his own story.)

LASCH, ROBERT, "*PM*, Post-Mortem," *Atlantic Monthly* 182:44, July, 1948. (An excellent analysis of the liberal tabloid.)

TEBBEL, JOHN, *The Marshall Fields*, New York: E. P. Dutton & Co., Inc., 1947. (Tells about the backer of *PM* and the *Chicago Sun*.)

NEW ENGLAND JOURNALISM

CANHAM, ERWIN, *Commitment to Freedom: The Story of the Christian Science Monitor*, Boston: Houghton Mifflin Company, 1958. (A highly readable history of the daily with ethical standards. Shows revisions in the paper made by Canham.)

CHILDS, MARQUIS, "The Christian Science Monitor," *Saturday Evening Post* 218:14, September 15, 1945.
See previous entries in Gilded Age era on Boston, Hartford and Springfield.

MIDDLE ATLANTIC PRESS

Philadelphia

STERN, J. DAVID, *Memoirs of a Maverick Publisher*, New York: Simon and Schuster, Inc., 1962. (Publisher Stern tells interesting inside story of the *Philadelphia Record* and its final closing.)
STROUSE, RICHARD, "Let's Look at the Record," *New Republic* 116:15-18, February 24, 1947. (Recounts story of *Philadelphia Record*.)
WITTELS, DAVID G., "The Paper That Was Tailored to a City," *Saturday Evening Post* vol. 217, April 7, 1945. (A sympathetic, yet objective account of William McLean and the *Philadelphia Evening Bulletin*.)

Baltimore

JOHNSON, GERALD *et al.*, *Sunpapers of Baltimore, op. cit.* Penny Press Era.
KEMLER, EDGAR, *The Irreverent Mr. Mencken*, Boston: Little, Brown and Company, 1950. (Has original material obtained from the editor.)
MANCHESTER, WILLIAM R., *Disturber of the Peace*, New York: Harper & Row, Publishers, 1950. (Gives an account of the life and writings of H. L. Mencken, an editor of the *Evening Sun*.)
MENCKEN, H. L., *The Days of H. L. Mencken*, New York: Alfred A. Knopf, Inc., 1947. (Combines several of Mencken's individual autobiographies.)

Washington

CATER, DOUGLASS, *Fourth Branch of Government*, Boston: Houghton Mifflin Company, 1959. (Deals fully with Washington correspondents, written by one of them.)
CHILDS, MARQUIS, "Squire of Washington," John Drewry's *op. cit.*
"Guest at Breakfast," *Time* 67:64, April 16, 1956. (A lengthy account of the *Washington Post* revitalized.)
PHILLIPS, CABELL *et al.*, *Dateline: Washington*, Garden City, N.Y.: Doubleday & Company, Inc., 1949. (Gives facts about Washington correspondents.)
See also magazines at time of merger of *Post* and *Times-Herald*, 1954, and on death of Eugene Meyer, July 17, 1959.

SOUTHERN PAPERS

DANIELS, JOSEPHUS, *Editor in Politics* vol. 2 of autobiography, Chapel Hill: University of North Carolina Press, 1941. (Has some material but not as useful for journalism history as first volume.)
———, *Shirt-Sleeve Diplomat*, Chapel Hill: University of North Carolina Press, 1947. (Deals with New Deal era.)
WHITE, LLEWELLYN, "Papers of Paradox," *The Reporter* 2:22, January 31, 1950. (Deals fully with *Louisville* (Ky.) *Courier-Journal*, plus the afternoon *Times*.)
See previous entries: Sass, *Outspoken*; biographies of Henry Watterson; Dabney, *One Hundred Great Years: The Story of the Times-Picayune.*

MIDWESTERN JOURNALISM

See entries in Part Four, Gilded Age Journalism, for Chicago, Detroit and Ohio newspapers.

Chicago

AKERS, MILBURN P., "Chicago's Newspaper Concentration," *Nieman Reports* 13:20, July, 1959. (Gives reasons for consolidations in Chicago.)

ALEXANDER, JACK, "Up From Akron," Drewry, *op. cit.* (Deals with publisher John S. Knight.)

BEASLEY, NORMAN, *Frank Knox, American,* New York: Doubleday, Doran, 1936. (Has some facts on newspaper career.)

BECKER, STEPHEN, *Marshall Field III, op. cit.* (Gives an account of life of liberal publisher of the Chicago *Sun* and New York *PM.*)

"The Challenger," *Time* 77:60, January 20, 1961. (Tells about Marshall Field, Jr., in Chicago journalism.)

"Knight of the Press," *Newsweek* 45:97, April 25, 1955. (A lengthy portrait of the publisher.)

LINN, JAMES W., *James Keeley, Newspaperman,* Indianapolis: The Bobbs-Merrill Company, Inc., 1937. (Only biography of important managing editor of *Chicago Tribune* at beginning of century.)

WALDROP, FRANK, *McCormick,* Englewood Cliffs, N.J.: Prentice-Hall, Inc., 1965. (Latest biography of Chicago publisher.)

Milwaukee

WHITE, LLEWELLYN, "A Good Paper Pays Off," *The Reporter* vol. 3, August 29, September 12, 1950. (Tells about Milwaukee newspapers.)

WITTELS, DAVID G., "Milwaukee's Dutch Uncle," *Saturday Evening Post* 220:36, September 20, 1947. (Concerns Harry Grant and the Milwaukee Journal; tells policies.)

See authors Kinsley, Tebbel and McPhaul in previous section. Stewart and Tebbel, in *Makers of Modern Journalism,* have up-to-date chapters on publishers. "Fair Lady of Milwaukee," *Time* 63:44, February 1, 1954. (Extensive study of *Milwaukee Journal.*)

Minneapolis

"The Cowles World," *Time* 72:55ff., December 8, 1959. (A detailed account of the Cowles journalistic enterprises.)

MORISON, BRADLEY L., *Sunlight on Your Doorstep,* Minneapolis: Ross & Haines, 1966. (First treatment of history of *Minneapolis Tribune.* Continues story begun in the Gilded Age.)

St. Louis

ALEXANDER, JACK, "The Last Shall Be First," Drewry, *op. cit.* (Deals with Joseph Pulitzer, Jr., and the *St. Louis Post-Dispatch.*)

HART, JIM ALLEN, *A History of the St. Louis Globe-Democrat,* Columbia: University of Missouri Press, 1961. (A thorough study with much detail.)

MARKHAM, JAMES, *Bovard of the Post-Dispatch,* Baton Rouge: Louisiana State University Press, 1954. (A particularly valuable biography of an expert newsman.)

See also special booklet, *Story of St. Louis Post-Dispatch,* issued in 1954 and other years by the daily. Gives an account of news, editorial operations and crusades.

SOUTHWEST JOURNALISM

SCHMITT, JO ANN, *Fighting Editors,* San Antonio: Naylor Company, 1958. (Deals with pioneer Arizona editors.)

See Acheson, Sharpe volumes on *Dallas News* and George Dealey. Also entries on *Oklahoma City Oklahoman* in previous Gilded Age period.

ROCKY MOUNTAIN NEWSPAPERS

ASHTON, WENDELL J., *Voice in the West,* New York: Duell, Sloan & Pearce, 1950. (Tells history of *Deseret News* in Salt Lake City.)

FOWLER, GENE, *Timber Line,* New York: Covici-Friede, 1933.

PERKIN, ROBERT L., *The First Hundred Years, An Informal History of Denver and the Rocky Mountain News,* Garden City, N. Y.: Doubleday and Company, Inc., 1959.

WALDROP, A. GAYLE, "A Chinook Blows on Champa Street," *Journalism Quarterly* 24:109ff., June, 1947. (Gives readable account of *Denver Post* rebirth.)

———, "Reborn *Denver Post* Has Prestige and Power," *Journalism Quarterly* 28:327ff., Summer, 1951. (Waldrop continues his account of the Denver daily.)

WEISS, LAWRENCE G., "Voice of Rocky Mountain Empire," *Nieman Reports* vol. 10, April, 1956. (Has useful analysis of the *Denver Post.*)

PACIFIC COAST

SMITH, PAUL C., *Personal File: An Autobiography,* New York: Appleton-Century-Crofts, 1964. (Gives account of Smith's newspaper experiences, especially with *San Francisco Chronicle.*)

TAYLOR, FRANK, "Man with a Borrowed Shoestring," *Saturday Evening Post,* December 2, 1944. (Tells lively story of Manchester Boddy.)

See entries in Part Four on Fremont Older, Ralph E. Dyar, *News for an Empire;* Turnbull, *History of Oregon Newspapers.*

REPORTERS, COLUMNISTS, PHOTOGRAPHERS

ALEXANDER, JACK, "Pugnacious Pearson," Drewry, *More Post Biographies, op cit.* (Facts and analysis of investigative reporter-columnist Drew Pearson.)

BULMAN, DAVID, ed., *Molders of Opinion,* Milwaukee: The Bruce Publishing Co., 1945. (Deals factually, critically with columnists.)

CARNES, CECIL, *Jimmy Hare, News Photographer,* New York: The Macmillan Company, 1940. (One of few biographies about news cameramen.)

DRISCOLL, CHARLES B., *Life of O. O. McIntyre,* New York: Greystone Corporation, 1938. (Story of a famous columnist who dealt with human interest material.)

FISHER, CHARLES, *The Columnists: A Clinical Survey,* New York: Howell, Soskin, 1944.

FUERBRINGER, OTTO, "Average Man's Columnist," (Raymond Clapper), Drewry, *More Post Biographies, op. cit.*
KRAMER, DALE, *Heywood Broun,* New York: Current Books, 1949. (Deals with founder of newspaper guild and the *World* columnist.)
See Lippmann under *New York World.*

WIRE SERVICES, FEATURE SYNDICATES

ALEXANDER, JACK, "Rip Roaring Baillie," *Saturday Evening Post* vol. 218, June 1, 8, 1946. (Reprinted Drewry, *op. cit.*)
"AP," *Fortune Magazine* vol. 15, February, 1937. (Has extended treatment.)
BAILLIE, HUGH, *High Tension,* New York: Harper & Row, Publishers, 1959. (A lively account of the UP's executive head and some of the wire service philosophy.)
COOPER, KENT, *Barriers Down,* New York: Farrar & Rinehart, 1942. (Tells AP general manager's story about getting foreign news without interference.)
———, *Kent Cooper and the Associated Press,* New York: Random House, Inc., 1959.
KOENIGSBERG, MOSES, *King News,* New York: Stokes, 1941. (Tells detailed development of International News Service.)
MORRIS, JO ALEX, *Deadline Every Minute,* Garden City, N.Y.: Doubleday & Company, Inc., 1957. (First complete history of United Press.)
STONE, MELVILLE E., *Fifty Years a Journalist,* Garden City, N.Y.: Doubleday, Page, 1922. (Associated Press story.)
See Gramling, AP previous listing in Part Four.

WAR REPORTING PROPAGANDA

World War I

CREEL, GEORGE, *How We Advertised America,* New York: Harper & Row, Publishers, 1920. (Creel, head of the Committee on Public Information, tells the inside story. See Mock and Larson entry.)
CROZIER, EMMET, *American Reporters on Western Front, 1914-1918,* New York: Oxford University Press, Inc., 1959.
MATHEWS, JOSEPH J., *Reporting the Wars,* Minneapolis: University of Minnesota Press, 1959.
MILLIS, WALTER, *Road to War,* Boston: Houghton Mifflin Company, 1935.
MOCK, JAMES R., *Censorship,* Princeton: Princeton University Press, 1941. (A standard work on the subject.)
———, and CEDRIC LARSON, *Words that Won the War,* Princeton: Princeton University Press, 1939. (Gives an account of Committee on Public Information. See Creel entry.)
NAFZIGER, RALPH, "World War Correspondents and Censorship of Belligerents," *Journalism Quarterly* 14:226ff., September, 1937.
TANSILL, CHARLES, *America Goes to War,* Boston: Little, Brown and Company, 1938. (A critical appraisal of U. S. war efforts and propaganda.)

World War II

CARROLL, WALLACE, *Persuade or Perish,* Boston: Houghton Mifflin Company, 1948. (Propaganda efforts in World War II.)

DAVIS, ELMER, "OWI Has A Job," *Public Opinion Quarterly* 7:8ff., spring, 1943.

KOOP, THEODORE F., *Weapon of Silence*, Chicago: University of Chicago Press, 1946. (This is an account of the Office of Censorship in World War II.)

LARSON, CEDRIC, "OWI's Domestic News Bureau: An Account and Appraisal," *Journalism Quarterly* vol. 26:3, March, 1949.

LAVINE, HAROLD and JAMES WECHSLER, *War Propaganda and the United States,* New Haven: Yale University Press, 1940.

MATHEWS, JOSEPH J., *Reporting the Wars.* Minneapolis: University of Minnesota Press, 1959.

MILLER, LEE G., *The Story of Ernie Pyle,* New York: The Viking Press, Inc., 1950. (A readable biography of a correspondent with human interest slant.)

MILLER, WEBB, *I Found No Peace,* New York: Simon and Schuster, Inc., 1936. (A distinguished war correspondent tells his story.)

MOTT, FRANK L., *Journalism in Wartime,* American Council on Public Affairs, 1943. (Has a number of articles on newspapers in the war.)

Korean War

MILLER, ROBERT G., "Censorship in Korea," *Nieman Reports* 6:3ff., July, 1952.

FREEDOM OF THE PRESS, SPEECH

BRUCKER, HERBERT, *Freedom of Information,* New York: The Macmillan Company, 1949.

CHAFEE, ZECHARIAH, JR., *Free Speech in the United States,* Cambridge: Harvard University Press, 1948.

COOPER, KENT, *The Right to Know: An Exposition of the Evils of News Suppression and Propaganda,* New York: Farrar, Straus, and Cudahy, 1956.

GERALD, J. EDWARD, *The Press and the Constitution,* Minneapolis: University of Minnesota Press, 1948. (Has free press cases.)

HOCKING, WILLIAM E., *Freedom of the Press: A Framework of Principle,* Chicago: University of Chicago Press, 1947. (See also *A Free and Responsible Press.*)

JOHNSON, GERALD W., *Peril and Promise: An Inquiry into Freedom of the Press,* New York: Harper & Row, Publishers, 1958.

MACDOUGALL, CURTIS D., *Press and Its Problems,* Dubuque, Iowa: William C. Brown Company Publishers, 1964.

SELDES, GEORGE, *Freedom of the Press,* Indianapolis: The Bobbs-Merrill Company, Inc., 1935. (A stimulating exposition by a newspaperman-critic.)

WIGGINS, JAMES RUSSELL, "The Right to News," *Nieman Reports* vol. 4, October, 1950; "Right to Know," *Nieman Reports* vol. 6, July, 1952. (Well-stated presentation of issue by managing editor.)

———, *Freedom or Secrecy,* New York: Oxford University Press, 1956.

CRITICISMS OF JOURNALISM

BLUMBERG, NATHAN, *One Party Press*? Lincoln: University of Nebraska Press, 1954. (A study of newspaper in political campaigns.)

CLARK, WESLEY C., *Journalism Tomorrow*, Syracuse, N.Y.: Syracuse University Press, 1958. (Peeks into future of newspapers; provocative.)

ERNST, MORRIS, *The First Freedom*, New York: The Macmillan Company, 1946. (A well-written, thoroughly documented piece of research.)

ICKES, HAROLD L., *America's House of Lords*, New York: Harcourt, Brace & World, Inc., 1939. (Typical of the attacks on the press by a member of President Franklin D. Roosevelt's cabinet.)

LINDSTROM, CARL E., *The Fading American Newspaper*, Garden City, N.Y.: Doubleday & Company, Inc., 1960. (Has sharp comments on the press today; written by former newspaper executive.)

ROWSE, ARTHUR E., *Slanted News*, Boston: The Beacon Press, 1957. (A carefully documented study of headlines and newswriting.)

SELDES, GEORGE, *Lords of the Press*, New York: Julian Messner, 1938. (A powerful indictment. See other volume on *Freedom of the Press*.)

SVIRSKY, LEON, ed., *Your Newspaper*, New York: The Macmillan Company, 1947. (Predictions for the future.)

CONSOLIDATIONS, CHAINS

NEURATH, PAUL, "One Publisher Communities, Factors Influencing the Trend," *Journalism Quarterly* 21:230ff., September, 1944.

NIXON, RAYMOND B., "Trends in Daily Newspaper Ownership Since 1945," *Journalism Quarterly* 31:3, winter, 1954.

———, and JEAN WARD, "Trends in Newspaper Ownership and Inter-Media Competition," *Journalism Quarterly* 38:3, winter, 1961.

RAY, ROYAL H., "Economic Forces as Factors in Daily Newspaper Concentration," *Journalism Quarterly* 29:31ff., winter, 1952.

PRESS AND THE PRESIDENTS

CORNWELL, ELMER E., Jr., "The Press Conferences of Woodrow Wilson," *Journalism Quarterly* 39:292ff., summer, 1962.

HUTCHISON, EARL R., "Kennedy and the Press; The First Six Months," *Journalism Quarterly* 38:453, autumn, 1961.

POLLARD, JAMES E., "Eisenhower and the Press," *Journalism Quarterly* 32:285, summer, 1955; 33:3, winter, 1956; 38:181, spring, 1961.

———, *The Presidents and the Press*, New York: The Macmillan Company, 1947. (An outstanding work; has relationships of press and the Presidents up to Franklin D. Roosevelt.)

———, "President Truman and the Press," *Journalism Quarterly* 28:457, fall, 1951.

———, "Truman and the Press," *Journalism Quarterly* 30:273, summer, 1953.

STARTT, JAMES D., "Early Press Reaction to Wilson's League Proposal," *Journalism Quarterly* 39:301ff., summer, 1962.

PRESS COVERAGE IN PRESIDENTIAL ELECTIONS

BEGEMAN, JEAN, "The One-Party Press Pays Off," *New Republic*, November 17, 1952, pp. 17-22.

"Campaign Coverage: An Appraisal of 1960–and Implications for 1964," *Columbia Journalism Review,* fall, 1961. (An extensive study of the election coverage.)

DANIELSON, WAYNE A. and JOHN B. ADAMS, "Completeness of Press Coverage of 1960 Campaign," *Journalism Quarterly* 38:441, autumn, 1961. (Covers ninety dailies in this extensive study.)

HIGBIE, JOHN, "Wisconsin Dailies in the 1952 Campaign: Space vs. Display," *Journalism Quarterly* 31:56, winter, 1954.

KOBRE, SIDNEY, "How Florida Dailies Handled the 1952 Presidential Campaign," *Journalism Quarterly* 30:163-169, spring, 1953.

MARKHAM, JAMES W. and GUIDO H. STEMPEL, III, *Pennsylvania Daily Press Coverage of the 1956 Election Campaign,* University Park, Pa.: School of Journalism, Pennsylvania State University, 1957.

"Page One Display Contradicts Authors on Press Bias," *Editor & Publisher,* October 25, 1952, p. 2.

"Post Election Roundup: News Held in Balance," *Editor & Publisher,* November 15, 1952, p. 10.

STEMPEL, GUIDO H., III, "Prestige Press Covers the 1960 Presidential Campaign," *Journalism Quarterly* 38:157ff., spring, 1961.

See Nathan Blumberg, *One Party Press*? Arthur Rowse, *Slanted News* listed under "Criticisms of Journalism."

MAGAZINES

BAGDIKIAN, BEN, "Newsmagazines," *New Republic* vol. 40, February 2, 16, 23, 1959. (Critical but authenticated articles on current newsmagazines.)

BAINBRIDGE, JOHN, *Little Wonder; Or, The Reader's Digest and How It Grew,* New York: Reynal & Company, Inc., 1946.

BAKER, RAY STANNARD, *An American Chronicle,* New York: Charles Scribner's Sons, 1945. (The autobiography of a magazine muckraker.)

BUSCH, NOEL F., *Briton Hadden: A Biography of the Co-Founder of Time,* New York: Farrar, Straus & Giroux, Inc., 1949. (See also Wolcott Gibbs, "Profile," *New Yorker,* November, 23, 1936.)

DREWRY, JOHN E., *Some Magazines and Magazine Makers,* Boston: Stratford, 1924. (An earlier but useful volume.)

FILLER, LOUIS, *Crusaders for American Liberalism,* New York: Harcourt, Brace & World, Inc., 1939. (A competent story of the muckrakers. Now in paperback edition, New York: Collier Books, 1961.)

KRAMER, DALE, *Ross and the New Yorker,* Garden City, N.Y.: Doubleday & Company, Inc., 1951. (Tells story of man behind the sophisticated magazine).

PHILLIPS, DAVID GRAHAM, *The Treason of the Senate,* edited by George E. Mowry and Judson A. Grenier, Chicago: Quadrangle Books, 1964. (Contains the muckraker's articles on the Senate plus the author's interpretive analysis.)

REIGER, C. C., *Era of the Muckrakers,* Chapel Hill: University of North Carolina Press, 1932. (First extended study of magazines; still solid.)

STEFFENS, LINCOLN, *Autobiography of Lincoln Steffens,* New York: Harcourt, Brace & World, Inc., 1931. (A leading muckraker gives an account of his own adventures in newspaper and magazine muckraking.)

TARBELL, IDA M., *All in the Day's Work: An Autobiography,* New York: The Macmillan Company, 1939. (A woman magazine writer tells how she developed her articles of exposure.)

TEBBEL, JOHN, *George Horace Lorimer and the Saturday Evening Post,* Garden City, N.Y., Doubleday & Company, Inc., 1948.

THURBER, JAMES, *The Years With Ross,* Boston: Little, Brown & Company, Inc., 1959. (A writer for the *New Yorker* tells about the publication and its editor.)

"U. S. Magazines: State of Their Progress," *Tide,* May 23, 1953. (Has excellent information and gives overall picture.)

WEINBERG, ARTHUR and LELA, *The Muckrakers,* New York: Simon and Schuster, Inc., 1961. (Contributes to the story of the early magazine and magazine writers who exposed corruption in American life. Has reprints of original articles.)

WOOD, JAMES P., *Of Lasting Interest: The Story of Reader's Digest,* Garden City, N.Y.: Doubleday & Company, Inc., 1958. (History of this little magazine which made a phenomenal success in the twentieth century.)

See Mott, Wood, Peterson listed in previous eras. Peterson's *Magazines in the Twentieth Century* (rev. 1964) is especially complete.

Journalism Quarterly 25:260, September, 1948. (Has extensive magazine references.)

ADVERTISING

BORDEN, NEIL, *National Advertising in Newspapers,* Cambridge: Harvard University Press, 1946. (A thorough study of the subject.)

PRESBREY, FRANK, *History of Advertising,* Garden City, N.Y.: Doubleday & Company, Inc., 1929. (An unusually complete account with many reproductions.)

UDELL, JON G., *The Growth of the American Daily Newspaper,* Madison: University of Wisconsin, 1965. (The latest study of newspaper trends, circulation and advertising.)

WOOD, JAMES P., *Story of Advertising,* New York: The Ronald Press Company, 1958. (A compressed, rapid survey of advertising growth.)

NEWSPAPER GUILD

BROUN, HEYWOOD, "An Army with Banners," *Nation* 140:184, February 13, 1935. (The founder of the guild tells the story of the union.)

Guild Reporter vol. 16, December 9, 1949. (Gives biography of Heywood Broun and the founding of the American Newspaper Guild.)

KEATING, ISABELLE, "Reporters Become of Age," *Harper's* 170:601ff., April, 1935.

KRAMER, DALE, *Heywood Broun,* New York: Current Books, 1941. (Only full biography of Newspaper Guild founder.)

Current material available at headquarters of American Newspaper Guild.

PRESS AND NEW DEAL

Editor & Publisher 66:3, August 12, 1933; also 67:3, 36, February 24, 1934.

LEE, ALFRED MCCLURE, *op. cit.* (Has extensive coverage of this subject.)

See also Emery, *Press and America,* Chapter 28.

RADIO, TELEVISION NEWS

AGEE, WARREN J., "A Study of Cross-Channel Ownership of Communication Media," M.A. Thesis, University of Minnesota, 1949. (Also in *Journalism Quarterly* 26:410, fall, 1949.)

BULMAN, DAVID, ed., *Molders of Opinion*, Milwaukee: The Bruce Publishing Company, 1945. (Has profiles of outstanding newscasters and commentators.)

BURLINGAME, ROGER, *Don't Let Them Scare You: The Life and Times of Elmer Davis*, Philadelphia: J. B. Lippincott Company, 1961. (The only biography of this penetrating, dry-wit news commentator.)

CHARNLEY, MITCHELL V., *News By Radio*, New York: The Macmillan Company, 1948. (Has considerable radio history.)

CLARK, DAVID G., "H. V. Kaltenborn's First Year on the Air," *Journalism Quarterly* 42:373-381, summer, 1965. (Tells Kaltenborn's problems in giving the news. See his autobiography.)

KALTENBORN, H. V., *Fifty Fabulous Years, 1900-1950: A Personal Review*, New York: G. P. Putnam's Sons, 1950.

———, *It Seems Like Yesterday*, New York: G. P. Putnam's Sons, 1956.

LEVIN, HARVEY J., *Cross Channel Ownership of Mass Media: A Study in Social Evaluation*, New York: Columbia University Press, 1953. (Ph.D. dissertation on microfilm.)

PRICE, WESLEY, "Murrow Sticks to the News," *Saturday Evening Post* 222:25ff., December 10, 1949. (A profile in depth of the leading newscaster.)

SIEPMANN, CHARLES A., *Radio's Second Choice*, Boston: Little, Brown & Company, Inc., 1946. (A critical view of radio.)

———, *Radio, Television, and Society*, Chicago: University of Chicago Press, 1950.

SHAPLEN, ROBERT, "A Farewell to Personal History," *Saturday Review* 43:46, December 10, 1960. (Gives radio and television coverage abroad in the 1950s.)

WERTENBAKER, CHARLES, "Profiles," *New Yorker* 29:28-30, December 26, 1953. (An account of Edward R. Murrow. See Price.)

WHITE, LLEWELLYN, *The American Radio*, Chicago: University of Chicago Press, 1947. (Tells history of big broadcasting companies in detail.)

PROFESSIONAL ADVANCES, SCHOOLS, ASSOCIATIONS

CLAYTON, CHARLES C., *Fifty Years of Freedom*, Carbondale: Southern Illinois University Press, 1959. (Story of Sigma Delta Chi.)

EMERY, EDWIN, *History of American Newspaper Publishers*, Minneapolis: University of Minnesota Press, 1950.

LEE, ALFRED MCCLUNG, *op. cit.*, pp. 666-71; also pp. 223ff.

See previous entries in Gilded Age period, especiallv Sutton, O'Dell; also *Journalism Quarterly*, March 1944, and March, 1947, special issues.

PHOTOGRAPHY HISTORY

FABER, JOHN, *Great Moments in News Photography*, New York: Thomas Nelson & Sons, 1960. (Outstanding news photos and the story behind them.)

NEWHALL, BEAUMONT, *History of Photography: From 1839 to the Present Day*, New York: Simon and Schuster, Inc., 1949.

TAFT, ROBERT, *Photography and the American Scene*, New York: Dover Publications, Inc., 1938. (Deals with illustrations in newspapers and magazines.)

PULITZER PRIZES

HOHENBERG, JOHN, *The Pulitzer Prize Story*, New York: Columbia University Press, 1959.

COMICS

BARCUS, FRANCIS E., "A Content Analysis of Trends in Sunday Comics," *Journalism Quarterly* 38:171ff., spring, 1961.

WHITE, DAVID M and ROBERT H. ABEL, *The Funnies*, Glencoe, Ill.: Free Press, 1963. (Analytical study of the comics in America.)

See previous entries in Part Four, Gilded Age Journalism, under Becker, Murrell and Waugh.

SUBURBAN PRESS

CARTER, ROY E. and PETER CLARKE, "Why Suburban News Attracts Reader Interest," *Journalism Quarterly* 39:522ff., autumn, 1962.

EDELSTEIN, ALEX S. and OTTO N. LARSEN, "The Weekly Press' Contribution to a Sense of Urban Community," *Journalism Quarterly* 37:489ff., autumn, 1960.

FORCE, JAMES, "The Daily Press in Surburbia: Trends in 15 Metropolitan Areas," *Journalism Quarterly* 39:457ff., autumn, 1962.

JANOWITZ, MORRIS, *The Community Press in an Urban Setting*, Glencoe, Ill.: Free Press, 1952.

JUDD, ROBERT P., "The Newspaper Reporter in a Suburban City," *Journalism Quarterly* 38:35ff., winter, 1961.

MACDOUGALL, CURTIS D., "Suburban Press Offers New Challenges," *Publishers' Auxiliary*, November, 1965, p. 1.

MECHANICS OF NEWSPAPER PRODUCTION

BARNHART, THOMAS F., "New Processes in Letterpress Printing: 'Cold Type' and Magnesium Plate," *Journalism Quarterly* 25:12, March, 1948. (An early account of the process.)

FLINT, C. U., "Report on Research Program Before ANPA Convention," reprinted in *Editor & Publisher*, April 24, 1949, p. 107.

TEBBEL, JOHN, "The Quiet Offset Revolution," *Saturday Review* vol. 44, December 9, 1961. (A summary of the developments in this new process.)

ZEISLER, KARL F., "The Revolution in Printing: A Critical Appraisal," *Journalism Quarterly*, 26:281, September, 1949.

See previous entries Sutton, Olson in Part Four, Gilded Age Journalism. *Editor & Publisher* and *Publishers' Auxiliary* carry articles on current developments in letterpress and offset printing.

Index